# PUBLIC INTERNATIONAL LAW

Public international law is a global legal system which regulates the conduct of countries and other actors, both in international relations and within states' territories. *Public International Law* offers Australian students a comprehensive and accessible introduction to international law.

Covering the fundamental topics of international law – including treaties, use of force and dispute settlement – this text also discusses specialised branches such as humanitarian law, criminal law and environmental law. The key principles and theories of international law are clearly explained and analysed, and their application is illustrated by succinct, carefully chosen extracts from cases and materials. These sources strike a balance between key international cases and important cases from domestic legal systems, with an emphasis on Australian cases and state practice.

Discussion questions at the end of each chapter encourage students to apply and test their understanding of each topic, while a glossary of key terms clearly explains complex concepts.

Written by an expert author team, *Public International Law* is a fundamental resource for Australian students of international law.

**Emily Crawford** is a Professor at the University of Sydney Law School.

**Alison Pert** is an adjunct Associate Professor at the University of Sydney.

**Ben Saul** is Challis Chair of International Law at the University of Sydney.

# PUBLIC INTERNATIONAL LAW

Edited by
Emily Crawford
Alison Pert
Ben Saul

Shaftesbury Road, Cambridge CB2 8EA, United Kingdom

One Liberty Plaza, 20th Floor, New York, NY 10006, USA

477 Williamstown Road, Port Melbourne, VIC 3207, Australia

314–321, 3rd Floor, Plot 3, Splendor Forum, Jasola District Centre, New Delhi – 110025, India

103 Penang Road, #05-06/07, Visioncrest Commercial, Singapore 238467

Cambridge University Press is part of Cambridge University Press & Assessment, a department of the University of Cambridge.

We share the University's mission to contribute to society through the pursuit of education, learning and research at the highest international levels of excellence.

www.cambridge.org
Information on this title: www.cambridge.org/highereducation/isbn/9781009055888

First published 2023

Cover designed by Shaun Jury
Typeset by Straive
Printed in Singapore by Markono Print Media Pte Ltd, March 2023

A catalogue record for this publication is available from the British Library

A catalogue record for this book is available from the National Library of Australia

ISBN 978-1-009-05588-8 Paperback

Additional resources for this publication at www.cambridge.org/highereducation/isbn/9781009055888/resources

*For Ivan Shearer (1938–2019) and James Crawford (1948–2021), who taught us to love international law, and to love teaching it.*

# CONTENTS

| | | |
|---|---|---|
| *About the authors* | page *xxii* | |
| *Preface* | *xxv* | |
| *Acknowledgements* | *xxvi* | |
| *Table of cases* | *xxviii* | |
| *Table of statutes* | *xli* | |
| *Table of treaties and other international instruments* | *xliv* | |
| *List of abbreviations* | *lxxiii* | |

**1  Overview of public international law**                                1

*Ben Saul*

| | | |
|---|---|---|
| **1.1** | Introduction | 2 |
| **1.2** | What is international law? | 2 |
| | 1.2.1  Historical context | 3 |
| |    1.2.1.1  Early origins | 3 |
| |    1.2.1.2  The 19th and early 20th centuries | 5 |
| |    1.2.1.3  The international order after 1945 | 6 |
| | 1.2.2  Participants | 7 |
| |    1.2.2.1  States | 7 |
| |    1.2.2.2  International organisations | 8 |
| |    1.2.2.3  Other actors | 9 |
| **1.3** | Implementation and enforcement | 12 |
| | 1.3.1  International level | 13 |
| |    1.3.1.1  State responsibility | 13 |
| |    1.3.1.2  Diplomatic claims | 13 |
| |    1.3.1.3  Dispute settlement methods | 13 |
| |    1.3.1.4  Other accountability procedures | 14 |
| |    1.3.1.5  Enforcement of international security | 14 |
| |    1.3.1.6  Self-help | 14 |
| |    1.3.1.7  Treaty law | 15 |
| |    1.3.1.8  Social processes | 15 |
| | 1.3.2  National level | 16 |
| **1.4** | The nature of international law as 'law' | 16 |
| | 1.4.1  International law is not 'law'? | 17 |
| | 1.4.2  Voluntarism: law by sovereign consent | 18 |

| | 1.4.3 | Hart: international law is law lacking a legal system | 19 |
| | 1.4.4 | Realists: international law is subordinate to power | 20 |
| | 1.4.5 | Pragmatists: international law is recognised and treated as law | 22 |
| | 1.4.6 | International law as process | 24 |
| | 1.4.7 | Theories of compliance with international law | 25 |
| **1.5** | | Critical theories | 26 |
| | 1.5.1 | Marxism | 26 |
| | 1.5.2 | Third World Approaches to International Law | 28 |
| | 1.5.3 | Feminism | 28 |
| | 1.5.4 | Postmodernism | 30 |
| | | Discussion questions | 31 |

**2   Sources of international law**                                            32

*Emily Crawford*

| **2.1** | | Introduction | 33 |
| **2.2** | | The traditional starting point: art 38 of the *Statute of the International Court of Justice* | 33 |
| | 2.2.1 | Treaties | 34 |
| | 2.2.2 | Custom | 34 |
| | | 2.2.2.1 State practice | 34 |
| | | 2.2.2.2 *Opinio juris* | 38 |
| | | 2.2.2.3 Local or regional custom | 40 |
| | | 2.2.2.4 The persistent and subsequent objector | 41 |
| | | 2.2.2.5 The interaction between treaties and custom | 42 |
| | | 2.2.2.6 *Jus cogens* | 43 |
| | 2.2.3 | General principles of law | 45 |
| | 2.2.4 | Judicial decisions and the teachings of highly qualified publicists | 47 |
| | | 2.2.4.1 A special subcategory of highly qualified publicists: the International Law Commission | 48 |
| **2.3** | | Another binding source of international law: unilateral declarations | 49 |
| **2.4** | | Soft law instruments | 50 |
| | 2.4.1 | Resolutions of international organisations and conferences | 51 |
| | 2.4.2 | Codes of conduct and manuals of instruction | 52 |
| | | Discussion questions | 53 |

**3   The law of treaties**                                            55

*Alison Pert and Meda Couzens*

| **3.1** | | Introduction | 56 |
| **3.2** | | What is a treaty, and the relationship of treaties with customary international law? | 56 |

**3.3** The *Vienna Convention on the Law of Treaties*                                57

3.3.1 Introduction and scope                                                         57

3.3.2 What is a treaty for the purposes of the *VCLT*?                               58

  3.3.2.1 An agreement between states                                               58

  3.3.2.2 In written form                                                           58

  3.3.2.3 Governed by international law                                             59

  3.3.2.4 Whether embodied in one or more instruments                              59

  3.3.2.5 Whatever its particular designation                                      59

**3.4** Treaty negotiation and conclusion                                            60

**3.5** Expressing the consent to be bound                                           61

**3.6** Entry into force of a treaty                                                 62

**3.7** Reservations to treaties                                                     62

3.7.1 Reservations vs interpretative declarations                                    63

3.7.2 Are reservations allowed?                                                      64

3.7.3 Effect of reservations                                                         67

**3.8** Legal effects of a treaty                                                    69

3.8.1 Obligation not to defeat the object and purpose of a treaty

  prior to its entry into force (art 18)                                            69

3.8.2 Observance of treaties: obligations after the treaty comes

  into effect                                                                       69

  3.8.2.1 *Pacta sunt servanda*                                                     69

  3.8.2.2 Internal law and observance of treaties                                  70

  3.8.2.3 Treaties and third states                                               70

**3.9** Application of treaties                                                      70

**3.10** Interpretation of treaties                                                  70

3.10.1 General rule of interpretation (art 31)                                       71

3.10.2 Supplementary means of interpretation (art 32)                               72

3.10.3 Role of resolutions of international organisations                           73

**3.11** Invalidity, termination, withdrawal from and suspension of a treaty         73

3.11.1 Invalidity                                                                    74

  3.11.1.1 Internal law                                                             74

  3.11.1.2 Error                                                                    75

  3.11.1.3 Fraud or corruption                                                     75

  3.11.1.4 Coercion                                                                 75

  3.11.1.5 Breach of good faith: a further ground of invalidity?                   76

3.11.2 Termination, withdrawal and suspension                                       76

  3.11.2.1 Termination or suspension by express or implied

    agreement                                                                       77

  3.11.2.2 Denunciation or withdrawal by express or

    implied agreement                                                               77

| | | 3.11.2.3 | Material breach | 77 |
| | | 3.11.2.4 | Impossibility | 78 |
| | | 3.11.2.5 | Fundamental change of circumstances | 79 |
| | 3.11.3 | Consequences of invalidity, termination and suspension | | 81 |
| | Discussion questions | | | 82 |

**4   International law and Australian law** 83

*Tim Stephens and Meda Couzens*

| **4.1** | Introduction | 84 |
| **4.2** | International law and domestic law: general concepts, theories and comparisons | 84 |
| **4.3** | Domestic law in international law | 86 |
| | 4.3.1   Municipal law as a source of international law | 86 |
| | 4.3.2   Deficiencies in municipal law no justification for breach of international law | 86 |
| **4.4** | Categorising the influence of international law on Australian law | 88 |
| **4.5** | Treaties and Australian law | 90 |
| | 4.5.1   The treaty-making process | 91 |
| | 4.5.2   Constitutional considerations | 92 |
| | 4.5.3   Legislative considerations | 94 |
| | 4.5.4   Treaties and administrative decision-making | 96 |
| **4.6** | International law and statutory interpretation | 97 |
| **4.7** | International law and constitutional interpretation | 100 |
| **4.8** | Customary international law in Australian law | 101 |
| | 4.8.1   Crimes in customary international law | 105 |
| **4.9** | Proof of international law in Australian courts | 105 |
| | Discussion questions | 106 |

**5   Statehood, self-determination and territory** 107

*Rowan Nicholson*

| **5.1** | Introduction | 108 |
| **5.2** | Statehood | 108 |
| | 5.2.1   The role of the statehood criteria | 108 |
| | | 5.2.1.1   The criteria of population, territory and government | 109 |
| | | 5.2.1.2   The criterion of independence | 110 |
| | | 5.2.1.3   The example of Australia | 111 |
| | 5.2.2   The role of recognition | 113 |
| | | 5.2.2.1   Recognition as a state | 113 |
| | | 5.2.2.2   Recognition as a government | 116 |

|  |  | 5.2.3 | The role of unlawfulness | 117 |
|  |  |  | 5.2.3.1 Entities created by unilateral secession | 117 |
|  |  |  | 5.2.3.2 Entities created by force | 119 |
|  |  |  | 5.2.3.3 Entities created by breaches of other peremptory norms | 121 |
|  | **5.3** | | Self-determination | 122 |
|  |  | 5.3.1 | The right to external self-determination | 123 |
|  |  |  | 5.3.1.1 The scope of the right to external self-determination | 123 |
|  |  |  | 5.3.1.2 How self-determination affects statehood | 126 |
|  |  | 5.3.2 | Other manifestations of self-determination | 128 |
|  | **5.4** | | Territory | 130 |
|  |  | 5.4.1 | The initial territory of new states | 130 |
|  |  | 5.4.2 | Territorial change | 131 |
|  |  |  | 5.4.2.1 Conquest | 132 |
|  |  |  | 5.4.2.2 Cession | 132 |
|  |  |  | 5.4.2.3 Occupation of terra nullius | 133 |
|  |  |  | 5.4.2.4 Prescription | 135 |
|  |  | 5.4.3 | Territorial disputes | 137 |
|  |  |  | 5.4.3.1 Effective occupation | 137 |
|  |  |  | 5.4.3.2 Critical date | 139 |
|  |  |  | 5.4.3.3 Relativity of title | 140 |
|  |  | 5.4.4 | Special types of territory | 140 |
|  |  | | Discussion questions | 141 |
| **6** | **Jurisdiction and immunities** | | | **142** |
| *Alison Pert* | | | | |
|  | **6.1** | | Introduction | 143 |
|  | **6.2** | | Jurisdiction | 143 |
|  |  | 6.2.1 | Meaning and scope | 143 |
|  |  | 6.2.2 | The *Lotus* case | 144 |
|  |  | 6.2.3 | Civil jurisdiction | 146 |
|  |  |  | 6.2.3.1 The *Alien Tort Statute of 1789* | 146 |
|  |  | 6.2.4 | Criminal jurisdiction | 147 |
|  |  |  | 6.2.4.1 The territoriality principle | 148 |
|  |  |  | 6.2.4.2 Extended territoriality and the 'effects doctrine' | 148 |
|  |  |  | 6.2.4.3 The nationality principle | 150 |
|  |  |  | 6.2.4.4 The passive personality principle | 150 |
|  |  |  | 6.2.4.5 The protective principle | 151 |
|  |  |  | 6.2.4.6 The universality principle | 153 |
|  |  |  | 6.2.4.7 'Prosecute or extradite' treaties | 154 |
|  |  |  | 6.2.4.8 Universal jurisdiction in national courts | 154 |
|  |  | 6.2.5 | Accused brought 'unlawfully' before the court | 154 |
|  |  | 6.2.6 | Extradition | 155 |

**6.3**    Diplomatic immunity    156
   6.3.1    Diplomatic relations    157
   6.3.2    Consular relations    158
   6.3.3    The *Vienna Convention on Diplomatic Relations*    158
     6.3.3.1    Immunities    159
     6.3.3.2    Appointments    161
     6.3.3.3    Duration of immunity    161
     6.3.3.4    Inviolability    162
     6.3.3.5    Duties of the sending state    163

**6.4**    Foreign state immunity    164
   6.4.1    Absolute vs restrictive immunity    165
   6.4.2    Who or what is entitled to immunity?    168
     6.4.2.1    The 'state'    168
     6.4.2.2    Agencies and instrumentalities, separate entities    169
     6.4.2.3    Political subdivisions    169
     6.4.2.4    Individuals representing the state: functional immunity    170
     6.4.2.5    Personal immunity for certain individuals: the 'Troika'    170
   6.4.3    Some questions not answered by the *Arrest Warrant* case    172
     6.4.3.1    Personal immunity from civil proceedings    172
     6.4.3.2    Personal immunity beyond the Troika?    173
   6.4.4    Immunity for *jus cogens* violations?    173
     6.4.4.1    Immunity from criminal proceedings for torture    174
     6.4.4.2    Immunity from criminal proceedings for other *jus cogens* violations    175
     6.4.4.3    Immunity from civil proceedings for torture and other international crimes    176
   6.4.5    Functional immunity of officials for other crimes    176

**6.5**    Immunity before international tribunals    177

**6.6**    Special mission immunity    177

**6.7**    Foreign act of state doctrine    178

   Discussion questions    179

**7    State responsibility and diplomatic protection**    180
*Chester Brown, Emily Crawford and Brett Williams*

**7.1**    Introduction    181

**7.2**    A brief history: custom and the work of the International Law Commission    181

**7.3**    Elements of state responsibility    183
   7.3.1    Attribution of conduct    183
     7.3.1.1    Conduct of state organs, and of persons or entities exercising elements of governmental authority    183

|  |  |  |
|---|---|---|
| 7.3.1.2 | Ultra vires or unauthorised acts | 184 |
| 7.3.1.3 | Acts by non-state actors or groups | 185 |
| 7.3.1.4 | Adoption by the state | 186 |
| 7.3.1.5 | Joint responsibility | 187 |
| 7.3.2 | Breach | 188 |
| 7.3.3 | Admissibility of claims | 188 |
| 7.3.4 | Circumstances precluding wrongfulness | 188 |
| 7.3.4.1 | Consent | 188 |
| 7.3.4.2 | Self-defence | 189 |
| 7.3.4.3 | Countermeasures | 190 |
| 7.3.4.4 | *Force majeure* | 190 |
| 7.3.4.5 | Distress | 191 |
| 7.3.4.6 | Necessity | 191 |
| 7.3.5 | Consequences of an internationally wrongful act | 192 |
| 7.3.5.1 | Cessation | 192 |
| 7.3.5.2 | Reparation | 193 |
| 7.3.6 | Consequences for a breach of a *jus cogens* norm | 195 |
| 7.3.7 | Invocation | 196 |

**7.4** Diplomatic protection — 198

**7.5** Content of a state's obligation regarding the treatment of foreign nationals — 200

| | | |
|---|---|---|
| 7.5.1 | National standard vs the international minimum standard | 200 |
| 7.5.2 | International minimum standard of treatment | 200 |
| 7.5.3 | Responsibility for direct and indirect injury to foreign nationals | 201 |
| 7.5.4 | Obligation to provide physical protection for foreign nationals | 202 |
| 7.5.5 | International minimum standard and obligations under investment treaties | 202 |
| 7.5.6 | Expropriation of the property of foreign nationals | 203 |

**7.6** Additional requirements for a claim in diplomatic protection — 206

| | | |
|---|---|---|
| 7.6.1 | Nationality of claims: natural persons | 206 |
| 7.6.2 | Nationality of claims: corporations and shareholders | 207 |
| 7.6.3 | Exhaustion of local remedies | 208 |

**7.7** State responsibility in the era of international human rights law — 209

Discussion questions — 210

**8 Use of force** — 212

*Alison Pert*

**8.1** Introduction — 213

**8.2** Pre-1945 — 213

**8.3** The *Charter of the United Nations* — 214

| | | |
|---|---|---|
| 8.3.1 | 'Force', 'in their international relations', 'any state' | 214 |
| 8.3.2 | 'Territorial integrity or political independence' | 214 |

| | | | |
|---|---|---|---|
| | 8.3.3 | What is prohibited? | 215 |
| | 8.3.4 | The prohibition is customary international law, and *jus cogens* | 216 |
| | | 8.3.4.1 The *Nicaragua* case | 216 |
| | 8.3.5 | Indirect use of force vs 'effective control' | 218 |
| | 8.3.6 | What is not a use of force? | 218 |
| | 8.3.7 | New challenges: cyber-attacks | 219 |
| | 8.3.8 | What is a threat of force? | 220 |
| **8.4** | | Self-defence | 221 |
| | 8.4.1 | Necessity and proportionality | 222 |
| | 8.4.2 | Procedural requirements for lawful self-defence | 223 |
| | | 8.4.2.1 Reporting to the Security Council | 223 |
| | | 8.4.2.2 Declaration by victim state: collective self-defence | 223 |
| | 8.4.3 | 'Armed attack' | 223 |
| | | 8.4.3.1 Meaning of 'armed attack' | 224 |
| | | 8.4.3.2 Timing of 'armed attack' | 225 |
| | | 8.4.3.3 Pre-emptive self-defence | 227 |
| | 8.4.4 | Protection of nationals abroad | 228 |
| | 8.4.5 | Self-defence against terrorism | 228 |
| | | 8.4.5.1 The 'unable or unwilling' doctrine | 229 |
| **8.5** | | Collective security: action authorised by the Security Council | 230 |
| | 8.5.1 | Collective security | 230 |
| | 8.5.2 | Sanctions | 230 |
| | 8.5.3 | Peacekeeping | 231 |
| | 8.5.4 | Authorisation of force | 232 |
| **8.6** | | Humanitarian intervention and the responsibility to protect | 233 |
| **8.7** | | Intervention by invitation | 235 |
| | 8.7.1 | The principle of non-intervention | 236 |
| | 8.7.2 | The right to intervene by invitation | 236 |
| | | Discussion questions | 237 |
| **9** | **International dispute settlement** | | 238 |
| | *Chester Brown* | | |
| **9.1** | | Introduction | 239 |
| **9.2** | | International dispute settlement: an overview | 239 |
| | 9.2.1 | Existence of a 'dispute' | 240 |
| | 9.2.2 | Legal and political disputes | 241 |
| **9.3** | | Evolution of the obligation to settle disputes peacefully and the *UN Charter* framework | 242 |
| **9.4** | | Diplomatic methods for the peaceful settlement of international disputes | 244 |
| | 9.4.1 | Negotiation | 244 |
| | 9.4.2 | Fact-finding and inquiry | 246 |

| | | | |
|---|---|---|---|
| | 9.4.3 | Good offices | 247 |
| | 9.4.4 | Mediation | 248 |
| | 9.4.5 | Conciliation | 249 |
| **9.5** | International arbitration | | 251 |
| **9.6** | International Court of Justice (ICJ) | | 252 |
| | 9.6.1 | History | 252 |
| | 9.6.2 | Composition | 252 |
| | 9.6.3 | Access to the Court | 253 |
| | 9.6.4 | Jurisdiction of the Court | 254 |
| | | 9.6.4.1 Contentious jurisdiction | 254 |
| | | 9.6.4.2 Admissibility of claims | 258 |
| | | 9.6.4.3 Provisional measures | 260 |
| | | 9.6.4.4 Third-party intervention | 261 |
| | | 9.6.4.5 Advisory jurisdiction | 261 |
| | 9.6.5 | Judgments | 262 |
| | 9.6.6 | Australia and the ICJ | 263 |
| **9.7** | Role of the United Nations and regional organisations in the settlement of international disputes | | 264 |
| | Discussion questions | | 264 |
| **10** | **International human rights law** | | 265 |

*Irene Baghoomians and Jacqueline Mowbray*

| | | | |
|---|---|---|---|
| **10.1** | Introduction | | 266 |
| | 10.1.1 | Histories of international human rights law | 266 |
| **10.2** | Substantive content of international human rights law | | 267 |
| | 10.2.1 | The major international human rights instruments | 267 |
| | | 10.2.1.1 The *Universal Declaration of Human Rights* | 267 |
| | | 10.2.1.2 The *ICCPR* and the *ICESCR* | 268 |
| | | 10.2.1.3 Other international human rights instruments | 269 |
| | | 10.2.1.4 International refugee law | 270 |
| | | 10.2.1.5 Regional human rights treaties | 270 |
| | 10.2.2 | Overview of rights and obligations | 272 |
| | | 10.2.2.1 Who has obligations under international human rights law? | 272 |
| | | 10.2.2.2 Who has rights under international human rights law? | 272 |
| | | 10.2.2.3 Jurisdictional scope | 272 |
| | | 10.2.2.4 Nature of obligations: respect, protect, fulfil | 273 |
| | | 10.2.2.5 Derogations and limitations | 273 |
| | | 10.2.2.6 Reservations to human rights treaties? | 274 |
| | | 10.2.2.7 Generations of rights? | 275 |

**10.3**  The institutional framework: international human rights bodies  275
    10.3.1  International bodies  275
        10.3.1.1  Human Rights Council  276
        10.3.1.2  Human rights treaty bodies  278
    10.3.2  Regional bodies and mechanisms  281
        10.3.2.1  ASEAN case study  284
    10.3.3  Civil society  285

**10.4**  Domestic implementation of international human rights law  286
    10.4.1  International overview  286
    10.4.2  Human rights law in Australian law  287
        10.4.2.1  Federal law  287
        10.4.2.2  State and territory human rights legislation  287
        10.4.2.3  A federal human rights Act?  288
    10.4.3  Australian institutions for the protection and promotion of
        human rights  289
        10.4.3.1  Parliamentary Joint Committee on Human Rights  289
        10.4.3.2  Australian Human Rights Commission  289

**10.5**  Human rights as a discourse and critiques  291

Discussion questions  293

**11  International humanitarian law**  294
*Emily Crawford*

**11.1**  Introduction  295

**11.2**  Sources of international humanitarian law  295

**11.3**  Types of armed conflict and scope of application of international
    humanitarian law  298
    11.3.1  International armed conflicts  298
    11.3.2  Non-international armed conflicts  299
    11.3.3  Parallel conflicts  301
    11.3.4  Transformation of conflicts and internationalised,
        transnational, hybrid and spillover conflicts  301
    11.3.5  Scope of application of international humanitarian law  302

**11.4**  Fundamental principles of international humanitarian law  303
    11.4.1  Distinction  303
    11.4.2  Proportionality  303
    11.4.3  Military necessity  305
    11.4.4  Humanity  305
    11.4.5  Prohibition on causing unnecessary suffering and
        superfluous injury  305

**11.5**  Persons and objects under international humanitarian law  306
    11.5.1  Combatants and attached non-combatants  306
    11.5.2  Civilians (including those taking direct part in hostilities)  308

|       | 11.5.3 | Objects |       | 310 |
|-------|--------|---------|-------|-----|
|       |        | 11.5.3.1 | Military objects and objectives | 310 |
|       |        | 11.5.3.2 | Civilian objects | 310 |

**11.6** The law of targeting and the rules on means and methods of
warfare — 311

11.6.1 The law of targeting — 312
11.6.2 Prohibited means and methods of warfare — 312
    11.6.2.1 Weapons — 312
    11.6.2.2 Methods — 313

**11.7** Special protection regimes — 314
11.7.1 Prisoners of war — 314
11.7.2 The law of occupation — 315
11.7.3 Wounded, sick and shipwrecked — 316
11.7.4 Cultural property — 317
11.7.5 The natural environment — 317

**11.8** Implementation and enforcement of international humanitarian law — 318

Discussion questions — 319

**12 International criminal law** — 320
*Rosemary Grey*

**12.1** Introduction — 321

**12.2** International criminal law and its aims — 321

**12.3** The development of international criminal law — 323

**12.4** The enforcement of international criminal law today — 325
12.4.1 International Criminal Court — 325
    12.4.1.1 Jurisdiction of the ICC — 326
    12.4.1.2 The ICC's admissibility rules — 327
12.4.2 National courts — 329
12.4.3 'Hybrid' criminal tribunals — 330

**12.5** Crimes under international law — 331
12.5.1 War crimes — 331
12.5.2 Crimes against humanity — 332
12.5.3 Genocide — 333
    12.5.3.1 Genocide in Australia? — 336
12.5.4 Aggression — 338

**12.6** Individual criminal responsibility — 341
12.6.1 Commission — 341
12.6.2 Command responsibility — 343
12.6.3 Defences — 344

Discussion questions — 345

**13    International law of the sea**                                          346

*Tim Stephens*

**13.1**    Introduction                                                        347

**13.2**    Origins and development                                            347

**13.3**    Coastal state maritime zones                                       349
    13.3.1    Baselines                                     351
    13.3.2    Territorial sea                               352
    13.3.3    Contiguous zone                               354
    13.3.4    Exclusive economic zone                       355
    13.3.5    Continental shelf                             357
    13.3.6    Archipelagic waters                           359

**13.4**    Maritime boundary delimitation                                     361
    13.4.1    Australia and Timor-Leste's maritime boundary  363

**13.5**    Maritime zones beyond national jurisdiction                        364
    13.5.1    High seas                                     364
    13.5.2    Deep seabed                                   365

**13.6**    Maritime environmental protection                                  367

**13.7**    Fisheries                                                          369

**13.8**    Dispute resolution                                                 370

Discussion questions                                                           371

**14    International environmental law**                                       372

*Ben Boer*

**14.1**    Introduction                                                       373

**14.2**    Development of international environmental law                      373
    14.2.1    International environmental law over five decades  373
    14.2.2    National level implementation                 375
    14.2.3    Remedies for violations                       375

**14.3**    Sources and drafting of IEL                                        375

**14.4**    International institutions                                          377
    14.4.1    United Nations Environment Programme           377
    14.4.2    United Nations Environment Assembly            377

**14.5**    Principles of international environmental law                       378
    14.5.1    The importance of principles                  378
    14.5.2    Established principles                         378
    14.5.3    Sustainable development                       380
        14.5.3.1    Sustainable Development Goals 2015    381
        14.5.3.2    Sustainable development in Australia  382

|  |  | 14.5.4 | Emergence of new principles | 382 |
|  |  |  | 14.5.4.1 Principles of IEL in a global instrument | 382 |
|  |  |  | 14.5.4.2 Environmental Rule of Law | 383 |
|  |  |  | 14.5.4.3 *In dubio pro natura* | 384 |
|  |  |  | 14.5.4.4 Principle of non-regression | 384 |
|  |  |  | 14.5.4.5 Principle of progression | 385 |
|  |  |  | 14.5.4.6 Human right to a safe, clean, healthy and sustainable environment | 385 |

**14.6** Selected environmental law issues — 388
  14.6.1 Greenhouse gases and climate change — 388
  14.6.2 Transboundary air pollution — 390
  14.6.3 Chemicals and wastes — 390
  14.6.4 Conservation of biological diversity — 392
  14.6.5 Land degradation — 394

**14.7** Heritage conservation — 395
  14.7.1 The heritage conventions — 395
  14.7.2 The *World Heritage Convention* — 396
      14.7.2.1 The *World Heritage Convention* in Australia — 397

Discussion questions — 399

**15  International organisations** — 400
*Ben Saul*

**15.1** Introduction — 401

**15.2** Origins and purposes of international organisations — 401
  15.2.1 League of Nations 1919 — 402
  15.2.2 Contemporary international organisations — 404

**15.3** What is an international organisation? — 405
  15.3.1 Established by international law — 405
  15.3.2 Membership including states — 406
  15.3.3 International legal personality — 407

**15.4** Powers of international organisations — 409

**15.5** Immunities from and privileges under national law — 411
  15.5.1 Immunities of the United Nations — 412
  15.5.2 Privileges of the United Nations — 413
  15.5.3 Immunities and privileges of UN personnel — 413
  15.5.4 Lifting of immunity — 414

**15.6** Responsibility and accountability of international organisations and member states — 415
  15.6.1 Breach of an international obligation — 416
  15.6.2 Attribution — 416

| 15.6.3 | Dual attribution | 417 |
| 15.6.4 | Responsibility for contributing to the acts of others | 418 |
| 15.6.5 | Responsibility of member states for a breach by an international organisation | 419 |
| 15.6.6 | Dispute settlement procedures | 419 |
| **15.7** | United Nations 1945 | 420 |
| 15.7.1 | General Assembly | 423 |
| 15.7.2 | Security Council | 424 |
| 15.7.3 | Other UN bodies | 425 |
| 15.7.3.1 | World Bank and International Monetary Fund | 426 |
| 15.7.3.2 | Other autonomous UN bodies | 426 |
| 15.7.3.3 | World Trade Organization | 426 |
| 15.7.4 | UN Secretariat | 426 |
| 15.7.5 | Criticisms of the United Nations | 427 |
| 15.7.6 | Reform of the United Nations | 428 |
| | Discussion questions | 429 |

**16   International economic law**                                              430

*Chester Brown and Alison Pert*

| **16.1** | Introduction | 431 |
| **16.2** | International trade law | 431 |
| 16.2.1 | The *General Agreement on Tariffs and Trade* 1947 | 431 |
| 16.2.2 | The World Trade Organization | 433 |
| 16.2.2.1 | The *General Agreement on Tariffs and Trade 1994* | 434 |
| 16.2.2.2 | The *General Agreement on Trade in Services* | 436 |
| 16.2.2.3 | The *Agreement on Trade-Related Aspects of Intellectual Property* | 437 |
| 16.2.2.4 | The *Understanding on Dispute Settlement* | 439 |
| 16.2.2.5 | Australia and the WTO | 441 |
| 16.2.3 | Other free trade agreements | 441 |
| **16.3** | International investment law | 442 |
| 16.3.1 | Introduction | 442 |
| 16.3.2 | Substantive obligations in investment treaties | 444 |
| 16.3.2.1 | Fair and equitable treatment | 444 |
| 16.3.2.2 | Full protection and security | 447 |
| 16.3.2.3 | Protection from expropriation | 448 |
| 16.3.2.4 | Most-favoured-nation treatment | 450 |
| 16.3.2.5 | National treatment | 451 |
| 16.3.2.6 | Umbrella clause | 452 |

16.3.3   Dispute settlement                                          453
          16.3.3.1   Investor–state dispute settlement               453
          16.3.3.2   Inter-state dispute settlement                  454

Discussion questions                                                 455

*Glossary*                                                           *456*
*Index*                                                              *465*

# ABOUT THE AUTHORS

## Editors

**Emily Crawford** is a Professor at the University of Sydney Law School, where she teaches and researches in international law and international humanitarian law. She has published widely in the field of international humanitarian law, including three monographs and a textbook, and is co-editor of the *Journal of International Humanitarian Legal Studies*.

**Alison Pert** (LLB (Hons), LLM, PhD) is an adjunct Associate Professor at the University of Sydney where she lectures in public international law and international law and the use of armed force. She has practised as a lawyer in government and in the private sector in London, Papua New Guinea and Australia, and has represented Australia at international organisations including Unidroit and UNCITRAL, and in treaty negotiations. She is the author of *Australia as a Good International Citizen* (Federation Press, 2014) and co-author of *International Humanitarian Law* (CUP, 3rd edition forthcoming, 2023, with Emily Crawford).

**Ben Saul** is Challis Chair of International Law at the University of Sydney, and an Associate Fellow at the Royal Institute of International Affairs (Chatham House) in London and the International Centre for Counter-Terrorism in The Hague. He has taught at Harvard, Oxford, The Hague Academy of International Law and in Italy, India, Nepal and Cambodia, and been a visitor at the Max Planck Institute for International Law and the Raoul Wallenberg Institute for Human Rights. He has published 20 books and hundreds of articles. His books include *Defining Terrorism in International Law* (2006), the *Oxford Commentary on the International Covenant on Economic, Social and Cultural Rights* (2014) (awarded a Certificate of Merit by the American Society of International Law), the *Research Handbook on International Law and Terrorism* (2020) and the *Oxford Guide to International Humanitarian Law* (2020). Ben has advised United Nations bodies, governments, militaries and security agencies, and NGOs; practised in international tribunals; and undertaken missions in over 35 countries. He has a doctorate from Oxford and honours degrees in Arts and Law from Sydney.

## Contributors

**Irene Baghoomians** has worked in the areas of public interest and human rights litigation, policy and research, including at the Australian Law Reform Commission and the Department of the Prime Minister and Cabinet. Irene was a legal policy adviser in the Race Discrimination Unit of the Human Rights and Equal Opportunity Commission (1998–2000). In New York, she studied for an LLM at Columbia University Law School (2000–01) and was designated a human rights fellow. Upon graduation she was granted a second human rights fellowship which she spent at the Center for Constitutional Rights. Irene is a Senior Lecturer at the University of Sydney Law School and is the coordinator of the clinical legal education program.

**Ben Boer** is an Emeritus Professor in the University of Sydney Law School. He was also the international Co-Director of the IUCN Academy of Environmental Law (2006–08) and Deputy Chair of the IUCN World Commission on Environmental Law (2012–16). He was a Distinguished Professor in the Research Institute of Environmental Law at Wuhan University, PRC (2011–20). He has served as a consultant to various intergovernmental and non-governmental organisations, and is a member of the Board of Governors of the International Council of Environmental Law. He continues to write on a range of environmental law and human rights topics. He is co-founder and co-editor of the *Chinese Journal of Environmental Law*.

**Chester Brown** is Professor of International Law and International Arbitration at the University of Sydney Law School. He is also a Barrister at 7 Wentworth Selborne Chambers, Sydney, and an Overseas Member of Essex Court Chambers, London. He teaches and researches in the fields of public international law, international dispute settlement, international arbitration, international investment law, and private international law. He also maintains a practice in these fields, and has been involved as counsel, expert and arbitrator in various proceedings, including before the International Court of Justice, the Iran–United States Claims Tribunal, inter-state and investor–state tribunals, as well as in inter-state conciliation proceedings, international commercial arbitrations and domestic court proceedings.

**Meda Couzens** is a Lecturer with the School of Law, Western Sydney University and an Honorary Research Fellow with the University of KwaZulu-Natal, South Africa. Meda holds a PhD from Leiden University, The Netherlands and other postgraduate degrees (legal and multidisciplinary) from universities in South Africa, the United Kingdom and Romania. Meda has taught public international law at the University of Sydney and Western Sydney University. Her main area of research is the rights of children.

**Rosemary Grey** is a Senior Lecturer at the University of Sydney Law School. Her research focuses on gender and international criminal law, with a focus on the International Criminal Court ('ICC') and the Extraordinary Chambers in the Courts of Cambodia ('ECCC'). She has taught courses in public international law, international criminal law and domestic criminal law, and has submitted amicus curiae observations in the ICC and ECCC.

**Jacqueline Mowbray** is an Associate Professor at the University of Sydney Law School, where she teaches international law, human rights, and legal theory. She is also the external legal adviser to the Commonwealth of Australia's Parliamentary Joint Committee on Human Rights, and she was a member of the drafting committee of the Abidjan Principles on the Right to Education. Her book, *The International Covenant on Economic, Social and Cultural Rights: Commentary, Cases, and Materials* (co-authored with Ben Saul and David Kinley), was winner of the 2015 American Society of International Law Certificate of Merit.

**Rowan Nicholson** teaches and researches in international law and public law. His book *Statehood and the State-Like in International Law* (Oxford University Press, 2019), adapted from his doctorate at the University of Cambridge, draws on colonial history and presents a theory about how political communities acquire legal rights and duties. His other research interests include the status of Indigenous Australians. He has worked on cases before the International Court of Justice and was previously co-director of the Sydney Centre for

International Law. He is now at Flinders University and also speaks and writes about international law in the media.

**Tim Stephens** is Professor of International Law at the University of Sydney Law School. He teaches and researches in public international law, with his work focusing on the international law of the sea, international environmental law and international dispute settlement. Tim holds a PhD in international law from the University of Sydney, an MPhil in geography from the University of Cambridge, and BA and LLB degrees (both with Honours) from the University of Sydney. He is a Fellow of the Australian Academy of Law and a past president of the Australian and New Zealand Society of International Law.

**Brett Williams** is the Principal of Williams Trade Law and is an Honorary Senior Lecturer at the Law School of the University of Sydney, where he is an associate of the Sydney Centre for International Law and the Centre for Asian and Pacific Law.

# PREFACE

From the earliest days of legal education in Australian universities, instruction in international law was considered critical for every law student. Early leadership was provided by the likes of Pitt Cobbett and Archibald Charteris. After World War II, international law dropped off the law curriculum for some decades, even as Australian international lawyers and diplomats were making an impact on the international stage – they included Kenneth Bailey, Joseph Starke, Julius Stone, Daniel O'Connell, William Webb, Herbert Vere Evatt and Percy Spender. By the 1980s, international law began to return to subject lists in Australian law schools, with an increasing trend towards making it a compulsory part of the law degree.[1]

However, despite the centrality of international law to studies of law in Australia, there have been only a handful of textbooks written by Australian scholars, with a focus on Australian students.[2] This has meant that teachers and scholars have sometimes struggled to incorporate Australian content and approaches into their teaching practice. Reliance on supplementary primary materials has often been ad hoc and inconsistent. This textbook is our contribution to the Australian perspective of international law, informed by our collective years of teaching and research, particularly in the curriculum at the University of Sydney. In approaching the vast field of international law, we chose to put together an edited collection, to draw on the wealth of scholarly and research expertise of our contributors.

This book is supplemented by a comprehensive set of online instructor resources designed to aid students in their study of the subject. In addition to case extracts and summaries, the resources include study guides, topic summaries, and practice exam and essay/discussion questions, with guided answers. The guided answers are intended to be used by students as scaffolds for formulating their own, more detailed responses, and to prompt critical thinking about this dynamic and engaging subject area.

**Emily Crawford, Alison Pert and Ben Saul**

---

1    See further Ivan A Shearer, 'The Teaching of International Law in Australian Law Schools' (1983) 9(1) *Adelaide Law Review* 61; JR Crawford, 'Teaching and Research in International Law in Australia' (1983) 10(1) *Australian Year Book of International Law* 176; Irene Baghoomians, Emily Crawford and Jacqueline Mowbray, 'The Teaching of Public International Law in Australian Law Schools: 2020 and Beyond' (2002) 43 *Adelaide Law Review* 7.

2    For example, Donald Rothwell et al, *International Law: Cases and Materials with Australian Perspectives* (Cambridge University Press, 3rd ed, 2018); Gillian Triggs, *International Law: Contemporary Principles and Practices* (LexisNexis Butterworths, 2nd ed, 2011); Stephen Hall, *Principles of International Law* (LexisNexis Butterworths, 6th ed, 2019); Anthony Cassimatis, *Public International Law* (Oxford University Press, 2021). Honorary mention should be made of James Crawford's *Brownlie's Principles of Public International Law* (Oxford University Press, 9th ed, 2019), not just because of Crawford's ties to Australia, but also because of the wealth of Australian case law and examples that Crawford draws upon.

# ACKNOWLEDGEMENTS

The editors and Cambridge University Press would like to thank the following for permission to reproduce material in this book.

**Figure 13.1:** © Commonwealth of Australia (Geoscience Australia) 2021. Reproduced under a CC BY 4.0 licence: https://creativecommons.org/licenses/by/4.0/.

**Figure 13.2:** © Commonwealth of Australia (Geoscience Australia) 2021. Reproduced under a CC BY 4.0 licence: https://creativecommons.org/licenses/by/4.0/. This map was produced using the Australian Marine Spatial Information System ('AMSIS') web mapping facility provided by Geoscience Australia. AMSIS incorporates data provided by various Commonwealth government agencies and private sector organisations. Maps produced using AMSIS may also incorporate information provided by end users of AMSIS.

Extracts from JL Brierly, *The Law of Nations*, rev Humphrey Waldock (Clarendon Press, 6th ed, 1963): © Oxford Publishing Limited. Reproduced with permission.

Extracts from Inspector-General of the Australian Defence Force, *Afghanistan Inquiry Report* (November 2020): © Commonwealth of Australia 2020.

Extract from the report of the Australian Human Rights Commission, *Use of Force in Immigration Detention*: © Australian Human Rights Commission 2019, reproduced under Creative Commons Attribution 4.0 International: https://creativecommons.org/licenses/by/4.0/.

Extracts from *Rome Statute of the International Criminal Court*: © ICC-CPI. Reproduced with permission.

Extracts from the *Charter of the United Nations, Final Report to the Prosecutor by the Committee Established to Review the NATO Bombing Campaign against the Federal Republic of Yugoslavia, Marrakesh Agreement Establishing the World Trade Organization, Protocol I Additional to the Geneva Conventions of 12 August 1949*, UN Doc A/56/10, UN Doc A/61/10, UN Doc A/73/10 and *Vienna Convention on the Law of Treaties*: © United Nations.

Extracts from *GATT 1994*: © World Trade Organization. Reproduced with permission.

Extract from *Australian Law Reports* (ALR): originally published by LexisNexis.

Extracts from *Commonwealth Law Reports* (CLR) and *Federal Court Reports* (FCR): reproduced with permission of Thomson Reuters (Professional) Australia Limited, legal.thomson reuters.com.au.

Extracts from *Supreme Court Reports* (SCR): reproduced with the permission of the Supreme Court of Canada.

Extracts from *Law Reports, Queen's Bench* (QB) (Third Series) and *Law Reports, Appeal Cases* (AC) (Third Series): reproduced with permission of the Incorporated Council of Law Reporting for England and Wales.

Extracts from *England and Wales Court of Appeal – Civil Division* (EWCA Civ): © Crown Copyright. Reproduced under the Open Government Licence: https://www.nationalarchives.gov.uk/doc/open-government-licence/version/3/.

Extracts from *International Law Reports* (ILR); ICSID Reports; and Michael Schmitt (ed), *Tallinn Manual 2.0 on the International Law Applicable to Cyber Operations* (Cambridge University Press, 2017): © Cambridge University Press. Reproduced with permission.

Extracts from the *International Court of Justice Reports of Judgments* (ICJ Rep), the Permanent Court of International Justice (PCIJ), the *Statute of the International Court of Justice* (ICJ Statute) and *Declaration Recognising the Jurisdiction of the Court as Compulsory: Australia*: reproduced with permission of the International Court of Justice.

Extracts from Australian Commonwealth legislation: sourced from the Federal Register of Legislation. Reproduced under Creative Commons Attribution 4.0 International. For the latest information on Australian Government law please go to https://www.legislation.gov.au.

*Every effort has been made to trace and acknowledge copyright. The publisher apologises for any accidental infringement and welcomes information that would redress this situation.*

# TABLE OF CASES

*Accordance with International Law of the Unilateral Declaration of Independence in Respect of Kosovo (Advisory Opinion)* [2010] ICJ Rep 403, **118–19**, **126**, **262**

*ADC Affiliate Ltd v Hungary (Award)* (ICSID Arbitral Tribunal, Case No ARB/03/16, 2 October 2006), **205**

*Alabama Claims (United States v Great Britain) (Award)* (1872) 29 RIAA 125, **87**, **242–3**

*Al-Adsani v United Kingdom* (2001) 34 EHRR 273, **176**

*Al-Jedda v United Kingdom* (European Court of Human Rights, Grand Chamber, Application No 2702/08, 7 July 2011), **417**

*Al-Kateb v Godwin* (2004) 219 CLR 562, **99–101**

*Alleged Violations of Sovereign Rights and Maritime Spaces in the Caribbean Sea (Nicaragua v Colombia) (Preliminary Objections)* [2016] ICJ Rep 3, **45**

*Al-Skeini v United Kingdom* (2011) 53 EHRR 18, **272**

*Ambatielos Claim (Greece v United Kingdom) (Award)* (1956) 12 RIAA 83, **208**

*Ameziane v United States* (Inter-American Commission on Human Rights, Merits Report 29/20, 22 April 2020), **272–3**

*Amoco International Finance Corporation v Iran* (1987) 15 Iran-US CTR 189, **205**

*Ampal-American Israel Corporation v Egypt (Decision on Liability and Heads of Loss)* (2022) 20 ICSID Rep 406, **447**

*Anglo-Norwegian Fisheries (United Kingdom v Norway) (Judgment)* [1951] ICJ Rep 116, **41–2**

*Anudo v United Republic of Tanzania* (African Court on Human and Peoples' Rights, Application No 12/2015, 22 March 2018), **284**

*Appeal against the Decision on the Authorisation of an Investigation into the Situation in the Islamic Republic of Afghanistan (Judgment)* (International Criminal Court, Appeals Chamber, Case No ICC-02/17-138, 5 March 2020), **327**

*Applicant A v Minister for Immigration and Ethnic Affairs* (1997) 190 CLR 225, **98**

*Application of the Convention on the Prevention and Punishment of the Crime of Genocide (Bosnia and Herzegovina v Serbia and Montenegro)* (International Court of Justice, General List No 91, 15 April 1994), **121**

*Application of the Convention on the Prevention and Punishment of the Crime of Genocide (Bosnia and Herzegovina v Serbia and Montenegro) (Judgment)* [2007] ICJ Rep 43, **58**, **121**, **186**, **335**

*Application of the Convention on the Prevention and Punishment of the Crime of Genocide (Bosnia and Herzegovina v Yugoslavia) (Preliminary Objections)* [1996] ICJ Rep 595, **44**, **47**

*Application of the Convention on the Prevention and Punishment of the Crime of Genocide (Bosnia and Herzegovina v Yugoslavia (Serbia and Montenegro)) (Provisional Measures)* [1993] ICJ Rep 325, **253**

*Application of the International Convention on the Elimination of All Forms of Racial Discrimination (Georgia v Russian Federation) (Provisional Measures)* [2008] ICJ Rep 353, **260**

*Application of the International Convention on the Elimination of All Forms of Racial Discrimination (Qatar v United Arab Emirates) (Order on 23 July 2018)* [2018] ICJ Rep 406, **260–1**

*Application of the International Convention on the Elimination of All Forms of Racial Discrimination (Qatar v United Arab Emirates) (Preliminary Objections)* [2021] ICJ Rep 71, **70–1**

*Arbitration under the Timor Sea Treaty (Timor-Leste v Australia)* (Permanent Court of Arbitration, Case No 2013-16), **76, 252, 363**

*Arbitration under the Timor Sea Treaty (Timor-Leste v Australia) (II)* (Permanent Court of Arbitration, Case No 2015-42), **252**

*Armed Activities on the Territory of the Congo (Democratic Republic of the Congo v Uganda) (Judgment)* [2005] ICJ Rep 168, **189, 214, 216–17, 222–4, 226–9, 236, 315–16**

*Arrest Warrant of 11 April 2000 (Democratic Republic of the Congo v Belgium) (Judgment)* [2002] ICJ Rep 3, **145, 151, 170–2, 174–5**

*Asian Agricultural Products Ltd v Sri Lanka (Award)* (ICSID Arbitral Tribunal, Case No ARB/87/3, 27 June 1990), **202, 447**

*Asylum (Colombia v Peru) (Judgment)* [1950] ICJ Rep 266, **40–1**

*Attorney-General (Israel) v Eichmann* (1968) 36 ILR 18, **152, 324**

*Attorney-General (UK) v Heinemann Publishers Australia Pty Ltd* (1987) 8 NSWLR 341, **178**

*Attorney-General (UK) v Heinemann Publishers Australia Pty Ltd* (1988) 165 CLR 30, **178**

*Australia – Certain Measures concerning Trademarks, Geographical Indications and Other Plain Packaging Requirements Applicable to Tobacco Products and Packaging*, WTO Cases DS435, DS441, DS458, DS467, **441**

*Australian Competition and Consumer Commission v PT Garuda Indonesia Ltd (No 9)* (2013) 212 FCR 406, **88–9, 106**

*Azurix v Argentina (Award)* (ICSID Arbitral Tribunal, Case No ARB/01/12, 14 July 2006), **448**

*Banković v Belgium (Admissibility)* [2001] ECHR 890, **72**

*Barcelona Traction, Light and Power Company Ltd (Belgium v Spain) (Judgment)* [1970] ICJ Rep 3, **150, 199, 207–8, 259**

*Basfar v Wong* [2022] 3 WLR 208, **160**

*Bayindir v Pakistan (Award)* (ICSID Arbitral Tribunal, Case No ARB/03/29, 27 August 2009), **450**

*Behrami v France; Saramati v France* (European Court of Human Rights, Grand Chamber, Application Nos 71412/01 and 78166/01, Admissibility, 2 May 2007), **417**

*Belhaj v Straw* [2017] AC 964, **178**

*Belilos v Switzerland* (1988) 88 ILR 635, **68, 275**

*Big Brother Watch v United Kingdom* (European Court of Human Rights, Grand Chamber, Application No 58170/13, 25 May 2021), **274, 282–3**

*Bilcon v Canada (Award on Jurisdiction and Liability)* (Permanent Court of Arbitration, Case No 2009-04, 17 March 2015), **452**

*Biwater Gauff (Tanzania) Ltd v Tanzania (Award)* (ICSID Arbitral Tribunal, Case No ARB/05/22, 24 July 2008), **445**

*Boundary Dispute (British Guiana v Venezuela) (Award)* (1899) 28 RIAA 331, **243**

*BP Exploration Co (Libya) Ltd v Libya* (1974) 53 ILR 297, **205**

*Bradley v Commonwealth* (1973) 128 CLR 557, **90–1**

*Caire Claim (France v Mexico) (Award)* (1929) 5 RIAA 516, **184–5**

*Case 002/01 (Appeal Judgment)* (Extraordinary Chambers in the Courts of Cambodia, Supreme Court Chamber, Case No 002/19-09-2007-ECCC-SC, 23 November 2016), **342**

*Case 002/02 (Trial Judgment)* (2020) 59 ILM 159, **335–6**

*Case No 2016 Ga-Hap 505092* (Seoul Central District Court, 8 January 2021), **174**

*Certain Activities Carried out by Nicaragua in the Border Area (Costa Rica v Nicaragua) and Construction of a Road in Costa Rica along the San Juan River (Nicaragua v Costa Rica) (Merits)* [2015] ICJ Rep 665, **218, 380**

*Certain Criminal Proceedings in France (Republic of the Congo v France) (Provisional Measures)* [2003] ICJ Rep 102, **258**

*Certain Expenses of the United Nations (Advisory Opinion)* [1962] ICJ Rep 151, **231, 410, 416, 423**

*Certain German Interests in Polish Upper Silesia (Germany v Poland) (Merits)* [1926] PCIJ (ser A) No 7, **204**

*Certain Norwegian Loans (France v Norway) (Preliminary Objections)* [1957] ICJ Rep 9, **255–6**

*Certain Phosphate Lands in Nauru (Nauru v Australia) (Preliminary Objections)* [1992] ICJ Rep 240, **125, 197, 263**

*Certain Questions of Mutual Assistance in Criminal Matters (Djibouti v France) (Judgment)* [2008] ICJ Rep 177, **58**

*Chow Hung Ching v The Queen* (1948) 77 CLR 449, **103**

*Chung Chi Cheung v The Queen* [1939] AC 160, **103**

*Claim of Finnish Shipowners against Great Britain in Respect of the Use of Certain Finnish Vessels during the War (Finland v United Kingdom) (Award)* (1934) 3 RIAA 1479, **209**

*Clipperton Island (France v Mexico) (Award)* (1932) 26 *American Journal of International Law* 390, **135, 138**

*CME Czech Republic BV (The Netherlands) v Czech Republic (Partial Award of 13 September 2001)* (2006) 9 ICSID Rep 113, **447**

*CMS Gas Transmission Co v Argentina (Award)* (ICSID Arbitral Tribunal, Case No ARB01/8, 12 May 2005), **449**

*Commonwealth v Human Rights and Equal Opportunity Commission* (1999) 95 FCR 218, **291**

*Commonwealth v Tasmania* (1983) 158 CLR 1, **92–4, 397**

*Comptroller-General of Customs v Pharm-A-Care Laboratories Pty Ltd* (2020) 270 CLR 494, **70**

*Continental Shelf (Tunisia v Libyan Arab Jamahiriya) (Judgment)* [1982] ICJ Rep 18, **256**

*Cooper v Stuart* (1886) 14 AC 286, **134**

*Corfu Channel (United Kingdom v Albania) (Merits)* [1949] ICJ Rep 4, **218, 354**

*Corfu Channel (United Kingdom v Albania) (Preliminary Objections)* [1948] ICJ Rep 15, **257–8**

*CPCF v Minister for Immigration and Border Protection* (2015) 255 CLR 514, **355**

*Crystallex International Corporation v Venezuela (Award)* (ICSID Arbitral Tribunal, Case No ARB(AF)/11/2, 4 April 2016), **445**

*Customs Régime between Germany and Austria (Advisory Opinion)* [1931] PCIJ (ser A/B) No 41, **110–11**

*Cyprus v Turkey* (2001) 120 ILR 11, **120**

*Daimler AG v Argentina (Award)* (ICSID Arbitral Tribunal, Case No ARB/05/1, 22 August 2012), **451**

*Delimitation of the Continental Shelf (United Kingdom v France)* (1977) 54 ILR 6, **67–8**

*Delimitation of the Maritime Boundary in the Bay of Bengal (Bangladesh v Myanmar) (Judgment)* [2012] ITLOS Rep 4, **61, 362**

*Delimitation of the Maritime Boundary in the Gulf of Maine Area (Canada v United States of America)* [1984] ICJ Rep 246, **136**

*Democratic Republic of Congo v FG Hemisphere Associates LLC* [2011] HKCFA 42, **165**

*Deutsche Continental Gas-Gesellschaft c État polonais* (1929) 9 Recueil des décisions des tribunaux arbitraux mixtes institués par les traités de paix 336, **109**

*Deutsche Continental Gas-Gesellschaft v Polish State* (1929) 5 ILR 11, **109**

*DG Khan Cement Co Ltd v Government of Punjab* (Supreme Court of Pakistan, Mansoor Ali Shah J, CP1290-L/2019, 2021), **384**

*Diallo (Republic of Guinea v Democratic Republic of the Congo) (Preliminary Objections)* [2007] ICJ Rep 582, **208**, **210**

*Dietrich v The Queen* (1992) 177 CLR 292, **90–1**

*Difference between New Zealand and France concerning the Interpretation or Application of Two Agreements Concluded on 9 July 1986 between the Two States and Which Related to the Problems Arising from the Rainbow Warrior Affair (New Zealand v France) (Decision)* (1990) 20 RIAA 215, **190–1**

*Difference Relating to Immunity from Legal Process of a Special Rapporteur of the Commission on Human Rights (Advisory Opinion)* [1999] ICJ Rep 62, **183**, **412**, **414**

*Differences between New Zealand and France Arising from the Rainbow Warrior Affair (New Zealand v France) (Ruling)* (1986) 19 RIAA 199, **191**, **195**

*Dispute regarding Navigational and Related Rights (Costa Rica v Nicaragua) (Judgment)* [2009] ICJ Rep 213, **71–2**

*East Timor (Portugal v Australia) (Judgment)* [1995] ICJ Rep 90, **126**, **259–60**, **263**

*Ecuador v United States (Award)* (Permanent Court of Arbitration, Case No 2012-5, 29 September 2012), **454**

*Effect of Awards of Compensation Made by the United Nations Administrative Tribunal (Advisory Opinion)* [1954] ICJ Rep 47, **45**, **410**

*Eichmann v Attorney-General (Israel)* (1968) 36 ILR 277, **152**, **155**, **324**

*El Paso v Argentina (Decision on Jurisdiction)* (ICSID Arbitral Tribunal, Case No ARB/03/15, 27 April 2006), **453**

*El Paso Energy International Co v Argentina (Award)* (ICSID Arbitral Tribunal, Case No ARB/03/15, 31 October 2011), **445**

*Electrabel SA v Hungary (Decision on Jurisdiction, Applicable Law and Liability)* (ICSID Arbitral Tribunal, Case No ARB/07/19, 30 November 2012), **449**

*Elettronica Sicula SpA (ELSI) (United States of America v Italy) (Judgment)* [1989] ICJ Rep 15, **209**, **259**, **447**

*Eritrea v Yemen (Award on Territorial Sovereignty and Scope of the Dispute)* (1998) 33 RIAA 209, **138**, **140**

*Eureko BV v Poland (Partial Award)* (Ad Hoc Arbitral Tribunal, 19 August 2005), **453**

*Factory at Chorzów (Germany v Poland) (Jurisdiction) (Judgment No 8)* [1927] PCIJ (ser A) No 9, **45**, **193**, **205**

*Factory at Chorzów (Germany v Poland) (Merits)* [1928] PCIJ (ser A) No 17, **45**

*Fedotova v Russia* (European Court of Human Rights, Third Section, Application No 40792/10, 13 July 2021), **282**

*Fisheries Jurisdiction (Spain v Canada) (Jurisdiction)* [1998] ICJ Rep 432, **219**

*Fisheries Jurisdiction (United Kingdom v Iceland) (Jurisdiction)* [1973] ICJ Rep 3, **79**, **132**

*Freedom and Justice Party v Secretary of State for Foreign and Commonwealth Affairs* [2018] EQCA Civ 1719, **176–7**

*Frontier Dispute (Burkina Faso v Republic of Mali) (Judgment)* [1986] ICJ Rep 554, **131, 137**

*Gabčíkovo-Nagymaros Project (Hungary v Slovakia) (Judgment)* [1997] ICJ Rep 7, **49, 58, 69, 77, 79–81, 131, 190, 192, 380–1, 386**

*Genin v Estonia (Award)* (ICSID Arbitral Tribunal, Case No ARB/99/2, 25 June 2001), **445**

*Glamis Gold Ltd v United States (Award)* (NAFTA Chapter 11 Arbitral Tribunal, IIC 380, 8 June 2009), **201**

*Guyana v Suriname (Award)* (2007) 139 ILR 566, **219, 221**

*Habib v Commonwealth* (2010) 183 FCR 62, **104, 179**

*Handyside v United Kingdom* (1979–80) 1 EHRR 737, **274**

*Hicks v Australia*, HRC Communication No 2005/2010 (19 February 2016), **281**

*Home Frontier and Foreign Missionary Society (United States v Great Britain)* (1920) 6 RIAA 42, **202, 447**

*Horta v Commonwealth* (1994) 181 CLR 183, **94**

*I Congresso del Partido* [1983] AC 244, **166**

*Ickale Insaat v Turkmenistan (Award)* (ICSID Arbitral Tribunal, Case No ARB/10/24, 8 March 2016), **451**

*Institute for Human Rights and Development in Africa v Democratic Republic of the Congo*, ACHPR Communication No 393/10 (9–18 June 2016), **283**

*Intel Corporation Inc v European Commission* (Court of Justice of the European Union, C-413/14 P, ECLI:EU:C:2017:632, 6 September 2017), **149**

*Interhandel (Switzerland v United State of America) (Preliminary Objections)* [1959] ICJ Rep 6, **256**

'International Military Tribunal (Nuremberg), Judgment and Sentences' (1947) 41(1) *American Journal of International Law* 172, **321, 334, 339, 345**

*Interpretation and Application of the 1971 Montreal Convention arising from the Aerial Incident at Lockerbie (Libyan Arab Jamahiriya v United Kingdom) (Preliminary Objections)* [1998] ICJ Rep 9, **230, 419**

*Interpretation of Peace Treaties with Bulgaria, Hungary and Romania (Advisory Opinion) (First Phase)* [1950] ICJ Rep 65, **240, 262**

*Interpretation of the Agreement of 25 March 1951 between the WHO and Egypt (Advisory Opinion)* [1980] ICJ Rep 73, **416**

*Investigation of Certain Incidents Affecting the British Trawler Red Crusader (Report of the Commission of Inquiry)* (1962) 29 RIAA 521, **247**

*Island of Palmas (Netherlands v United States of America) (Award)* (1928) 2 RIAA 829, **47, 130–1, 135, 140, 251**

*Italy v Cuba (Final Award of 1 January 2008)* (2012) 106(2) *American Journal of International Law* 341, **454**

*Jan de Nul NV v Egypt (Award)* (ICSID Arbitral Tribunal, Case No ARB/04/13, 6 November 2008), **186**

*JH v Australia*, CRPD Communication No 35/2016 (20 December 2018), **281**

*Jones v Saudi Arabia* [2007] 1 AC 270, **165, 170, 174–5**

*Jones v United Kingdom* (2017) 168 ILR 364, **170, 176**

*Jorgić*, Bundesverfassungsgericht [German Constitutional Court], 2 BvR 1290/99, 30 April 1999, **336**

*Jorgić v Germany* [2007] III Eur Court HR 263, **336**

*Joyce v Director of Public Prosecutions* [1946] AC 347, **152**

*Jumbunna Coal Mine NL v Victorian Coal Miners' Association* (1908) 6 CLR 309, **99**

*Jurisdictional Immunities of the State (Germany v Italy) (Judgment)* [2012] ICJ Rep 99, **143, 148, 165, 174, 176, 261**

*Jurisdictional Immunities of the State (Germany v Italy) (Order on Application by Hellenic Republic for Permission to Intervene)* [2011] ICJ Rep 494, **261**


*Kartinyeri v Commonwealth* (1998) 195 CLR 337, **99**

*Kasikili/Sedudu Island (Botswana v Namibia) (Judgment)* [1999] ICJ Rep 1045, **136**

*Kiobel v Royal Dutch Petroleum* Co, 569 US 108 (2013), **147–8**

*Kruger v Commonwealth* (1997) 190 CLR 1, **336**

*Kuwait Airways Corporation v Iraq* [2010] 2 SCR 571, **166–7**

*Kuwait Airways Corporation v Iraqi Airways Co (Nos 4 and 5)* [2002] 2 AC 883, **179**


*LaGrand (Germany v United States) (Provisional Measures)* [1999] ICJ Rep 9, **184**

*LaGrand (Germany v United States of America) (Judgment)* [2001] ICJ Rep 466, **58, 71, 192–3, 260**

*Lake Lanoux (Spain v France) (Award)* (1957) 12 RIAA 281, **244**

*Land and Maritime Boundary between Cameroon and Nigeria (Cameroon v Nigeria) (Judgment)* [2002] ICJ Rep 303, **63, 75, 136–7**

*Land and Maritime Boundary between Cameroon and Nigeria (Cameroon v Nigeria) (Preliminary Objections)* [1998] ICJ Rep 275, **241**

*Land, Island and Maritime Frontier Dispute (El Salvador v Honduras) (Application by Nicaragua for Permission to Intervene)* [1990] ICJ Rep 92, **261**

*Land, Island and Maritime Frontier Dispute (El Salvador v Honduras) (Judgment)* [1992] ICJ Rep 351, **131, 139**

*Land Reclamation by Singapore in and around the Straits of Johor (Malaysia v Singapore) (Order of 8 October 2003)* [2003] ITLOS Rep 10, **245**

*Legal Consequences for States of the Continued Presence of South Africa in Namibia (South West Africa) notwithstanding Security Council Resolution 276 (1970) (Advisory Opinion)* [1971] ICJ Rep 16, **125, 128, 226**

*Legal Consequences of the Construction of a Wall in the Occupied Palestinian Territory (Advisory Opinion)* [2004] ICJ Rep 136, **9, 125, 132, 195–6, 229, 262–3, 272, 319**

*Legal Consequences of the Separation of the Chagos Archipelago from Mauritius in 1965 (Advisory Opinion)* [2019] ICJ Rep 95, **123, 126, 132, 263**

*Legal Status of Eastern Greenland (Denmark v Norway) (Judgment)* [1933] PCIJ (ser A/B) No 53, **45, 47, 137–40**

*Legality of the Threat or Use of Nuclear Weapons (Advisory Opinion)* [1996] ICJ Rep 226, **38, 220, 222–3, 263, 303, 305, 319**

*Legality of the Use of Nuclear Weapons in Armed Conflict (Advisory Opinion)* [1996] ICJ Rep 66, **410**

*Legality of Use of Force (Serbia and Montenegro v Belgium)* (International Court of Justice, General List No 105, 10 May 1999), **234**

*Liangsiripasert v United States* [1991] 1 AC 225, **148**

*Loizidou v Turkey* (1997) 23 EHRR 513, **275**

*López Soto v Venezuela (Judgment)* (Inter-American Court of Human Rights, Series C No 362, 26 September 2018), **282**

*Love v Commonwealth* (2020) 270 CLR 152, **90**

*Mabo v Queensland (No 2)* (1992) 175 CLR 1, **104**, **134**

*'Maduro Board' of the Central Bank of Venezuela v 'Guaidó Board' of the Central Bank of Venezuela* [2022] 2 WLR 167, **178**

*Maffezini v Spain (Decision on Jurisdiction)* (ICSID Arbitral Tribunal, Case No 97/7, 25 January 2000), **451**

*Maloney v The Queen* (2013) 252 CLR 168, **98**

*Mamidoil Jetoil Greek Petroleum Products SA v Albania (Award)* (ICSID Arbitral Tribunal, Case No ARB/11/24, 30 March 2015), **447**

*Maritime Delimitation and Territorial Questions (Qatar v Bahrain) (Jurisdiction and Admissibility)* [1994] ICJ Rep 112, **59–60**

*Maritime Delimitation in the Black Sea (Romania v Ukraine) (Judgment)* [2009] ICJ Rep 61, **362**

*Maritime Delimitation in the Indian Ocean (Somalia v Kenya) (Preliminary Objections)* [2017] ICJ Rep 3, **58–9**, **61**, **370**

*Mavrommatis Palestine Concessions (Greece v Great Britain) (Jurisdiction)* [1924] PCIJ (ser A) No 2, **198–9**, **240**

*Mergé Claim* (1955) 22 ILR 443, **206–7**

*Metalclad Corporation v Mexico (Award)* (ICSID Arbitral Tribunal, Case No ARB(AF)/97/1, 30 August 2000), **204**, **449**

*Methanex Corporation v United States (Final Award on Jurisdiction and Merits)* (2005) 44 ILM 1345, **450**

*Micula v Romania (Final Award)* (ICSID Arbitral Tribunal, Case No ARB/05/20, 11 December 2013), **446**

*Milirrpum v Nabalco Pty Ltd* (1971) 17 FLR 141, **134**

*Military and Paramilitary Activities in and against Nicaragua (Nicaragua v United States of America) (Merits)* [1986] ICJ Rep 14, **36–7**, **40**, **43**, **57**, **119**, **185–6**, **216–18**, **221–4**, **226–7**, **236–7**, **257**

*Military and Paramilitary Activities in and against Nicaragua (Nicaragua v United States of America) (Provisional Measures)* [1984] ICJ Rep 169, **260**

*Minister for Foreign Affairs v Magno* (1992) 37 FCR 298, **162–3**

*Minister for Immigration and Border Protection v WZARH* (2015) 256 CLR 326, **97**

*Minister for Immigration and Ethnic Affairs v Teoh* (1995) 183 CLR 273, **97**, **100**

*Minister for Immigration and Multicultural and Indigenous Affairs v B* (2004) 219 CLR 365, **100**

*Minquiers and Ecrehos (France v United Kingdom) (Judgment)* [1953] ICJ Rep 47, **131**, **140**

*Mondev International v United States (Award)* (ICSID Arbitral Tribunal, Case No ARB(AF)/99/2, 11 October 2002), **445**

*Monetary Gold Removed from Rome (Italy v France) (Preliminary Objection)* [1954] ICJ Rep 19, **259**

*Mortensen v Peters* (1906) 14 Scots LTR 227, **99**

*Mothers of Srebrenica v The Netherlands* (Dutch Supreme Court, ECLI:NL:HR:2012:BW1999, Judgment, 13 April 2012), **415**

*Mothers of Srebrenica v The Netherlands* (Hague District Court, ECLI:NL:RBDHA:2014:8562, Judgment, 16 July 2014), **418**

*Moti v The Queen* (2011) 245 CLR 456, **155**

*Neer (United States v Mexico) (Award)* (1926) 4 RIAA 60, **200–2, 209, 443, 445**

*Nestlé USA v Doe*, 141 S Ct 1931 (2021), **147**

*Netherlands v Stichting Mothers of Srebrenica* (Dutch Supreme Court, ECLI:NL:HR:2019:1284, Judgment, 19 July 2019), **418**

*New South Wales v Commonwealth* (1975) 135 CLR 337, **351**

*North Sea Continental Shelf (Federal Republic of Germany v Denmark) (Merits)* [1969] ICJ Rep 3, **37–9, 42–3, 45, 140, 357, 361**

*Northern Cameroons (Cameroon v United Kingdom) (Preliminary Objections)* [1963] ICJ Rep 15, **240, 258**

*Norwegian Shipowners' Claims (Norway v United States) (Award)* (1922) 1 RIAA 307, **251**

*Nottebohm (Liechtenstein v Guatemala) (Judgment)* [1955] ICJ Rep 4, **206**

*Nottebohm (Liechtenstein v Guatemala) (Second Phase)* [1955] ICJ Rep 4, **259**

*Noyes (United States v Mexico)* (1933) 6 RIAA 308, **447**

*Nuclear Tests (Australia v France) (Judgment)* [1974] ICJ Rep 253, **49–50, 240, 258–9, 263**

*Nuhanović v The Netherlands* (Dutch Court of Appeal, Interim Judgment, 5 July 2011 and 26 June 2012), **418**

*Nulyarimma v Thompson* (1999) 96 FCR 153, **104–5, 329, 336, 338**


*Obligations concerning Negotiations Relating to Cessation of the Nuclear Arms Race and to Nuclear Disarmament (Marshall Islands v United Kingdom) (Preliminary Objections)* [2016] ICJ Rep 833, **241**

*Oil Platforms (Islamic Republic of Iran v United States of America) (Merits)* [2003] ICJ Rep 161, **57, 72, 189, 222–5, 227**

*Oppenheimer v Cattermole* [1976] AC 249, **179**


*Pantechniki SA v Albania (Award)* (ICSID Arbitral Tribunal, Case No ARB/07/21, 30 July 2009), **447**

*Parking Privileges for Diplomats* (1971) 70 ILR 396, **34**

*Philip Morris Brands Sàrl v Uruguay (Award)* (ICSID Arbitral Tribunal, Case No ARB/10/7, 8 July 2016), **446**

*Pious Fund Case (United States v Mexico) (Award)* (1902) 9 RIAA 1, **251**

*Plama Consortium Ltd v Bulgaria (Decision on Jurisdiction)* (ICSID Arbitral Tribunal, Case No ARB/03/24, 8 February 2005), **451**

*Polites v Commonwealth* (1945) 70 CLR 60, **99, 103**

*Polyukhovich v Commonwealth* (1991) 172 CLR 501, **153**

*Project Blue Sky v Australian Broadcasting Authority* (1998) 194 CLR 355, **96**

*Prosecutor v Akayesu (Judgment)* (International Criminal Tribunal for Rwanda, Trial Chamber I, Case No ICTR-96-4-T, 2 September 1998), **302, 325**

*Prosecutor v Al-Bashir (Decision on the Prosecution's Application for a Warrant of Arrest)* (International Criminal Court, Pre-Trial Chamber I, Case No ICC-02/05-01/09-3, 4 March 2002), **343**

*Prosecutor v Al-Bashir (Second Decision on the Prosecution's Application for a Warrant of Arrest)* (International Criminal Court, Pre-Trial Chamber I, Case No ICC-02/05-01/09-95, 12 July 2010), **336, 343**

*Prosecutor v Al Mahdi (Judgment and Sentence)* (International Criminal Court, Trial Chamber VIII, Case No ICC-01/12-01/15-171, 27 September 2016), **317, 328**

*Prosecutor v Bemba (Corrected Version of Prosecution's Closing Brief)* (International Criminal Court, Office of the Prosecutor, Case No ICC-01/05-01/08-3079-Corr-Red, 22 April 2016), **344**

*Prosecutor v Bemba (Judgment on the Appeal against Trail Chamber III's 'Judgment Pursuant to Article 74 of the Statute')* (International Criminal Court, Appeals Chamber, Case No ICC-01/05-01/08-3636-Red, 8 December 2018), **344**

*Prosecutor v Bemba (Judgment Pursuant to Article 74 of the Statute)* (International Criminal Court, Trial Chamber III, Case No ICC-01/05-01/08, 21 March 2016), **313**

*Prosecutor v Bemba (Trial Judgment)* (International Criminal Court, Trial Chamber III, Case No ICC-01/05001/08-3343, 21 March 2016), **344**

*Prosecutor v Blagojević (Judgment)* (International Criminal Tribunal for the Former Yugoslavia, Trial Chamber I, Case No IT-02-60-T, 17 January 2005), **335**

*Prosecutor v Chui (Judgment on the Prosecutor's Appeal against the Decision of Trial Chamber II Entitled 'Judgment Pursuant to Article 74 of the Statute')* (International Criminal Court, Appeals Chamber, Case No ICC-01/04-02/12-271-Corr, 7 April 2015), **328**

*Prosecutor v Gbabgo (Judgment in the Appeal of the Prosecutor against Trial Chamber I's Decision on the No Case to Answer Motions)* (International Criminal Court, Appeals Chamber, Case No ICC-02/11-01/15-1400, 31 March 2021), **328**

*Prosecutor v Katanga* (International Criminal Court, Trial Chamber II, Case No ICC-01/04-01/07-3436-tENG, 7 March 2014), **328, 342**

*Prosecutor v Katanga (Decision on the Confirmation of Charges)* (International Criminal Court, Pre-Trial Chamber I, Case No ICC-01/04-01/07-717, 30 September 2008), **342**

*Prosecutor v Katanga (Judgment on the Appeal against the Oral Decision of Trial Chamber II of 12 June 2009 on the Admissibility of the Case)* (International Criminal Court, Appeals Chamber, Case No ICC-01/04-01/07-1497, 25 September 2009), **327**

*Prosecutor v Kenyatta (Appeal Judgment on Admissibility)* (International Criminal Court, Appeals Chamber, Case No ICC-01/09-02/11-274, 30 August 2011), **327**

*Prosecutor v Krajišnik (Judgment)* (International Criminal Tribunal for the Former Yugoslavia, Trial Chamber I, Case No IT-00-39-T, 27 September 2006), **335**

*Prosecutor v Krstić (Appeal Judgment)* (International Criminal Tribunal for the Former Yugoslavia, Appeals Chamber, Case No IT-98-33-A, 19 April 2004), **335**

*Prosecutor v Krstić (Judgment)* (International Criminal Tribunal for the Former Yugoslavia, Trial Chamber, Case No IT-98-33-T, 2 August 2001), **335**

*Prosecutor v Kupreškić (Judgment)* (International Criminal Tribunal for the Former Yugoslavia, Appeals Chamber, Case No IT-95-16-T, 14 January 2000), **305**

*Prosecutor v Limaj (Judgment)* (International Criminal Tribunal for the Former Yugoslavia, Trial Chamber II, Case No IT-03-66-T, 30 November 2005), **299**

*Prosecutor v Lubanga (Judgment on the Appeal against Conviction)* (International Criminal Court, Appeals Chamber, Case No ICC-01/04-01/06-3121-Red, 2 December 2014), **328**

*Prosecutor v Nahimana (Judgment)* (International Criminal Tribunal for Rwanda, Appeals Chamber, Case No ICTR-99-52-A, 28 November 2007), **325**

*Prosecutor v Ntaganda (Judgment on Appeal against the Decision of Trial Chamber VI of 8 July 2019 Entitled 'Judgment')* (International Criminal Court, Appeals Chamber, Case No ICC-01/04-02/06-2666-Red, 20 March 2021), **328**

*Prosecutor v Ongwen (Appeal Judgment)* (International Criminal Court, Appeals Chamber, Case No ICC-02/04-01/15-2022-Red, 15 December 2022), **328**

*Prosecutor v Ongwen (Trial Judgment)* (International Criminal Court, Trial Chamber IX, Case No ICC-02/04-01/15-1762-Red, 4 February 2021), **344**

*Prosecutor v Strugar (Judgment)* (International Criminal Tribunal for the Former Yugoslavia, Appeals Chamber, Case No IT-01-42-A, 17 July 2008), **309**

*Prosecutor v Tadić (Appeal against Conviction)* (1999) 124 ILR 61, **121, 301, 332, 341**

*Prosecutor v Tadić (Decision on the Defence Motion for Interlocutory Appeal on Jurisdiction)* (International Criminal Tribunal for the Former Yugoslavia, Appeals Chamber, Case No IT-94-1, 2 October 1995), **298–9, 301–3, 317, 331**

*Prosecutor v Tadić (Opinion and Judgment)* (International Criminal Tribunal for the Former Yugoslavia, Trial Chamber, Case No IT-94-1-T, 7 May 1997), **299**

*PT Garuda Indonesia Ltd v Australian Competition and Consumer Commission* (2011) 192 FCR 393, **169**

*PT Garuda Indonesia Ltd v Australian Competition and Consumer Commission* (2012) 247 CLR 240, **169**

*Public Committee against Torture in Israel v Israel* (Supreme Court of Israel, Case No HCJ 769/02, 14 December 2006), **309**

*Pulp Mills on the River Uruguay (Argentina v Uruguay) (Judgment)* [2010] ICJ Rep 14, **59, 245, 380**

*Questions Relating to the Obligation to Prosecute or Extradite (Belgium v Senegal) (Judgment)* [2012] ICJ Rep 422, **44, 70, 87, 154, 197–8**

*Questions Relating to the Seizure and Detention of Certain Documents and Data (Timor-Leste v Australia)* [2015] ICJ Rep 572, **76**

*Quiborax SA v Bolivia (Award)* (ICSID Arbitral Tribunal, Case No ARB/06/2, 16 September 2015), **446**

*R v Bow Street Metropolitan Stipendiary Magistrate; Ex parte Pinochet Ugarte (No 3)* [2000] 1 AC 147, **48, 174–5**

*R v Disun* (2003) 27 WAR 146, **103**

*R v Jones* [2007] 1 AC 136, **105**

*R v Turnbull; Ex parte Petroff* (1971) 17 FLR 438, **162**

*R (Abbasi) v Secretary of State for Foreign and Commonwealth Affairs* [2002] EWCA Civ 1598, **200**

*R (Al Rawi) v Secretary of State for Foreign and Commonwealth Affairs* [2008] QB 289, **200**

*R (Freedom and Justice Party) v Secretary of State for Foreign and Commonwealth Affairs* [2018] EWCA Civ 1719, **49**

*Re Al M (Immunities)* [2021] EWHC 660 (Fam), **173**

*Re Bo Xilai* (2005) 128 ILR 713, **173**

*Re Minister for Immigration and Multicultural Affairs; Ex parte Lam* (2003) 214 CLR 1, **90, 97**

*Re Mofaz* (2004) 128 ILR 709, **173**

*Re Secession of Quebec* [1998] 2 SCR 217, **123–6, 128**

*Re Thompson; Ex parte Nulyarimma* (1998) 136 ACTR 9, **338**

*Re Westinghouse Electric Corporation Uranium Contract Litigation*, 563 F 2d 992 (10th Cir, 1977), **149**

*Reference re Secession of Quebec* (1998) 115 ILR 536, **48**

*Reparation for Injuries Suffered in the Service of the United Nations (Advisory Opinion)* [1949] ICJ Rep 174, **8, 404, 407–11, 416**

*Request for an Advisory Opinion Submitted by the Sub-Regional Fisheries Commission (Advisory Opinion)* [2015] ITLOS Rep 4, **364, 369**

*Request for Authorisation of an Investigation Pursuant to Article 15* (International Criminal Court, Office of the Prosecutor, Case No ICC-02/17-7-Red, 20 November 2017), **327**

*Reservations to the Convention on the Prevention and Punishment of the Crime of Genocide (Advisory Opinion)* [1951] ICJ Rep 15, **66**

*Responsibilities and Obligations of States Sponsoring Persons and Entities with Respect to Activities in the Area (Advisory Opinion)* [2011] ITLOS Rep 10, **366, 368, 379**

*Right of Passage over Indian Territory (Portugal v India)* [1960] ICJ Rep 6, **41**

*Rights of Jurisdiction of United States in the Bering's Sea and the Preservation of Fur Seals (United States v United Kingdom) (Award)* (1893) 28 RIAA 263, **243**

*Rio Tinto plc v Sarei*, 569 US 945 (2013), **147**

*Roberts (United States v Mexico)* (1926) 4 RIAA 77, **201, 209, 443, 445**


*Salem (Egypt v United States)* (1932) 2 RIAA 1161, **206**

*Salini Costruttori SpA v Jordan (Decision on Jurisdiction)* (ICSID Arbitral Tribunal, Case No ARB/02/13, 29 November 2004), **451**

*Saluka Investments BV v Czech Republic (Partial Award)* (ICSID Arbitral Tribunal, Case No 2001-04, 17 March 2006), **210, 446–50**

*Sandline International Inc v Papua New Guinea* (2000) 117 ILR 552, **87–8**

*Saudi Arabia v Arabian American Oil Company (Aramco)* (1963) 27 ILR 117, **205**

*Seizure and Detention of Certain Documents and Data (Timor-Leste v Australia) (Provisional Measures)* [2014] ICJ Rep 147, **260–1**

*SGS v Pakistan (Decision on Jurisdiction)* (ICSID Arbitral Tribunal, Case No ARB/01/13, 6 August 2003), **452**

*SGS SA v Philippines (Decision on Jurisdiction)* (ICSID Arbitral Tribunal, Case No ARB/02/6, 29 January 2004), **452–3**

*SH v Australia*, CAT Communication No 761/2016 (17 January 2019), **281**

*Siemens AG v Argentina* (ICSID Arbitral Tribunal, Case No ARB/02/8, 3 August 2004), **451**

*Siemens AG v Argentina (Award)* (ICSID Arbitral Tribunal, Case No ARB/02/8, 6 February 2007), **448**

*Simoncioni v Repubblica Federale di Germania*, Judgment No 238/2014, Corte Costituzionale [Italian Constitutional Court], 29 October 2014, **173**

*Simsek v MacPhee* (1982) 148 CLR 636, **90**

*Snedden v Minister for Justice* (2014) 230 FCR 82, **156**

*Somalia v Woodhouse, Drake & Carey (Suisse) SA* (1992) 94 ILR 609, **110**

*South China Sea Arbitration (Republic of the Philippines v People's Republic of China) (Award)* (Permanent Court of Arbitration, Case No 2013-19, 12 July 2016), **22, 349–50**

*South China Sea Arbitration (Republic of Philippines v People's Republic of China) (Award on Jurisdiction and Admissibility)* (Permanent Court of Arbitration, Case No 2013-19, 29 October 2015), **59**

*South West Africa (Ethiopia v South Africa) (Preliminary Objections)* [1962] ICJ Rep 319, **240–1**

*South West Africa (Ethiopia v South Africa) (Second Phase)* [1966] ICJ Rep 6, **259**

*Southern Bluefin Tuna (New Zealand v Japan) (Provisional Measures)* [1999] ITLOS Rep 280, **367**

*Sovereignty over Pedra Branca/Palau Batu Puteh, Middle Rocks and South Ledge (Malaysia v Singapore) (Judgment)* [2008] ICJ Rep 12, **133, 136**

*Sovereignty over Pulau Ligitan and Pulau Sipadan (Indonesia v Malaysia) (Application by the Philippines for Permission to Intervene)* [2001] ICJ Rep 575, **261**

*Sovereignty over Pulau Ligitan and Pulau Sipadan (Indonesia v Malaysia) (Judgment)* [2002] ICJ Rep 625, **138**

*SP v Australia*, CAT Communication No 718/2015 (26 December 2019), **281**

*SS 'Lotus' (France v Turkey) (Judgment)* [1927] PCIJ (ser A) No 10, **18, 143–6, 148–9, 151, 364**

*Starrett Housing Corporation v Iran* (1983) 4 Iran US CTR 122, **204**

*State v Ebrahim* (1991) 31 ILM 888, **155**

*State Obligations concerning Change of Name, Gender Identity, and Rights Derived from a Relationship between Same-Sex Couples (Advisory Opinion)* (Inter-American Court of Human Rights, Series A No 24, 24 November 2017), **282**

*State Obligations in Relation to the Environment in the Context of the Protection and Guarantee of the Rights to Life and to Personal Integrity (Advisory Opinion)* (Inter-American Court of Human Rights, Series A No 23, 15 November 2017), **273, 282**

*Stichting Mothers of Srebrenica v The Netherlands* (European Court of Human Rights, Section III, Application No 65521/12, Decision, 11 June 2013, **415**

*Strabag SE v Libya (Award)* (ICSID Arbitral Tribunal, Case No ARB(AF)/15/1, 29 June 2020), **447**

*Sunday Times v United Kingdom* (1980) EHRR 317, **272**

*SWR v Australia*, CAT Communication No 855/2017 (10 December 2019), **281**


*Tecmed v Mexico (Award)* (ICSID Arbitral Tribunal, Case No ARB(AF)/00/2, 29 May 2003), **445**

*Teinver SA v Argentina (Decision on Jurisdiction)* (ICSID Arbitral Tribunal, Case No ARB/11/20, 3 July 2013), **451**

*Temple of Preah Vihear (Cambodia v Thailand) (Merits)* [1962] ICJ Rep 6, **45, 75, 140**

*Territorial Dispute (Libyan Arab Jamahiriya v Chad) (Judgment)* [1994] ICJ Rep 6, **71**

*Texaco Overseas Petroleum Co v Libya (Merits)* (1978) 17 ILM 1, **10, 35**

*The 'Enrica Lexie' Incident (Italy v India) (Award)* (Permanent Court of Arbitration, Case No 2015-28, 21 May 2020), **176**

*The Institution of Asylum and Its Recognition as a Human Right in the Inter-American Protection System (Advisory Opinion)* (Inter-American Court of Human Rights, Series A No OC-25, 30 May 2018), **162**

*The M/V Saiga (No 2) (St Vincent and the Grenadines v Guinea) (Judgment)* [1999] ITLOS Rep 10, **357**

*The M/V Virginia G (Panama v Guinea-Bissau) (Judgment)* [2014] ITLOS Rep 4, **357, 364**

*The Netherlands v Nuhanović* (Dutch Supreme Court, Case No 12/03324, Judgment, 6 September 2013), **417–18**

*The Paquete Habana*, 175 US 677 (1900), **47**

*The Volga (Russian Federation v Australia) (Prompt Release)* [2002] ITLOS Rep 10, **356**

*Timor Sea Conciliation (Timor-Leste v Australia) (Report and Recommendations)* (Permanent Court of Arbitration, Case No 2016-10, 9 May 2018), **249, 251, 363**

*Tinoco (Great Britain v Costa Rica)* (1923) 1 RIAA 369, **116**

*Toonen v Australia*, HRC Communication No 488/1992 (31 March 1994), **280**

*Trail Smelter (United States of America v Canada) (Awards)* (1938-1941) 3 RIAA 1905, **378**

*Trendtex Trading Corporation v Central Bank of Nigeria* [1977] QB 529, **102**


*UAB E Energija (Lithuania) v Latvia (Award)* (ICSID Arbitral Tribunal, Case No ARB/12/33, 22 December 2017), **448**

*United Parcel Service Inc v Canada (Merits)* (North American Free Trade Agreement Chapter 11 Arbitral Tribunal, 24 May 2007), **451**

*United States v Alvarez Machain*, 504 US 655 (1992), **155**

*United States v Benitez*, 741 F 2d 1312 (1984), **151–2**

*United States v Yunis*, 924 F 2d 1086 (1991), **151**

*United States Diplomatic and Consular Staff in Tehran (United States of America v Iran) (Judgment)* [1980] ICJ Rep 3, **186, 194, 241**

*Ure v Commonwealth* (2016) 236 FCR 458, **45–6, 135**

*VCL v United Kingdom* (European Court of Human Rights, Fourth Section, Application Nos 77587/12 and 74603/12, 16 February 2021), **282**

*Victoria v Commonwealth* (1996) 187 CLR 416, **92, 112**

*VM v Australia*, CAT Communication No 723/2015 (21 August 2019), **281**

*Waite v Germany; Beer v Germany* (European Court of Human Rights, Grand Chamber, Application Nos 26083/94 and 28934/95, Judgment, 18 February 1999), **415**

*Ward v The Queen* (1980) 142 CLR 308, **148**

*Waste Management v Mexico (No 2) (Award)* (ICSID Arbitral Tribunal, Case No ARB(AF)/00/2, 30 April 2004), **445–6**

*Western Sahara (Advisory Opinion)* [1975] ICJ Rep 12, **123, 133–4**

*Whaling in the Antarctic (Australia v Japan) (Judgment)* [2014] ICJ Rep 226, **71, 73, 261, 263, 368–9**

*XYZ v Commonwealth* (2006) 227 CLR 532, **150**

*Youmans (United States v Mexico)* (1926) 4 RIAA 110, **202**

*Yugoslavia Peace Conference Opinion No 1* (1991) 92 ILR 162, **110**

*Yugoslavia Peace Conference Opinion No 2* (1991) 92 ILR 167, **128**

*Yugoslavia Peace Conference Opinion No 3* (1992) 92 ILR 170, **131**

*Yugoslavia Peace Conference Opinion No 8* (1992) 92 ILR 199, **110**

*Yugoslavia Peace Conference Opinion No 11* (1993) 96 ILR 719, **118**

*Zhang v Zemin* (2010) 243 FLR 299, **170**

*Zongo v Burkina Faso* (African Court on Human and Peoples' Rights, Application No 13/2011, 28 March 2014), **283**

# TABLE
# OF STATUTES

## Australia

*Acts Interpretation Act 1901*, **98**
  s 15AB(1), **98**
  s 15AB(2), **98**
*Administrative Decisions (Judicial Review) Act 1977*, **291**
*Age Discrimination Act 2004*, **287**
*Aged Care Legislation Amendment (Royal Commission Response No 1) Principles 2021*, **289**
*Air Services Act 1995*
  s 9(3), **96**
*Australia Act 1986*, **113**
*Australian Human Rights Commission Act 1986*, **95**
  s 3(1), **290**
  s 11, **95**
  s 11(f), **290**
  s 11(1), **290**
  s 11(1)(aa), **290**
  s 11(1)(f), **290**
  s 29, **290**
  s 31(b), **290**
*Autonomous Sanctions Act 2011*, **231**
*Charter of the United Nations Act 1945*, **90**
*Chemical Weapons (Prohibition) Act 1994*
  s 95(2), **97**
*Civil Aviation Act 1988*
  s 11, **96**
*Coastal Waters (State Powers) Act 1980*, **351**
*Coastal Waters (State Title) Act 1980*, **351**
*Constitution*, **84, 100, 287, 397**
  s 51, **86, 92**
  s 51(i), **92**

  s 51(vi), **99**
  s 51(xix), **90, 99**
  s 51(xxix), **92, 351**
  s 61, **86, 92**
*Crimes (Aviation) Act 1991*, **95**
*Crimes (Child Sex Tourism) Amendment Act 1994*, **150**
*Criminal Code Act 1995*, **329**
  s 228, **297**
  sch 1 div 14, **149**
  sch 1 divs 14–16, **149**
  sch 1 div 15, **149**
  sch 1 div 104, **150**
  sch 1 s 15.4, **329**
  sch 1 s 16.2, **149**
  sch 1 s 80.4, **152**
  sch 1 s 91.7, **152**
  sch 1 s 91.10, **152**
  sch 1 s 91.14, **152**
  sch 1 s 268, **91**
  sch 1 s 268.117(1), **329**
  sch 1 s 268.121(1), **329**
  sch 1 s 268.35, **308**
  sch 1 s 268.77, **308**
*Customs Act 1901*
  s 268SK, **96**
*Diplomatic Privileges and Immunities Act 1967*, **96, 158**
  s 7, **158**
  s 7(1), **96**
  s 11, **161**
*Enhancing Online Safety Act 2015*
  s 12(1), **97**
*Environment Protection (Sea Dumping) Act 1981*
  s 19(8A), **97**

*Environment Protection and Biodiversity*
    *Conservation Act 1999*, **397**
  s 3A, **382**
  s 137, **97**
  ss 137–140, **97**
*Extradition Act 1998*, **156**
*Fisheries Management Act 1991*, **369**
*Foreign Proceedings (Excess of Jurisdiction)*
    *Act 1984*, **149**
  ss 9–14, **149**
*Foreign States Immunities Act 1985*, **165**
  s 3, **168–9**
  s 3(1), **168–9**
  s 3(3), **169**
  s 3(3)(b), **173**
  s 3(3)(c), **170**
  s 9, **167, 173**
  ss 10–20, **167**
  s 11(1), **167**
  s 11(3), **167**
  s 12(1), **167**
  s 13, **167**
  s 36, **173**
*Geneva Conventions Act 1957*, **297**
  s 15, **314**
*Genocide Convention Act 1949*, **91**
*Human Rights (Parliamentary Scrutiny) Act*
    *2011*, **88, 289**
  s 3(1), **289**
  s 7(a), **289**
*Human Rights (Sexual Conduct) Act 1994*
  s 4, **280**
*International Criminal Court Act 2002*, **326**
*International Criminal Court (Consequential*
    *Amendments) Act 2002*, **326**
*Maritime Powers Act 2013*, **355**
*Migration Act 1958*, **100**
*National Greenhouse and Energy Reporting*
    *Act 2007*, **96**
*Nuclear Non-Proliferation (Safeguards) Act*
    *1987*
  s 70, **97**
*Protection of the Environment*
    *Administration Act 1991*
  s 6, **382**
*Quality of Care Amendment (Minimising the*
    *Use of Restraints) Principles 2019*, **289**

*Racial Discrimination Act, 1975*, **98, 287**
*Seas and Submerged Lands Act 1973*,
    **351**
  s 6, **351**
  s 12, **358**
*Sex Discrimination Act 1984*, **287**
*Statute of Westminster Adoption Act 1942*,
    **113**
*Telecommunications Act 1997*
  s 580, **97**
*World Heritage Properties Conservation Act*
    *1983*, **93, 397**

**AUSTRALIAN CAPITAL TERRITORY**
*Human Rights Act 2004*, **95, 287**
  s 32, **288**
  s 40B, **288**
  s 40C, **288**

**NEW SOUTH WALES**
*Crimes Act 1900*
  s 10B(3), **149**
  s 10C, **149**

**QUEENSLAND**
*Human Rights Act 2019*, **95, 287**
  art 53, **288**
  s 54, **288**
  s 58, **288**
  s 59, **288**

**TASMANIA**
*Criminal Code Amendment Act 1997*
  s 4, **280**
  s 5, **280**

**VICTORIA**
*Charter of Human Rights and Responsibilities*
    *Act 2006*, **95, 287**
  s 36, **288**
  s 38, **288**
  s 39, **288**

**Denmark**

*Act on Greenland Self-Government 2009*, **133**

## European Union

*Council Regulation (EC) No 2271/96 of 22
November 1996 Protecting against the
Effects of the Extra-Territorial
Application of Legislation Adopted by
a Third Country,* **149**

## France

*Code de l'environnement*
art L.110-1(II)(9), **385**
*Declaration of the Rights of Man and of the
Citizen,* **266**
*La Constitution du 4 octobre 1958*
art 55, **84**

## Papua New Guinea

*Constitution*
s 200, **87**

## Singapore

*State Immunity Act 1979,* **165, 167**
s 16, **169**
s 16(2), **169**

## South Africa

*Constitution of the Republic of South Africa
Act 1996*
s 39(1)(b), **100**

s 231(4), **85**
s 232, **84–5**

## United Kingdom

*Bill of Rights,* **266**
*Commonwealth of Australia Constitution Act
1900,* **111**
*Human Rights Act 1998,* **286**
*Protecting against the Effects of the
Extraterritorial Application of Third
Country Legislation (Amendment)
(EU Exit) Regulations 2020,* **149**
*Protection of Trading Interests Act 1980,*
**149**
*State Immunity Act 1978,* **165, 167**
s 14, **169**
*Statute of Westminster 1931,* **113**

## United States of America

*Alien Tort Claims Act of 1789,* **146–7**
*Constitution,* **266**
art VI, **84**
*Foreign Sovereign Immunities Act of 1976,*
**165**
*Sherman Antitrust Act of 1890,* **149**

### CALIFORNIA

*California Global Warming Solutions Act of
2006,* **385**

# TABLE OF TREATIES AND OTHER INTERNATIONAL INSTRUMENTS

*Activation of the Jurisdiction of the Court over the Crime of Aggression*, **326, 340**

*Additional Protocol to the American Convention on Human Rights in the Area of Economic, Social and Cultural Rights*, **271**
  art 11, **387**

*Additional Protocol to the Convention on Prohibitions or Restrictions on the Use of Certain Conventional Weapons Which May Be Deemed to Be Excessively Injurious or to Have Indiscriminate Effects (Protocol (IV), Entitled Protocol on Blinding Laser Weapons*, **296**

*Additional Protocol to the European Social Charter Providing for a System of Collective Complaints*, **283**

*African Charter on Human and Peoples' Rights*, **271, 283, 386**
  arts 19–24, **271–2**
  arts 27–29, **271**
  art 30, **283**
  arts 47–52, **283**
  arts 55–59, **283**
  art 62, **283**

*African Convention on the Conservation of Nature and Natural Resources*, **376**

*Agreement between Australia and the Republic of Poland on the Reciprocal Promotion and Protection of Investments*
  art 10, **452**

*Agreement between Australia and Timor-Leste on Taxation Information Exchange*, **96**

*Agreement between the Government of Australia and the Government of Hong Kong for the Promotion and Protection of Investments*
  art 10, **454**

*Agreement between the Government of the Commonwealth of Australia and the Government of the Republic of Indonesia for Air Services between and beyond Their Respective Territory*, **88**

*Agreement between the Republic of Indonesia and the Kingdom of the Netherlands concerning West New Guinea (West Irian)*, **124**

*Agreement between the United Kingdom and the Republic of Sri Lanka for the Promotion and Protection of Investments*, **452**

*Agreement between the United Nations and the Government of Sierra Leone on the Establishment of a Special Court for Sierra Leone*
  art 1, **330**

*Agreement between the United Nations and the Royal Government of Cambodia concerning the Prosecution under Cambodian Law of Crimes Committed during the Period of Democratic Kampuchea*, **330**

*Agreement for the Implementation of the Provisions of the United Nations Convention on the Law of the Sea Relating to the Conservation and Management of Straddling Fish Stocks and Highly Migratory Fish Stocks*, **348**

    art 5(d), **370**
    art 5(e), **370**
    art 6, **370**

*Agreement for the Prosecution and Punishment of the Major War Criminals of the European Axis*, **324, 333**

    art 1(2), **334**
    art 1(2)[1], **334**
    art 1(2)[2], **334**
    art 1(2)[3], **334**
    art 6, **323**
    art 6(a), **339**
    art 8, **345**

*Agreement for the Surrender of Accused and Convicted Persons between the Government of Australia and the Government of Hong Kong*, **79**

*Agreement on Trade-Related Aspects of Intellectual Property*

    annex IC, **437**
    arts 1–12, **438**
    art 2(1), **438**
    art 3, **438**
    art 4, **438**
    art 7, **438**
    art 9, **438**
    arts 9–40, **437**
    art 10, **438**
    art 11, **438**
    art 12, **438**
    art 14, **438**
    art 16, **439**
    art 18, **439**
    art 19, **438**
    arts 27–34, **439**
    art 35, **439**
    arts 35–38, **439**
    art 39, **439**
    arts 41–50, **439**
    Preamble, **437**

*Agreement Relating to the Implementation of Part XI of the United Nations Convention on the Law of the Sea*, **348, 366**

*Amendment to the Montreal Protocol on Substances That Deplete the Ozone Layer*, **390–1**

*Amendments to the Rome Statute of the International Criminal Court: Adoption of the Crime of Aggression*, **340**

*American Convention on Human Rights*, 271, 281
    art 1(2), 272
    arts 34–51, 281
    art 44, 11, 281
    art 45(2), 281
    art 61, 282
    art 62, 282
    art 64, 282
*American Declaration of the Rights and Duties of Man*, 270, 281
*American Treaty on Pacific Settlement*, 248
*Antarctic Treaty*, 197, 359
    art I, 140
    art IV, 140–1, 359
*Arab Charter on Human Rights*, 271
    art 45, 284
    art 48(2), 284
*Articles on Diplomatic Protection*
    art 1, 199
    art 3, 206
    art 6, 206
    art 7, 207
    art 8, 206
    art 9, 207
    art 12, 208
    art 14, 208
    art 15, 209
    art 19, 199
*ASEAN Agreement on the Conservation of Nature and Natural Resources*, 376
*ASEAN Human Rights Declaration*, 271, 285
    art 28(f ), 387

*Bangkok Declaration*, 284
    para 3, 284
    para 8, 284
    Preamble, 284
*Basel Convention on the Control of Transboundary Movements of Hazardous Wastes and Their Disposal*, 377, 391
*Berne Convention for the Protection of Literary and Artistic Works*, 437–8
    arts 1–21, 438
*Brasília Declaration of Judges on Water Justice*, 384

*Cartagena Protocol on Biosafety to the Convention on Biological Diversity*, 393
*Cessation of the Transmission of Information under Article 73(e) of the Charter in respect of Greenland*, 133
*Charter of Fundamental Rights and Freedoms*, 283, 420
*Charter of the Association of Southeast Asian Nations*, 285
    art 3, 408
    art 14(1), 285

*Charter of the United Nations*, 6, 11, 18–19, 23, 90, 117, 122, 132, 215, 239–40, 243, 266, 340, 404, 408–10, 420, 425, 429
    art 1, 266, 420–1
    art 1(1), 214, 239
    art 1(2), 129, 421
    art 1(3), 424
    art 2, 421
    art 2(1), 421
    art 2(3), 117, 214, 239, 243
    art 2(4), 6, 15, 57, 119, 179, 214–17, 219–22, 224–6, 228, 233, 421
    art 2(7), 404, 422
    art 4, 406, 420
    art 4(2), 424
    art 7, 252, 423
    art 7(2), 423
    art 9(1), 423
    art 10, 423–4
    art 11, 423
    art 12(1), 423
    art 13, 266, 276
    art 13(1)(a), 48
    art 14, 423
    art 15, 423
    art 16, 423
    art 17, 423
    art 17(1), 424
    art 18(1), 423
    art 19, 423
    art 24, 230
    art 24(2), 424
    art 25, 35, 128, 230, 424
    art 27, 226
    art 33, 117, 239–40, 264, 421
    art 33(1), 240, 243, 246–9
    art 34, 264
    art 35(1), 264
    art 35(2), 70
    art 36, 264
    art 36(2), 219
    art 37, 264
    art 38(1), 240
    art 39, 215, 230, 340
    art 41, 230
    art 42, 232
    arts 43–47, 232
    art 51, 15, 132, 189, 215, 221–3, 225–6, 228–9, 421
    art 52(1), 264
    art 52(2), 264

*Charter of the United Nations* (cont.)
  art 53, **264**
  art 55, **129, 266, 422**
  art 56, **266**
  art 62(2), **266**
  art 68, **266**
  art 73, **421**
  art 76, **266**
  art 92, **252**
  art 93(1), **253**
  art 93(2), **253**
  art 94, **263**
  art 94(1), **263**
  art 94(2), **263**
  art 96, **261**
  art 97, **427**
  art 99, **248**
  art 102, **60–1**
  art 103, **424**
  art 104, **9, 409**
  art 105, **9, 409, 411**
  arts 107–108, **429**
  ch VI, **214, 231, 240, 264, 421**
  ch VII, **14, 214, 230–1, 239, 264, 421, 424**
  ch VIII, **264**
  ch IX, **423**
  ch X, **422–3**
  ch XI, **9, 125, 421**
  ch XII, **421, 423**
  ch XIII, **421**
  ch XV, **423**
  Preamble, **215, 266**
*Chatham House Principles of International Law on the Use of Force by States in Self-Defence*,
  **226**
*Comprehensive and Progressive Agreement for Trans-Pacific Partnership*
  annex 9-B art 3(b), **450**
  art 9.4, **452**
  art 9.8, **448**
  arts 9.18–9.30, **454**
  art 27.1, **245**
*Consideration of Principles of International Law concerning Friendly Relations and
  Co-operation among States in accordance with the Charter of the United Nations*,
  **244**
*Consolidated Version of the Treaty on the Functioning of the European Union*
  art 263, **11, 420**
*Constitution of the International Labour Organization*
  art 3, **406**
  art 7, **406**

*Convention against Torture and Other Cruel, Inhuman or Degrading Treatment or Punishment*, 154, 175, 197, 269, 278
  art 1, 174
  art 1(1), 153
  art 3(1), 270
  art 3(2), 270
  art 4(1), 95
  art 5(1)(c), 151
  art 21, 280
  art 22, 280
*Convention concerning Discrimination in Respect of Employment and Occupation (No 111)*, 290
*Convention concerning Indigenous and Tribal Peoples in Independent Countries (No 169)*, 269
  art 1, 129
*Convention concerning the Protection of the World Cultural and Natural Heritage*, 93, 97, 376, 392
  art 5, 396
  art 5(d), 396
  art 11(4), 397
  art 12, 396
*Convention for the Protection of Cultural Property in the Event of Armed Conflict*, 296, 317, 395
  art 1(a), 317
  art 4(1), 317
*Convention for the Protection of Human Rights and Fundamental Freedoms*, 197, 271, 282, 286
  art 34, 11
*Convention for the Suppression of Unlawful Acts against the Safety of Maritime Navigation*, 365
*Convention for the Suppression of Unlawful Seizure of Aircraft*
  art 2, 95
*Convention of the World Meteorological Organization*
  art 3(d)–(f), 406
*Convention on Biological Diversity*, 376–7, 392–3
  art 9, 393
  art 15, 393
  art 19, 393
  art 30(1), 59
*Convention on Cluster Munitions*, 296
*Convention on International Civil Aviation*
  art 1, 141
*Convention on International Liability for Damage Caused by Space Objects*, 415
*Convention on International Trade in Endangered Species of Wild Fauna and Flora*, 376–7, 392, 394
*Convention on Long-Range Transboundary Air Pollution*, 390–1
*Convention on Political Asylum*, 41
*Convention on Prohibitions or Restrictions on the Use of Certain Conventional Weapons Which May Be Deemed to Be Excessively Injurious or to Have Indiscriminate Effects*, 296
  para 5, 305

*Convention on Special Missions*
art 1, **177**
*Convention on the Conservation of Species of Migratory Animals*, **377**, **392**
*Convention on the Continental Shelf*, **67**
art 6, **67**
art 6(2), **37**
*Convention on the Elimination of All Forms of Discrimination against Women*,
**269**, **278**
art 9, **206**
*Convention on the Means of Prohibiting and Preventing the Illicit Import, Export and Transfer
of Ownership of Cultural Property*, **396**
*Convention on the Prevention and Punishment of the Crime of Genocide*, **7**, **64**, **194**, **269**, **321**,
**324**, **330**, **334–5**, **337**
art I, **334**
art II, **335**
art III, **335**
art IV, **153**
art VI, **330**
art IX, **65**
*Convention on the Privileges and Immunities of the Specialized Agencies*, **411**
*Convention on the Privileges and Immunities of the United Nations*, **411**
art II(2), **412**
art II(3), **412**
art II(3)–(4), **413**
art II(5)–(8), **413**
art II(8), **413**
art II(10), **413**
art IV, **414**
art V(18), **413**
art V(18)(a), **413**
art V(19), **413**
art V(20), **414**
art V(21), **414**
art VI(22), **414**
art VI(23), **414**
art VIII(29), **412**
*Convention on the Prohibition of Military or Any Other Hostile Use of Environmental
Modification Techniques*, **296**, **317**
art 1(1), **318**
*Convention on the Prohibition of the Development, Production and Stockpiling of
Bacteriological (Biological) and Toxin Weapons and on Their Destruction*,
**296**
*Convention on the Prohibition of the Development, Production, Stockpiling and Use of
Chemical Weapons and on Their Destruction*, **296**
art 2, **313**
*Convention on the Prohibition of the Use, Stockpiling, Production and Transfer of Anti-
Personnel Mines and on Their Destruction*, **64**, **296**

*Convention on the Protection and Promotion of the Diversity of Cultural Expressions*, 395
*Convention on the Protection of the Underwater Cultural Heritage*, 395
*Convention on the Rights of Persons with Disabilities*, 269, 272, 278, 280
   art 9, 279
*Convention on the Rights of the Child*, 97, 269, 278, 280, 290
   art 45, 11
*Convention on the Safeguarding of the Intangible Heritage*, 395
*Convention on the Settlement of Investment Disputes between States and Nationals of Other States*, 444, 454
*Convention on Wetlands of International Importance Especially as Waterfowl Habitat*, 392, 394
*Convention Relating to the Status of Refugees*, 269
   art 1A(2), 270
   art 33(1), 270
*Covenant of the League of Nations*, 112, 213, 239, 243
   art 3(3), 403
   art 4(1), 403
   art 4(4), 403
   art 5(1), 403
   arts 8–9, 403
   art 10, 215
   art 12, 243
   arts 12–15, 213
   art 13, 243
   art 13(1), 243
   art 13(2), 243
   art 14, 252, 403
   art 16, 213
   art 22, 403
   art 23(a)–(f), 403
   Preamble, 402

*Declaration by United Nations* (1 January 1942), 420
*Declaration of Legal Principles Governing the Activities of States in the Exploration and Use of Outer Space*, 35
*Declaration of Principles on Interim Self-Government Arrangements*, 9
*Declaration of the Government of the Democratic and Popular Republic of Algeria*, 181
*Declaration of the Government of the Democratic and Popular Republic of Algeria concerning the Settlement of Claims by the Government of the United States of America and the Government of the Islamic Republic of Iran*, 181
   principle 1, 216
*Declaration of the Rights of Man and of the Citizen*, 291
*Declaration of the United Nations Conference on the Human Environment*, 374, 378
   principle 1, 385–6
   principle 21, 379
*Declaration on Principles Guiding Relations between Participating States*, 51

*Declaration on Principles of International Law concerning Friendly Relations and Co-operation among States in accordance with the Charter of the United Nations*, 35, 215, 217, 236, 244

  principle (a), 132

  principle (e), 124–6

  principle 1, 225, 228, 237

  principle 3, 237

*Declaration on the Granting of Independence to Colonial Countries and Peoples*, 35, 123

*Declaration on the Inadmissibility of Intervention in the Domestic Affairs of States and the Protection of Their Independence and Sovereignty*, 236

*Declaration on the Right to Development*, 270

*Declaration on the Rights of Indigenous Peoples*, 270, 277

*Declaration Renouncing the Use, in Time of War, of Explosive Projectiles under 400 Grammes Weight*, 306

*Definition of Aggression*, 216

  art 3, 216

  art 3(g), 224, 228

*Differential and More Favourable Treatment, Reciprocity and Fuller Participation of Developing Countries*, 435

Draft Articles on Diplomatic Protection, 182, 199

  art 11, 208

Draft Articles on Prevention of Transboundary Harm from Hazardous Activities, 182

Draft Articles on the Responsibility of International Organizations, 182, 405, 415

  art 2(a), 405

  arts 3–4, 416

  art 6, 416

  arts 6–9, 415

  art 7, 416, 418

  art 9, 416

  arts 14–16, 418

  arts 14–19, 416

  art 17, 418

  arts 20–27, 415

  arts 28–42, 415

  arts 43–57, 415

  art 48, 415, 417

  arts 58–60, 419

  arts 58–63, 416

  art 61, 419

  art 62, 419

  art 66, 420

Draft Convention on the Crime of Genocide

  art 1(2), 334

Draft Model Status-of-Forces Agreement between the United Nations and Host Countries, 413–14

Draft Principles of the Allocation of Loss in the Case of Transboundary Harm Arising out of Hazardous Activities, 182

*Energy Charter Treaty*
    art 13(1), **205**
*Establishment of Bantustans*, **121**
*European Convention on State Immunity*, **165**
    art 27, **169**
*European Social Charter*, **271, 283**
*European Social Charter (Revised)*, **271**


*General Agreement on Tariffs and Trade* (1947), **426, 432, 434, 439**
    art II, **432**
    art XX, **452**
    art XXVIII*bis*, **432**
    art XXIX, **432**
*General Agreement on Tariffs and Trade 1994*, **434, 437**
    art 1, **434**
    art I(2)–(4), **434**
    art III, **435**
    art III(1), **435**
    art VI, **435**
    art IX, **435**
    art XVI, **435**
    art XIX, **435**
    art XX, **436**
    art XX(b), **436**
    art XXI, **436**
*General Agreement on Trade in Services*, **436–7**
    Annex on Air Transport Services, **436**
    art II, **436**
    art III, **436**
    art XVII, **436**
    art XX, **436**
    Preamble, **436**
*General Claims Convention*, **181**
*General Treaty for Renunciation of War as an Instrument of National Policy*, **6, 132, 213, 243,**
    **339**
    art I, **243**
    art II, **243**
*Geneva Convention (I) for the Amelioration of the Condition of the Wounded and Sick in*
    *Armed Forces in the Field*, **7, 12, 295, 297–8, 305–6, 324**
    art 1, **318**
    art 2, **299**
    art 3, **12, 300, 308, 316**
    art 15, **313**
    art 38, **314**
    art 47, **318**
    art 48, **318**
    art 49, **330**
    art 50, **318**
    art 63(4), **305**

*Geneva Convention (II) for the Amelioration of the Condition of Wounded, Sick and Shipwrecked Members of Armed Forces at Sea*, 7, 12, 295, 297–8, 305–6, 324
art 1, 318
art 3, 12, 300, 308, 316
art 18, 313
arts 36–40, 316
art 41, 314
art 48, 318
art 49, 318
art 50, 330
art 51, 318
art 62(4), 305
*Geneva Convention (III) Relative to the Treatment of Prisoners of War*, 7, 12, 295, 297–8, 305–6, 314, 324
art 1, 318
art 3, 12, 300, 308, 316
art 4A(1), 306
art 4A(4), 307
art 4A(5), 307
art 4A(6), 306–7
art 5(1), 302
arts 8–10, 315
arts 12–13, 314
arts 12–14, 314
arts 19–28, 314
art 23, 314
art 28, 318
arts 29–32, 314
arts 49–57, 314
arts 69–77, 315
arts 82–108, 315
arts 109–121, 314
art 126, 319
art 127, 318
art 129, 330
art 130, 318
art 142(4), 305
*Geneva Convention (IV) Relative to the Protection of Civilian Persons in Time of War*, 7, 12, 295, 297–8, 300, 305–6, 315, 324
art 1, 318
art 2, 302
art 3, 12, 300, 308, 316
art 6(1), 302
art 6(2), 302
art 6(3), 303
arts 13–26, 315
art 15, 302
art 16, 313

art 17, 313
art 23, 319
art 27, 315
arts 31–34, 315
art 42, 316
arts 47–63, 315
arts 47–75, 315
art 55, 319
arts 79–135, 316
art 143, 319
art 144, 318
art 145, 318
art 146, 330
art 147, 318
art 158(4), 305
*Geneva Convention on Fishing and Conservation of the Living Resources of the High Seas*, 348
*Geneva Convention on the Continental Shelf*, 348, 357
art 1, 357
*Geneva Convention on the High Seas*, 348
*Geneva Convention on the Territorial Sea and the Contiguous Zone*, 348

*Hague Convention (I) for the Pacific Settlement of International Disputes* (1899), 6, 213, 243, 246–7, 249, 251
art 2, 248
art 3, 248
art 4, 248
art 5, 249
art 15, 251
art 16, 251
art 20, 251
art 21, 251
art 31, 251
*Hague Convention (I) for the Pacific Settlement of International Disputes* (1907), 247–9, 251
art 2, 248
art 3, 248
art 4, 248
art 5, 249
art 22, 247
art 44, 253
*Hague Convention (II) with Respect to the Laws and Customs of War on Land* (1899), 296–7, 311
art 1, 306, 318
art 22, 312
art 23(b), 313
art 23(d), 313
art 26, 317
art 28, 313
art 29, 307
art 42, 315

*Hague Convention (II) with Respect to the Laws and Customs of War on Land* (1899) (cont.)
  art 47, **313**
  art 56, **317**
  arts 48–56, **315**
*Hague Convention (IV) respecting the Laws and Customs of War on Land* (1907), **296–7, 311**
  art 1, **306**
  art 22, **312**
  art 23, **305**
  art 23(b), **313**
  art 23(d), **313**
  art 26, **317**
  art 28, **313**
  art 29, **307**
  art 42, **303, 315**
  art 47, **313**
  arts 48–56, **315**
  art 56, **317**
Harvard Draft Convention on the International Responsibility of States for Injuries to Aliens, **443**
  art 10(1), **203**
  art 10(2), **203**
  art 10(3)(a), **203**
  art 10(5), **449**
*Havana Charter for an International Trade Organization*, **432**

*Illegal Occupation by Portuguese Military Forces of Certain Sectors of the Republic of Guinea-Bissau and Acts of Aggression Committed by Them against the People of the Republic*, **127**
*Immunities from Jurisdiction and Execution of Heads of State and of Government in International Law*, **173**
*Information from Non-Self-Governing Territories Transmitted under Article 73e of the Charter*, **421**
*International Coffee Agreement*, **406**
*International Convention against the Recruitment, Use, Financing and Training of Mercenaries*, **308**
*International Convention against the Taking of Hostages*
  art 5(1)(d), **151**
*International Convention for the Protection of All Persons from Enforced Disappearance*, **269, 278**
  art 31, **280**
*International Convention for the Regulation of Whaling*, **71, 73, 368**
  art VII(1), **71**
  art VIII, **368**
*International Convention for the Suppression of Acts of Nuclear Terrorism*, **63**
*International Convention on the Elimination of All Forms of Racial Discrimination*, **98, 269, 278, 290**
  art 1(4), **98**
  art 4(a), **274**
  arts 11–13, **280**

art 14, 257, 280

art 22, 257

*International Convention on the Protection of the Rights of All Migrant Workers and Members of Their Families*, 269, 278, 280

art 74, 280

art 77, 280

*International Convention Relative to the Opening of Hostilities*, 213

*International Convention respecting the Limitation of the Employment of Force for the Recovery of Contract Debts*, 213

International Court of Justice, *Rules of Court*

art 38(5), 258

*International Covenant on Civil and Political Rights*, 268–9, 274, 278–9, 290

art 1, 272

art 1(1), 122, 130

art 1(2), 130

art 2, 10, 268

art 2(1), 272

art 4, 274

art 4(1), 274

art 4(2), 274

art 4(3), 274

art 7, 7, 274

art 8, 274

art 9, 281, 316

art 10, 7, 290

art 11, 274

art 14, 315

art 14(3)(d), 91

art 15(1), 274

art 16, 274

art 17, 274

art 18(3), 274

art 27, 334

art 40(1), 279

arts 41–43, 280

*International Covenant on Economic, Social and Cultural Rights*, 268–9, 278–9

art 1, 272

art 1(1), 122, 130

art 1(2), 130

art 2, 268

art 2(2), 268

art 11, 279

art 12, 279

art 16(1), 279

art 17, 280

International Criminal Court, *Elements of Crimes* (2011)

art 8, 331

*Israeli–Palestinian Interim Agreement on the West Bank and the Gaza Strip*, 9

*Kyoto Protocol to the United Nations Framework Convention on Climate Change*, 388

*Law on the Establishment of Extraordinary Chambers in the Courts of Cambodia for the Prosecution of Crimes Committed during the Period of Democratic Kampuchea, with Inclusion of Amendments as Promulgated on 27 October 2004*, 330
    art 4, 335

*Maastricht Principles on Extraterritorial Obligations of States in the Area of Economic, Social and Cultural Rights*
    principle 9(b), 273
*Mandate of the Special Rapporteur on the Promotion and Protection of Human Rights in the Context of Climate Change*, 389
*Manila Declaration on the Peaceful Settlement of International Disputes between States*, 244
*Marrakesh Agreement Establishing the World Trade Organization*, 433, 439
    annex 1A, 435
    annexes 1A–4, 433–4
    annex 2, 439
    annex 2 art 13, 11
    art I, 405
    art II, 433
    art VIII, 408
    art VIII(1), 408
    art XI, 406
    art XI(2), 435
    art XII, 433
    art XII(1), 406
*Minamata Convention on Mercury*, 377, 391–2
*Montevideo Convention on the Rights and Duties of States*, 2, 109
    art 1, 8, 109
    art 1(d), 110
*Montreal Protocol on Substances That Deplete the Ozone Layer*, 377, 390

*Nagoya Protocol on Access to Genetic Resources and the Fair and Equitable Sharing of the Benefits Arising from Their Utilisation to the Convention on Biological Diversity*, 393
*North American Free Trade Agreement*, 446
    art 1103(1), 450

OECD Draft Convention on the Protection of Foreign Property, 443
*Operational Guidelines for the Implementation of the World Heritage Convention*, 396
*Optional Protocol to the Convention on the Elimination of All Forms of Discrimination against Women*, 280
*Optional Protocol to the Convention on the Rights of Persons with Disabilities*, 280
*Optional Protocol to the Convention on the Rights of the Child on a Communications Procedure*, 280
*Optional Protocol to the Convention on the Rights of the Child on the Involvement of Children in Armed Conflict*, 297

*Optional Protocol to the International Covenant on Civil and Political Rights*, 280
*Optional Protocol to the International Covenant on Economic, Social and Cultural Rights*, 280

*Paris Agreement*, 376, 388
  art 2(1)(a), 388
  art 2(2), 389
  art 4(2), 389
  art 4(3), 385
  art 7(1), 389
  Preamble, 389
*Paris Convention for the Protection of Industrial Property*, 437
*Paris Convention for the Protection of Intellectual Property*, 438–9
  art 1(2), 438
*Permanent Sovereignty over Natural Resources*, 130, 204, 374
*Preferential Tariff Treatment for Least-Developed Countries*, 435
*Principles Relating to the Status of National Institutions*, 287
*Principles Which Should Guide Members in Determining Whether or Not an Obligation Exists to Transmit the Information Called for in Article 73(e) of the Charter of the United Nations*, 124
*Protocol Additional (I) to the Geneva Conventions of 12 August 1949, and Relating to the Protection of Victims of International Armed Conflicts*, 295, 297–8, 305–6, 311, 313
  art 1(2), 305
  art 1(4), 9, 299
  art 3(b), 302
  art 6, 318
  art 8(1), 314
  art 11(4), 318
  arts 21–31, 316
  art 35, 317
  art 35(1), 312
  art 35(3), 317
  art 36, 305, 313
  art 37, 312
  art 37(1), 313
  art 40, 313
  arts 41–44, 312
  art 43(1), 307
  art 44(3), 307
  art 46, 307
  art 47(2)(c), 308
  art 47(2)(d)–(e), 308
  art 48, 303, 311
  art 49, 311
  art 50, 308
  art 50(1), 308
  art 51(2), 308, 311
  art 51(3), 308, 311–12
  art 51(4), 303

*Protocol Additional (I) to the Geneva Conventions of 12 August 1949, and Relating to the Protection of Victims of International Armed Conflicts* (cont.)
art 51(4)–(5), **311**
art 51(5)(b), **303**
art 51(7), **312**
art 52, **311–12**
art 52(1), **310**
art 52(2), **310, 312**
art 53, **317**
art 54, **311, 313**
art 54(2), **311**
art 55, **317**
art 56, **311**
art 57, **311**
art 57(2), **311**
art 57(2)(a)(ii), **311**
art 58, **312**
art 70, **313**
art 75, **315**
art 80, **318**
art 81, **319**
art 82, **318**
art 83, **318**
art 84, **318**
art 85, **318**
art 87(2), **318**
art 96, **9**
*Protocol Additional (II) to the Geneva Conventions of 12 August 1949, and Relating to the Protection of Victims of Non-International Armed Conflicts*, **295, 297, 300, 305–6, 308, 311**
art 1(1), **300**
art 2(2), **303**
art 4, **313**
arts 4–6, **300, 316**
art 4(2)(g), **313**
arts 7–8, **316**
arts 7–12, **300**
arts 10–11, **316**
art 12, **314**
arts 13–18, **300**
art 18, **319**
art 19, **318**
Preamble, **305**
*Protocol Additional (III) to the Geneva Conventions of 12 August 1949, and Relating to the Adoption of an Additional Distinctive Emblem*, **296–7, 305–6, 311**
art 2(2), **314**
*Protocol Amending the Marrakesh Agreement Establishing the World Trade Organization*, **433**

*Protocol between the Government of Australia and the Government of the Hong Kong Special Administrative Region of the People's Republic of China Amending the Agreement for the Surrender of Accused and Convicted Persons of 15 November 1993*, 79
*Protocol for the Prohibition of the Use of Asphyxiating, Poisonous or Other Gases, and of Bacteriological Methods of Warfare*, 296
*Protocol for the Protection of Cultural Property in the Event of Armed Conflict*, 395
*Protocol on Prohibitions or Restrictions on the Use of Incendiary Weapons (Protocol III)*, 296
   art 2(4), 317
*Protocol on Prohibitions or Restrictions on the Use of Mines, Booby-Traps and Other Devices (Protocol II)*, 296
*Protocol Relating to the Status of Refugees*, 270
*Protocol to the African Charter on Human and Peoples' Rights on the Establishment of an African Court on Human and Peoples' Rights*, 283
   art 4, 283
   art 5, 283
   art 5(3), 283
   art 34(6), 283
*Protocol to the Convention for the Protection of Human Rights and Fundamental Freedoms*, 271
*Protocol to the Hague Convention for the Protection of Cultural Property in the Event of Armed Conflict*, 317
*Protocol to the London Convention on the Prevention of Marine Pollution by Dumping of Wastes and Other Matter*, 367

*Question of Niue*, 124
*Question of the Cook Islands*, 124

*Regional Comprehensive Economic Partnership Agreement*, 442
   art 1(3), 442
*Resolution on Amendments to Article 8 of the Rome Statute of the International Criminal Court*, 331
*Resolution on Limits to Evolutive Interpretation of the Constituent Instruments of the Organizations within the United Nations System by their Internal Organs*, 411
*Responsibility of States for Internationally Wrongful Acts*, 2, 78, 86, 182, 187, 191, 194–5, 197
   art 2, 183, 188
   art 3, 16, 86, 188
   art 4, 183–4
   arts 4–11, 116, 183
   art 4(1), 183
   art 4(2), 183
   art 5, 184
   art 7, 184
   art 8, 185–6, 418
   art 11, 186
   art 12, 188
   art 16, 187
   art 17, 187
   art 20, 188

*Responsibility of States for Internationally Wrongful Acts* (cont.)
    art 21, 189
    art 22, 190
    art 23, 190
    art 24, 191
    art 24(2)(b), 191
    art 26, 188
    art 29, 192
    art 30, 192
    art 31, 193
    art 34, 193
    art 35(a), 193
    art 35(b), 194
    art 36, 194
    art 36(1), 194
    art 39, 193
    art 40, 119–20, 195
    art 41, 120, 182, 195
    art 42, 196–7
    art 42(b)(ii), 197
    art 44, 206
    art 46, 197
    art 46(2), 194
    art 47, 187, 197
    art 47(1), 187
    art 47(2), 187
    art 48, 182, 197
    art 48(1)(a), 197
    art 48(1)(b), 197
    arts 49–54, 15
    art 55, 198
    ch V, 188
*Restoration of the Lawful Rights of the People's Republic of China in the United Nations*, 117, 407
*Rio Declaration on Environment and Development*, 378, 381
    annex I, 378
    principle 2, 378–9
    principle 15, 379
    principle 17, 379
*Rome Statute of the International Criminal Court*, 58, 63, 91, 105, 297, 321–2, 326–8, 330–1, 339
    art 3, 325
    art 4, 408
    art 5, 335
    art 7, 153, 332–3
    art 7(1), 333
    art 7(1)(g), 331
    art 8, 153, 331
    art 8 *bis*, 153, 340

art 8 *bis*(1), **340**
art 8 *bis*(2), **340**
art 8(2)(b)(i), **308**
art 8(2)(b)(iv), **331**
art 8(2)(b)(xxii), **331**
art 8(2)(b)(xxv), **331**
art 8(2)(b)(xxvi), **331**
art 8(2)(e)(i), **308**
art 8(2)(e)(vi), **331**
art 8(2)(e)(vii), **331**
art 11, **326**
art 12(2), **327**
art 12(3), **327**
art 13(c), **326**
art 15, **326**
art 15 *bis*, **326**
art 15 *bis*(5), **327, 340**
art 15 *bis*(6)–(8), **340**
art 15 *bis*(9), **340**
art 15 *ter*(4), **340**
art 16, **340**
art 17, **327**
art 17(1)(a)–(b), **327**
art 17(2)–(3), **328**
art 25(3), **341**
art 25(3) *bis*, **340**
art 25(3)(a), **342**
art 25(3)(d), **342**
art 27, **177**
art 28, **343**
art 28(a), **343–4**
art 28(a)(i), **343**
art 28(a)(ii), **343**
art 28(b), **343**
art 28(b)(iii), **343**
art 31(1)–(2), **344**
art 33, **345**
art 48, **414**
art 68(3), **326**
art 75, **326**
art 125, **58**
Preamble, **325**
*Rotterdam Convention on the Prior Informed Consent Procedure for Certain Hazardous Chemicals and Pesticides in International Trade*, **377, 391**

*San Remo Manual on International Law Applicable to Armed Conflicts at Sea*, **297**
*Second Protocol to the Hague Convention of 1954 for the Protection of Cultural Property in the Event of Armed Conflict*, **296, 298, 317, 395**

*Special Agreement for Submission to the International Court of Justice of the Differences concerning the Gabčikovo-Nagymaros Project*
   art 2, **256**
*Special Agreement for Submission to the International Court of Justice of the Dispute between Indonesia and Malaysia concerning Sovereignty over Pulau Ligitan and Pulau Sipadan*
   art 4, **256**
*Special Agreement for the Submission to Arbitration of Pecuniary Claims Outstanding between the United States and Great Britain,* **181**
*Special Proclamation by the Supreme Commander for the Allied Powers: Establishment of an International Military Tribunal for the Far East,* **323–4**
   art 5(a), **339**
   art 5(c), **332**
*Standing Mandate for a General Assembly Debate when a Veto is Cast in the Security Council,* **429**
*Status of Palestine in the United Nations,* **115, 406**
*Statute of the International Court of Justice,* **240–1, 252–3**
   art 2, **252**
   art 3, **252**
   art 3(1), **252**
   art 4(1), **252**
   art 13(1), **252**
   art 19, **414**
   art 31(1), **253**
   art 31(1)–(3), **253**
   art 34, **253**
   art 35, **253**
   art 36(1), **256**
   art 36(2), **217, 254–5**
   art 36(3), **254**
   art 36(5), **257**
   art 36(6), **256**
   art 37, **257**
   art 38, **19, 33, 43, 47, 49–50, 256**
   art 38(1), **2**
   art 38(1)(a), **56**
   art 38(1)(b), **34, 86**
   art 38(1)(c), **45–6, 86**
   art 38(1)(d), **3, 33, 47–8, 86**
   art 38(2), **45**
   art 41, **260**
   art 41(1), **260**
   art 59, **47, 262**
   art 60, **263**
   art 62, **261**
   art 63, **261**
   art 65, **261**
   art 66, **262**
*Statute of the Permanent Court of International Justice,* **45, 47, 252, 257**
   art 38, **240**

*Statute of the River Uruguay*
  arts 7–12, **245**
*Statute of the World Tourism Organization*
  art 7, **406**
*Stockholm Convention on Persistent Organic Pollutants*, **377**, **391**
*Strengthening the Role of Mediation in the Peaceful Settlement of Disputes, Conflict Prevention and Resolution*, **249**
*Study by the International Law Commission of the Question of an International Criminal Jurisdiction*, **324**

*Territorial Integrity of Ukraine*, **22**, **120**
*The Charter and Judgment of the Nürnberg Tribunal*
  art 6(a), **153**
  art 6(b), **153**
*The Crime of Genocide*, **334**
*The Human Right to a Clean, Healthy and Sustainable Environment*, **373**, **387**
*The Situation with Regard to the Implementation of the Declaration on the Granting of Independence to Colonial Countries and Peoples*, **422**
*Timor Sea Treaty between the Government of Australia and the Government of East Timor*, **251**, **362–3**
*Treaty between Australia and the Democratic Republic of Timor-Leste on Certain Maritime Arrangements in the Timor Sea*, **76**
  art 4, **362**
  art 12, **362**
*Treaty between Australia and the Republic of Indonesia on the Zone of Cooperation in an Area between the Indonesian Province of East Timor and Northern Australia*, **94**, **259**, **362**
*Treaty between Sweden and Chile concerning the Establishment of a Permanent Enquiry and Conciliation Commission*, **250**
*Treaty for an Amicable Settlement of All Causes of Difference between the Two Countries*, **242**
*Treaty of Amity, Commerce and Navigation*, **242**
*Treaty of Amity, Economic Relations, and Consular Rights*
  art I, **189**
  art XX, **72**
*Treaty of Peace between the Allied and Associated Powers and Germany*, **112**, **323**, **402**
*Treaty of Saint-Germain*
  art 88, **111**
*Treaty on European Union*
  art 47, **408**
*Treaty on Intellectual Property in Respect of Integrated Circuits*, **439**
*Treaty on Political Asylum and Refuge*, **41**
*Treaty on Principles Governing the Activities of States in the Exploration and Use of Outer Space, Including the Moon and Other Celestial Bodies*
  art 2, **141**
*Treaty on the Prohibition of Nuclear Weapons*, **296–7**

UN Security Council, SC Res 827, UN Doc S/RES/827 (25 May 1993), **322**
  art 4, **335**

UN Security Council, SC Res 827, UN Doc S/RES/827 (25 May 1993) (cont.)
  art 5, **332**
  art 7(1), **341**
  art 7(3), **343**
  art 7(4), **345**
UN Security Council, SC Res 955, UN Doc S/RES/955 (8 November 1994)
  annex, **322**
  art 2, **335**
  art 3, **332**
  art 6(1), **341**
  art 6(3), **343**
  art 6(4), **345**
UN Security Council, SC Res S/RES/1593, UN Doc S/RES/1593 (31 March 2005), **326**
UN Security Council, SC Res 1877, UN Doc S/RES/1877 (7 July 2009), **322**
UN Security Council, SC Res S/RES/1970, UN Doc S/RES/1970 (26 February 2011), **326**
*Understanding on Dispute Settlement*
  app 3, **440**
  art 1, **439**
  art 4, **440**
  arts 6–8, **440**
  art 10, **440**
  art 12, **440**
  art 16, **440**
  art 17, **440**
  art 19, **440**
  art 20, **440**
  art 21, **440**
  art 22, **440**
*UNIDROIT Convention on Stolen or Illegally Exported Cultural Objects*, **396**
*United Nations Convention against Corruption*, **63**
*United Nations Convention on Jurisdictional Immunities of States and Their Property*,
    **165**
  art 1(b), **168**
  art 2(1)(b), **169**
  art 2(1)(b)(iii), **169**
*United Nations Convention on the Law of the Sea*, **48, 196, 252, 347–9, 356, 367, 369, 415, 426**
  annex II art 4, **358**
  annex V, **363**
  annex VII, **371**
  annex VIII, **371**
  art 1(a), **365**
  art 2, **141, 352**
  art 3, **352**
  art 5, **350**
  art 7(1), **351**
  art 7(3), **351**
  art 7(4), **351**
  art 10, **351**

art 11, **349**

art 13, **349**

art 15, **361**

art 17, **352**

art 18(1), **353**

art 18(2), **353**

art 19(1), **353**

art 19(2), **353**

art 21, **352**

art 25(1), **353**

art 25(2), **353**

art 27, **352**

art 33, **354–5**

art 37, **353**

art 39(1), **353**

art 39(1)(c), **354**

art 39(2), **353**

art 40, **353**

art 42(2), **353**

art 44, **353**

art 46(a), **359**

art 46(b), **359**

art 47(1), **359**

art 47(2), **361**

art 47(3), **361**

art 48, **359**

art 49, **141**

art 55, **355**

art 56, **355**

art 56(1)(b), **356**

art 57, **355**

art 58(1), **356**

art 60(8), **349**

art 63(1), **369**

art 74(1), **361**

art 74(3), **362**

art 76, **357**

art 76(4), **358**

art 76(5), **358**

art 76(8), **358**

art 77, **358**

art 77(3), **358**

art 77(4), **358**

art 80, **349, 358**

art 81, **358**

art 83(1), **361**

art 83(3), **362**

art 86, **364**

*United Nations Convention on the Law of the Sea* (cont.)
    art 87, 364
    art 89, 364
    art 90, 364
    art 91, 364
    art 92(1), 364
    art 94, 364
    art 97, 145, 364
    art 97(1), 148
    art 101, 153, 365
    art 105, 365
    art 110, 364
    art 111, 365
    art 121, 349–50
    art 136, 366
    art 137, 366
    art 137(1), 366
    art 157, 366
    art 192, 367
    art 211, 367
    art 283(1), 244
    art 287, 371
    art 298(1)(a)(i), 250
    art 309, 348, 370
    art 312, 370
    pt VII, 364
    pt XI, 348, 365–6
    pt XV, 370
*United Nations Convention to Combat Desertification in Those Countries Experiencing Serious Drought and/or Desertification Particularly in Africa*, 395
*United Nations Declaration on the Rights of Indigenous Peoples*, 90, 380, 386
    arts 3–4, 129
    art 29(1), 386
    art 46(1), 129
*United Nations Forest Instrument*, 393–4
*United Nations Framework Convention on Climate Change*, 96, 250, 388, 392
*United Nations Millennium Declaration*, 381
*Uniting for Peace*, 423
*Universal Declaration of Human Rights*, 6, 35, 266, 268, 270–1, 284
    art 3, 268
    art 14, 270
    art 17, 268
    art 22, 268
    art 24, 268
    art 26, 268

*Vienna Convention for the Protection of the Ozone Layer*, 377, 390
*Vienna Convention on Consular Relations*, 48, 158, 186, 241
    art 5, 158

art 36, 192
art 70, 158
*Vienna Convention on Diplomatic Relations*, 48, 96, 157, 163, 186, 241, 414
art 1, 159
art 1(i), 162
art 3, 157
art 4, 161
art 5, 159
art 7, 161
art 8(1), 161
art 8(2), 161
art 8(3), 161
art 9, 164
art 9(1), 161
art 9(2), 161
art 10, 159, 161
art 22, 162
art 22(2), 162
art 24, 163
art 27(4), 163
art 29, 160, 162, 414
arts 29–30, 414
art 30, 162
art 31, 159–60, 173
art 31(1), 159
art 31(3), 160
art 32, 159
art 34, 160
art 36, 160
art 37, 160
art 37(2), 160
art 37(3), 160
art 37(4), 160
art 38(1), 161
art 38(2), 161
art 39(1), 161
art 39(2), 161
art 41, 163
art 43, 161
art 44, 157
art 45, 157
*Vienna Convention on Succession of States in Respect of Treaties*, 56
art 11, 131
art 12, 131
*Vienna Convention on the Law of Treaties*, 2, 34, 48, 56–8, 76, 250
art 2, 59, 62, 274
art 2(1)(a), 34, 58
art 2(1)(c), 60

*Vienna Convention on the Law of Treaties* (cont.)

art 3, **57, 59**

art 4, **57**

art 6, **58**

art 7, **58, 60, 75**

arts 7–19, **60**

art 7(2), **60**

art 8, **60**

art 9, **60**

art 10, **60**

art 11, **61**

art 12, **61**

art 12(1), **61**

art 14, **61**

art 16, **62**

art 18, **61, 69**

art 19, **66–7, 274**

arts 19–21, **66**

art 19(a), **66**

art 19(b), **66**

art 20(1), **66**

art 20(2), **66**

art 20(4)(a), **66**

art 20(4)(b), **66–7**

art 20(5), **67**

art 21, **67**

art 21(1), **67**

art 21(3), **67–8**

art 24(1), **62**

art 26, **15, 34, 58, 69, 73**

art 27, **15–16, 58, 70, 86–7, 163**

art 28, **70**

art 29, **70**

art 30, **70**

art 31, **70–2**

arts 31–32, **58**

art 31(2), **71**

art 31(3), **71–3**

art 31(3)(c), **72**

art 32, **70–3**

art 33, **58, 70**

arts 34–36, **70**

art 35, **70**

art 36, **70**

art 37, **68**

art 38, **70**

art 42, **74**

art 46, **74**

arts 46–50, 74
arts 46–51, 74
arts 46–53, 74
art 46(2), 75
art 48, 74–5
arts 48–51, 74
art 49, 74–5
art 50, 74–5
art 51, 74–5
arts 51–53, 74
art 52, 74–5, 132
art 53, 43–4, 74
arts 54–63, 74, 76
art 54(a), 77
art 54(b), 77
art 56, 77, 407
art 56(1)(a), 77
art 56(1)(b), 77
art 56(2), 77
art 57(a), 77
art 57(b), 77
art 58(a), 77
art 58(b), 77
art 59, 77
art 60, 78, 80
arts 60–62, 58, 77, 80
art 60(1), 78
art 60(2)(a), 78
art 60(2)(a)(i), 78
art 60(2)(a)(ii), 78
art 60(2)(b), 78
art 60(2)(c), 78
art 60(5), 78
art 61, 78, 80–1
art 61(2), 79
art 62, 79–80
art 62(1)(a), 79
art 62(1)(b), 79
art 64, 74
art 65, 58, 74
arts 65–66, 74
art 67, 74
art 69, 74
art 69(1), 81
art 69(2), 81
art 69(4), 81
art 70, 81
art 71, 81

*Vienna Convention on the Law of Treaties* (cont.)
    art 72, **81**
    art 75, **74**
    art 76(1), **60**
    art 77(1), **60**
    art 80(1), **60**
    art 81, **61**
    art 84(1), **62**
    art 84(2), **62**
    pt V, **15**
*Vienna Convention on the Law of Treaties between States and International Organizations or between International Organizations*, **9, 56, 409**
*Vienna Declaration and Programme of Action*, **275**
    art 5, **284**
    art 37, **285**

*World Declaration on the Environmental Rule of Law*, **376, 383**
    principle 3, **386**
    principle 5, **384**
    principle 7, **385**
    principle 12, **384**

# ABBREVIATIONS

| | |
|---|---|
| **ACHR** | *American Convention on Human Rights* |
| **ADP** | *Articles on Diplomatic Protection* |
| **ARSIWA** | *Articles on Responsibility of States for Internationally Wrongful Acts* |
| **BIT** | bilateral investment treaty |
| **CAT** | *Convention against Torture and Other Cruel, Inhuman or Degrading Treatment or Punishment* |
| **CED** | *International Convention for the Protection of All Persons from Enforced Disappearance* |
| **CEDAW** | *Convention on the Elimination of All Forms of Discrimination against Women* |
| **CERD** | *International Convention on the Elimination of All Forms of Racial Discrimination* |
| **CITES** | *Convention on International Trade in Endangered Species* |
| **CLCS** | Commission on the Limits of the Continental Shelf |
| **CMW** | *International Convention on the Protection of the Rights of All Migrant Workers and Members of Their Families* |
| **CRC** | *Convention on the Rights of the Child* |
| **CRPD** | *Convention on the Rights of Persons with Disabilities* |
| **DARIO** | Draft Articles on the Responsibility of International Organisations |
| **DPH** | direct participation in hostilities |
| **DRC** | Democratic Republic of the Congo |
| **DSB** | Dispute Settlement Body |
| **DSU** | *Dispute Settlement Understanding* |
| **ECCC** | Extraordinary Chambers in the Courts of Cambodia |
| **EEZ** | exclusive economic zone |
| **EIA** | environmental impact assessment |
| **EROL** | Environmental Rule of Law |
| **FET** | fair and equitable treatment |
| **FPS** | full protection and security |
| **FTA** | free trade agreement |
| **GATS** | *General Agreement on Trade in Services* |
| **GATT** | *General Agreement on Tariffs and Trade* |
| **GATT 1994** | *General Agreement on Tariffs and Trade 1994* |
| **IAC** | international armed conflict |
| **ICC** | International Criminal Court |
| **ICCPR** | *International Covenant on Civil and Political Rights* |
| **ICESCR** | *International Covenant on Economic, Social and Cultural Rights* |

| | |
|---|---|
| **ICJ** | International Court of Justice |
| **ICL** | international criminal law |
| **ICSID** | International Centre for Settlement of Investment Disputes |
| **ICTR** | International Criminal Tribunal for Rwanda |
| **ICTY** | International Criminal Tribunal for the Former Yugoslavia |
| **IEL** | international environmental law |
| **IHL** | international humanitarian law |
| **IHRL** | international human rights law |
| **ILC** | International Law Commission |
| **ILO** | International Labour Organization |
| **IMF** | International Monetary Fund |
| **IMO** | International Maritime Organization |
| **IO** | international organisation |
| **ISA** | International Seabed Authority |
| **ISDS** | investor–state dispute settlement |
| **ITLOS** | International Tribunal for the Law of the Sea |
| **IUCN** | International Union for the Conservation of Nature |
| **IWC** | International Whaling Commission |
| **JSCOT** | Joint Standing Committee on Treaties |
| **LOAC** | law of armed conflict |
| **MEA** | multilateral environmental agreement |
| **MFN** | most favoured nation |
| **MOU** | memorandum of understanding |
| **NGO** | non-governmental organisation |
| **NIAC** | non-international armed conflict |
| **OAS** | Organization of American States |
| **OSCE** | Organization for Security and Co-operation in Europe |
| **P5** | Permanent Five members of the UN Security Council |
| **PCA** | Permanent Court of Arbitration |
| **PCIJ** | Permanent Court of International Justice |
| **SDGs** | Sustainable Development Goals |
| ***TRIPS*** | *Agreement on Trade-Related Aspects of Intellectual Property* |
| **TWAIL** | Third World Approaches to International Law |
| **UN** | United Nations |
| **UNCITRAL** | United Nations Commission on International Trade Law |
| ***UNCLOS*** | *United Nations Convention on the Law of the Sea* |
| **UNEP** | United Nations Environment Programme |
| **UNESCO** | United Nations Educational, Scientific and Cultural Organization |
| **UPR** | universal periodic review |
| ***VCCR*** | *Vienna Convention on Consular Relations* |
| ***VCDR*** | *Vienna Convention on Diplomatic Relations* |
| ***VCLT*** | *Vienna Convention on the Law of Treaties* |
| **WIPO** | World Intellectual Property Organization |
| **WTO** | World Trade Organization |

# 1

# OVERVIEW OF PUBLIC INTERNATIONAL LAW

Ben Saul

# 1.1   Introduction

Public international law is a worldwide legal system which regulates the conduct of states (countries) and other actors, both in their international relations and within states' territories. It governs many areas, such as sovereignty over territory; rights and responsibilities at sea; environmental protection; human rights and the suppression of international crimes; trade and investment; the use of military force; responsibility for breaches of the law; and the settlement of disputes. This chapter introduces the main features of public international law, including its history, sources and purposes. It outlines what the law regulates, who has rights and bears obligations under it, and how it is implemented and enforced. The chapter then considers jurisprudential debates about the nature of public international law as 'law' and the reasons for compliance with it, and concludes with discussion of some key critical theories.

# 1.2   What is international law?

Public international law (hereafter 'international law') is a global legal system collectively created by states through its distinctive legal sources which include treaties, customary international law, and 'general principles of law'.[1] It recognises states as its principal subjects or 'international legal persons' – those who bear international rights and obligations, and have the capacity to make international claims and be held responsible for their breaches – but also other actors with more limited personality. International law is implemented and enforced through international processes (bilateral, regional and multilateral) and national legal systems.

In addition to regulating a wide variety of substantive conduct (discussed in Section 1.2.1), international law includes 'background' rules which enable it to function as a legal system. These include the law on statehood (determining which entities qualify as states; see Chapter 5) and on legal personality (discussed in Section 1.2.2); the sources of law (specifying what is valid law);[2] the law of treaties (addressing the formation, validity, interpretation, breach and termination of treaties);[3] and the law of state responsibility (identifying when states are legally responsible for breaches of obligations and the consequences, including remedies).[4] While international law is a universal legal *system*, not every international rule applies universally and the system provides for contextual flexibility: treaties can be made between as few as two states; particular states can contract out of customary law between themselves; and custom can form at a local or regional level.

Public international law is distinct from states' national ('domestic' or 'municipal') laws, although it interacts closely with them (see Chapter 4). It is also distinguishable from 'private

---

1    See *Statute of the International Court of Justice* ('*ICJ Statute*') art 38(1). In addition, the article refers to 'subsidiary means for the determination' of law, being judicial decisions (national or international) and the views of the 'most highly qualified publicists' (jurists and scholars).

2    See, eg, *Montevideo Convention on the Rights and Duties of States*, opened for signature 26 December 1933, 165 LNTS 19 (entered in force 26 December 1934). See Chapter 2.

3    See, eg, *Vienna Convention on the Law of Treaties*, opened for signature 23 May 1969, 1155 UNTS 331 (entered into force 27 January 1980) ('*VCLT*'). See Chapter 3.

4    See, eg, *Responsibility of States for Internationally Wrongful Acts*, GA Res 56/83, UN Doc A/RES/56/83 (28 January 2002, adopted 12 December 2001) annex ('*Responsibility of States for Internationally Wrongful Acts*') ('*ARSIWA*'). See Chapter 7.

international law' (or 'conflict of laws') which consists of mainly national rules that determine which national laws will apply ('choice of law') and which national courts will decide ('choice of forum') in relation to a private, national-law dispute with a 'foreign' element.[5]

## 1.2.1 Historical context

### 1.2.1.1 Early origins

Historically the interaction of different pre-modern political communities stimulated efforts to regularise and stabilise relations, whether among ancient civilisations of the Middle East (from Mesopotamia to Egypt), Greece and Rome, or China and India.[6] These early measures included practices relating to the sanctity of treaties, respect for envoys, trade cooperation and restraints on war. Many practices were, however, ad hoc and bilateral rather than part of a systematic or universal legal system; some occurred in the context of imperial relations of subordination and inequality; and they sometimes reflected political, moral or religious commitments more than strict legal ones.

Modern international law originated 400–500 years ago in late medieval Europe's public 'law of nations' (*jus gentium*), which governed relations between political entities. This law itself derived from the *jus gentium* of the Roman Empire,[7] which had been more narrowly concerned with 'private law' relations with foreigners, Christian canon law and 'natural law' theories. More so than in domestic law, writers played a prominent role in the early formulation of international law – and jurists are still a 'subsidiary means' of determining international law today.[8] The 'law of nature',[9] with roots in classical Greek and Roman philosophy and revived during the Renaissance, was believed to establish universal, immutable principles governing humanity, which transcended particular political orders and religions. Later, in medieval Christian Europe, natural law was understood as derived from divine will, as in the influential work of 13th century scholar Thomas Aquinas.[10]

From the 16th century, natural law was gradually separated from religion and became grounded in human nature, reason and justice, evident in the writings of early founders of

---

5   Examples are where a contract made in one country is breached in another, or a tort committed in one country produces damage in another.
6   See, eg, Arthur Nussbaum, *A Concise History of the Law of Nations* (Macmillan, 2nd ed, 1954); David Bederman, *International Law in Antiquity* (Cambridge University Press, 2001); RP Anand, *Development of Modern International Law and India* (Nomos, 2005); CH Alexandrowicz, *An Introduction to the History of the Law of Nations in the East Indies* (Clarendon Press, 1967); Taslim Elias, *Africa and the Development of International Law* (AW Sijthoff, 1972); Shin Kawashima, 'China' in Bardo Fassbender and Anne Peters (eds), *The Oxford Handbook of the History of International Law* (Oxford University Press, 2012) 451.
7   See Randall Lesaffer, 'Roman Law and the Intellectual History of International Law' in Anne Orford and Florian Hoffmann (eds), *The Oxford Handbook of the Theory of International Law* (Oxford University Press, 2016) 38.
8   *ICJ Statute* (n 1) art 38(1)(d).
9   See generally Alexander Orakhelashvili, 'Natural Law and Justice' in Rüdiger Wolfrum (ed), *The Max Planck Encyclopedia of Public International Law* (Oxford University Press, online, August 2007); Geoff Gordon, 'Natural Law in International Legal Theory' in Anne Orford and Florian Hoffmann (eds), *The Oxford Handbook of the Theory of International Law* (Oxford University Press, 2016) 279.
10  See Thomas Aquinas, *Summa Theologica*, tr Fathers of the English Dominican Province (Benziger Bros, 1947–48) [trans of: *Summa Theologiae* (1485)].

international law such as the Spaniards Francisco de Vitoria and Cristóbal Suárez de Figueroa, the Italian Alberico Gentili and, in the 17th century, the Dutch Protestant Hugo Grotius and the German Samuel von Pufendorf.[11] Grotius's foundational book, *The Law of War and Peace* (*De Jure Belli ac Pacis*), written during the bitter religious violence of Europe's Thirty Years War, sought to moderate war between sovereigns; it also focused on the law of the sea. Alongside natural law, Grotius acknowledged the human-made 'positive' law of treaties and custom. Grotius is often called the 'founding father of international law' – but is also known as 'the godfather of Dutch imperialism',[12] since international law also legitimised European expansion in the colonial era.

The settlement of the Thirty Years War in the Treaties of Westphalia in 1648–49 embodied a tectonic geopolitical shift in Europe, marking the decline of the Holy Roman Empire and supranational papal authority across Europe, and giving further impetus to the rise of the modern, independent sovereign state.[13] By the 18th century, writers imagined different trajectories for international law: whereas the Germans Christian Wolff and Immanuel Kant foreshadowed an eventual supreme or international state uniting and ruling sovereigns under supranational authority,[14] the Prussian Emer de Vattel and Genevan Jean-Jacques Rousseau foresaw more modest collective cooperation in the common interest, underpinned by the balance of power.[15]

Much early international law primarily addressed relations between states on the international plane and sought to safeguard sovereignty. Rules emerged governing the acquisition of sovereign legal title to territory and sovereign rights within territory (see Chapter 5), such as the exercise of jurisdiction to make and enforce laws regulating behaviour (see Chapter 6). To maintain free communication between governments, norms developed to ensure respect for envoys (see Chapter 7); and to preclude equal sovereigns from judging each other, norms developed to guarantee the immunity of state officials before foreign domestic courts (see Chapter 6). The law of treaties emerged to stabilise political agreements between states (see Chapter 3). Freedom of navigation of ships on the high seas (an area beyond national sovereignty) was recognised (see Chapter 13) to enable all states to benefit from trade – but also to 'discover' and colonise distant lands. War too became subject to norms, albeit of a more religious or moral than legal quality, evident in medieval Christian 'just war theory', and territory could still be lawfully conquered by force as late as 1928 (see Chapter 8).

---

11    Martti Koskenniemi, 'International Law in the World of Ideas' in James Crawford and Martti Koskenniemi (eds), *The Cambridge Companion to International Law* (Cambridge University Press, 2012) 47, 50–2.

12    Martine van Ittersum, 'Hugo Grotius: The Making of a Founding Father of International Law' in Anne Orford and Florian Hoffmann (eds), *The Oxford Handbook of the Theory of International Law* (Oxford University Press, 2016) 82, 99.

13    See historically Henry Wheaton, *History of Law of Nations in Europe and America since the Peace of Westphalia* (Gould, Banks, 1841).

14    Christian Wolff, *The Law of Nations Treated According to the Scientific Method*, tr Joseph Drake (Liberty Fund, 2017) [trans of: *Jus Gentium Methodo Scientifica Pertractum* (1749)]; Immanuel Kant, 'Perpetual Peace: A Philosophical Sketch', tr HB Nisbet in Hans Reiss (ed), *Kant: Political Writings* (Cambridge University Press, 2nd ed, 1991) [trans of: 'Zum ewigen Frieden: Ein philosophischer Entwurf' (1795)].

15    See, eg, Emer de Vattel, *The Law of Nations*, tr Charles G Fenwick (Hein, 1995) [trans of: *Le Droit des Gens* (1758)]; Jean-Jacques Rousseau, *A Lasting Peace through the Federation of Europe*, tr CE Vaughan (Constable, 1917) [trans of: *Extrait du Projet de Paix Perpétuelle de Monsieur l'Abbé de Saint-Pierre* (1782)].

While international law originated in Europe, colonialism from the 15th to the early 20th centuries caused 'European' international law to be exported to govern relations with the rest of the world,[16] including to enable acquisition of territory, treaty making and trade. Non-European entities were generally not, however, regarded as sovereign equals; their rights depended on their perceived level of 'civilisation', in part due to ideas about natural law.[17] From the 19th century, 'semi-civilized' powers enjoyed considerable rights, starting with the Ottoman Empire and later including Persia, China, Japan, Korea, Siam, Morocco, Muscat and Zanzibar.[18] At the 'lowest' level were indigenous peoples, although (unequal) 'treaties' were still made with some in Africa, the Americas and New Zealand, but not Australia. European power thus 'universalised' international law, particularly as a tool of domination.

## 1.2.1.2   The 19th and early 20th centuries

In the 19th century,[19] legal positivism became the dominant lens of international law.[20] Positivism recognises only law declared by states (regardless of morality), rather than what emanates from a higher 'natural' or divine source. Relations between equal, independent sovereigns were understood as based on consent to legal rules – either specifically in the adoption of treaties, or tacitly through the formation of customary rules based on collective consent over time. This left little room for natural law as law 'above' (as opposed to 'between') states,[21] although vestiges of natural law were codified in treaties.[22]

The 19th century saw a proliferation of treaty making, and the establishment of early international organisations (discussed in Chapter 15) to promote cooperation in response to the accelerating phenomena of globalisation. These included the increasing interaction of states and their peoples, rapid industrialisation, expanding trade and commerce, and new technologies of communications, transport, energy and war.[23] A spirit of multilateralism was evident in the Hague Peace Conferences of 1899 and 1907, which codified international humanitarian law and strengthened the peaceful settlement of international disputes by

---

16     See generally Anthony Anghie, *Imperialism, Sovereignty and the Making of International Law* (Cambridge University Press, 2004). For a contemporaneous legal account of Spanish colonisation, see Francisco de Vitoria, *On the Indians and on the Law of War* (Carnegie Institution, 1917) [trans of: *De Indis et De Ivre Belli Relectiones* (1557)].

17     Orakhelashvili (n 9) [17].

18     Umut Özsu, 'The Ottoman Empire, the Origins of Extraterritoriality, and International Legal Theory' in Anne Orford and Florian Hoffmann (eds), *The Oxford Handbook of the Theory of International Law* (Oxford University Press, 2016) 123, 125.

19     See generally Martii Koskenniemi, *The Gentle Civilizer of Nations: The Rise and Fall of International Law 1870–1960* (Cambridge University Press, 2001).

20     For a critical account of this narrative see Jörg Kammerhofer, 'International Legal Positivism' in Anne Orford and Florian Hoffmann (eds), *The Oxford Handbook of the Theory of International Law* (Oxford University Press, 2016) 407.

21     James Crawford, *Brownlie's Principles of Public International Law* (Oxford University Press, 9th ed, 2019) 9.

22     As in international humanitarian law moderating the conduct of war, and – in the 20th century – the shift from 'natural' to 'human' rights, and the 'inherent' right of national self-defence.

23     See generally Hans-Ulrich Scupin, 'History of International Law: 1815 to World War I' in Rüdiger Wolfrum (ed), *The Max Planck Encyclopedia of Public International Law* (Oxford University Press, online, May 2011).

establishing the Permanent Court of Arbitration.[24] Agreement could not, however, be reached there on disarmament[25] in an era when war was lawful and Great Power rivalry later culminated in World War I.[26]

The end of World War I was characterised by the ambitious liberal internationalism of US president Woodrow Wilson, culminating in the establishment of the League of Nations, and the embedding of global values such as self-determination and procedural limits on resort to war within the League Covenant 1919. The Permanent Court of International Justice was established in 1922 and war was banned in 1928,[27] except for national self-defence.

Whereas traditional international law was concerned with coexistence among states and largely left undisturbed the power of sovereigns within their own territory, international law in this period became more concerned with protecting individuals. In addition to international humanitarian law, this was evident in the outlawing of slavery and human trafficking, protection of minorities, and the social work of the League of Nations to advance the rights of workers, women and refugees, and to promote economic prosperity and public health.[28]

### 1.2.1.3 The international order after 1945

Despite the League's many successes, its perceived failure to ensure peace in the face of fascist expansion and Great Power conflict in World War II led to a more sober view of internationalism and greater pragmatism in the design of the *Charter of the United Nations* ('*UN Charter*') of 1945. The Charter embodies a more realistic understanding of international politics by according the five permanent members of the UN Security Council (the war victors – Russia, United States, United Kingdom, France and China) special, unequal, binding powers to ensure international security. Nonetheless, a strong internationalism persists. The use of armed force, and intervention in foreign states, is prohibited.[29] The UN General Assembly has a broad competence to address most human problems and issues requiring international cooperation. The Charter also establishes the International Court of Justice ('ICJ'), albeit it is dependent on state consent to its jurisdiction (see Chapter 9).

Two key post-war trends are evident. The first is intensified concern for the human person within states' territories (thus limiting sovereign power). This is evident in human rights protection under the *UN Charter*, the *Universal Declaration of Human Rights* 1948,[30] international refugee law, and new international humanitarian law. The new collective right of self-determination entitled colonised peoples to become independent, thus shaping sovereignty

---

24    *Hague Convention for the Pacific Settlement of International Disputes*, opened for signature 29 July 1899, [1901] ATS 130 (entered into force 4 September 1900).

25    See Andrew Webster, 'Reconsidering Disarmament at the Hague Peace Conference of 1899, and After' in Maartje Abbenhuis, Christopher Barber and Annalise Higgins (eds), *War, Peace and International Order? The Legacies of the Hague Conferences of 1899 and 1907* (Routledge, 2017) 69.

26    See, eg, Margaret MacMillan, *The War That Ended Peace: How Europe Abandoned Peace for the First World War* (Profile Books, 2012); Christopher Clark, *The Sleepwalkers: How Europe Went to War in 1914* (Allen Lane, 2012).

27    *General Treaty for Renunciation of War as an Instrument of National Policy*, opened for signature 27 August 1928, 94 LNTS 57 (entered into force 24 July 1929) art 1. The treaty is also known as the *Kellogg–Briand Pact*.

28    See generally FP Walters, *A History of the League of Nations* (Oxford University Press, 1952).

29    *Charter of the United Nations* art 2(4) ('*UN Charter*').

30    GA Res 217A (III), UN GAOR, UN Doc A/810 (10 December 1948).

and statehood in new ways. This led to the rapid creation of a large number of new states from the 1950s to the early 1980s, shifting the balance of power in the General Assembly – and in law-making – from the West to developing states. Related to the enforcement of both international humanitarian law and human rights was the creation of international criminal liability of individuals for war crimes, crimes against humanity and genocide through the post-war international Nuremberg trials, the 1948 *Genocide Convention*[31] and the four *Geneva Conventions* 1949 on armed conflict.[32]

The second trend is the specialisation of international law, in areas not limited to traditional concerns for coexistence and sovereignty, to promote coordination and cooperation in areas of mutual interest. In addition to those mentioned above, specialised areas now regulate, for example, development and the international economy; international transport and communications; the environment; the oceans; other special areas, such as Antarctica and the Moon and outer space; and international organisations. Many of these are considered in other chapters of this book. International law is constantly adapting to new challenges, whether climate change, transnational terrorism, cyber activities or pandemics.

These trends are further evidence of international law's increasing regulation of conduct that was historically regarded as a purely 'internal' matter for states. Now, the way a government treats its own people, manages its environment or regulates its economy can be of direct concern to international law, even if states retain much freedom of action. Thus, national criminal trials must be fair and police detention must be humane;[33] biodiversity must be preserved, and pollution and carbon emissions limited (see Chapter 14); and foreign investors must be protected from arbitrary interference, while domestic industries must not be unfairly protected from competition by foreign imports (see Chapter 16). The bargains struck by states can be domestically controversial. Some international rules or practices, particularly economic ones, can potentially undermine others, such as those on human rights, labour or the environment.[34]

## 1.2.2   Participants

### 1.2.2.1   States

States are the central actors or participants in international law. They are commonly described as 'subjects' of international law or as 'international legal persons', meaning that they possess

---

31    *Convention on the Prevention and Punishment of the Crime of Genocide*, opened for signature 9 December 1948, 78 UNTS 277 (entered into force 12 January 1951).

32    *Geneva Convention (I) for the Amelioration of the Condition of the Wounded and Sick in Armed Forces in the Field*, opened for signature 12 August 1949, 75 UNTS 31 (entered in force 21 October 1950); *Geneva Convention (II) for the Amelioration of the Condition of Wounded, Sick and Shipwrecked Members of Armed Forces at Sea*, opened for signature 12 August 1949, 75 UNTS 85 (entered in force 21 October 1950); *Geneva Convention (III) Relative to the Treatment of Prisoners of War*, opened for signature 12 August 1949, 75 UNTS 135 (entered in force 21 October 1950); *Geneva Convention (IV) Relative to the Protection of Civilian Persons in Time of War*, opened for signature 12 August 1949, 75 UNTS 287 (entered in force 21 October 1950) (together, *'Geneva Conventions 1949'*).

33    *International Covenant on Civil and Political Rights*, opened for signature 16 December 1966, 999 UNTS 171 (entered into force 23 March 1976) art 14 (trial), arts 7 and 10 (treatment in detention).

34    See, eg, Mac Darrow, *Between Light and Shadow: The World Bank, the International Monetary Fund and International Human Rights Law* (Hart Publishing, 2003); Sarah Joseph, *Blame it on the WTO? A Human Rights Critique* (Oxford University Press, 2011).

international legal rights and obligations, have the capacity to maintain their rights by bringing international claims, and can be held internationally responsible for breaches of obligations.[35] International law specifies the rules governing which entities qualify as states (see Chapter 5). The starting point is that the entity must possess a permanent population, a defined territory, an effective and independent government, and the capacity to enter into relations with other states.[36] The acquisition of legal personality can be a gradual process that takes time; in Australia's case, its limited personality after Federation in 1901 evolved into full independent statehood over some decades (see Chapter 5). States are continuing legal persons, notwithstanding that those who represent them on the international plane – their governments – frequently change over time. As such, current governments are responsible for the acts of past ones (see Chapter 7).

## 1.2.2.2   International organisations

While international law remains state-centric, since the late 19th century a variety of other actors has proliferated. The ICJ considered the nature of international personality in its advisory opinion *Reparation for Injuries Suffered in the Service of the United Nations*.[37] The case concerned whether the United Nations could claim against Israel regarding its responsibility for the murder, by a non-state Zionist group, of a senior UN official on mission in Israel. The ICJ recognised that not only states but also the United Nations possesses international legal personality, as an international organisation distinct from the individual personalities of its member states:

> The subjects of law in any legal system are not necessarily identical in their nature or in the extent of their rights, and their nature depends upon the needs of the community. Throughout its history, the development of international law has been influenced by the requirements of international life, and the progressive increase in the collective activities of States has already given rise to instances of action upon the international plane by certain entities which are not States. This development culminated in the establishment in June 1945 of an international organization whose purposes and principles are specified in the *Charter of the United Nations*. But to achieve these ends the attribution of international personality is indispensable.[38]

As the Court suggests, international legal personality is relative. While the United Nations is the 'supreme type' of international organisation,[39] there are hundreds of others with varying capacities, from regional organisations to the World Trade Organization to the International Criminal Court (see Chapter 15). Next to states they are the most important international persons, as forums for intensifying and broadening cooperation and coordination, and in developing, implementing and enforcing international law. While the personality of the United Nations is objective, with consequences for all states, the personality of organisations with less than universal membership is more likely to be subjective, meaning that its personality depends on recognition by individual states.[40]

---

35    *Reparation for Injuries Suffered in the Service of the United Nations (Advisory Opinion)* [1949] ICJ Rep 174, 179 ('*Reparation for Injuries*'). See also Crawford (n 21) 105.
36    See, eg, *Montevideo Convention on the Rights and Duties of States* (n 2) art 1.
37    *Reparation for Injuries* (n 35).
38    Ibid 178.
39    Ibid 179.
40    Ibid.

In the case of the United Nations, evidence of its personality (which grounded its right to claim against Israel) included the requirements on its member states under the *UN Charter* to recognise its legal capacity[41] and to confer immunities and privileges on it[42] under domestic law. The endowment of the United Nations with organs and powers independent of its members, and the conferral of functions, could only be effective if the United Nations bore international personality. Depending on the actor, other evidence of international personality may include the capacities to enter into treaties,[43] to send and receive diplomatic missions, and to bring and receive international claims.[44] These capacities are distinct from whatever legal status actors may have under domestic law, including their rights and obligations and ability to sue or be sued in national courts.

### 1.2.2.3   Other actors

Whether other actors have international personality depends on how stringently or loosely the concept is understood. If it is accepted that international personality is relative and contextual, then an actor need not be able to do all the things states can do, such as make treaties or bring claims. While personality in principle arises under customary international law, it is heavily influenced by the treaties which give rise to the rights, obligations and capacities of the actor. This is particularly so for non-state entities, including international organisations (which are usually created by treaty), peoples, individuals, corporations and non-governmental organisations.

### PEOPLES

'Peoples' have had a strong claim to international personality since at least 1945. The term foremost means the populations of territories under colonial rule, including but not limited to those in 'non-self-governing territories' under the *UN Charter*.[45] Peoples are entitled to choose independence from foreign state control (see Chapter 5). Their personality is, however, restricted and context dependent. For example, they have been: able to enter into treaties with states;[46] recognised under international humanitarian law, including in procedures to trigger its application;[47] and accorded observer status at the United Nations and the possibility to be heard before the ICJ in advisory proceedings.[48] They do not, however, enjoy a general capacity to claim against states or bear international responsibility for breaches of international law.

---

41    See, eg, *UN Charter* (n 29) art 104.

42    See, eg, ibid art 105.

43    See *Vienna Convention on the Law of Treaties between States and International Organizations or between International Organizations*, opened for signature 21 March 1986, UN Doc A/CONF.129/15 (not in force).

44    Jan Klabbers, *An Introduction to International Institutional Law* (Cambridge University Press, 2002) 44–8.

45    *UN Charter* (n 29) ch XI. See the list of territories in United Nations, 'Non-Self-Governing Territories', *The United Nations and Decolonization* (Web Page, 10 May 2022) <www.un.org/dppa/decolonization/en/nsgt>.

46    See, eg, the Oslo Accords between Israel and the Palestine Liberation Organisation: *Declaration of Principles on Interim Self-Government Arrangements*, signed 13 September 1993, and *Israeli–Palestinian Interim Agreement on the West Bank and the Gaza Strip*, signed 28 September 1995.

47    *Protocol Additional (I) to the Geneva Conventions of 12 August 1949, and Relating to the Protection of Victims of International Armed Conflicts (Protocol I)*, opened for signature 8 June 1977, 1125 UNTS 3 (entered in force 7 December 1978) arts 1(4), 96.

48    For example, Palestine in *Legal Consequences of the Construction of a Wall in the Occupied Palestinian Territory (Advisory Opinion)* [2004] ICJ Rep 136.

## INDIVIDUALS

Individuals can likewise be seen as having limited international personality. Their human rights have been recognised under numerous international and regional treaties, some of which confer rights to access binding or supervisory procedures to vindicate their rights.[49] Individuals and private entities also have certain rights to protection and to access international arbitration under international investment law, and communities can bring non-binding complaints about development financing against the World Bank (see Chapter 15). Individuals are also liable under international criminal law. Again, however, their international rights, obligations and capacities are limited and specific. Also, they obviously lack the capacities of states or international organisations to make treaties or assert immunities or privileges against national jurisdiction.

## CORPORATIONS

Corporations too cannot make treaties; at most, some contracts under national law between states and foreign companies may be created, and partly governed, by international law, and vest specific international capacities in private parties.[50] Investment treaties recognise certain rights of corporations and give them access to international arbitration (as through the International Centre for Settlement of Investment Disputes) to sue states beyond national courts and applying international, not national, law.[51] There is also the sui generis personality of private corporations created under national law but accorded powers and immunities by states under treaties; they include organs for making rules and decisions ('intergovernmental corporations of private law').[52]

Corporations have rights under investment treaties to sue states, but individuals or communities have not been given international rights to sue corporations in relation to, for example, harm to human rights or the environment. Since human rights treaties only provide remedies against state violations,[53] victims must rely indirectly on domestic law for the regulation of corporations. This is often inadequate, particularly where powerful transnational corporations operate in weak states and their home states of incorporation do not regulate their extraterritorial activities. In recent decades there have been influential 'soft law' efforts to hold corporations accountable for such harms;[54] these efforts involve corporations voluntarily committing to non-binding standards and procedures.

---

49    See Section 1.2.1.3.

50    See, eg, *Texaco Overseas Petroleum Co v Libya (Merits)* (1978) 17 ILM 1, 11–19 [22]–[52] (arbitration concerning a 'stabilisation' clause in a resource concession contract, which limited the state's capacity to infringe contractual rights).

51    See Chapters 9 (dispute settlement) and 16 (international economic law).

52    Robert Jennings and Arthur Watts, *Oppenheim's International Law* (Oxford University Press, 9th ed, 1992) 22; Crawford (n 21) 112 (an example is the Swiss rolling stock financing company EUROFIMA, established by treaty).

53    States must provide effective remedies for violations of obligations owed by the state: see, eg, *International Covenant on Civil and Political Rights*, opened for signature 16 December 1966, 999 UNTS 171 (entered into force 23 March 1976) art 2. They must also ensure respect for the human rights of private actors, but individuals cannot claim directly against non-state actors.

54    See, eg, *Human Rights Council, Report of the Special Representative of the Secretary-General on the Issue of Human Rights and Transnational Corporations and Other Business Enterprises, John Ruggie*, UN Doc A/HRC/17/31 (21 March 2011) annex (*'Guiding Principles on Business and Human Rights'*),

## NON-GOVERNMENTAL ORGANISATIONS

Non-governmental organisations ('NGOs'), of which there are over 10 million globally,[55] have lesser capacities than individuals or corporations. They are established under national, not international, law; they cannot make treaties; they do not enjoy immunities or generally bear international rights or obligations; and they cannot claim or be held responsible under international law. They are, however, recognised in limited contexts, such as the representation of trade unions in the governing structure of the International Labour Organization (alongside representatives of states and employers' organisations).

More generally, the *UN Charter* provides for 'consultation' between NGOs and the UN Economic and Social Council (but not other UN organs) and almost 6,000 NGOs are registered with 'consultative status'. Depending on their type, this may entitle them to attend conferences, submit agenda items, make statements, organise events, and network. They cannot, however, vote in decisions. Yet NGOs are still influential in international law-making: examples include their campaigns for (and expert inputs during) treaty negotiations to ban landmines and cluster munitions, combat climate change and establish the International Criminal Court.[56] Their 'soft law' standards have also influenced rules adopted by states and international organisations.[57]

In international dispute settlement, NGOs *as victims* can participate in International Criminal Court proceedings and receive reparation;[58] and other NGOs can file amicus curiae briefs there and in other international courts or dispute procedures.[59] Further, NGOs can bring cases in some regional bodies.[60] Information from NGOs is often admitted in UN human rights procedures, including under treaty.[61]

## ACTORS WITH LIMITED PERSONALITY

Finally, mention should be made of the eclectic range of other actors with limited personality. For example, formally the International Committee of the Red Cross is simply a Swiss NGO, but the universally ratified four *Geneva Conventions* 1949 empower it to protect people in armed

---

endorsed by *Human Rights and Transnational Corporations and Other Business Enterprises*, HRC Res 17/4, UN Doc A/HRC/RES/17/4 (16 June 2011); Organisation for Economic Co-operation and Development, *OECD Guidelines for Multinational Enterprises* (2011 ed).

55    Stephan Hobe, 'Non-Governmental Organizations' in Rüdiger Wolfrum (ed), *The Max Planck Encyclopedia of Public International Law* (Oxford University Press, online, June 2019) [6].

56    See generally Christine Chinkin and Alan Boyle, *The Making of International Law* (Oxford University Press, 2007) ch 2; Hobe ibid [14]–[18].

57    Hobe (n 55) [14]–[18].

58    International Criminal Court, *Rules of Procedure and Evidence*, Doc No ICC-ASP/1/3 (adopted 9 September 2002) r 85 and following.

59    See, eg, Extraordinary Chambers in the Courts of Cambodia, *Internal Rules* (adopted 16 January 2015) r 33; Special Tribunal for Lebanon, *Rules of Procedure and Evidence* (adopted 10 December 2020) r 131; *Marrakesh Agreement Establishing the World Trade Organization*, opened for signature 15 April 1994, 1867 UNTS 3 (entered into force 1 January 1995) annex 2 ('*Understanding on Rules and Procedures Governing the Settlement of Disputes*') art 13.

60    *Consolidated Version of the Treaty on the Functioning of the European Union*, opened for signature 13 December 2007, [2012] OJ C 326/47 (entered into force 1 December 2009) art 263; *Convention for the Protection of Human Rights and Fundamental Freedoms*, opened for signature 4 November 1950, 213 UNTS 221 (entered into force 3 September 1953) art 34; *American Convention on Human Rights*, opened for signature 22 November 1969, 1144 UNTS 123 (entered into force 18 July 1978) art 44.

61    *Convention on the Rights of the Child*, opened for signature 20 November 1989, 1577 UNTS 3 (entered into force 2 September 1990) art 45 (committee can request NGO information).

conflicts.[62] International humanitarian law also imposes obligations on organised non-state armed groups, such as rebels or guerrillas.[63] Insurgents can also bear limited international personality, and a capacity to act internationally,[64] particularly if 'recognised' by a state.[65]

Sui generis state-like entities also have limited personality. Most states and the United Nations regard the territory of Taiwan (the Republic of China) as part of mainland China (the People's Republic of China) and not as a state. However, Taiwan has its own effective government and enters into a variety of international relations that evidence a limited personality: it is a party to treaties, it sends and receives actual or de facto diplomats, and it participates (not as a state) in some international organisations such as the World Trade Organization and World Health Organization, and fisheries arrangements.[66] More controversial is the argument that it has a right of self-defence.

Also approximating a state, but not quite, is the international religious order of the Holy See, which enters into treaties and diplomatic relations with some states; and its territorial administrative nucleus, the Vatican City, which lacks a permanent population and has a limited religious purpose.[67] Its personality is likely subjective and thus dependent on recognition by states, similar to less-than-universal international organisations. The same is true of the more tenuous personality of the Sovereign Military Hospitaller Order of Saint John of Jerusalem, of Rhodes and of Malta, a humanitarian actor which has had no territory or population since it lost Malta in 1798, but maintains relations with over 100 states and has concluded treaties.[68] Mention should also be made of 'governments in exile', which may sustain certain international capacities at least for a time after losing control of their territories.[69]

Another kind of limited legal person is a UN 'transitional administration', an entity established by the Security Council to temporarily govern a territory pending a resolution of its status, as in East Timor (1999–2002) and Kosovo (1999–2008).[70]

# 1.3    Implementation and enforcement

In the absence of any 'global police' or universal machinery for its application, international law is implemented and enforced in layered, decentralised and intersecting ways. These operate at the international, regional and national levels; through administrative and judicial measures and social processes; and involves a multitude of actors – states, international organisations, regional bodies, civil society and business. These methods of securing compliance have grown in number, breadth and sophistication over time. Critical gaps and deficiencies nonetheless remain and are largely explained by an insufficient number of states being

---

62    *Geneva Conventions* 1949 (n 32).
63    See, eg, Common Article 3 of the four *Geneva Conventions* 1949 (n 32).
64    Jennings and Watts (n 52) 553.
65    Crawford (n 21) 108.
66    See Kuan-Hsiung Wang, 'Current International Legal Issues: Taiwan' (2017) 23 *Asian Yearbook of International Law* 61.
67    Crawford (n 21) 114.
68    Ibid.
69    Ibid 115.
70    SC Res 1272, UN Doc S/RES/1272 (25 October 1999) (East Timor); SC Res 1244, UN Doc S/RES/1244 (10 June 1999) (Kosovo).

willing to cede more sovereignty to international enforcement or dispute settlement. Some states also flout the procedures that do exist. That said, some groups of states at the regional level, where mutual confidence and identity are often strongest, have pioneered stronger mechanisms than at the universal level.

## 1.3.1    International level

Like national law, international law is implemented and enforced through a multitude of processes and mechanisms. Some of these are familiar to national law, such as non-binding and binding dispute settlement procedures, with the important caveat that binding enforcement under international law is limited by the consent of states (with the important exception of action by the UN Security Council to maintain international security). International law is also more decentralised than national law in relying more heavily on methods of 'self-help'. International law structures issues of compliance through two overarching frameworks: the law of state responsibility and the law of treaties.

### 1.3.1.1    State responsibility

The law of state responsibility (discussed in Chapter 7) is a regime of rules which provides that states are responsible for breaches of their international obligations. It specifies whose conduct can be attributed to a state, and recognises circumstances precluding the wrongfulness of conduct (defences). It also addresses the consequences of a breach, including the duty to make reparation, and sets out when one state can invoke the responsibility of another. The regime only provides for inter-state complaints and is not available to any other injured actors, including individuals.

### 1.3.1.2    Diplomatic claims

The law of state responsibility does not itself establish any concrete procedures for making and pursuing a claim. At a minimum, it is usually possible for an injured state to diplomatically present its claim to the responsible state, and many international disputes are settled through this negotiated bilateral process. States are also able to make such diplomatic claims to protect their nationals injured by a foreign state, but only where domestic remedies have been exhausted before the courts of the responsible state.[71] Diplomatic protection is, however, at the discretion of the state of nationality and is not a right of the injured person. Under Australian law too, citizens at risk abroad have no right to protection by the Australian government.

### 1.3.1.3    Dispute settlement methods

Whether other specific methods of dispute settlement are available depends on the subject of the dispute, the governing treaty regime (if any), the states involved, and the extent to which those states have accepted settlement procedures. Dispute settlement is discussed in detail in Chapter 9. In brief, there are numerous possibilities which are commonly used by states. Informal, non-binding methods include negotiation, mediation, conciliation, or use of the

---

71    See Chapter 7.

'good offices' of a trusted intermediary such as the UN Secretary-General. More formal methods are binding arbitration (including through the Permanent Court of Arbitration and the International Centre for the Settlement of Investment Disputes), and adjudication in an international court or tribunal (such as the ICJ, the International Tribunal for the Law of the Sea, or the dispute panels of the World Trade Organization). There is also the International Criminal Court to prosecute individuals. Further, various regional courts can settle inter-state economic or other disputes. There is, however, no international court with binding universal jurisdiction to hear all inter-state disputes, let alone all violations of international law, including those affecting individuals.

### 1.3.1.4    Other accountability procedures

Binding procedures in international law are supplemented by many non-binding, treaty-based mechanisms for monitoring, supervising or critiquing state compliance. They include, for example, human rights procedures such as the UN Human Rights Council, the UN Human Rights Committee, 'special rapporteurs', and fact-finding commissions of inquiry or investigative mechanisms (including of the UN General Assembly and Security Council); International Labour Organization mechanisms; World Bank inspection panels to hear complaints about the Bank's development financing; verification procedures for chemical and nuclear weapons; and compliance procedures under environmental treaties.[72]

While many procedures empower states to complain but are not available to other actors, there are exceptions, as for individuals in relation to human rights, labour, the environment and investment and development. However, procedures empowering individuals or communities tend to involve non-binding outcomes, while those that provide binding decisions tend to favour economic interests, such as investor–state arbitration. The picture is different at the regional level, with binding individual remedies available before regional human rights courts in Africa, the Americas and Europe;[73] there are none in Australia's region, Asia and the Pacific.

### 1.3.1.5    Enforcement of international security

One special means of enforcement, discussed in Chapter 8, deserves mention. The UN Security Council has powers under Chapter VII of the *UN Charter* to require states to take binding enforcement action to maintain international security, for instance to combat aggression by one state against another, counter atrocities such as genocide or war crimes, or suppress terrorism. Such measures can include, for example, sanctions (such as arms embargoes or asset freezing) or military force. Action by the Council depends, however, on the political agreement of the five permanent members, any of whom can veto action.

### 1.3.1.6    Self-help

While the international system remains under-institutionalised, it preserves states' rights to resort to 'self-help' in some circumstances. Before 1928, war was permitted as a means of

---

72    Malgosia Fitzmaurice and Catherine Redgwell, 'Environmental Non-Compliance Procedures and International Law' (2009) 31 *Netherlands Yearbook of International Law* 35.

73    The African Court of Human and People's Rights, the Inter-American Court of Human Rights, and the European Court of Human Rights, respectively.

enforcing a state's rights against violations of treaties or custom. The *UN Charter* now prohibits resort to any armed force to vindicate rights,[74] except in self-defence against an armed attack.[75] While this deprives states of a historically important means of enforcing international law, the costs were judged to be worth it: risks of escalation are inherent in forcible self-help; innocent civilians may suffer; threats less than armed attack may be addressed collectively by the UN Security Council; and the Charter strengthened possibilities for the peaceful settlement of disputes.

Non-forcible self-help remains available. 'Retorsion' involves an unfriendly, but not unlawful, act in response to another state's breach; it may be designed to pressure the state to cease a continuing violation, punish it for a past violation or deter future violations.[76] Examples include withdrawing diplomats, restricting trade and halting law enforcement cooperation.

'Countermeasures' are more drastic. They involve non-forcible, ordinarily *unlawful* measures designed not to punish or deter but to induce the state in breach to comply with its obligations – where the unlawfulness of the measures is excused by its legitimate enforcement purpose. An example is refusing to honour a treaty obligation. Strict conditions apply: countermeasures must be notified, endure only while the wrongful act continues, be proportionate to the injury, and comply with fundamental rules including human rights and the ban on use of force.[77]

### 1.3.1.7   Treaty law

In concert with the law of state responsibility, which applies to the breach of any international obligation (including under a treaty) and requires reparation for breaches, the law of treaties also addresses implementation and enforcement (see Chapter 3). The fundamental principle *pacta sunt servanda* – treaties are binding and must be implemented in good faith[78] – highlights the importance of the contractual basis of treaties in securing compliance with them. Treaty law further emphasises that any inconsistency of domestic law with a treaty does not excuse violation of the treaty.[79]

Like the law of state responsibility, the law of treaties does not itself establish mechanisms for resolving disputes. A particular treaty may, however, specify the procedures that apply to a breach, including dispute settlement methods and the consequences of a breach (including remedies); such clauses are common. In addition, the general rules of treaty law address the further consequences of 'material' (particularly important) breaches, the possibility to suspend, terminate, withdraw from or denounce a treaty, and disputes about a treaty's validity.[80]

### 1.3.1.8   Social processes

Non-governmental organisations are very active in investigating, researching, documenting, monitoring, verifying, 'naming and shaming' and advocating in relation to violations in many

---

74      *UN Charter* (n 29) art 2(4).
75      Ibid art 51.
76      'Draft Articles on Responsibility of States for Internationally Wrongful Acts, with Commentaries' [2001] II(2) *Yearbook of the International Law Commission* 1, 128.
77      *ARSIWA* (n 4) arts 49–54.
78      *VCLT* (n 3) art 26.
79      Ibid art 27.
80      Ibid pt V.

areas, from human rights to the environment to arms control.[81] States are often responsive to the reputational risks of adverse global publicity, although some states suppress NGOs precisely to avoid such scrutiny.

### 1.3.2   National level

Where international law regulates state conduct on the international plane – whether ensuring respect for freedom of navigation on the high seas, or non-intervention in internal affairs – there may be no need to transform such rules into domestic law. On the other hand, the many contemporary international rules which regulate conduct in a state's territory often require domestic legislation to put them into effect, whether protecting foreign investors, respecting the immunities of diplomats, establishing liability for international crimes, or protecting human rights or the environment. In this way international law is enforced through national laws and courts.

The different ways in which international law is brought into domestic legal systems is considered in Chapter 4 – whether treating international and domestic law as a single integrated system ('monism'), as separate systems ('dualism'), or as a mixture (as in Australia). Importantly, international law emphasises that domestic law cannot excuse a violation of international law.[82] Consequently, to avoid being in breach of their obligations, states must ensure that their domestic laws are consistent with international law. At the same time, there is a symbiotic relationship between the two systems in that national laws, including judicial decisions, can themselves contribute to making international law, as evidence of customary international law, the interpretation of treaties, or 'general principles of law'.[83] International lawyers within government play a vital role in advising on compliance with international law, such as those in Australia's Attorney-General's Department and Department of Foreign Affairs and Trade.

# 1.4   The nature of international law as 'law'

In the past there was much debate about whether international law is really 'law' and, relatedly, why states should obey it. These days it is broadly accepted that it is indeed law, but explanations differ for compliance with it.[84] Whether international law is 'law', and if so what kind it is, depends on the jurisprudential starting point for considering what is 'law' generally. As we saw in Section 1.2.1, explanations for the quality of international law as 'law', including its binding force, have depended on the historical moment. Older explanations grounded in divine will or natural law are no longer sufficient, the former because international law is now secular and universal and the latter because it is too subjective and amorphous in a plural, heterogenous world.

---

81    Hobe (n 55) [22]–[24].
82    *ARSIWA* (n 4) art 3; *VCLT* (n 3) art 27.
83    The sources of international law are discussed in Chapter 2.
84    See Section 1.4.7.

# 1.4.1    International law is not 'law'?

One pessimistic answer to the question whether international law is truly law came in the early 19th century. The English domestic law positivist John Austin denied that international law was law at all, regarding it as merely 'positive morality':[85]

> [T]he law obtaining between nations is not positive law[,] for every positive law is set by a given sovereign to a person or persons in a state of subjection to its author. ... the law obtaining between nations is law (improperly so called) set by general opinion [among nations]. The duties which it imposes are enforced by moral sanctions: by fear on the part of nations, or by fear on the part of sovereigns, of provoking general hostility, and incurring its probable evils, in case they shall violate maxims generally received and respected.[86]

Austin's view was later discredited for simplistically equating law (including domestic law) with sovereign commands backed by threats. Earlier English positivists, such as William Blackstone – who wrote of the 'law of nations' – and Jeremy Bentham – who coined the term 'international law'[87] – viewed international law as law,[88] and Blackstone showed how it was treated as automatically part of English law.[89]

In the 1960s, the influential positivist HLA Hart showed that not all rules emanate from a central sovereign (such as sub-national community, tribal, or religious customary laws) or coercively direct behaviour (such as rules conferring powers), and that obedience to law cannot be explained by Austin's view of sovereignty.[90] Hart did not see the lack of centralised sanctions as fatal to international law since even in domestic law legal obligation is distinct from enforceability[91] – even if the latter is desirable. He saw the international order as qualitatively different from domestic systems, since forcible sanctions between states carry 'fearful risks' of unpredictable violence without necessarily deterring powerful states.[92] For Hart, it is enough that

> what these rules require is thought and spoken of as obligatory; there is general pressure for conformity to the rules; claims and admissions are based on them and their breach is held to justify not only insistent demands for compensation, but reprisals and counter-measures. When the rules are disregarded, it is not on the footing that they are not binding; instead efforts are made to conceal the facts.[93]

Hart also disagreed with the view that international law is mere morality, since in practice states treat it and publicly formulate it in legal terms, including by reference to rights, obligations,

---

85    John Austin, *The Province of Jurisprudence Determined* (John Murray, 1832) 132.
86    Ibid 208; see also 147–51.
87    Jeremy Bentham, *An Introduction to the Principles of Morals and Legislation* (Methuen, 1970) 6, 293–300.
88    See Mark Weston Janis, *America and the Law of Nations 1776–1939* (Oxford University Press, 2010) ch 1.
89    William Blackstone, *Commentaries on the Laws of England: A Facsimile of the First Edition of 1765–1769* (University of Chicago Press, 1979) vol 4, 67.
90    HLA Hart, *The Concept of Law* (Clarendon, 2nd ed, 1994) 27–48.
91    Ibid 218.
92    Ibid 219.
93    Ibid 220.

criticism of wrongdoing, demands for compensation, and retaliation; they also distinguish it from moral claims, including from habitual courtesies or politeness in international relations known as 'international comity'.[94] Further, some international law is morally indifferent, such as convenient or technical rules – for example, about the width of the territorial sea.[95] Even international law as a whole does not depend on an overall moral obligation to obey it, given states' diverse motives for adherence, such as tradition, long-term interest, or altruism.[96]

## 1.4.2 Voluntarism: law by sovereign consent

In contrast to Austin's approach which was rooted in domestic law, 19th century positivism in international law was associated with 'voluntarism' (or 'auto-limitation'). This view held that the legal quality of international law arose from the will of states, expressed in their consent to be bound. In the *Lotus* case in the 1920s, the Permanent Court of Justice declared that '[t]he rules of law binding upon States therefore emanate from their own free will ... Restrictions upon the independence of States therefore cannot be presumed'.[97] That approach appears helpful in reconciling the contradiction between 'sovereignty' as freedom from external constraints and the limits imposed by international law. It is, however, insufficient.

It is true that treaties are entered into by each state giving specific consent and do not normally have effects for non-party states. However, some treaties, such as the *UN Charter*, do have legal consequences for non-parties, whether in relation to the Security Council's enforcement powers or the objective international personality of the United Nations. In other situations, consent is attenuated or nominal, as where international organisations are empowered by their treaties to 'make' law for member states, or where 'framework' treaties, as in environmental law, presume consent to new rules through opt-out procedures.[98]

In the case of customary law, voluntarism is even more problematic. Custom is supposed to reflect the practices and legal beliefs of states collectively, but does not require each state's specific consent, other than negatively through 'persistent objection' during its formation. Further, peremptory rules (*jus cogens*) are not subject to objection at all, and cannot be contracted out of by treaties. In addition, new states are automatically bound by customs they had no role in creating;[99] even a relatively old state like Australia had no role in forming centuries of international law before its establishment. A similar problem applies in relation to new territories acquired by existing states.[100]

There thus exist rules of international law which are not based on consent, and reasons other than voluntarism are necessary to explain their binding nature. For Hart, earlier positivists asked the wrong question. The issue is not how to reconcile sovereign freedoms with international legal constraints, but how international law itself constitutes the scope of sovereignty.[101]

---

94    Ibid 228, 231.
95    Ibid 229–30.
96    Ibid 231–2.
97    *SS 'Lotus' (France v Turkey) (Judgment)* [1927] PCIJ (ser A) No 10, 18.
98    Frauke Lachenmann, 'Legal Positivism' in Rüdiger Wolfrum (ed), *The Max Planck Encyclopedia of Public International Law* (Oxford University Press, online, July 2011) [34].
99    Hart (n 90) 226.
100   Ibid.
101   Ibid 223–4. See also Jennings and Watts (n 52) 12.

## 1.4.3   Hart: international law is law lacking a legal system

Hart developed his own concept of law, involving 'primary rules' which direct behaviour and 'secondary rules' which confer powers and are the 'rules about rules'.[102] The latter are threefold: there are *rules of recognition*, such as rules in a constitution, which identify valid primary rules; *rules of change* which authorise changes in the primary rules, as by a legislature; and *rules of adjudication* which provide for authoritative decision-making about breaches of primary rules, as through the courts.[103] Hart evaluates international law in the light of this concept. He acknowledges the obvious differences between international and domestic law:

> International law lacks a legislature, states cannot be brought before international courts without their prior consent, and there is no centrally organized effective system of sanctions. Certain types of primitive law, including those out of which some contemporary legal systems may have gradually evolved, similarly lack these features ...[104]

International law also lacks *rules of recognition* for identifying valid sources of law.[105] However, Hart does not conclude that international law is not law, since *rules of recognition* are not essential for law to be binding: 'if rules are in fact accepted as standards of conduct, and supported with appropriate forms of social pressure distinctive of obligatory rules, nothing more is required to show that they are binding rules'.[106] For Hart, international law is a simple social structure consisting of a set of primary rules – and the next closest thing to domestic law[107] – but it is not a 'legal system' because it lacks secondary rules.[108]

While partly redeeming international law from the 'Austinian handicap', Hart's influential account has also been criticised. One response accepts Hart's concept of law but challenges how he applies his 'domestic analogy' to international law. Thus, Hart underestimates how *rules of recognition* are cumulatively supplied by art 38 of the *Statute of the International Court of Justice* which identifies sources of law, the *pacta sunt servanda* principle, and techniques for resolving conflicts of norms – including priority for *jus cogens* norms, *UN Charter* obligations, *lex specialis* (special law, which prevails over general law), and treaties later in time. Since the 1960s when Hart wrote, enforcement has become much more institutionalised, with more binding adjudication and post–Cold War possibilities for Security Council action. And *rules of change* are evident in the law of treaties, the rules on custom formation, and the law-making powers of international organisations. None of this makes for a perfect domestic analogy, but it moves international law and domestic law closer together than Hart supposed.

A more fundamental response challenges Hart's concept of legal systems as the standard for evaluating international law, and law in general. Hart conceives of legal systems as occupying positions on a continuum of primitive to sophisticated, based on a historically

---

102    Hart (n 90) 80–1.
103    Ibid 94–8.
104    Ibid 3–4.
105    Ibid 233.
106    Ibid 234.
107    Ibid 237.
108    Ibid 234.

and culturally contingent, ideal type of English law (particularly private and criminal law)[109] and its separation of powers. In practice many national legal systems do not fully satisfy his model, including so-called 'advanced' ones like those of the United Kingdom or the United States. For instance, certain legislative and executive acts can be non-reviewable,[110] and constitutions may not specify the validity of all primary rules, rules of interpretation,[111] or powers of judicial review.[112] A more contextual account of law would be more receptive to the plurality of 'legal' cultures – and different 'systems' – and the different reasons explaining their normativity, rather than offering a singular common law or statist 'domestic analogy' as the gold standard. It would also not fixate on rules but consider other sources of norms, such as principles and policies as suggested by Dworkin,[113] or legal processes.[114]

Of course, positivist accounts are unable to *legally* explain the binding force of *rules of recognition*. In the early 20th century, the German jurist Hans Kelsen argued that legal norms depend for their validity on a chain of prior superior norms that reaches back until a basic norm (*Grundnorm*) is reached,[115] a view reflected in Hart's *rules of recognition*. However, a lacuna remains: what validates a constitution, which is ultimately a political convention whose binding quality and observance depend not on law but politics? In the same vein, what is the basis of the meta-rule that 'treaties are binding' other than a political belief or natural law supposition that this is so? Legal systems are only as strong as the political and social customs in which they are embedded; law is not autonomously authoritative, as numerous coups d'état in many states demonstrate. Judges cannot stop governments of gunmen, even if they possess ostensibly 'binding' jurisdiction to enforce laws validated by *rules of recognition*. In this sense, international law has proved more stable and law-like than many national legal orders.[116]

## 1.4.4   Realists: international law is subordinate to power

A more existential critique comes from outside the discipline of law, from international relations scholars in the broad 'realist' school.[117] The perceived 'utopian' failures of the interwar, neo-Kantian internationalism of the League of Nations, and the onset of the Cold War and UN paralysis, led many US scholars[118] to characterise the international system as an

---

109    Mehrdad Payandeh, 'The Concept of International Law in the Jurisprudence of HLA Hart' (2011) 21(4) *European Journal of International Law* 967, 980.

110    Ibid 985–6.

111    Ibid 990.

112    Ibid 992.

113    Ronald Dworkin, *Taking Rights Seriously* (Harvard University Press, 1977).

114    See Section 1.4.6.

115    Hans Kelsen, *General Theory of Law and State*, tr A Wedberg (Russell & Russell, 1961) 110–11. See also Joseph Raz, 'Kelsen's Theory of the Basic Norm' (1974) 19 *American Journal of Jurisprudence* 94.

116    Iain Brownlie, 'The Reality and Efficacy of International Law' (1981) 52 *British Yearbook of International Law* 1, 8.

117    See generally Oliver Jütersonke, 'Realist Approaches to International Law' in Anne Orford and Florian Hoffmann (eds), *The Oxford Handbook of the Theory of International Law* (Oxford University Press, 2016) 327, 340. See, eg, Hans Morgenthau, *Politics among Nations: The Struggle for Power and Peace* (McGraw-Hill, 6th ed, 1985).

118    Harold Kongju Koh, 'Why Do Nations Obey International Law?' (1997) 106 *The Yale Law Journal* 2599, 2615.

anarchic theatre of conflict, in which rational decisions about state survival, military power and balance-of-power politics decisively drive state behaviour. Hobbes had likewise emphasised sovereign competition in the 17th century – although he accepted that there is also a place for beneficial horizontal cooperation in '[l]eagues between Common-wealths'.[119] Realists view international law either as a strictly consensual instrument of national self-interest whose uses include solving mutual coordination problems and reducing transaction costs[120] (in which case it reflects but does not constrain power)[121] or as irrelevant.[122] It is only enforced if the powerful desire. The influential realist Hans Morgenthau regards the subordinate role of international law as follows:

> The great majority of rules of international law are generally observed by all nations without actual compulsion, for it is generally in the interest of all nations concerned to honour their obligations under international law. . . . It is for this reason that they generally enforce themselves, as it were, and that there is generally no need for a specific enforcement action. In most cases [of violations] . . . satisfaction is given to the wronged party either voluntarily or in consequence of adjudication.
>
> . . . The problem of enforcement becomes acute, however, in that minority of important and generally spectacular cases . . . in which compliance and its enforcement have a direct bearing upon the relative power of the nations concerned. In those cases . . . considerations of power rather than of law determine compliance and enforcement.[123]

Related to realism is 'international law and economics' scholarship since the 1970s which explains state behaviour by rational economic choice analysis and game theory.[124] International law is thus an expression of states (and individuals) maximising their interests, including in areas of mutual interest and through consensual coordination and cooperation.[125] Rationalist, 'institutionalist' approaches likewise see some (albeit limited) scope for self-interested, rational cooperation through international institutions.[126]

Realists fail, however, to adequately account for the many instances where powerful states adhere to international law, not only when there is no self-interest in doing so, but even when it conflicts with their interests.[127] International law often exerts normative force that is distinct from calculations about power. The end of the Cold War further challenged realist assumptions, with a renewed liberal internationalism in a more active UN Security Council, a revival of

---

119    Thomas Hobbes, *Leviathan* (Penguin, 1986) 286.
120    Stephen Krasner, 'Realist Views of International Law' (2002) *ASIL Proceedings* 265, 266.
121    Anne-Marie Slaughter and Thomas Hale, 'International Relations, Principal Theories' in Rüdiger Wolfrum (ed), *The Max Planck Encyclopedia of Public International Law* (Oxford University Press, online, September 2013) [6].
122    Other than indirectly in influencing domestic foreign policy constituencies and choices: Krasner (n 120) 266.
123    Morgenthau (n 117) 312–13.
124    See Dan Danielsen, 'International Law and Economics' in Anne Orford and Florian Hoffmann (eds), *The Oxford Handbook of the Theory of International Law* (Oxford University Press, 2016) 452. See, eg, Jack Goldsmith and Eric Posner, *The Limits of International Law* (Oxford University Press, 2005).
125    Danielsen (n 124) 454.
126    Slaughter and Hale (n 121) [8]–[13].
127    Shirley Scott, 'International Law as Ideology: Theorizing the Relationship between International Law and International Politics' (1994) 5(3) *European Journal of International Law* 313, 313–14.

international criminal justice (including establishment of the International Criminal Court), humanitarian intervention, and creation of the World Trade Organization.[128]

These debates are, however, cyclical. Since the 2000s realism has revived, and internationalism has been dampened, by several developments: the illegal US–UK–Australian invasion of Iraq in 2003 (a *jus cogens* violation, and an international crime),[129] renewed competition between the West and Russia and China at the United Nations, Russia's aggression in Ukraine,[130] China's illegal maritime activities in the South China Sea,[131] and the relative rise of China and decline of the United States.

## 1.4.5    Pragmatists: international law is recognised and treated as law

Given the theoretical challenges of articulating the binding nature of international law, and the post–World War II divorce of international relations realists from international lawyers,[132] many international lawyers after the war resorted, like Hart, to sociological, empirical or 'commonsense' explanations. A mainstream account is provided by Humphrey Waldock, writing in the 1960s:

> [Q]uestions of international law are invariably treated as legal questions by the foreign offices which conduct our international business, and in the courts, national or international, before which they are brought … It is significant too that when a breach of international law is alleged … the act impugned is practically never defended by claiming the right of private judgment, which would be the natural defence if the issue concerned the morality of the act, but always by attempting to prove that no rule has been violated.
>
> …
>
> If … as probably most competent jurists would today agree, the only essential conditions for the existence of law are the existence of a political community, and the recognition by its members of settled rules binding upon them in that capacity, international law seems on the whole to satisfy these conditions. …
>
> Violations of law are rare … For the law is normally observed because … the demands that it makes on states are generally not exacting, and on the whole states find it convenient to observe it …[133]

Philip Jessup similarly emphasises that breaches are the exception, not the rule, and that the disproportionate attention attracted by spectacular breaches such as war overshadows routine compliance in most areas: 'The record proves that there is a "law habit" in international relations'.[134] For Louis Henkin, too, '[a]lmost all nations observe almost all principles of

---

128    Martti Koskenniemi, 'International Legal Theory and Doctrine' in Rüdiger Wolfrum (ed), *The Max Planck Encyclopedia of Public International Law* (Oxford University Press, online, November 2007) [11].

129    See, eg, Sean Murphy, 'Assessing the Legality of Invading Iraq' (2004) 92(2) *Georgetown Law Journal* 173.

130    *Territorial Integrity of Ukraine*, GA Res 68/262, UN Doc A/RES/68/262 (adopted 27 March 2014).

131    *South China Sea Arbitration (Republic of the Philippines v People's Republic of China) (Award)* (Permanent Court of Arbitration, Case No 2013-19, 12 July 2016).

132    Koh, 'Why Do Nations Obey' (n 118) 2615–16.

133    JL Brierly, *The Law of Nations*, rev Humphrey Waldock (Clarendon Press, 6th ed, 1963) 68–69, 71, 71–2.

134    Philip Jessup, *A Modern Law of Nations* (Macmillan, 1948) 6–8.

international law and almost all of their obligations almost all of the time'.[135] Henkin acknowledges that international law is not necessarily the 'paramount' or even a dominant motivation of state behaviour;[136] consider, for instance, whether nuclear deterrence and 'mutually assured destruction', or the *UN Charter*'s prohibition on the use of force, prevented the Cold War from turning hot. But Henkin emphasises:

> Because of the requirements of law ... nations modify their conduct in significant respects and in substantial degrees. It takes an extraordinary and substantially more important interest to persuade a nation to violate its obligations. Foreign policy is far from free; even the most powerful nations have learned that there are forces ... in the society of nations that limit their freedom of choice.[137]

International law is binding because it is recognised as law by its participants, and this in turn may derive from many factors: positivistic consent, realist self-interest (including the rational need to cooperate,[138] reciprocity and concern for reputation), morality (including natural law, and altruism), or the social need to cooperate in an interdependent world.[139]

It remains true, however, that powerful states occasionally violate international law with relative impunity. This occurs even in relation to such fundamental rules as the prohibitions on the use of force (such as the Iraq invasion in 2003), or torture (as in US practices after 9/11), or the acquisition of territory by force (as in Russia's annexation of Crimea since 2014, or Israel's annexation of Palestine's East Jerusalem and Syria's Golan Heights). In certain areas many less powerful states also enjoy impunity, as in relation to domestic human rights, where other states may be relatively uninterested in their enforcement. Australia, for example, is notorious for violating international law by unlawfully detaining thousands of asylum seekers.[140] Elsewhere, it is sadly true that most international crimes in most conflicts will never be punished.

Again, however, to some extent this is a difference of degree not of kind. In many domestic legal systems, law enforcement is weak, selective, arbitrary, corrupt or ineffective. Even in strong legal systems like Australia's, noncompliance is endemic in some areas and enforcement is limited, tokenistic or arbitrary. Consider, for example, that most people (representing millions of violations) did not comply with public health restrictions during the COVID-19 pandemic,[141] and that almost 80% of Australian drivers break the road speed limit.[142] Consider also the prevalence of tax evasion,[143] the small chance that sexual assault will be

---

135    Louis Henkin, *How Nations Behave* (Columbia University Press, 2nd ed, 1979) 47.
136    Ibid 321.
137    Ibid.
138    Koskenniemi, 'International Legal Theory and Doctrine' (n 128) [18].
139    Ibid [19].
140    See, eg, Human Rights Committee, 59th sess, *Views: Communication No 560/1993*, UN Doc CCPR/C/59/D/560/1993 (3 April 1997) ('*A v Australia*').
141    See, eg, Kristina Murphy, Harley Williamson and Elise Sargeant, 'Why People Comply with COVID-19 Social Distancing Restrictions: Self-Interest or Duty?' (2020) 53(3) *Journal of Criminology* 477 (only 21% of surveyed people reported they complied with all COVID-19 restrictions).
142    'The Staggering Number of Australians Who Admit to Speeding', *3AW News* (Radio 3AW, 30 April 2021) (findings of the Australian Road Safety Foundation survey).
143    There is an annual 'tax gap' of $31 billion, or 7% of total tax owed: 'Tax Gap Program Summary Findings', *Australian Taxation Office* (Web Page, 30 August 2021) <www.ato.gov.au/About-ATO/Research-and-statistics/In-detail/Tax-gap/Australian-tax-gaps-overview/?anchor=Summaryfindings#Summaryfindings>.

punished,[144] the miniscule chance that thieves will be caught,[145] the fact that federal environmental assessments were not sought for 93% of the vast threatened species habitat cleared from 2000 to 2019[146] or that 'the cost of legal representation is beyond the reach of many, probably most, ordinary Australians'.[147]

Pragmatists have also punctured the claim sometimes made by domestic lawyers that international law is too indeterminate to be legally binding. As Waldock observes:

> It is a natural consequence of the absence of authoritative law-declaring machinery that many of the principles of international law . . . are uncertain. But on the whole the layman tends to exaggerate this defect. It is not in the nature of any law to provide mathematically certain solutions . . . so long as the possible conjunctions of facts remain infinitely various. . . . Therefore the difference between international law and the law of a state in this respect . . . is one of degree and not of kind, and it tends to be reduced as . . . resorting to international courts . . . becomes more common.[148]

Many treaty rules in particular are highly specific. The vagueness of some international rules can, however, allow them to be stretched to suit the political purposes of powerful states,[149] as debates about the use of force and self-defence often illustrate. Conversely, ambiguity can also be 'constructive', as when it enables a larger number of states to agree to a treaty than if its provisions were specific and thus disagreeable.

## 1.4.6    International law as process

Beyond the mainstream of practising international lawyers, theoretical debate was taken in new directions by American 'legal process' schools in the 1960s, namely the 'international legal process' and 'New Haven' approaches. Contrary to realists, the proponents elucidated the constraining and constitutive roles of international law in policy decision-making.[150]

---

144     About 87% of sexual assaults are not reported to police: Australian Institute of Health and Welfare, 'Sexual Assault in Australia' (28 August 2020) 5 <www.aihw.gov.au/reports/domestic-violence/sexual-assault-in-australia/contents/summary>. Of those reported, police take no action in 25% of cases; 35% remain unsolved; and legal action is taken in 30% of cases: Inga Ting, Nathanael Scott and Alex Palmer, 'Rough Justice: How Police Are Failing Survivors of Sexual Assault', *ABC News* (online, 28 January 2020) <www.abc.net.au/news/2020-01-28/how-police-are-failing-survivors-of-sexual-assault/11871364>. About half of prosecutions result in a conviction: Nicole Precel, Rachael Dexter and Eleanor Marsh, 'Are We Failing Victims of Sexual Violence?', *The Sydney Morning Herald* (online, 13 September 2019) <www.smh.com.au/interactive/2019/are-we-failing-victims-of-sexual-violence/nowebgl/smh.html>.

145     Charles Hymas, 'Police Fail to Solve a Single Theft in More Than Eight out of 10 Neighbourhoods', *The Telegraph* (online, 7 August 2022) (no thefts solved by UK police in 84% of 21,000 UK neighbourhoods in three years) <www.telegraph.co.uk/news/2022/08/07/police-fail-solve-single-theft-eight-10-neighbourhoods>.

146     Michelle Ward et al, 'Environment Laws Have Failed to Tackle the Extinction Emergency', *The Conversation* (online, 9 September 2019) <theconversation.com/environment-laws-have-failed-to-tackle-the-extinction-emergency-heres-the-proof-122936>.

147     Productivity Commission, *Access to Justice Arrangements* (Inquiry Report, No 72, September 2014) 5 (quoting Chief Justice of Western Australia, Wayne Martin).

148     Brierly (n 133) 75–6.

149     Barbara Delcourt, 'Compliance, Theory of' in Rüdiger Wolfrum (ed), *The Max Planck Encyclopedia of Public International Law* (Oxford University Press, online at September 2013) [25].

150     Koh, 'Why Do Nations Obey' (n 118) 2599; Mary Ellen O'Connell, 'Legal Process School' in Rüdiger Wolfrum (ed), *The Max Planck Encyclopedia of Public International Law* (Oxford University Press, online, November 2006).

The New Haven school focuses on how international law involves the making of policy-oriented choices by legal experts, ideally grounded in values of public order and human dignity.[151] It also opened up a discussion about how the legitimacy of legal processes, including in international institutions, affects compliance.[152]

## 1.4.7  Theories of compliance with international law

A variety of 'compliance' theories have proliferated since the 1990s, bridging international relations and international law. For the regime theory 'managerialists' Abram Chayes and Antonia Chayes, participation in multilateral treaty regimes generates dynamics that induce compliance,[153] including because compliance is efficient and avoids the transaction costs of recalculating routine decisions.[154] Another writer in this rationalist tradition, Andrew Guzman, for whom self-interest is still a critical determinant,[155] emphasises the importance of reputational concerns and the risk of sanctions in shaping behaviour.[156]

A different, liberal explanation is offered by Thomas Franck, who argues that compliance depends on the legitimacy of rules and the fairness of legal processes.[157] Legitimacy in turn depends on the determinacy of rules, how they are symbolically validated in the international social order or international community, their coherence or consistency in application, and adherence to a 'right' international legal process in the making and enforcement of rules. A risk in this approach is that it may prioritise procedural legitimacy over substantive outcomes and redistributive justice.[158]

In contrast to Franck's procedural model, a different strand of liberal internationalism suggests that compliance depends on domestic political and legal structures,[159] although it is also interested in stronger international institutionalisation. If states are democratic, respect rights and abide by the rule of law, they are more likely to comply. Such claims may be verifiable in some fields, but they do not account for noncompliance by some powerful democracies in certain areas, from the use of force to human rights; and the unpredictability

---

151    Harold Kongju Koh, 'Is There a "New Haven" School of International Law?' (2007) 32(2) *The Yale Journal of International Law* 559, 562–4; W Michael Reisman, 'The View from the New Haven School of International Law' (1992) 86 *ASIL Proceedings* 118–25. See especially Harold Lasswell and Myers McDougal, *Jurisprudence for a Free Society* (New Haven Press, 1992).

152    Delcourt (n 149) [6].

153    Abram Chayes and Antonia Handler Chayes, *The New Sovereignty: Compliance with International Regulatory Agreements* (Harvard University Press, 1995).

154    Delcourt (n 149) 9 (referring to Chayes and Chayes ibid).

155    Koh, 'Why Do Nations Obey' (n 118) 2632–4.

156    Andrew Guzman, 'A Compliance-Based Theory of International Law' (2002) 90(6) *California Law Review* 1823; Andrew Guzman, *How International Law Works: A Rational Choice Theory* (Oxford University Press, 2008).

157    Thomas Franck, *The Power of Legitimacy among Nations* (Oxford University Press, 1990); Thomas Franck, *Fairness in International Law and Institutions* (Oxford University Press, 1995). See also Jutta Brunnée and Stephen Toope, *Legitimacy and Legality in International Law* (Cambridge University Press, 2010).

158    Gerry Simpson, 'Is International Law Fair?' (1996) 17(3) *Michigan Journal of International Law* 563, 641.

159    Koh, 'Why Do Nations Obey' (n 118) 2633. See, eg, Anne-Marie Slaughter, 'International Law in a World of Liberal States' (1995) 6(4) *European Journal of International Law* 503. See generally Daniel Joyce, 'Liberal Internationalism' in Anne Orford and Florian Hoffmann (eds), *The Oxford Handbook of the Theory of International Law* (Oxford University Press, 2016) 471.

of domestic politics makes it difficult to generalise about compliance over time.[160] They are also vulnerable to imperialism, whether through humanitarian intervention or neoliberal economic governance,[161] as powerful domestic orders project their values onto the world.

Like liberalism, 'constructivist' approaches contrast with rationalist accounts but explore how states' interests and practices are socially constructed by their identities and beliefs, and their exposure, through international interactions, to common principles, social norms, and legal argumentation.[162] Rules are not simply made by states to advance their self-interest, but are constitutive of state behaviour. Compliance with human rights law, for example, arises from a combination of inducements, persuasion, sanctions, and acculturation or socialisation.[163]

Finally, the 'transnational legal process' approach, associated with Harold Koh, expands the analysis of compliance beyond purely international law-based reasons which focus on inter-state and vertical (international to domestic level) processes. It examines how norms are internalised in state behaviour through more plural, horizontal and interactive processes involving state and non-state actors, including international organisations, NGOs, multinational corporations, and individuals; public and private law, such as a cross-border commercial law; and domestic, transnational and international law mechanisms.[164] Compliance is considered to be more likely where international rules are domestically internalised.[165]

# 1.5    Critical theories

Various critical approaches to international law are not necessarily concerned with its quality as 'law' or compliance; rather, they critique its norms, discourses, assumptions or effects. These approaches include Marxism, Third World Approaches to International Law, feminism and postmodernism.[166]

## 1.5.1    Marxism

Marxism entails not only a theory of law but also, through socialist states, its practice. It understands law (and political order) as the 'superstructure' built atop the 'foundation' of society's evolving economic structure, including its relations of production between capital and workers.[167] At the international level, international law is thus part of the superstructure of the global economic order,[168] whether during colonialism or contemporary globalisation.

---

160    Guzman, 'A Compliance-Based Theory' (n 156) 1839.
161    Joyce (n 159) 475.
162    Slaughter and Hale (n 121) [19]–[23].
163    See, eg, Thomas Risse, Stephen Ropp and Kathryn Sikkink (eds), *The Power of Human Rights: International Norms and Domestic Change* (Cambridge University Press, 1999); Ryan Goodman and Derek Jinks, *Socializing States: Promoting Human Rights through International Law* (Oxford University Press, 2013).
164    See Harold Kongju Koh, 'Transnational Legal Process' (1996) 75(1) *Nebraska Law Review* 181.
165    Ibid 203–5.
166    These are not exhaustive of the array of contemporary theories; another, for instance, is critical race theory: HJ Richardson III, 'To the Co-Editors in Chief' (2000) 94(1) *American Journal of International Law* 99.
167    Karl Marx, *A Contribution to the Critique of Political Economy* (International Publishers, 1970) 20.
168    GI Tunkin (ed), *International Law* (Progress Publishers, 1986) 16.

Marxists recognise that international law is relatively autonomous from the states which create it (which themselves reflect bourgeois interests, not society as a whole), and thus constrains states' behaviour, but they critique its relations of power, exploitation and exclusion.[169] A leading Indian Marxist scholar, BS Chimni, explains:

> First, a Marxist approach to international law is inextricably related to its theory of international relations whose essence is in the final analysis determined by the manner in which states are internally organised. . . . Second, it follows, the foreign policy of a state is integrally linked to its domestic policy and is articulated and executed in the matrix of a specific socio-economic formation based on a definite and dominant mode of production. . . . Third, it . . . contends that the state in its external relations does not seek to realise 'national interests' but rather the interests of particular groups and classes. Fourth, it does not view the contemporary international system as a mere sum of its parts but as possessing a distinct identity created by the supranational character of capitalism which is rooted in a world market and an international division of labour which together constitute the world economy. Together, these propositions point towards a perception of international law and institutions as a device which serves sectional global interests.[170]

These concerns have led to critiques of specific areas of international law, such as the liberal economic, hegemonic influence of international organisations, Western imperial abuse of military force, an emphasis on strong sovereignty as a shield against intervention, and a suspicion of international adjudication as a tool of the bourgeoisie.[171] Since the 1990s, the focus has been on the hegemonic and exploitative impacts of globalisation, including the neoliberal co-option of developing states, as in the deep reform of developing economies through international finance, investment, and trade law, and the disempowerment of resistance movements.[172]

In practice, Marxist views, including those advanced by some developing countries, influenced the international development agenda; the activities of UN bodies; and the recognition of the right to development, of the economic rights and duties of states, and of individual economic, social and labour rights.[173] At the same time, the Marxist-Leninist socialist internationalism of the Soviet Union justified unlawful forcible interventions in other socialist states to protect socialism, as part of a regional socialist international law.[174] For Marxism ultimately also sees law as an instrument of revolution and as subordinate to socialism's ideological goals.[175] In contrast, communist China's approach after 1949 was less influenced by Marxism and was more pragmatic, including while it embraced the international economy from the 1980s.

---

169    Bhupinder Chimni, 'Marxism' in Rüdiger Wolfrum (ed), *The Max Planck Encyclopedia of Public International Law* (Oxford University Press, online, July 2011) [4], [15].
170    BS Chimni, 'Marxism and International Law: A Contemporary Analysis' (1999) 34(6) *Economic and Political Weekly* 337.
171    See Chimni, 'Marxism' (n 169).
172    Chimni, 'Marxism and International Law' (n 170).
173    Ibid.
174    Chimni, 'Marxism' (n 169) (as in, for example, Hungary and Czechoslovakia).
175    See, eg, Martin Krygier, 'Marxism and the Rule of Law: Reflections after the Collapse of Communism' (1990) 15(4) *Law and Social Inquiry* 633.

## 1.5.2   Third World Approaches to International Law

Related to Marxism is the movement 'Third World Approaches to International Law' (or 'TWAIL'), which crystallised in the 1990s but had roots in the earlier practices of postcolonial developing states. Based on self-determination under the *UN Charter*, rapid decolonisation from 1945 to the 1970s led to newly independent developing states gaining a majority in the General Assembly, overtaking the Western bloc. These states, often allied with socialist states, challenged aspects of the international legal order, including in regard to control over natural resources and the global liberal economic model. These pressures led to modest reforms in UN development practices and institutions, but failed to secure a transformative 'New International Economic Order' as some had hoped.[176] Makau Mutua explains TWAIL as follows:

> The regime of international law is illegitimate. It is a predatory system that legitimizes, reproduces and sustains the plunder and subordination of the Third World by the West. Neither universality nor its promise of global order and stability make international law a just, equitable, and legitimate code of global governance for the Third World. The construction and universalization of international law were essential to the imperial expansion that subordinated non-European peoples and societies to European conquest and domination. Historically, the Third World has generally viewed international law as a regime and discourse of domination and subordination, not resistance and liberation. This broad dialectic of opposition to international law is defined and referred to here as Third World Approaches to International Law ...
>
> TWAIL is driven by three basic, interrelated and purposeful objectives. The first is to understand, deconstruct, and unpack the uses of international law as a medium for the creation and perpetuation of a racialized hierarchy of international norms and institutions that subordinate non-Europeans to Europeans. Second, it seeks to construct and present an alternative normative legal edifice for international governance. Finally, TWAIL seeks through scholarship, policy, and politics to eradicate the conditions of underdevelopment in the Third World.[177]

Like Marxism, TWAIL constructively seeks to reform international law. Chimni, for example, has argued for greater accountability of international institutions and transnational corporations; shifting permanent sovereignty over natural resources from states to their peoples; using human rights and environmental law to challenge the economic order; and promoting human mobility from the Third World.[178]

## 1.5.3   Feminism

Feminist theories have also been applied to international law since the 1990s, but like TWAIL are grounded in earlier legal activism, whether for women's rights at the League of Nations in

---

176    See Giorgio Sacerdoti, 'New International Economic Order' in Rüdiger Wolfrum (ed), *The Max Planck Encyclopedia of Public International Law* (Oxford University Press, online, September 2015).

177    Makau Mutua, 'What is TWAIL?' (2000) 94 *ASIL Proceedings* 31, 31.

178    See BS Chimni, 'Third World Approaches to International Law: A Manifesto' (2006) 8 *International Community Law Review* 3.

the 1920s[179] or the post-war UN human rights movement. They have been concerned not only with traditional 'women's issues' such as gender violence and reproductive rights, but increasingly also 'mainstream' topics including economic and governance structures and international security. There is much diversity in feminist theory, for instance, as between liberal, cultural[180] and radical approaches; and differences between Western/Northern feminism, with its risks of imperialism, including at the United Nations, and feminism from the South/developing states. There is also growing attention to the intersection of identity and experience, including in relation to factors such as ethnicity, disability and age.

Leading feminist scholars Hilary Charlesworth, Christine Chinkin and Shelley Wright argue that the international legal order is 'virtually impervious to the voices of women' for two reasons. The first is because of its organisational structure:

> The [organisational] structure of the international legal order reflects a male perspective and ensures its continued dominance. The primary subjects of international law are states and, increasingly, international organizations. In both … the invisibility of women is striking. Power structures … are overwhelmingly masculine …
>
> Long-term domination of all bodies wielding political power … means that issues traditionally of concern to men become seen as general human concerns, while 'women's concerns' are relegated to a special, limited category.

The second reason is because of international law's normative structure:

> International jurisprudence assumes that international law norms directed at individuals within states are universally applicable and neutral. It is not recognized, however, that such principles may impinge differently on men and women; consequently, women's experiences of the operation of these laws tend to be silenced or discounted. …
>
> [T]he definition of certain principles of international law rests on and reproduces the public/private distinction. It thus privileges the male world view and supports male dominance …
>
> This division, however, is an ideological construct rationalizing the exclusion of women from the sources of power. It also makes it possible to maintain repressive systems of control over women without interference from human rights guarantees, which operate in the public sphere.[181]

Feminist accounts have shown, for example, how even human rights discourse has not produced substantive equality or addressed patriarchal practices that subordinate women; and that collective rights, such as to development and self-determination, have been impeded by the public/private dichotomy.[182] Feminist theories present incremental but also radical suggestions to reconstruct the law, from challenging the centrality of the state and the

---

179    Christine Chinkin, 'Feminism, Approaches to International Law' in Rüdiger Wolfrum (ed), *The Max Planck Encyclopedia of Public International Law* (Oxford University Press, online, October 2010) [1].
180    Carol Gilligan, *In a Different Voice: Psychological Theory and Women's Development* (Harvard University Press, 1982) (women have a naturally different voice).
181    Hilary Charlesworth, Christine Chinkin and Shelley Wright, 'Feminist Approaches to International Law' (1991) 85(4) *American Journal of International Law* 613, 621–9.
182    Ibid.

sources of law to creating regimes to address structural abuses and revise state responsibility.[183]

## 1.5.4   Postmodernism

Postmodern critiques suggest that international law is indeterminate, value-laden and arbitrarily applied, not certain, objective or neutral as is often supposed, and that it is accordingly prone to abuse by the powerful.[184] One leading theorist, Martti Koskenniemi, argues that international lawyers oscillate between attempting to demonstrate the normativity of international law (that it tells states what they 'ought' to do, and is thus not simply an apology for state interests) and its concreteness (that it is grounded in state behaviour, and is not simply idealistic or utopian). He sees no way of ultimately explaining the binding force of international law because

> [t]heories that seek binding force from beyond sovereignty seem utopian and unverifiable, unable to explain their content unless they refer back to what it is that States do or say or what lies in their interest. Theories that base binding force on sovereign behaviour, will or interest cannot distinguish between power and authority, a band of robbers and legitimate sovereigns, unless they refer to a criterion that tells which 'will' is normative, what 'interest' is lawful and where the boundary between conforming behaviour and breach lies.[185]

Koskenniemi thus concludes that

> international law is singularly useless as a means for justifying or criticizing international behaviour. Because it is based on contradictory premises it remains both over- and underlegitimizing: it is overlegitimizing as it can be ultimately invoked to justify any behaviour (apologism), it is underlegitimizing because it is incapable of providing a convincing argument on the legitimacy of any practices (utopianism).[186]

He argues that international lawyers should abandon their pretentions that law is more objective than politics and 'admit that if they wish to achieve justifications, they have to take a stand on political issues without assuming that there exists a privileged rationality which solves such issues for them'.[187]

Such subjectivity and relativity produce a crisis of legal authority, since law is reduced to politics disguised as legal argument, 'political actors have no reason at all to listen to it', and all that is left is raw political power and a triumph of realism.[188] An alternative is the deliberate politicisation of international law by lawyers, but that raises questions of legitimacy and

---

183   Ibid.
184   Andreas Paulus, 'International Law after Postmodernism: Towards Renewal or Decline of International Law?' (2001) 14(4) *Leiden Journal of International Law* 727, 731–2. See, eg, David Kennedy, *International Legal Structure* (Nomos Verlagsgesellschaft, 1987).
185   Koskenniemi, 'International Legal Theory and Doctrine' (n 128) [17].
186   Martti Koskenniemi, *From Apology to Utopia: The Structure of International Legal Argument* (Cambridge University Press, 1989) 48.
187   Ibid.
188   Paulus (n 184) 735.

democracy,[189] not to mention why other more powerful political actors, namely states, would listen. In some quarters, postmodernism and other critical theories have contrarily stimulated a rigid positivist backlash designed to shore up law against its reduction to subjective politics – and thus its risks of neoliberal abuses and state violence.[190]

# DISCUSSION QUESTIONS

(1)   What did the United Nations learn from the experience of the League of Nations?

(2)   To what extent are actors other than states recognised under international law?

(3)   How adequate are the various means of implementing and enforcing international law?

(4)   How does the international legal order compare with domestic legal orders?

(5)   What factors best explain compliance or noncompliance with international law?

---

189     Ibid 736–7.
190     Ibid 745–6.

# SOURCES OF
# INTERNATIONAL LAW

Emily Crawford

## 2.1    Introduction

The starting point for discussion and analysis of the sources of international law is almost invariably art 38 of the *Statute of the International Court of Justice* ('*ICJ Statute*'), the International Court of Justice being the primary judicial organ of the United Nations. Article 38 lists the sources of international law as comprising treaties, custom, general principles of law, and – as subsidiary means for determining the law – judicial decisions and academic writing. However, in the 75 years since the adoption of the *ICJ Statute*, newer sources of legal obligation have emerged for the international community. These often involve non-state and intergovernmental actors in their creation. This chapter explores both the traditional and newer sources of international law and assesses how they are adopted and created.

## 2.2    The traditional starting point: art 38 of the *Statute of the International Court of Justice*

Article 38 of the *ICJ Statute* provides:

1.  The Court, whose function is to decide in accordance with international law such disputes as are submitted to it, shall apply:
    a.  international conventions, whether general or particular, establishing rules expressly recognized by the contesting states;
    b.  international custom, as evidence of a general practice accepted as law;
    c.  the general principles of law recognized by civilized nations;
    d.  subject to the provisions of Article 59, judicial decisions and the teachings of the most highly qualified publicists of the various nations, as subsidiary means for the determination of rules of law.
2.  This provision shall not prejudice the power of the Court to decide a case *ex aequo et bono*, if the parties agree thereto.

Though the article lists those sources in order, there is no significance to this. The Court is not bound to apply sources in the order in which they appear in art 38 – that is to say, there is no requirement for the Court, or indeed any international judicial or arbitral body, to look first to a treaty before turning to examine customary international law.[1] However, the sources listed in art 38(1)(d) (judicial decisions and the writings of publicists) are 'subsidiary' rather than direct sources, as discussed in Section 2.2.2.4.

---

1    See Samantha Besson, 'Theorising the Sources of International Law' in Samantha Besson and John Tasioulas (eds), *The Philosophy of International Law* (Oxford University Press, 2010) 163, 181–2. Compare Pellet, who states that in practice the Court does tend to use the article in successive order: Alain Pellet, 'Article 38' in Andreas Zimmerman et al (eds), *The Statute of the International Court of Justice: A Commentary* (Oxford University Press, 2nd ed, 2012) 731, 841; James Crawford, *Brownlie's Principles of Public International Law* (Oxford University Press, 9th ed, 2019) 20.

## 2.2.1   Treaties

An 'international convention' is defined in the 1969 *Vienna Convention on the Law of Treaties* (*'VCLT'*) as 'an international agreement concluded between states in written form and governed by international law, whether embodied in a single instrument or in two or more related instruments and whatever its particular designation'.[2] Regardless of the nomenclature – treaty, convention, accord, agreement, covenant, pact or charter – a treaty is one of the clearest and most common ways in which states (and indeed other entities with international legal personality) can create binding obligations. Treaties can be either bilateral (between two parties) or multilateral (between more than two parties).

The binding quality of the agreement is paramount: the fundamental principle of treaty law is *pacta sunt servanda* – agreements must be kept. This is codified in art 26 of the *VCLT* which provides that 'every treaty in force is binding upon the parties to it and must be performed by them in good faith'. Treaties are somewhat similar to contracts in that they are binding written documents between two or more parties which clearly outline the parties' obligations. However, while treaties are only binding on the parties to the treaty, their terms can reflect customary international law at the time they are adopted, or come to reflect custom over time. In either case, this can mean that states are bound by separate but similar (or identical), parallel regimes: the rules expressed in the treaty, and rules that have customary status. This is discussed further in Section 2.2.2.5.

## 2.2.2   Custom

Article 38(1)(b) of the *ICJ Statute* refers to 'international custom, as evidence of a general practice accepted as law'. Customary international law generally refers to a recurring practice that is recognised and accepted by the community as a form of obligation.[3] In the international legal system, customary law involves recognition that the practice of states on a particular subject, over a sufficient period of time, can become a source of binding obligations and be treated as such. Unlike treaties, which bind only their parties, customary international law can bind all states if the custom is universal. It is also possible to have bilateral and regional custom (explored in Section 2.2.2.3).

Not all practice will become customary international law, however. It must be accompanied by a belief that the practice is legally required (*opinio juris*) – and not motivated by a non-legal reason, such as international practice based on comity.[4] Thus, to determine whether a particular practice is customary law, one must look to two elements: state practice and *opinio juris*.

### 2.2.2.1   State practice

The first element of custom – that of general practice – relates to the practice of states in their international relations. What *kinds* of state practice are considered relevant was first considered in 1950 by the International Law Commission ('ILC').[5] The ILC proposed a

---

2   *Vienna Convention on the Law of Treaties*, opened for signature 23 May 1969, 1155 UNTS 331 (entered into force 27 January 1980) art 2(1)(a) (*'VCLT'*). The *VCLT* is discussed in detail in Chapter 3.

3   See generally Amanda Perreau-Saussine and James Murphy, *The Nature of Customary Law: Legal, Historical and Philosophical Perspectives* (Cambridge University Press, 2007).

4   The tradition of granting visiting foreign dignitaries a 21-gun salute is an example of 'international comity' – a practice that is political in nature and not carried out with a sense of legal obligation: see, eg, *Parking Privileges for Diplomats* (1971) 70 ILR 396, 402–4.

5   See further Section 2.2.4.1 on the status of International Law Commission reports.

non-exhaustive list of possible evidence of state practice – including treaty collections, decisions of international and national courts, national legislation, diplomatic correspondence, opinions of national legal advisers, and the practice of international organisations.[6] For example, it is possible for practice to be evidenced in UN General Assembly resolutions. Unlike decisions of the UN Security Council,[7] General Assembly resolutions are typically not binding on states and cannot necessarily create customary law as such.[8] However, voting records on resolutions are important evidence of state practice.

General Assembly resolutions may also influence or even become declaratory of customary law because they 'provide a basis for the progressive development of the law and, if substantially unanimous, for the speedy consolidation of customary rules'.[9] Examples of such resolutions include the *Universal Declaration of Human Rights*,[10] the *Friendly Relations Declaration*,[11] the *Declaration on the Granting of Independence to Colonial Countries and Peoples*[12] and the *Declaration of Legal Principles Governing the Activities of States in the Exploration and Use of Outer Space*.[13] In determining the evidentiary weight of a General Assembly resolution, important factors to assess have included the voting record on the resolution (the number of votes in favour, against and abstaining); the clarity of the language used in the resolution; and whether the resolution has been affirmed in later resolutions.[14]

The ILC re-examined the question of identifying customary international law in 2018, stating as follows:

**Conclusion 4**

**Requirement of practice**

1.  The requirement of a general practice, as a constituent element of customary international law, refers primarily to the practice of States that contributes to the formation, or expression, of rules of customary international law.

---

6   'Ways and Means for Making the Evidence of Customary International Law More Readily Available' [1950] II *Yearbook of the International Law Commission* 1, 367, 368–72 [33]–[78]. Note that International Law Commission reports and studies, which are highly influential, are not necessarily declaratory of the law: see further Section 2.2.4.1.

7   *Charter of the United Nations* art 25 states: 'The Members of the United Nations agree to accept and carry out the decisions of the Security Council in accordance with the present Charter.'

8   Not all General Assembly resolutions are non-binding but most are recommendatory only. For an assessment of the legal weight of General Assembly resolutions, see further Jorge Castañeda, *Legal Effects of United Nations Resolutions*, tr Alba Amoia (Columbia University Press, 1969).

9   Crawford (n 1) 39.

10  *Universal Declaration of Human Rights*, GA Res 217A (III), UN GAOR, UN Doc A/810 (10 December 1948).

11  *Declaration on Principles of International Law concerning Friendly Relations and Co-operation among States in accordance with the Charter of the United Nations*, GA Res 2625, UN Doc A/RES/2625 (adopted 24 October 1970).

12  *Declaration on the Granting of Independence to Colonial Countries and Peoples*, GA Res 1514 (XV), UN Doc A/RES/1514(XV) (adopted 14 December 1960).

13  *Declaration of Legal Principles Governing the Activities of States in the Exploration and Use of Outer Space*, GA Res 1962 (XVIII), UN Doc A/RES/1962(XVIII) (adopted 13 December 1963).

14  *Texaco Overseas Petroleum Co v Libya (Merits)* (1978) 17 ILM 1, 27. See also Stephen Schwebel, 'The Effect of Resolutions of the UN General Assembly on Customary International Law' (1979) 73 *ASIL Proceedings* 301.

2. In certain cases, the practice of international organizations also contributes to the formation, or expression, of rules of customary international law.
3. Conduct of other actors is not practice that contributes to the formation, or expression, of rules of customary international law, but may be relevant when assessing the practice referred to in paragraphs 1 and 2.

**Conclusion 5**
**Conduct of the State as State practice**
State practice consists of conduct of the State, whether in the exercise of its executive, legislative, judicial or other functions.

**Conclusion 6**
**Forms of practice**
1. Practice may take a wide range of forms. It includes both physical and verbal acts. It may, under certain circumstances, include inaction.
2. Forms of State practice include, but are not limited to: diplomatic acts and correspondence; conduct in connection with resolutions adopted by an international organization or at an intergovernmental conference; conduct in connection with treaties; executive conduct, including operational conduct 'on the ground'; legislative and administrative acts; and decisions of national courts.
3. There is no predetermined hierarchy among the various forms of practice.[15]

The practice in question must also be of sufficient duration, consistency and generality to have the weight needed to prove the existence of a customary norm. To make a case for universal custom, one would need to demonstrate practice from all the relevant geographical regions of the world, as well as relevant diversity in political and legal systems – for example, from both the developed and developing world, and from common and civil law systems. (The case for bilateral or regional custom is discussed in Section 2.2.2.3.)

The practice need not be absolutely uniform, but it must exhibit some general consistency. Deviations from the practice must be justifiable either as allowable exceptions or as not being relevant practice at all, as stated in *Military and Paramilitary Activities in and against Nicaragua* ('*Nicaragua*').[16] At issue in that case was whether the fact that states had repeatedly used force in their international relations would undermine the alleged customary status of the prohibition on the use of force and the rule on non-intervention.[17] For the International Court of Justice ('ICJ'):

> It is not to be expected that in the practice of States the application of the rules in question should have been perfect, in the sense that States should have refrained, with complete consistency, from the use of force or from intervention in each other's internal affairs. The Court does not consider that, for a rule to be established as customary, the corresponding practice must be in absolutely rigorous conformity with the rule. In order to deduce the

---

15   *Report of the International Law Commission on the Work of Its Seventieth Session*, UN GAOR, 73rd sess, Supp No 10, UN Doc A/73/10 (2018) 119–20 ('*Draft Conclusions on Identification of Customary International Law*'). For analysis of the status of ILC reports as a potential source of international law, see Section 2.2.4.1.
16   *Military and Paramilitary Activities in and against Nicaragua (Nicaragua v United States of America) (Merits)* [1986] ICJ Rep 14, 98 [186] ('*Nicaragua*').
17   For the facts of the *Nicaragua* case see Chapter 8.

existence of customary rules, the Court deems it sufficient that the conduct of States should, in general, be consistent with such rules, and that instances of State conduct inconsistent with a given rule should generally have been treated as breaches of that rule, not as indications of the recognition of a new rule. If a State acts in a way prima facie incompatible with a recognized rule, but defends its conduct by appealing to exceptions or justifications contained within the rule itself, then whether or not the State's conduct is in fact justifiable on that basis, the significance of that attitude is to confirm rather than to weaken the rule.[18]

Usually, practice needs to be evidenced over a considerable period of time in order to be considered useful for proving the existence of custom. However, what was proposed in the *North Sea Continental Shelf* cases[19] was that it is possible for a customary rule to develop over only a short period of time. That being said, if the time elapsed is short, the amount of practice required may change. Precisely how this could happen was explored in *North Sea Continental Shelf*, where three states – the Netherlands, Germany and Denmark – were in dispute over how to divide their shared continental shelf. The Netherlands and Denmark were parties to the 1958 *Convention on the Continental Shelf* which provided:

> Where the same continental shelf is adjacent to the territories of two adjacent States, the boundary of the continental shelf shall be determined by agreement between them. In the absence of agreement, and unless another boundary line is justified by special circum-stances, the boundary shall be determined by application of the principle of equidistance from the nearest points of the baselines from which the breadth of the territorial sea of each State is measured.[20]

However, Germany was not a party to that treaty and advocated instead that the continental shelf should be divided more equitably, at least as Germany perceived it. The equidistance approach would give Germany, with its concave coastline, a notably smaller portion of the shared continental shelf and its resources. For the Netherlands and Denmark to prevail and claim a larger portion of the continental shelf, they had to prove that the equidistance approach under the Convention was customary. The Court suggested that it was possible to do this, but difficult:

> With respect to the other elements usually regarded as necessary before a conventional rule can be considered to have become a general rule of international law, it might be that, even without the passage of any considerable period of time, a very widespread and representative participation in the convention might suffice of itself, provided it included that of States whose interests were specially affected. ...
>
> Although the passage of only a short period of time is not necessarily, or of itself, a bar to the formation of a new rule of customary international law on the basis of what was originally a purely conventional rule, an indispensable requirement would be that within the period in question, short though it might be, State practice, including that of States

---

18    *Nicaragua* (n 16) 98 [186].

19    *North Sea Continental Shelf (Federal Republic of Germany v Denmark) (Merits)* [1969] ICJ Rep 3 ('*North Sea Continental Shelf*').

20    *Convention on the Continental Shelf*, opened for signature 29 April 1958, 499 UNTS 311 (entered into force 10 June 1964) art 6(2).

whose interests are specially affected, should have been both extensive and virtually uniform in the sense of the provision invoked; – and should moreover have occurred in such a way as to show a general recognition that a rule of law or legal obligation is involved.[21]

*North Sea Continental Shelf* also raised an additional point of consideration – the 'specially affected' state. This is a concept based on the idea that, when examining state practice for the purpose of customary law, the practice of states with specific subject-matter interest should be given more weight.[22] This would seem uncontroversial in some areas – for example, a landlocked state will have limited state practice regarding the territorial sea. However, the rule has been criticised due to concern about it being used as a 'respectable disguise'[23] by powerful states to impose their will on smaller states. The possibility for manipulation of the concept for political means seems apparent: powerful states could potentially always 'be "specially affected" by all or almost all political–legal developments within the international community'.[24] An example of this would be the continued practice by a handful of states of possessing nuclear weapons while at the same time promoting non-proliferation by other states.[25]

### 2.2.2.2   *Opinio juris*

The second element needed for the establishment of a customary rule is *opinio juris sive necessitatis* – the belief that the conduct is legally required. This element separates acts undertaken by states for reasons of courtesy, which are not relevant practice for determining customary law, from acts done out of a sense of obligation – which *are* relevant. As the ICJ noted in *North Sea Continental Shelf*:

> Not only must the acts concerned amount to a settled practice, but they must also be such, or be carried out in such a way, as to be evidence of a belief that this practice is rendered obligatory by the existence of a rule of law requiring it. The need for such a belief, i.e., the existence of a subjective element, is implicit in the very notion of the *opinio juris sive necessitatis*. The States concerned must therefore feel that they are conforming to what amounts to a legal obligation. The frequency, or even habitual character of the acts is not in itself enough.[26]

*Opinio juris* is a complex concept. In the first instance, it should be acknowledged that the state is an abstract construct; therefore, determining what states 'feel' and 'think' is something of an artificial process. Second, the entire concept of *opinio juris* relies on reasoning that is essentially circular. As Anthea Roberts and Sandesh Sivakumaran ask: 'how can practice ever

---

21   *North Sea Continental Shelf* (n 19) 42–3 [73]–[74].

22   See further *Legality of the Threat or Use of Nuclear Weapons (Advisory Opinion)* [1996] ICJ Rep 226.

23   Gennadiĭ Mikhaĭlovich Danilenko, *Law-Making in the International Community* (Martinus Nijhoff, 1993) 96. See also Anthea Roberts and Sandesh Sivakumaran, 'The Theory and the Reality of the Sources of International Law' in Malcolm Evans (ed), *International Law* (Oxford University Press, 5th ed, 2018) 95.

24   Danilenko (n 23) 96.

25   For example, see the regular condemnation by the United States of other states acquiring nuclear weapons: Ju-min Park and Jack Kim, 'North Korea's Largest Nuclear Test Draws Global Condemnation', *The Huffington Post* (online, 10 January 2017) <www.huffpost.com/entry/north-korea-nuclear-test-condemnation_n_57d2a93de4b03d2d4599dcbb>.

26   *North Sea Continental Shelf* (n 19) 44 [77].

develop into a customary rule if States have to believe the rule already exists before their practice can be significant for the creation of the rule?'[27] One possible answer to this paradox is that the initial acts of a state, done before a customary rule emerges, are evidence of the state asserting its position on what the law should be.[28] From there, other states may choose to accept or reject the act, or indeed not respond at all, from which point the customary practice either does or does not develop.

Finding *opinio juris* is also difficult – it is almost unheard of for a state to proclaim that it is acting in a particular way because it considers itself bound to do so under a customary rule. Faced with the difficulty of proving the existence of a subjective state of mind held by an abstract entity, some courts have taken the approach of presuming or inferring the existence of *opinio juris*. As noted by Judge Tanaka in his dissenting opinion in *North Sea Continental Shelf*:

> [S]o far as the qualitative factor, namely *opinio juris sive necessitatis* is concerned, it is extremely difficult to get evidence of its existence in concrete cases. This factor, relating to internal motivation and being of a psychological nature, cannot be ascertained very easily, particularly when diverse legislative and executive organs of a government participate in an internal process of decision-making in respect of ratification or other State acts. There is no other way than to ascertain the existence of *opinio juris* from the fact of the external existence of a certain custom and its necessity felt in the international community, rather than to seek evidence as to the subjective motives for each example of State practice, which is something which is impossible of achievement.[29]

Therefore, *opinio juris* must usually be deduced from the acts of states. As outlined in the ILC report on customary law:

**Conclusion 10**

**Forms of evidence of acceptance as law (*opinio juris*)**

1. Evidence of acceptance as law (*opinio juris*) may take a wide range of forms.
2. Forms of evidence of acceptance as law (*opinio juris*) include, but are not limited to: public statements made on behalf of States; official publications; government legal opinions; diplomatic correspondence; decisions of national courts; treaty provisions; and conduct in connection with resolutions adopted by an international organization or at an intergovernmental conference.
3. Failure to react over time to a practice may serve as evidence of acceptance as law (*opinio juris*), provided that States were in a position to react and the circumstances called for some reaction.[30]

---

27    Roberts and Sivakumaran (n 23) 96.
28    James Crawford and Thomas Viles, 'International Law on a Given Day' in Konrad Ginther et al (eds), *Völkerrecht zwischen normativen Anspruch und politischer Realität [International Law between Normative Claim and Political Reality]* (Duncker & Humblot, 1994) 45; reprinted in James Crawford, *International Law as an Open System: Selected Essays* (Cameron & May, 2002) 92. See also John Tasioulas, 'Opinio Juris and the Genesis of Custom: A Solution to the "Paradox"' (2007) 26 *Australian Year Book of International Law* 199, 204.
29    *North Sea Continental Shelf* (n 19) 175–6 (Judge Tanaka).
30    *Draft Conclusions on Identification of Customary International Law*, UN Doc A/73/10 (n 15) 120 (Draft Conclusion 10).

Controversially, the ICJ has treated General Assembly resolutions as evidence of *opinio juris*. In the *Nicaragua* case, it stated:

> The Court has ... to be satisfied that there exists in customary international law an *opinio juris* as to the binding character of such abstention [from the threat or use of force against another state]. This *opinio juris* may, though with all due caution, be deduced from, inter alia, the attitude of the Parties and the attitude of States towards certain General Assembly resolutions, and particularly resolution 2625 (XXV) entitled *Declaration on Principles of International Law concerning Friendly Relations and Co-operation among States in accordance with the Charter of the United Nations*. The effect of consent to the text of such resolutions cannot be understood as merely that of a 'reiteration or elucidation' of the treaty commitment undertaken in the Charter. On the contrary, it may be understood as an acceptance of the validity of the rule or set of rules declared by the resolution by themselves.[31]

In this instance, the controversy arose from treating resolutions as evidence of *opinio juris*. This may be problematic because states may vote in favour of resolutions for reasons other than their belief in the binding legal nature of the statements contained in the resolution. General Assembly resolutions are 'often the results of political compromises and arrangements and, comprehended in that sense, never intended to constitute binding norms. Great care must be taken in moving from a plethora of practice to the identification of legal norms'.[32]

## 2.2.2.3   Local or regional custom

It is possible for custom to be limited to a group of states – for instance, those from a specific geographical region – and even to as few as two states. Likewise, regional custom can exist among states that are not geographically proximate but nonetheless share common goals or interests – for example, the League of Arab States and the North Atlantic Treaty Organization ('NATO').

The possibility of a regional customary practice was acknowledged by the ICJ in the *Asylum* case,[33] where Colombia argued that a regional custom of granting diplomatic asylum for political reasons could be evidenced in the practice of Latin American states. The *Asylum* case was triggered by Colombia granting political asylum to a Peruvian citizen, Victor Raúl Haya de la Torre, who had led an unsuccessful rebellion against the Peruvian government. Haya de la Torre had fled to the Colombian embassy in Lima and the Colombian authorities had sought Peruvian permission to transport him across Peruvian territory to Colombia. Peru denied permission and rejected Colombia's assertions that it (and not Peru) retained the right to determine political refugee status and that such determination was binding on Peru.

In support of its claim before the ICJ, Colombia cited several treaties and 'American international law in general':

> The Colombian Government has finally invoked 'American international law in general'. In addition to the rules arising from agreements which have already been considered, it has relied on an alleged regional or local custom peculiar to Latin-American States.

---

31    *Nicaragua* (n 16) 99 [188].
32    Malcolm Shaw, *International Law* (Cambridge University Press, 9th ed, 2021) 99.
33    *Asylum (Colombia v Peru) (Judgment)* [1950] ICJ Rep 266 ('*Asylum*').

The Colombian Government must prove that the rule invoked by it is in accordance with a constant and uniform usage practised by the States in question, and this usage is the expression of a right appertaining to the State granting asylum and a duty incumbent on the territorial State.

. . .

The Court cannot . . . find that the Colombian Government has proved the existence of such a custom. But even if it could be supposed that such a custom existed between certain Latin-American states only, it could not be invoked against Peru which far from having by its attitude adhered to it, has, on the contrary, repudiated it by refraining from ratifying the Montevideo Conventions of 1933 [the regional *Convention on Political Asylum*] and 1939 [the regional *Treaty on Political Asylum and Refuge*], which were the first to include a rule concerning the qualification of the offence in matters of diplomatic asylum.[34]

The ICJ, though not finding a regional custom in the *Asylum* case, acknowledged that it could exist. In *Right of Passage over Indian Territory*,[35] the ICJ acknowledged the existence of bilateral custom. Portugal claimed that there was a bilateral custom allowing for free passage between Portuguese enclaves in India. The ICJ noted:

With regard to Portugal's claim of a right of passage as formulated by it on the basis of local custom, it is objected on behalf of India that no local custom could be established between only two States. It is difficult to see why the number of States between which a local custom may be established on the basis of long practice must necessarily be larger than two. The Court sees no reason why long continued practice between two States accepted by them as regulating their relations should not form the basis of mutual rights and obligations between the two States.[36]

As with general customary international law, local or regional customary international law requires evidence of state practice and *opinio juris*.

## 2.2.2.4   The persistent and subsequent objector

Though customary international law binds all states once it has been established, it is possible that a state may exempt itself from the application of a rule if, from the time of formation of the rule, the state persistently objects to the rule as it emerges.[37] The principle was acknowledged by the ICJ in *Anglo-Norwegian Fisheries*.[38] That case was based on a complaint by the United Kingdom about the Norwegian practice of drawing straight baselines across the fjords that line the Norwegian coast. The geography of the Norwegian coast, indented as it is with numerous bays, fjords, islands, islets and reefs – some of which form a continuous archipelago known as

---

34   Ibid 276–8. *Convention on Political Asylum*, opened for signature 26 December 1933 (entered into force 28 March 1935); *Treaty on Political Asylum and Refuge*, opened for signature 4 August 1939 (entered into force 29 December 1954).

35   *Right of Passage over Indian Territory (Portugal v India) (Merits)* [1960] ICJ Rep 6 ('*Right of Passage*').

36   Ibid 39.

37   See generally Jonathan Charney, 'The Persistent Objector Rule and the Development of Customary International Law' (1986) 56 *British Yearbook of International Law* 1; James Green, *The Persistent Objector Rule in International Law* (Oxford University Press, 2016).

38   *Anglo-Norwegian Fisheries (United Kingdom v Norway) (Judgment)* [1951] ICJ Rep 116.

*skjaergaard* – means it is difficult to clearly delimit water and land. Norwegian practice had, at the time of the case, always been to draw straight baselines across the fjords and *skjaergaard*. This would result in significant waters being enclosed within Norway's territorial sea, and thus within its exclusive jurisdiction for, among other things, fishing.

The United Kingdom argued that, under existing international law, Norway was not entitled to draw straight baselines longer than 10 miles across the openings of the fjord. The ICJ disagreed:

> In these circumstances the Court deems it necessary to point out that although the ten-mile rule has been adopted by certain States both in their national law and in their treaties and conventions, and although certain arbitral decisions have applied it as between these States, other States have adopted a different limit. Consequently, the ten-mile rule has not acquired the authority of a general rule of international law. In any event the ten-mile rule would appear to be inapplicable as against Norway inasmuch as she has always opposed any attempt to apply it to the Norwegian coast.[39]

For a claim of persistent objection to be successful, the state must clearly and publicly express its objection on a consistent basis.[40] A state cannot validly object to a rule once the rule has been established, and a subsequent objection has no legal effect. However, subsequent objection can potentially create a new rule – initial state practice may violate the rule but, if the conduct is supported by enough states, it may gradually become a new rule. Research on the doctrine of the persistent objector demonstrates that, while accepted as law, the doctrine is not regularly invoked by states.[41]

### 2.2.2.5   The interaction between treaties and custom

As noted in Section 2.2.2.1, state participation in a treaty regime may be evidence of state practice. Additionally, a treaty may itself contribute to the formation of custom in one of three ways: it may codify existing custom; crystallise emerging or developing custom (by the process of states agreeing to a particular wording or formulation of an emergent rule); or lay down a rule that eventually becomes customary.

In order for a treaty norm to become customary, certain requirements must be met. First, as noted by the ICJ in *North Sea Continental Shelf*, the rule in question must be of a 'fundamentally norm-creating character'[42] – that is, it must be a generally applicable rule of international law. Then, the treaty rule in question must be accompanied by relevant state practice and *opinio juris* – both from the parties to the treaty and, more crucially, from non-parties. It is this last element that is most relevant. To determine whether a treaty rule has achieved customary status, one must look to the behaviour of states that are *not* parties to the treaty: states that *are*

---

39      Ibid 131.

40      See *Draft Conclusions on Identification of Customary International Law*, UN Doc A/73/10 (n 15) 121–2 (Draft Conclusion 15): 'Persistent objector: 1. Where a State has objected to a rule of customary international law while that rule was in the process of formation, the rule is not opposable to the State concerned for so long as it maintains its objection. 2. The objection must be clearly expressed, made known to other States, and maintained persistently.'

41      Ted Stein, 'The Approach of the Different Drummer: The Principle of the Persistent Objector in International Law' (1985) 26(2) *Harvard International Law Journal* 457; Gleider Hernández, *International Law* (Oxford University Press, 2019) 42.

42      *North Sea Continental Shelf* (n 19) 42 [72].

parties might simply be acting in accordance with their obligations under the treaty – actions from which 'no inference could legitimately be drawn as to the existence of a rule of customary law'.[43] Mere widespread participation in a treaty regime is insufficient to prove customary status – compliance with the purported rule must arise out of a sense of customary obligation, not because a separate parallel treaty regime compels such compliance.

In any event, when a customary norm is codified in a treaty, the customary norm endures and is not subsumed by the treaty. As noted by the ICJ in *Nicaragua*, 'even if a treaty norm and a customary norm relevant to the present dispute were to have exactly the same content, this would not be a reason for the Court to take the view that the operation of the treaty process must necessarily deprive the customary norm of its separate applicability'.[44]

Finally, while customary rules will typically bind all states (excluding persistent objectors), it was noted in *North Sea Continental Shelf* that a customary rule can be derogated from by agreement – two or more states could agree that, as between themselves, a particular custom-ary rule would not apply in certain circumstances.[45]

### 2.2.2.6  *Jus cogens*

While practice demonstrates that there is no hierarchy in the sources enumerated in art 38 of the *ICJ Statute*, there is one source of international law, not explicitly referenced in art 38, that *does* claim hierarchical supremacy over all other norms: *jus cogens* norms. *Jus cogens* – literally, compelling law – are peremptory norms of international law from which no derogation is permitted.

*Jus cogens* norms were first enunciated in treaty form in art 53 of the *VCLT*. However, their origins can be traced back to the 17th century when scholars such as Hugo Grotius[46] argued for the existence of a stratum of law to which all other law was subordinate. This was 'natural law', considered to be 'unchangeable – even in the sense that it cannot be changed by God. Measureless as is the power of God, nevertheless it can be said that there are certain things over which that power does not extend'.[47] While early authors did not use the term *jus cogens*, they were, nevertheless, making the case that 'there were rules of international law that protected the interests of the international community ... which it was not possible to contract out of, that is, from which no derogation was permitted'.[48]

The notion of *jus cogens* was initially debated primarily in academic literature, with some very limited judicial notice of the concept.[49] However, in the immediate post–World War II era, the ILC began its program of work on the law of treaties. It was here that the notion of *jus cogens* became more firmly established in international law. Reports from the ILC's Special

---

43    Ibid 43–4 [76].
44    *Nicaragua* (n 16) 94 [175]. However, the Court in this case found only that there was partial convergence of treaty and customary norms on self-defence, noting that, for instance, the Charter's procedural reporting requirements on self-defence were not necessarily customary.
45    *North Sea Continental Shelf* (n 19) 42 [72].
46    Hugo Grotius, *The Law of War and Peace*, tr Francis Kelsey (Clarendon Press, 1925) bk 1, [10] [trans of: *De Jure Belli ac Pacis Libri Tres* (1646)].
47    Ibid.
48    Dire Tladi, Special Rapporteur, *First Report on Jus Cogens*, UN Doc A/CN.4/693 (8 March 2016) 11 [22].
49    See ibid 9–23 [18]–[41] for a history of the development of the concept of *jus cogens*.

Rapporteurs proposed that, among the other rules on the law of treaties, it should be stated that a treaty would be invalid if 'its object and its execution involves the infringement of a general rule or principle of international law having the character of *jus cogens*'.[50]

While the early reports from the ILC acknowledged that the concept of *jus cogens* was controversial,[51] what was essentially undisputed by states was the notion that there are certain illegal activities under international law – such as slavery and piracy – in which no state could justifiably agree to engage.[52] Therefore, when art 53 of the *VCLT* was adopted, it enshrined the notion that states were not free to conclude treaties that violated certain fundamental principles of international law. However, despite there being general acceptance of the *concept* of *jus cogens*, for a long time there was dispute over what norms could be considered fundamental to international law. Indeed, there is still debate over what norms can be considered as having attained *jus cogens* status,[53] though recent work by the ILC has done much to provide clarity.[54] There is widespread acknowledgement that the prohibitions on genocide[55] and torture[56] have achieved *jus cogens* status, as have the prohibitions on slavery, war crimes, crimes against humanity, aggression, racial discrimination and apartheid, and the right to self-determination.[57]

Only a new norm of *jus cogens* can modify an existing *jus cogens* norm. However, there is still dispute among states and practitioners as to the nature and scope of norms having *jus cogens* status, with theoretical debates over how and why they emerge, whether they are simply another form of consent-based law, or whether they instead exist as a source of law separate from state consent (due to their 'higher status' as fundamental principles of the international legal order).[58]

---

50    Sir Humphrey Waldock, Special Rapporteur, *Second Report on the Law of Treaties*, UN Doc A/CN.4/156 (20 March 1963) 52 (Draft Article 13).

51    See, eg, ibid 52 (Draft Article 13 Commentary [1]).

52    Ibid. See further Tladi (n 48) [11]–[22], for a summary of state responses to the work of the ILC, both before and during the conference that eventually adopted the *VCLT*.

53    Waldock (n 50) 52 (Draft Article 13 Commentary [2]).

54    See further 'Analytical Guide to the Work of the International Law Commission: Peremptory Norms of General International Law (*Jus Cogens*)', *International Law Commission* (Web Page) <https://legal.un .org/ilc/guide/1_14.shtml>.

55    See, eg, *Application of the Convention on the Prevention and Punishment of the Crime of Genocide (Bosnia and Herzegovina v Yugoslavia) (Preliminary Objections)* [1996] ICJ Rep 595, 615–16 [31] ('*Genocide*').

56    *Questions Relating to the Obligation to Prosecute or Extradite (Belgium v Senegal) (Judgment)* [2012] ICJ Rep 422, 457 [99].

57    See further 'Draft Articles on Responsibility of States for Internationally Wrongful Acts, with Commentaries' [2001] II(2) *Yearbook of the International Law Commission* 1, 85 (Draft Article 26 Commentary [5]). This list of *jus cogens* norms was affirmed by the ILC in 2019 in its draft conclusions on peremptory norms of general international law (*jus cogens*): see *Report of the International Law Commission on the Work of Its Seventy-First Session*, UN GAOR, 74th sess, Supp No 10, UN Doc A/74/10 (2019) 208.

58    See generally Robert Kolb, *Peremptory International Law – Jus Cogens: A General Inventory* (Hart, 2015); Alexander Orakhelashvili, *Peremptory Norms in International Law* (Oxford University Press, 2006); Erika de Wet, 'Sources and the Hierarchy of International Law: The Place of Peremptory Norms and Article 103 of the UN Charter within the Sources of International Law' in Samantha Besson and Jean d'Aspremont (eds), *The Oxford Handbook on the Sources of International Law* (Oxford University Press, 2017) 625.

## 2.2.3   General principles of law

Article 38(1)(c) of the *ICJ Statute* provides that the ICJ, in its deliberations, is entitled to look to 'the general principles of law recognised by civilised nations'. The intention behind the inclusion of 'general principles' in both the *Statute of the Permanent Court of International Justice ('PCIJ Statute')* and the *ICJ Statute* was to address a particular concern noted by the Committee of Jurists when drafting the *PCIJ Statute*:[59] the possibility of a *non liquet* – a determination that no positive law exists on the matter. The concern was that, in the absence of specific customary or treaty law, the Court might feel obliged to declare that the claim could be neither supported nor rejected, due to a lack of law. General principles are therefore available for the Court to draw on in its decision-making.

While there is debate about what 'general principles' are, the case law of the ICJ suggests that the phrase refers to a general principle of law commonly applied in domestic legal systems. According to this approach, 'general principles of law are those which can be derived from a comparison of the various systems of domestic law and the extraction of such principles as appear to be shared by all, or a majority of them'.[60] For example, the ICJ has noted that certain legal principles are common in domestic judicial systems the world over: they include the doctrine of finality (*res judicata*),[61] the principle that any breach of an obligation also involves the obligation to make reparation,[62] and the principles of acquiescence and estoppel.[63] Equitable principles, such as reasonableness and fairness, have also been used by the Court. Indeed, art 38(2) of the *ICJ Statute* notes that parties to a dispute may agree to have the case decided *ex aequo et bono* – according to principles of fairness rather than law. While equitable principles are not, of themselves, a source of law, they are relevant for decision-making processes – for example, with equity seen in the reasoning in *North Sea Continental Shelf*.[64]

Proving the existence of a general principle is difficult, and the ICJ has only ever drawn sparingly on general principles. An Australian case that highlights the complexity of the concept is *Ure v Commonwealth*.[65] The case turned on whether a private individual can acquire proprietary rights, recognised by international law, in land considered *terra nullius*. Traditionally, under international law, land can only be claimed by sovereign states.[66] Ure claimed that there was both a customary right and a general principle of law that allowed

---

59    Permanent Court of International Justice, Advisory Committee of Jurists, *Procès-Verbaux of the Proceedings of the Committee* (1920) 318, 338 (Descamps), 311 (Loder), 312–3 (La Pradelle), 307, 317 (Hagerup).

60    Roberts and Sivakumaran (n 23) 98. An alternative approach would limit general principles to those found in international law, such as the doctrine of *pacta sunt servanda* or the sovereign equality of states: see, eg, Grigoriĭ Ivanovich Tunkin, *Theory of International Law*, ed and tr William Butler (Harvard University Press, 1974) ch 7.

61    *Effect of Awards of Compensation Made by the United Nations Administrative Tribunal (Advisory Opinion)* [1954] ICJ Rep 47; *Alleged Violations of Sovereign Rights and Maritime Spaces in the Caribbean Sea (Nicaragua v Colombia) (Preliminary Objections)* [2016] ICJ Rep 3, 29 [58].

62    *Factory at Chorzów (Germany v Poland) (Jurisdiction) (Judgment No 8)* [1927] PCIJ (ser A) No 9, 31; *Factory at Chorzów (Germany v Poland) (Merits)* [1928] PCIJ (ser A) No 17, 29.

63    *Legal Status of Eastern Greenland (Denmark v Norway) (Judgment)* [1933] PCIJ (ser A/B) No 53, 52–4, 62, 69; *Temple of Preah Vihear (Cambodia v Thailand) (Merits)* [1962] ICJ Rep 6, 26.

64    *North Sea Continental Shelf* (n 21) 32–4 [46]–[52].

65    (2016) 236 FCR 458.

66    See further Chapter 5 on statehood and title to territory.

such a proprietary claim over, in this instance, Elizabeth and Middleton Reefs – small, uninhabited islands located about 80 nautical miles north of Lord Howe Island. In coming to its decision, the Federal Court of Australia looked to the operation of art 38(1)(c) of the *ICJ Statute*:

> [128] There exists a debate about the operation of Art 38(1)(c) which [Ure] largely sought to evade but which is significant for the disposition of this appeal. It concerns the need for the principles concerned to be general principles recognised by civilized nations. It is understood in contemporary times that the reference to 'civilized nations' is a reference to all nations, but the words suggest a necessary focus, nevertheless, upon municipal systems. . . .
>
>> While the intentions of the drafters of the Statute are less obscure than sometimes alleged, international lawyers have never reached agreement on the definition of the general principles mentioned in Art 38. There is, however, little doubt that they are:
>> • unwritten legal norms of a wide-ranging character and
>> • recognized in the municipal laws of States;
>> • moreover, they must be transposable at the international level.
>
> . . .
>
> [129] Further, this focus is certainly on municipal law . . .
>
> . . .
>
> [131] Before this Court there was some debate about the role of natural law under Art 38(1)(c). The express reference in the article to municipal legal systems suggests that natural law concepts can have no direct application under it, unless the posited natural law principle is recognised in the laws of the various nations. It was, after all, precisely to avoid resort to moral precepts that the alternate final drafting of Art 38(1)(c) was eventually adopted. Thus Zimmerman et al have remarked:
>
>> Moreover, as seen previously, the Court itself has made an (intellectually) clear distinction between legal rules and 'moral principles' which can be taken into account 'only in so far as these are given a sufficient expression in legal form'. It might be true that 'in Art 38, para 1(c) some natural law elements are inherent', but these 'elements' have to be 'legalized' by their incorporation in the legal systems of States. This requirement of recognition of the general principles in *foro domestico* is the criterion which differentiates the principles of Art 38, para 1(c) from both the equitable or moral principles and from the general principles of international law.
>
> [132] Consequently, in establishing the principle of international law for which she contends, [Ure] is faced with the unenviable task of proving that the principle – or a municipal analogue of the principle – is recognised by the laws of civilised nations.[67]

The ILC has also commenced a program of work on general principles of law.[68] The first reports note that ascertaining what amounts to general principles of law has been a process

---

67   *Ure v Commonwealth* (n 65) [128]–[132] (citations omitted).
68   'Analytical Guide to the Work of the International Law Commission: General Principles of Law', *International Law Commission* (Web Page, 28 September 2022) <https://legal.un.org/ilc/guide/1_15 .shtml>.

marked by ambiguity and a lack of clarity since before the adoption of the *PCIJ Statute*, and that 'the abundance of literature devoted to general principles of law shows not only the continuing relevance of the topic, but also the diversity of views that exist and the need for clarification'.[69]

## 2.2.4    Judicial decisions and the teachings of highly qualified publicists

Article 38(1)(d) of the *ICJ Statute* provides that 'judicial decisions and the teachings of the most highly qualified publicists of the various nations [may be used] as subsidiary means for the determination of rules of law'.[70] Judicial decisions and academics' writings are not formal sources of law; rather, they are a means of helping the Court determine the exact contours of existing law. Indeed, domestic courts around the world have long referred to decisions of *other* courts, and the laws of other nations, to help in their decision-making processes. For example, well before the creation of the PCIJ and the ICJ, the US Supreme Court in *The Paquete Habana* noted:

> [W]here there is no treaty and no controlling executive or legislative act or judicial decision, resort must be had to the customs and usages of civilized nations, and, as evidence of these, to the works of jurists and commentators who by years of labor, research and experience have made themselves peculiarly well acquainted with the subjects of which they treat. Such works are resorted to by judicial tribunals, not for the speculations of their authors concerning what the law ought to be, but for trustworthy evidence of what the law really is.[71]

Article 38(1)(d) is subject to the application of art 59 of the *ICJ Statute* which provides that '[t]he decision of the Court has no binding force except between the parties and in respect of that particular case'. Article 59 affirms that the ICJ is not bound by the principle of *stare decisis* – there is in international law no doctrine of precedent as understood in common law jurisdictions. However, in practice the ICJ (like other international courts and tribunals) will closely examine previous decisions of relevant international (and, to a lesser extent, domestic) courts, and take steps to clarify if and why a different conclusion was reached in the instant case.[72]

The 'judicial decisions' referred to in art 38 encompass decisions of the ICJ itself, as well as those of other international courts and tribunals, such as international criminal tribunals and arbitral tribunals.[73] Judicial decisions have a double value: they are subsidiary means, but can also be evidence of state practice for the formation of customary international law. Whether a court or tribunal is cited in the ICJ depends greatly on the 'status' of the particular body – its

---

69    Marcelo Vázquez-Bermúdez, Special Rapporteur, *First Report on General Principles of Law*, UN Doc A/CN.4/732 (5 April 2019) 5 [11].

70    *ICJ Statute* art 38(1)(d).

71    *The Paquete Habana*, 175 US 677, 700 (1900).

72    See, eg, the *Genocide* case (n 55), where the ICJ reviewed and disagreed with the jurisprudence of the International Criminal Tribunal for the Former Yugoslavia when considering the standard for state responsibility.

73    See, eg, *Legal Status of Eastern Greenland (Denmark v Norway) (Judgment)* [1933] PCIJ (ser A/B) No 53 (n 63) 45–6, where the Court referred to the decision of the Permanent Court of Arbitration in *Island of Palmas (Netherlands v United States of America) (Award)* (1928) 2 RIAA 829.

area of competence, its members, and the quality of its reasoning in any given case.[74] The decisions of domestic courts are also of value – they often provide significant interpretations of important international issues such as the immunity of heads of state,[75] or the right to self-determination and its relationship to secession.[76]

With regard to the 'teachings of publicists', courts and tribunals make use of the writings of scholars and, more frequently, counsel appearing before the courts will cite leading scholars in support of their arguments. However, the ICJ cites authors less often, in part 'because of the process of collective drafting of judgments, and the need to avoid an invidious selection of citations'.[77] Article 38 refers to 'highly qualified publicists', but sets out no additional criteria. Research into citations by the ICJ indicates that the authors most frequently cited tend not to be current writers, but instead scholars from previous generations[78] who were responsible for landmark publications on international law – figures such as Julius Stone, Lassa Oppenheim and Hersch Lauterpacht. That being said, more specialised tribunals, such as the International Tribunal on the Law of the Sea, do tend to cite living authors.

### 2.2.4.1  A special category of highly qualified publicists: the International Law Commission

The work of the ILC is technically considered within art 38(1)(d), categorised as writings of highly qualified publicists. However, the ILC, established in 1947 as a subsidiary body of the General Assembly, occupies a more authoritative position than other highly qualified publicists. In part this is due to its mandate under art 13(1)(a) of the *Charter of the United Nations* to 'initiate studies and make recommendations for the purpose of . . . encouraging the progressive development of international law and its codification'.

The ILC comprises 34 independent experts in international law drawn from across the globe, nominated by state governments and elected by the General Assembly.[79] It has been responsible for spearheading and shepherding significant instruments through the United Nations, such as conventions on the law of the sea,[80] diplomatic and consular relations[81] and the law of treaties.[82]

---

74    See generally André Nollkaemper, 'The Role of Domestic Courts in the Case Law of the International Court of Justice' (2006) 5(2) *Chinese Journal of International Law* 301.

75    See, eg, the decision of the UK House of Lords in *R v Bow Street Metropolitan Stipendiary Magistrate; Ex parte Pinochet Ugarte (No 3)* [2000] 1 AC 147.

76    See, eg, the decision of the Canadian Supreme Court in *Reference re Secession of Quebec* (1998) 115 ILR 536.

77    Crawford (n 1) 40.

78    See generally Sondre Torp Helmersen, 'Finding "the Most Highly Qualified Publicists": Lessons from the International Court of Justice' (2019) 30(2) *European Journal of International Law* 509; Sandesh Sivakumaran, 'The Influence of Teachings of Publicists on the Development of International Law' (2017) 66(1) *International and Comparative Law Quarterly* 1.

79    See 'Membership', *International Law Commission* (Web Page) <https://legal.un.org/ilc/ilcmembe.shtml>.

80    *United Nations Convention on the Law of the Sea*, opened for signature 10 December 1982, 1833 UNTS 3 (entered into force 16 November 1994).

81    *Vienna Convention on Diplomatic Relations*, opened for signature 18 April 1961, 500 UNTS 95 (entered into force 24 April 1964); *Vienna Convention on Consular Relations*, opened for signature 24 April 1963, 596 UNTS 261 (entered into force 19 March 1967).

82    *VCLT* (n 2).

The ILC has adopted 'articles'[83] on state responsibility[84] and diplomatic protection,[85] and conducted important studies on principles of *jus cogens*,[86] and the fragmentation of international law[87] (due in part to the proliferation of specialised international courts and tribunals).

The work of the ILC, which has been cited extensively by international courts and tribunals, has been influential in ICJ decision-making.[88] For example, in a 2018 decision the England and Wales Court of Appeal noted the importance of the ILC's draft conclusions on the identification of customary international law:

> We are mindful ... of the fact that they are the writings of some of the most qualified jurists drawn from across the world who have debated the matter most thoroughly between themselves over an extended period of time. We have found them a valuable source of the principles on this subject and, since they are not controversial between the parties, this judgment should be read on the basis that we have sought to follow them in our consideration of this appeal in view of their importance and scholarship.[89]

# 2.3   Another binding source of international law: unilateral declarations

In addition to the binding sources of law outlined in art 38 of the *ICJ Statute*, in certain circumstances unilateral declarations made by a state can bind that state. For example, in the *Nuclear Tests* cases,[90] Australia and New Zealand had brought an application to the ICJ to compel France to cease atmospheric nuclear testing in the South Pacific. Before the Court could hear the merits of the case, the president of France made a public statement declaring that France had completed its tests and would not undertake any more atmospheric testing. At issue was whether this unilateral undertaking created a binding obligation on France, such that the application by Australia and New Zealand was rendered moot because their objective of stopping the tests had been achieved. The ICJ stated:

> [43] It is well recognized that declarations made by way of unilateral acts, concerning legal or factual situations, may have the effect of creating legal obligations. Declarations of this

---

83    Though the ILC adopts draft articles, those documents are not treaties and have no binding effect as such – but they can be highly influential.

84    'Draft Articles on Responsibility of States for Internationally Wrongful Acts' [2001] II(2) *Yearbook of the International Law Commission* 1, 26–30. See Chapter 7.

85    'Draft Articles on Diplomatic Protection' [2006] II(2) *Yearbook of the International Law Commission* 1, 24–6.

86    'Analytical Guide to the Work of the International Law Commission: Peremptory Norms of General International Law (*Jus Cogens*)' (n 54).

87    'Analytical Guide to the Work of the International Law Commission: Fragmentation of International Law', *International Law Commission* (Web Page, 6 June 2022) <https://legal.un.org/ilc/guide/1_9.shtml>.

88    See, eg, *Gabčíkovo-Nagymaros Project (Hungary v Slovakia) (Judgment)* [1997] ICJ Rep 7, which made extensive reference to the then draft Articles on State Responsibility.

89    *R (Freedom and Justice Party) v Secretary of State for Foreign and Commonwealth Affairs* [2018] EWCA Civ 1719, [18].

90    *Nuclear Tests (Australia v France) (Judgment)* [1974] ICJ Rep 253.

kind may be, and often are, very specific. When it is the intention of the State making the declaration that it should become bound according to its terms, that intention confers on the declaration the character of a legal undertaking, the State being thenceforth legally required to follow a course of conduct consistent with the declaration. An undertaking of this kind, if given publicly, and with an intent to be bound, even though not made within the context of international negotiations, is binding. In these circumstances, nothing in the nature of a *quid pro quo* nor any subsequent acceptance of the declaration, nor even any reply or reaction from other States, is required for the declaration to take effect, since such a requirement would be inconsistent with the strictly unilateral nature of the juridical act by which the pronouncement by the state was made.

. . .

[45] With regard to the question of form, it should be observed that this is not a domain in which international law imposes any special or strict requirements. Whether a statement is made orally or in writing makes no essential difference, for such statements made in particular circumstances may create commitments in international law, which does not require that they should be couched in written form. Thus, the question of form is not decisive. . . .

[46] One of the basic principles governing the creation and performance of legal obligations, whatever their source, is the principle of good faith. Trust and confidence are inherent in international co-operation, in particular in an age when this co-operation in many fields is becoming increasingly essential. Just as the very rule of *pacta sunt servanda* in the law of treaties is based on good faith, so also is the binding character of an international obligation assumed by unilateral declaration. Thus interested States may take cognizance of unilateral declarations and place confidence in them, and are entitled to require that the obligation thus created be respected.[91]

The approach of the ICJ in the *Nuclear Tests* cases was codified by the ILC in its Guiding Principles on Unilateral Acts,[92] which highlight that such a statement must be made publicly,[93] by a person authorised to bind the state,[94] either in writing or orally,[95] and in clear and specific terms.[96]

# 2.4   Soft law instruments

Since its adoption in 1945, art 38 of the *ICJ Statute* has been subject to significant criticism regarding its limitations.[97] For example, the article makes no reference to *jus cogens* or

91    Ibid 267–8 [43]–[46].
92    'Guiding Principles Applicable to Unilateral Declarations of States Capable of Creating Legal Obligations, with Commentaries' [2006] II(2) *Yearbook of the International Law Commission* 1, 159.
93    Ibid (Guiding Principle 1).
94    Ibid (Guiding Principle 4).
95    Ibid (Guiding Principle 5).
96    Ibid (Guiding Principle 7).
97    See, eg, Harlan Grant Cohen, 'Finding International Law: Rethinking the Doctrine of Sources' (2007) 93(1) *Iowa Law Review* 65; Gerald Fitzmaurice, 'Some Problems regarding the Formal Sources of International Law' in Martti Koskenniemi (ed), *Sources of International Law* (Routledge, 2017) 153; Jean d'Aspremont, 'Towards a New Theory of Sources' in Anne Orford and Florian Hoffman (eds), *The Oxford Handbook of the Theory of International Law* (Oxford University Press, 2016) 545.

unilateral declarations as binding sources of law. In addition, it ignores a significant source of materials that are relevant for determining the scope of international obligations – these can be broadly termed 'soft law'. Soft law is a contentious term[98] and there is dispute over how to define it,[99] but, generally speaking, soft law is any provision or instrument that provides instruction or guidance on a particular course of action, but does not create formal legal obligations for its addressee.[100] Soft law is widely used in international practice and is seen in instruments such as resolutions of the UN General Assembly (see Section 2.2.2.1) and draft articles or reports of the ILC (see Section 2.2.4.1), as well as recommendations of UN organs or other bodies, resolutions of international conferences, and international codes of conduct or manuals of instruction (see Section 2.4.1).

## 2.4.1   Resolutions of international organisations and conferences

As noted in Section 2.2.2.1, resolutions of the General Assembly can influence and shape state behaviour while having no binding status. Likewise, Final Acts and resolutions of international conferences may prove influential in setting out emerging customary law, contributing to the process of crystallisation. Often, these Final Acts and resolutions closely resemble treaties and set out clear positions on the law, as agreed by the conference participants (that is, states). An example is the *Declaration on Principles Guiding Relations between Participating States*, embodied in the Final Act of the 1975 Conference on Security and Cooperation in Europe ('*Helsinki Final Act*'). The Declaration outlined 10 principles of inter-state relations, including respect for:

    I.     Sovereign equality, respect for the rights inherent in sovereignty

    II.    Refraining from the threat or use of force

    III.   Inviolability of frontiers

    IV.   Territorial integrity of States

    V.    Peaceful settlement of disputes

    VI.   Non-intervention in internal affairs

    VII.   Respect for human rights and fundamental freedoms, including the freedom of thought, conscience, religion or belief

    VIII.  Equal rights and self-determination of peoples

    IX.   Co-operation among States

    X.    Fulfilment in good faith of obligations under international law.[101]

---

98    Robert Baxter, 'International Law in "Her Infinite Variety"' (1980) 29(4) *International and Comparative Law Quarterly* 549; Jaye Ellis, 'Shades of Grey: Soft Law and the Validity of Public International Law' (2012) 25(3) *Leiden Journal of International Law* 313; Andrew Guzman and Timothy Meyer, 'Soft Law' in Eugene Kontorovich and Francesco Parisi (eds), *Economic Analysis of International Law* (Elgar, 2015) 123.

99    See, eg, Francesco Francioni, 'International "Soft Law": A Contemporary Assessment' in Vaughan Lowe and Malgosia Fitzmaurice (eds), *Fifty Years of the International Court of Justice: Essays in Honour of Sir Robert Jennings* (Cambridge University Press, 1996) 167; Guzman and Meyer (n 98) 123; Ulrika Mörth, 'Introduction' in Ulrika Mörth (ed), *Soft Law in Governance and Regulation: An Interdisciplinary Analysis* (Elgar, 2004) 5.

100  Oscar Schachter, 'The Twilight Existence of Nonbinding International Agreements' (1977) 71(2) *American Journal of International Law* 296, 300.

Though never intended to be binding,[102] the *Helsinki Final Act* was pivotal in leading to the creation of the Organization for Security and Co-operation in Europe ('OSCE'). It has been hailed as having 'enormous influence in the subsequent "progress" and demise of the Cold War'.[103]

Such non-binding documents are significant because they can provide clear statements of principle that, while not binding, serve as important guidance. Their non-binding status may also make them more appealing to states, as they do not entail sanctions for noncompliance. As noted by Malcolm Shaw:

> [I]t may be advantageous for states to reach agreements with each another or through international organisations which are not intended to be binding and thus subject to formal legal implementation, but which reflect a political intention to act in a certain way. Such agreements may be more flexible, easier to conclude and easier to adhere to for domestic reasons.[104]

## 2.4.2   Codes of conduct and manuals of instruction

Soft law instruments also include documents such as manuals of instruction and codes of conduct. These instruments may originate from any number of sources, including non-government organisations,[105] civil society organisations such as the International Committee of the Red Cross,[106] expert groups drawn from academia and practice,[107] and intergovernmental organisations.[108] Regardless of their origin, the instruments that emerge are designed to provide guidance in areas of international law where the existing law may be underdeveloped. For example, an expert process, comprising academics and practitioners, was responsible for

---

102    The *Final Act* specifically notes that while the 'Government of the Republic of Finland is requested to transmit to the Secretary-General of the United Nations the text of this Final Act', the document is 'not eligible for registration under Article 102 of the Charter of the United Nations' – that is, it is not considered a treaty and therefore is not binding.

103    Wade Mansell and Karen Openshaw, *International Law: A Critical Introduction* (Hart, 2013) 36.

104    Shaw (n 32) 100.

105    See, eg, Geneva Call, a non-government organisation committed to engaging with non-state armed groups to train those groups to respect international law: *Geneva Call* (Web Page) <www.genevacall.org>.

106    The mandate of the International Committee of the Red Cross is 'ensuring humanitarian protection and assistance for victims of armed conflict and other situations of violence. It takes action in response to emergencies and at the same time promotes respect for international humanitarian law and its implementation in national law': *International Committee of the Red Cross* (Web Page) <www.icrc.org/en>.

107    See, eg, the Institute of International Humanitarian Law which provides training courses and seminars in international humanitarian law and has spearheaded non-binding instruments of instruction in areas such as the law of naval warfare: *Institute of International Humanitarian Law* (Web Page) <www.iihl.org>.

108    See, eg, the Association of Southeast Asian Nations which aims to 'promote regional peace and stability through abiding respect for justice and the rule of law in the relationship among countries of the region and adherence to the principles of the *United Nations Charter*': *Association of Southeast Asian Nations* (Web Page) <https://asean.org>.

drafting the *Tallinn Manual 2.0 on the International Law Applicable to Cyber Operations*,[109] a guide for government legal and policy advisers on how international law applies to state military and intelligence operations in cyberspace. These manuals are not binding but are frequently influential and useful guides for interested stakeholders when applying international law to new and complex situations. They are frequently drafted with real-life examples, so that advisers and practitioners can better theorise how the law applies, as seen in this extract:

> **Rule 6 – Due diligence (general principle)**
>
> A State must exercise due diligence in not allowing its territory, or territory or cyber infrastructure under its governmental control, to be used for cyber operations that affect the rights of, and produce serious adverse consequences for, other States.
>
> 1.  This Rule is based on the general international law principle that States must exercise due diligence in ensuring territory and objects over which they enjoy sovereignty are not used to harm other States. For the purposes of this Manual, the principle shall be referred to as the 'due diligence principle', as that is the term most commonly used with respect to the obligation of States to control activities on their territory. Properly understood, due diligence is the standard of conduct expected of States when complying with this principle. It is a principle that is reflected in the rules, and interpretation thereof, of numerous specialised regimes of international law.
>
> . . .
>
> 8.  The obligation of due diligence applies throughout the sovereign territory of the territorial State. It encompasses any cyber infrastructure used for, as well as people carrying out, cyber operations in that territory. Note that the party launching the cyber operation in question may be operating remotely from a third State. As an example, consider a hacker group located in State A that carries out a destructive cyber operation against State B using cyber infrastructure located in State C. If State C knows of said usage and fails to take feasible measures to put an end to the operation, it is in violation of the due diligence principle.[110]

# DISCUSSION QUESTIONS

(1)  It has been argued that there is no such thing as soft law – that something is either law or not, and that there is no intermediate stage of legality between the two. Do you agree?

(2)  How does one reconcile the binding nature of customary international law, with the fundamental notion of consent under international law?

(3)  Given there is no doctrine of precedent in international law, why should decisions of the International Court of Justice ('ICJ') be given any consideration?

---

109    Michael Schmitt (ed), *Tallinn Manual 2.0 on the International Law Applicable to Cyber Operations* (Cambridge University Press, 2017).

110    Ibid 30–2 (citations omitted).

**(4)**    A number of scholars have, over the years, remarked on (or called for) the 'death' of customary international law. Why do you think this has happened and do you agree?

**(5)**    In his consideration of *Military and Paramilitary Activities in and against Nicaragua*, Frederic Kirgis theorised that the ICJ approached customary international law as existing on a 'sliding scale', whereby the Court could be justified in finding for a customary rule in the absence of *opinio juris* if there was sufficient state practice (and vice versa).[111] Do you agree with this argument?

---

111    Frederic Kirgis, 'Custom on a Sliding Scale' (1987) 81(1) *American Journal of International Law* 146.

# 3

# THE LAW
# OF TREATIES

Alison Pert and
Meda Couzens

## 3.1   Introduction

Before the 20th century, most rules of international law were in the form of customary international law. Since then, the increased complexity of international relations and rapid international development have led to a substantial growth in the number and diversity of treaties.[1] Article 38(1)(a) of the *Statute of the International Court of Justice ('ICJ Statute')* recognises treaties as a (material) source of international law by referring to 'international conventions, whether general or particular, establishing rules expressly recognized by the contesting states'. Treaties now regulate trade, communications, environmental protection, military cooperation and defence, and human rights, to name but a few of the myriad topics. International environmental law, for example, is almost entirely governed by treaties, and international trade, investment and communications 'are unimaginable without treaties'.[2]

The main rules in the law of treaties are contained in the 1969 *Vienna Convention on the Law of Treaties ('VCLT')*,[3] which governs treaty relations between states and is the focus of this chapter. Other relevant international instruments include the 1978 *Vienna Convention on Succession of States in Respect of Treaties*,[4] which addresses the legal implications of the succession of states in relation to existing treaties, and the 1986 *Vienna Convention on the Law of Treaties between States and International Organizations or between International Organizations*,[5] which is not yet in force.

## 3.2   What is a treaty, and the relationship of treaties with customary international law?

Treaties are agreements between states and/or international organisations, and can be entered into on a wide variety of matters. They can be bilateral or multilateral, global or regional, of limited duration or perpetual, and can create rights and obligations, sets of rules and inter-national institutions.[6]

The significant growth of treaties does not make customary international law obsolete. Some topics, such as state responsibility (see Chapter 7), are not covered by treaties, making

1     See 'United Nations Treaty Series Online', *United Nations Treaty Collection* (Web Page) <https://treaties.un.org/Pages/AdvanceSearch.aspx?tab=UNTS&clang=_en>.
2     Malgosia Fitzmaurice, 'The Practical Working of Treaties' in Malcolm Evans (ed), *International Law* (Oxford University Press, 5th ed, 2018) 138, 138.
3     *Vienna Convention on the Law of Treaties*, opened for signature 23 May 1969, 1155 UNTS 331 (entered into force 27 January 1980) ('*VCLT*').
4     *Vienna Convention on Succession of States in Respect of Treaties*, opened for signature 23 August 1978, 1946 UNTS 3 (entered into force 6 November 1996).
5     *Vienna Convention on the Law of Treaties between States and International Organizations or between International Organizations*, opened for signature 21 March 1986, UN Doc A/CONF.129/15 (not yet in force).
6     James Crawford, *Brownlie's Principles of Public International Law* (Oxford University Press, 9th ed, 2019) 355.

reliance on customary international law necessary. Further, an obligation can exist both in a treaty and in customary international law. In *Military and Paramilitary Activities in and against Nicaragua*,[7] for example, the International Court of Justice ('ICJ') held that the prohibition on the use of force continued to exist in customary law and had not, as argued by the United States, been displaced by art 2(4) of the *Charter of the United Nations* ('*UN Charter*') (see Chapter 8). Thus, the relationship between treaties and custom is often one of complementarity.

# 3.3    The *Vienna Convention on the Law of Treaties*

## 3.3.1    Introduction and scope

The core aspects of the law of treaties are contained in the *VCLT*, which had 116 parties at the time of writing.[8] The *VCLT* 'acts as a residual rule'[9] in that it applies unless the particular treaty provides otherwise.

The *VCLT* is the result of nearly 20 years' work by the International Law Commission ('ILC'). In 1966 the ILC adopted draft articles on the law of treaties[10] and recommended that the UN General Assembly convene a conference to conclude a convention on the subject.[11] This it did, resulting in the *VCLT* in 1969, based closely on the ILC draft.

Not all treaties fall within the scope of the *VCLT*.[12] Oral agreements, and agreements between states and other entities (such as international organisations), or between such entities, may be treaties but are not covered by the *VCLT*. Agreements that are not intended to create international legal obligations are also outside its scope, as explained in Section 3.3.2.3.

The *VCLT* only applies to those treaties concluded after the *VCLT*'s entry into force for the states concerned.[13] However, many *VCLT* provisions reflect customary international law,[14] and so the content of those provisions may apply as custom to treaties that are outside the scope of the *VCLT*.[15]

---

7    *Military and Paramilitary Activities in and against Nicaragua (Nicaragua v United States of America) (Merits)* [1986] ICJ Rep 14, 93–7 [174]–[182].

8    United Nations Treaty Collection, '1. Vienna Convention on the Law of Treaties', *Multilateral Treaties Deposited with the Secretary-General: Chapter XXIII Law of Treaties* (Web Page) <https://treaties.un .org/Pages/ViewDetailsIII.aspx?src=TREATY&mtdsg_no=XXIII-1&chapter=23&Temp=mtdsg3&clang=_ en>. Australia acceded to the *VCLT* in 1974.

9    Fitzmaurice (n 2) 143.

10    'Draft Articles on the Law of Treaties, with Commentaries' [1966] II *Yearbook of the International Law Commission* 1, 187.

11    'Report of the International Law Commission on the Work of the Second Part of its 17th Session' [1966] II *Yearbook of the International Law Commission* 1, 177.

12    *VCLT* (n 3) art 3.

13    Ibid art 4.

14    See the online instructor resources for a table on the customary status of *VCLT* provisions.

15    *VCLT* (n 3) arts 3, 4; Anthony Aust, *Modern Treaty Law and Practice* (Cambridge University Press, 2013) 347–8. In *Oil Platforms (Islamic Republic of Iran v United States of America) (Merits)* [2003] ICJ Rep 161, the *VCLT* was applied even though the United States and Iran were not parties to it.

Provisions that have been explicitly recognised as reflecting customary international law include arts 7,[16] 26,[17] 27,[18] 31–32,[19] 33,[20] 60–62,[21] 65 and 67.[22]

## 3.3.2    What is a treaty for the purposes of the *VCLT*?

Article 2(1)(a) of the *VCLT* defines a treaty as 'an international agreement concluded between States in written form and governed by international law, whether embodied in a single instrument or in two or more related instruments and whatever its particular designation'. Each element of this definition is discussed in the following sections.

### 3.3.2.1    An agreement between states

According to art 6 of the *VCLT*, '[e]very State possesses capacity to conclude treaties'.[23] 'State' here refers to sovereign, independent states,[24] but the range of entities that may become parties to a treaty depends on the particular treaty.[25] The 'all states' formula is the most common – under it the treaty is open to all states (or any state) – but difficulties arise when an entity's statehood is contested. The UN Secretary-General, who is the depositary[26] for over 500 multilateral treaties, takes the view that it is beyond the competence of the role to determine whether a particular entity is a 'state' for this purpose; the practice of the Secretary-General is to follow the advice of the General Assembly on the issue.[27] The state of Palestine, whose statehood is not universally recognised, has become party to a number of treaties under an 'all states' clause – for example, the *Rome Statute of the International Criminal Court*.[28]

### 3.3.2.2    In written form

The *VCLT* applies only to written treaties. Oral treaties are still treaties, but they are not governed by the *VCLT*. However, as explained in Section 3.3.1, many of the *VCLT* provisions

---

16    *Maritime Delimitation in the Indian Ocean (Somalia v Kenya) (Preliminary Objections)* [2017] ICJ Rep 3, 22 [43].

17    *Gabčíkovo-Nagymaros Project (Hungary v Slovakia) (Judgment)* [1997] ICJ Rep 7, 78 [142].

18    *Certain Questions of Mutual Assistance in Criminal Matters (Djibouti v France) (Judgment)* [2008] ICJ Rep 177, 222–3 [124].

19    *Application of the Convention on the Prevention and Punishment of the Crime of Genocide (Bosnia and Herzegovina v Serbia and Montenegro) (Judgment)* [2007] ICJ Rep 43, 109–10 [160].

20    *LaGrand (Germany v United States of America) (Judgment)* [2001] ICJ Rep 466, 502 [101].

21    *Gabčíkovo-Nagymaros Project* (n 17) 38 [46].

22    Ibid 66 [109].

23    For special cases such as Vatican City, Taiwan and Western Sahara, see Aust (n 15) 57–60.

24    Ibid 56; 'Draft Articles on the Law of Treaties, with Commentaries' (n 10) 192 (Draft Article 5 Commentary [4]).

25    For examples of the different types of participation clause, see Duncan Hollis (ed), *The Oxford Guide to Treaties* (Oxford University Press, 2nd ed, 2020) 651–9.

26    See Section 3.4.

27    United Nations, *Final Clauses of Multilateral Treaties: Handbook* (2003) 14 <https://treaties.un.org/doc/source/publications/FC/English.pdf> ('*UN Final Clauses Handbook*'); United Nations, *Summary of Practice of the Secretary-General as Depositary of Multilateral Treaties*, UN Doc ST/LEG/7/Rev.1 (1999) 23 [81]–[83] <https://treaties.un.org/doc/source/publications/practice/summary_english.pdf>.

28    *Rome Statute of the International Criminal Court*, opened for signature 17 July 1998, 2187 UNTS 3 (entered into force 1 July 2002) art 125.

reflect customary international law, so the substance of those provisions will apply as custom-ary international law to oral treaties.[29]

### 3.3.2.3    Governed by international law

To be a treaty as defined by the *VCLT*, the agreement must be governed by international law. Thus, for example, a treaty is not formed if states choose to enter into an agreement that is governed by domestic law[30] or that is a political rather than legal agreement (such as a non-binding memorandum of understanding ('MOU'); see Section 3.3.2.5).

Whether an agreement is intended to be legally binding is '[o]ne of the most difficult and unresolved problems'[31] in the law of treaties, one question being whether the test of intention is objective or subjective. The objective test considers the text of the agreement to be the sole determinant, while the subjective test considers the parties' intentions to be relevant.[32] The ICJ tends to follow the objective approach,[33] while other tribunals have favoured a more subject-ive test. In the *South China Sea Arbitration*,[34] the Arbitral Tribunal Constituted under Annex VII to the 1982 United Nations Convention on the Law of the Sea decided that to establish such intent it was necessary to consider the terms of the agreement, the circumstances of its adoption, and, possibly, the subsequent conduct of the parties.[35]

### 3.3.2.4    Whether embodied in one or more instruments

Some treaties consist of more than one instrument, and include schedules, annexes or maps, which together with the text form the treaty.[36]

### 3.3.2.5    Whatever its particular designation

Whether an international agreement is a treaty depends not on its name but on whether it creates international obligations. Terms used to designate treaties to which the *VCLT* applies include 'treaty', 'covenant', 'convention', 'protocol', 'agreement' and 'pact'. Even joint communiqués, exchanges of letters and minutes of meetings can be treaties if they create international rights and obligations and otherwise satisfy the requirements of art 2.[37]

Australia increasingly uses the phrase 'instruments of less-than-treaty status'.[38] These instruments reflect political commitments but do not create binding legal obligations, and thus

---

29    *VCLT* (n 3) art 3.
30    'Draft Articles on the Law of Treaties, with Commentaries' (n 10) 189 (Draft Article 2 Commentary [6]).
31    Fitzmaurice (n 2) 139.
32    Duncan Hollis, 'Defining Treaties' in Duncan Hollis (ed), *The Oxford Guide to Treaties* (Oxford University Press, 2nd ed, 2020) 11, 25–30.
33    Ibid 27. See, eg, *Maritime Delimitation and Territorial Questions (Qatar v Bahrain) (Jurisdiction and Admissibility)* [1994] ICJ Rep 112, 121 [27]; *Pulp Mills on the River Uruguay (Argentina v Uruguay) (Judgment)* [2010] ICJ Rep 14, 62 [128]; *Maritime Delimitation in the Indian Ocean* (n 16) 21 [42].
34    *South China Sea Arbitration (Republic of Philippines v People's Republic of China) (Award on Jurisdiction and Admissibility)* (Permanent Court of Arbitration, Case No 2013-19, 29 October 2015).
35    Ibid [213].
36    See, eg, *Convention on Biological Diversity*, opened for signature 5 June 1992, 1760 UNTS 79 (entered into force 29 December 1993) art 30(1).
37    See, eg, *Maritime Delimitation and Territorial Questions* (n 33) 121 [24]–[25].
38    'Australia's Practice for Concluding Less-than-Treaty Status Instruments', *Department of Foreign Affairs and Trade* (Web Page) <www.dfat.gov.au/international-relations/treaties/australias-practice-concluding-less-than-treaty-status-instruments>.

do not go through the same parliamentary scrutiny as treaties.[39] They are therefore faster to conclude and more flexible as tools of inter-state cooperation. The instrument most commonly given this label is the MOU. But labelling an agreement an MOU does not determine its status. In *Maritime Delimitation in the Indian Ocean*,[40] the ICJ found that the MOU in question was a binding international agreement because it contained a provision regarding its entry into force (illustrating its binding nature) and Kenya had requested its registration under art 102 of the *UN Charter* unopposed by Somalia.[41]

## 3.4    Treaty negotiation and conclusion

Treaty negotiation and conclusion are addressed in arts 7–19 of the *VCLT*. Multilateral treaties are often negotiated over many years at international conferences. The text might be adopted in the same forum, or a separate 'diplomatic conference' may be arranged where the final negotiations take place. A state representative must be duly authorised to adopt the text, or to express the consent of their state to be bound (see Section 3.5),[42] although even an unauthorised act can subsequently be validated by the state.[43]

Certain individuals such as the head of state, foreign minister and ambassador are assumed to be authorised,[44] but others must produce 'full powers' (in older parlance, showing they are 'plenipotentiaries') unless it appears that the relevant states have dispensed with this requirement.[45] 'Full powers' are formal documents, usually provided by the state's foreign affairs department, 'designating a person or persons to represent the State for negotiating, adopting or authenticating the text of a treaty, for expressing the consent of the State to be bound by a treaty, or for accomplishing any other act with respect to a treaty'.[46]

Upon finalisation of the negotiations, the treaty is 'adopted' by consensus or by a relevant majority[47] and the text is 'authenticated'[48] – 'some act or procedure which certifies the text as the correct and authentic text' such as initialling or signature by the negotiating states.[49] It is then placed with a depositary, which can be a state or an international organisation.[50] The UN Secretary-General serves as the depositary for numerous multilateral treaties.[51] Under art 80(1) of the *VCLT*, after a treaty has entered into force it must be transmitted to the UN Secretariat for

---

39      Ibid.
40      *Maritime Delimitation in the Indian Ocean* (n 16).
41      Ibid 17 [36], 22 [42].
42      *VCLT* (n 3) art 7.
43      Ibid art 8.
44      Ibid art 7(2).
45      Ibid arts 2(1)(c), 7.
46      Ibid art 2(1)(c). See also Aust (n 15) 72–8.
47      *VCLT* (n 3) art 9.
48      Ibid art 10.
49      'Draft Articles on the Law of Treaties, with Commentaries' (n 10) 195 (Draft Article 9 Commentary [1]).
50      The depositary can be the head of the international organisation (eg the Secretary-General of the United Nations): *VCLT* (n 3) art 76(1). The functions of the depositary include keeping custody of the treaty and receiving ratifications and accessions: at art 77(1).
51      Over 560 such treaties at the time of writing: see 'Overview: Depositary of Treaties', *United Nations Treaty Collection* (Web Page) <https://treaties.un.org/pages/Overview.aspx?path=overview/overview/page1_en.xml>.

registration and publication.[52] The registration requirement is to discourage secret treaties,[53] and although failure to register a treaty does not affect its validity, registration may be an indication that the agreement is a binding international instrument.[54]

Generally, a multilateral treaty is said to be 'concluded' when the text is adopted or it is opened for signature, whichever is later; a bilateral treaty is concluded when signed by both states.[55]

# 3.5   Expressing the consent to be bound

Once a treaty is concluded, states may decide whether they wish to become bound by it. States can express their consent to be bound 'by signature, exchange of instruments constituting a treaty, ratification, acceptance, approval or accession, or by any other means if so agreed'.[56]

A multilateral treaty is usually 'open for signature' for a specified period (12–18 months is common) during which states can physically sign the treaty at the nominated place.[57] Signature alone is rarely sufficient to express a state's consent to be bound, but this depends on what the treaty requires and the intention of the negotiating states.[58] If the treaty provides that signature is subject to ratification, acceptance or approval,[59] a signature alone will not be sufficient to bind a state.[60] A state that signs a treaty has no obligation to ratify it – many signatures are never ratified – but the signature has some limited legal consequences, for example under art 18 of the *VCLT*.[61]

Ratification is a formal procedure for confirming an earlier signature.[62] The period between signature and ratification can be days or years, and is commonly used by a state to ensure that any necessary internal laws and policies are in place before it becomes bound by the treaty. This is the practice in Australia, for instance, which has the added complication of being a federation: even where the Commonwealth has the constitutional power to legislate to implement a treaty,[63] it prefers a cooperative approach, with the States and Territories passing uniform legislation.[64]

---

52    *VCLT* (n 3) art 80(1). See also *Charter of the United Nations* ('*UN Charter*') art 102.

53    Megan Donaldson, 'The Survival of the Secret Treaty: Publicity, Secrecy, and Legality in the International Order' (2017) 111(3) *American Journal of International Law* 575; F Seymour Cocks, *The Secret Treaties and Understandings* (Union of Democratic Control, 1918) <www.gwpda.org/comment/secrettreaties .html>.

54    *Delimitation of the Maritime Boundary in the Bay of Bengal (Bangladesh v Myanmar) (Judgment)* [2012] ITLOS Rep 4 [97]; *Maritime Delimitation in the Indian Ocean* (n 16) 21 [42].

55    Aust (n 15) 86.

56    *VCLT* (n 3) art 11.

57    For example, the *VCLT* was open for signature in, unusually, two places: Vienna for six months and then New York for five months: ibid art 81.

58    Ibid art 12(1).

59    The terms 'acceptance' and 'approval' are preferred by some states and are equivalent to ratification or accession depending on the context: 'Draft Articles on the Law of Treaties, with Commentaries' (n 10) 198 (Draft Article 11 Commentary [9]).

60    *VCLT* (n 3) arts 12, 14, 16.

61    Discussed in Section 3.8.1.

62    For a model instrument of ratification, acceptance or approval, see United Nations, *Treaty Handbook* (2012) 52 <https://treaties.un.org/doc/source/publications/THB/English.pdf>.

63    See Chapter 4 on international law and domestic law.

64    Ibid. See also Treaties Council, *Principles and Procedures for Commonwealth–State Consultation on Treaties* (1996) <https://arp.nsw.gov.au/assets/ars/attachments/Principles-and-Procedures-for-Commonwealth-State-Consultation-on-Treaties.pdf>.

Entering into treaties is an executive act in Australia, with Parliament having no formal role. However, it is now the practice that before any 'treaty action' is taken Parliament is consulted.[65]

A multilateral treaty may also be open for 'accession'; it may specify that states can accede to it at any time, or after it closes for signature.[66] This is a one-step procedure for expressing consent to be bound, and does not require a prior signature.

Unless the treaty provides differently, the instruments of ratification, accession or approval establish the consent to be bound on exchange, on deposit with the depositary, or when the depositary or the contracting states are notified.[67]

# 3.6   Entry into force of a treaty

A treaty enters into force in the manner and at the date provided by the treaty or agreed by the negotiating states,[68] usually after a certain number of states have ratified or acceded to it. For example, art 84(1) of the *VCLT* provides: 'The present Convention shall enter into force on the thirtieth day following the date of deposit of the thirty-fifth instrument of ratification or accession.'

If a state consented to be bound *before* the treaty came into force, the state will be bound when the treaty comes into force. For a state that consents to be bound *after* the treaty has come into force, the state will be bound when its consent to be bound takes effect, unless the treaty provides differently.[69]

# 3.7   Reservations to treaties

A state may want to become a party to a treaty but not like or be able to comply with a particular provision. It may therefore seek to exclude or modify the provision as it applies to that state, by submitting a reservation. This section discusses when reservations are permitted, and what their effects are.[70]

The *VCLT* defines a reservation as

> a unilateral statement, however phrased or named, made by a State, when signing, ratifying, accepting, approving or acceding to a treaty, whereby it purports to exclude or to modify the legal effect of certain provisions of the treaty in their application to that State.[71]

65   See Chapter 4; 'Australia's Treaty-Making Process', *Department of Foreign Affairs and Trade* (Web Page) <www.dfat.gov.au/international-relations/treaties/treaty-making-process>.
66   *Treaty Handbook* (n 62) 10 [3.3.4], 53 (model instrument of accession).
67   *VCLT* (n 3) art 16.
68   Ibid art 24(1).
69   See, eg, ibid art 84(2).
70   The *United Nations Treaty Collection* website maintains a searchable list of all reservations, declarations and other depositary notifications for treaties deposited with the Secretary-General: see 'Depositary Notifications' (Web Page) <https://treaties.un.org/Pages/CNs.aspx?cnTab=tab2&clang=_en> ('*UN Depositary Notifications*').
71   *VCLT* (n 3) art 2.

This definition reflects customary international law.[72] Note that a reservation can only be made at the point when a state is consenting to be bound by the treaty – it cannot be made at a later date.[73] One consequence of this requirement is that reservations are only relevant to multilateral treaties: if one party tried to submit a reservation to a bilateral treaty, it would simply be continuing the treaty negotiations.

## 3.7.1 Reservations vs interpretative declarations

A reservation must be distinguished from an interpretative declaration, which is a statement declaring how a state interprets a particular provision. Given that a multilateral treaty might be negotiated by more than 190 states, and the language of the treaty must be acceptable to all, the words used can be somewhat general – hence the need felt by some states to clarify their understanding of certain provisions. The distinction between a reservation and an interpretative declaration is usually, but not always, clear, and does not depend on the label used by the submitting state.[74] Australia submitted a 'declaration' when ratifying the *Rome Statute of the International Criminal Court*,[75] but it was arguably a reservation because it asserted that the Australian Attorney-General maintained complete discretion as to whether to surrender an accused to the Court:

> **Declaration:**
>
> The Government of Australia, having considered the Statute, now hereby ratifies the same, for and on behalf of Australia, with the following declaration, the terms of which have full effect in Australian law, and which is not a reservation:
>
> [T]he procedure under Australian law implementing the *Statute of the Court* provides that no person can be surrendered to the Court unless the Australian Attorney-General issues a certificate allowing surrender. Australian law also provides that no person can be arrested pursuant to an arrest warrant issued by the Court without a certificate from the Attorney-General.[76]

Some declarations are very specific; Canada submitted several declarations in relation to the *United Nations Convention against Corruption*,[77] including this:

---

72   *Land and Maritime Boundary between Cameroon and Nigeria (Cameroon v Nigeria) (Judgment)* [2002] ICJ Rep 303, 429 [263].

73   See, eg, the Netherlands' regarding as void Bhutan's reservation because it was deposited seven months after ratification: 'United Nations Convention against Corruption: Objections (Netherlands)' (17 April 2018), *UN Depositary Notifications* (n 70) <https://treaties.un.org/Pages/ViewDetails.aspx?src= TREATY&mtdsg_no=XVIII-14&chapter=18&clang=_en>.

74   For example, many states submitted declarations and reservations to the *International Convention for the Suppression of Acts of Nuclear Terrorism*. China submitted what was clearly a reservation but titled it a 'declaration': 'International Convention for the Suppression of Acts of Nuclear Terrorism: Declarations and Reservations (China)', *UN Depositary Notifications* (n 70) <https://treaties.un.org/Pages/ ViewDetailsIII.aspx?src=TREATY&mtdsg_no=XVIII-15&chapter=18&Temp=mtdsg3&clang=_ en#EndDec>.

75   *Rome Statute of the International Criminal Court*, opened for signature 17 July 1998, 2187 UNTS 3 (entered into force 1 July 2002).

76   'Rome Statute of the International Criminal Court: Declarations and Reservations (Australia)', *UN Depositary Notifications* (n 70) <https://treaties.un.org/Pages/ViewDetails.aspx?src=TREATY&mtdsg _no=XVIII-10&chapter=18&clang=_en#EndDec>.

77   *United Nations Convention against Corruption*, opened for signature 31 October 2003, 2349 UNTS 41 (entered into force 14 December 2005).

> It is the understanding of the Government of Canada that in relation to Article 17 the word 'diversion' means embezzlement and misappropriation, which constitute the criminal offences of theft and fraud under current Canadian law.[78]

Other declarations can be much broader. The *Ottawa Convention on Anti-Personnel Mines*,[79] for example, caused many states some difficulties because of their military cooperation with the United States, which refused to become a party to the treaty and continued to manufacture and use anti-personnel mines. The parties feared that engaging in military activities with the United States could be interpreted as 'assisting' the use or development of such mines, contrary to the Convention. Several states therefore submitted similar declarations,[80] including Australia:

> **Declarations:**
>
> It is the understanding of Australia that, in the context of operations, exercises or other military activity authorised by the United Nations or otherwise conducted in accordance with international law, the participation by the Australian Defence Force, or individual Australian citizens or residents, in such operations, exercises or other military activity conducted in combination with the armed forces of States not party to the Convention which engage in activity prohibited under the Convention would not, by itself, be considered to be in violation of the Convention.[81]

## 3.7.2 Are reservations allowed?

The whole purpose of a reservation is to change the way a treaty applies to a particular state. If all states submitted reservations, therefore, a painstakingly negotiated treaty could fragment into a patchwork of mismatched obligations. International law has developed rules which try to balance these competing aims: on the one hand, preserving the integrity of the treaty, and on the other, encouraging as many states as possible to adhere to the treaty, by allowing reservations under certain conditions. These rules were articulated by the ICJ in the *Reservations* advisory opinion in 1951.[82] The *Convention on the Prevention and Punishment of the Crime of Genocide*[83] had been concluded in 1948 and several states had

---

78    'United Nations Convention against Corruption: Declarations and Reservations (Canada), *UN Depositary Notifications* (n 70) <https://treaties.un.org/Pages/ViewDetails.aspx?src=TREATY&mtdsg_no=XVIII-14&chapter=18&clang=_en>; full text in UN Reference CN.981.2007.TREATIES-25 (Depositary Notification) (2 October 2007).

79    *Convention on the Prohibition of the Use, Stockpiling, Production and Transfer of Anti-Personnel Mines and on Their Destruction*, opened for signature 18 September 1897, 2056 UNTS 211 (entered into force 1 March 1999).

80    See, eg, declarations by Canada, Czech Republic, Montenegro, Poland, Serbia and the United Kingdom: 'Convention on the Prohibition of the Use, Stockpiling, Production and Transfer of Anti-Personnel Mines and on Their Destruction: Declarations', *UN Depositary Notifications* (n 70) <https://treaties.un.org/Pages/ViewDetails.aspx?src=TREATY&mtdsg_no=XXVI-5&chapter=26&clang=_en#EndDec>.

81    Ibid; full text in UN Reference CN.95.1999.TREATIES-7 (Depositary Notification) (11 February 1999) <https://treaties.un.org/doc/Publication/CN/1999/CN.95.1999-Eng.pdf>.

82    *Reservations to the Convention on the Prevention and Punishment of the Crime of Genocide (Advisory Opinion)* [1951] ICJ Rep 15 ('*Reservations Advisory Opinion*').

83    *Convention on the Prevention and Punishment of the Crime of Genocide*, opened for signature 9 December 1948, 78 UNTS 277 (entered into force 12 January 1951).

submitted reservations, particularly to the article requiring states to refer any dispute under the Convention to the ICJ (art IX).[84] These reservations had been objected to by other states. The UN General Assembly requested an advisory opinion from the Court on, essentially, the legal effect of such reservations.[85]

The Court began by affirming the importance of consent:

> It is well established that in its treaty relations a State cannot be bound without its consent, and that consequently no reservation can be effective against any State without its agreement thereto. It is also a generally recognized principle that a multilateral convention is the result of an agreement freely concluded upon its clauses and that consequently none of the contracting parties is entitled to frustrate or impair, by means of unilateral decisions or particular agreements, the purpose and *raison d'être* of the convention.[86]

In the Court's opinion, reservations were permitted if they were compatible with the object and purpose of the Convention, and each state would have to form its own view of this in the circumstances:

> The object and purpose of the *Genocide Convention* imply that it was the intention of the General Assembly and of the States which adopted it that as many States as possible should participate. The complete exclusion from the Convention of one or more States would not only restrict the scope of its application, but would detract from the authority of the moral and humanitarian principles which are its basis. It is inconceivable that the contracting parties readily contemplated that an objection to a minor reservation should produce such a result. But even less could the contracting parties have intended to sacrifice the very object of the Convention in favour of a vain desire to secure as many participants as possible. The object and purpose of the Convention thus limit both the freedom of making reservations and that of objecting to them. It follows that it is the compatibility of a reservation with the object and purpose of the Convention that must furnish the criterion for the attitude of a State in making the reservation on accession as well as for the appraisal by a State in objecting to the reservation. ...
>
> Any other view would lead either to the acceptance of reservations which frustrate the purposes which the General Assembly and the contracting parties had in mind, or to recognition that the parties to the Convention have the power of excluding from it the author of a reservation, even a minor one, which may be quite compatible with those purposes.
>
> It has nevertheless been argued that any State entitled to become a party to the *Genocide Convention* may do so while making any reservation it chooses by virtue of its sovereignty. The Court cannot share this view. It is obvious that so extreme an application of the idea of State sovereignty could lead to a complete disregard of the object and purpose of the Convention.[87]

---

84    For the text of the reservations, see ibid 301–23 <https://treaties.un.org/doc/Publication/UNTS/Volume%2078/volume-78-I-1021-English.pdf>.

85    *Reservations Advisory Opinion* (n 82) 16.

86    Ibid 21.

87    Ibid 24.

As to the effect of other states' objections to a reservation, the Court said that that would be a matter for the objecting state:

> [E]ach State which is a party to the Convention is entitled to appraise the validity of the reservation and it exercises this right individually and from its own standpoint. As no State can be bound by a reservation to which it has not consented, it necessarily follows that each State objecting to it will or will not, on the basis of its individual appraisal within the limits of the criterion of the object and purpose stated above, consider the reserving State to be a party to the Convention.[88]

The Court's views were codified in arts 19–21 of the *VCLT*. These articles are quite brief and, in some respects, unclear and incomplete. The ILC endeavoured to remedy this with its 2011 *Guide to Practice on Reservations to Treaties*.[89] Article 19 of the *VCLT* provides that a reservation will be allowed unless it is prohibited by the treaty itself, either expressly or impliedly (by specifying that only certain other reservations may be made), or it is 'incompatible' with the object and purpose of the treaty. In its Guide, the ILC elaborates on art 19 and explains that the test of compatibility with the object and purpose of the treaty also applies to reservations impliedly permitted by the treaty under art 19(a) and (b), but not to a reservation *expressly* permitted by the treaty.[90]

The ILC defines incompatibility as follows:

> A reservation is incompatible with the object and purpose of the treaty if it affects an essential element of the treaty that is necessary to its general tenor, in such a way that the reservation impairs the *raison d'être* of the treaty.[91]

If reservations are expressly permitted by the treaty, then acceptance by other parties is not necessary.[92] Acceptance by all parties is required if there is only a limited number of negotiating states, and the object and purpose of the treaty indicate that application of treaty in its entirety is an essential condition of each party's consent to be bound.[93] This may be the case, for example, with a small regional treaty governing the use of water resources. In all other cases:

- acceptance by another contracting state makes the reserving state a party to the treaty in relation to the accepting state;[94] and
- if another contracting state objects, whether the treaty comes into force between them depends on the objecting state: if it expressly says the treaty is not to apply, it will not apply between the two states; if the objecting state is silent, the treaty will apply (the effect of the reservation is explained in Section 3.7.3).[95]

---

88    Ibid 26.
89    'Guide to Practice on Reservations to Treaties' [2011] II(3) *Yearbook of the International Law Commission* 1, 23.
90    Ibid 208–11 (Guidelines 3.1.3–3.1.4 Commentary).
91    Ibid 211 (Guideline 3.1.5).
92    *VCLT* (n 3) art 20(1).
93    Ibid art 20(2).
94    Ibid art 20(4)(a).
95    Ibid art 20(4)(b). For example, the United Kingdom objected to Tunisia's reservation to the *VCLT* in 1972, saying '[t]he United Kingdom ... does not accept the entry into force of the Convention as between the

If a state does not object within 12 months of consenting to be bound, or being notified of the reservation, it is deemed to have accepted the reservation.[96]

### 3.7.3   Effect of reservations

Article 21 of the *VCLT* sets out the effect of reservations. Although not expressly stated, it is clear that art 21 relates only to permissible reservations – the *VCLT* does not address the effects of an impermissible reservation (that is, one which does not comply with art 19).[97] Where a permissible reservation is made by a reserving state ('R'), the effects are:

- if State A *accepts the reservation* – the treaty is modified as between R and A, as provided for in the reservation (art 21(1));
- if State B *objects* and *says the treaty is not to apply* as between R and B – there is no treaty at all between R and B (art 20(4)(b)); and
- if State C *objects* but *does not say the treaty is not to apply* as between R and C – the treaty applies as between R and C, but 'the provisions to which the reservation relates do not apply ... to the extent of the reservation' (art 21(3)).

This last provision is intended to mean that the parts affected by the reservation will not apply, at all, between the two states. As the ILC noted in its 2011 Guide:

> [T]he objective of this provision – which derives from the same principle of mutuality of consent – is to safeguard as much as possible the agreement between the parties. One should not exclude the application of the entirety of the provision or provisions to which a reservation relates, but only of the parts of those provisions concerning which the parties have expressed disagreement.[98]

Confusingly, the result of this in many cases will be to give effect to the reservation, despite the objection.[99] In *Anglo-French Continental Shelf*,[100] for example, France submitted a reservation rejecting the principle of equidistance in art 6 of the *Convention on the Continental Shelf* except on certain conditions;[101] the United Kingdom objected and the matter went to arbitration. The arbitral tribunal held that under art 21(3) of the *VCLT*, art 6 did not apply as between France and the United Kingdom to the extent excluded by the reservation; therefore, France

---

United Kingdom and Tunisia': 'Vienna Convention of the Law of Treaties: Declarations and Reservations (United Kingdom)', *UN Depositary Notifications* (n 70) <https://treaties.un.org/Pages/ViewDetailsIII .aspx?src=TREATY&mtdsg_no=XXIII-1&chapter=23&Temp=mtdsg3&clang=_en>.

96    *VCLT* (n 3) art 20(5).
97    'Guide to Practice on Reservations to Treaties' (n 89) 294–8 (Guideline 4.5 Commentary).
98    Ibid 287 (Guideline 4.3.6 Commentary [27]).
99    Ibid 288 (Guideline 4.3.6 Commentary [39]).
100   *Delimitation of the Continental Shelf (United Kingdom v France)* (1977) 54 ILR 6 ('*Anglo-French Continental Shelf*').
101   *Convention on the Continental Shelf*, opened for signature 29 April 1958, 499 UNTS 311 (entered into force 10 June 1964).

could not rely on the reservation, but the United Kingdom could not rely on art 6 except on the conditions stated in France's reservation. The practical effect was that France succeeded in preventing the principle of equidistance being applied, notwithstanding the United Kingdom's objection.[102]

The ILC explains this in more detail in its 2011 Guide by distinguishing between a reservation that excludes a provision, and one that modifies the effect of a provision. If the reservation purports to *exclude* a provision – for example, 'article 37 shall not apply' – the effect is that art 37 does not apply between the reserving state and an objecting state. This has the same practical effect as if the objecting state had accepted the reservation.[103] If the reservation purports to *modify* an obligation in a provision, then neither the original, nor the modified, obligation applies between the reserving and objecting states.[104] To illustrate, suppose a treaty contains the following provision:

> Article 2. The parties agree to settle any dispute by negotiation or, failing agreement, by submission to the International Court of Justice.

State R lodges a reservation asserting 'State R accepts Article 2 on the condition that any dispute will be submitted to international arbitration and not to the International Court of Justice', and another state objects. Applying the ILC analysis, the original obligation is to submit any dispute to the ICJ and the modified obligation is to submit any dispute to international arbitration. The effect of art 21(3) of the *VCLT* is that neither obligation applies between the reserving and objecting states, so that the objecting state cannot insist on ICJ dispute settlement, and State R cannot insist on international arbitration.

The ILC Guide also fills the gaps left by the *VCLT* in relation to impermissible reservations. Before this, opinion was (and to some extent remains) divided on their legal effect. One school of thought was that an impermissible reservation should be severed from the consent to be bound (ratification, accession, etc) so that the reserving state would be bound, in full, without the benefit of the reservation.[105] The other school was that such reservations were an integral part of a state's consent and so were not severable; the reserving state would not be a party to the treaty at all. The ILC Guide makes it clear, first, that an impermissible reservation is null and void, and so has no legal effect regardless of the reactions of other contracting states.[106] It then proposes that where a state makes an impermissible reservation, that state will be bound by the treaty, without the benefit of the reservation, unless it has clearly made its consent to be bound conditional upon the reservation.[107] If it has done this, the state will not be a party to the treaty at all.[108]

---

102    *Anglo-French Continental Shelf* (n 100) 110.
103    'Guide to Practice on Reservations to Treaties' (n 89) 32 (Guideline 4.3.6(2)).
104    Ibid 289 (Guideline 4.3.6(3) Commentary [41]).
105    See, eg, *Belilos v Switzerland* (1988) 88 ILR 635.
106    'Guide to Practice on Reservations to Treaties' (n 89) 32 (Guidelines 4.5.1, 4.5.2).
107    Ibid 32 (Guideline 4.5.3).
108    Ibid.

# 3.8    Legal effects of a treaty

## 3.8.1    Obligation not to defeat the object and purpose of a treaty prior to its entry into force (art 18)

Article 18 of the *VCLT* creates a limited obligation for states that have signed a treaty or expressed their consent to be bound. The obligation applies before the treaty becomes binding on that state,[109] and requires that the state 'must not, therefore, do anything that would prevent it from being able to fully comply with the treaty once it has entered into force'.[110] For example, if a treaty provides for the return of certain objects, art 18 of the *VCLT* prohibits the possessor state destroying the objects before the treaty comes into force.[111] Importantly, art 18 is *not* an obligation to give effect to the treaty itself.

The obligation under art 18 ceases when a state makes clear its intention not to become a party to the treaty (known as 'unsigning'),[112] or when the entry into force of the treaty is unduly delayed. Both the United States and Russia 'unsigned' the *Rome Statute of the International Criminal Court* by notification to the depositary.[113]

## 3.8.2    Observance of treaties: obligations after the treaty comes into effect

### 3.8.2.1    *Pacta sunt servanda*

Article 26 of the *VCLT* states that once a treaty comes into force, it is binding on the parties and must be performed by them in good faith – *pacta sunt servanda*. This article reflects customary international law.[114] It is a 'fundamental principle of treaty law' and 'arguably the oldest principle of international law'.[115] In *Gabčíkovo-Nagymaros Project*, the ICJ applied this rule strictly and decided that the treaty between Hungary and Slovakia could not be terminated simply because both parties breached their obligations arising from it:

> [T]his reciprocal wrongful conduct did not bring the Treaty to an end nor justify its termination. The Court would set a precedent with disturbing implications for treaty relations and the integrity of the rule *pacta sunt servanda* if it were to conclude that a treaty in force between States, which the parties have implemented in considerable measure and at great cost over a period of years, might be unilaterally set aside on grounds of reciprocal noncompliance.[116]

---

109    Paul Gragl and Malgosia Fitzmaurice, 'The Legal Character of Article 18 of the Vienna Convention on the Law of Treaties' (2019) 68(3) *International and Comparative Law Quarterly* 699.

110    Aust (n 15) 108.

111    Ibid 109.

112    Gragl and Fitzmaurice (n 109) 704.

113    See, eg, the full text of the Russian Federation communication in UN Reference CN.886.2016.TREATIES-XVIII.10 (Depositary Notification) (30 November 2016) <https://treaties.un.org/doc/Publication/CN/2016/CN.886.2016-Eng.pdf>.

114    *Gabčíkovo-Nagymaros Project* (n 17) 78 [142].

115    Malcolm Shaw, *International Law* (Cambridge University Press, 9th ed, 2021) 788.

116    *Gabčíkovo-Nagymaros Project* (n 17) 68 [114].

### 3.8.2.2   Internal law and observance of treaties

Article 27 of the *VCLT* provides: 'A party may not invoke the provisions of its internal law as justification for its failure to perform a treaty.' Therefore, when a claim is made in an international forum that a state has breached its obligations under a treaty, it is no defence for the state to argue that its conduct is justified by its domestic law.[117]

### 3.8.2.3   Treaties and third states

Treaties do not create rights or obligations for a non-party ('third') state without the third state's consent.[118] The parties must intend to confer the right or impose the obligation, and the third state must consent – in writing in the case of an obligation.[119] Conditions may be imposed on the third state's exercise of a right.[120] Importantly, this does not preclude 'a rule set forth in a treaty from becoming binding upon a third State as a customary rule of international law, recognized as such'.[121]

## 3.9   Application of treaties

Unless otherwise intended by parties, a treaty does not apply to acts, facts or situations which occurred or existed before the treaty came into force for those parties.[122] A treaty is binding on a state in relation to its entire territory (including its airspace and territorial waters), unless the parties intended differently.[123]

Article 30 of the *VCLT* regulates the application of successive treaties on the same subject matter.[124] The general rule is that as between those states that are parties to both treaties, the later treaty applies; the earlier treaty will also apply, but only to the extent that it is compatible with the later treaty. Between a state that is party to both treaties and a state that is party to only one, only the treaty to which both states are parties applies.

## 3.10   Interpretation of treaties

Articles 31 and 32 of the *VCLT* deal with the interpretation of treaties; art 33 deals with the interpretation of treaties authenticated in more than one language.[125] These articles reflect customary international law.[126]

---

117    *Questions Relating to the Obligation to Prosecute or Extradite (Belgium v Senegal) (Judgment)* [2012] ICJ Rep 422, 460 [113]. See also Human Rights Committee, 59th sess, *Views: Communication No 560/1993*, UN Doc CCPR/C/59/D/560/1993 (3 April 1997) ('*A v Australia*').
118    *VCLT* (n 3) arts 34–36.
119    Ibid art 35.
120    Ibid art 36. Article 35(2) of the *UN Charter* is an example.
121    *VCLT* (n 3) art 38; see Section 3.2. For more detail and discussion on possible exceptions, such as 'objective regimes', see David Bederman, 'Third Party Rights and Obligations in Treaties' in Duncan Hollis (ed), *The Oxford Guide to Treaties* (Oxford University Press, 2012) 328 (not included in 2nd edition).
122    *VCLT* (n 3) art 28.
123    Ibid art 29.
124    See Shaw (n 115) 809.
125    Article 33 was recently applied in *Comptroller-General of Customs v Pharm-A-Care Laboratories Pty Ltd* (2020) 270 CLR 494, where the Australian High Court read words into the authentic English text of a treaty in order to give it the same meaning as the authentic French text: at [36], [37].
126    See, eg, *Application of the International Convention on the Elimination of All Forms of Racial Discrimination (Qatar v United Arab Emirates) (Preliminary Objections)* [2021] ICJ Rep 71,

In drafting what became arts 31 and 32, the ILC considered the principal approaches to interpretation asserted by jurists: that primacy should be given, variously, to the actual words (textual approach), the intention of the parties (subjective approach), or the object and purpose of the treaty (teleological approach). The ILC concluded that all were relevant, and they are encompassed by art 31.[127] As the ICJ has noted, '[i]nterpretation must be based above all upon the text of the treaty', but 'the Court's interpretation must take account of all [the art 31(1)] elements considered as a whole'.[128]

## 3.10.1    General rule of interpretation (art 31)

The focus of art 31 is on the 'ordinary meaning' of a treaty, but the context and the object and purpose of a treaty are also important.[129] The term 'context' includes the text of the treaty, the preamble and annexes, and any agreements or other instruments emanating from the parties in connection with the conclusion of the treaty.[130] In the *Territorial Dispute* case, the ICJ relied on the preamble, the object and purpose of the treaty, and other agreements between the parties, to confirm the interpretation of the ordinary meaning of the treaty under consideration.[131]

The preamble is not part of the operational or enforceable part of a treaty but can inform its interpretation.[132] The *Whaling in the Antarctic* case[133] concerned the meaning of art VIII(1) of the *International Convention for the Regulation of Whaling*.[134] The article provides that all state parties may grant their nationals a special permit for whaling for purposes of scientific research. Australia argued that it should be interpreted as favouring the conservation of whales, while Japan argued that it should be interpreted in favour of freedom of whaling enjoyed by states under customary international law.[135] The ICJ relied on the preamble to establish the purpose of the Convention, which was that of 'ensuring the conservation of all species of whales while allowing for their sustainable exploitation'.[136] Thus the Court rejected both parties' approaches to interpretation.

Article 31(3), concerning the relevance of the parties' subsequent agreements and practice, can support a dynamic interpretation of a treaty. In *Dispute regarding Navigational and Related Rights*,[137] the ICJ had to decide the navigational rights of Costa Rica in relation to the San Juan River, which separates that state from Nicaragua. An 1858 treaty granted free navigational rights to Costa Rica provided this was done *con objetos de comercio* (for the

95–6 [75]–[76] ('*Qatar v United Arab Emirates*'), and the cases cited there. For art 33 see, eg, *LaGrand* (n 20) 502 [101].

127    'Draft Articles on the Law of Treaties, with Commentaries' (n 10) 219 (Draft Articles 27 and 28 Commentary [8]).

128    *Qatar v United Arab Emirates* (n 126) 96 [78], 98 [81].

129    See, eg, *Territorial Dispute (Libyan Arab Jamahiriya v Chad) (Judgment)* [1994] ICJ Rep 6, 22–7 [43]–[55].

130    *VCLT* (n 3) art 31(2).

131    *Territorial Dispute* (n 129) 25–6 [52]–[53].

132    *Qatar v United Arab Emirates* (n 126) 98 [84].

133    *Whaling in the Antarctic (Australia v Japan) (Judgment)* [2014] ICJ Rep 226.

134    *International Convention for the Regulation of Whaling*, opened for signature 2 December 1946, 161 UNTS 72 (entered into force 10 November 1948) ('*Whaling Convention*').

135    *Whaling in the Antarctic* (n 133) 251–2 [57].

136    Ibid 251 [56].

137    *Dispute regarding Navigational and Related Rights (Costa Rica v Nicaragua) (Judgment)* [2009] ICJ Rep 213, 237 [47].

purposes of commerce).[138] Nicaragua argued that the term *comercio* included only the purchase and sale of merchandise or physical goods, but not services such as passenger transport, because in 1858 'commerce' did not include services. To respect the intent of the drafters, the treaty should be interpreted according to the meaning of the terms at the time of its conclusion.[139] Applying customary international law as reflected in art 31(3) of the *VCLT*, the Court agreed that the common intention of the parties was important,[140] but when the meaning of a term changes over time, the meaning at the time of application cannot be ignored.[141] Thus,

> where the parties have used generic terms in a treaty, the parties necessarily having been aware that the meaning of the terms was likely to evolve over time, and where the treaty has been entered into for a very long period or is 'of continuing duration', the parties must be presumed, as a general rule, to have intended those terms to have an evolving meaning.[142]

Consequently, as the meaning of the term 'commerce' had changed since 1858, the present meaning applied: *comercio* included the commercial transport of persons (including tourists) as well as goods.[143] A dynamic interpretation of treaties is often used in a human rights context, with the relevant treaties being called 'living instruments'.[144]

Article 31(3)(c) allows a treaty to be interpreted in the context of *other* obligations that states parties may have under international law. This article was controversially applied (as customary international law) in the *Oil Platforms* case,[145] in which Iran accused the United States of breaching the 1955 *Treaty of Amity, Economic Relations, and Consular Rights* by using force. The United States argued that its actions were justified under art XX of the treaty, which permitted 'measures … necessary to protect its essential security interests'. Rather than confining itself to interpreting the words of art XX, the Court relied on art 31(3)(c) of the *VCLT* to view the United States' actions through the lens of the law on the use of force under the *UN Charter* and customary international law.[146]

The Court was criticised, in two separate opinions, for not paying sufficient attention to the economic and commercial context of the treaty[147] and for using the *VCLT* interpretation rules to 'improperly transform the case into a dispute relating to the use of force under international law rather than one calling for the interpretation and application of a bilateral treaty with regard to which it alone had jurisdiction'.[148]

## 3.10.2   Supplementary means of interpretation (art 32)

Supplementary means of interpretation, such as preparatory works of a treaty (*travaux préparatoires*) and the circumstances of its conclusion, can be relied on to confirm the meaning

138    Ibid 240 [56].
139    Ibid 240–1 [57]–[58].
140    Ibid 242 [63].
141    Ibid 242 [64].
142    Ibid 243 [66].
143    Ibid 244 [70]–[71].
144    *Banković v Belgium (Admissibility)* [2001] ECHR 890, [64].
145    *Oil Platforms* (n 15).
146    Ibid 182–3 [41]–[42].
147    See, eg, ibid 237 [46], 238 [49] (Judge Higgins).
148    Ibid 281 [28], 283 [32] (Judge Buergenthal).

which results from applying the primary rules of interpretation, or to determine the meaning of a treaty when the application of the primary rules leaves the meaning ambiguous, obscure, manifestly absurd or unreasonable.[149] Preparatory works include the records of negotiation, successive drafts of the treaty, conference records, and statements made by parties.[150] However, records of conferences are not always complete because negotiations also take place informally, without agreed records being kept.[151] Also, even extensive records may simply reveal competing views rather than a definitive interpretation. Anthony Aust cautions that '[t]ravaux must therefore always be approached with care. Their investigation is time-consuming, their usefulness often being marginal and very seldom decisive'.[152]

### 3.10.3  Role of resolutions of international organisations

Article 31(3) of the *VCLT* requires any subsequent agreement or subsequent practice between the parties to be taken into account when interpreting a treaty. In *Whaling in the Antarctic*, the ICJ confirmed that resolutions of international organisations can constitute such agreement or practice.[153] Australia argued that certain resolutions of the International Whaling Commission ('IWC') supported an interpretation of the *Whaling Convention* that precluded the use of lethal methods of scientific research.[154] The ICJ accepted that IWC resolutions, 'when they are adopted by consensus or by a unanimous vote ... may be relevant for the interpretation of the Convention or its Schedule'.[155] However, the resolutions relied on by Australia were either not adopted by consensus (and therefore did not reflect the parties' agreement) or did not support Australia's interpretation.[156]

The UN human rights treaty bodies have given comprehensive interpretations of the treaties they monitor through a wide range of views, general comments, and concluding observations. Such interpretations are not binding, but some are authoritative.[157]

# 3.11   Invalidity, termination, withdrawal from and suspension of a treaty

This section considers when and how a state may cease to be bound by a treaty. The starting point is art 26 of the *VCLT* and the principle of *pacta sunt servanda* – treaties are binding and

---

149    See, eg, Fitzmaurice (n 2) 156.
150    Aust (n 15) 218. For an example of preparatory works, see Office of the UN High Commissioner for Human Rights, *Legislative History of the Convention on the Rights of the Child* (2007).
151    Aust (n 15) 218.
152    Ibid 219.
153    See also 'Draft Conclusions on Subsequent Agreements and Subsequent Practice in Relation to the Interpretation of Treaties, with Commentaries' [2018] II(2) *Yearbook of the International Law Commission* 1, 92–3 (Draft Conclusion 11 Commentary [38]) <https://legal.un.org/ilc/texts/instruments/english/commentaries/1_11_2018.pdf>.
154    *Whaling in the Antarctic* (n 133) 256 [78]–[79], 257 [83].
155    Ibid 248 [46].
156    Ibid 257 [83].
157    For discussion, see Rosanne Van Alebeek and André Nollkaemper, 'The Legal Status of Decisions by Human Rights Treaty Bodies in National Law' in Hellen Keller and Gert Ulfstein (eds), *UN Human Rights Treaty Bodies: Law and Legitimacy* (Cambridge University Press, 2012) 356, 396.

must be performed in good faith. One consequence of this fundamental principle is that it is, in general, very difficult for a state to avoid or terminate its treaty obligations.

Article 42 of the *VCLT* stipulates that a treaty can only be invalidated, terminated, suspended or withdrawn from in accordance with the *VCLT*. As always, most *VCLT* rules operate only if the specific treaty is silent on the issue. Articles 46–53 of the *VCLT* deal with invalidity, while arts 54–63 deal with termination and suspension.

## 3.11.1   Invalidity

A treaty is void if its conclusion was procured by the threat or use of force,[158] if it violates a rule of *jus cogens*,[159] or if it is 'invalid'.[160]

If a state only enters into a treaty because it is under a threat of force, the whole treaty is void. This would include a peace treaty imposed on a victim state, but does not apply to one imposed on an aggressor state.[161] Articles 53 and 64 render void any provision which conflicts with a *jus cogens* norm, such as an agreement to invade a third state or to commit piracy.

There are several grounds listed in the *VCLT* on which a treaty may be declared invalid.[162] The invalidity of a treaty flows from the invalidity of a state's consent to be bound, which can be based on any of the following grounds:

- internal law (art 46);
- error (art 48);
- fraud (art 49);
- corruption (art 50); or
- coercion of a state representative (art 51).

The common element in these situations, particularly evident in arts 48–51, is that the state has not truly consented to the treaty.

Articles 46–50 are sometimes said to concern *relative invalidity*: a state must invoke the ground in order to invalidate its consent to be bound.[163] The state must also formally notify the other parties of this,[164] and give at least three months' notice of its intended action.[165] If another party objects, the matter must go to dispute resolution.[166] By contrast, arts 51–53 concern *absolute invalidity*: if the ground is established the treaty is automatically vitiated.

### 3.11.1.1   Internal law

A state's consent to be bound can be invalidated if the consent manifestly violated a municipal law relating to the state's competence to enter into treaties.[167] The law in question must be of

---

158   *VCLT* (n 3) art 52.
159   Ibid arts 53, 64.
160   Ibid art 69.
161   Ibid art 75.
162   Ibid arts 42, 46–51.
163   Compare ibid arts 46–50 and art 51; Fitzmaurice (n 2) 148.
164   *VCLT* (n 3) art 67.
165   Ibid art 65.
166   Ibid arts 65–66.
167   Ibid art 46.

fundamental importance, and 'objectively evident' to other states.[168] In *Land and Maritime Boundary between Cameroon and Nigeria*,[169] Nigeria claimed that its consent to be bound by a boundary treaty with Cameroon was invalid because, although the treaty had been signed by the Nigerian head of state, the signature had not been ratified by the Supreme Military Council as required by the Nigerian Constitution. The ICJ held that this internal law was not 'manifest' because it had not been properly publicised, especially since heads of state are recognised in art 7 of the *VCLT* as representing their states for the purpose of concluding treaties. Further, 'there is no general legal obligation for States to keep themselves informed of legislative and constitutional developments in other States which are or may become important for the international relations of those States'.[170]

### 3.11.1.2   Error

A state's consent to be bound can be invalidated where it was based on an error which:

- relates to a fact or situation which was assumed by that state to exist at the time the treaty was concluded; and
- formed an essential basis of its consent to be bound by the treaty.[171]

A state cannot plead error where it was on notice of a possible error, or contributed to it. The classic case on error is *Temple of Preah Vihear*,[172] on which this part of art 48 is based.[173] Cambodia and Thailand both claimed sovereignty over the Temple of Preah Vihear. Thailand argued that a 1907 boundary map, clearly placing the temple in Cambodia, was incorrect because the boundary did not follow the watershed line agreed in a 1904 treaty. The ICJ found that Thailand had received the map and had said nothing to suggest it was inaccurate: the Thai authorities had 'accepted it without any independent investigation, and cannot now therefore plead any error vitiating the reality of their consent'.[174]

### 3.11.1.3   Fraud or corruption

A state's consent to be bound may be invalidated if it has been induced to enter into a treaty by the fraudulent conduct of another negotiating state,[175] or if its consent was procured through the corruption of its representative by another negotiating state.[176] There seem to be no recorded cases of either fraud or corruption in this context to date.[177]

### 3.11.1.4   Coercion

Articles 51 and 52 deal with different forms of coercion. Under art 51, consent procured by the coercion of a state's representative will be 'without any legal effect', rendering the

---

168    Ibid art 46(2).
169    *Land and Maritime Boundary between Cameroon and Nigeria* (n 72).
170    Ibid 430.
171    *VCLT* (n 3) art 48.
172    *Temple of Preah Vihear (Cambodia v Thailand) (Merits)* [1962] ICJ Rep 6.
173    'Draft Articles on the Law of Treaties, with Commentaries' (n 10) 244 (Draft Article 46 Commentary [8]).
174    *Temple of Preah Vihear* (n 172) 26–7.
175    *VCLT* (n 3) art 49.
176    Ibid art 50.
177    See, eg, Aust (n 15) 276–7.

consent – and therefore the treaty – automatically void.[178] Coercion might be of any kind, from a physical threat to blackmail.[179] Under art 52, a treaty procured by the threat or use of force against the state will also be void.

### 3.11.1.5   Breach of good faith: a further ground of invalidity?

Although not yet tested, it is possible (but unlikely) that a breach of good faith by one negotiating party might render the subsequent treaty invalid or void. Timor-Leste argued this in the arbitral proceedings it brought against Australia in 2013,[180] seeking to set aside a 2006 treaty on maritime arrangements.[181] It argued that the treaty was procured in bad faith because Australia had planted listening devices in the office used by the Timor-Leste negotiating team, allowing Australia to hear their private discussions. Timor-Leste likened this to fraud or corruption under the *VCLT*.[182] The matter was settled before hearing and so the issue was not determined; some commentators at the time predicted difficulty in proving that an additional ground of invalidity exists, outside the *VCLT*.[183] But it is at least arguable that if Australia had been aware of Timor-Leste's negotiating position, and was able to take advantage of that, then Timor-Leste's consent – the core of all the *VCLT* grounds of invalidity – was tainted.

## 3.11.2   Termination, withdrawal and suspension

It is important when reading arts 54–63 of the *VCLT* to note whether each article permits:

- termination – the treaty ceases to exist;
- denunciation or withdrawal (these terms are usually used interchangeably) – one party can denounce or withdraw from a treaty which, if multilateral, remains in existence for the other parties; or
- suspension – the treaty remains on foot, but its performance is suspended for a time.

---

178    'Draft Articles on the Law of Treaties, with Commentaries' (n 10) 246 (Draft Article 48 Commentary [3]).
179    Ibid 246 (Draft Article 48 Commentary [2]).
180    *Arbitration under the Timor Sea Treaty (Timor-Leste v Australia)* (Permanent Court of Arbitration, Case No 2013-16) ('*TST Arbitration*').
181    *Treaty between Australia and the Democratic Republic of Timor-Leste on Certain Maritime Arrangements in the Timor Sea*, signed 12 January 2006, 2438 UNTS 359 (entered into force 23 February 2007).
182    *TST Arbitration* (n 180) Statement of Claim of Timor-Leste, 18 February 2014, reproduced in part in 'Memorial of Timor-Leste' (28 April 2014) 17–19 [3.4] in *Questions Relating to the Seizure and Detention of Certain Documents and Data (Timor-Leste v Australia)* [2015] ICJ Rep 572 <www.icj-cij.org/en/case/156/written-proceedings>.
183    See, eg, Kate Mitchell and Dapo Akande, 'Espionage and Good Faith in Treaty Negotiations: *East Timor v Australia*', *EJIL:Talk!* (Blog Post, 20 January 2014) <www.ejiltalk.org/espionage-fraud-good-faith-in-treaty-negotiations-east-timor-v-australia-in-the-permanent-court-of-arbitration>. Cf Donald Anton, 'The Timor Sea Treaty Arbitration: Timor-Leste Challenges Australian Espionage and Seizure of Documents' (2014) 18(6) *ASIL Insights* <www.asil.org/insights/volume/18/issue/6/timor-sea-treaty-arbitration-timor-leste-challenges-australian-espionage>.

### 3.11.2.1   Termination or suspension by express or implied agreement

Subject, as always, to the terms of the particular treaty, a treaty will terminate in accordance with its provisions,[184] or by the consent of all parties,[185] or where it is replaced by a later treaty between the same parties and on the same subject matter and the later treaty is intended to supersede, or is incompatible with, the earlier.[186]

A treaty may be suspended by all the parties in regard either to all the parties or to a particular party – if the treaty so provides[187] or if all parties agree.[188] Two or more parties to a multilateral treaty can agree to suspend the operation of a treaty as between themselves, if:

- it is expressly permitted by the treaty;[189] or
- it is not prohibited by the treaty, provided suspension will not affect the rights and obligations of the other parties under the treaty, and suspension is not incompatible with the object and purpose of the treaty.[190]

### 3.11.2.2   Denunciation or withdrawal by express or implied agreement

An individual party may denounce or withdraw from[191] a treaty if the treaty permits it,[192] all the parties consent,[193] the parties intended the possibility of denunciation or withdrawal,[194] or such a right can be inferred from the nature of the treaty.[195]

Unless otherwise specified, a party denouncing or withdrawing from a treaty under art 56 must give 12 months' notice.[196] Importantly, the denunciation or withdrawal of an individual party does not terminate a multilateral treaty, which remains on foot between all the other parties.

As the headings suggest, these bases for termination, suspension or withdrawal stem from the treaty itself, or rather the will of the parties. Articles 60–62, on the other hand (discussed in Sections 3.11.2.3 to 3.11.2.5), address external factors that may result in termination, suspension or withdrawal. The ICJ affirmed the customary international law status of these articles in *Gabčíkovo-Nagymaros Project* (discussed in Section 3.11.2.5).

### 3.11.2.3   Material breach

If a state violates a treaty obligation, it commits an internationally wrongful act under the rules of state responsibility (see Chapter 7). Under customary law, codified in the ILC's articles on

184    *VCLT* (n 3) art 54(a).
185    Ibid art 54(b).
186    Ibid art 59.
187    Ibid art 57(a).
188    Ibid art 57(b).
189    Ibid art 58(a).
190    Ibid art 58(b).
191    'Denunciation' and 'withdrawal' are used interchangeably: see, eg, Laurence Helfer, 'Terminating Treaties' in Duncan Hollis (ed), *The Oxford Guide to Treaties* (Oxford University Press, 2nd ed, 2020) 624, 635; *UN Final Clauses Handbook* (n 27) 109.
192    *VCLT* (n 3) art 54(a).
193    Ibid art 54(b).
194    Ibid art 56(1)(a).
195    Ibid art 56(1)(b).
196    Ibid art 56(2).

state responsibility,[197] certain legal consequences flow from that wrongfulness, such as the right of an injured state to impose countermeasures, and the obligation of the wrongdoing state to cease the wrongful act and make reparation (see Chapter 7).

In addition to these rules, the *VCLT* sets out particular consequences under the law of treaties, if the breach of the treaty obligation is a 'material' breach. Article 60 defines a material breach as a repudiation of the treaty that is not permitted under the *VCLT*, or a violation of a provision which is essential to the accomplishment of the object and purpose of the treaty.

A material breach of a bilateral treaty committed by one party entitles the other party to terminate or suspend the treaty.[198] If there is a material breach of a multilateral treaty, the other parties, acting unanimously, may terminate or suspend the treaty,[199] either between all the parties[200] or only between the defaulting state and the other parties.[201] In the latter instance, the treaty remains in place between the other parties.

Certain parties may be specially affected by a breach, for example where breach of a treaty on the prevention of oil pollution results in damage to the beaches and marine life of that party. A 'specially affected' party can suspend – not terminate – the operation of all or part of the treaty as between that state and the defaulting state.[202]

Any party other than the defaulting party can suspend – not terminate – the treaty if a material breach 'radically changes the position of every party with respect to the further performance of its obligations under the treaty'.[203] A material breach of a disarmament treaty, for example, would usually mean that the defaulting state was either re-arming or failing to dispose of existing weapons. As the ILC put it, in such a case 'a breach by one party tends to undermine the whole regime of the treaty as between all the parties';[204] each of the other parties might need to suspend its obligations under the treaty, because otherwise 'it may be unable to protect itself against the threat resulting from the arming of the defaulting State'.[205]

Article 60(5) provides an exception for 'provisions protecting the human person', especially those prohibiting reprisals, contained in treaties of a humanitarian nature (such as those in the field of international humanitarian law). These provisions cannot be suspended or terminated.

### 3.11.2.4   Impossibility

Article 61 of the *VCLT* permits a state to terminate or withdraw from a treaty if performance has become impossible because 'an object indispensable for the execution of the treaty' has permanently disappeared or been destroyed. This will be rare in practice; the ILC suggests as examples 'the submergence of an island, the drying up of a river or the destruction of a dam or hydro-electric installation' where these are essential to the performance of the treaty.[206]

---

197    *Responsibility of States for Internationally Wrongful Acts*, GA Res 56/83, UN Doc A/RES/56/83 (28 January 2002, adopted 12 December 2001) annex (*'Responsibility of States for Internationally Unlawful Acts'*).
198    *VCLT* (n 3) art 60(1).
199    Ibid art 60(2)(a).
200    Ibid art 60(2)(a)(ii).
201    Ibid art 60(2)(a)(i).
202    Ibid art 60(2)(b).
203    Ibid art 60(2)(c).
204    'Draft Articles on the Law of Treaties, with Commentaries' (n 10) 255 (Draft Article 57 Commentary [8]).
205    Ibid.
206    Ibid 256 (Draft Article 58 Commentary [2]).

Impossibility cannot be relied on by a party if it is the result of a breach by that party – either of the particular treaty, or of any other international obligation owed by it to any of the other parties to the treaty.[207]

## 3.11.2.5   Fundamental change of circumstances

Article 62 permits a state to terminate or withdraw from (or suspend) a treaty if there has been 'a fundamental change of circumstances' since the conclusion of the treaty. This is sometimes referred to as the principle of *rebus sic stantibus*, a principle known to many legal systems.

Article 62 requires several conditions to be satisfied. First, the circumstances as they existed at the time the treaty was concluded must have been an essential basis of the parties' consent.[208] Second, the change must be one that was not foreseen by the parties.[209] Third, the change must be one that radically transforms the extent of obligations still to be performed under the treaty.[210] In other words, the condition will not be satisfied by a change of circumstances that has little or no effect on the parties' continuing obligations under the treaty. This was illustrated in the *Fisheries Jurisdiction* case[211] between the United Kingdom and Iceland. When a fisheries dispute arose, Iceland claimed that a 1961 agreement with the United Kingdom to refer disputes to the ICJ had been validly terminated because of a fundamental change of circumstances in relation to fishing techniques, and that the Court therefore had no jurisdiction. The Court affirmed the principle:

> International law admits that a fundamental change in the circumstances which deter-
> mined the parties to accept a treaty, if it has resulted in a radical transformation of the
> extent of the obligations imposed by it, may, under certain conditions, afford the party
> affected a ground for invoking the termination or suspension of the treaty. This principle,
> and the conditions and exceptions to which it is subject, have been embodied in Article 62
> of the [*VCLT*], which may in many respects be considered as a codification of existing
> customary law on the subject of the termination of a treaty relationship on account of
> change of circumstances.[212]

However, the Court noted that a change in fishing techniques was irrelevant to the obligation to submit disputes to the Court, which remained the same.[213]

A recent example of a fundamental change of circumstances being used as a ground for suspension is the decision by Australia (and other states) to suspend its extradition treaty with Hong Kong[214] based on a fundamental change of circumstances, when China imposed its

---

207   *VCLT* (n 3) art 61(2).
208   *VCLT* (n 3) art 62(1)(a).
209   Ibid art 62(1); *Gabčíkovo-Nagymaros Project* (n 17) 64 [104].
210   *VCLT* (n 3) art 62(1)(b).
211   *Fisheries Jurisdiction (United Kingdom v Iceland) (Jurisdiction)* [1973] ICJ Rep 3.
212   Ibid 18.
213   Ibid 20.
214   *Agreement for the Surrender of Accused and Convicted Persons between the Government of Australia
      and the Government of Hong Kong*, signed 15 November 1993, [1997] ATS 11 (entered into force 29 June
      1997); *Protocol between the Government of Australia and the Government of the Hong Kong Special
      Administrative Region of the People's Republic of China Amending the Agreement for the Surrender of
      Accused and Convicted Persons of 15 November 1993*, signed 19 March 2007, [2008] ATS 6 (entered into
      force 7 May 2008) ('*Hong Kong Extradition Protocol*').

highly restrictive National Security Law on Hong Kong in 2020.[215] No details of the fundamental change were made public, but it can be inferred that the criminal justice system in place in Hong Kong in 1993 had been an essential basis of Australia's consent to be bound. That system had dramatically changed under the new Law, which created new and vaguely defined offences with severe penalties, and provided for suspects to be tried in mainland China; as the Canadian government put it, the new Law was seen as violating the 'one country, two systems' framework promised by China in 1997.[216]

The fourth condition in art 62 (similar to art 61) is that a fundamental change of circumstances cannot be relied on by a party if it is the result of a breach by that party of the particular treaty or of any other international obligation owed to any other party to the treaty.[217]

Finally, the plea of a fundamental change of circumstances cannot be invoked in relation to a treaty establishing a boundary.[218]

Articles 60–62, as reflected in customary international law, were considered by the ICJ in *Gabčíkovo-Nagymaros Project*.[219] In 1977, Hungary and Czechoslovakia (now Slovakia) entered into a treaty to build a system of locks along a 200-kilometre section of the River Danube, aimed at producing hydroelectricity, improving navigation and mitigating flooding. Over the next 10 years, against a background of profound political and economic changes in socialist European countries, the cost and environmental effects of the project attracted intense criticism in Hungary, leading it to suspend work on the project in 1989.[220] By 1991 both states recognised that the project would be an ecological disaster, but Czechoslovakia had already completed much of the work and wanted to proceed in a modified way to mitigate both its losses and the damage to the environment.[221] It therefore built 'Variant C', a canal diverting the Danube over its territory, despite Hungary's protests. In May 1992, Hungary purported to terminate the treaty, and in October 1992, Czechoslovakia put Variant C into operation. In 1993 the states agreed to submit their differences to the ICJ.

The *VCLT* did not apply to the 1977 treaty because Hungary and Czechoslovakia only became parties to the *VCLT* in 1987, but the Court applied the relevant provisions of the *VCLT* as customary international law. Hungary submitted that its termination of the treaty was justified on three grounds: Czechoslovakia's material breach (art 60), impossibility of performance (art 61), and a fundamental change of circumstances (art 62). The Court rejected each of these pleas.

215    Joint Statement of the Prime Minister, Minister for Foreign Affairs, and Attorney-General, 'Extradition Treaty with Hong Kong' (9 July 2020) <www.foreignminister.gov.au/minister/marise-payne/media-release/extradition-treaty-hong-kong>. The suspension took effect on 9 October 2020: Department of Foreign Affairs and Trade, Australian Treaties Database, '*Hong Kong Extradition Protocol*' (n 214) <https://info.dfat.gov.au/Info/Treaties/Treaties.nsf/AllDocIDs/6317F90BCFF0F235CA2572A500214DC0>.
216    Minister of Foreign Affairs, 'Canada Takes Action Following Passage of National Security Legislation for Hong Kong', *CBC News* (online, 3 July 2020) <https://www.cbc.ca/news/politics/canada-suspending-extradition-treaty-hong-kong-over-security-law-1.5636479>.
217    *VCLT* (n 3) art 62(2)(b).
218    Ibid art 62(3).
219    *Gabčíkovo-Nagymaros Project* (n 17).
220    *Gabčíkovo-Nagymaros Project* (n 17) 31–2 [33].
221    Ibid 51–2 [68], 52–3 [72].

First, it found that Czechoslovakia had not breached the treaty at the time Hungary purported to terminate it, because building Variant C was a lawful countermeasure.[222] The Court found that the subsequent implementation of Variant C was a breach, but it occurred after Hungary's purported termination.[223] As to impossibility, Hungary submitted that the 'object' that had disappeared, within the meaning of art 61 of the *VCLT*, was the project itself – an economic joint investment.[224] But the Court held that even if 'object' in art 61 could include a legal regime rather than a physical object, that legal regime had not ceased to exist.[225] Further, if joint work on the project were no longer possible, it was because of Hungary's conduct in failing to carry out its works under the treaty.[226]

As to a fundamental change of circumstances, Hungary argued unsuccessfully that there had been profound political and economic changes, and changes in environmental knowledge and law, since the conclusion of the treaty.[227] The Court found that the political and economic situation in 1977 was not an essential basis of the parties' consent to be bound, the environmental changes were not unforeseen, and the obligations still to be performed were not radically different.[228]

## 3.11.3   Consequences of invalidity, termination and suspension

If a treaty is invalid or contrary to a *jus cogens* norm, it is void – that is, of no legal effect – but prior acts done in good faith are generally unaffected.[229] That usually applies to the whole treaty, but art 44 allows for partial invalidity if the affected clauses are severable, they were not an essential basis of the consent of the other party or parties to be bound, and continued performance of the remainder of the treaty would not be unjust. If a state's consent to be bound to a multilateral treaty is found to have been invalid, the treaty is invalid only as between that state and the other parties; the treaty remains on foot for all other parties.[230] Again, prior acts done in good faith are generally unaffected.[231]

If the treaty is terminated, the parties are released from further obligations, but rights, obligations and legal situations created under the treaty are unaffected.[232] If the treaty is suspended, the parties must not do anything to obstruct the resumption of operation of the treaty.[233]

222     Ibid 54 [79], 57 [88].
223     Ibid 57 [88], 66 [108].
224     Ibid 63–4 [103].
225     Ibid.
226     Ibid.
227     Ibid 64–5 [104].
228     Ibid.
229     *VCLT* (n 3) arts 69(1), 71.
230     Ibid art 69(4).
231     Ibid art 69(2).
232     Ibid art 70.
233     Ibid art 72.

# DISCUSSION QUESTIONS

(1)  Should entities whose statehood is not universally recognised or corporations be allowed to become parties to international treaties?

(2)  Are the rules of treaty interpretation in arts 31 and 32 of the *Vienna Convention on the Law of Treaties* ('*VCLT*') adequate for the interpretation of human rights treaties?

(3)  Some states, such as New Zealand, have entered into 'treaties' with their Indigenous people. Does the *VCLT* apply to such agreements? If not, should the *VCLT* apply to them, and what would be the legal implications?

(4)  Should there be any limits on a state's ability to make reservations to a treaty?

(5)  Should a state party be able to terminate a bilateral treaty for any breach, rather than only a material breach?

# 4

# INTERNATIONAL LAW AND AUSTRALIAN LAW

Tim Stephens and
Meda Couzens

# 4.1   Introduction

The Australian legal system is not an island, and Australian law[1] has felt the influence of law and legal ideas from other jurisdictions, particularly other common law countries. Australian law has also been shaped by public international law both directly and indirectly and this interaction has become increasingly important as the scope and content of international law have grown. The relationship between Australian law and international law is mediated by Australia's constitutional framework in which the separation of powers between the executive, legislature and the courts holds central place. Unlike the constitutions in many other legal systems,[2] the *Australian Constitution* does not address the relationship between international and domestic law, and most of the relevant legal principles are to be found in the common law. This chapter examines how each arm of government in Australia has engaged with international law, identifying areas where the relationship is well settled (as it is in relation to treaties) and areas where there remains some uncertainty (as in relation to customary international law).

# 4.2   International law and domestic law: general concepts, theories and comparisons

The relationship between municipal law and international law raises many interesting conceptual and practical questions. Are both bodies of law components of one and the same legal system, or are they distinct? If distinct, and if there is conflict, which rule prevails – the municipal or the international? How can municipal law influence international law? How can international law influence municipal law? What steps, if any, must be taken to enable rules of international law to operate in domestic law?

In order to address these and other questions, legal theorists have suggested several possible frameworks for understanding the relationship between municipal and international law.[3] The two dominant theories are *monism* and *dualism*. Monism is the notion that international law and municipal law form part of a singular legal system and are inseparable. The Austrian legal philosopher Hans Kelsen was one of the best-known exponents of monism, and argued that all law, including municipal law, could be derived from a fundamental rule of international law (which he called the *Grundnorm*).[4] While Kelsen was a legal positivist, the

---

1   'Australian law' refers to the legal system introduced following British colonisation in 1788 which largely displaced a sophisticated body of law that was developed over tens of thousands of years by Australia's Indigenous peoples: Australian Law Reform Commission, *Recognition of Aboriginal Customary Laws* (Report No 31, 1986) 28–9 [37]–[38].

2   See, eg, *La Constitution du 4 octobre 1958* [French Constitution of 4 October 1958] art 55; *United States Constitution* art VI; *Constitution of the Republic of South Africa Act 1996* (South Africa) s 232 ('*Constitution of South Africa*').

3   See Ivan Shearer, 'The Relationship between International Law and Domestic Law' in Brian Opeskin and Donald Rothwell (eds), *International Law and Australian Federalism* (Melbourne University Press, 1997) 34.

4   Hans Kelsen, *The Problem of Sovereignty and the Theory of International Law* (1920), tr Paul Silverman (Oxford University Press, 2021).

monist approach has tended to be linked with natural law approaches which see all law as one and deduced from human reason or divine will.[5]

An alternative view of the relationship between municipal law and international law is the concept of dualism which holds that the two legal orders are independent. According to the dualist conception, of which German jurist Heinrich Triepel was a central exponent,[6] the two bodies of law differ in their origins: the will of the people or the state is the basis of domestic law, while for international law, it is state consent that is critical. They also differ in the subjects they regulate: domestic law is concerned primarily with individuals, while international law is concerned primarily with states. Dualist theories have been strongly influenced by positivist approaches which hold that legal rules are derived from real-world practice, rather than being deduced at an abstract level.

Monism is associated with *incorporation* – the idea that international law is automatically received or made a part of domestic law without the Parliament passing a law that 'absorbs' the international standards.[7] The effect is that international law then applies like other domestic laws.[8] On the other hand, dualism is associated with the concept of *transformation* – the idea that international law has no effect on domestic law unless and until it is implemented in some way, for example through legislation or by a court judgment.

Monism and dualism, and the connected ideas of incorporation and transformation, invite us to think about how domestic and international legal systems can, do and should relate. However, these two notions in their pure forms are caricatures, and neither provides a satisfactory account of what happens in practice in Australia, or any other jurisdiction.[9] In reality, it is possible to discern various monist and dualist elements in the interface between international law and domestic law in Australia and other countries. As Eileen Denza explains:

> There are almost as many ways of giving effect to international law as there are national legal systems. To classify a State as 'monist' or 'dualist' does not greatly assist in describing its constitutional approach to international obligations, in determining how its government and parliament will proceed in order to adopt or implement a new treaty, or in predicting how its courts will approach the complex questions which arise in litigation involving international law.[10]

---

5    See, eg, Hersch Lauterpacht, *International Law and Human Rights* (Stevens & Sons, 1950) 70.
6    Heinrich Triepel, *Völkerrecht unde Landesrecht* [International Law and National Law] (Hirschfeld, 1899).
7    Even in states that embrace a monist approach, constitutions typically require that Parliaments pass special ratification statutes that endorse the treaty and bring its content into the domestic law. This parliamentary involvement largely alleviates separation of powers concerns, which are central to arguments against the automatic incorporation of ratified treaties in the domestic law of states taking a dualist approach.
8    The consequences of automatic incorporation can be far-reaching, potentially leading to the direct application of a treaty; however, there are numerous obstacles that prevent the direct application or the direct effect of international treaties in monist systems. In relation to the French legal system, see Emmanuel Decaux, 'Le Régime du Droit International en Droit Interne' [The Regime of International Law in Domestic Law] (2010) 62 *Revue Internationale de Droit Comparé* 467.
9    A good example is that of South Africa. This state is cautiously monist in relation to customary international law (*Constitution of South Africa* (n 2) s 232), and primarily dualist in relation to treaties, although self-executing provisions can nonetheless be applied directly (see s 231(4)).
10   Eileen Denza, 'The Relationship between International and National Law' in Malcolm Evans (ed), *International Law* (Oxford University Press, 5th ed, 2018) 383, 388.

James Crawford similarly observed that *pluralism* better describes the complexity of practice, 'in which it falls to each system to regulate its own relationship with other legal systems' including the international legal system.[11]

Separation of powers considerations resulting from Australia's constitutional structure have a major influence on the way international law affects Australian law. Under s 61 of the *Australian Constitution*, the executive represents Australia internationally and has sole authority to enter into treaties in exercise of the Crown's prerogative powers. Under s 51, only the Parliament has power to implement treaties in Australian law (that is, to give a treaty or its provisions the force of domestic law). The courts have a less defined function when it comes to international law, but central roles include applying and interpreting the legislation that gives effect to Australia's international legal obligations.

# 4.3   Domestic law in international law

## 4.3.1   Municipal law as a source of international law

In Chapter 2 we saw that domestic law provides evidence of state practice and *opinio juris* and can therefore give rise to norms of customary international law.[12] It can also be evidence of general principles of law.[13] Furthermore, the decisions of domestic courts may be referred to as subsidiary means for the determination of rules of international law.[14]

## 4.3.2   Deficiencies in municipal law no justification for breach of international law

While domestic law may have some influence on international law, it is a fundamental principle of international law that a state may not invoke the absence of or inconsistent provisions in its domestic law as justification for failing to perform its international legal obligations. Hence art 27 of the *Vienna Convention on the Law of Treaties* ('*VCLT*') provides that a party to a treaty 'may not invoke the provisions of its internal law as justification for its failure to perform a treaty'.[15] Similarly, art 3 of the *Articles on Responsibility of States for Internationally Wrongful Acts* provides that '[t]he characterization of an act of a State as internationally wrongful is governed by international law' and that '[s]uch characterization is not affected by the characterization of the same act as lawful by internal law'.[16]

---

11    James Crawford, *Brownlie's Principles of Public International Law* (Oxford University Press, 9th ed, 2019) 102 ('*Brownlie's Principles*').

12    *Statute of the International Court of Justice* art 38(1)(b) ('*ICJ Statute*').

13    Ibid art 38(1)(c).

14    Ibid art 38(1)(d).

15    *Vienna Convention on the Law of Treaties*, opened for signature 23 May 1969, 1155 UNTS 331 (entered into force 27 January 1980 ('*VCLT*').

16    *Responsibility of States for Internationally Wrongful Acts*, GA Res 56/83, UN Doc A/RES/56/83 (28 January 2002, adopted 12 December 2001) annex ('*Responsibility of States for Internationally Wrongful Acts*').

There is longstanding authority for this proposition, stretching back to the US Civil War.[17] In the *Alabama Claims* arbitration,[18] the United States successfully claimed damages from Great Britain for breach of the latter's obligations as a neutral power during the Civil War. Britain had not prevented the construction of Confederate vessels in British ports, in violation of its obligation of neutrality, and these vessels were used during the conflict. The Tribunal rejected the British argument that it had not acted contrary to international law as there was no domestic legislation preventing the construction of Confederate vessels, holding that 'the government or Her Britannic Majesty cannot justify itself for a failure in due diligence on the plea of insufficiency of the legal means of action which it possessed'.[19]

The interaction between domestic and international obligations was also explored in *Sandline International Inc v Papua New Guinea*.[20] The dispute concerned a contract between Sandline, a company that provided military and security services, and the Papua New Guinea ('PNG') government. The contract was to supply personnel, services and equipment to assist the PNG Defence Force in operations against the Bougainville Revolutionary Army. Under the contract, which had been signed by the PNG deputy prime minister, Papua New Guinea paid Sandline USD18 million on signature, with a subsequent payment of USD18 million to be made following the deployment of Sandline personnel. However, after the personnel arrived there was a mutiny in the PNG Defence Force and the Sandline team were arrested and ejected from the country. Sandline claimed the outstanding USD18 million. Papua New Guinea argued that the contract was illegal as it contravened s 200 of the *Constitution of the Independent State of Papua New Guinea* which forbade the raising of military forces without parliamentary approval. The arbitration tribunal, which was applying international law under an international contract, found for Sandline:

> 10.2 In international law, in relation to contracts to which a State is a party and which are to be performed within the territory of that State, the principle and the authorities referred to in paragraph 9.1 above have no application or must at any rate give way to a fundamental qualification. This is that a State cannot rely upon its own internal laws as the basis for a plea that a contract concluded by it is illegal. It is a clearly established principle of international law that acts of a State will be regarded as such even if they are *ultra vires* or unlawful under the internal law of the State. Of course, a State is a juristic person and can only act through its institutions, officials or employees (commonly referred to in international law as organs). But their acts or omissions when they purport to act in their capacity as organs of the State are regarded internationally as those of the State even though they contravene the internal law of the State.
>
> . . .
>
> **11. Application of International Law**
>
> 11.1 Upon the basis of the facts . . . there can be no doubt that in executing the agreement between Sandline and PNG, the Deputy Prime Minister, Mr Haiveta, purported to act on

---

17    See also reliance on *VCLT* art 27 in *Questions Relating to the Obligation to Prosecute or Extradite (Belgium v Senegal) (Judgment)* [2012] ICJ Rep 422, 460 [113].

18    *Alabama Claims (United States v Great Britain) (Award)* (1872) 29 RIAA 125.

19    Ibid 131.

20    *Sandline International Inc v Papua New Guinea* (Award, Sir Edward Somers, Sir Michael Kerr and Sir Daryl Dawson, 9 October 1998) reported in (2000) 117 ILR 552.

behalf of PNG. .... The agreement was not illegal or unlawful under international law or under any established principle of public policy. A political decision having been made by PNG to enter into it, its execution by a person with apparent authority to bind the State gave rise to a valid contract in the eyes of international law.[21]

# 4.4    Categorising the influence of international law on Australian law

International law has several direct and indirect effects on Australian law. The most direct effects are felt when treaties to which Australia is a party are implemented in Australian law by legislation, or when Australian courts draw upon norms of customary international law to develop the Australian common law. There may be less direct, but no less important, effects when Australian courts are called upon to interpret legislation whose application may place Australia in breach of its international legal obligations. International law may also influence official policies, professional guidelines or codes, and the like. In such cases, although international law does not become domestic law, it nonetheless has some domestic impact. Further, the *Human Rights (Parliamentary Scrutiny) Act 2011* (Cth) requires that proposed legislation is assessed against core human rights treaties. Inconsistency with these treaties does not prevent the passing of the statute, but it can generate robust debates and, if political support can be garnered, may lead to changes to the proposed law.

In *Australian Competition and Consumer Commission v PT Garuda Indonesia Ltd (No 9)* ('*Garuda*'),[22] the Federal Court described the multiple ways international law and Australian law interact. The case was part of long-running proceedings brought by the Australian Competition and Consumer Commission against an Indonesian state-owned airline for entering into anti-competitive arrangements with other airlines in respect of commercial air freight services to Australia. This particular judgment in the proceedings concerned the interpretation of a bilateral air services agreement between Australia and Indonesia.[23] In the course of the judgment, Perram J considered the interaction between foreign, domestic and international law in relation to evidence in the proceedings, and offered the following examples of circumstances in which questions of international law may arise before Australian courts:

(a)    situations where a question of domestic common law overlaps with an area of customary international law. The former common law obtaining to [foreign] sovereign immunity ... is an example of this situation. In such cases, prior to the matter being dealt with explicitly by statute, it was natural to think that the common law on the topic ought to align with the customary international law on the same issue. ...

---

21    Ibid 562–3 [10.2]–[11.1].
22    (2013) 212 FCR 406 ('*Garuda*').
23    *Agreement between the Government of the Commonwealth of Australia and the Government of the Republic of Indonesia for Air Services between and beyond Their Respective Territory*, signed 7 March 1969, [1969] ATS 4 (entered into force 7 March 1969).

The original doctrine of terra nullius was an aspect of customary international law upon which came to rest a corresponding common law concept. When the High Court came to consider the scope of that doctrine at common law it inevitably invited a consideration of the customary international law position of the doctrine: see *Mabo v Queensland [No 2]* (1992) 175 CLR 1, 32–41;

(b)    a conceptually similar class of case arises where the common law operates in the same area as a treaty. Here the considerations are largely the same;

(c)    situations where a domestic statute evinces an intention to give effect to a treaty in its own terms: cf *NBGM v Minister for Immigration and Multicultural and Indigenous Affairs* (2006) 231 CLR 52, 71–2 [61];

(d)    situations where a choice arises for a court between an interpretation of a statute which causes Australia to infringe international law and one which does not: every statute is 'to be so interpreted and applied as far as its language admits as not to be inconsistent with the comity of nations or with the established rules of international law': *Jumbunna Coal Mine NL v Victorian Coal Miners' Association* (1908) 6 CLR 309, 363; *Chu Kheng Lim v Minister of State for Immigration, Local Government and Ethnic Affairs* (1992) 176 CLR 1, 38; *Minister for Immigration and Ethnic Affairs v Teoh* (1995) 183 CLR 273, 287 [('*Teoh*')];

(e)    situations (perhaps) where the Commonwealth's ratification of a treaty gives rise, in domestic administrative law, to a legitimate expectation: *Teoh*;

(f)    situations involving the act of State doctrine where it is said that the State in question has acted in breach of international law and thereby taken itself outside the doctrine: see *Kuwait Airways Corporation v Iraqi Airways Co (Nos 4 and 5)* [2002] 2 AC 883, 1081 [27]–[29] [('*Kuwait Airways*')];

(g)    situations (perhaps) where a domestic court declines to give effect to a foreign law because it infringes international law or a *jus cogens* obligation: *Kuwait Airways* 883, 1081 [27]–[29];

(h)    situations in constitutional law where a question arises as to whether a Commonwealth law, in fact, sufficiently implements a treaty obligation under s 51(xxix) of the *Constitution* to be a valid law: *Victoria v Commonwealth* (1996) 187 CLR 416, 487.[24]

This list is not exhaustive, and there are a wide variety of ways in which Australian courts engage with international law, especially where international law is relevant to the exercise of judicial discretion.[25] In relation to the United Kingdom, Shaheed Fatima has similarly observed that around a 'nucleus' of established categories of engagement with international law, there is a 'hazily defined – and ever expanding – penumbra where unincorporated treaties are used freely and creatively' within constitutional limits 'as aids in construing legislation ... providing background and context for legislation and as points of comparison and analogy'.[26]

Furthermore, it is not only binding norms of international law that can have relevance for Australian law. For instance, soft law instruments have been referred to in a number of cases to

---

24    *Garuda* (n 22) 417 [38].

25    Wendy Lacey, 'Judicial Discretion and Human Rights: Expanding the Role of International Law in the Domestic Sphere' (2004) 5(1) *Melbourne Journal of International Law* 108, 123–4.

26    Shaheed Fatima, *Using International Law in Domestic Courts* (Hart Publishing, 2005) 293–340.

support the reasoning of a court. For example, in *Love v Commonwealth*,[27] Bell J and Nettle J in their separate judgments relied on the 2007 *United Nations Declaration on the Rights of Indigenous Peoples* to strengthen their argument that there is a special relationship between Aboriginal Australians and Australia.[28] A majority of the High Court held that Aboriginal Australians have a unique cultural, historical and spiritual connection with the territory of Australia, one that is central to their traditional laws and customs and is recognised by the common law. Because of this connection, an Indigenous Australian cannot be an alien within the meaning of s 51(xix) of the *Constitution*.

## 4.5    Treaties and Australian law

The relationship between treaties and Australian law is relatively straightforward. The Commonwealth executive possesses exclusive power to enter into treaties on any subject matter in exercise of Crown prerogative powers. However, a treaty is not directly incorporated in Australian law simply by entry into the agreement.[29] Treaties have no legal effect on the rights and duties of individuals,[30] because otherwise the executive would effectively have the power of legislation merely by ratifying or acceding to a treaty.[31] In order to be given full domestic effect, treaties must be implemented into Australian law, and it is Parliament which possesses exclusive (but not unlimited) power to do so through legislation.

It also follows that the executive cannot give domestic legal effect to international obligations in the absence of legislation. In *Bradley v Commonwealth*,[32] the Commonwealth made regulations to give effect to UN Security Council resolutions concerning the illegal state of Rhodesia. On the basis of these regulations the Australian government shut down communications to and from the 'Rhodesian Information Centre' operated by Rhodesia in Sydney. While this was consistent with Australia's obligations under the *Charter of the United Nations*, the High Court found that '[s]ince the Charter and the resolutions of the Security Council have not been carried into effect in Australia by appropriate legislation, they cannot be relied upon as a justification for executive acts that would otherwise be unjustified'.[33]

*Bradley v Commonwealth* also made clear that legislation that merely purported to 'approve' a treaty, such as the *Charter of the United Nations Act 1945* (Cth), does not make

---

27    (2020) 270 CLR 152.
28    Ibid 190 [73] (Bell J), 255 [274] (Nettle J).
29    With the exception of peace treaties and maritime boundary agreements which may be given automatic effect: James Crawford and William Edeson, 'International Law and Australian Law' in Kevin Ryan (ed), *International Law in Australia* (Law Book Co, 2nd ed, 1984) 71, 94. In *Re Minister for Immigration and Multicultural Affairs; Ex parte Lam* (2003) 214 CLR 1, McHugh and Gummow JJ stated that 'a peace treaty will, without legislation, change the status of enemy aliens in Australian courts': at 33 [100].
30    A ratified but unincorporated treaty does not create rights or obligations that can be claimed or enforced in Australian courts, as illustrated in *Dietrich v The Queen* (1992) 177 CLR 292. Instead, those interested in invoking unincorporated treaties will need to base their claims on the domestic law (statute or common law) and then find a way to bring the international law into the interpretation or development of the domestic law.
31    *Simsek v MacPhee* (1982) 148 CLR 636, 641–2.
32    (1973) 128 CLR 557.
33    Ibid 583 (Barwick CJ and Gibbs J).

the treaty itself part of Australian law.[34] Another example of legislation which 'approved' a treaty but did not carry it into effect in Australian law was the *Genocide Convention Act 1949* (Cth). It was not until the enactment of amendments to Commonwealth criminal law, following Australia's entry into the *Rome Statute of the International Criminal Court*,[35] that genocide was specifically criminalised under Australian law.[36] The practice of 'approving' treaties has now lapsed.

In *Dietrich v The Queen*,[37] the accused contended that he had a right to publicly funded legal representation, and in support of this argument he cited art 14(3)(d) of the *International Covenant on Civil and Political Rights* ('*ICCPR*'),[38] which provides for such an entitlement. However, while Australia had ratified the *ICCPR* it had not (and has still not) passed legislation implementing the treaty. In their joint judgment, Mason CJ and McHugh J set out the effect of a ratified but not legislated treaty:

> Ratification of the *ICCPR* as an executive act has no direct legal effect upon domestic law; the rights and obligations contained in the *ICCPR* are not incorporated into Australian law unless and until specific legislation is passed implementing the provisions.[39]

## 4.5.1   The treaty-making process

In formal constitutional terms it is purely a matter for the executive to decide whether to enter into a treaty. This is not ideal as it allows limited oversight of treaty making. In the 1990s there were a number of reforms to treaty-making practice in Australia to address this 'democratic deficit'. These reforms, which expanded the role of Parliament in scrutinising treaty action, followed a major report prepared by a Senate committee and titled *Trick or Treaty?*[40] Key elements of these reforms included the requirements that signed treaties, together with an accompanying National Interest Analysis, be tabled in Parliament well in advance of their ratification; that there be scrutiny of treaties by the parliamentary Joint Standing Committee on Treaties ('JSCOT'); and that an online treaties database be established. In adopting these reforms, provision was made to accommodate urgent treaty action in exceptional circumstances.

Since its establishment, JSCOT has issued over 200 reports on hundreds of treaties and other treaty actions (such as treaty amendments).[41] In almost all cases, JSCOT has recommended that the executive proceed with binding treaty action.[42] Following JSCOT's report, and

---

34    Ibid.

35    *Rome Statute of the International Criminal Court*, opened for signature 17 July 1998, 2187 UNTS 3 (entered into force 1 July 2002). It was signed by Australia on 9 December 1998, and ratified on 1 July 2002.

36    See *Criminal Code Act 1995* (Cth) sch 1 s 268.

37    (1992) 177 CLR 292.

38    *International Covenant on Civil and Political Rights*, opened for signature 16 December 1966, 999 UNTS 171 (entered into force 23 March 1976).

39    *Dietrich v The Queen* (1992) 177 CLR 292, 305. While this aspect of the case was rejected, the majority held that the absence of representation rendered the trial unfair, and Dietrich's conviction was quashed.

40    Senate Legal and Constitutional References Committee, Parliament of Australia, *Trick or Treaty? Commonwealth Power to Make and Implement Treaties* (Report, November 1995).

41    See 'Joint Standing Committee on Treaties', *Parliament of Australia* (Web Page) <www.aph.gov.au/Parliamentary_Business/Committees/Joint/Treaties>.

42    Hilary Charlesworth et al, *No Country Is an Island: Australia and International Law* (UNSW Press, 2006) 152.

before a treaty is ratified, any legislative changes necessary to implement the treaty must be passed by Parliament. It is only once all domestic procedures are completed that arrangements can be made for the formal entry into force of the treaty in Australia. For bilateral treaties this usually occurs through an exchange of diplomatic notes; for multilateral treaties Australia needs to deposit an instrument of ratification with the treaty depositary.[43]

## 4.5.2   Constitutional considerations

The executive power to enter into treaties is conferred by s 61 of the *Constitution* and is largely unconfined. The exercise of the treaty-making power is a matter of Australia's international relations reserved for the executive, and may not be challenged in Australian courts.[44]

The executive power to enter into treaties is very broad and so is the legislative power to implement treaties in Australian law. The Parliament's legislative power is set out in s 51 of the *Constitution*, and there are a number of heads of power that are relevant to the implementation of treaties. For instance, if Australia enters into a free trade agreement, the 'trade and commerce' power in s 51(i) will support legislation implementing the treaty. However, the legislative power that has come to have the greatest significance for the implementation of treaties is the 'external affairs power' in s 51(xxix). This power is not limited to any particular subject matter, which means the Parliament can legislate on any matter relating to 'external affairs' even if it is not covered by another head of power.

The external affairs power has been interpreted in successive High Court decisions from the 1980s onwards to support legislation concerning Australia's relations with other countries and matters physically external to Australia, and legislation which implements Australia's international obligations assumed under customary international law or through treaties. These decisions have substantially transformed the distribution of power in Australia's federation, allowing the Commonwealth to step into areas that fall under the legislative powers of the states. If this were not the case, Australia would be placed in the difficult position of being able to enter many treaties but not give effect to them.

The external affairs power will support legislation implementing a treaty if the treaty is 'itself defined with sufficient specificity to direct the general course to be taken by the signatory states'.[45] Second, the legislation 'must be capable of being reasonably considered to be appropriate and adapted to achieving' the treaty provision.[46] While there must be a sufficiently close relationship between the treaty provision and the implementing legislation, it is not the case that the legislation will have to enact all aspects of the treaty into Australian law. The legislature has considerable discretion and, as Brennan J observed in *Commonwealth v Tasmania* ('*Tasmanian Dam Case*'),[47] if the Parliament chooses to exercise its legislative power to implement a treaty obligation only to a limited extent this does not affect the validity

43    'Australia's Treaty-Making Process', *Department of Foreign Affairs and Trade* (Web Page) <www.dfat .gov.au/international-relations/treaties/treaty-making-process>.

44    *Victoria v Commonwealth* (1996) 187 CLR 416, 476 (Brennan CJ, Toohey, Gaudron, McHugh and Gummow JJ).

45    Ibid 487 (Brennan CJ, Toohey, Gaudron, McHugh and Gummow JJ).

46    *Commonwealth v Tasmania* (1983) 158 CLR 1, 545 (Deane J) ('*Tasmanian Dam Case*').

47    Ibid.

of the law.[48] Furthermore, legislation will be constitutional even if it is not concerned with implementing a specific treaty obligation but rather allows Australia to 'facilitate the enjoyment of the benefits promised by [a] treaty'.[49]

In the *Tasmanian Dam Case*, the Tasmanian government had challenged the constitutionality of the *World Heritage Properties Conservation Act 1983* (Cth) which was used to prevent Tasmania from constructing a large hydroelectricity project on the Gordon River in South West Tasmania. The area had been placed on the World Heritage List under the *World Heritage Convention*.[50] The majority of the Court held the legislation valid under the external affairs power, and several of the majority justices made observations concerning the legislative power to implement treaties:

### Mason J

[22] If the carrying out of, or the giving effect to, a treaty or convention to which Australia is a party is a matter of external affairs, and so much is now accepted, it is very difficult to see why a law made under s 51(xxix) [of the *Australian Constitution*], that is, a law with respect to the matter of external affairs, should be limited to the implementation of an obligation. To say this is to import an arbitrary limitation into the exercise of the power, one which might deprive Australia of the benefits which a treaty or convention seeks to secure ...

...

[26] The extent of the Parliament's power to legislate so as to carry into effect a treaty will, of course, depend on the nature of the particular treaty, whether its provisions are declaratory of international law, whether they impose obligations or provide benefits and, if so, what the nature of these obligations or benefits are, and whether they are specific or general or involve significant elements of discretion and value judgment on the part of the contracting parties. I reject the notion that once Australia enters into a treaty Parliament may legislate with respect to the subject matter of the treaty as if that subject matter were a new and independent head of Commonwealth legislative power. The law must conform to the treaty and carry its provisions into effect. The fact that the power may extend to the subject matter of the treaty before it is made or adopted by Australia, because the subject matter has become a matter of international concern to Australia, does not mean that Parliament may depart from the provisions of the treaty after it has been entered into by Australia and enact legislation which goes beyond the treaty or is inconsistent with it.[51]

### Deane J

[19] Circumstances could well exist in which a law which procured or ensured observance within Australia of the spirit of a treaty or compliance with an international recommendation or pursuit of an international objective would properly be characterized as a law with respect to external affairs notwithstanding the absence of any potential breach of defined international obligations or of the letter of international law.

---

48    Ibid 534 (Brennan J).
49    Ibid 488 (Mason J).
50    *Convention concerning the Protection of the World Cultural and Natural Heritage*, opened for signature 16 November 1972, 1037 UNTS 151 (entered into force 17 December 1975) ('*World Heritage Convention*').
51    *Tasmanian Dam Case* (n 46) 488 [22], 489 [26].

[20] On the other hand, . . . a law would not properly be characterized as a law with respect to external affairs if it failed to carry into effect or to comply with the particular provisions of a treaty which it was said to execute or if the treaty which the law was said to carry into effect was demonstrated to be no more than a device to attract domestic legislative power. More importantly, while the question of what is the appropriate method of achieving a desired result is a matter for the Parliament and not for the Court, the law must be capable of being reasonably considered to be appropriate and adapted to achieving what is said to impress it with the character of a law with respect to external affairs.

[21] Implicit in [this] requirement . . . is a need for there to be a reasonable proportionality between the designated purpose or object and the means which the law embodies for achieving or procuring it. Thus, to take an extravagant example, a law requiring that all sheep in Australia be slaughtered would not be sustainable as a law with respect to external affairs merely because Australia was a party to some international convention which required the taking of steps to safeguard against the spread of some obscure sheep disease which had been detected in sheep in a foreign country and which had not reached these shores. . . . The law must be seen, with 'reasonable clearness', upon consideration of its operation, to be 'really, and not fancifully, colourably, or ostensibly, referable' to and explicable by the purpose or object which is said to provide its character . . .[52]

The external affairs power supports legislation implementing a treaty relating to matters external to Australia even in circumstances where the treaty may be contrary to international law. In *Horta v Commonwealth*,[53] the plaintiffs asked the High Court to declare invalid legislation that gave effect to the *Timor Gap Treaty* between Australia and Indonesia.[54] That treaty provided for access to the oil and gas resources of parts of the Timor Sea between Australia and East Timor (as it then was) pending a settlement of a maritime boundary between Australia and Indonesia. The plaintiffs argued that the *Timor Gap Treaty* was invalid because Indonesia had occupied East Timor unlawfully in 1975.[55] The High Court found that 'even if the Treaty were void under international law' and even if 'Australia's entry into or performance of the Treaty involved a breach of Australia's obligations under international law', the implementing legislation would 'not thereby be deprived of their character as laws with respect to "External affairs"'.[56]

## 4.5.3  Legislative considerations

Considerable discretion is usually left to the parties to a treaty to determine the legislative and other measures that will be needed to give effect to the treaty in domestic law. International

52    Ibid 545 [19]–[20].
53    (1994) 181 CLR 183.
54    *Treaty between Australia and the Republic of Indonesia on the Zone of Cooperation in an Area between the Indonesian Province of East Timor and Northern Australia*, signed 11 December 1989, 1654 UNTS 105 (entered into force 9 February 1991).
55    The treaty was alleged to be invalid because Indonesia was not the sovereign of East Timor and therefore did not have the power to enter into the treaty; and because it violated the East Timorese people's right to self-determination. See further Kristen Walker, 'Case Note: *Horta v Commonwealth*' (1994) 19 *Melbourne University Law Review* 1114.
56    *Horta v Commonwealth* (n 53) 195.

law is generally concerned with *whether* rather than *how* states give effect to their inter-national obligations.[57] This discretion exists so that the implementation of a treaty can be tailored to the particular characteristics and requirements of the relevant domestic legal system. Some treaties are more specific and actually require parties to adopt specific legisla-tive measures. For instance, a number of treaties require parties to criminalise certain offences: the *Convention for the Suppression of Unlawful Seizure of Aircraft* requires parties to make hijacking an 'offence punishable by severe penalties',[58] and the *Convention against Torture* requires that a state party 'shall ensure that all acts of torture are offences under its criminal law'.[59]

There are a variety of ways treaties have been implemented in Australian law. In some circumstances legislation is not considered necessary. For example, Australia is a party to all the main human rights treaties; however, these have only been partially implemented in Commonwealth legislation, with successive governments taking the view (which is open to criticism) that the rights which they contain are adequately protected by existing state and federal legislation and by the common law. Ivan Shearer described the effect given to core human rights treaties in Australia as 'quasi-incorporation'.[60] This consists of treaties being made 'declared instruments' under the *Australian Human Rights Commission Act 1986* (Cth) and being scheduled to the Act. Although this does not amount to full legislative implementation, the Australian Human Rights Commission has certain functions in relation to the rights contained in the declared instruments.[61]

The reluctance of the Commonwealth to give legislative effect to human rights treaties has been described by Hilary Charlesworth and colleagues as a 'Janus-faced' approach to some areas of international law: 'the international face smiles and accepts obligations, while the domestic-turned face frowns and refrains from giving them legal force'.[62] Three Australian states and territories – the Australian Capital Territory, Victoria and Queensland – have enacted human rights statutes which give some effect to some provisions of the core human rights treaties.[63] This increases the opportunities for human rights treaties to be relied on in the relevant state and territory courts.[64]

Less controversial examples of non-implementation include where Australia joins a treaty on a matter that is already extensively addressed under Australian law, or which can be addressed through regulations made under existing legislation. An example is the *Agreement*

---

57  One way of conceptualising this discretion is using the 'margin of appreciation' doctrine: Jean-Pierre Cot, 'Margin of Appreciation' in Rüdiger Wolfrum (ed), *The Max Planck Encyclopedia of Public International Law* (Oxford University Press, online, June 2007).

58  *Convention for the Suppression of Unlawful Seizure of Aircraft*, opened for signature 16 December 1970, 860 UNTS 105 (entered into force 14 October 1971) art 2. See *Crimes (Aviation) Act 1991* (Cth).

59  *Convention against Torture and Other Cruel, Inhuman or Degrading Treatment or Punishment*, opened for signature 10 December 1984, 1465 UNTS 85 (entered into force 26 June 1987) art 4(1).

60  Shearer (n 3) 34, 55.

61  On the functions of the Commission, see *Australian Human Rights Commission Act 1986* (Cth) s 11.

62  Hilary Charlesworth et al, 'Deep Anxieties: Australia and the International Legal Order' (2003) 25(4) *Sydney Law Review* 423, 436.

63  *Human Rights Act 2004* (ACT); *Charter of Human Rights and Responsibilities Act 2006* (Vic); *Human Rights Act 2019* (Qld).

64  See further Chapter 10 on Australia's approach to, and reception of, international human rights law.

*between Australia and Timor-Leste on Taxation Information Exchange*,[65] which may be implemented under existing Australian taxation law without the need for new legislation.[66]

The National Interest Analyses that accompany the tabling of treaties in Parliament usually contain statements about the need or otherwise for new legislation to implement the treaty. If legislation is required, there are several different forms it can take.[67] For a small number of treaties it may be possible simply to give the treaty 'the force of law'. This method is appropriate where the provisions of the treaty have been drafted in such a way that they are amenable to statutory incorporation. An example is the *Vienna Convention on Diplomatic Relations*,[68] which formulates obligations regarding diplomatic privileges and immunities with such clarity and specificity that many of its provisions are given direct force by the *Diplomatic Privileges and Immunities Act 1967* (Cth).[69]

The much more common practice is to 'translate' treaty provisions into precise statutory language that suits the Australian legal system. For example, the *National Greenhouse and Energy Reporting Act 2007* (Cth) gives effect to Australia's obligations under the *United Nations Framework Convention on Climate Change*[70] to obtain and report information relating to greenhouse gas emissions. This type of approach may retain a number of references to treaty terms but avoids the uncertainty which may result from the direct incorporation of general, and sometimes ambiguous, treaty language.

## 4.5.4   Treaties and administrative decision-making

International law has become increasingly relevant to many administrative decisions. Often this is because the applicable legislation itself directs decision-makers to consider international law when exercising powers or functions.[71] Andrew Edgar and Rayner Thwaites catalogue a growing number of statutes 'where powers granted to administrators by legislation are qualified by reference to Australia's treaty commitments'.[72] This includes legislation on civil aviation,[73] customs,[74] nuclear

---

65    *Agreement between Australia and Timor-Leste on Taxation Information Exchange*, opened for signature 20 March 2020, [2020] ATNIF 15 (not yet in force).

66    *National Interest Analysis* [2020] ATNIA 12 <www8.austlii.edu.au/au/other/dfat/ATNIA/2020/12.pdf>.

67    See Bill Campbell, 'The Implementation of Treaties in Australia' in Brian Opeskin and Donald Rothwell (eds), *International Law and Australian Federalism* (Melbourne University Press, 1997) 132.

68    *Vienna Convention on Diplomatic Relations*, opened for signature 18 April 1961, 500 UNTS 95 (entered into force 24 April 1964).

69    'Subject to this section, the provisions of Articles 1, 22 to 24 (inclusive) and 27 to 40 (inclusive) of the Convention [*on Diplomatic Relations*] have the force of law in Australia and in every external Territory': *Diplomatic Privileges and Immunities Act 1967* (Cth) s 7(1).

70    *United Nations Framework Convention on Climate Change*, opened for signature 9 May 1992, 1771 UNTS 107 (entered into force 21 March 1994).

71    An important case dealing with this method of giving legislative effect to international treaties is *Project Blue Sky v Australian Broadcasting Authority* (1998) 194 CLR 355. In their joint judgment, McHugh, Gummow, Kirby and Hayne JJ found that if a statutory provision requires an administrative decision-maker to act consistently with Australia's international obligations, failing to do so would result in the decision being unlawful.

72    Andrew Edgar and Rayner Thwaites, 'Implementing Treaties in Domestic Law: Translation, Enforcement and Administrative Law' (2018) 19(1) *Melbourne Journal of International Law* 24, 26.

73    *Civil Aviation Act 1988* (Cth) s 11; *Air Services Act 1995* (Cth) s 9(3).

74    *Customs Act 1901* (Cth) s 269SK.

materials,[75] telecommunications,[76] chemical weapons,[77] online safety[78] and the environment.[79] For instance, s 137 of the *Environment Protection and Biodiversity Conservation Act 1999* (Cth) requires the Minister, when making a decision on whether to approve a project, not to act inconsistently with Australia's obligations under the *World Heritage Convention*.[80] These kinds of provisions do not incorporate international law into Australian law, but they do make treaties relevant to administrative decision-making and they provide litigants with a way to challenge those decisions by reference to treaties to which Australia is a party.

A different issue was raised in *Minister for Immigration and Ethnic Affairs v Teoh* ('*Teoh*'),[81] in which the High Court held that Australia's ratification of the *Convention on the Rights of the Child*,[82] which it was yet to implement in Australian law, gave rise to a legitimate expectation that the government decision-maker would take the best interests of the child into account as a primary consideration. *Teoh* stands for this fairly narrow proposition and nothing more, and it is accepted that 'unenacted international obligations' are 'not mandatory relevant considerations attracting judicial review for jurisdictional error'.[83] Although the High Court subsequently abandoned the legitimate expectation doctrine, finding it unnecessary and unhelpful in determining whether procedural fairness has been accorded to a person affected by a decision,[84] *Teoh* has not been overruled within the narrow confines of its operation.

*Teoh* gave rise to considerable speculation that it would open the door on Australia's engagement with international law, giving ratified but unimplemented treaties much greater influence on administrative decision-making and Australian law more generally. However, this has not occurred.[85] Accordingly, the primary relevance of international law to administrative decision-making remains in situations where an international legal obligation is directly incorporated in legislation, or in those situations, discussed in this section, where the applicable statutory framework requires decision-makers to act consistently with treaty obligations, or more generally to have regard to Australia's international legal obligations.

# 4.6 International law and statutory interpretation

The High Court has held that where a domestic statute incorporates text from an international treaty then, absent contrary intention, the text should be interpreted in accordance with its

---

75    *Nuclear Non-Proliferation (Safeguards) Act 1987* (Cth) s 70.

76    *Telecommunications Act 1997* (Cth) s 580.

77    *Chemical Weapons (Prohibition) Act 1994* (Cth) s 95(2).

78    *Enhancing Online Safety Act 2015* (Cth) s 12(1).

79    *Environment Protection and Biodiversity Conservation Act 1999* (Cth) ss 137–140; *Environment Protection (Sea Dumping) Act 1981* (Cth) s 19(8A).

80    *World Heritage Convention* (n 50).

81    (1995) 183 CLR 273 ('*Teoh*').

82    *Convention on the Rights of the Child*, opened for signature 20 November 1989, 1577 UNTS 3 (entered into force 2 September 1990).

83    *Re Minister for Immigration and Multicultural Affairs; Ex parte Lam* (2003) 214 CLR 1, 33 [101] (McHugh and Gummow JJ).

84    *Minister for Immigration and Border Protection v WZARH* (2015) 256 CLR 326, 334–5 [28]–[30] (Kiefel, Bell and Keane JJ).

85    Edgar and Thwaites (n 72) 44.

meaning in the treaty and the *VCLT* rules of interpretation, rather than the narrower rules of statutory interpretation that govern the interpretation of the statutory provisions.[86]

The *Acts Interpretation Act 1901* (Cth) includes a provision relating to the broader use of treaties by Australian courts when interpreting legislation. Under s 15AB(1), consideration may be given to extrinsic material to confirm the ordinary meaning of the provision, taking into account its context in the relevant Act and the purpose or object of the Act; or to determine the meaning of the provision when it is ambiguous or obscure, or its ordinary meaning leads to a result that is manifestly absurd or is unreasonable. Included in the non-exhaustive list of extrinsic materials that may be considered in this way is 'any treaty or other international agreement that is referred to in the Act'.[87]

An example of how Australian courts have applied this principle is *Maloney v The Queen*.[88] An Indigenous woman in Queensland was convicted of an offence of possessing alcohol contrary to Queensland legislation that imposed restrictions on the possession of alcohol in certain areas. She appealed against the conviction on the grounds that the legislation was inconsistent with the *Racial Discrimination Act 1975* (Cth) which implements the 1965 *Convention on the Elimination of All Forms of Racial Discrimination*.[89] The High Court held unanimously that the discrimination was a 'special measure' taken for the advancement of Indigenous people and was not contrary to the Act. Under art 1(4) of the *Convention*, 'special measures' could be taken for the protection of certain racial and ethnic groups. Indigenous people were such a group in this case. Several comments were made on the approach to be taken to international legal materials when interpreting the *Racial Discrimination Act*:

### French CJ

[23] An interpretation of a treaty provision adopted in international practice, by the decisions of international courts or tribunals, or by foreign municipal courts may illuminate the interpretation of that provision where it has been incorporated into the domestic law of Australia. That does not mean that Australian courts can adopt 'interpretations' which rewrite the incorporated text or burden it with glosses which its language will not bear.[90]

### Gageler J

[327] The Convention is, and always has been, firmly understood to be based on the principles of the dignity and equality of all human beings and to have as its objective the securing of equality in fact in the enjoyment of human rights by persons of all races. The international understanding of its content has nevertheless evolved ...

[328] The purpose of s 10 [of the *Racial Discrimination Act*] would not be achieved were constructional choices now presented by its text not to be made consistently with that contemporary international understanding.[91]

---

86    *Applicant A v Minister for Immigration and Ethnic Affairs* (1997) 190 CLR 225, 349. See further Chapter 3 on treaties and treaty interpretation.

87    *Acts Interpretation Act 1901* (Cth) s 15AB(2).

88    (2013) 252 CLR 168.

89    *International Convention on the Elimination of All Forms of Racial Discrimination*, opened for signature 21 December 1965, 660 UNTS 195 (entered into force 4 January 1969).

90    *Maloney v The Queen* (2013) 252 CLR 168, 185 [23].

91    Ibid 292–3 [327]–[328].

In addition to these principles or approaches to interpretation is a longstanding common law rule that, in the absence of express words to the contrary, it is presumed that legislation is intended to be in conformity with international law and should be interpreted as such.[92] In *Al-Kateb v Godwin*, McHugh J questioned the cogency of the presumption, and observed that '[g]iven the widespread nature of the sources of international law under modern conditions, it is impossible to believe that, when parliament now legislates, it has in mind or is even aware of all the rules of international law'.[93] His Honour concluded nonetheless that the rule was 'too well established to be repealed by judicial decision'.[94]

The principle was first expressed by the High Court in 1908 in relation to customary law in *Jumbunna Coal Mine NL v Victorian Coal Miners' Association*,[95] with O'Connor J observing that 'every statute is to be so interpreted and applied as far as its language admits as not to be inconsistent with the comity of nations or with the established rules of international law'.[96] It is only a presumption, and it will not operate if the language of the legislation is clear.[97] It is often referred to as the '*Polites* principle'. In *Polites v Commonwealth*,[98] the plaintiffs, two Greek nationals residing in Australia, were given notices requiring them to enlist in the Australian defence forces. The plaintiffs challenged the constitutionality of the regulations under which they were conscripted, arguing that there was a rule of customary international law preventing states from conscripting aliens. The High Court held that the legislation was supported by the defence and aliens powers in the *Constitution*, s 51(vi) and s 51(xix) respectively, even if the powers were contrary to international law:

### Latham CJ

It must be held that legislation otherwise within the power of the Commonwealth Parliament does not become invalid because it conflicts with a rule of international law, though every effort should be made to construe Commonwealth statutes so as to avoid breaches of international law and of international comity.

### Dixon J

It is a rule of construction that, unless a contrary intention appear, general words occurring in a statute are to be read subject to the established rules of international law and not as intended to apply to persons or subjects which, according to those rules, a national law of the kind in question ought not to include.

### McTiernan J

There is a presumption that the legislature does not intend to violate by a statute any established rule of international law. But the presumption does not govern the construction of a statute if its language shows that it was not the intention of the legislature that the statute should be in harmony with international law ...[99]

---

92    See, eg, *Kartinyeri v Commonwealth* (1998) 195 CLR 337, 384 (Gummow and Hayne JJ).
93    (2004) 219 CLR 562, 591 [65].
94    Ibid.
95    (1908) 6 CLR 309.
96    Ibid 363.
97    *Mortensen v Peters* (1906) 14 Scots LTR 227 (High Court of Justiciary, Scotland).
98    (1945) 70 CLR 60 ('*Polites*').
99    Ibid 69 (Latham CJ), 77 (Dixon J), 79 (McTiernan J).

In *Teoh* the High Court accepted that the *Polites* principle would operate in relation to treaty obligations where the legislation being interpreted is ambiguous, but rejected a 'narrow conception of ambiguity', holding that '[i]f the language of the legislation is susceptible of a construction which is consistent with the terms of the international instrument ... then that construction should prevail'.[100] According to *Teoh*, this presumptive interpretation should apply 'at least in those cases in which the legislation is enacted after, or in contemplation of, entry into, or ratification of, the relevant international instrument'.[101]

When inconsistency between an Australian statute and international law cannot be resolved by way of interpretation, Australian courts are bound to apply domestic law. As Kirby J said in *Minister for Immigration and Multicultural and Indigenous Affairs v B*:

> Mandatory detention of unlawful non-citizens who are children is the will of the Parliament of Australia. It is expressed in clear terms in ss 189 and 196 of the [*Migration Act 1958*]. Those sections are constitutionally valid. In the face of such clear provisions, the requirements of international law ... cannot be given effect by a court such as this. This Court can note and call attention to the issue. However, it cannot invoke international law to override clear and valid provisions of Australian national law.[102]

Nonetheless, should the inconsistency between Australian and international law cause a breach of international obligations, Australia could be held responsible by other governments under the rules of state responsibility (see Chapter 7).

# 4.7    International law and constitutional interpretation

While international law may be relevant to statutory interpretation, the High Court has not accepted its use when reading the *Australian Constitution*. This sets Australian jurisprudence apart from other jurisdictions which have been more open to the influence of international law.[103] The issue was addressed by several justices in *Al-Kateb v Godwin*,[104] in which the High Court found that the indefinite immigration detention of a stateless person was lawful under the *Migration Act 1958* (Cth):

### McHugh J

[68] If Australian courts interpreted the *Constitution* by reference to the rules of international law now in force, they would be *amending* the Constitution in disregard of the direction in s 128 of the *Constitution*. Section 128 declares that the *Constitution* is to be amended only by legislation that is approved by a majority of the States and 'a majority of all the electors voting'. Attempts to suggest that a rule of international law is merely a factor that can be taken into account in interpreting the Constitution cannot hide the fact

---

100    *Teoh* (n 81) 287–8 [27].
101    Ibid 287 [26] (Mason CJ and Deane J).
102    (2004) 219 CLR 365, 525 [171].
103    See, eg, *Constitution of South Africa* (n 2) s 39(1)(b): 'When interpreting the Bill of Rights, a court, tribunal or forum ... must consider international law'. See Devika Hovell and George Williams, 'A Tale of Two Systems: The Use of International Law in Constitutional Interpretation in Australia and South Africa' (2005) 29(1) *Melbourne University Law Review* 95.
104    (2004) 219 CLR 562.

that, if that is done, the meaning of the Constitution is changed whenever that rule changes what would otherwise be the result of the case.

. . .

[71] Failure to see the difference between taking into account political, social and economic developments since 1900 and taking into account the *rules* of international law is the error in the approach of those who assert that the *Constitution* must be read in conformity with or in so far as it can be read conformably with the rules of international law. Rules are specific. If they are taken into account as *rules*, they amend the *Constitution*.[105]

. . .

**Kirby J**

[175] The complete isolation of constitutional law from the dynamic impact of international law is neither possible nor desirable today. That is why national courts, and especially national constitutional courts such as this, have a duty, so far as possible, to interpret their constitutional texts in a way that is generally harmonious with the basic principles of international law, including as that law states human rights and fundamental freedoms.

[176] In practice, this development presents no significant difficulty for a legal system such as Australia's. In part, this is because of the profound influence on the most basic statements of international law (and specifically of the law of human rights and fundamental freedoms) of Anglo-American lawyers and the concepts that they derived from the common law. In part, it is because such rights and freedoms express the common rights of all humanity. They pre-existed their formal expression.[106]

James Crawford commented on the High Court's approach to international law and constitutional interpretation, noting that

there is a certain tendency for the High Court to pass by, metaphorically, on the other side, saying in effect that we are not as other final courts are. Of course, each final court retains the last word in its own system, and one should be wary of facile comparativism as much as of facile internationalism. But the proposition that the executive is legally required to keep someone in administrative detention in Australia for the rest of his life – so compelled by a statutory provision containing the word 'until' – is amazing and, frankly, disreputable. . . . We must always remember that it is a Constitution we are interpreting; and new developments at the international level may have to be taken into account without usurping the role of the Australian people under section 128.[107]

# 4.8  Customary international law in Australian law

Australia, like all states, is bound by rules of customary international law. This does not mean that these rules automatically form part of Australian law, although, as discussed in Section 4.6,

---

105    Ibid [68], [71] (emphasis in original).
106    Ibid [175]–[176].
107    James Crawford, 'International Law in the House of Lords and the High Court of Australia 1996–2008: A Comparison' (2009) 28 *Australian Year Book of International Law* 1, 20–1 (citations omitted).

a presumption operates that statutes should be interpreted, as far as their language permits, consistently with customary international law. In relation to custom, Australian courts have not accepted the approach of some other jurisdictions in which international law is regarded as being automatically incorporated into domestic law.

One jurisdiction that traditionally automatically accepted customary international law is the United Kingdom, notably in *Trendtex Trading Corporation v Central Bank of Nigeria*.[108] The case concerned contracts entered into by the Nigerian government to purchase cement. Payment was made by a letter of credit issued by the Central Bank of Nigeria. So much cement was ordered that the port of Lagos was overwhelmed. After a new military government took office, cement imports were limited, with special governmental approval required before shipments could sail or letters of credit would be honoured. Trendtex, a Swiss corporation, sued the Central Bank of Nigeria in respect of two cement shipments for which payment was refused. At issue were whether the bank was a state entity protected by immunity, and whether foreign state immunity applied to commercial transactions.

The Court found that the bank was separate from the state and not entitled to immunity. In his judgment, Lord Denning MR also found that the restrictive doctrine of state immunity[109] applied in English law, and made observations about the relationship between international law and domestic law:

> A fundamental question arises for decision. What is the place of international law in our English law? One school of thought holds to the doctrine of incorporation. It says that the rules of international law are incorporated into English law automatically and considered to be part of English law unless they are in conflict with an Act of Parliament. The other school of thought holds to the doctrine of transformation. It says that the rules of international law are not to be considered as part of English law except in so far as they have been already adopted and made part of our law by the decisions of the judges, or by Act of Parliament, or long established custom. The difference is vital when you are faced with a change in the rules of international law. Under the doctrine of incorporation, when the rules of international law change, our English law changes with them. But, under the doctrine of transformation, the English law does not change. It is bound by precedent. . . . It cannot develop as international law develops.
>
> . . .
>
> Which is correct? As between these two schools of thought, I now believe that the doctrine of incorporation is correct. Otherwise I do not see that our courts could ever recognise a change in the rules of international law. . . . International law does change: and the courts have applied the changes without the aid of any Act of Parliament. Thus, when the rules of international law were changed (by the force of public opinion) so as to condemn slavery, the English courts were justified in applying the modern rules of international law.[110]

A contrast is often drawn between the approach of Australian and UK courts, with the latter more open to the direct influence of customary international law on the common law. However, as Roger O'Keefe points out, the position in the United Kingdom was not, and is

---

108   [1977] QB 529 ('*Trendtex*').
109   See Chapter 6 on immunity.
110   *Trendtex* (n 108) 553, 554.

not, as clear as Lord Denning's dictum above suggests.[111] The doctrine of incorporation in the United Kingdom is 'really a doctrine of judicial transformation or judicial adoption, whereby the courts ... are empowered and even directed to fashion rules of common law by reference to rules of customary international law'.[112] Both Australia and the United Kingdom have a shared heritage, and when it comes to common law approaches to international law the jurisdictions are in fact very similar.[113]

While Australian courts have rejected the incorporation approach (that customary international law is automatically part of Australian law unless the Parliament legislates to the contrary), they have also not clearly adopted the transformation approach (that customary international law does not become part of domestic law until adopted by judicial decision or parliamentary enactment). The dominant Australian approach appears to be that customary international law is but one 'source' of or 'influence' on domestic law. However, discerning the position is challenging because there have only been a handful of cases and there is no conclusive High Court authority. In *Polites v Commonwealth*, Williams J supported the incorporation approach and observed that '[i]t is clear that such a [customary] rule, when it has been established to the satisfaction of the courts, is recognized and acted upon as part of English municipal law so far as it is not inconsistent with rules enacted by statutes or finally declared by the courts'.[114]

There were additional dicta in *Chow Hung Ching v The Queen*,[115] a few years later. That case related to convictions of Chinese army labourers for assault in Papua New Guinea (which was at the time administered by Australia under UN mandate). The question for the Court was whether, as a matter of international law and Australian law, the labourers enjoyed immunity as 'visiting armed forces'. On the evidence, the Court found that they were not members of the military forces of China and so no immunity applied. However, several justices remarked on the place of customary international law in Australian law. For Latham CJ, '[i]nternational law is not as such part of the law of Australia, but a universally recognised principle of international law would be applied by our courts'.[116] Justice Dixon referred to the competing views of William Blackstone and JL Brierly in England, and found that the 'true view' is that international law is not a part, but is one of the sources, of Australian law.[117] The meaning of these statements has been subject to much speculation and not clarified by subsequent authority.[118]

---

111   Roger O'Keefe, 'The Doctrine of Incorporation Revisited' (2008) 79 *British Year Book of International Law* 7, 84.
112   Ibid. See also Crawford, *Brownlie's Principles* (n 11) 63–8.
113   See Crawford, 'International Law in the House of Lords' (n 107) 5.
114   *Polites* (n 98) 80 citing *Chung Chi Cheung v The Queen* [1939] AC 160.
115   (1948) 77 CLR 449.
116   Ibid 462.
117   Ibid 477.
118   Support for these different approaches can be found in the case law. Justice Merkel (dissenting) in *Nulyarimma v Thompson* (1999) 96 FCR 153 endorsed the 'source' approach which he said could be 'loosely described as the common law adoption approach': at 190 [132]. The 'incorporation' approach (in relation to immunity) was supported by Anderson J in *R v Disun* (2003) 27 WAR 146: 'Whether the ship was or was not a "floating island" of Norway is a question which falls to be answered by reference to the customary rule of international law recognised as part of the common law of Australia and the answer is that there is no rule of international law which is to the effect that persons on board private ships entering Australian territorial waters are immune from local jurisdiction ...': at 151 [18] (Murray and Templeman JJ agreeing).

Justice Wilcox in the Full Federal Court decision in *Nulyarimma v Thompson* noted that the approach might differ according to the type of customary law rule (that is, civil or criminal):

> [I]t is difficult to make a general statement covering all the diverse rules of international customary law. It is one thing, it seems to me, for courts of a particular country to be prepared to treat a civil law rule like the doctrine of foreign sovereign immunity as part of its domestic law, whether because it is accepted by those courts as being 'incorporated' in that law or because it has been 'transformed' by judicial act. It is another thing to say that a norm of international law criminalising conduct that is not made punishable by the domestic law entitles a domestic court to try and punish an offender against that law.[119]

In *Mabo v Queensland (No 2)*,[120] Brennan J lent credence to the view that international law, including customary international law, could be a source for the development of the common law, observing:

> The common law does not necessarily conform with international law, but international law is a legitimate and important influence on the development of the common law, especially when international law declares the existence of universal human rights. A common law doctrine founded on unjust discrimination in the enjoyment of civil and political rights demands reconsideration. It is contrary both to international standards and to the fundamental values of our common law to entrench a discriminatory rule which, because of the supposed position on the scale of social organization of the indigenous inhabitants of a settled colony, denies them a right to occupy their traditional lands.[121]

A similar approach was suggested in the Full Federal Court in *Habib v Commonwealth*.[122] That case concerned whether proceedings by the plaintiff against the Commonwealth for alleged torture he suffered in foreign states could proceed, given that they would involve scrutiny of the actions of foreign governments in their territory. Ordinarily the common law 'act of state' doctrine (see Chapter 6) would make such a claim non-justiciable. The Court found that the prohibition against torture was a peremptory (*jus cogens*) norm of public international law from which no derogation is permitted. It also found that the act of state doctrine does not prevent judicial scrutiny by an Australian court of the conduct of an agent of a foreign state, within the territory of the foreign state, where that conduct 'involves alleged acts of torture constituting grave breaches of human rights, serious violations of international law and conduct made illegal by Australian laws having extra-territorial effect'.[123] Chief Justice Black observed:

> It is not to the point that Mr Habib's proceeding is a civil claim for damages and not a criminal proceeding under the *Crimes (Torture) Act*, the *Geneva Conventions Act* or the *Criminal Code*. The point is that, if a choice were indeed open, in determining whether or not the act of state doctrine operates to deny a civil remedy contingent upon breach of those Acts, the common law should develop congruently with emphatically expressed ideals of public policy, reflective of universal norms.[124]

---

119   *Nulyarimma v Thompson* (1999) 96 FCR 153, 164 [25].
120   (1992) 175 CLR 1.
121   Ibid 42.
122   (2010) 183 FCR 62.
123   Ibid [135] (Jagot J, Black CJ agreeing).
124   Ibid [13].

## 4.8.1    Crimes in customary international law

While there is uncertainty about the general influence of customary international law on Australian common law, there is clarity when it comes to whether customary international crimes are automatically incorporated in Australian law. The Full Federal Court of Australia in *Nulyarimma v Thompson* held that the *jus cogens* prohibition on genocide was not automatically part of Australian law.[125] The case involved claims by Indigenous plaintiffs that certain named Commonwealth Ministers and Members of Parliament had committed genocide by making changes to native title laws. Justices Wilcox and Whitlam held that genocide was a crime under customary international law but was not a crime under Australian law in the absence of implementing or adopting legislation. Justice Merkel, in dissent, held that universal crimes under customary international law, such as genocide, could give rise to criminal jurisdiction in Australia even in the absence of implementing legislation. Justices Wilcox and Whitlam took similar approaches in their separate judgments, emphasising separation of power issues and the need for criminal law to be made through legislation. Justice Wilcox observed that if custom could create a common law crime, 'it would lead to the curious result that an international obligation incurred pursuant to customary law has greater domestic consequences than an obligation incurred, expressly and voluntarily, by Australia signing and ratifying an international convention'.[126]

The approach taken by the majority in *Nulyarimma v Thompson* was cited with approval by the House of Lords in *R v Jones*.[127] The case concerned criminal proceedings against Margaret Jones and others for causing damage to air force equipment as part of an anti-war protest. The defendants argued that they were acting with legal justification in seeking to impede the commission of the customary international law crime of aggression by the United Kingdom and the United States. The House of Lords held that although the crime of aggression was part of customary international law, it did not form part of English law in the absence of specific statutory authority.

The High Court refused leave to appeal against the decision in *Nulyarimma v Thompson*. Accordingly, the decision currently remains the last word on the status of customary crimes in the Australian common law. However, there has been subsequent statutory reform, and genocide was criminalised under the *Criminal Code 1995* (Cth) when Australian ratified the *Rome Statute of the International Criminal Court*.[128]

# 4.9    Proof of international law in Australian courts

When international law is raised in proceedings in an Australian court, what needs to be done to establish the rule being relied upon? Is international law to be treated like foreign law which requires proof, or can the court take judicial notice of international law? There is not a great deal of authority on this point, but it appears to be accepted that Australian '[c]ourts

---

125    (1999) 96 FCR 153.
126    Ibid 162 [20].
127    [2007] 1 AC 136.
128    *Rome Statute of the International Criminal Court* (n 35).

acknowledge the existence of a body of international law, whose content is not a matter of evidence but of argument'.[129] As noted by Perram J in *Garuda*:

> There is no doubt that domestic law cannot be proved law by evidence. . . .
>
> Does a similar principle apply to international law? Despite authority to this effect being scarce, it seems that the answer is that it does.
>
> . . .
>
> International law is then a normative system having a significant impact on the content of domestic public law whilst, at the same time, Australian courts are themselves potential sources of the same international norms. It is natural in such circumstances to treat international law as if it were domestic law for the purpose of its proof. This is not to make, what I think would be, the unrealistic suggestion that Australian law includes international law (eg, as opposed to the latter being a source in the limited sense discussed above, of the former). Rather, it is to accept its inherent legal nature, its domestic legal consequences, the practicality of it being dealt with as legal material and the qualification of domestic courts to engage in such an exercise. These matters mark it out as qualitatively different to foreign law.[130]

# DISCUSSION QUESTIONS

(1) 'The High Court of Australia should hold, when the appropriate case arises, that customary international law is automatically part of the Australian common law.' Discuss.

(2) What is the process by which Australia enters into a treaty? Could the process be improved and made more democratic?

(3) Australia has ratified a number of treaties which have then not been fully or even partly implemented by legislation. Why is this the case, and is it a problem? Provide examples.

(4) 'Dualist states such as Australia are inherently hostile to international law.' Do you agree with this statement? Critically discuss.

(5) What is the '*Polites* principle' and should it be extended to the interpretation of the *Australian Constitution*?

---

129    Crawford, 'International Law in the House of Lords' (n 107) 6.
130    *Garuda* (n 22) 413–4 [31]–[32], 417 [47].

# 5

# STATEHOOD, SELF-DETERMINATION AND TERRITORY

Rowan Nicholson

# 5.1   Introduction

This chapter covers three areas of international law that, though distinct, are interconnected. The law of statehood defines which entities qualify as states, the most important actors on the world stage and the international legal persons with the most rights, duties and functions. The law of self-determination accords rights to 'peoples' rather than to states, but in limited circumstances it enables peoples to create new states for themselves. That can be a way for a people to seize control of its own destiny, especially if it has been subject to colonialism or oppression. Finally, the law of territory determines the geographical borders within which many of the rights, duties and functions of states are applicable, including how those borders can change.

# 5.2   Statehood

States are by far the most important entities with international legal personality.[1] Virtually every area of international law gives them rights, duties or functions of some sort (as discussed in other chapters): the rules about how states produce customary law or make treaties; the law of state jurisdiction, state immunity, and state responsibility; the rules about the unlawful use of force; and so on. Some rights are perceived as being inextricably connected – or at least historically associated – with the very idea of statehood; an example is territorial sovereignty, which is a state's right to exercise exclusive jurisdiction over its territory (see Section 5.4). The law of statehood is basically definitional: it defines which entities qualify as states in the first place. Since other areas of international law give rights, duties and functions to states, the definition is of enormous significance.

This section of the chapter will discuss three factors that are relevant to statehood. The first is that, generally, an entity qualifies as a state if it meets certain criteria: population, territory, government and independence. As the word 'generally' hints, this is not enough to explain every case. The second factor is recognition, which is significant in various ways and may be decisive in special situations. The third is unlawfulness, which may underpin exceptions to the criteria.

## 5.2.1   The role of the statehood criteria

It is widely accepted that, generally, an entity qualifies as a state if it meets certain criteria that have been described in summary as criteria of 'effectiveness'.[2] They are sometimes also called the 'Montevideo criteria' after a treaty of 1933, the *Montevideo Convention on the Rights and Duties of States* ('*Montevideo Convention*'). That can be misleading, because the criteria do not derive from the treaty, which has only a few parties.[3] They derive from customary international law. But the treaty is seen as reflecting customary international law:

---

1    On other international legal persons, see Chapter 1.
2    James Crawford, *The Creation of States in International Law* (Oxford University Press, 2nd ed, 2006) ch 2.
3    Thomas Grant, 'Defining Statehood: The Montevideo Convention and Its Discontents' (1999) 37(2) *Columbia Journal of Transnational Law* 403, 456.

***Article 1***

The state as a person of international law should possess the following qualifications:

(a)   a permanent population;

(b)   a defined territory;

(c)   government; and

(d)   capacity to enter into relations with the other states.[4]

The criterion referred to in the treaty as 'capacity to enter into relations with the other states' is often expressed more straightforwardly as a requirement of 'independence' from other states. Thus, in short, the four criteria are population, territory, government and independence.

## 5.2.1.1   The criteria of population, territory and government

Many aspirant states meet the criteria of population and territory with little difficulty. In other instances, these criteria are elastic. Nauru has a population of hardly more than 10,000 and a land territory of 21 km$^2$, yet it is a state. Moreover, although the *Montevideo Convention* refers to a 'defined' territory, a state need not have *fully* defined borders. It may lack them either because it has territorial disputes with its neighbours or because it is a new state that has emerged in conditions of war or disorder. An example is the new state of Poland that emerged at the end of World War I on territory previously ruled by Germany and Russia. Its statehood was considered by a tribunal in *Deutsche Continental Gas-Gesellschaft v Polish State*, which observed:

> [T]he applicant has expressed the opinion that the Polish State could not be considered as having had *de jure* the territory designated as Congress Poland [a previously Russian territory] as long as the borders of that territory were not fixed. But, whatever may be the importance of the delimitation of borders, one cannot go so far as to maintain that, as long as that delimitation has not been legally settled, the State in question cannot be considered as having had any territory at all. Here, again, the practice of international law and the historical precedents demonstrate the contrary. In order for a State to exist ... with a territory that is necessary to its existence ... it is enough that the territory has a sufficiently certain coherence (even if its borders have not yet been delimited precisely) and that, over the territory, the State in reality exercises national public power in an independent manner. There are numerous examples of cases in which States have indisputably existed ... in a period during which the border between them was not yet precisely fixed.[5]

Many states today have unsettled or disputed borders, such as Israel and India, and it remains true that this does not undermine the existence of a territory.

Whether the criterion of government is similarly elastic is a more complex issue. There are certain circumstances in which the requirement is more or less suspended. One is where a state

---

4     *Montevideo Convention on the Rights and Duties of States*, opened for signature 26 December 1933, 165 LNTS 19 (in force 26 December 1934) art 1 ('*Montevideo Convention*').

5     *Deutsche Continental Gas-Gesellschaft c État polonais* (1929) 9 Recueil des décisions des tribunaux arbitraux mixtes institués par les traités de paix [Reports of the Mixed Arbitral Tribunals Established by the Peace Treaties] 336, 346 [tr author]. Although the decision is in French, a summary in English can be found at *Deutsche Continental Gas-Gesellschaft v Polish State* (1929) 5 ILR 11.

comes under belligerent occupation or unlawful annexation by a foreign power. For example, the various states occupied by Nazi Germany during World War II did not thereby cease to be states; nor did Kuwait when Iraq purported to annex it in 1990–91.[6] Another circumstance is where a government collapses for internal reasons, as in a civil war. A state can survive 'even a period of anarchy and absence of government, provided that such period is temporary'.[7]

There is a debate, however, about how far this elasticity goes, which is illustrated by Somalia's collapse into anarchy in the 1990s. In 1991, a British judge noted that the United Kingdom did not consider that there was 'any effective government in Somalia'.[8] The case differs from others in that the period of anarchy went beyond what can confidently be described as temporary; the United States, for instance, did not recognise any Somalian government between 1991 and 2013.[9] Despite this, no state ceased to treat Somalia as a state.[10]

On one side of the debate, some scholars have argued that the 'road to Statehood is a one-way street' in that once 'an entity has become a State it will remain one, no matter how useless and ineffectual its government might become'.[11] On the other side of the debate, one can point to observations made by the Arbitration Commission of the Peace Conference on Yugoslavia (known as the Badinter Commission), a body established to give advice on the collapse of Yugoslavia into multiple new states in the 1990s. It described not only 'the existence' but also 'the disappearance' of a state as 'a question of fact' and concluded that Yugoslavia – unlike, apparently, Somalia – disappeared as a state by reason of the fact that it ceased to exercise effective federal authority.[12] An alternative explanation of how Somalia may have continued to qualify as a state, regardless of whether or not it had a government, is given below in the discussion of recognition (see Section 5.2.2.1).

One reason the criteria of population, territory and government may be elastic is that they are seldom decisive in any event. A great many entities meet all three of these criteria and yet are not states. Consider, say, South Australia (which is a 'state' in the somewhat different sense of a constituent state of a federation, rather than on the international legal definition of the word) or Scotland (which is a 'country' in the sense of a historically distinctive part of the United Kingdom). What these entities lack is the fourth criterion: independence.

## 5.2.1.2   The criterion of independence

Independence (or, in the formulation from the *Montevideo Convention*, the 'capacity to enter into relations with the other states')[13] is the 'central criterion for statehood'.[14] The word was

---

6       Krystyna Marek, *Identity and Continuity of States in Public International Law* (Librairie Droz, 2nd ed, 1968) 73–125, 189; Crawford (n 2) 688–90.

7       Marek (n 6) 188.

8       *Somalia v Woodhouse, Drake & Carey (Suisse) SA* (1992) 94 ILR 609, 619 (High Court England and Wales, Queen's Bench).

9       US Department of State, 'Somalia President Hassan Sheikh Mohamud's Visit to Washington, DC' (Press Release, 17 January 2013). See also SC Res 2067, UN Doc S/RES/2067 (18 September 2012).

10      John Dugard, *The Secession of States and Their Recognition in the Wake of Kosovo* (Hague Academy of International Law, 2013) 60.

11      Vaughan Lowe, *International Law* (Oxford University Press, 2007) 165.

12      *Yugoslavia Peace Conference Opinion No 1* (1991) 92 ILR 162, 164–5; *Yugoslavia Peace Conference Opinion No 8* (1992) 92 ILR 199, 201–2.

13      *Montevideo Convention* (n 4) art 1(d).

14      Crawford (n 2) 62; see further 63–89.

defined in a related context by Judge Anzilotti in the advisory opinion *Customs Régime between Germany and Austria* in 1931.[15] The case concerned whether a proposed customs union with Germany was compatible with art 88 of the *Treaty of Saint-Germain* of 1919, which provided that the 'independence of Austria is inalienable otherwise than with the consent of the League of Nations'.[16] Judge Anzilotti remarked in his separate opinion:

> [T]he independence of Austria within the meaning of Article 88 is nothing else but the existence of Austria, within the frontiers laid down by the *Treaty of Saint-Germain*, as a separate State and not subject to the authority of any other State or group of States. Independence as thus understood is really no more than the normal condition of States according to international law; it may also be described as *sovereignty* (*suprema potestas*), or *external sovereignty*, by which is meant that the State has over it no other authority than that of international law . . .
>
> It follows that the legal conception of independence has nothing to do with a State's subordination to international law or with the numerous and constantly increasing states of *de facto* dependence which characterize the relation of one country to other countries.
>
> It also follows that the restrictions upon a State's liberty, whether arising out of ordinary international law or contractual engagements, do not as such in the least affect its independence. As long as these restrictions do not place the State under the legal authority of another State, the former remains an independent State however extensive and burdensome those obligations may be.[17]

This definition essentially sums up the meaning of independence in the context of the criteria. As Stefan Talmon articulates the criterion, it refers 'to *legal* independence; that is, the State must only be subject to international law, not to the laws of any other State'.[18] James Crawford has concluded that 'independence for the purposes of statehood should be presumed where an entity is formally independent' but that 'where formal independence masks a lack of any actual independence at all, the entity should be regarded as not independent'.[19]

Sections 5.2.3 and 5.3.1.2 will illustrate how the criterion of independence operates in distinctive scenarios involving unlawfulness or self-determination. What follows in Section 5.2.1.3 is a discussion of how it operated in one situation without those distinctive features: Australia.

## 5.2.1.3  The example of Australia

The Commonwealth of Australia was created by the federation of six British colonies in 1901.[20] That is not, however, the date at which Australia became a state in international law. Although it clearly met the criteria of population, territory and government, it was not yet independent; it was merely a self-governing dominion within the British Empire. Alison Pert explains:

---

15    *Customs Régime between Germany and Austria (Advisory Opinion)* [1931] PCIJ (ser A/B) No 41.
16    Ibid 42–4.
17    Ibid 57–8.
18    Stefan Talmon, 'The Constitutive versus the Declaratory Theory of Recognition: *Tertium Non Datur?*' (2005) 75 *British Yearbook of International Law* 101, 110 (emphasis in original).
19    Crawford (n 2) 88–9.
20    *Commonwealth of Australia Constitution Act 1900* (UK).

First, the Imperial Parliament retained the power to legislate for the whole Empire and any colonial legislation repugnant to an Imperial Act was void. Indeed, self-government could be withdrawn at any time if the Imperial Parliament so decided ... Secondly, the Judicial Committee of the Privy Council [of the United Kingdom], rather than an Australian court, was the final court of appeal in many matters. Thirdly, the [Australian] *Constitution* was itself an Imperial Act and while it could be amended by Australia in accordance with its terms, the Imperial Parliament retained at least the theoretical power to amend or repeal it. Fourthly, and of more practical significance, Australia had no power in its own right to enter into treaties with foreign states ... Thus its international relations, and therefore its foreign policy, were largely controlled by the Imperial government.[21]

The difficulty with Australia's legal history is that these things changed by degrees and at different times, such that it is far from obvious precisely when Australia qualified as a state.

In 1919, Australia – along with its fellow dominions of Canada, New Zealand and South Africa – was a signatory in its own right of the peace treaty with Germany made at Versailles and also became a member in its own right of the new League of Nations.[22] The High Court of Australia has suggested that Australia 'had assumed international personality' by 1919.[23] But that may not necessarily imply statehood; there are many cases of colonies or constituent parts of states acquiring a degree of international legal personality, in particular under treaties.[24] Thus British India, which was very much a colony, also had separate membership of the League.

In 1923, an Imperial Conference stated, among other things, that the 'ratification of treaties imposing obligations on one part of the Empire is effected at the instance of the government of that part'.[25] Alison Pert comments that, even if this fell short of 'fully sovereign, independent statehood', it was enough to enable Australia 'to act autonomously on the international plane, and to be treated by the international community, as if it were a fully independent state'.[26]

In 1926, a further Imperial Conference issued a report (sometimes called the Balfour Report) that began by referring to 'the group of self-governing communities composed of Great Britain and the Dominions' and by declaring them to be 'autonomous Communities within the British Empire, equal in status, in no way subordinate one to another in any aspect of their domestic or external affairs, though united by a common allegiance to the Crown, and freely associated as members of the British Commonwealth of Nations'.[27] Although this equality had, 'as regards all vital matters, reached its full development', the report noted that 'administrative, legislative, and judicial' formalities of domestic law were 'not wholly in accord'

21    Alison Pert, 'The Development of Australia's International Legal Personality' (2017) 34 *Australian Year Book of International Law* 149, 160–1.
22    *Treaty of Peace between the Allied and Associated Powers and Germany*, signed 28 June 1919, 225 CTS 188 (entered into force 10 January 1920) (commonly known as the *Treaty of Versailles*); *Covenant of the League of Nations*.
23    *Victoria v Commonwealth* (1996) 187 CLR 416, 477 [12].
24    See further Rowan Nicholson, *Statehood and the State-Like in International Law* (Oxford University Press, 2019) 195–201.
25    See JG Latham, *Australia and the British Commonwealth* (Macmillan, 1929) 131–3.
26    Pert (n 21) 189.
27    'Report of Inter-Imperial Relations Committee of the Imperial Conference, 1926' (18 November 1926) (1927) 21(S) *American Journal of International Law* 21, 21.

with it, because most of them dated 'back to a time well antecedent to the present stage' of development.[28] In other words, the formalities had not kept pace with the convention that the dominions were independent.

From 1931, the *Statute of Westminster 1931* (UK) in some respects formalised the equality that the Imperial Conferences had declared.[29] Along with legislation from as late as 1986 that further tidied up links with the United Kingdom, it is important to Australian constitutional law.[30]

In sum, the equality between Australia and its parent state was established as a convention between the two entities in the period 1919–26 and formalised in legislation from 1931 onward. It has been suggested that international law, unlike domestic law, has no reason to insist on legislative formalities when the position is already clear as a matter of substance.[31] On that view, Australia met the criterion of independence and became a state at the latest by 1926.

## 5.2.2   The role of recognition

The role of the statehood criteria cannot be fully understood without reference to the next factor: recognition. The word 'recognition' has multiple meanings. Most importantly, it refers to recognition as a state, which, subject to some scholarly controversy, is significant in various ways and may be decisive in special situations. The word may also refer to recognition as a government, which will also be covered here to clarify the distinction between states and governments.

### 5.2.2.1   Recognition as a state

Recognition as a state is an act by which an existing state acknowledges or asserts that another entity also qualifies as a state.[32] Existing states may disagree with each other about whether to recognise an entity. For example, the majority of states recognise Palestine as a state; other states, including Australia, do not.[33] Recognition may take the form of, among other things, an explicit spoken or written declaration, a message of congratulations on independence, a decision to accredit diplomats, or even a treaty provision.[34] There has been some debate about whether admission to the United Nations amounts to recognition by each existing member state, but the dominant view is that it does not and that UN membership is technically distinct from both statehood and recognition.[35]

The following discussion will mainly relate to the scholarly controversy about how recognition fits into the law of statehood. But a preliminary point is that acts of recognition may be

---

28      Ibid 21, 23.

29      This was not formally adopted by Australia until the enactment of the *Statute of Westminster Adoption Act 1942* (Cth), which had retroactive effect from the date Australia entered World War II.

30      *Australia Act 1986* (Cth).

31      Crawford (n 2) 363; see further 358–66.

32      See further Victor Rodríguez Cedeño, Special Rapporteur, 'Sixth Report on Unilateral Acts of States' [2003] II(1) *Yearbook of the International Law Commission* 1, 53 [67].

33      See further Security Council, *Report of the Committee on the Admission of New Members concerning the Application of Palestine for Admission to Membership in the United Nations*, UN Doc S/2011/705 (11 November 2011).

34      Przemysław Saganek, *Unilateral Acts of States in International Law* (Brill, 2016) 551–8.

35      David Raič, *Statehood and the Law of Self-Determination* (Kluwer, 2002) 45–7.

significant in several ways regardless of what position is taken in that controversy. First, recognition may provide evidence that an entity meets the statehood criteria, especially if the recognising state cites the criteria to justify recognition. For example, when Australia recognised Kosovo in 2008, it affirmed that the criteria were 'a permanent population, a defined territory, a capacity for effective government and a capacity to have relations with other [states]' and that 'these criteria are met in the case of Kosovo'.[36] Second, an entity may not enjoy the benefits of statehood in practice if other states refuse to recognise and engage with it as a state. It will have no partners with which to make treaties or to exchange diplomatic representatives and will not be welcomed into international organisations.[37] An example of a state that was ostracised like this is Haiti, which was established in 1804 by former slaves who had revolted against France. The United Kingdom refused to recognise Haiti until 1825, France until 1838, and the United States until the 1860s.[38] Third, recognition may have significance in the domestic law of recognising states. For example, a recognised state may be able to own property and to sue or be sued in domestic courts.

The controversy is about whether, in addition, recognition affects which entities qualify as states in the first place. In particular, it is about how recognition interacts with the criteria. There are two traditional theories – 'constitutive' and 'declaratory' – and there are also hybrid views.[39]

The traditional constitutive theory is nowadays rejected by most international lawyers but is of historical interest. It claimed that recognition by other states was what 'constituted' an entity as a state; that is to say, recognition was necessary and sufficient for statehood. If this were correct, it would transform the statehood criteria into a mere optional standard. Existing states might *choose* to recognise entities based on whether they met the criteria. In principle, however, each state could decide for itself 'not only whether or not a given community fulfils the requirements of international existence' but also 'what those requirements are'.[40] One reason most international lawyers reject this view is its destabilising theoretical implications. If international law could never apply between any given pair of states unless that pair of states recognised each other, then it would not be a single, universal legal system. It would be a network of bilateral contracts by which a pair of states agreed to apply certain rules relative to each other.[41] Another reason for rejecting this theory is that it sits uneasily with state practice and *opinio juris*, especially with instances in which a state treats an entity as a state despite not recognising that entity. For example, in 1968, the United States accused North Korea of breaching international law by attacking a US naval vessel, the *Pueblo*, even though it did not recognise North Korea.[42]

---

36    Stephen Smith, Minister for Foreign Affairs, 18 February 2008, speech extracted in 'Australian Practice in International Law' (2010) 29 *Australian Year Book of International Law* 307, 315 ('Kosovo').

37    Thomas Grant, *The Recognition of States: Law and Practice in Debate and Evolution* (Praeger, 1999) 24.

38    Charles Wesley, 'The Struggle for the Recognition of Haiti and Liberia as Independent Republics' (1917) 2(4) *Journal of Negro History* 369, 376.

39    Generally on theories of recognition, see Nicholson, *Statehood and the State-Like* (n 24) ch 3.

40    James Lorimer, *The Institutes of the Law of Nations: A Treatise of the Jural Relations of Separate Political Communities* (Blackwood & Sons, 1883–84) 107.

41    See, eg, Hersch Lauterpacht, *Recognition in International Law* (Cambridge University Press, 2013) 78. The book was first published in 1947.

42    UN SCOR, 23rd sess, 1388th mtg, UN Doc S/PV.1388 (26 January 1968); 'The Crisis in Korea' (1968) 58 *US Department of State Bulletin* 189.

The traditional declaratory theory is at the opposite extreme. It claims that meeting the statehood criteria is necessary and sufficient for an entity to qualify as a state. If the entity is recognised, then the act of recognition merely 'declares' that it has a status that it already has anyway by operation of the criteria. Recognition functions mainly as a political rather than a legal act.[43] In short, it is not necessary, though it is still significant in the ways mentioned earlier.

It is also possible to take a hybrid view that is basically declaratory but that moderates the traditional declaratory theory by acknowledging two special situations. In these situations, recognition may create duties and other legal consequences for the recognising state.[44]

One special situation is where an entity that fails the statehood criteria is recognised by some states but not all states. Since the entity does not have the rights and duties of a state relative to non-recognising states, the entity cannot be a state in a full sense. But it functions as a state relative to recognising states and, as a result of that recognition, within certain international organisations or treaty regimes.[45] This is arguably true of Palestine. Although Palestine has purported to be a state since 1988, whether it meets the criteria is open to doubt given the control exercised by Israel over its claimed territory.[46] But regardless of whether or not Palestine is a state on the basis of the criteria, at a minimum it functions as a state in particular legal contexts on the basis of recognition. For example, a majority of states in the UN General Assembly recognise Palestine, with the result that the General Assembly treats it as a 'non-member observer State'.[47]

In the other special situation, an entity that fails the criteria is recognised by all states. Since that makes it functionally equivalent to an entity that meets the criteria, it can meaningfully be described as a state. This is relevant to how Somalia could have continued to qualify as a state regardless of whether or not, in the 1990s, it ceased to meet the criterion of having a government (see Section 5.2.1.1). Somalia has been described as 'a nail in the coffin of the [traditional] declaratory theory'.[48] It can readily be explained, however, on the basis that ongoing recognition by all states was an alternative means of legally sustaining its statehood.

These two situations are rare, because in most cases recognition of an entity that does not already have statehood is a breach of the ostensible parent state's territorial integrity or a breach of the collective duty of non-recognition (discussed in Section 5.2.3) and, being unlawful, cannot have the consequences just described.[49]

The key points are as follows. International lawyers mostly reject the traditional constitutive theory and agree that recognition is merely declaratory – meaning it is not necessary for statehood, which depends instead on the statehood criteria. But it is still significant. It may

---

43    See *Yugoslavia Peace Conference Opinion No 10* (1992) 92 ILR 206, 208.
44    Nicholson, *Statehood and the State-Like* (n 24) especially 127–45. See also Crawford (n 2) 93.
45    Nicholson, *Statehood and the State-Like* (n 24) 143–5.
46    *Letter of 18 November 1988 from the Permanent Representative of Jordan to the United Nations*, UN Doc A/43/827 (18 November 1988) annex III (*'Declaration of Independence of Palestine'*); Security Council, *Report of the Committee on the Admission of New Members concerning the Application of Palestine*, UN Doc S/2011/705 (11 November 2011).
47    *Status of Palestine in the United Nations*, GA Res 67/19, UN Doc A/RES/67/19 (4 December 2012, adopted 29 November 2012).
48    Gerard Kreijen, *State Failure, Sovereignty and Effectiveness: Legal Lessons from the Decolonization of Sub-Saharan Africa* (Nijhoff, 2004) 355.
49    Nicholson, *Statehood and the State-Like* (n 24) 146–65.

be evidence of the criteria, may be a precondition for participating in treaties or other aspects of international life, and may have domestic legal significance. Further, on a hybrid view, recognition may have legal consequences for the recognising state in the two special situations described in this section.

### 5.2.2.2   Recognition as a government

A state acts through its government; conduct by its government is attributable to it under the law of state responsibility.[50] If a state holds an election, the identity of its government may change. If it adopts a new constitution or experiences a revolution or coup, it may even change the form of its government. But this does not affect the legal continuity of the state. It follows that recognising a new government of an existing state is very different from recognising a new state.[51]

Recognition as a government is also a more settled legal issue. The seminal case is *Tinoco*.[52] A former military government of Costa Rica had granted oil concessions to a British company. The United Kingdom had not recognised that government but argued that the concessions were nonetheless valid. The arbitrator indicated that the standard for the existence of a government is '*de facto* sovereignty and complete governmental control'.[53] Where non-recognition is based on a failure to meet that standard, it may be evidence of the non-existence of a government. But where non-recognition is based instead on 'illegitimacy or irregularity of origin' (as where a state refuses to recognise a government that came to power in a military coup), it loses 'evidential weight'.[54] In this case, it could not outweigh evidence that the military government met the standard.

Since governments exist anyway without recognition, and since recognising a government that is seen as having an illegitimate origin may be misinterpreted as a gesture of support, some states have indicated that they will no longer formally recognise governments at all. This is sometimes called the 'Estrada doctrine' after the Mexican secretary for foreign affairs who enunciated it in 1930.[55] For example, in 1988, Australia indicated that it would simply 'conduct relations with new regimes to the extent and in the manner which may be required in the circumstances of each case'.[56]

There is some potential for confusion between recognition as a state and recognition as a government. This is illustrated by the complex dispute about Taiwan.

The dispute began between two rival governments of China. After the Chinese Civil War ended in 1949, a new communist government (the People's Republic of China) controlled mainland China, but the old nationalist government (the Republic of China) controlled the

---

50    *Responsibility of States for Internationally Wrongful Acts*, GA Res 56/83, UN Doc A/RES/56/83 (28 January 2002, adopted 12 December 2001) annex ('*Responsibility of States for Internationally Wrongful Acts*') arts 4–11 ('*ARSIWA*').

51    See generally MJ Peterson, *Recognition of Governments: Legal Doctrine and State Practice, 1815–1995* (Palgrave Macmillan, 1997); Stefan Talmon, *Recognition of Governments in International Law with Particular Reference to Governments in Exile* (Oxford University Press, 1998).

52    *Tinoco (Great Britain v Costa Rica)* (1923) 1 RIAA 369.

53    Ibid 381.

54    Ibid.

55    Peterson (n 51) 37–8, 88.

56    Bill Hayden, Minister for Foreign Affairs and Trade, quoted in 'Recognition of Governments: Change in Australian Policy' (1987) 11 *Australian Year Book of International Law* 205, 357.

island of Taiwan.[57] Each side claimed to be, legally, the sole government of the single state of China. Many states – primarily on the side of the West in the Cold War – were slow to recognise the People's Republic of China, but in 1971 the General Assembly declared that it was now 'the only legitimate representative of China to the United Nations'.[58] For practical purposes, Taiwan as governed by the Republic of China has functioned for several decades like a separate state, with its own population, territory and government. Its claims about whether it is a separate state or just a rival government of the single state of China have also become more ambiguous.[59] Nonetheless, it has never formally and explicitly declared that it is independent of the rest of China.

Even if Taiwan is merely a part of the state of China with a separate government, that does not mean it cannot act on the world stage. It was observed earlier that constituent parts of states can acquire a degree of personality, in particular under treaties (see Section 5.2.1.3). Taiwan has joined bodies such as the World Trade Organization on terms that are vague about its status; there, it is known as the 'Separate Customs Territory of Taiwan, Penghu, Kinmen and Matsu'. Moreover, some scholars have argued that, even if Taiwan is a part of China, the People's Republic of China may be prohibited from using force against it by provisions of the *Charter of the United Nations* ('*UN Charter*') that require states to seek peaceful solutions to disputes (as distinct from the prohibition on using force against a foreign state).[60]

## 5.2.3   The role of unlawfulness

It has been seen that, generally, an entity qualifies as a state if it meets the statehood criteria. But if the entity emerges in circumstances that are tainted by unlawfulness, that raises the issue of whether the unlawfulness creates an exception to the criteria, precluding statehood.[61] This section of the chapter will cover three topics: unilateral secession, which does not in itself create an exception to the criteria; the emergence of an entity due to a use of force by an existing state, which does; and breaches of other peremptory norms, such as the prohibition of racial discrimination.

### 5.2.3.1   Entities created by unilateral secession

Unilateral secession is the acquisition of statehood by an entity whose territory was previously part of an existing state without that parent state's consent. For example, in the late 18th and early 19th centuries – a period of rising nationalism in Europe and the Americas – many entities seceded unilaterally, including Greece from the Ottoman Empire, Belgium from the

---

57    See generally Frank Chiang, *The One-China Policy: State, Sovereignty, and Taiwan's International Legal Status* (Elsevier, 2018).

58    *Restoration of the Lawful Rights of the People's Republic of China in the United Nations*, GA Res 2758 (XXVI), UN Doc A/RES/2758(XXVI) (25 October 1971).

59    See, eg, Republic of China (Taiwan), Mainland Affairs Council, 'The Official Position of the Republic of China (Taiwan) on the People's Republic of China's Anti-Secession (Anti-Separation) Law' (29 March 2005).

60    Christine Gray, *International Law and the Use of Force* (Oxford University Press, 4th ed, 2018) 74, citing *Charter of the United Nations* art 2(3) ('*UN Charter*'); Crawford (n 2) 220–1, citing *UN Charter* art 33.

61    This reflects the principle *ex injuria jus non oritur* (no law arises from unlawfulness).

Netherlands, and several Latin American republics from Spain.[62] Recent examples are scarce but arguably include the unilateral secession of Slovenia from Yugoslavia in October 1991, when Yugoslavia had not yet ceased to exist as a state.[63] One reason recent examples are scarce is that an entity sometimes begins by attempting to secede unilaterally but instead, at the end of a conflict, attains statehood with the parent state's consent. For instance, Sudan eventually consented to the secession of South Sudan in 2011.[64] Another reason is that true unilateral secession is extremely difficult, because the parent state often resists with military force, which may prevent a secessionist entity from demonstrating that it meets the criteria and in particular the criterion of independence.

Taking certain steps towards unilateral secession may involve crimes in domestic law, such as sedition. Whether taking those steps is unlawful in international law is a separate question. In 2008, a majority of the Assembly of Kosovo unilaterally declared Kosovo to be independent from Serbia, and some states argued that such a declaration was prohibited in international law by the principle of territorial integrity.[65] In the *Kosovo* advisory opinion, the International Court of Justice ('ICJ') recalled 'that the principle of territorial integrity is an important part of the international legal order and is enshrined in the *Charter of the United Nations*', but it added that 'the scope of the principle of territorial integrity is confined to the sphere of relations between States'.[66] This broad statement suggests that, when an entity is trying to secede and does not yet qualify as a state, the entity and any individuals associated with it are not yet bound by the principle of territorial integrity, which means that the principle does not prohibit actions such as a unilateral declaration of independence. There may not necessarily be an issue of unlawfulness at the international level.

There are caveats to this. Although a unilaterally seceding entity may not have a specific legal duty to respect its parent state's territorial integrity, other existing states do. That duty prohibits them from recognising the entity as a state before it has acquired statehood (what is known as 'premature recognition').[67] For example, in 1967–70, five states recognised Biafra, a part of Nigeria that tried unsuccessfully to secede, and those recognitions were described as premature and therefore unlawful.[68] In addition, the ICJ indicated in *Kosovo* that, though unilaterally declaring independence is not in itself unlawful, it may be connected with other conduct that *is* unlawful:

> Several participants have invoked resolutions of the Security Council condemning particular declarations of independence: see, *inter alia*, Security Council resolutions 216

62    On these and other examples, see further Mikulas Fabry, *Recognizing States: International Society and the Establishment of New States since 1776* (Oxford University Press, 2010) chs 1–3.
63    *Yugoslavia Peace Conference Opinion No 11* (1993) 96 ILR 719, [4]. In the case of other successor states of Yugoslavia, the exact date of the acquisition of statehood involves more complexity and controversy.
64    Jure Vidmar, 'Explaining the Legal Effects of Recognition' (2012) 61(2) *International and Comparative Law Quarterly* 361, 368–70.
65    *Accordance with International Law of the Unilateral Declaration of Independence in Respect of Kosovo (Advisory Opinion)* [2010] ICJ Rep 403, 434–5 [74]–[77], 437 [80] ('*Kosovo*').
66    Ibid 437 [80].
67    Lauterpacht (n 41) 8. See also Christian Tomuschat, 'Recognition of New States: The Case of Premature Recognition' in Peter Hipold (ed), *Kosovo and International Law: The ICJ Advisory Opinion of 22 July 2010* (Nijhoff, 2012) 31, 35.
68    David Ijalaye, 'Was "Biafra" at Any Time a State in International Law?' (1971) 65 *American Journal of International Law* 551, 558–9.

(1965) and 217 (1965), concerning Southern Rhodesia; Security Council resolution 541 (1983), concerning northern Cyprus; and Security Council resolution 787 (1992), concerning the Republika Srpska.

    The Court notes, however, that in all of those instances the Security Council was making a determination as regards the concrete situation existing at the time that those declarations of independence were made; the illegality attached to the declarations of independence thus stemmed not from the unilateral character of these declarations as such, but from the fact that they were, or would have been, connected with the unlawful use of force or other egregious violations of norms of general international law, in particular those of a peremptory character (*jus cogens*). In the context of Kosovo, the Security Council has never taken this position. The exceptional character of the resolutions enumerated above appears to the Court to confirm that no general prohibition against unilateral declarations of independence may be inferred from the practice of the Security Council.[69]

Exceptional cases such as Northern Cyprus, Republika Srpska, and Rhodesia will be discussed in the sections of that follow.

## 5.2.3.2   Entities created by force

The duty to respect territorial integrity, in a broad sense, dates back many centuries.[70] Today, states also have the more specific duty, reflected in the *UN Charter*, to refrain 'from the threat or use of force against the territorial integrity or political independence of any state'.[71] This is a peremptory norm of customary international law (*jus cogens*).[72] It is relevant in the scenario where one state uses force against another state and an entity makes an attempt to secede from the latter state that is facilitated by the use of force. For example, in 1974, Turkey occupied the northern part of Cyprus by force; in 1983, with Turkey's support, an entity calling itself the Turkish Republic of Northern Cyprus purported to secede unilaterally.[73] This scenario raises three issues.

    First, in this scenario involving force, states have a collective duty not to recognise the entity as a state. This duty of non-recognition arises under customary international law and is codified in *Articles on Responsibility of States for Internationally Wrongful Acts*:

> **Article 40. Application of this chapter**
> 1.   This chapter applies to the international responsibility which is entailed by a serious breach by a State of an obligation arising under a peremptory norm of general international law.

---

69    *Kosovo* (n 65) 437–8 [81].

70    See, eg, Emer de Vattel, *The Law of Nations*, tr TJ Hochstrasser (Liberty Fund, 2008) pt II.93 [trans of: *Le Droit des Gens* (1758)].

71    *UN Charter* art 2(4). See further Chapter 8.

72    *Military and Paramilitary Activities in and against Nicaragua (Nicaragua v United States of America) (Merits)* [1986] ICJ Rep 14, 100–1 [190]; 'Draft Articles on Responsibility of States for Internationally Wrongful Acts, with Commentaries' (2001) II(2) *Yearbook of the International Law Commission* 1, 112 (Draft Article 40 Commentary [4]). See further Chapter 2.

73    See Crawford (n 2) 143–7.

2.   A breach of such an obligation is serious if it involves a gross or systematic failure by the responsible State to fulfil the obligation.

***Article 41. Particular consequences of a serious breach of an obligation under this chapter***

. . .

2.   No State shall recognize as lawful a situation created by a serious breach within the meaning of article 40, nor render aid or assistance in maintaining that situation.[74]

The Security Council may also call on states not to recognise an entity created by force, as it did with Northern Cyprus.[75] In any case, since statehood generally depends on the statehood criteria rather than recognition, non-recognition may not necessarily indicate a lack of statehood.

Second, an entity cannot meet the criteria if it is not sufficiently independent of the state whose use of force facilitated its attempt at secession. A classic example is Manchukuo, which purported to secede unilaterally from China in 1931 and which most states refused to recognise.[76] According to a League of Nations report, the 'Manchurian independence movement' was able to succeed only 'owing to the presence of Japanese troops'; moreover, political authority in the territory remained 'in the hands of Japanese officials and advisors'.[77] Similarly, the European Court of Human Rights observed in a 2001 decision that Turkey retained 'effective overall control over northern Cyprus'.[78] There is 'a presumption against the independence of entities created by the use of force or during a period of belligerent occupation'.[79]

Third, even if the entity were able to meet the criteria, it still might not qualify as a state.[80] The customary rule that a state cannot acquire territory by the use of force (discussed in Section 5.4.2.1) might be undermined if a state could achieve that outcome informally or indirectly by facilitating the creation of a friendly new state. By way of illustration, in 2014, facilitated by Russia, an entity calling itself the Republic of Crimea purported to secede unilaterally from Ukraine; two days later, it signed a treaty with Russia in which it agreed to Russian annexation.[81] The General Assembly denied that the status of Crimea had changed and called on 'all States' – necessarily including Russia – to desist from 'attempts to modify Ukraine's borders through the threat or use of force'.[82] This hints that Russia's use of force was enough to invalidate the purported secession and hence that, where an entity emerges due to such a use of force, it is not a state regardless of whether it meets the statehood criteria – in other

74    *ARSIWA* (n 50) arts 40–41. See further Chapter 7.
75    SC Res 541, UN Doc S/RES/541 (18 November 1983).
76    See, notably, Henry Stimson, 'Letter to William Forbes, 7 January 1932' in *Foreign Relations of the United States: Japan, 1931–1941* (US GPO, 1943) vol 1, 76 (the 'Stimson doctrine').
77    'Report Provided for in Article 15(4) of the Covenant on Manchuria' (1933) 112 *League of Nations Official Journal Special Supplement* 56, 72.
78    *Cyprus v Turkey* (2001) 120 ILR 11, [77] (European Court of Human Rights).
79    Crawford (n 2) 132–3.
80    Ibid 131–48; Nicholson, *Statehood and the State-Like* (n 24) 165–8.
81    Thomas Grant, *Aggression against Ukraine: Territory, Responsibility, and International Law* (Palgrave Macmillan, 2015) 13–21.
82    *Territorial Integrity of Ukraine*, GA Res 68/262, UN Doc A/RES/68/262 (adopted 27 March 2014).

words, that there is an exception to the criteria. A possible exception to this exception, illustrated by Bangladesh, will be discussed in Section 5.3.1.2.

### 5.2.3.3  Entities created by breaches of other peremptory norms

The same reasoning might be applied to entities created by breaches of other peremptory norms. Possible examples are, however, rare and idiosyncratic. In one instance, between 1976 and 1981, South Africa purported to transform four parts of its territory, known as Bantustans, into new states: Transkei, Bophuthatswana, Venda and Ciskei.[83] Supposedly, these were homelands for parts of South Africa's black population; in reality, they were a way of pursuing the racially discriminatory policy known as apartheid.[84] The prohibition of racial discrimination is a peremptory norm.[85] In another instance, in 1992, ethnic Serbs unilaterally created an ostensible new state, Republika Srpska, out of part of Bosnia.[86] Bosnia later argued that this entity

> came about as a result ... of the genocidal practice of ethnic cleansing. As the United Nations Security Council has made clear in numerous other cases, the creation or maintenance of an entity purporting to be a state in violation of the prohibition of the use of force, or all other rules of *jus cogens*, such as the prohibition of apartheid, and it is submitted, the obligation not to perpetrate genocide, cannot have legal consequences.[87]

The Bantustans and Republika Srpska raise the same issues as cases involving the use of force. First, other states have a collective duty not to recognise a situation created by a serious breach of a peremptory norm. Second, it is doubtful whether the entities were independent of, respectively, South Africa and Serbia-Montenegro.[88] Finally, it is plausible that, in any event, an entity created by a breach of a peremptory norm such as the prohibition of racial discrimination or genocide cannot qualify as a state even if meets the statehood criteria.

The next section will discuss how another norm that has been described as peremptory,[89] self-determination, can actually enable the creation of a state in some circumstances.

---

83    John Dugard, *Recognition and the United Nations* (Grotius, 1987) 98–108.

84    See, among other resolutions, *Establishment of Bantustans*, GA Res 2775 (XXVI)[E], UN Doc A/RES/
      2775(XXVI) (29 November 1971).

85    'Draft Articles on Responsibility of States for Internationally Wrongful Acts, with Commentaries' (n 72)
      112–13 (Draft Article 40 Commentary [4]).

86    *Application of the Convention on the Prevention and Punishment of the Crime of Genocide (Bosnia
      and Herzegovina v Serbia and Montenegro) (Judgment)* [2007] ICJ Rep 43, 138 [233] ('*Genocide*').

87    'Memorial of Bosnia', *Application of the Convention on the Prevention and Punishment of the Crime of
      Genocide (Bosnia and Herzegovina v Serbia and Montenegro)* (International Court of Justice, General
      List No 91, 15 April 1994) 263–4 [6.3.2.8]. See also Martin Dawidowicz, 'The Obligation of Non-
      Recognition of an Unlawful Situation' in James Crawford, Alain Pellet and Simon Olleson (eds), *The Law
      of International Responsibility* (Oxford University Press, 2010) 677, 683.

88    *Prosecutor v Tadić (Appeal against Conviction)* (1999) 124 ILR 61, [160]. Cf *Genocide* case (n 86) 202–6
      [385]–[395]. Serbia-Montenegro officially called itself Yugoslavia until 2003. Serbia and Montenegro
      became separate states in 2006.

89    'Draft Articles on Responsibility of States for Internationally Wrongful Acts, with Commentaries' (n 72) 85
      (Draft Article 26 Commentary [5]).

# 5.3   Self-determination

In the early 20th century, the notion of the self-determination of peoples was invoked by two figures writing from different political perspectives: the revolutionary Russian leader Vladimir Lenin and US president Woodrow Wilson.[90] Despite differences, both argued that a people was entitled to exercise its free will over certain questions, including whether to create a state of its own rather than being ruled by others.[91] For a long time, this was primarily a political aspiration rather than a legal principle.[92] Today, however, it is a principle of international law, reflected in the *UN Charter*, human rights treaties, and General Assembly declarations.[93]

A difficulty that international law has not fully resolved is how to determine when a group of individuals with a shared identity qualifies as a 'people'. The difficulty is illustrated by the 'onion problem' of the former state of Yugoslavia.[94] The outermost layer of the onion was the people of Yugoslavia as a whole, defined as the people of an existing state or by a degree of common history; next were the peoples of its constituent republics, including Slovenia, Croatia, Bosnia and Serbia; and then there were the minorities within each republic, such as the ethnic Serbs within Bosnia who tried to create a new state of their own. Any of these units might plausibly be considered a people, but if they were all considered peoples then their entitlements to self-determination would be in conflict. Such attempts as have been made to specify general characteristics of peoples, such as a 'racial or ethnic identity' or 'the conscious-ness of being a people', have often been imprecise.[95] The African Commission on Human and Peoples' Rights has defined 'peoples' for its own purposes as 'any groups or communities of people that have an identifiable interest in common, whether this is from the sharing of an ethnic, linguistic or other factor', and has clarified that they are 'not to be equated solely with nations or states'.[96]

Instead of fully resolving the difficulty, international law has largely sidestepped it. Self-determination has a variety of legal manifestations that apply to specific categories of peoples,

90      See especially Vladimir Lenin, 'The Socialist Revolution and the Right of Nations to Self-Determination' in
        *Collected Works* (Lawrence & Wishart, 1964) vol 22, 143 (essay first published in 1916); Woodrow
        Wilson, *Address of the President of the United States, Delivered at a Joint Session of the Two Houses of
        Congress, January 8, 1918* (US GPO, 1918) (the 'Fourteen Points').
91      Antonio Cassese, *Self-Determination of Peoples: A Legal Reappraisal* (Cambridge University Press, 1995)
        14–20.
92      'Report of the International Committee of Jurists upon the Legal Aspects of the Aaland Islands Question'
        (1920) 3 *League of Nations Official Journal Special Supplement* 3, 5–6.
93      See, eg, *International Covenant on Economic, Social and Cultural Rights*, opened for signature
        16 December 1966, 993 UNTS 3 (entered into force 3 January 1976) art 1(1) ('*ICESCR*'); *International
        Covenant on Civil and Political Rights*, opened for signature 16 December 1966, 999 UNTS 1 (entered
        into force 23 March 1976) art 1(1) ('*ICCPR*').
94      Martti Koskenniemi, 'National Self-Determination Today: Problems of Legal Theory and Practice' (1994)
        43(2) *International and Comparative Law Quarterly* 241, 260.
95      These are among the characteristics that a group of experts identified as 'inherent in a description (but
        not a definition)' of a people, in International Meeting of Experts on Further Study of the Concept of the
        Rights of Peoples, *Final Report and Recommendations*, UNESCO Doc SHS-89/CONF.602/7 (22
        February 1990).
96      African Union, African Commission on Human and Peoples' Rights, *Principles and Guidelines on the
        Implementation of Economic, Social and Cultural Rights in the African Charter on Human and
        Peoples' Rights* (24 October 2011) guideline 1(c).

and international law provides definitions of some of those categories. This is true in particular of the most important manifestation: external self-determination.

## 5.3.1    The right to external self-determination

The evolution of the law of self-determination was driven by the movement for European colonial powers – including the United Kingdom, France and Portugal – to grant independence to their colonies in Africa, Asia and elsewhere.[97] In 1960, the General Assembly issued the *Declaration on the Granting of Independence to Colonial Countries and Peoples*, which reflects customary international law[98] and provides in part:

1.   The subjection of peoples to alien subjugation, domination and exploitation consti-
     tutes a denial of fundamental human rights, is contrary to the *Charter of the United
     Nations* and is an impediment to the promotion of world peace and co-operation.
2.   All peoples have the right to self-determination; by virtue of that right they freely
     determine their political status and freely pursue their economic, social and
     cultural development.

  . . .

5.   Immediate steps shall be taken, in Trust and Non-Self-Governing Territories or all
     other territories which have not yet attained independence, to transfer all powers to
     the peoples of those territories, without any conditions or reservations, in accordance
     with their freely expressed will and desire, without any distinction as to race, creed or
     colour, in order to enable them to enjoy complete independence and freedom.[99]

'External' self-determination (as distinct from other manifestations of self-determination) is the right by which certain peoples, primarily colonised peoples, can choose to become independent.[100]

### 5.3.1.1    The scope of the right to external self-determination

Three issues require discussion here: the meaning of 'external', the categories of peoples entitled to this type of self-determination, and the scope of the relevant international legal duty.

On the first issue, this type of self-determination is external in that it entitles peoples to exercise free will over their status relative to the outside world. Typically, a people expresses its choice about that status through a vote (a plebiscite or referendum) or another consultation process – though the ICJ noted in *Western Sahara* that sometimes a consultation may be 'totally unnecessary, in view of special circumstances'.[101] Another General Assembly resolution from 1960 (resolution 1541) details the options from among which a people is entitled to choose:

---

97    See generally Martin Shipway, *Decolonization and Its Impact: A Comparative Approach to the End of
      the Colonial Empires* (Wiley, 2008).
98    *Legal Consequences of the Separation of the Chagos Archipelago from Mauritius in 1965 (Advisory
      Opinion)* [2019] ICJ Rep 95, 130–5 [140]–[162] ('*Chagos Archipelago*').
99    *Declaration on the Granting of Independence to Colonial Countries and Peoples*, GA Res 1514 (XV), UN
      Doc A/RES/1514 (14 December 1960) arts 1–6.
100   *Re Secession of Quebec* [1998] 2 SCR 217 [126] (Supreme Court of Canada).
101   *Western Sahara (Advisory Opinion)* [1975] ICJ Rep 12, 33 [59].

A Non-Self-Governing Territory can be said to have reached a full measure of self-government by:

(a)   Emergence as a sovereign independent State;

(b)   Free association with an independent State; or

(c)   Integration with an independent State.[102]

A later General Assembly resolution, the *Friendly Relations Declaration* of 1970, mentions an additional option: 'emergence into any other political status freely determined by a people'.[103]

Of the various options, the most commonly chosen is emergence into a new state. This is how most European colonies in Africa, Asia and elsewhere achieved statehood. Examples of peoples who have instead chosen free association are those of the Cook Islands and Niue, which are in free association with New Zealand.[104] This is a sort of intermediate status in which a territory relies heavily on an existing state (for example, in foreign affairs or defence) while retaining 'the right to determine its internal constitution without outside interference, in accordance with due constitutional processes and the freely expressed wishes of the people'.[105] As for the option of integration with an existing state, it is sometimes uncontroversial, but it may also raise doubts about whether the choice was truly free, as with the western part of New Guinea. Previously this was a colony of the Netherlands. In 1969, a small group of individuals chosen by Indonesia voted for integration, and it is now divided into multiple Indonesian provinces.[106]

The next issue is the identity of the peoples entitled to external self-determination. In *Re Secession of Quebec*, which concerned the possibility of the province of Quebec seceding from Canada, the Supreme Court of Canada explained why external self-determination is restricted to specific categories of peoples:

> The recognized sources of international law establish that the right to self-determination of a people is normally fulfilled through *internal* self-determination – a people's pursuit of its political, economic, social and cultural development within the framework of an existing state. A right to *external* self-determination (which in this case potentially takes the form of the assertion of a right to unilateral secession) arises only in the most extreme of cases and, even then, under carefully defined circumstances . . .
>
> The international law principle of self-determination has evolved within a framework of respect for the territorial integrity of existing states. The various international documents that support the existence of a people's right to self-determination also contain

---

102   *Principles Which Should Guide Members in Determining Whether or Not an Obligation Exists to Transmit the Information Called for in Article 73(e) of the Charter of the United Nations*, GA Res 1541 (XV), UN Doc A/RES/1541(XV) (15 December 1960) annex, principle VI ('*Principles Which Should Guide Members*').

103   *Declaration on Principles of International Law concerning Friendly Relations and Co-operation among States in accordance with the Charter of the United Nations*, GA Res 2625 (XXV), UN Doc A/RES/2625(XXV) (24 October 1970) annex, principle (e) ('*Friendly Relations Declaration*').

104   *Question of the Cook Islands*, GA Res 2064 (XX), UN Doc A/RES/2064(XX) (16 December 1965); *Question of Niue*, GA Res 3285 (XXIX), UN Doc A/RES/3285(XXIV) (13 December 1974).

105   *Principles Which Should Guide Members* (n 102) principle VII.

106   *Agreement between the Republic of Indonesia and the Kingdom of the Netherlands concerning West New Guinea (West Irian)*, GA Res 2504 (XXIV), UN Doc A/RES/2504(XXIV) (20 November 1969).

parallel statements supportive of the conclusion that the exercise of such a right must be sufficiently limited to prevent threats to an existing state's territorial integrity or the stability of relations between sovereign states.[107]

As this passage indicates, international law attempts to strike a balance between self-determination and the broad value of territorial integrity.[108]

The right to external self-determination certainly applies to two specific categories of peoples: a colonial category and a smaller non-colonial category. It may additionally apply to a third, more controversial category of peoples: cases involving 'remedial secession'.

First, reflecting its origin in the decolonisation movement, the right vests in peoples under colonial rule.[109] Historically, these included the peoples of UN trust territories, most of which were former German colonies that were confiscated after World War I to be administered by other states, initially under mandates granted by the League of Nations.[110] Nauru and the north-eastern part of New Guinea were UN trust territories under Australian administration.[111] Also included in this category are the peoples of 'non-self-governing' territories, of which the United Nations maintains an official list.[112] This list embraced the great majority of European colonies in Africa, Asia and elsewhere. Since the creation of the United Nations in 1945, more than 80 former colonies have gained independence and joined the organisation (a huge number when compared with the mere 51 original members). Although there are no UN trust territories left today, a few non-self-governing territories still remain. One that is near to Australia is the French territory of New Caledonia, which has held a series of referendums on whether to secede.[113]

Second, the right also vests in peoples who are 'subject to alien subjugation, domination or exploitation outside a colonial context'.[114] This has historically been a much smaller category. The most prominent example is the Palestinian people.[115] The Palestinian territories have largely – though subject to complexities and qualifications that cannot be detailed here – been under occupation by Israel for over half a century.[116] The ICJ alluded to the Palestinian people's right to self-determination in *Wall in the Occupied Palestinian Territory* in 2004.[117]

---

107    *Re Secession of Quebec* (n 100) [126]–[127] (emphasis in original).
108    This does not mean that an entity seeking statehood has a specific legal duty to respect territorial integrity, on which see Section 5.2.3.1.
109    *Re Secession of Quebec* (n 100) [131]–[132].
110    Crawford (n 2) ch 13. Also included was South West Africa, formerly German, which remained under a mandate and was never converted into a UN trust territory: *Legal Consequences for States of the Continued Presence of South Africa in Namibia (South West Africa) notwithstanding Security Council Resolution 276 (1970) (Advisory Opinion)* [1971] ICJ Rep 16 ('*Namibia*').
111    On Nauru, see further *Certain Phosphate Lands in Nauru (Nauru v Australia) (Preliminary Objections)* [1992] ICJ Rep 240.
112    *UN Charter* ch XI.
113    John Connell, 'The 2020 New Caledonia Referendum: The Slow March to Independence?' (2021) 56 *Journal of Pacific History* 144.
114    *Re Secession of Quebec* (n 100) [133], citing the similar language in *Friendly Relations Declaration* (n 103) principle (e).
115    Cassese (n 91) 230–48.
116    See, eg, Victor Kattan (ed), *The Palestine Question in International Law* (British Institute of International and Comparative Law, 2008).
117    *Legal Consequences of the Construction of a Wall in the Occupied Palestinian Territory (Advisory Opinion)* [2004] ICJ Rep 136, 171–2 [88], 182–3 [118], 199 [155]–[156], 200 [159] ('*Wall in the Occupied Palestinian Territory*').

The third, more controversial category of peoples was described in *Re Secession of Quebec* as follows:

> [T]he underlying proposition is that, when a people is blocked from the meaningful exercise of its right to self-determination internally, it is entitled, as a last resort, to exercise it by secession ...
>
> Clearly, such a circumstance parallels the other two recognized situations in that the ability of a people to exercise its right to self-determination internally is somehow being totally frustrated ... [I]t remains unclear whether this third proposition actually reflects an established customary international law standard ...[118]

Since few peoples now remain that fall into the first two categories, disputes about external self-determination often relate to this third category. If it exists at all, it is limited to exceptional cases. The Canadian Supreme Court held that a people such as that of Quebec could not even be said to approach the threshold of oppression that would be required, given that 'Quebecers occupy prominent positions within the government of Canada' and 'freely make political choices and pursue economic, social and cultural development within Canada'.[119] Arguable examples, such as Bangladesh and Kosovo, feature allegations of crimes against humanity, genocide or other grave wrongs.[120] These are often described as cases of 'remedial secession', on the basis that the creation of a new state functions as a remedy for wrongs or injustice.[121]

A final issue is the nature of the duty that attaches to external self-determination. The ICJ has indicated that 'respect for the right to self-determination is an obligation *erga omnes* [towards all]'.[122] This means that the duty of respect for self-determination is owed not just to particular peoples but to the international community as a whole. The *Friendly Relations Declaration* fills out its content: '[e]very state has the duty to promote, through joint and separate action, realization of the principle of equal rights and self-determination of peoples, in accordance with the relevant provisions of the [UN] *Charter* ... in order ... [t]o bring a speedy end to colonialism, having due regard to the freely expressed will of the peoples concerned'.[123] Although this duty falls on every state, it is of special relevance to states that administer the territories concerned, such as France in New Caledonia, which may be expected to organise voting and grant independence.

## 5.3.1.2    How self-determination affects statehood

A right to create a new state is not the same as a *power* to create a new state. A new state does not come into being automatically; instead, a people's exercise of external self-determination must generally be implemented by creating a new entity that meets the criteria of population,

---

118    *Re Secession of Quebec* (n 100) [134]–[135].
119    Ibid [135]–[136].
120    Alain Pellet, 'Kosovo – The Questions Not Asked: Self-Determination, Secession, and Recognition' in Marko Milanović and Michael Wood (eds), *The Law and Politics of the Kosovo Advisory Opinion* (Oxford University Press, 2015) 268.
121    *Kosovo* (n 65) 438 [82]; Michel Seymour, 'Remedial Secession' in Gëzim Visoka, John Doyle and Edward Newman (eds), *Routledge Handbook of State Recognition* (Routledge, 2019).
122    *Chagos Archipelago* (n 98) 139 [180]. See also *East Timor (Portugal v Australia) (Judgment)* [1995] ICJ Rep 90, 102 [29]. On duties *erga omnes*, see Chapter 7.
123    *Friendly Relations Declaration* (n 103) principle (e).

territory, government and independence.[124] Thus the law of self-determination does not supersede or replace the law of statehood described earlier (see Section 5.2). Its function is to establish a regime of rights and duties that, if complied with, will result in the creation of new states. There are, however, three special scenarios in which self-determination may affect statehood directly.

The first is where an administering state forcibly breaches its duty to respect external self-determination, as when Portugal refused to relinquish its African colonies in the 1960s and 1970s. In Guinea-Bissau, insurgents declared statehood unilaterally and won partial control.[125] Since Guinea-Bissau was still in a military struggle against Portugal over its territory, it might not have met the statehood criteria *if* this were an ordinary case. Nonetheless, in 1973, the General Assembly affirmed it was 'an independent state'.[126] James Crawford offers this explanation:

> Where ... the metropolitan State forcibly denies self-determination to the territory ... the principle of self-determination operates in favour of the statehood of the seceding territory, provided that the seceding government can properly be regarded as representative of the people of the territory ... [T]he criterion in this type of case would appear to be one of qualified effectiveness: the metropolitan government cannot rely on the advantages of incumbency against a liberation movement which is supported by the population and controls substantial territory (eg, Guinea-Bissau). In such a case the principle of self-determination legitimizes what might otherwise be premature recognition ...[127]

In other words, self-determination renders the criteria less onerous. This might be justified on the ground that a parent state that denies external self-determination is more like a foreign aggressor than a state lawfully protecting its own territorial integrity.[128]

The second scenario is similar in that self-determination may make statehood easier to acquire. It is a possible exception to the notion, discussed earlier in Section 5.2.3.2, that a new state cannot be created by the use of force by an existing state. A case in point is the territory known in the past as East Pakistan and nowadays as Bangladesh. In 1971, Bangladesh purported to secede unilaterally from Pakistan; India forcibly intervened in support of its secession; and Pakistan eventually surrendered to Indian troops.[129] Unlike in other cases involving force, many states quickly recognised Bangladesh, and the General Assembly did not call on states to withhold recognition.[130] This has been explained on the basis that Pakistan

---

124    On the criteria, see Section 5.2.1.
125    Bunyan Bryant et al, 'Recognition of Guinea (Bissau)' (1974) 15(3) *Harvard International Law Journal* 482; Dugard, *Recognition and the United Nations* (n 83) 73–4.
126    *Credentials of Representatives to the Twenty-Eight Session of the General Assembly*, GA Res 3181 (XXVIII), UN Doc A/RES/3181(XXVIII) (17 December 1973). See also *Illegal Occupation by Portuguese Military Forces of Certain Sectors of the Republic of Guinea-Bissau and Acts of Aggression Committed by Them against the People of the Republic*, GA Res 3061 (XXVIII) , UN Doc A/RES/3061(XXVIII) (2 November 1973).
127    Crawford (n 2) 387.
128    Nicholson, *Statehood and the State-Like* (n 24) 180–4.
129    Dugard, *Recognition and the United Nations* (n 83) 75–6.
130    Ved Nanda, 'Self-Determination in International Law: The Tragic Tale of Two Cities – Islamabad (West Pakistan) and Dacca (East Pakistan)' (1972) 66 *American Journal of International Law* 321, 336.

was forcibly suppressing a right to external self-determination.[131] It is, however, debatable whether the people of Bangladesh had such a right. Since Pakistan had already been decolonised, the case does not unambiguously fall into the established categories discussed earlier; and although it has features of 'remedial secession', that category is controversial.

In the third scenario, self-determination may make acquiring statehood *more* difficult. In 1965, the white minority government of the British colony of Southern Rhodesia unilaterally declared independence. The purported state of Rhodesia lasted until 1979 and appeared to meet the statehood criteria, though – in accordance with Security Council resolutions – it was never recognised.[132] Some scholars have argued that in a case such as Rhodesia, which excluded its black majority population from political participation, 'self-determination ... operates as a peremptory requirement, suspending statehood until the constitutional and governmental structure of the territory is brought into line with the principle'.[133] Others have suggested that Rhodesia was a state, albeit one that could not be recognised, with the result that it was burdened by the duties of statehood while being denied all the benefits.[134] Thus the Security Council ascribed responsibility to it for aggression and other breaches of international law against neighbouring states.[135] In 1980, Rhodesia became the state of Zimbabwe, with a government from the black majority.

## 5.3.2   Other manifestations of self-determination

In addition to external self-determination, there are other manifestations of the principle, which apply internally, to indigenous peoples, to peoples of existing states, or in the economic realm.

'Internal' self-determination is 'a people's pursuit of its political, economic, social and cultural development within the framework of an existing state'.[136] One possible consequence of this was mentioned earlier: in exceptional cases, it might – controversially – be transformed into external self-determination (remedial secession). Internal self-determination applies more broadly to some peoples within existing states. For instance, it gives racial groups such as black South Africans a right to take part in the national decision-making process; moreover, groups within a state that constitute distinct ethnic, religious or linguistic communities may have a right to recognition of their identity.[137] Some of the other manifestations of self-determination discussed below may be considered further aspects of internal self-determination.

131    Jean Salmon, 'Naissance et reconnaissance du Bangla-Desh' [Birth and Recognition of Bangladesh] in Josef Tittel (ed), *Multitudo Legum Ius Unum: Festschrift für Wilhelm Wengler* [*Essays in Honour of Wilhelm Wengler*] (Interrecht, 1973) vol 1, 467, 490; Crawford (n 2) 142.

132    James Fawcett, 'Note' (1971) 34(3) *Modern Law Review* 417; Vera Gowlland-Debbas, *Collective Responses to Illegal Acts in International Law: United Nations Action in the Question of Southern Rhodesia* (Nijhoff, 1990). See, among other resolutions, SC Res 277, UN Doc S/RES/277 (18 March 1970), which '[*decided*] that Member States shall refrain from recognizing this illegal régime'. On the binding force of Security Council decisions, see *UN Charter* art 25; *Namibia* (n 110) 52–4 [111]–[116].

133    Crawford (n 2) 388; see further 129–31.

134    Talmon, 'The Constitutive versus the Declaratory Theory' (n 18) 103, 123; Nicholson, *Statehood and the State-Like* (n 24) 175–80.

135    SC Res 424, UN Doc S/RES/424 (17 March 1978); SC Res 445, UN Doc S/RES/445 (8 March 1979); SC Res 455, UN Doc S/RES/455 (23 November 1979).

136    *Re Secession of Quebec* (n 100) [126].

137    See, respectively, Cassese (n 91) 124; *Yugoslavia Peace Conference Opinion No 2* (1991) 92 ILR 167, 168.

Indigenous peoples have distinctive characteristics, some of which are summarised in a 1989 treaty: they are 'peoples in independent countries'; they 'are regarded as indigenous on account of their descent from the populations who inhabited' a country 'at the time of conquest or colonisation or the establishment of present state boundaries'; they retain 'some or all of their own social, economic, cultural and political institutions'; and a 'fundamental criterion' is '[s]elf-identification as indigenous'.[138] The concept of indigenous self-determination is still evolving, but it appears to emphasise autonomy within existing states, which amounts to less than a right to external self-determination but possibly to more than the internal self-determination accorded to other peoples. The *United Nations Declaration on the Rights of Indigenous Peoples* of 2007 provides:

> ***Article 3***
>
> Indigenous peoples have the right to self-determination. By virtue of that right they freely determine their political status and freely pursue their economic, social and cultural development.
>
> ***Article 4***
>
> Indigenous peoples, in exercising their right to self-determination, have the right to autonomy or self-government in matters relating to their internal and local affairs, as well as ways and means for financing their autonomous functions.
>
> . . .
>
> ***Article 46***
>
> 1. Nothing in this Declaration may be . . . construed as authorizing or encouraging any action which would dismember or impair, totally or in part, the territorial integrity or political unity of sovereign and independent States.[139]

Although the declaration is not binding as such, it is likely that art 3 reflects custom.[140] In the Uluru Statement from the Heart of 2017, representatives of the Aboriginal and Torres Strait Islander peoples of Australia aspired to 'a fair and truthful relationship with the people of Australia and a better future for our children based on justice and self-determination'.[141]

The *UN Charter* alludes to 'the principle of equal rights and self-determination of peoples'.[142] A committee involved in drafting this explained that it entails 'a free and genuine expression of the will of the people, which avoids cases of the alleged expression of the popular will, such as those used for their own ends by [Nazi] Germany and [Fascist] Italy'.[143]

---

138    International Labour Organization, *Convention Concerning Indigenous and Tribal Peoples in Independent Countries (No 169)*, opened for signature 27 June 1989, 1650 UNTS 383 (entered into force 5 September 1991) art 1. See further Ben Saul, *Indigenous Peoples and Human Rights* (Bloomsbury, 2016) ch 1.

139    *United Nations Declaration on the Rights of Indigenous Peoples*, GA Res 61/295, UN Doc A/RES/61/295 (2 October 2007, adopted 13 September 2007) annex.

140    Martin Scheinin and Mattias Åhrén, 'Relationship to Human Rights, and Related International Instruments' in Jessie Hohmann and Marc Weller (eds), *The UN Declaration on the Rights of Indigenous Peoples: A Commentary* (Oxford University Press, 2018) 63, 64.

141    'Uluru Statement from the Heart' (Statement, First Nations National Constitution Convention, 26 May 2017).

142    *UN Charter* (n 60) arts 1(2), 55.

143    *Documents of the United Nations Conference on International Organization, San Francisco, 1945* (United Nations Information Organizations, 1945) vol 6, 396.

This suggests that the people of an existing state has a continuing right to self-determination that takes 'the well-known form of the rule preventing intervention in the internal affairs of a State, the central element of which is the right of the people to choose for themselves their own form of government'.[144] Note that this is not necessarily a right to democracy; it is a right against *foreign* intervention.[145]

Finally, many instruments refer to 'economic' self-determination. For example, the two human rights covenants of 1966 provide that, by virtue of the right of self-determination, peoples 'freely pursue their economic, social and cultural development'.[146] They add:

> All peoples may, for their own ends, freely dispose of their natural wealth and resources without prejudice to any obligations arising out of international economic co-operation, based upon the principle of mutual benefit, and international law. In no case may a people be deprived of its own means of subsistence.[147]

This is often described as 'permanent sovereignty over natural resources'.[148]

# 5.4   Territory

One of the most important rights that attaches to statehood – and one of the reasons it is desired by peoples exercising self-determination – is territorial sovereignty: a state's right to exercise exclusive jurisdiction within its territory.[149] This right 'has as corollary a duty' to respect the territorial integrity of other states.[150] Although it vests in states, in some cases the United Nations has exercised administrative functions over territory in place of the sovereign, as in East Timor from 1999 to 2002.[151] The significance of the international law of territory is that it determines the boundaries within which territorial sovereignty and various other rights, duties and functions of states are applicable. This section of the chapter will begin with a few words about new states; it will deal at more length with territorial change and the closely related topic of territorial disputes; and finally, it will mention some special types of territory.

## 5.4.1   The initial territory of new states

Historically, there were few rules about how a new state acquires its initial territory other than those already discussed as part of the law of statehood.[152] But there is one established principle: *uti possidetis* (so that you may possess). This principle originated in cases involving

---

144    Crawford (n 2) 114, 126.

145    See Cassese (n 91) 102.

146    *ICESCR* (n 93) art 1(1); *ICCPR* (n 93) art 1(1).

147    *ICESCR* (n 93) art 1(2); *ICCPR* (n 93) art 1(2).

148    See, eg, *Permanent Sovereignty over Natural Resources*, GA Res 1803 (XVII), UN Doc A/RES/1803(XVII) (14 December 1962).

149    *Island of Palmas (Netherlands v United States of America) (Award)* (1928) 2 RIAA 829, 838.

150    Ibid 839. See also Section 5.2.3.1.

151    See Carsten Stahn, *The Law and Practice of International Territorial Administration: Versailles to Iraq and beyond* (Cambridge University Press, 2010). On East Timor, see SC Res 1272, UN Doc S/RES/1272 (25 October 1999).

152    Robert Jennings, *The Acquisition of Territory in International Law* (Manchester University Press, 1963) 6–12.

former European colonies. It transforms pre-existing internal and external boundaries, which may have been 'intended originally for quite other purposes', into the borders of a new state at the moment it becomes independent.[153] Thus, after the collapse of Yugoslavia, both its external borders with other states and the internal boundaries between its constituent republics were transformed into the borders of the new states of Slovenia, Croatia and so on.[154]

Also applicable is the law of state succession, under which the creation of a new state 'does not as such affect … a boundary established by a treaty' or certain types of rights and duties established by a treaty that relate to a boundary or to the use of territory.[155] For instance, when Slovakia became a new state in 1993, it inherited from its parent state, Czechoslovakia, rights and duties under a treaty about a dam project on its inherited border with Hungary.[156]

## 5.4.2   Territorial change

International law has traditionally distinguished between five methods or 'modes' by which a state can acquire additional territory or lose territory. One is 'where the shape of land is changed by the processes of nature', either by avulsion (sudden change, as where a new volcanic island emerges within a state's territorial sea or a flood deposits silt or washes away land) or accretion (gradual change, as through sedimentation or erosion of a coast or river).[157] The other four modes will be discussed in more detail: conquest, cession, occupation of terra nullius, and prescription.

It will be seen that international law has evolved over time such that, of these traditional modes, conquest is no longer possible at all and cession is possible only in narrower circumstances than in the past. These developments, however, are not retrospective. That follows from what the arbitrator in *Island of Palmas* called the principle of 'intertemporal' law: 'a juridical fact must be appreciated in the light of the law contemporary with it, and not of the law in force at the time when a dispute in regard to it arises or falls to be settled'.[158] A corollary to this is that the law might evolve so as to impose conditions on the continuing existence of territorial title:

> [A] distinction must be made between the creation of rights and the existence of rights. The same principle which subjects the act creative of a right to the law in force at the time the right arises, demands that the existence of the right, in other words its continued manifestation, shall follow the conditions required by the evolution of law.[159]

Despite that corollary, if a state acquired territory in the past by a method that was valid at the time, generally it can retain sovereignty. Since the answers to territorial questions often depend on acquisition long ago in the past, knowledge of those methods remains important.

---

153    *Land, Island and Maritime Frontier Dispute (El Salvador v Honduras) (Judgment)* [1992] ICJ Rep 351, 387–8 [43] ('*El Salvador v Honduras*'). See also *Frontier Dispute (Burkina Faso v Republic of Mali) (Judgment)* [1986] ICJ Rep 554, 566 [23] ('*Burkina Faso v Mali*').
154    *Yugoslavia Peace Conference Opinion No 3* (1992) 92 ILR 170.
155    *Vienna Convention on Succession of States in Respect of Treaties*, opened for signature 23 August 1978, 1946 UNTS 3 (entered into force 6 November 1996) arts 11, 12.
156    *Gabčíkovo-Nagymaros Project (Hungary v Slovakia) (Judgment)* [1997] ICJ Rep 7, 69–72 [117]–[123].
157    Jennings (n 152) 6.
158    *Island of Palmas* (n 149) 845.
159    Ibid. See also *Minquiers and Ecrehos (France v United Kingdom) (Judgment)* [1953] ICJ Rep 47, 56.

### 5.4.2.1    Conquest

In the past, international law permitted territorial acquisitions by force. But some states renounced war under the *Kellogg–Briand Pact* of 1928;[160] and the threat or use of force has been generally prohibited since the adoption of the *UN Charter* in 1945. Accordingly, the *Friendly Relations Declaration* of 1970, reflecting custom, affirms that '[n]o territorial acquisition resulting from the threat or use of force shall be recognized as legal'.[161] Conquest is not only unlawful but also invalid. Thus, in 1990, the Security Council declared that the 'annexation of Kuwait by Iraq under any form and whatever pretext has no legal validity, and is considered null and void'.[162] The rule invalidating conquest is actually wider than the prohibition on the threat or use of force, because it applies not only to unlawful force but even in exceptional cases where force is lawful, as with self-defence.[163] In 1967, Israel occupied East Jerusalem (and other territories, including the rest of the West Bank and Gaza) as the result of a use of force that it characterised as lawful self-defence against Arab states.[164] In 1980, after Israel declared the whole of Jerusalem to be its capital, the Security Council affirmed 'that the acquisition of territory by force is inadmissible' and that measures taken by Israel to change the status of Jerusalem were 'null and void'.[165]

### 5.4.2.2    Cession

Cession – consensual transfer – by treaty has historically been common and remains available as a mode of territorial change. There are two developments that may restrict its availability.

First, in the period when a state could conquer territory *directly*, it could also use force to gain territory *indirectly* by coercing another state – perhaps the losing side in a war – into accepting a treaty of cession. Nowadays, under the *Vienna Convention on the Law of Treaties*, reflecting custom, a 'treaty is void if its conclusion has been procured by the threat or use of force in violation of the principles of international law embodied in the *Charter of the United Nations*'.[166]

Second, there have been hints that cession may now require the consent of the people of the territory, at least where the people has a right to self-determination. The ICJ held in *Legal Consequences of the Separation of the Chagos Archipelago*, albeit in a somewhat different context that did not involve cession, that 'any detachment by the administering Power of part of a non-self-governing territory, unless based on the freely expressed and genuine will of the people of the territory concerned, is contrary to the right to self-determination'.[167] In 2019,

---

160    *General Treaty for Renunciation of War as an Instrument of National Policy*, opened for signature 27 August 1928, 94 LNTS 57 (entered into force 25 July 1929) (commonly known as the *Kellogg–Briand Pact* of 1928).

161    *Friendly Relations Declaration* (n 103) principle (a); *Wall in the Occupied Palestinian Territory* (n 117) 171 [87].

162    SC Res 662, UN Doc S/RES/662 (9 August 1990).

163    *UN Charter* (n 60) art 51.

164    Gray (n 60) 161.

165    SC Res 478, UN Doc S/RES/478 (20 August 1980). See also *Wall in the Occupied Palestinian Territory* (n 117) 166–7 [75], 167 [78].

166    *Vienna Convention on the Law of Treaties*, opened for signature 23 May 1969, 1155 UNTS 331 (entered into force 27 January 1980) art 52 (see also arts 51, 53); *Fisheries Jurisdiction (United Kingdom v Iceland) (Jurisdiction)* [1973] ICJ Rep 3, 14 [24]. See Chapter 3.

167    *Chagos Archipelago* (n 98) 134 [160]. Rather than ceding territory, the administering state (the United Kingdom) had retained part of the territory (Chagos) when the remainder achieved statehood (as Mauritius).

when US president Donald Trump expressed interest in buying Greenland from Denmark, Denmark reacted negatively.[168] Although Greenland was removed from the UN list of non-self-governing territories in 1954, Danish legislation recognises its people as having a right to self-determination (though without specifying whether the right is external or internal).[169]

Cession by treaty is not the only form of the cession of territory by consent, merely the most obvious and explicit. In *Sovereignty over Pedra Branca/Pulau Batu Puteh, Middle Rocks and South Ledge* ('*Malaysia v Singapore*'), the ICJ commented that a

> passing of sovereignty might be by way of agreement between the two States in question. Such an agreement might take the form of a treaty ... The agreement might instead be tacit and arise from the conduct of the Parties. International law does not, in this matter, impose any particular form. Rather it places its emphasis on the parties' intentions ...[170]

### 5.4.2.3   Occupation of terra nullius

Occupation of terra nullius (no one's land) also remains available as a mode of territorial change, at least in principle. In practice, now that states have extended sovereignty across more or less Earth's entire land surface, virtually no territories remain that qualify as terrae nullius.[171] There are two relevant legal issues: which territories qualify, and how states can acquire them.

On the first issue, uninhabited land that lacks an existing sovereign is terra nullius. That is not controversial. More controversially, in past centuries, some international lawyers also placed certain inhabited territories into the category, in particular territories that were inhabited but lacked governments with characteristics akin to those of Western states.[172] This expanded view of terra nullius was always dubious, because in practice states seldom purported to acquire inhabited territory on this basis. In the colonial period, the main modes by which Western states acquired territory in other parts of the world were conquest and cession.[173] In 1926, MF Lindley concluded from a survey of practice that all that was needed for a territory to escape being terra nullius was that it be inhabited by a 'political society'.[174] The ICJ took basically the same view in *Western Sahara* in 1975, when it was asked whether part of north Africa had once been terra nullius:

---

168    Joseph Blocher and Mitu Gulati, 'Transferable Sovereignty: Lessons from the History of the Congo Free State' (2020) 69(6) *Duke Law Journal* 1219, 1269–71.

169    *Cessation of the Transmission of Information under Article 73(e) of the Charter in respect of Greenland*, GA Res 849 (IX), UN Doc A/RES/849(IX) (22 November 1954); *Act on Greenland Self-Government 2009* (Denmark).

170    *Sovereignty over Pedra Branca/Pulau Batu Puteh, Middle Rocks and South Ledge (Malaysia v Singapore) (Judgment)* [2008] ICJ Rep 12, 50 [120] (citations omitted) ('*Malaysia v Singapore*').

171    But on the special case of Antarctica, see Section 5.4.4.

172    See, eg, de Vattel (n 70) pt I.VII.81; John Westlake, *Chapters on the Principles of International Law* (Cambridge University Press, 1894) 141; Lassa Oppenheim, *International Law: A Treatise* (Longmans, Green & Co, 1905) vol 1, 276.

173    On, for example, treaties with African peoples, see CH Alexandrowicz, 'The Afro-Asian World and the Law of Nations (Historical Aspects)' (1968) 123 *Recueil des cours* 117, 172–82.

174    MF Lindley, *The Acquisition and Government of Backward Territory in International Law* (Longmans, Green & Co, 1926) 22–3.

> Whatever differences of opinion there may have been among jurists, the State practice of
> the relevant period indicates that territories inhabited by tribes or peoples having a social
> and political organization were not regarded as *terrae nullius*. It shows that in the case of
> such territories the acquisition of sovereignty was not generally considered as effected
> unilaterally through 'occupation' of *terra nullius* by original title but through agreements
> concluded with local rulers. ... In the present instance ... at the time of colonization
> Western Sahara was inhabited by peoples which, if nomadic, were socially and politically
> organized in tribes and under chiefs competent to represent them.[175]

For a long time, the British colonisation of Australia was justified on the basis of terra
nullius. In 1837, a select committee of the UK House of Commons observed that the Aboriginal
peoples of Australia were 'so entirely destitute ... even of the rudest forms of civil polity, that
their claims, whether as sovereigns or proprietors of the soil, have been utterly disregarded'.[176]
But the view that they lacked social and political organisation was not factually correct.[177] As
observed, for instance, in *Milirrpum v Nabalco Pty Ltd*, Aboriginal Australians had 'a subtle and
elaborate system' of law 'highly adapted to the country in which the people led their lives'.[178]
The issue remained practically important because the international legal test of terra nullius
corresponded with a domestic legal test concerning whether precolonial property rights
survived colonisation.[179] In 1992 in *Mabo v Queensland (No 2)* ('*Mabo*'), the High Court of
Australia cited *Western Sahara* and indicated that, on a correct application of the test, Australia
was not terra nullius before British colonisation.[180] The High Court did not go so far as to say
that the Aboriginal and Torres Strait Islander peoples of Australia had sovereignty before
colonisation. But arguably they were sovereign under the international law of the period.[181]
This also reflects their own practice as between one people and another. In 1910, relying on
evidence gathered in earlier times, one Western scholar concluded:

> The evidence we have been able to collect from the Australian tribes shows us many of
> the ideas of International Law clearly developed – territorial sovereignty, the sacredness of
> messengers and envoys, a normal and recognized intercourse over wide areas through
> intermarriage and the exchange of commodities, and the existence in many cases of the
> rights of asylum, domicilement, and hospitality ... It would seem that in Australia we have
> a very early stage in the differentiation of intergroup from intragroup justice ...[182]

Another question not answered in *Mabo*, given that Australia was not terra nullius, is how else
the British could have acquired territorial sovereignty. The main mode of acquisition was

---

175   *Western Sahara* (n 101) 39 [80]–[81].
176   *Report from the Select Committee on Aborigines (British Settlements)* (House of Commons Papers
      No 425, Session 1837) 82. See also *Cooper v Stuart* (1886) 14 AC 286, 291.
177   See generally Nii Lante Wallace-Bruce, 'Two Hundred Years on: A Reexamination of the Acquisition of
      Australia' (1989) 19(1) *Georgia Journal of International and Comparative Law* 87, 96–100; Henry
      Reynolds, *Aboriginal Sovereignty: Reflections on Race, State and Nation* (Allen & Unwin, 1996) ch 2.
178   (1971) 17 FLR 141, 276.
179   *Mabo v Queensland (No 2)* (1992) 175 CLR 1, 36 (Brennan J).
180   See among other relevant passages ibid, 40–1 (Brennan J), 109 (Deane and Gaudron JJ).
181   Rowan Nicholson, 'Was the Colonisation of Australia an Invasion of Sovereign Territory?' (2019) 20(2)
      *Melbourne Journal of International Law* 493. See also Henry Reynolds, *Truth-Telling: History,
      Sovereignty and the Uluru Statement* (NewSouth, 2021) ch 5.
182   Gerald Wheeler, *The Tribe, and Intertribal Relations in Australia* (John Murray, 1910) 160, 163.

probably conquest, with the result that the British may not have acquired sovereignty over each part of Australia until they had conquered that particular part, a process that began in 1788 and may have still been ongoing in the late 19th century in some parts of Western Australia.[183]

The second issue to consider here is what states must do to acquire terra nullius, at least in the uncontroversial case of uninhabited land that lacks an existing sovereign. Practice from the 15th and 16th centuries suggests that at one time mere discovery may have been sufficient; but in *Island of Palmas* it was held that, at least from the 19th century, 'discovery alone, without any subsequent act,' could not 'suffice to prove sovereignty'.[184] In *Clipperton Island*, the arbitrator accepted that an uninhabited island had been terra nullius before 1858, when a French naval officer had proclaimed French sovereignty over it.[185] He went on:

> It is beyond doubt that by immemorial usage having the force of law, besides the *animus occupandi* [intention to occupy], the actual, and not the nominal, taking of possession is a necessary condition of occupation. This taking of possession consists in the act, or series of acts, by which the occupying state reduces to its possession the territory in question and takes steps to exercise exclusive authority there.[186]

In short, occupation must be 'effective'. In other contexts, this requires a state to establish 'an organization capable of making its laws respected'; but the arbitrator noted that if a territory is 'completely uninhabited' and hence, 'from the first moment when the occupying state makes its appearance there, at the absolute and undisputed disposition of that state', then that may suffice, and in this case it did suffice.[187] Since the notion of effective occupation is also relevant in other contexts, further discussion of it will be deferred until those contexts have been introduced (see Section 5.4.3.1).

A final clarification is that only existing states can acquire terra nullius by occupation. In *Ure v Commonwealth*, it was argued that 'individuals can acquire proprietary rights over terra nullius' under international law and that, on that basis, an individual had acquired two reefs to the east of Australia in 1970; but the Federal Court of Australia rejected that argument.[188]

### 5.4.2.4  Prescription

The final mode of territorial change is prescription.[189] This is similar to adverse possession in domestic property law. It is where a usurping state exercises sovereign rights over another state's territory in a way that 'either rests upon a demonstrably defective title or is even in origin wrongful' and where that 'exercise of sovereign rights over a period of time is allowed to cure a

---

183  Gerry Simpson, '*Mabo*, International Law, *Terra Nullius* and the Stories of Settlement: An Unresolved Jurisprudence' (1993) 19(1) *Melbourne University Law Review* 195; Nicholson, 'Colonisation of Australia' (n 181) 493–4, 525–8.
184  *Island of Palmas* (n 149) 846.
185  *Clipperton Island (France v Mexico) (Award)* (1932) 26 *American Journal of International Law* 390.
186  Ibid 393.
187  Ibid 394.
188  *Ure v Commonwealth* (2016) 236 FCR 458, 462 [9], 498 [161]–[162].
189  More precisely, 'acquisitive prescription', because the term 'prescription' sometimes has other meanings in international law: Jennings (n 152) 20–2.

defect in title' and, correspondingly, to extinguish the title of the other state.[190] In argument before the ICJ in *Kasikili/Sedudu Island*, Namibia summarised the requirements that the usurping state must meet in order for its possession 'to mature into a prescriptive title' (and the other party, Botswana, accepted that these were the requirements while denying that Namibia had met them):

1. The possession of the ... state must be exercised *à titre de souverain* [in a sovereign capacity].
2. The possession must be peaceful and uninterrupted.
3. The possession must be public.
4. The possession must endure for a certain length of time.[191]

The first requirement is embraced by the concept of effective occupation that has already been mentioned in the context of terra nullius and that will be discussed in Section 5.4.3.1.

There is also yet another requirement, which relates to the conduct of the other state – the state whose territory has been usurped. It must give its 'acquiescence': silence or inaction that the ICJ has indicated is 'equivalent to tacit recognition manifested by unilateral conduct which the other party may interpret as consent'.[192] In *Malaysia v Singapore*, the ICJ remarked:

> Under certain circumstances, sovereignty over territory might pass as a result of the failure of the State which has sovereignty to respond to conduct *à titre de souverain* of the other State or, as Judge Huber put it in the *Island of Palmas* case, to concrete manifestations of the display of territorial sovereignty by the other State. Such manifestations of the display of sovereignty may call for a response if they are not to be opposable to the State in question. The absence of reaction may well amount to acquiescence ... That is to say, silence may also speak, but only if the conduct of the other State calls for a response.
>
> Critical for the Court's assessment of the conduct of the Parties is the central importance in international law and relations of State sovereignty over territory and of the stability and certainty of that sovereignty. Because of that, any passing of sovereignty over territory on the basis of the conduct of the Parties, as set out above, must be manifested clearly and without any doubt by that conduct and the relevant facts. That is especially so if what may be involved, in the case of one of the Parties, is in effect the abandonment of sovereignty over part of its territory.[193]

Consistent with the emphasis on territorial stability, acquiescence is hard to establish. In *Land and Maritime Boundary between Cameroon and Nigeria*, the ICJ held that, even though Cameroon had 'engaged in only occasional direct acts of administration in [the Bakassi Peninsula], having limited material resources to devote to this distant area', that could not 'be

---

190    Ibid 21.
191    *Kasikili/Sedudu Island (Botswana v Namibia) (Judgment)* [1999] ICJ Rep 1045, 1103–5 [94]–[95], quoting Namibia. The ICJ itself did not express a view on whether these were the requirements, because Namibia had not met them anyway: at 1105 [97]. But see the joint dissenting opinion of Judges Simma and Abraham in *Malaysia v Singapore* (n 170) at 122.
192    *Delimitation of the Maritime Boundary in the Gulf of Maine Area (Canada v United States of America)* [1984] ICJ Rep 246, 305 [130].
193    *Malaysia v Singapore* (n 170) 50–1 [121]–[122] (citations omitted).

viewed as an acquiescence in the loss' of the territory to Nigeria.[194] It may be, then, that the state whose territory has been usurped must have done virtually nothing.

## 5.4.3  Territorial disputes

A territorial dispute occurs when two (or more) states claim the same territory. As such disputes have increasingly come before international courts and tribunals, it has become clear that the law of territory as outlined so far – although not incorrect – is inadequate. One reason is practical: although the traditional modes of territorial change may seem rigidly distinct, in practice it is sometimes too difficult to untangle the exact events by which territory was acquired. A more basic reason is that many disputes are not about territorial change at all. It may be, for instance, that the border between two states has been in the same location for a very long time, but the two states disagree about precisely where that location is, and a court is called upon to decide.

For these reasons, much of the case law focuses, not on the question of territorial *change* over time, but on the subtly different question of which state currently has title to territory. In answering that question, courts may have regard to the law already outlined, but they also tend to employ broader underlying concepts.

### 5.4.3.1  Effective occupation

The most important of those underlying concepts, effective occupation, has been encountered already as one of the requirements of territorial change by occupation of terra nullius or by prescription. In *Burkina Faso v Mali*, the ICJ summarised the ways in which effective occupation is relevant to the question of which state currently has title to territory.

First, in some cases, there is an unambiguous 'legal title' such as a treaty of cession, a boundary treaty, or some other instrument that explicitly defines territorial boundaries, either directly or by operation of the *uti possidetis* principle or the law of state succession (see Section 5.4.1). That is generally decisive of which state currently has title to the territory. Thus, on the one hand, if a state has title to territory under a treaty and has also effectively occupied that territory, then 'the only role of [effective occupation] is to confirm the exercise of the right derived from a legal title'; and, on the other hand, if the territory 'is effectively administered by a State other than the one possessing the legal title, preference should be given to the holder of the title'.[195]

Second, in other cases, the 'legal title is not capable of showing exactly the territorial expanse to which it relates'.[196] This may occur where treaties define borders by reference to vague geographical features or with thick or fuzzy lines drawn on maps. Here, effective occupation can 'play an essential role in showing how the title is interpreted in practice'.[197]

Third, if effective occupation 'does not co-exist with any legal title, it must invariably be taken into consideration'.[198] The same idea was expressed in another way in *Legal Status of*

---

194    *Land and Maritime Boundary between Cameroon and Nigeria (Cameroon v Nigeria) (Judgment)*
       [2002] ICJ Rep 303, 415 [223].
195    *Burkina Faso v Mali* (n 153) 586–7 [63].
196    Ibid.
197    Ibid.
198    Ibid.

*Eastern Greenland*: 'a claim to sovereignty not based on some particular act or title such as a treaty of cession' may be based instead on 'continued display of authority'.[199] This accords with the notion that effective occupation is necessary to acquire territory by occupation of terra nullius or by prescription (see Sections 5.4.2.3 and 5.4.2.4). Territory that is attributed to a state based on effective occupation may, historically, have been acquired in one of those ways. But it may have been acquired in time immemorial in some way that is no longer known or even knowable. In practice, in determining which state currently has title to territory, courts often do not distinguish between those historical situations.

The issue that remains to be considered is what constitutes evidence of effective occupation. The tribunal in *Eritrea v Yemen* held that the 'law of the acquisition (or attribution) of territory generally requires that there be: an intentional display of power and authority over the territory, by the exercise of jurisdiction or State functions, on a continuous and peaceful basis'.[200] In *Legal Status of Eastern Greenland*, this was split into 'two elements each of which must be shown to exist: the intention and will to act as sovereign, and some actual exercise or display of such authority'.[201]

The first element is also known as the *animus occupandi* (intention to occupy). In *Clipperton Island*, there was 'ground to hold as incontestable, the regularity of the act by which France in 1858 made known in a clear and precise manner, her intention to consider the island as her territory'.[202] This element excludes, for instance, situations where a state exercises authority in territory but with the consent of another state that it acknowledges to be sovereign.

The second element is usually more decisive. Activities 'of the administrative authorities as proof of the effective exercise of territorial jurisdiction' are often known as *effectivités* (the plural of the French word for effectiveness).[203] They must be performed *à titre de souverain* (in a sovereign capacity). That means that 'activities by private persons cannot be seen as *effectivités* if they do not take place on the basis of official regulations or under governmental authority'.[204] For example, in a dispute with Malaysia, Indonesia argued that the waters around certain disputed islands had 'traditionally been used by Indonesian fisherman', but the ICJ held that those acts 'did not constitute acts *à titre de souverain* reflecting the intention and will to act in that capacity'.[205] Beyond that principle, the case law shows that the quantity and nature of the *effectivités* that are required varies greatly from one factual situation to another. In *Legal Status of Eastern Greenland*, the Permanent Court of International Justice explained this, partly, by reference to the characteristics of the particular territory:

> [I]n many cases the tribunal has been satisfied with very little in the way of the actual exercise of sovereign rights, provided that the other State could not make out a superior claim. This is particularly true in the case of claims to sovereignty over areas in thinly populated or unsettled countries [such as the uncolonized east of Greenland] . . .

---

199    *Legal Status of Eastern Greenland (Denmark v Norway) (Judgment)* [1933] PCIJ (ser A/B) No 53, 45.
200    *Eritrea v Yemen (Award on Territorial Sovereignty and Scope of the Dispute)* (1998) 33 RIAA 209, 268 [239].
201    *Eastern Greenland* (n 199) 45–6; see further 63.
202    *Clipperton Island* (n 185) 393.
203    *Burkina Faso v Mali* (n 153) 586–7 [63].
204    *Sovereignty over Pulau Ligitan and Pulau Sipadan (Indonesia v Malaysia) (Judgment)* [2002] ICJ Rep 625, 683 [140].
205    Ibid 683 [140]–[141].

[Denmark has relied] on the concession granted in 1863 . . . of exclusive rights on the East coast for trading, hunting, mining, etc. The result of all the documents connected with the grant of the concession is to show that, on the one side, it was granted upon the footing that the King of Denmark was in a position to grant a valid monopoly on the East coast and that his sovereign rights entitled him to do so, and, on the other, that the concessionnaires in England regarded the grant of a monopoly as essential to the success of their projects and had no doubt as to the validity of the rights conferred . . . The concessions granted for the erection of telegraph lines and the legislation fixing the limits of territorial waters in 1905 are also manifestations of the exercise of sovereign authority.

In view of the above facts, when taken in conjunction with the legislation she had enacted applicable to Greenland generally, the numerous treaties in which Denmark, with the concurrence of the other contracting Party, provided for the non-application of the treaty to Greenland in general, and the absence of all claim to sovereignty over Greenland by any other Power, Denmark must be regarded as having displayed during this period of 1814 to 1915 her authority over the uncolonized part of the country to a degree sufficient to confer a valid title to the sovereignty.[206]

### 5.4.3.2    Critical date

In looking for evidence of effective occupation, a court often restricts itself to evidence from before a 'critical date': the date 'falling at the end of a period within which the material facts of a dispute are said to have occurred' and 'after which the actions of the parties to a dispute can no longer affect the issue'.[207] This depends on the facts but tends to occur when the court satisfies itself that the territorial boundaries, wherever they may turn out to be, must have solidified by that date. In *El Salvador v Honduras*, the ICJ gave some non-exhaustive examples.[208] First, in some cases, the critical date is the date when a new state emerged with boundaries determined by the *uti possidetis* principle.[209] A court may look for evidence of effective occupation predating the emergence of the new state (that is to say, evidence of effective occupation by the parent state, from which the new state has inherited its boundaries). Second, a later critical date may arise from a tribunal decision, in which case the tribunal's 'view of the *uti possidetis juris* position prevails and cannot now be questioned juridically, even if it could be questioned historically'.[210] It may also arise from a boundary treaty or perhaps from 'acquiescence or recognition' where the parties have 'accepted a variation, or at least an interpretation, of the *uti possidetis juris* position'.[211]

---

206    *Legal Status of Eastern Greenland* (n 199) 46, 52–4. Further on thinly populated territory, see ibid 682 [134].

207    LFE Goldie, 'The Critical Date' (1963) 12(4) *International and Comparative Law Quarterly* 1251, 1251. See also Hugh Thirlway, *The Law and Procedure of the International Court of Justice: Fifty Years of Jurisprudence* (Oxford University Press, 2013) vol 1, pt III.B.IV; vol 2, pt III.B.IV.

208    *El Salvador v Honduras* (n 153) 401 [67].

209    On *uti possidetis*, see Section 5.4.1.

210    *El Salvador v Honduras* (n 153) 401 [67].

211    Ibid.

### 5.4.3.3 Relativity of title

The *effectivités* that a state must establish may vary depending on whether the other party to the dispute can 'make out a superior claim'.[212] That is because, when faced with two states that claim the same territory, a court generally limits itself to the question of which of those two states has a stronger claim *relative to the other* and may ignore the possibility that neither has title.[213] A caveat, given by the tribunal in *Eritrea v Yemen*, is 'there must be some absolute minimum requirement' for title 'and that in principle it ought not normally to be merely a relative question'.[214]

Relativity of title reinforces the potential importance of estoppel. Estoppel precludes a state from denying a situation if that state has engaged in 'conduct, declarations, etc., which not only clearly and consistently evidence acceptance' of that situation but have also caused another state, 'in reliance on such conduct, detrimentally to change position or suffer some preju-dice'.[215] This overlaps with the notion that territorial change by prescription requires acquies-cence (see Section 5.4.2.4). But estoppel does not necessarily transfer territory from one state to another. What it may do is preclude the estopped state from maintaining a claim to territory relative to another state, regardless of which state would otherwise have the stronger claim.

## 5.4.4 Special types of territory

This chapter has focused on ordinary land territory. One area of land, Antarctica, is unique. Several states, including Australia, claim parts of it as their own territory, but they and other states have agreed to a special regime governed by the Antarctic Treaty (see Chapter 14). It provides that 'Antarctica shall be used for peaceful purposes only'.[216] It also precludes new territorial claims:

> ***Article IV***
> 1. Nothing contained in the present treaty shall be interpreted as:
>     (a) a renunciation by any Contracting Party of previously asserted rights of or claims to territorial sovereignty in Antarctica;
>     (b) a renunciation or diminution by any Contracting Party of any basis of claim to territorial sovereignty in Antarctica which it may have whether as a result of its activities or those of its nationals in Antarctica, or otherwise;
>     (c) prejudicing the position of any Contracting Party as regards its recognition or non-recognition of any other State's right of or claim or basis of claim to territorial sovereignty in Antarctica.
> 2. No acts or activities taking place while the present treaty is in force shall constitute a basis for asserting, supporting or denying a claim to territorial sovereignty in

---

212    *Legal Status of Eastern Greenland* (n 199) 46.
213    See, eg, *Island of Palmas* (n 149) 869; *Minquiers and Ecrehos* (n 159) 52.
214    *Eritrea v Yemen* (n 200) 313 [453].
215    *North Sea Continental Shelf (Federal Republic of Germany v Denmark) (Merits)* [1969] ICJ Rep 3, 26 [30]. See also *Temple of Preah Vihear (Cambodia v Thailand) (Merits)* [1962] ICJ Rep 6, especially 22–7, 30–1.
216    *Antarctic Treaty*, opened for signature 1 December 1959, 402 UNTS 71 (entered into force 23 June 1961) art I.

Antarctica or create any rights of sovereignty in Antarctica. No new claim, or enlargement of an existing claim, to territorial sovereignty in Antarctica shall be asserted while the present treaty is in force.[217]

There are also types of territory other than land. Maritime zones are covered in Chapter 13. Among these, a state has sovereignty over internal waters; the territorial sea, including its bed and subsoil; and, if 'an archipelagic State', the archipelagic waters (other maritime zones, in contrast, are not considered state territory).[218] Further, under the *Convention on International Civil Aviation*, 'every State has complete and exclusive sovereignty over the airspace above its territory', though the upper limit of this is not universally agreed, and treaty provisions enable air traffic.[219] As for the cosmos beyond Earth, many states are parties to the *Outer Space Treaty*, under which '[o]uter space, including the moon and other celestial bodies, is not subject to national appropriation by claim of sovereignty, by means of use or occupation, or by any other means'.[220]

# DISCUSSION QUESTIONS

(1)    Should the law require an entity to be a democracy in order to qualify as a state?

(2)    In 2022, Russia recognised two Ukrainian regions, Donetsk and Luhansk, as new states; it then cited their defence to justify invading Ukraine. Do cases like this suggest it is futile to regulate statehood, because states will just interpret or manipulate the law to suit their objectives?

(3)    Should the law permit any people living in an identifiable region (such as the Catalans in Spain, the Kurds divided among countries including Turkey and Iraq, or the residents of Western Australia) to declare independence and create a new state, with no restrictions?

(4)    If the British acquired territorial sovereignty over Australia by conquest rather than by the occupation of terra nullius, what significance might that have in the present day?

(5)    Should the law permit states or individuals to claim territory on the moon or elsewhere in outer space, or should those areas remain the common province of all humankind?

---

217    Ibid art 4.
218    *United Nations Convention on the Law of the Sea*, opened for signature 10 December 1982, 1833 UNTS 3 (entered into force 16 November 1994) arts 2, 49.
219    *Convention on International Civil Aviation*, opened for signature 7 December 1944, 15 UNTS 295 (entered into force 4 April 1947) art 1.
220    *Treaty on Principles Governing the Activities of States in the Exploration and Use of Outer Space, Including the Moon and Other Celestial Bodies*, opened for signature 27 January 1967, 610 UNTS 205 (entered into force 10 October 1967) art 2.

# 6

# JURISDICTION AND IMMUNITIES

Alison Pert

# 6.1   Introduction

The previous chapter described the extent of a state's physical territory; this chapter looks at how far a state's legal power extends. As will be seen, international law places certain limits on the right of a state to make, apply and enforce its laws – its jurisdiction – and these limits are considered in Section 6.2. International law also recognises two principal bars to the exercise of that jurisdiction: diplomatic immunity and state immunity; these are covered in Sections 6.3 and 6.4. Two other bars to jurisdiction, namely special mission immunity and the foreign act of state doctrine, are also briefly covered in Sections 6.6 and 6.7.

# 6.2   Jurisdiction
## 6.2.1   Meaning and scope

The meaning of the term 'jurisdiction' will vary according to the context. For lawyers, one of the most common usages is in relation to a court: the legal powers given to a court to hear particular kinds of cases. When we speak of state jurisdiction, however, we are referring to the power of a state to affect persons and property by prescribing, applying and enforcing its laws. Jurisdiction can be classified as legislative/prescriptive (the power to make laws), judicial/adjudicative (the power to hear and adjudicate cases) and executive/enforcement (the power to punish or ensure compliance with the law), although many jurists regard judicial jurisdiction as an aspect of enforcement jurisdiction, rather than as a separate category.[1]

State jurisdiction is an attribute of sovereignty: as Henry Wheaton noted in 1836, '[t]he supreme, exclusive power of civil and criminal legislation is ... an essential right of every independent state'.[2] More recently, the International Court of Justice ('ICJ') referred to the principle that 'each State possesses sovereignty over its own territory and that there flows from that sovereignty the jurisdiction of the State over events and persons within that territory'.[3] As a matter of domestic law, a state is free to make, apply and enforce whatever laws it likes, but as a matter of international law, a state's jurisdiction is limited by the principles of sovereignty and non-intervention in the affairs of other states. A fundamental aspect of sovereignty is that no state may exercise its power in another state, without that state's consent.[4] Thus, for example, a person in State A could not be arrested by a police officer from State B; nor could State B tax State A's citizens in State A. But less dramatic exercises of jurisdiction can also cause tension between states, such as when a state criminalises conduct occurring in other states, or when two or more states claim the right to prosecute the same crime.

The precise extent of a state's jurisdiction has not yet been defined in international law. Lassa Oppenheim lamented in 1905 that 'the matter ought to be thoroughly regulated by the

---

1    FA Mann, 'The Doctrine of Jurisdiction in International Law' (1964) 3 *Collected Courses of the Hague Academy of International Law* 1, 13; James Crawford (ed), *Brownlie's Principles of Public International Law* (Oxford University Press, 9th ed, 2019) ('*Brownlie's Principles*') 440; Roger O'Keefe, 'Universal Jurisdiction: Clarifying the Basic Concept' (2004) 2(3) *Journal of International Criminal Justice* 735, 737–8.

2    Henry Wheaton, *Elements of International Law* (Carey, Lea & Blanchard, 1836) 98.

3    *Jurisdictional Immunities of the State (Germany v Italy) (Judgment)* [2012] ICJ Rep 99, 123–4 [57].

4    See, eg, *SS 'Lotus' (France v Turkey) (Judgment)* [1927] PCIJ (ser A) No 10, 18 ('*Lotus*').

Law of Nations . . . [b]ut such regulation has as yet only partially grown up',[5] and over a century later, that is still the case. There have been attempts to codify the law, such as by the Institute of International Law in the late 19th and early 20th centuries,[6] and the Harvard Draft Research Project in 1935.[7] These have had some influence, but the parameters of state jurisdiction have largely been developed by states themselves, in the scope of their legislation, and the interpretation of that legislation in domestic courts.[8] Despite – or perhaps because of – this lack of clarity, many jurists assert that there is an underlying, basic principle: that for a state to exercise jurisdiction, there must be a genuine link between the state and the conduct or situation being regulated.[9]

## 6.2.2   The *Lotus* case

Mention should be made here of the famous case *SS 'Lotus'* (*'Lotus'*),[10] decided by the Permanent Court of International Justice in 1927. The *SS Lotus* was a French steamship, which collided on the high seas with a Turkish ship, the *Boz-Kourt*. The *Boz-Kourt* sank, with the loss of eight Turkish lives. When the *SS Lotus* arrived in Constantinople, the French officer of the watch was charged with manslaughter.[11] France protested that Turkey did not have jurisdiction to prosecute a French national for a crime committed on the high seas. It argued that the onus lay on Turkey to prove 'some title to jurisdiction recognised by international law', while Turkey argued the opposite: that it was free to exercise jurisdiction unless there was a principle of international law preventing it.[12] The Court agreed with Turkey, in the famous dictum:

> International law governs relations between independent States. The rules of law binding upon States therefore emanate from their own free will as expressed in conventions or by usages generally accepted as expressing principles of law and established in order to regulate the relations between these co-existing independent communities or with a view to the achievement of common aims. Restrictions upon the independence of States cannot therefore be presumed.[13]

This statement has become known as the '*Lotus* principle' – that states are free to act unless there is a rule of international law prohibiting the action. Its correctness continues to be debated, both as a general principle and in the specific context of jurisdiction,[14] and many

---

5    Lassa Oppenheim, *International Law* (Longmans, Green, 1905) vol 1, 194.
6    Institute of International Law, *Yearbook: Volume 7* [1883–85] 156–60; Institute of International Law, *Yearbook: Volume 36* [1931] 235–6.
7    Harvard Draft Research Project, 'Draft Convention on Jurisdiction with Respect to Crime' (1935) 29(S) *American Journal of International Law* 437.
8    See, eg, Robert Jennings and Arthur Watts (eds), *Oppenheim's International Law* (Longman, 1992) vol 1, 457.
9    This is discussed in Section 6.2.2. See, eg, Mann (n 1) 31; Crawford, *Brownlie's Principles* (n 1) 441. Brownlie has long maintained the need for such a connection: see, eg, Ian Brownlie, *Principles of International Law* (Oxford University Press, 3rd ed, 1979) 305.
10   *Lotus* (n 4) 3.
11   Ibid 10–11.
12   Ibid 18.
13   Ibid.
14   In their joint separate opinion, Judges Higgins, Kooijmans and Buergenthal described this dictum as 'represent[ing] the high water mark of *laissez-faire* in international relations . . . from an era that has been

of the specific findings in the case have been reversed by treaties.[15] As some writers have noted, the Court's broad assertion of a state's power is at odds with consistent state practice: when challenged, states endeavour to prove their entitlement to exercise jurisdiction.[16] It is also at odds with the view, described in Section 6.2.1, that some genuine or effective link must be shown before a state can exercise jurisdiction. The issue has not been authoritatively decided, but an increasing number of jurists appear to agree on the need for an effective link.[17]

The exercise of jurisdiction based on territory or nationality, as detailed in Section 6.2.4, clearly satisfies this requirement, if it exists. Problems arise in practice only where there is some foreign element – one or more of the parties is a foreign national, or the relevant conduct occurred outside the forum state. Similarly, the mere passing of legislation tends not to attract criticism from other states;[18] but applying and enforcing that legislation in cases with a foreign element may well do.[19]

Section 6.2.4 considers the different bases, generally accepted by the international community, on which jurisdiction can be exercised in such cases. The words 'generally accepted' are used because it is often not easy to characterise the rules on jurisdiction as being founded in customary international law, or general principles, or any other recognised source of international law. Some, such as jurisdiction based on territory, are simply an aspect of sovereignty; others depend on which view is taken of the '*Lotus* principle': are states free to act unless there is an international law prohibition against it, or must states first find a rule of international law permitting them to act in that way? Judge van den Wyngaert, in her dissenting opinion in *Arrest Warrant of 11 April 2000* ('*Arrest Warrant*'), explained her view of the *Lotus* principle:

> A distinction must be made between *prescriptive jurisdiction* and *enforcement jurisdiction*. The above-mentioned [*Lotus*] *dictum* concerns *prescriptive jurisdiction*: it is about what a State may do *on its own territory* when investigating and prosecuting crimes committed abroad, not about what a State may do *on the territory of other States* when prosecuting such crimes. Obviously, a State has no *enforcement jurisdiction* outside its territory: a State may, failing permission to the contrary, not exercise its power on the territory of another State. This is 'the first and foremost restriction imposed by international law upon a State'. In other words, the permissive rule only applies to prescriptive jurisdiction, not to enforcement jurisdiction: failing a prohibition, State A *may*, on its own territory, prosecute offences committed in State B *(permissive rule)*; failing a permission, State A *may not* act on the territory of State B.[20]

---

significantly overtaken by other tendencies': *Arrest Warrant of 11 April 2000 (Democratic Republic of the Congo v Belgium) (Judgment)* [2002] ICJ Rep 3, 78–9 [51] ('*Arrest Warrant*').

15   For example, following a collision on the high seas, the master or crew can only be prosecuted in the flag state of the vessel or their state of nationality: *United Nations Convention on the Law of the Sea*, opened for signature 10 December 1982, 1833 UNTS 397 (entered into force 16 November 1994) art 97 ('*UNCLOS*').

16   See, eg, Christopher Staker, 'Jurisdiction' in Malcolm Evans (ed), *International Law* (Oxford University Press, 5th ed, 2018) 295.

17   Ibid; Mann (n 1); Jennings and Watts (n 8) vol 1, 457.

18   Although, as Mills points out, the mere existence of legislation may still cause foreign nationals to modify their behaviour, and therefore be objectionable: Alex Mills, 'Rethinking Jurisdiction' (2014) 87 *British Yearbook of International Law* 197, 201.

19   See, eg, *Lotus* (n 4).

20   *Arrest Warrant* (n 14) 168 [49] (emphasis in original).

On this analysis, the 'permissive rule' of prescriptive jurisdiction is again simply an integral aspect of sovereignty, while the 'permission' required for a state to exercise enforcement jurisdiction outside its territory must be found in the consent of the other state or in some rule of international law, whether custom or treaty.

## 6.2.3   Civil jurisdiction

There are two schools of thought on whether international law imposes any limits on the exercise of a state's civil jurisdiction – that is, the regulation of all non-criminal matters, from marriage and nationality to torts and contracts. On one view, there is no substantive difference between civil and criminal jurisdiction: excessive civil jurisdiction might be just as much a violation of another state's sovereignty as excessive criminal jurisdiction, and many enforcement measures (such as fines, or seizure of property) are as coercive as those in the criminal sphere.[21] The other view is that there are no such limits: cases involving a foreign element are resolved according to the rules of private international law, or conflict of laws,[22] and states rarely lodge diplomatic protests complaining of excessive civil jurisdiction. Michael Akehurst argued that:

> The acid test of the limits of jurisdiction in international law is the presence or absence of diplomatic protests ... In practice the assumption of jurisdiction by a State does not seem to be subject to any requirement that the defendant or the facts of the case need have any connection with that State; and this practice seems to have met with acquiescence by other States. .... It is hard to resist the conclusion that (apart from the well-known rules of immunity for foreign States, diplomats, international organizations, etc.) customary international law imposes no limits on the jurisdiction of municipal courts in civil trials.[23]

### 6.2.3.1   The *Alien Tort Statute of 1789*

This argument loses some force when it is remembered that Akehurst was writing in 1972, before some very prominent cases were decided under the US *Alien Tort Statute*.[24] This one-sentence statute was virtually ignored for 200 years but rediscovered in the late 1970s, when it began to be used by non-US plaintiffs suing foreign individuals and corporations in the US courts for human rights violations committed anywhere in the world. As the number of cases increased, other states started objecting: Australia, for example, submitted *amicus curiae* briefs to the US Supreme Court on several occasions, stating its view that the statute should be confined to cases with an appropriate connection with the United States or involving US nationals:

> The primary basis for jurisdiction under international law is territorial. Each state may regulate activity that occurs in its own territory (the 'territorial principle'). It may also

---

21    Mills (n 18) 201; Mann (n 1) 73; Ian Brownlie, *Principles of Public International Law* (Oxford University Press, 6th ed, 2003), 298. Cf Crawford, *Brownlie's Principles* (n 1) 455–60, expressing no conclusion.
22    Crawford, *Brownlie's Principles* (n 1) 455.
23    Michael Akehurst, 'Jurisdiction in International Law' (1972–73) 46 *British Yearbook of International Law* 145, 176–7.
24    28 USC § 1350. Also known as the *Alien Tort Claims Act of 1789*, it provides: 'The district courts shall have original jurisdiction of any civil action by an alien for a tort only, committed in violation of the law of nations or a treaty of the United States.'

exercise prescriptive jurisdiction in relation to the conduct of its citizens, wherever located (the 'nationality principle'). These 'are parts of a single broad principle according to which the right to exercise jurisdiction depends on there being *between the subject matter and the state exercising jurisdiction a sufficiently close connection* to justify that state in regulating the matter and perhaps also to override any competing rights of other states.[25]

In *Kiobel v Royal Dutch Petroleum Co*,[26] the US Supreme Court dramatically reduced the scope of the statute, finding that there was nothing in the *Alien Tort Statute* to rebut the strong presumption against the extraterritorial application of US statutes. This was refined in *Nestlé USA v Doe*,[27] where the US Supreme Court held that since the statute does not operate extraterritorially, it will only apply where the specific impugned conduct occurred in the United States – general corporate activity or 'mere corporate presence' in the United States is insufficient.[28]

## 6.2.4   Criminal jurisdiction

It is generally accepted that a state can exercise criminal jurisdiction on one (or more) of five bases:

- territory;
- nationality;
- passive personality;
- protection/security of the state; and
- universality.

While they have never been codified, these bases can be gleaned from the nature of sovereignty itself, state practice, and the contributions of jurists. They were listed, for example (with varying degrees of approval), in the Harvard Draft Research Project in 1935, in which a group of eminent jurists working on the codification of international law concluded:

> An analysis of modern national codes of penal law and penal procedure, checked against the conclusions of reliable writers and the resolutions of international conferences or learned societies, and supplemented by some exploration of the jurisprudence of national courts, discloses five general principles on which a more or less extensive penal jurisdiction is claimed by States at the present time.[29]

The bases are not mutually exclusive, and one state might have jurisdiction over the same crime on two or more bases. Similarly, one state may have jurisdiction based on territory, another on nationality, and so on. There is no hierarchy between the bases of jurisdiction: in such cases the state in which the accused is present has the practical advantage, but another

---

25    'Brief of the Governments of Australia and the United Kingdom ... as Amici Curiae in Support of the Petitioners on Certain Questions in Their Petition for Certiorari', *Rio Tinto plc v Sarei*, 569 US 945 (2013), 14 (citations omitted) (emphasis in original).

26    569 US 108 (2013) ('*Kiobel*').

27    US Supreme Court, 141 S Ct 1931 (2021).

28    Ibid 3–5.

29    Harvard Draft Research Project (n 7) 445.

state could also prosecute the accused, if its domestic law permits trials *in absentia*, or it could request the accused's extradition to that state.[30]

### 6.2.4.1    The territoriality principle

Every state has jurisdiction over crimes committed in its territory, including by non-nationals. This is an integral part of sovereignty, as noted by the ICJ in *Jurisdictional Immunities of the State*,[31] and uncontroversial. Also, a crime can begin in one state and be completed in another, such as where a shot is fired in State A and kills a person across the river in State B. State A (where the offence began) has jurisdiction based on what is known as subjective territoriality, and State B (where the offence was completed) on the basis of objective territoriality.[32]

The *Lotus* case is often cited as an example of objective territoriality because the 'effect' of the alleged crime was felt on the Turkish ship, and the Court assimilated the Turkish ship to Turkish territory.[33] This is a useful illustration of objective territoriality but not one that would hold today: art 97(1) of the *United Nations Convention on the Law of the Sea*[34] provides that where there is a collision on the high seas, criminal proceedings against the master or crew of a vessel can only be instituted by the flag state of that vessel – in the *Lotus* case, France.

The principle applies equally to conspiracy and other 'inchoate' offences as in *Liangsiriprasert v United States*,[35] where the UK Privy Council confirmed the jurisdiction of the Hong Kong courts over a conspiracy to import drugs from Thailand into the United States. The accused had been arrested in Hong Kong and challenged his extradition to the United States. The Privy Council reasoned:

> [I]nchoate crimes of conspiracy, attempt and incitement developed with the principal object of frustrating the commission of a contemplated crime by arresting and punishing the offenders before they committed the crime. … If evidence is obtained that a terrorist cell operating abroad is planning a bombing campaign in London what sense can there be in the authorities holding their hand and not acting until the cell comes to England to plant the bombs, with the risk that the terrorists may slip through the net?[36]

### 6.2.4.2    Extended territoriality and the 'effects doctrine'

It is a principle of statutory interpretation in Australia, the United Kingdom, the United States and many other countries that legislation is not intended to have extraterritorial effect unless it says so expressly or by necessary implication.[37] It is quite common for legislation to do this, and for states to extend the notion of objective territoriality to include not just offences committed partly on their territory, but those committed outside the state but which have an

---

30    Extradition is explained in Section 6.2.6.
31    *Jurisdictional Immunities of the State* (n 3) 123–4 [57].
32    *Ward v The Queen* (1980) 142 CLR 308.
33    *Lotus* (n 4) 23.
34    *UNCLOS* (n 15).
35    [1991] 1 AC 225.
36    Ibid 250.
37    See, eg, Dennis Pearce, *Statutory Interpretation in Australia* (LexisNexis Butterworths, 9th ed, 2019) 218; Mann (n 1) 64 (United Kingdom); *Kiobel* (n 26) (United States).

effect,[38] or result,[39] within the state. The New South Wales Crimes Act, for example, creates certain offences with a 'geographical nexus', including where 'the offence is committed wholly outside the State, but the offence has an effect in the State'.[40]

In this example, the 'effect' does not have to be physical; it can be a threat to the 'peace, order or good government' of the state.[41] As generally applied, these kinds of provisions cause few problems in practice, but US anti-trust legislation in particular has attracted international criticism because of its very broad reach.[42] The legislation provides for civil and criminal penalties for anti-competitive conduct by foreign corporations outside the United States which has an adverse effect on US imports or exports – potentially including any loss suffered by any importing or exporting US corporation.[43] This somewhat tenuous connection is sometimes referred to as the 'effects doctrine', although the term is not always used uniformly. The 'effects doctrine' could be regarded as an (extremely) extended form of objective territoriality, where acts commenced outside the state have economic rather than physical effects in the state.

In the 1970s *Westinghouse* litigation,[44] 29 foreign uranium producers (including four Australian companies) were sued by Westinghouse, a US corporation, in the US courts. Westinghouse alleged that the foreign corporations, who all operated outside the United States, had agreed to fix the price of uranium in violation of US law, and it claimed USD6 billion in damages.[45] Concerned that proceedings might be taken in Australia to enforce any judgment, the Commonwealth passed the *Foreign Proceedings (Excess of Jurisdiction) Act 1984*. This permits the Attorney-General to issue orders preventing the enforcement of a judgment in certain circumstances, such as foreign anti-trust suits.[46]

The European Union[47] and several countries (including the United Kingdom[48] and China[49]) have enacted similar blocking legislation to protect their nationals from US sanctions

---

38    The Permanent Court of International Justice in *Lotus* (n 4) referred to an offence having 'produced its effects' in another state: at 23.
39    See, eg, *Criminal Code Act 1995* (Cth) sch 1 ('*Criminal Code*') divs 14–16.
40    *Crimes Act 1900* (NSW) s 10C. Similarly, *Criminal Code* ibid divs 14 and 15 provide for 'standard' and 'extended' geographical jurisdiction, covering different categories ranging from conduct by anyone wholly or partly in Australia, to conduct by Australian citizens or residents anywhere in the world, to conduct by anyone anywhere. If the conduct occurs wholly outside Australia by a person who is not an Australian citizen, the Attorney-General's consent is required for the prosecution: at s 16.2.
41    *Crimes Act 1900* (NSW) s 10B(3). Examples might range from economic effects to civil unrest stirred by sedition.
42    The European Union has similar but less far-reaching competition laws: *Intel Corporation Inc v European Commission* (Court of Justice of the European Union, C-413/14 P, ECLI:EU:C:2017:632, 6 September 2017).
43    *Sherman Antitrust Act of 1890*, 15 USC §§ 1–7 (1992) and related legislation.
44    *Re Westinghouse Electric Corporation Uranium Contract Litigation*, 563 F 2d 992, 996 (10th Cir, 1977).
45    Explanatory Memorandum, Foreign Proceedings (Excess of Jurisdiction) Bill 1983 (Cth) 5 [8].
46    *Foreign Proceedings (Excess of Jurisdiction) Act 1984* (Cth) ss 9–14.
47    See *Council Regulation (EC) No 2271/96 of 22 November 1996 Protecting against the Effects of the Extra-Territorial Application of Legislation Adopted by a Third Country* [1996] OJ L 309/1. See also 'Guidance Note – Questions and Answers: Adoption of Update of the Blocking Statute' [2018] OJ C 2771/4.
48    See *Protection of Trading Interests Act 1980* (UK); *Protecting against the Effects of the Extraterritorial Application of Third Country Legislation (Amendment) (EU Exit) Regulations 2020* (UK). See also 'Guidance: Protection of Trading Interests (Retained Blocking Regulation)', *GOV.UK* (Web Page, 19 November 2020) <www.gov.uk/guidance/protection-of-trading-interests-retained-blocking-regulation>.
49    See «号 阻断外国法律与措施不当域外适用办法» [Rules on Counteracting Unjustified Extra-Territorial Applications of Foreign Legislation and Other Measures] (People's Republic of China) Ministry of Commerce, 9 January 2021.

regimes, many of which apply extraterritorially to non-US nationals. The European Union has stated publicly that it 'does not recognise the extra-territorial application of laws adopted by third countries and considers such effects to be contrary to international law'.[50]

### 6.2.4.3   The nationality principle

A state has jurisdiction over its nationals for crimes wherever committed, although that jurisdiction cannot be enforced extraterritorially.[51] In Australia, the nationality principle has been confirmed in cases such as *XYZ v Commonwealth*.[52] XYZ, an Australian citizen, was charged under the *Crimes (Child Sex Tourism) Amendment Act 1994* (Cth) with offences committed in Thailand. He challenged the constitutional validity of the legislation, arguing that a law which applied to conduct outside Australia was beyond the legislative competence of the Parliament.[53] In the course of rejecting this argument, Gleeson CJ stated:

> The territorial principle of legislative jurisdiction over crime is not the exclusive source of competence recognised by international law. Of primary relevance to the present case is the nationality principle, which covers conduct abroad by citizens or residents of a state. . . .
>
> . . .
>
> Where a state legislates with respect to the conduct abroad of its citizens and residents, and exercises judicial power only upon their return, there is ordinarily no invasion of the domestic concerns of the place where the conduct occurred.[54]

Jurisdiction based on nationality is premised on the duty of allegiance owed by a national to his or her state.[55] Most states restrict the exercise of this jurisdiction to varying degrees, but '[b]oth the crimes abroad for which it will punish its nationals and the circumstances under which it will exercise jurisdiction are matters which international law leaves each State free to decide according to local needs and conditions'.[56] The nationality principle extends to legal as well as natural persons; corporations generally have the nationality of the state where they are incorporated.[57] Many states, such as Australia, also extend their legislation to permanent residents of the state, as well as citizens. The international legality of this was doubted in 1935,[58] but is now widely accepted.[59]

### 6.2.4.4   The passive personality principle

Some states, including Australia, apply their legislation to crimes where the victim is a national of that state.[60] This is known as the passive personality principle. The authors of the Harvard

---

50    'Extraterritoriality (Blocking Statute)', *European Commission* (Web Page) <https://ec.europa.eu/info/business-economy-euro/banking-and-finance/international-relations/blocking-statute_en>.

51    See, eg, Mann (n 1) 29.

52    *XYZ v Commonwealth* (2006) 227 CLR 532.

53    Ibid [8].

54    Ibid [4], [16].

55    Harvard Draft Research Project (n 7) 519.

56    Ibid 531.

57    *Barcelona Traction, Light and Power Company Ltd (Belgium v Spain) (Judgment)* [1970] ICJ Rep 3, 42.

58    Harvard Draft Research Project (n 7) 533.

59    See, eg, Staker (n 16) 301; Crawford, *Brownlie's Principles* (n 1) 443.

60    See, eg, *Criminal Code* (n 39) div 104.

Draft Convention in 1935 found it was not supported widely enough to be accepted in international law.[61] One objection was expressed by Judge Moore in his dissenting opinion in the *Lotus* case in 1927:

> In substance, it means that the citizen of one country, when he visits another country, takes with him for his 'protection' the law of his own country and subjects those with whom he comes into contact to the operation of that law. In this way an inhabitant of a great commercial city, in which foreigners congregate, may in the course of an hour unconsciously fall under the operation of a number of foreign criminal codes. ...
>
> No one disputes the right of a State to subject its citizens abroad to the operations of its own penal laws, if it sees fit to do so. This concerns simply the citizen and his own government, and no other government can properly interfere. But the case is fundamentally different where a country claims either that its penal laws apply to other countries and to what takes place wholly within such countries or, if it does not claim this, that it may punish foreigners for alleged violations, even in their own country, of laws to which they were not subject.[62]

Nearly a century later, the principle has gained greater acceptance, but is usually confined to very serious offences. It was applied, for example, in two US cases: *United States v Benitez*[63] in 1984 (for conspiracy to murder a US government agent) and *United States v Yunis*[64] in 1991 (for aircraft hijacking). The principle appears in some treaties, such as the *International Convention against the Taking of Hostages*[65] and the *Convention against Torture and Other Cruel, Inhuman or Degrading Treatment or Punishment* ('*Convention against Torture*'),[66] and was considered uncontroversial by Judges Higgins, Kooijmans and Buergenthal in their joint separate opinion in the *Arrest Warrant* case:

> The movement is towards bases of jurisdiction other than territoriality. 'Effects' or 'impact' jurisdiction is embraced both by the United States and, with certain qualifications, by the European Union. Passive personality jurisdiction, for so long regarded as controversial, is now reflected ... in the legislation of various countries ... and today meets with relatively little opposition, at least so far as a particular category of offences is concerned.[67]

## 6.2.4.5   The protective principle

Under the protective, or security, principle states may proscribe and punish acts which threaten or injure their national interest or security, even when committed outside the state

---

61    Harvard Draft Research Project (n 7) 579.
62    *Lotus* (n 4) 92–3.
63    741 F 2d 1312 (1984).
64    924 F 2d 1086 (1991).
65    *International Convention against the Taking of Hostages*, opened for signature 17 December 1979, 1316 UNTS 205 (entered into force 3 June 1983) art 5(1)(d), and most other counter-terrorism conventions.
66    *Convention against Torture and Other Cruel, Inhuman or Degrading Treatment or Punishment*, opened for signature 10 December 1984, 1465 UNTS 85 (entered into force 26 June 1987) art 5(1)(c) ('*Convention against Torture*').
67    *Arrest Warrant* (n 14) 76–7 [47].

by non-nationals.[68] These are acts against the vital interests of the state (as opposed to its nationals), such as treason, counterfeiting,[69] terrorism and espionage. The Australian *Criminal Code* has extensive provisions on treason, espionage and similar offences, covering conduct by any person within or outside Australia.[70]

The cases of *Joyce v Director of Public Prosecutions* (*'Joyce'*)[71] and *Attorney-General (Israel) v Eichmann* (*'Eichmann'*)[72] are often invoked as examples of this jurisdiction, although neither is a particularly clear example. In the UK case of *Joyce*, William Joyce was prosecuted for treason – broadcasting pro-German propaganda – committed in Germany during World War II.[73] He was not a British citizen, but he had obtained a British passport by fraud and had used that passport to travel to Germany. His prosecution was challenged on the basis that, as neither a British citizen nor an alien resident in Britain, Joyce did not owe allegiance to the British Crown, and a person cannot be guilty of treason if they do not owe allegiance. The House of Lords concluded that as long as he held a British passport, Joyce owed allegiance to Britain and was therefore capable of committing treason. It was only in passing that one of the Law Lords mentioned the protective principle to reinforce this conclusion:

> No principle of comity demands that a state should ignore the crime of treason committed against it outside its territory. On the contrary a proper regard for its own security requires that all those who commit that crime, whether they commit it within or without the realm should be amenable to its laws.[74]

In *Eichmann*, the wartime head of the Gestapo's Jewish office, in charge of the Holocaust, was prosecuted in the Israeli District Court for war crimes and crimes against the Jewish people. The Court held that it had jurisdiction to try the case, in part under the protective principle: 'this crime very deeply concerns the vital interests of the State of Israel, and pursuant to the "protective principle," this State has the right to punish the criminals'.[75] The state of Israel did not exist at the time of the crimes but the Court, in reasoning that is very hard to follow, found that the legislation was validly retrospective.[76]

In *United States v Benitez*,[77] a charge of conspiracy to murder a US government official (in the Drug Enforcement Agency) was upheld on the basis of both the protective and the passive personality principles: 'Under the protective principle, the crime certainly had a potentially adverse effect upon the security or governmental functions of the nation.'[78]

While the principle is well accepted, its limits are unclear, and it is open to abuse. A state may defend its arrest of, say, foreign journalists critical of the government,

---

68    Harvard Draft Research Project (n 7) 543.
69    For example, of currency or passports.
70    *Criminal Code* (n 39) ss 80.4, 91.7, 91.10, 91.14.
71    [1946] AC 347.
72    *A-G (Israel) v Eichmann* (1968) 36 ILR 18 (District Court, Jerusalem, 12 December 1961); *Eichmann v A-G (Israel)* (1968) 36 ILR 277 (Supreme Court of Israel, 29 May 1962).
73    The broadcasts were heard in Great Britain where he gained the nickname 'Lord Haw-Haw' because of his upper-class British accent.
74    *Joyce v DPP* [1946] AC 347, 372 (Lord Howitt LC).
75    *A-G (Israel) v Eichmann* (n 72) 54 [35] (District Court, Jerusalem).
76    Ibid 54–5 [36]–[38].
77    741 F 2d 1312 (1984).
78    Ibid 1316.

claiming that they are threatening national security, when on another view the journalists are simply reporting the facts.

### 6.2.4.6   The universality principle

In its purest form, the universality principle – or universal jurisdiction – permits a state to exercise jurisdiction where there is no link at all between that state and the crime. The conduct takes place in another state; neither the offender nor the victim is a national of the state; and there is no threat to the state's security or vital interests. In practice, the exercise of universal jurisdiction is usually limited to cases where the offender is present in the forum state.

International law permits a state to exercise universal jurisdiction in relation to 'the most serious crimes under international law'.[79] Whether a state does actually exercise such jurisdiction depends on that state's domestic law. While there is no agreed list of such crimes, they are the handful of crimes which are so serious that they are of concern to the whole international community, and are universally condemned.[80] They include[81] piracy,[82] slavery,[83] war crimes,[84] crimes against peace,[85] crimes against humanity,[86] genocide[87] and torture.[88] In addition to being international crimes, their prohibition has *jus cogens* status.[89]

---

79    Sixth Committee (Legal), 'The Scope and Application of the Principle of Universal Jurisdiction', *General Assembly of the United Nations* (Web Page) <www.un.org/en/ga/sixth/75/universal_jurisdiction.shtml>. The Sixth Committee has been studying this subject since 2009 and gathers reports from states (and organisations) on their views and practice in relation to universal jurisdiction.

80    See, eg, Canada, 'The Scope and Application of the Principle of Universal Jurisdiction', Submission to the Sixth Committee, 3 November 2020 <www.un.org/en/ga/sixth/75/pdfs/statements/universal_jurisdiction/11mtg_canz_e.pdf>.

81    See, eg, *The Princeton Principles on Universal Jurisdiction* (2001) principle 2(1) <https://lapa.princeton.edu/hosteddocs/unive_jur.pdf>. See also Chapter 12.

82    Wheaton in 1836 wrote that a state's judicial power extended to 'the punishment of piracy and other offences against the law of nations, by whomsoever and wheresoever committed': Wheaton (n 2) 110. Piracy is defined narrowly in *UNCLOS* (n 15) art 101.

83    Slavery is often included within crimes against humanity: see, eg, *Rome Statute of the International Criminal Court*, opened for signature 17 July 1998, 2187 UNTS 3 (entered into force 1 July 2002) art 7 ('*Rome Statute*').

84    There is no single definition of war crimes: see, eg, *The Charter and Judgment of the Nürnberg Tribunal*, Memorandum by the Secretary-General, UN Doc A/CN.4/5 (1949) app 2 ('*Charter of the International Military Tribunal*') art 6(b) ('War crimes: namely, violations of the laws or customs of war') <https://legal.un.org/ilc/documentation/english/a_cn4_5.pdf>; *Rome Statute* ibid art 8; *Polyukhovich v Commonwealth* (1991) 172 CLR 501, 664 (Toohey J): 'War crimes in international law are contraventions of the laws and customs of war recorded in such documents as the Hague Conventions of 1907 and in military manuals.'

85    See, eg, *Charter of the International Military Tribunal* (n 84) art 6(a) ('Crimes against peace: planning, preparation, initiation or waging of a war of aggression, or a war in violation of international treaties, agreements or assurances'). See now the definition of aggression in the *Rome Statute* (n 83) art 8 *bis* ('the planning, preparation, initiation or execution . . . of an act of aggression which, by its character, gravity and scale, constitutes a manifest violation of the *Charter of the United Nations*').

86    *Report of the International Law Commission on the Work of Its Seventy-First Session*, UN GAOR, 74th sess, Supp No 10, UN Doc A/74/10 (2019) ch IV(E)(2) ('*Draft Articles on Prevention and Punishment of Crimes against Humanity, with Commentary*') art 2; *Rome Statute* (n 83) art 7.

87    *Convention on the Prevention and Punishment of the Crime of Genocide*, opened for signature 9 December 1948, 78 UNTS 277 (entered into force 12 January 1951) art IV.

88    *Convention against Torture* (n 66) art 1(1).

89    *Report of the International Law Commission on the Work of Its Seventy-Third Session*, UN GAOR, 77th sess, Supp No 10, UN Doc A/77/10 (2022) ch IV ('*Draft Conclusions on Peremptory Norms of General International Law (Jus Cogens), with Commentary*') 16 (Draft Conclusion 23).

### 6.2.4.7    'Prosecute or extradite' treaties

There is a growing number of treaties on particular crimes, such as war crimes, torture and terrorism, aimed at ending impunity by reducing the places where those who commit atrocities can find refuge.[90] The treaties typically prohibit the relevant act, and require states parties to establish jurisdiction over the crime,[91] and to arrest and either prosecute an accused found on their territory, or extradite the person to another state possessing jurisdiction ('*aut dedere aut judicare*'). Whereas the principle of universal jurisdiction *permits* a state to prosecute, these treaties *require* a state to do so (or extradite). The ICJ confirmed this in its 2012 decision in *Questions relating to the Obligation to Prosecute or Extradite*.[92] The former Head of State of Chad, Hissène Habré, was accused of crimes against humanity and torture while in office and had taken refuge in Senegal in 1990. The Court found that Senegal was in breach of the *Convention against Torture* for not having passed the laws necessary to establish jurisdiction over Habré, and for failing to prosecute him or to extradite him to Belgium (a party to the Convention that was willing and able to prosecute).[93]

### 6.2.4.8    Universal jurisdiction in national courts

Many states choose to exercise universal jurisdiction over international crimes. Spain and Belgium originally had extremely wide laws, enabling prosecutions with no connection to the crime, victim or perpetrator, but Belgium now requires that either the victim or perpetrator be a Belgian national or resident.[94] The Netherlands is equally active, albeit subject to similar jurisdictional limits,[95] for example in 2021 convicting a Syrian man of war crimes committed during the Syrian civil war.[96] Many countries are still extraditing or prosecuting *génocidaires* from the Rwandan genocide in 1994.[97]

## 6.2.5    Accused brought 'unlawfully' before the court

Where the accused has been brought unlawfully before the court, for example by abduction, or not in compliance with an extradition agreement, this may constitute a violation of

---

90    See, eg, *Convention against Torture* (n 66). See also the list of treaties in Zdzislaw Galicki, Special Rapporteur, *Preliminary Report on the Obligation to Extradite or Prosecute (Aut Dedere aut Judicare)*, UN Doc A/CN.4/571 (7 June 2006) 11 [37].

91    In most states, establishing jurisdiction over a crime entails making the act a crime under the state's laws, and making provision for its prosecution.

92    *Questions relating to the Obligation to Prosecute or Extradite (Belgium v Senegal) (Judgment)* [2012] ICJ Rep 422.

93    Ibid.

94    Steven Ratner, 'Belgium's War Crimes Statute: A Postmortem' (2003) 97(4) *American Journal of International Law* 888. See also Center for Justice and Accountability, 'Spanish Congress Enacts Bill Restricting Spain's Universal Jurisdictions Law' (Web Page, 2009) <https://cja.org/spanish-congress-enacts-bill-restricting-spains-universal-jurisdiction-law/?id=740>; TRIAL International, *Universal Jurisdiction Database* <https://trialinternational.org/resources/universal-jurisdiction-database>.

95    The accused must be on Dutch soil or the offender or victim must be a Dutch national: Human Rights Watch, *The Legal Framework for Universal Jurisdiction in the Netherlands* (Report, 2014) <www.hrw.org/sites/default/files/related_material/IJ0914Netherlands_0.pdf>.

96    Alina Rizvi, 'Hague Court Convicts Syrian Man for War Crimes and Membership in Terrorist Organization', *Jurist* (Blog Post, 22 April 2021) <www.jurist.org/news/2021/04/hague-court-convictssyrian-man-for-war-crimes-and-membership-in-terrorist-organization>.

97    For example, Canada and France: see TRIAL International (n 94).

sovereignty, or a breach of the treaty. But at the domestic level, courts' responses vary.[98] In *State v Ebrahim*,[99] the South African Supreme Court found that the trial court had no jurisdiction to hear the prosecution of an accused abducted from Swaziland, apparently by South African agents, holding:

> When the state is a party to a dispute, as for example in criminal cases, it must come to court with 'clean hands'. When the state itself is involved in an abduction across international borders, as in the present case, its hands are not clean.[100]

In *Moti v The Queen*,[101] the Australian High Court stayed the prosecution of the former Attorney-General of the Solomon Islands. His deportation by the Solomon Islands to Australia, facilitated by the Australian government, was unlawful under local law because the statutory period for judicial review of the deportation order had not expired. The High Court held that the involvement of Australian government officials rendered the prosecution an abuse of process.[102]

By contrast, the US Supreme Court in *United States v Alvarez-Machain*[103] held that the accused's abduction from Mexico, with US government approval, was no bar to his prosecution in the United States; any violation of Mexico's sovereignty was a diplomatic matter concerning the executive arm of government, not the judiciary.[104] For similar reasons, the abduction from Argentina of Adolf Eichmann, one of the Nazi officials overseeing the Holocaust, did not oust the jurisdiction of the Israeli courts to try him for crimes against the Jewish people.[105]

## 6.2.6 Extradition

In stark contrast to abduction, extradition is the formal process whereby a person can be lawfully sent from one state to another where he or she has been accused or convicted of an offence. There is no duty to extradite in customary international law; there are, however, hundreds of extradition treaties in which the parties agree to surrender individuals on certain conditions.[106] Commonly, the offence must be of a minimum severity; the conduct must be an offence in both the requesting and the requested states ('double criminality'); and the requesting state promises to prosecute the individual only for the specified offence ('speciality'). Frequent reasons for refusing extradition are that the offence is a political offence rather than a common crime;[107] that if extradited the person faces torture or

---

98    See also Malcolm Shaw, *International Law* (Cambridge University Press, 9th ed, 2021) 585–7.
99    (1991) 31 ILM 888.
100   Ibid 896.
101   (2011) 245 CLR 456.
102   Ibid 461 [2].
103   504 US 655 (1992).
104   Ibid 669.
105   *Eichmann v A-G (Israel)* (n 72) 304–8 (Supreme Court of Israel).
106   See, eg, 'Countries with Which Australia Has a Bilateral Extradition Treaty', *Attorney-General's Department* (Web Page, 3 December 2019) <www.ag.gov.au/international-relations/publications/countries-which-australia-has-bilateral-extradition-treaty>.
107   There is no general definition of 'political offence' but the term is usually taken to mean offences against the state (eg espionage, rebellion and treason) rather than against the person.

persecution,[108] or the death penalty; that the person has already been punished for or acquitted of substantially the same offence; or that extradition will have exceptionally serious consequences because of the person's age or health.[109]

Many states have a procedure that is followed when an extradition request is received. In Australia, for example, this is set out in the *Extradition Act 1998* (Cth). The Attorney-General has discretion whether to accept the request. If the request is accepted, it is referred to a magistrate; the person is arrested; and the magistrate holds a hearing to determine whether the person is eligible for surrender.[110] The alleged guilt or innocence of the person is irrelevant: the magistrate determines only whether the procedural requirements have been satisfied, whether the offence is an extradition offence (double criminality, etc), and whether there are any 'extradition objections' (political offence, possibility of persecution, etc). If the magistrate decides that these conditions are satisfied, the Attorney-General may order the person's extradition.[111] The individual can appeal against the decision of the magistrate, up to the High Court. This happened in the case of 'Captain Dragan' who was wanted by Croatia for alleged war crimes committed there in the early 1990s; he fought extradition from Australia for nine years and through 13 appeals before finally being extradited in 2015.[112]

# 6.3   Diplomatic immunity

As seen in Section 6.2, in principle a state has complete and exclusive jurisdiction within its territory. However, certain *foreign* entities or individuals have immunity from that jurisdiction. The two principal classes of immunity are diplomatic immunity, covered in this section, and state (or sovereign) immunity, covered in Section 6.4. Immunity operates as a bar to jurisdiction: the local law still applies to the person or entity, but no proceedings can be taken against them for as long as they hold that immunity.

'Diplomatic immunity' in this section is a shorthand term for the body of rules governing the privileges, immunities and duties of diplomatic personnel sent by one state (the 'sending state') to another (the 'receiving state'). This area of law is one of the oldest in international law: rulers have always needed to communicate with each other, and would therefore send envoys to foreign lands. It was in their mutual interest to ensure that their envoys were protected from harm, and able to complete their mission without hindrance. From the 17th century it became more common for states to establish permanent missions to other states, instead of relying on envoys for particular communications.[113]

---

108   This international law obligation exists even without an extradition treaty: see, eg, UN Human Rights Committee, *General Comment No 31 [80]: The Nature of the General Legal Obligation Imposed on States Parties to the [International] Covenant [on Civil and Political Rights]*, UN Doc CCPR/C/21/Rev.1/Add 13 (adopted 29 March 2004).
109   See, eg, *Extradition Act 1988* (Cth) s 23(3)(f); *Extradition Act 2003* (UK) s 91.
110   *Extradition Act 1998* (Cth) ss 12–19. See also 'Extradition', *Attorney-General's Department* (Web Page) <www.ag.gov.au/international-relations/international-crime-cooperation-arrangements/extradition>.
111   *Extradition Act 1988* (Cth) s 22.
112   *Snedden v Minister for Justice* (2014) 230 FCR 82.
113   Wheaton (n 2) 167.

## 6.3.1   Diplomatic relations

Each state is free to decide whether, and with what other states, to establish diplomatic relations. One prerequisite is that the two states must recognise each other as states (see Chapter 5). For example, within a month of Kosovo declaring its independence from Serbia in 2008, over 30 states recognised it as a new, independent state: at the time of writing, 117 states recognise Kosovo.[114] The United States, the United Kingdom and Australia were among the first to do so, and almost immediately established diplomatic relations with it. Kosovo has an embassy in each of these states; the United States and United Kingdom have embassies in the Kosovo capital, Pristina, and the Australian embassy in Croatia is accredited to Kosovo.[115] As this illustrates, a physical presence in a country is not necessary for the existence of diplomatic relations. Few countries can afford a diplomatic mission in every other state, and it is very common for one ambassador to be accredited to several states in the region.[116]

While recognition is a prerequisite for diplomatic relations, the converse is not true: very rarely, two states can recognise each other but not have diplomatic relations. The United States recognises North Korea and Iran, but has no diplomatic relations with either.[117] Similarly when a state breaks off diplomatic relations with another, as the United Kingdom did with Libya in 1984,[118] this has no effect on recognition. In these situations, the two states accept each other's existence, but have no direct dealings. If they do need to communicate with each other, this is often done through a third state, which may also perform consular services on their behalf – as Sweden has done, for example, on behalf of the United States, Canada and Australia in North Korea.[119]

The international legal framework governing diplomatic relations is contained in the *Vienna Convention on Diplomatic Relations* ('*VCDR*'),[120] which has 193 parties – almost the whole international community. According to the *VCDR*, the functions of a diplomatic mission include representing the sending state, protecting its interests, reporting on developments in the receiving state, and promoting friendly relations.[121] These could be loosely described as the conduct of political, state-to-state relations.

---

114    See *Kosovo Thanks You* (Web Page) <www.kosovothanksyou.com>.

115    By contrast, neither state recognises Palestine, a non-member observer state of the United Nations recognised by nearly 140 states: 'Countries That Recognize Palestine 2022', *World Population Review* (Web Page) <https://worldpopulationreview.com/country-rankings/countries-that-recognize-palestine>.

116    See, eg, 'Foreign Embassies and Consulates in Australia', *Department of Foreign Affairs and Trade* (Web Page) <https://protocol.dfat.gov.au/Public/MissionsInAustralia>; 'Find a British Embassy, High Commission or Consulate', *GOV.UK* (Web Page) <www.gov.uk/world/embassies>.

117    'Countries', *Office of the Historian* (Web Page) <https://history.state.gov/countries>.

118    'On This Day: 17 April', *BBC* (Web Page) <http://news.bbc.co.uk/onthisday/hi/dates/stories/april/17/newsid_2488000/2488369.stm>; Geoffrey Marston (ed), 'UK Materials on International Law 1984' (1984) 55 *British Yearbook of International Law* 405, 471.

119    See, eg, 'North Korea', *Department of Foreign Affairs and Trade: Smartraveller* (Web Page) <www.smartraveller.gov.au/destinations/asia/north-korea-democratic-peoples-republic-korea>; Canada, 'North Korea', *Canada.ca* (Web Page) <https://travel.gc.ca/assistance/embassies-consulates/north-korea>; Department of State (US), 'North Korea Travel Advisory', *Travel.State.Gov* (Web Page) <https://travel.state.gov/content/travel/en/traveladvisories/traveladvisories/north-korea-travel-advisory.html>. See also *Vienna Convention on Diplomatic Relations*, opened for signature 14 April 1961, 500 UNTS 95 (entered into force 24 April 1964) arts 44, 45 ('*VCDR*').

120    *VCDR* (n 119).

121    Ibid art 3.

## 6.3.2   Consular relations

Consular functions are different. They are set out at length in the *Vienna Convention on Consular Relations* 1963 ('*VCCR*'), but essentially comprise the promotion of commercial, economic, cultural and scientific relations, issuing passports and visas, and assisting nationals in need.[122] The *VCCR* codifies the international law rules on consular relations, in much the same way that the *VCDR* codifies those on diplomatic relations; the basic rules of consular relations are regarded as customary international law and are therefore of general application.[123]

Individual consular arrangements vary considerably. Some sending states, with only a small presence in the receiving state, might have the same personnel performing diplomatic and consular functions.[124] The embassy of Tajikistan in London, for example, has a diplomatic staff of four, one of whom is also designated 'Consul'.[125] Larger missions will have designated consular sections within the mission – which is almost always in the receiving state's capital – and may also have consulates in other cities.

One of the most important consular functions is helping nationals in distress. Consular officials cannot 'solve' the problem in the sense of getting the person released from arrest or detention, but as the Australian government puts it:

> We do what we can to ensure Australians arrested or detained overseas are treated fairly under the laws of the country where they were arrested. This may include providing details of local lawyers, checking on the person's wellbeing, liaising with local authorities and helping to communicate with family members or nominated contacts.[126]

Consular officials and premises generally have similar, but less extensive, privileges and immunities to those of diplomatic personnel, which are detailed in the next section.

## 6.3.3   The *Vienna Convention on Diplomatic Relations*

The *VCDR* codifies the law on diplomatic immunity, and many of its provisions reflect customary international law.[127] It is implemented in Australia by the *Diplomatic Privileges and Immunities Act 1967*.[128] The *VCDR* deals with the privileges, immunities and inviolability of diplomatic personnel, their families and other staff of a diplomatic mission, and the

---

122   *Vienna Convention on Consular Relations*, opened for signature 24 April 1963, 596 UNTS 261 (entered into force 19 March 1967) art 5 ('*VCCR*').

123   Anne Dienelt, 'Vienna Convention on Consular Relations (1963)' in Rüdiger Wolfrum (ed), *The Max Planck Encyclopedia of Public International Law* (Oxford University Press, online, April 2011) [9]; Department of State (US), *Consular Notification and Access* (Manual, September 2018) 37 <https://travel.state.gov/content/dam/travel/CNAtrainingresources/CNA%20Manual%205th%20Edition_September%202018.pdf>.

124   This is expressly contemplated by *VCCR* (n 122) art 70.

125   Foreign and Commonwealth Office (UK), *London Diplomatic List* (2020) <www.gov.uk/government/publications/foreign-embassies-in-the-uk>.

126   Department of Foreign Affairs and Trade, *Consular State of Play: 2018–19* (2019) 11 <www.dfat.gov.au/about-us/our-services/consular-services/Pages/consular-state-of-play-2018-19>.

127   See the online instructor resources for a summary of which provisions reflect custom.

128   *Diplomatic Privileges and Immunities Act 1967* (Cth) s 7.

inviolability of the mission's premises, documents, archives and diplomatic bag. Article 1 defines some relevant terms:

    (a)   The 'head of the mission' is the person charged by the sending State with the duty of acting in that capacity;

    (b)   The 'members of the mission' are the head of the mission and the members of the staff of the mission;

    . . .

    (d)   The 'members of the diplomatic staff' are the members of the staff of the mission having diplomatic rank;

    (e)   A 'diplomatic agent' is the head of the mission or a member of the diplomatic staff of the mission . . .

The head of the mission is generally an ambassador (or as between Commonwealth countries, a High Commissioner).[129] It will usually be clear which other members of staff have diplomatic rank because their appointment, arrival and departure must be notified to the receiving state (*VCDR* art 10), and many countries publish a diplomatic list with the names and positions of all foreign diplomats accredited to that state.[130] As mentioned, it is very common for a sending state to accredit a head of mission based in one state to several other states; if a mission is established in those other states it is headed by a *chargé d'affaires ad interim* (*VCDR* art 5).[131]

### 6.3.3.1    Immunities

Diplomatic agents have the broadest immunity. They have complete immunity from criminal proceedings (art 31) – they cannot be prosecuted in the receiving state for any crime, no matter how serious. They also have immunity from civil proceedings, except where the suit concerns private immovable property, private wills and probate, or a professional or commercial activity outside their official functions (art 31(1)). The only exception to these broad protections is waiver: the sending state may decide to waive the immunity (art 32), but is under no obligation to do so.

The blanket criminal immunity in particular is much criticised, for two main reasons. First, it can easily be abused, as when foreign diplomats refuse to obey local traffic and parking rules and accrue millions of dollars in unpaid parking tickets,[132] or violate local labour laws when employing staff. Second, it protects the diplomat even if they have committed an international crime such as genocide or torture – a *jus cogens* violation. The argument that immunity should not prevail over such *jus cogens* violations is discussed in Section 6.4.4.

---

129    This is a historical quirk from the days when most Commonwealth countries were British colonies within a unified British Empire; as between themselves they were not 'foreign' and so the term 'ambassador' was considered inappropriate: Robert Stewart, *Treaty Relations of the British Commonwealth of Nations* (MacMillan, 1939) 328.

130    See, eg, 'Foreign Embassies and Consulates in Australia', *Department of Foreign Affairs and Trade* (Web Page) <https://protocol.dfat.gov.au/Public/Display>; Foreign and Commonwealth Office (UK) (n 125).

131    See, eg, 'Foreign Embassies and Consulates in Australia' (n 116).

132    The US government has introduced a policy of not renewing the registration of repeat-offender diplomatic vehicles: Department of State (US), *Diplomatic Parking Ticket Programs in New York and the District of Columbia* (Web Page) <www.state.gov/diplomatic-parking-ticket-programs-in-new-york-and-the-district-of-columbia-2>.

The usual answer to these criticisms is that immunity exists to protect the envoy from any interference in the performance of his or her functions and that any legal proceedings, and particularly a criminal prosecution, would seriously interfere with those functions.[133] Another consideration is the reciprocal nature of diplomatic relations: if a receiving state does not respect immunity, or exceptions are introduced, its own diplomats are vulnerable to similar, but perhaps politically motivated, treatment in another state.

However, in an important recent case, the UK Supreme Court (by a slim majority) held that a foreign diplomat was not immune from civil proceedings concerning the employment of a domestic worker in conditions tantamount to modern slavery.[134] The Court examined the 'commercial activity' exception in art 31 of the *VCDR*,[135] and agreed that it did not apply to ordinary contracts, such as hiring domestic staff, that were 'incidental to the daily life of a diplomat'.[136] But this was not such a contract, and the diplomat enjoyed a substantial personal financial gain from not paying the worker her entitlements.[137] The arrangement was, therefore, a commercial activity not protected by diplomatic immunity.

A diplomatic agent cannot be required to give evidence in court (art 31(3)), and is inviolable – he or she cannot be arrested or detained and must be treated with respect (art 29). He or she is immune from customs duties and most taxes in the receiving state (arts 34, 36). Family members of a diplomatic agent enjoy the same privileges and immunities, if they are part of the diplomat's household (art 37). This is not defined; in its commentary to the draft articles that formed the basis of the *VCDR*, the International Law Commission stated:

> The Commission did not feel it desirable to lay down either a criterion for determining who should be regarded as a member of the family, or a maximum age for children. The spouse and children under age at least, are universally recognized as members of the family, but cases may arise where other relatives too come into the matter ... close ties and special circumstances are necessary qualifications.[138]

Large embassies can employ hundreds of people performing different functions. The *VCDR* classifies them into four categories (art 37) – diplomatic agents, administrative and technical staff, service staff, and private servants – with decreasing degrees of immunity. The administrative and technical staff – such as information technology staff, technicians and secretaries – and their families have essentially the same privileges and immunities as diplomats, except that in civil proceedings they are immune only for acts performed in the course of their duties ('official acts') (art 37(2)). Service staff would include drivers, gardeners and cooks; these have immunity (both criminal and civil) only for their official acts, as well as exemption from income tax (art 37(3)). Private servants of the members of the mission, such as privately employed cooks, nannies and gardeners, have no immunity but are exempt from income tax (art 37(4)).

---

133    *VCDR* (n 119) Preamble.
134    *Basfar v Wong* [2022] 3 WLR 208.
135    Implemented in UK legislation by the *Diplomatic Privileges Act 1964* (UK).
136    *Basfar v Wong* (n 134) [37].
137    Ibid [56].
138    ILC, 'Draft Articles Concerning Diplomatic Intercourse and Immunities' [1957] II *Yearbook of the International Law Commission* 1, 141 (Draft Article 28 Commentary [8]). Some states have their own definition: see, eg, Department of State (US), 'Privileges and Immunities' <www.state.gov/privileges-and-immunities>.

Special rules apply if the person is a national or permanent resident of the receiving state. In principle, diplomatic agents should be nationals of the sending state (art 8(1)), and they cannot be nationals of the receiving state (or a third state) unless the receiving state agrees (art 8(2), (3)). A diplomatic agent who is a national or permanent resident of the receiving state is only entitled to immunity in respect of their official acts, unless the receiving state grants additional benefits (art 38(1)).

There is no restriction on the nationality of other staff, but if they are nationals or permanent resident of the receiving state, it is a matter for that state what if any privileges and immunities to afford them (art 38(2)). Australia, for example, grants immunity and inviolability in respect of their official acts to administrative and technical staff, and service staff, who are Australian citizens or permanent residents, and to private servants of the members of the mission.[139]

### 6.3.3.2   Appointments

The sending state must obtain the agreement of the receiving state to the proposed head of mission (art 4). The sending state is generally free to appoint other staff of the mission, but it may be required to submit the names of military, naval or air attachés for approval beforehand (art 7). As mentioned, the appointment, arrival and departure of members of the mission must be notified to the receiving state, as well as the arrival and departure of family members and private servants and the employment of residents of the receiving state (art 10).

### 6.3.3.3   Duration of immunity

The privileges and immunities begin at the moment the person enters the receiving state or, if they are already in receiving state, at the moment their appointment is notified to the receiving state (art 39(1)). They continue until the person leaves the receiving state, or on the expiry of a reasonable period in which to leave; importantly, immunity for official acts continues forever (art 39(2)).

Immunity also ceases on the expiry of a reasonable period after a person is declared *persona non grata* (literally, 'person not welcome') (art 43). The receiving state can do this at any time, even before the person has taken up their appointment, and without giving a reason; it can similarly declare other members of the mission 'not acceptable' (art 9(1)). The sending state must then recall the person, or terminate their functions; if it refuses to do so within a reasonable period, the receiving state may refuse to recognise the individual as a member of the mission (art 9(2)). This is the procedure being followed when we hear of a state 'expelling' diplomats, such as occurred in 2018 when many states 'expelled' over 150 Russian diplomats in response to the poisoning, allegedly by Russian agents, of a Russian dissident on UK territory.[140] Russia responded in kind.[141]

---

139    *Diplomatic Privileges and Immunities Act 1967* (Cth) s 11.

140    'Spy Poisoning: Nato Expels Russian Diplomats', *BBC News* (online, 27 March 2018) <www.bbc.com/news/world-asia-43550938>; 'United States, Europe Expel Russian Diplomats', *ABC News* (online, 27 March 2018) <www.abc.net.au/news/2018-03-27/donald-trump-orders-expulsion-of-60-russian-diplomats/9589922>.

141    'Russia 'Spy Poisoning: 23 UK Diplomats Expelled from Moscow', *BBC News* (online, 17 March 2018) <www.bbc.com/news/uk-43440992>.

## 6.3.3.4    Inviolability

As mentioned, a diplomatic agent is inviolable, as are their private residence, papers and property (arts 29, 30). The premises of the mission[142] and ancillary land such as a garden (art 1(i)) are also inviolable; the receiving state cannot enter without the permission of the head of the mission (art 22). Contrary to popular belief, the diplomatic and consular premises of foreign states are not an extension of the foreign state's territory; the law of the receiving state applies to them except as provided for in the *VCDR*.[143] This inviolability is why Julian Assange, an Australian citizen, was able to stay in the Ecuadorian embassy in London for seven years despite being wanted by the British authorities: the British police could not enter until 2019 when the Ecuadorean Ambassador gave his consent. This 'diplomatic asylum' is quite commonly granted, in both diplomatic and consular premises (which have the same inviolability), particularly when the sending state considers that the person seeking refuge is being prosecuted for political reasons.[144]

The complete inviolability of the mission is respected even when the premises are clearly being used for unlawful purposes. In 1984 a British police officer was shot from inside the Libyan embassy in London, but the British government nevertheless refrained from forcing entry to arrest those responsible.[145] A spectacular and extremely rare exception was the storming of the Bahraini embassy in London in 2019, when British police feared for the life of a demonstrator on the embassy roof.[146] Bahrain did not protest publicly, and indeed the embassy issued a statement thanking the police for their 'cooperation'.[147] Such incidents have led to debates about whether inviolability should be subject to exceptions, for example to save life, and whether international law already allows this through pleas of distress or necessity as a circumstance precluding wrongfulness.[148] For now, however, inviolability would seem to prevail.

A related obligation on the receiving state is the 'special duty to take all appropriate steps to protect the premises of the mission against any intrusion or damage and to prevent any disturbance of the peace of the mission or impairment of its dignity' (art 22(2)). In *Minister*

---

142    These include all buildings used for mission purposes and the residence of the head of the mission.

143    *R v Turnbull; Ex parte Petroff* (1971) 17 FLR 438. Earlier writers sometimes referred to ambassadors and their residences being 'extraterritorial', but this was a fiction that is now more accurately rendered as 'inviolable': see, eg, Lassa Oppenheim, *International Law* (Longmans, Green, 2nd ed, 1912) vol 1, 430; Henry Wheaton, *Elements of International Law* (Little, Brown, 8th ed, 1866) 304.

144    For more on diplomatic asylum see, eg, *The Institution of Asylum and Its Recognition as a Human Right in the Inter-American Protection System (Advisory Opinion)* (Inter-American Court of Human Rights, Series A No OC-25, 30 May 2018) <www.refworld.org/cases,IACRTHR,5c87ec454.html>.

145    United Kingdom, *Parliamentary Debates*, House of Commons, 25 April 1984, vol 58, col 739 (Leon Brittan) ('Statement on Libyan People's Bureau (Shooting Incident)') <https://api.parliament.uk/historic-hansard/commons/1984/apr/25/libyan-peoples-bureau-shooting-incident>.

146    'Police Storm Bahrain Embassy', *4 News* (Channel 4, 7 August 2019) <www.channel4.com/news/police-break-down-door-of-bahrain-embassy-in-uk-after-roof-protester-threatened>.

147    @BahrainEmbUK (Bahrain Embassy UK) (Twitter, 8 August 2019, 4:26am AEST) <https://twitter.com/BahrainEmbUK/status/1159168964762767360/photo/1>.

148    See, eg, the arguments in Miles Jackson, 'Inviolability and the Protest at the Bahraini Embassy', *EJIL: Talk!* (Blog Post, 9 August 2019) <www.ejiltalk.org/inviolability-and-the-protest-at-the-bahraini-embassy>; Eileen Denza, *Diplomatic Law: Commentary on the Vienna Convention on Diplomatic Relations* (Oxford University Press, 4th ed, 2016). See Chapter 7 for distress and necessity.

*for Foreign Affairs v Magno*,[149] the Federal Court of Australia upheld the validity of regulations authorising the removal of 124 white wooden crosses that had been placed outside the Indonesian embassy in Canberra in protest at Indonesian forces' actions in East Timor. The majority avoided deciding whether the crosses impaired the dignity of the mission, but suggested:

> Offensive or insulting behaviour in the vicinity of and directed to the mission may fall into this category. The burning of the flag of the sending State or the mock execution of its leader in effigy if committed in the immediate vicinity of the mission could well be construed as attacks on its dignity. So too might the depositing of some offensive substances and perhaps also the dumping of farm commodities outside mission premises.[150]

Also inviolable are the mission's documents, archives, official correspondence, diplomatic bag and diplomatic courier (arts 24 and 27). The diplomatic bag can be any shape or size, but 'the packages constituting the diplomatic bag must bear visible external marks of their character and may contain only diplomatic documents or articles intended for official use' (art 27(4)). However, since it cannot be opened or detained, the receiving state has little control over the use or abuse of the diplomatic bag, and notorious examples of abuse have occurred. One of the most commonly cited is the 1984 kidnapping in London of a former Nigerian government minister; he was drugged and placed in a crate for shipping to Nigeria as the diplomatic bag. The crate was not correctly labelled, so there was no violation of the *VCDR* when the British authorities opened the crate before it left the United Kingdom, but the UK government subsequently stated that it would have acted in the same way even if the crate had in fact constituted a diplomatic bag.[151]

There is growing acceptance of a right to subject the bag to electronic scanning, provided the contents of any communications in the bag are not revealed,[152] but the bag remains protected even if the scanning reveals illicit items.[153]

### 6.3.3.5 Duties of the sending state

Sending states must respect the laws of the receiving state, not interfere in its internal affairs, and not use the mission premises in any manner incompatible with the functions of the mission or with international law generally (art 41). One of the strongest criticisms of diplomatic asylum is that the sending state is interfering in the internal affairs of the receiving state by harbouring a fugitive from justice. Similarly, using the embassy or diplomatic bag for unlawful

---

149    (1992) 37 FCR 298.
150    Ibid 326.
151    United Kingdom, *Parliamentary Debates*, House of Commons, 6 July 1984, vol 63, col 609 (Leon Brittan) ('Mr Umaru Dikko (Abduction)') <https://api.parliament.uk/historic-hansard/commons/1984/jul/06/mr-umaru-dikko-abduction>; Denza (n 148) 203–4. For an amusing account of some of the more egregious abuses of diplomatic immunity, see 'The 6 Most Ridiculous Abuses of Diplomatic Immunity', *Cracked* (Web Page, 30 December 2011) <www.cracked.com/article_19591_6-most-ridiculous-abuses-diplomatic-immunity.html>.
152    Denza (n 148) 200–2.
153    It is accepted that an airline could refuse to carry a diplomatic bag carrying explosives, for example, but in other cases a solution would have to be negotiated between the sending and receiving states: ibid 203–4.

purposes such as drug smuggling would clearly be contrary to art 41. The perennial question is whether breach of art 41 entitles the receiving state to suspend or withdraw the privileges and immunities under the *VCDR*. It could be argued that the law of countermeasures (see Chapter 7), for example, would permit a receiving state to violate the *VCDR* as a proportionate response to the sending state's breach. However, the overwhelming consensus at present is that the duty to respect immunity is paramount. There is at least one sound policy reason for this: reciprocity. As mentioned earlier, once exceptions to immunity are introduced, particularly those capable of subjective assessment, they can be used or misused by all states.

What the receiving state can do in these – or any – circumstances is to declare one of more of the sending state's diplomatic staff *persona non grata* (art 9), or to break off diplomatic relations altogether. Either of these can be done at any time and do not require a prior violation of the *VCDR* by the other state, but they are unfriendly acts and signal, at the very least, disapproval of the other state's actions.[154] Breaking off diplomatic relations is extremely rare, even in times of armed conflict, but recent examples involve Taiwan: in 2019 Taiwan terminated diplomatic relations with Kiribati[155] shortly after the Solomon Islands withdrew its recognition of Taiwan.[156] In each case, the issue was the choice between recognising Taiwan or the People's Republic of China ('PRC'); neither will tolerate recognition of both, so when the South Pacific nations, heavily dependent on foreign aid, switched recognition from Taiwan to the PRC, diplomatic relations with Taiwan were severed. Taiwan maintains diplomatic relations with 15 states.[157]

# 6.4   Foreign state immunity

Foreign state immunity (also known as state immunity, sovereign immunity or foreign sovereign immunity) is the other main bar to the exercise of state jurisdiction. This section considers who or what is entitled to state immunity, and for what acts.

Like diplomatic immunity, state immunity has ancient roots. Nineteenth-century writers wrote about the immunity of a foreign sovereign, and his or her armed forces, public vessels and other public property,[158] but by the early 20th century they were making express reference to the immunity of the state itself.[159] The fundamental premise of this immunity is sovereign equality; because all states (and sovereigns) are equal, no state can claim jurisdiction over another state: *par in parem non habet jurisdictionem*[160] (literally, an equal does not have jurisdiction over equals). The effect is that a sovereign state cannot be sued in the courts of a

---

154   When one state breaks off diplomatic relations, it will usually specify the period allowed for the departure of mission staff (eg one week); the premises of the mission remain inviolable until then: Denza (n 148) 400–1.

155   Melissa Clarke, 'Kiribati Cuts Ties with Taiwan to Switch to China, Days after Solomon Islands', *ABC News* (online, 20 September 2019) <www.abc.net.au/news/2019-09-20/kiribati-to-switch-diplomatic-ties-from-taiwan-to-china/11532192>.

156   ABC/Reuters, 'Solomon Islands Breaks Ties with Taiwan after Chinese "Dollar Diplomacy"', *ABC News* (online, 17 September 2019) <www.abc.net.au/news/2019-09-16/solomon-islands-cuts-taiwan-ties-after-china-dollar-diplomacy/11510898>.

157   Taiwan Government, 'Foreign Affairs', *Taiwan.gov.tw* (Web Page) <https://taiwan.gov.tw/content_5.php>.

158   See, eg, WE Hall, *Treatise on International Law* (MacMillan, 3rd ed, 1890) 165–98; Wheaton (n 2) 153.

159   Oppenheim, *International Law*, 169.

160   Sometimes rendered as *par in parem non habet dominium*: ibid.

foreign state, subject to certain exceptions. The principle is customary international law,[161] but its precise extent and application are unclear. This is partly because unlike diplomatic immunity, state immunity has not been codified. The only treaties are the 1972 *European Convention on State Immunity*,[162] which is restricted to the 46 members of the Council of Europe and has only eight parties anyway, and the 2004 *United Nations Convention on Jurisdictional Immunities of States and Their Property*,[163] which is not yet in force. The detailed application of state immunity is therefore left largely to domestic courts, and it becomes essential to distinguish, where necessary, the position in international law (where there is one) from the position in domestic law; they will not always be the same.

Some states have legislation on state immunity, such as Australia (under the *Foreign States Immunities Act 1985* ('*FSIA*'))[164], the United Kingdom (*State Immunity Act 1978* ('*UK SIA*'))[165], the United States (*Foreign Sovereign Immunities Act of 1976*)[166] and Singapore (*State Immunity Act 1979* ('*Singapore SIA*'))[167]. Most domestic statutes, and the two treaties mentioned, cover only immunity from civil jurisdiction; immunity from criminal jurisdiction is largely left to customary international law, as discussed in the following sections. In international law, states cannot commit crimes,[168] but criminal jurisdiction is relevant when considering the acts of individuals.

## 6.4.1    Absolute vs restrictive immunity

There are two broad views of state immunity: the absolute approach and the restrictive approach. Under the absolute approach, a state has immunity for all acts, while under the restrictive approach, it is only immune for sovereign, or governmental, acts. Originally the absolute approach (which in practice was never completely absolute)[169] dominated, but during the 20th century it was gradually replaced by the restrictive approach because of the increasing engagement by governments in commerce and international trade: it was felt that litigants should not be deprived of a remedy in a commercial dispute just because the other party was a government.[170] China maintains the absolute approach,[171] but most other states have adopted the restrictive approach.[172]

The restrictive approach means that the relevant act must be characterised as, on the one hand, sovereign or governmental (*acta jure imperii*) or, on the other, commercial or non-

---

161    *Jurisdictional Immunities of the State* (n 3) 123 [56], confirming the conclusions of the ILC in 'Draft Articles on Jurisdictional Immunities of States and Their Property [with Commentary]' [1980] II(2) *Yearbook of the International Law Commission* 1, 147 (Draft Article 6 Commentary [26].

162    *European Convention on State Immunity*, opened for signature 16 May 1972, [1972] ETS 74 (entered into force 11 June 1976).

163    *United Nations Convention on Jurisdictional Immunities of States and Their Property*, opened for signature 2 December 2004 (not yet in force).

164    *Foreign States Immunities Act 1985* (Cth) ('*FSIA*').

165    *State Immunity Act 1978* (UK) ('*UK SIA*').

166    28 USC §§ 1330, 1441, 1602–11.

167    *State Immunity Act 1979* (Singapore) ('*Singapore SIA*').

168    *Jones v Saudi Arabia* [2007] 1 AC 270, 290 [31].

169    Hersch Lauterpacht, 'The Problem of Jurisdictional Immunities of Foreign States' (1951) 28 *British Yearbook of International Law* 220, 247; Australian Law Reform Commission, *Foreign State Immunity* (Report No 24, October 1984) 8–9.

170    Australian Law Reform Commission, *Foreign State Immunity* (n 169) 9.

171    *Democratic Republic of Congo v FG Hemisphere Associates LLC* [2011] HKCFA 42.

172    See, eg, Australian Law Reform Commission, *Foreign State Immunity* (n 169) 11–12.

governmental (*acta jure gestionis*): the latter will not be protected by immunity. The distinction is not always easy to draw, one question being whether it is the nature or the purpose of the act which should be determinative. In the landmark English case of *I Congreso del Partido*,[173] the House of Lords confirmed that the United Kingdom followed the restrictive approach and that the whole context of the case had to be considered. The simplified facts are that two Cuban ships were on their way to deliver sugar to Chile in 1973 when the Chilean régime changed (the right-wing Augusto Pinochet overthrew the left-wing Salvador Allende). The Cuban government, not willing to deal with Pinochet, ordered the ships not to deliver their cargo, with some of it instead donated to North Vietnam. The Chilean owners of the cargo brought an action for damages in the UK courts against *I Congreso del Partido*, another ship owned by the Cuban government,[174] and Cuba claimed sovereign immunity.

The Court had to decide whether the act giving rise to the claim – the failure to deliver the cargo – was sovereign, or commercial. It approved the lower court's test: 'it is not just that the purpose or motive of the act is to serve the purposes of the state, but that the act is of its own character a governmental act, as opposed to an act which any private citizen can perform'.[175] The Court concluded that while the decision not to deliver the cargo was politically motivated (the purpose of the act), it was an action that any commercial actor could take (the nature or character of the act), and was therefore not protected by immunity.[176]

The Canadian case of *Kuwait Airways Corporation v Iraq*[177] was one of many cases associated with Kuwait Airways' attempts to retrieve aircraft seized by Iraq during the 1990 invasion of Kuwait. The facts are best summarised in the headnote to the case:

> At the time of the invasion and occupation of Kuwait in 1990, the Iraqi government ordered its national airline, the Iraqi Airways Company ('IAC'), to appropriate the aircraft and equipment of the Kuwait Airways Corporation ('KAC'). After the war, KAC recovered only some of its aircraft. KAC brought an action for damages against IAC in the United Kingdom. After lengthy and difficult proceedings, IAC was ordered to pay over one billion Canadian dollars to KAC. Alleging that Iraq had controlled, funded and supervised IAC's defence throughout the proceedings, which had been marked by perjury and by tactics on the part of IAC and Iraq that were intended to deceive the British courts, KAC also claimed costs totalling approximately $84 million in Canadian currency from Iraq. In 2008, the High Court of Justice ordered Iraq to pay the amount in question. According to the English judge, Iraq's acts in controlling IAC's defence were not sovereign acts, but instead fell, under the *State Immunity Act 1978* (UK), within the commercial exception to the principle of state immunity. KAC applied for recognition of that judgment in the Quebec Superior Court. Iraq, relying on the *State Immunity Act* ('SIA'), moved for dismissal of the application for recognition on the ground that the impugned acts were sovereign acts and that it was accordingly entitled to immunity under Canadian law.[178]

173    *I Congreso del Partido* [1983] AC 244.
174    In UK maritime law, a breach by the owners of one ship can be remedied by an action against a sister ship: see, eg, Peter Glover, 'Sister Ship Arrest and the Application of the Doctrine of Attachment in Australia' (2008) 22(1) *Australian and New Zealand Maritime Law Journal* 99.
175    *I Congreso del Partido* (n 173) 269, citing *I Congreso del Partido* [1978] QB 500, 528 (Robert Goff J).
176    *I Congreso del Partido* (n 173) 245.
177    [2010] 2 SCR 571.
178    Ibid 572.

The Canadian Supreme Court rejected the claim of immunity, finding that the commercial activity exception did indeed apply:

> The nature of the acts must be examined in their full context, which includes the purpose of the acts. To this end, it is necessary to accept the English judge's findings of fact to the effect that Iraq was responsible for numerous acts of forgery, concealing evidence and lies that misled the English courts. Furthermore, the litigation in which Iraq intervened to defend IAC concerned the retention of KAC's aircraft after they had been seized. There was no connection between that commercial litigation and the initial sovereign act of seizing the aircraft.[179]

The restrictive approach is codified in the legislation of many states including Australia, the United Kingdom, Singapore and Canada, the general scheme of the legislation being to provide for foreign state immunity subject to a number of exceptions. The Australian *FSIA*, for example, which is almost identical to the *Singapore SIA* and the *UK SIA*, provides:

**9 General immunity from jurisdiction**

Except as provided by or under this Act, a foreign State is immune from the jurisdiction of the courts of Australia in a proceeding.

Sections 10–20 then set out the exceptions, including commercial contracts, certain contracts of employment, and actions for personal injury, death or damage occurring in forum state (sometimes called the 'territorial tort exception'):

**11 Commercial transactions**

(1)   A foreign State is not immune in a proceeding in so far as the proceeding concerns a commercial transaction.

. . .

(3)   In this section, *commercial transaction* means a commercial, trading, business, professional or industrial or like transaction into which the foreign State has entered or a like activity in which the State has engaged

. . .

**12 Contracts of employment**

(1)   A foreign State, as employer, is not immune in a proceeding in so far as the proceeding concerns the employment of a person under a contract of employment that was made in Australia or was to be performed wholly or partly in Australia.

. . .

**13 Personal injury and damage to property**

A foreign State is not immune in a proceeding in so far as the proceeding concerns:

(a)   the death of, or personal injury to, a person; or

(b)   loss of or damage to tangible property;

caused by an act or omission done or omitted to be done in Australia.

---

179      Ibid 573.

## 6.4.2    Who or what is entitled to immunity?

Sections 6.4.2.1–6.4.2.3 outline what comprises 'the state', and what other entities are entitled to state immunity in a foreign court. Here we are referring only to immunity from civil proceedings, because it is still generally accepted that the state itself cannot commit a crime.[180]

Sections 6.4.2.4–6.4.5 explain the different factors that determine the immunity of individuals – whether the proceedings are civil or criminal, the position held by the individual, and the functions being performed.

### 6.4.2.1    The 'state'

State immunity encompasses all the elements of a state: the Head of State, the legal person of the state itself, the executive government and its departments or organs, and individuals acting on behalf of the government. This is reflected in national legislation and the *United Nations Convention on Jurisdictional Immunities of States and Their Property*:

1.    For the purposes of the present Convention:

    . . .

    (b)    'State' means:

        (i)    the State and its various organs of government;

        (ii)    constituent units of a federal State or political subdivisions of the State, which are entitled to perform acts in the exercise of sovereign authority, and are acting in that capacity;

        (iii)    agencies or instrumentalities of the State or other entities, to the extent that they are entitled to perform and are actually performing acts in the exercise of sovereign authority of the State;

        (iv)    representatives of the State acting in that capacity . . .

Section 3 of the Australian *FSIA* is broadly to the same effect but in several provisions:

(1)    *foreign State* means a country the territory of which is outside Australia, being a country that is:

    (a)    an independent sovereign state; or

    (b)    a separate territory (whether or not it is self-governing) that is not part of an independent sovereign state.

    . . .

(3)    Unless the contrary intention appears, a reference in this Act to a foreign State includes a reference to:

    (a)    a province, state, self-governing territory or other political subdivision (by whatever name known) of a foreign State;

    (b)    the head of a foreign State, or of a political subdivision of a foreign State, in his or her public capacity; and

---

180    Although many states now impose criminal responsibility on corporations, making a prosecution of a separate entity possible: see, eg, Australian Law Reform Commission, *Corporate Criminal Responsibility* (Report No 136, April 2020).

(c) the executive government or part of the executive government of a foreign State or of a political subdivision of a foreign State, including a department or organ of the executive government of a foreign State or subdivision;

but does not include a reference to a separate entity of a foreign State.

## 6.4.2.2   Agencies and instrumentalities, separate entities

The terms 'agencies' and 'instrumentalities' refer to entities which have a legal identity separate from the state itself, such as a statutory commission, or a state-owned corporation; Garuda Airlines, for example, was recognised as a separate entity of the Indonesian government in *Pt Garuda Indonesia Ltd v Australian Competition and Consumer Commission*.[181] The Australian *FSIA*[182] treats separate entities essentially the same as states, defining a separate entity as follows:

> **3 Interpretation**
>
> (1)  ...
>
> > ***separate entity***, in relation to a foreign State, means a natural person (other than an Australian citizen), or a body corporate or corporation sole (other than a body corporate or corporation sole that has been established by or under a law of Australia), who or that:
> >
> > (a)   is an agency or instrumentality of the foreign State; and
> >
> > (b)   is not a department or organ of the executive government of the foreign State.
> >
> > . . .

Other instruments are more direct, allowing immunity to separate entities only to the extent that they are performing sovereign functions.[183]

## 6.4.2.3   Political subdivisions

The position of a province, constituent unit of a federation, self-governing territory or other political subdivision (such as an Australian state or territory) is unclear, and varies between instruments. In the Australian *FSIA* and the *United Nations Convention on Jurisdictional Immunities of States and Their Property*, they are included in the definition of a foreign state;[184] in the *European Convention on State Immunity* they have no immunity unless the federal state declares otherwise;[185] and the UK and Singapore Acts afford them the same immunity as a separate entity.[186]

---

181   (2011) 192 FCR 393. This finding was not challenged on appeal to the High Court, which held that Garuda was not entitled to immunity because the matter concerned a commercial transaction: *PT Garuda Indonesia Ltd v Australian Competition and Consumer Commission* (2012) 247 CLR 240, 255 [47].

182   *FSIA* (n 164) s 22.

183   *UK SIA* (n 165) s 14; *United Nations Convention on Jurisdictional Immunities of States and Their Property* (n 163) art 2(1)(b)(iii); *European Convention on State Immunity* (n 162) art 27; *Singapore SIA* (n 167) s 16(2).

184   *FSIA* (n 164) s 3(3); *United Nations Convention on Jurisdictional Immunities of States and Their Property* (n 163) art 2(1)(b).

185   *European Convention on State Immunity* (n 162) art 27.

186   Unless declared otherwise: *UK SIA* (n 165) s 14; *Singapore SIA* (n 167) s 16.

### 6.4.2.4   Individuals representing the state: functional immunity

Australia's *FSIA*, which is closely modelled on the *UK SIA*, does not specifically refer to individuals acting on behalf of the state, but 'executive government' in s 3(3)(c) has been confirmed as including such individuals.[187] This follows the UK case of *Jones v Saudi Arabia*[188] where the House of Lords upheld the immunity of Saudi government officials alleged to have committed torture, on the basis that

> [t]he foreign state's right to immunity cannot be circumvented by suing its servants or agents . . .
>
> A State can only act through servants and agents; their official acts are the acts of the State; and the State's immunity in respect of them is fundamental to the principle of State immunity.[189]

State immunity extends to such individuals only because they are acting on behalf of the state, and it therefore protects only their official acts, and not anything done in their personal capacity; this is known as immunity *ratione materiae*, or functional immunity.

Note that we are still considering only immunity from civil proceedings because, as mentioned, state legislation and the two treaties on immunity cover only immunity from civil jurisdiction; immunity from criminal jurisdiction is a less developed area of the law at both the domestic and the international level. Sections 6.4.2.5–6.4.5 deal with the immunity of individuals from criminal proceedings, as well as the particular issues of personal immunity and immunity for *jus cogens* violations.

### 6.4.2.5   Personal immunity for certain individuals: the 'Troika'

While all individuals acting on behalf of the state have functional immunity, certain very high ranking individuals have personal immunity – immunity *ratione personae* – from both criminal proceedings and, largely, from civil proceedings. They have immunity because of their status: the position that they hold. The ICJ in the *Arrest Warrant* case confirmed that this immunity attaches to 'certain holders of high-ranking office in a State, such as the Head of State, Head of Government and Minister for Foreign Affairs',[190] nicknamed the 'Troika' in the literature. Personal immunity and functional immunity can apply at the same time; the difference between them is that personal immunity lasts only as long as the person holds the relevant office, but is (virtually) complete, and covers criminal and (probably) civil proceedings, as explained in Sections 6.4.3–6.4.4.3; functional immunity applies only to official acts, but lasts forever.

The *Arrest Warrant* case concerned personal immunity from criminal proceedings. In 2000, Belgium issued a warrant for the arrest of the Foreign Minister of the Democratic Republic of the Congo ('DRC'), under Belgium's (then) very expansive universal jurisdiction laws. The Minister was alleged to have committed grave breaches of the 1949 Geneva Conventions and crimes against humanity by making radio broadcasts in 1998 inciting the massacre of Tutsis in

---

187    *Zhang v Zemin* (2010) 243 FLR 299, 313–14 [71]–[77].
188    *Jones v Saudi Arabia* (n 168) affirmed in *Jones v United Kingdom* (2017) 168 ILR 364 (European Court of Human Rights).
189    *Jones v Saudi Arabia* (n 168) 281 [10], 290 [30].
190    *Arrest Warrant* (n 14) 20–1 [51].

Kinshasa. The ICJ upheld the DRC's complaint that the arrest warrant violated the Minister's immunity. It first confirmed the wide personal immunity enjoyed by the 'Troika':

> The Court would observe at the outset that in international law it is firmly established that, as also diplomatic and consular agents, certain holders of high-ranking office in a State, such as the Head of State, Head of Government and Minister for Foreign Affairs, enjoy immunities from jurisdiction in other States, both civil and criminal.[191]

The Court then focused on the immunity of a serving Foreign Minister from criminal proceedings, noting that as there were no treaties specifically on point, the matter fell to be determined under customary international law:

> [53] In customary international law, the immunities accorded to Ministers for Foreign Affairs are not granted for their personal benefit, but to ensure the effective performance of their functions on behalf of their respective States. In order to determine the extent of these immunities, the Court must therefore first consider the nature of the functions exercised by a Minister for Foreign Affairs. He or she is in charge of his or her Government's diplomatic activities and generally acts as its representative in international negotiations and intergovernmental meetings. .... In the performance of these functions, he or she is frequently required to travel internationally, and thus must be in a position freely to do so whenever the need should arise. He or she must also be in constant communication with the Government, and with its diplomatic missions around the world, and be capable at any time of communicating with representatives of other States. ....
>
> [54] The Court accordingly concludes that the functions of a Minister for Foreign Affairs are such that, throughout the duration of his or her office, he or she when abroad enjoys full immunity from criminal jurisdiction and inviolability. That immunity and that inviolability protect the individual concerned against any act of authority of another State which would hinder him or her in the performance of his or her duties.
>
> [55] In this respect, no distinction can be drawn between acts performed by a Minister for Foreign Affairs in an 'official' capacity, and those claimed to have been performed in a 'private capacity', or, for that matter, between acts performed before the person concerned assumed office as Minister for Foreign Affairs and acts committed during the period of office. Thus, if a Minister for Foreign Affairs is arrested in another State on a criminal charge, he or she is clearly thereby prevented from exercising the functions of his or her office. The consequences of such impediment to the exercise of those official functions are equally serious, regardless of whether the Minister for Foreign Affairs was, at the time of arrest, present in the territory of the arresting State on an 'official' visit or a 'private' visit, regardless of whether the arrest relates to acts allegedly performed before the person became the Minister for Foreign Affairs or to acts performed while in office, and regardless of whether the arrest relates to alleged acts performed in an 'official' capacity or a 'private' capacity. Furthermore, even the mere risk that, by travelling to or transiting another State a Minister for Foreign Affairs might be exposing himself or herself to legal proceedings could deter the Minister from travelling internationally when required to do so for the purposes of the performance of his or her official functions.[192]

---

191    Ibid.
192    Ibid 21–2 [53]–[55].

In short, the immunity was complete, for as long as the Minister held that office: it did not matter whether the acts in question took place before or during the Minister's tenure, or were performed in an official or private capacity, or were crimes under international law. For as long as he held office, he could not be prosecuted. The Court was at pains, however, to emphasise that this immunity did not amount to impunity, noting that:

- immunity in international law did not prevent such Ministers being prosecuted in their own states;
- their own state could decide to waive the immunity (remembering that the immunity is always that of the state, even though it benefits the individual);
- after leaving office, they could be prosecuted for:
  - any acts committed before or after their period of office; and
  - private acts committed while in office; and
- they could be prosecuted before an international criminal tribunal (if it had jurisdiction).[193]

The result was that in issuing an arrest warrant, Belgium had failed to respect the Minister's immunity, thereby violating its obligations to the DRC, and was required to cancel the warrant.[194] Thus while in office, the Minister was protected by personal immunity; once he left office, he would lose that broad personal immunity but would continue to benefit from functional immunity – immunity in respect of the official acts he had done when in office.

Different justifications have been suggested for personal immunity, falling into two broad categories. One is functional necessity – ensuring that legal proceedings do not interfere with the performance of the person's official functions, as described by the ICJ in the *Arrest Warrant* case.[195] The other, relevant particularly to the Head of State, is based on the sovereign equality of states and the dignity and respect due to that office as representative of the state.[196]

## 6.4.3    Some questions not answered by the *Arrest Warrant* case

The decision in *Arrest Warrant* is clear so far as criminal proceedings, and the Troika, are concerned. It raises questions, however, about civil proceedings, and whether personal immunity attaches to other 'high-ranking' officials.

### 6.4.3.1    Personal immunity from civil proceedings

It is unclear whether the Troika's complete immunity extends to civil jurisdiction. The move towards the restrictive immunity approach in many states suggests that a similar narrowing of immunity should apply to the Troika. It might be questioned, for example, why a Head of State should be free to engage in private commercial activities and yet be immune from suit from an

---

193    See ibid 25 [61].
194    Ibid 32 [76].
195    Ibid 21–2 [53], [54].
196    Arthur Watts, 'The Legal Position in International Law of Heads of States, Heads of Governments and Foreign Ministers' (1994) 247 *Recueil des cours* 1, 36.

aggrieved creditor.[197] Notwithstanding the traditional rationales for personal immunity mentioned in Section 6.4.2.5, there appears to be a growing acceptance that personal immunity is not absolute.[198]

Some states make specific provision for a serving Head of State. In Australia and the United Kingdom, a foreign Head of State has restrictive immunity in civil proceedings for public acts,[199] but for all private acts, and in criminal proceedings for public acts, they have the same immunity as an ambassador in post (see Section 6.3.3.1).[200]

There is no special provision in Australian law for the other members of the Troika; these would have the same functional immunity as other state officials, and may also be entitled to special mission immunity (see Section 6.6). The position in international law remains unsettled; the English courts recently concluded that there is no rule of customary international law that recognises immunity for a Head of Government, in civil proceedings, for private acts.[201]

### 6.4.3.2 Personal immunity beyond the Troika?

Personal immunity beyond the Troika is also unsettled. Other ministers whose duties require international travel have been granted personal immunity on that basis in some states, such as a Minister for Defence[202] and a Minister for Trade.[203] The International Law Commission recommends confining this personal immunity from criminal jurisdiction to the Troika, and that it should cover both public and private acts.[204] However, Ministers visiting another state would usually be covered by special mission immunity (discussed in Section 6.6).

## 6.4.4 Immunity for *jus cogens* violations?

There are growing calls for immunity to be denied in cases involving international crimes. Several domestic courts have taken that approach, often on the basis that granting immunity for violations of *jus cogens* norms was contrary to the forum state's constitution or other laws. For this reason the Italian Constitutional Court denied immunity to Germany in suits for *jus cogens* violations committed during its occupation of Italy in World War II,[205] as did a South Korean

---

197  See, eg, ibid; Hazel Fox, 'The Resolution of the Institute of International Law on the Immunities of Heads of State and Government' (2002) 51(1) *International and Comparative Law Quarterly* 119; *Immunities from Jurisdiction and Execution of Heads of State and of Government in International Law*, Institute of International Law resolution (26 August 2001) <www.idi-iil.org/app/uploads/2017/06/2001_van_02_en.pdf>.

198  See, eg, Hazel Fox and Philippa Webb, *The Law of State Immunity* (Oxford University Press, 3rd ed, 2015) 543–76.

199  *FSIA* (n 164) ss 3(3)(b), 9.

200  Ibid s 36; *VCDR* (n 119) art 31. The reference to the *VCDR* in s 36 is just a convenient drafting device: a Head of State is not a diplomat.

201  *Re Al M (Immunities)* [2021] EWHC 660 (Fam).

202  *Re Mofaz* (2004) 128 ILR 709 (UK Magistrates' Court).

203  *Re Bo Xilai* (2005) 128 ILR 713 (UK Magistrates' Court).

204  Concepción Escobar Hernández, Special Rapporteur, *Eighth Report on Immunity of State Officials from Foreign Criminal Jurisdiction*, UN Doc A/CN.4/739 (28 February 2020). Note that the ILC's work in this area is continuing.

205  *Simoncioni v Repubblica Federale di Germania*, Judgment No 238/2014, Corte Costituzionale [Italian Constitutional Court], 29 October 2014; translation at <www.cortecostituzionale.it/documenti/download/doc/recent_judgments/S238_2013_en.pdf>.

court in suits against Japan for wartime sexual slavery of South Korean women,[206] while other domestic courts have upheld immunity.[207] The current position in international law is that immunity applies to states even if the acts for which they are responsible amount to international crimes. For individuals in civil proceedings, functional immunity applies, even if the acts amount to international crimes, but it does not apply in criminal proceedings, at least for torture. This much is clear from the cases of *Pinochet, Jones v Saudi Arabia, Arrest Warrant* and *Jurisdictional Immunities of the State*, as explained in Sections 6.4.4.1–6.4.4.3.

### 6.4.4.1    Immunity from criminal proceedings for torture

Immunity from criminal proceedings for torture was the central issue in *R v Bow Street Magistrates; Ex parte Pinochet (No 3)* ('*Pinochet*').[208] Augusto Pinochet was the president of Chile from 1973 to 1990. While visiting London for medical treatment in 1998, he was arrested in answer to an extradition request from Spain. The Spanish authorities wanted to prosecute him for torture and other atrocities allegedly committed by him in Chile while president. He challenged the extradition on a number of grounds including Head of State immunity. The House of Lords agreed that had he still been president at the time of the hearing, he would have been protected by the absolute personal immunity that attaches to a Head of State (as explained in Section 6.4.2.5). However, as a *former* Head of State, he was entitled only to functional immunity – that is, immunity for the acts he had done in an official capacity while in office. The House of Lords therefore had to determine whether torture – specifically, state torture – was an official act or a private act.

The difficulty facing the Court was that state torture is, by its very definition, an official act: it is only if torture is committed or sanctioned by the state that it is prohibited in international law.[209] Six of the seven Law Lords agreed that Pinochet was not entitled to immunity, but discerning a single *ratio decidendi* is difficult because they each gave a separate judgment. All agreed that immunity *ratione materiae* was inconsistent with the *Convention against Torture*, to which Chile, Spain and the United Kingdom were parties, since the principal purpose of the Convention is to criminalise state torture and ensure those who commit it are prosecuted. But they disagreed on how to resolve the inconsistency. One view was that acts of torture could not be official functions: 'How can it be for international law purposes an official function to do something which international law itself prohibits and criminalises?'[210] The other view was that these were indeed official acts, but that international law, and specifically the *Convention against Torture*, had removed that immunity:

> The only conduct covered by this Convention is conduct which would be subject to immunity *ratione materiae*, if such immunity were applicable. The Convention is thus

---

206    *Case No 2016 Ga-Hap 505092* (Seoul Central District Court, 8 January 2021); unofficial translation at <http://minbyun.or.kr/wp-content/uploads/2021/01/ENG-2016_Ga_Hap_505092_23Feb2021.pdf>.
207    See, eg, *Jones v Saudi Arabia* (n 168).
208    [2000] 1 AC 147 ('*Pinochet*').
209    See *Convention against Torture* (n 66) art 1.
210    *Pinochet* (n 208) 205 (Lord Browne-Wilkinson), 262 (Lord Hutton); see also Lord Phillips' alternative conclusion at 292.

incompatible with the applicability of immunity *ratione materiae*. There are only two possibilities. One is that the States Parties to the Convention proceeded on the premise that no immunity could exist *ratione materiae* in respect of torture, a crime contrary to international law. The other is that the States Parties to the Convention expressly agreed that immunity *ratione materiae* should not apply in the case of torture. I believe that the first of these alternatives is the correct one, but either must be fatal to the assertion by Chile and Senator Pinochet of immunity in respect of extradition proceedings based on torture.[211]

This latter view has come to be accepted as the better interpretation of *Pinochet*, as confirmed for example in the subsequent case of *Jones v Saudi Arabia*:

> The reason why General Pinochet did not enjoy immunity *ratione materiae* was not because he was deemed not to have acted in an official capacity; that would have removed his acts from the Convention definition of torture. It was because, by necessary implication, international law had removed the immunity.[212]

Although it is binding only in England and Wales, the *Pinochet* decision is widely viewed as confirming a change in international law: there is now an exception to functional immunity, in criminal proceedings, for officials who commit torture.[213]

### 6.4.4.2   Immunity from criminal proceedings for other *jus cogens* violations

It is arguable that by analogy with *Pinochet*, there should be no immunity for other *jus cogens* violations. However, a critical factor in the *Pinochet* case was the direct conflict between immunity for official acts and the obligation under the *Convention against Torture* to prosecute those accused of a particular official act – state torture. To allow immunity in those circumstances would render the Convention pointless.

Whether the same could be said of other international crimes is uncertain. Dapo Akande and Sangeeta Shah suggest that it should, at minimum 'where extra-territorial jurisdiction exists in respect of an international crime and the rule providing for jurisdiction expressly contemplates prosecution of the crimes committed in an official capacity', because in such a case, 'immunity *ratione materiae* cannot logically co-exist with such a conferment of jurisdiction'.[214] As examples they cite, in addition to torture, the crime of enforced disappearance and war crimes committed in an international armed conflict,[215] and – less confidently – genocide, crimes against humanity, and war crimes in a non-international armed conflict.[216]

---

211   Ibid 290 (Lord Phillips).
212   *Jones v Saudi Arabia* (n 168) 302 [81] (Lord Hoffman).
213   The ICJ in *Arrest Warrant* (n 14) rejected the submission that customary international law recognised this exception as extending to the personal immunity of a serving member of the Troika, which remains absolute: at 23–4 [56]–[58].
214   Dapo Akande and Sangeeta Shah, 'Immunities of State Officials, International Crimes, and Foreign Domestic Courts' (2011) 21(4) *European Journal of International Law* 815, 843.
215   Ibid 842–6.
216   For these crimes, Akande and Shah concede that the universal jurisdiction conferred is not 'practically co-extensive' with functional immunity, but argue that their approach furthers the goal of avoiding impunity: ibid at 846.

### 6.4.4.3   Immunity from civil proceedings for torture and other international crimes

The *'Pinochet* exception' applies only to criminal proceedings for torture; it does not apply to civil proceedings arising out of torture and other international crimes. The European Court of Human Rights confirmed this in *Al-Adsani v United Kingdom*[217] and *Jones v United Kingdom*.[218] Similarly, the ICJ in *Jurisdictional Immunities of the State*[219] found insufficient state practice and *opinio juris* to support Italy's argument that customary international law now recognised an exception from immunity in civil proceedings for *jus cogens* violations. In each case, the Court also rejected the 'normative hierarchy' argument: that because *jus cogens* norms are normatively superior, they should prevail over the 'ordinary' rule of state immunity.[220] The ICJ said:

> [T]here is no conflict between those [*jus cogens*] rules and the rules on State immunity. The two sets of rules address different matters. The rules of State immunity are procedural in character and are confined to determining whether or not the courts of one State may exercise jurisdiction in respect of another State. They do not bear upon the question whether or not the conduct in respect of which the proceedings are brought was lawful or unlawful.[221] . . .
>
> A *jus cogens* rule is one from which no derogation is permitted but the rules which determine the scope and extent of jurisdiction and when that jurisdiction may be exercised do not derogate from those substantive rules which possess *jus cogens* status, nor is there anything inherent in the concept of *jus cogens* which would require their modification or would displace their application.[222]

In other words, one is substantive (*jus cogens*) and the other is procedural (immunity) so there is no conflict between the two.[223]

## 6.4.5   Functional immunity of officials for other crimes

State practice in prosecuting foreign state officials for any crime, international or ordinary, is inconsistent. Some states[224] refuse to grant immunity at all; others refuse it if the offence is committed on their territory. For these reasons, the International Law Commission has produced draft articles on the immunity of state officials from foreign criminal jurisdiction in which it recommends that immunity should apply in principle, with exceptions for genocide, crimes against humanity, war crimes, apartheid, torture and enforced disappearances.[225]

---

217    (2001) 34 EHRR 273.

218    *Jones v United Kingdom* (n 188).

219    *Jurisdictional Immunities of the State* (n 3).

220    Ibid 140 [92]; *Jones v United Kingdom* (n 188) 425 [198].

221    *Jurisdictional Immunities of the State* (n 3) 140 [93].

222    Ibid 141 [95].

223    This reasoning has been followed in cases such as *Freedom and Justice Party v Secretary of State for Foreign and Commonwealth Affairs* [2018] EWCA Civ 1719. The strongly held contrary views are noted in, for example, Akande and Shah (n 214) 832.

224    See, eg, India's prosecution of the Italian marines in *The 'Enrica Lexie' Incident (Italy v India) (Award)* (Permanent Court of Arbitration, Case No 2015-28, 21 May 2020) [830]–[837].

225    *Report of the International Law Commission on the Work of Its Seventy-Third Session*, UN GAOR, 77th sess, Supp No 10, UN Doc A/77/10 (2022) ch VI ('*Immunity of State Officials from Foreign Criminal Jurisdiction*') 188.

# 6.5   Immunity before international tribunals

It should just be noted here that foreign state immunity arises only in domestic courts. International courts and tribunals invariably stipulate in their constituent document that immunity (of any kind) is no bar to prosecution of the individual.[226]

# 6.6   Special mission immunity

After many years in relative obscurity, special mission immunity has been recognised in some recent cases. The UN *Convention on Special Missions* has gained little support, but its definition of a special mission is helpful:

> a temporary mission, representing the State, which is sent by one State to another State with the consent of the latter for the purpose of dealing with it on specific questions or of performing in relation to it a specific task.[227]

Special mission immunity is a form of personal immunity that attaches to the members of the special mission for the duration of the mission. The Convention applies privileges and immunities very similar to those applicable to diplomatic agents – indeed, special missions have been referred to as 'ad hoc diplomacy'. Its detailed provisions bind only the few states parties, but its 'core immunities' were held to reflect customary international law in *Freedom and Justice Party v Secretary of State for Foreign and Commonwealth Affairs*.[228] In this UK case it was found that a visiting Egyptian delegation was immune from the criminal jurisdiction of the UK courts. After an exhaustive survey of state practice, the Court of Appeal found 'a very considerable amount of evidence of different types to satisfy these two elements [state practice and *opinio juris*] and very little against',[229] concluding that:

> Special missions have performed the role of *ad hoc* diplomats across the world for generations. They are an essential part of the conduct of international relations: there can be few who have not heard, for instance, of special envoys and shuttle diplomacy. Special missions cannot be expected to perform their role without the functional protection afforded by the core immunities. No state has taken action or adopted a practice inconsistent with the recognition of such immunities. No state has asserted that they do not exist. We do not, therefore, doubt but that an international court would find that there is a rule of customary international law to that effect.[230]

Accordingly:

> [A] rule of customary international law has been identified which now obliges a state to grant to the members of a special mission, which the state accepts and recognises as such, immunity from arrest or detention (ie, personal inviolability) and immunity from criminal proceedings for the duration of the special mission's visit.[231]

---

226    See, eg, *Rome Statute* (n 83) art 27.
227    *Convention on Special Missions*, opened for signature 8 December 1969, 1400 UNTS 231 (entered into force 21 June 1985) art 1.
228    *Freedom and Justice Party v Secretary of State for Foreign and Commonwealth Affairs* (n 223).
229    Ibid [78].
230    Ibid [79].
231    Ibid [136].

# 6.7   Foreign act of state doctrine

The foreign act of state doctrine is not a form of immunity but is included here because it operates as a bar to jurisdiction in some states. Because of its vagueness and complexity, space permits only a brief description of the doctrine. It is a common law principle to the effect that '[i]n general, courts will not adjudicate upon the validity of acts and transactions of a foreign sovereign State',[232] especially within that sovereign's own territory. It has a number of strands and sub-strands which have developed over the centuries and which are very difficult to rationalise or summarise in any coherent way.

The UK Supreme Court tried to remedy this in *Belhaj v Straw*.[233] The claimants alleged that they had been subjected to unlawful rendition, detention and torture in various countries with the assistance of UK officials. The UK government's defence included foreign act of state: that 'adjudication of the issues now before the court in favour of the claimants would necessarily involve a finding by the English courts that foreign states had acted illegally under the laws of the places where the conduct complained of occurred'.[234] Lord Neuberger, with whom three judges agreed, set out 'three rules or aspects of the doctrine of foreign act of state pursuant to which the court will not readily adjudicate upon the lawfulness or validity of sovereign acts of foreign states':[235]

> [121] The first rule is that the courts of this country will recognise, and will not question, the effect of a foreign state's legislation or other laws in relation to any acts which take place or take effect within the territory of that state.
>
> [122] The second rule is that the courts of this country will recognise, and will not question, the effect of an act of a foreign state's executive in relation to any acts which take place or take effect within the territory of that state.
>
> [123] The third rule has more than one component, but each component involves issues which are inappropriate for the courts of the United Kingdom to resolve because they involve a challenge to the lawfulness of the act of a foreign state which is of such a nature that a municipal judge cannot or ought not rule on it. Thus, the courts of this country will not interpret or question dealings between sovereign states; '[o]bvious examples are making war and peace, making treaties with foreign sovereigns, and annexations and cessions of territory' ... Similarly, the courts of this country will not, as a matter of judicial policy, determine the legality of acts of a foreign government in the conduct of foreign affairs. ... This third rule is justified on the ground that domestic courts should not normally determine issues which are only really appropriate for diplomatic or similar channels ...[236]

The UK Supreme Court has also confirmed that the act of state doctrine may apply to a foreign state's legislation and executive acts, but not to judicial acts (judgments); these are judged by the judicial standards of the forum state.[237]

---

232   *A-G (UK) v Heinemann Publishers Australia Pty Ltd* (1988) 165 CLR 30, 40 (on appeal from the 'Spycatcher case', *A-G (UK) v Heinemann Publishers Australia Pty Ltd* (1987) 8 NSWLR 341).

233   [2017] AC 964.

234   Ibid 1071 [32].

235   *Deutsche Bank AG v Central Bank of Venezuela* [2020] EWHC 1721 (Comm) [55].

236   *Belhaj v Straw* (n 233) 1111 [121]–[123] (citations omitted).

237   *'Maduro Board' of the Central Bank of Venezuela v 'Guaidó Board' of the Central Bank of Venezuela* [2022] 2 WLR 167, [159]–[161].

What has become clear in recent years is that even when the act of state doctrine would otherwise apply, it will be rejected if the foreign government act is a serious violation of international law, or is otherwise repugnant to the public policy of the forum state. An early example of this was *Oppenheimer v Cattermole*,[238] where the House of Lords refused to recognise a Nazi decree depriving non-resident Jews of their German nationality and confiscating their property: 'a law of this sort constitutes so grave an infringement of human rights that the courts of this country ought to refuse to recognise it as a law at all'.[239] This was developed in *Kuwait Airways v Iraqi Airways*,[240] where an Iraqi law purporting to extinguish Kuwait as an independent state and confiscating all its assets was not recognised as it was in clear breach of art 2(4) of the *Charter of the United Nations* and numerous Security Council resolutions. In *Habib v Commonwealth*,[241] the Australian (Full) Federal Court found the act of state doctrine inapplicable because the case turned on domestic law, but noted that it would not have applied in any event because the alleged foreign government conduct – torture – was a serious violation of international law: 'Torture offends the ideal of a common humanity' and is *jus cogens*, and public policy demands that the common law develop 'congruently with emphatically expressed ideals of public policy, reflective of universal norms'.[242]

## DISCUSSION QUESTIONS

(1)  As set out in Section 6.2, it is broadly accepted that international law limits the exercise of a state's jurisdiction to the five bases described in Section 6.2.4. How, if at all, can this be reconciled with the *Lotus* principle (see Section 6.2.2)?

(2)  Should states be free to exercise 'pure' universal jurisdiction – that is, where there is no link between that state and the crime, victim or perpetrator?

(3)  Would it be possible, or desirable, to refuse diplomatic immunity in certain cases?

(4)  If you could revise the rules on state immunity, what changes would you make to the current law, and why?

(5)  Critically analyse the competing arguments relating to state immunity for international crimes (see Sections 6.4.4.2 and 6.4.4.3). Which do you find more persuasive, and why?

---

238    [1976] AC 249.
239    Ibid 278.
240    *Kuwait Airways Corporation v Iraqi Airways Co (Nos 4 and 5)* [2002] 2 AC 883.
241    (2010) 183 FCR 62.
242    Ibid [8], [13].

# 7

# STATE RESPONSIBILITY AND DIPLOMATIC PROTECTION

Chester Brown,
Emily Crawford
and Brett Williams

# 7.1    Introduction

To explain the law of state responsibility and diplomatic protection, it helps to distinguish between primary rules and secondary rules. The primary rules of international law provide that certain acts or omissions are unlawful – for example, the law on the use of force would be considered primary rules of international law, a breach of which would be an internationally wrongful act. When those primary rules are breached, it is the secondary rules – the law of state responsibility – that come into play, to determine inter alia the consequences of that initial wrongful act, whether the wrongful act was committed by a state (thereby entailing that state's responsibility), and what action the 'wronged state' may take in reply.[1] The rules on state responsibility cover wrongful acts committed against another state, as well as certain wrongful acts committed against nationals of the state, including corporations; the law of diplomatic protection solely concerns how a state may raise a claim against another state for a wrong committed against one of its nationals, rather than against the state itself.

# 7.2    A brief history: custom and the work of the International Law Commission

Prior to about 1980, the sources of the law of state responsibility were primarily found in customary international law, often reflected in arbitral awards (including compensation) made by various tribunals. Most of the latter were established to peacefully settle disputes between two states, often after military or other hostilities, such as those between the United Kingdom and the United States,[2] Mexico and the United States,[3] and Iran and the United States.[4]

The evolution of the law on state responsibility has been strongly influenced by the International Law Commission ('ILC'), which worked on state responsibility and diplomatic protection from 1949 until 2004.[5] Due to the complexity of the topic, the ILC was the forum for protracted analysis and debate, resulting in numerous reports and draft articles (essentially, draft treaties). For some time, it seemed as if progress would languish forever in the ILC.

However, in 1995, the ILC decided to create separate work programs for several topics that had been part of the ILC's study on state responsibility: diplomatic protection, which

---

1    Importantly, however, the primary rules themselves may also specify the consequences of the wrong; for example, under the law on the use of force, an armed attack gives rise to a right of self-defence of the victim state, in addition to the other consequences specified by the law of state responsibility.

2    The Arbitral Tribunal (Great Britain–United States) was constituted by the *Special Agreement for the Submission to Arbitration of Pecuniary Claims Outstanding between the United States and Great Britain*, signed 18 August 1910, 6 RIAA 9 (entered into force 26 April 1912).

3    The US–Mexican Claims Commission was constituted by the *General Claims Convention*, signed 8 September 1923, 4 RIAA 11 (entered into force 1 March 1924).

4    The Iran–United States Claims Tribunal was constituted by the *Declaration of the Government of the Democratic and Popular Republic of Algeria* ('*General Declaration*') and the *Declaration of the Government of the Democratic and Popular Republic of Algeria concerning the Settlement of Claims by the Government of the United States of America and the Government of the Islamic Republic of Iran* ('*Claims Settlement Declaration*'), together known as the 'Algiers Declarations' (19 January 1981) <https://iusct.com/documents/>.

5    'Summaries of the Work of the International Law Commission: State Responsibility', *International Law Commission* (Web Page, 15 July 2015) <https://legal.un.org/ilc/summaries/9_6.shtml>.

became the 2006 Draft Articles on Diplomatic Protection (discussed in Section 7.4); the responsibility of states for acts not unlawful under international law, which became the 2001 Draft Articles on Prevention of Transboundary Harm from Hazardous Activities[6] and the 2006 Draft Principles of the Allocation of Loss in the Case of Transboundary Harm Arising out of Hazardous Activities;[7] and the responsibility of international organisations under international law, which led to the 2011 Draft Articles on the Responsibility of International Organizations (discussed in Chapter 15). A question that was 'shelved' was whether a state could be held responsible for the commission of international criminal acts, such as genocide. The ILC chose not to recognise the concept of international crimes of the state in its work on state responsibility[8] but instead suggested that specific rules should apply to breaches of *jus cogens* norms.[9]

Once these contentious areas were dealt with, the ILC quickly completed its work. In 2001, the ILC submitted the Draft Articles on Responsibility of States for Internationally Wrongful Acts to the UN General Assembly, which passed Resolution 56/83 of 12 December 2001 taking note of the articles and annexing them to the resolution.[10] Though not a treaty, the *Articles on Responsibility of States for Internationally Wrongful Acts* ('ARSIWA') have become increasingly prominent. They have been cited many times, including by the International Court of Justice ('ICJ'), and it seems that, over time, more of the articles are coming to be regarded as representing customary international law.[11] States remain divided over whether to adopt the articles as a treaty.[12] Some are concerned that, if adopted as a treaty, the articles may be subject to the usual reservations, interpretative declarations, and outright refusals to participate attendant to nearly all treaties, thus potentially diluting their impact; other states have argued that the rules are so important that only a treaty would give them their due recognition.[13] Regardless, both *ARSIWA* and the Draft Articles on Diplomatic Protection and their commentaries are the standard starting point when dealing with questions of state responsibility and diplomatic protection. This chapter turns now to the elements of state responsibility.

---

6    'Draft Articles on Prevention of Transboundary Harm from Hazardous Activities' [2001] II(2) *Yearbook of the International Law Commission* 1, 146.
7    'Draft Principles of the Allocation of Loss in the Case of Transboundary Harm Arising out of Hazardous Activities' (2006) II(2) *Yearbook of the International Law Commission* 1, 58.
8    'Draft Articles on Responsibility of States for Internationally Wrongful Acts, with Commentaries' [2001] II(2) *Yearbook of the International Law Commission* 1, 111 (Draft Chapter III of Part Two Commentary [7]) ('*ARSIWA Commentary*').
9    See further Section 7.3.6; Nina Jørgensen, *The Responsibility of States for International Crimes* (Oxford University Press, 2000).
10   *Responsibility of States for Internationally Wrongful Acts*, GA Res 56/83, UN Doc A/RES/56/83 (28 January 2002, adopted 12 December 2001) annex ('*Responsibility of States for Internationally Wrongful Acts*') ('*ARSIWA*').
11   More of the articles, but not all – some articles remain contested, in particular the regime for responsibility for serious breaches of obligations arising under *jus cogens* norms (*ARSIWA* art 41) and invocation in situations of responsibility for obligations owed erga omnes (art 48).
12   See Federica Paddeu, 'To Convene or Not to Convene? The Future Status of the Articles on State Responsibility: Recent Developments' (2017) 21 *Max Planck Yearbook of United Nations Law Online* 83.
13   For more detailed analysis of this debate, see further James Crawford and Simon Olleson, 'The Continuing Debate on a UN Convention on State Responsibility' (2005) 54(4) *International and Comparative Law Quarterly* 959.

# 7.3    Elements of state responsibility

There are two essential requirements of state responsibility: there is conduct (an act or an omission) by a state or by other entities whose conduct can be attributed to the state (see Section 7.3.1); and the conduct is wrongful under international law (see Section 7.3.2).[14]

## 7.3.1    Attribution of conduct

The first question is whether the conduct is attributable to the state under international law,[15] because it was the conduct either of the state itself or of a person or entity whose conduct can be attributed to the state.[16] Attribution is dealt with in arts 4–11 of *ARSIWA*.

### 7.3.1.1    Conduct of state organs, and of persons or entities exercising elements of governmental authority

The first situation in which conduct can be attributed to the state is where it is carried out by state organs. Under art 4 of *ARSIWA*:

> The conduct of any State organ shall be considered an act of that State under international law, whether the organ exercises legislative, executive, judicial or any other functions, whatever position it holds in the organization of the State, and whatever its character as an organ of the central Government or of a territorial unit of the State.[17]

An 'organ' includes 'any person or entity that has that status in accordance with the internal law of that State',[18] including the executive (such as government departments, the police or the armed forces), the courts and the legislature. The term 'state organ' is also not limited to organs or high-level officials of the central government; rather, it is to be understood broadly as including 'organs of government of whatever kind or classification, exercising whatever functions, and at whatever level in the hierarchy'.[19] The state organ may carry out 'legislative, executive, judicial or any other functions', which is to be read non-exhaustively, and the state conduct in question need not be of a sovereign character; rather, it can be commercial in nature.[20]

Article 4 also makes it clear that the term 'state organs' includes 'territorial units' such as provincial, regional and local government entities. This means that the acts and omissions of (for instance) New South Wales, and the City of Perth, are attributable to the Commonwealth of

---

14    *ARSIWA* (n 10) art 2.
15    Ibid.
16    Ibid arts 4–11.
17    Ibid art 4(1).
18    Ibid art 4(2).
19    *ARSIWA Commentary* (n 8) 40 (Draft Article 4 Commentary [6]). The ICJ has confirmed the customary character of the broad concept of the term 'state organ', holding that '[a]ccording to a well-established rule of international law, the conduct of any organ of a state must be regarded as an act of that State': see *Difference Relating to Immunity from Legal Process of a Special Rapporteur of the Commission on Human Rights (Advisory Opinion)* [1999] ICJ Rep 62, 87–8 [62].
20    *ARSIWA Commentary* (n 8) 41 (Draft Article 4 Commentary [6]).

Australia. This was illustrated by the *LaGrand* case, where the ICJ affirmed that the United States was responsible in international law for the conduct of the Governor of Arizona.[21]

Article 5 of *ARSIWA* provides for the attribution of conduct of persons or entities exercising elements of governmental authority:

> The conduct of a person or entity which is not an organ of the State under article 4 but which is empowered by the law of that State to exercise elements of the governmental authority shall be considered an act of the State under international law, provided the person or entity is acting in that capacity in the particular instance.

This provision applies to the conduct of persons or entities which are not covered by art 4 because they are not state organs, but they nonetheless exercise elements of governmental authority. Such persons or entities may include 'parastatal entities' such as public corporations, public agencies and private corporations which exercise certain public or regulatory functions.[22] For instance, states may authorise private security firms to operate prisons, or to carry out customs inspections and manage immigration or quarantine facilities. The characterisation of the person's or entity's status under the state's domestic law is not decisive. What matters is that the person or entity must be empowered by the law of the state to exercise those functions, and the conduct of the person or entity must relate to that exercise of governmental authority.[23]

### 7.3.1.2   Ultra vires or unauthorised acts

Under art 7 of *ARSIWA*, the conduct of a state organ (under art 4) or a person or entity empowered to exercise governmental authority (under art 5) 'shall be considered an act of the State under international law if the organ, person or entity acts in that capacity, even if it exceeds its authority or contravenes instructions'.[24] Thus, the state cannot deny its responsibility on the basis that the conduct was contrary to its domestic law, or to instructions given to the person or entity.[25]

The rule in art 7 was articulated in *Caire Claim*, decided by the Franco–Mexican Claims Commission in 1929.[26] A French national, Jean-Baptiste Caire, was murdered by two Mexican military officers who were acting ultra vires. The Commission held that

> the two officers, even if they are deemed to have acted outside their competence ... and even if their superiors countermanded an order, have involved the responsibility of the State, since they acted under cover of their status as officers and used means placed at their disposal on account of that status.[27]

As appears from the text of art 7, the main issue is whether the state organs or persons are acting in their official capacity when they carry out the internationally wrongful act. In *Caire Claim*, the Commission noted that the Mexican soldiers had 'acted under cover of their status

21    *LaGrand (Germany v United States) (Provisional Measures)* [1999] ICJ Rep 9, 16 [28]. The conduct in question was the impending execution of a German national who had been denied access to consular assistance: see Section 7.3.5.1.
22    *ARSIWA Commentary* (n 8) 42–3 (Draft Article 5 Commentary [1]–[2]).
23    Ibid 42–3 (Draft Article 5 Commentary [2]–[3]).
24    *ARSIWA* (n 10) art 7.
25    *ARSIWA Commentary* (n 8) 45 (Draft Article 7 Commentary [2]).
26    *Caire Claim (France v Mexico) (Award)* (1929) 5 RIAA 516.
27    Ibid 531.

as officers and used means placed at their disposal on account of that status',[28] such as wearing their uniforms, taking Caire to the army barracks and using their army weapons. By contrast, conduct will not be attributable where it is so far removed from the scope of the person's official functions that 'it should be assimilated to that of private individuals, not attributable to the State'.[29] Ultimately, the question is whether the organ, person or entity is 'acting with apparent authority'.[30]

### 7.3.1.3  Acts by non-state actors or groups

The conduct of private persons is not normally attributable to a state. However, art 8 of *ARSIWA* provides that the conduct of non-state actors can be attributed to a state if it is performed on the instructions of, or under the direction or control of, the state.

The first of these situations is comparatively straightforward, and commonly arises where an organ of the state (such as the state's military forces) engages private persons as auxiliary troops which remain outside the formal structure of the state[31] but still act on the state's instructions.

The second situation is more complex, and has given rise to issues concerning the level of direction or control which is necessary for the conduct to be attributed to the state. The leading case is *Military and Paramilitary Activities in and against Nicaragua* ('*Nicaragua*'), where the ICJ considered whether certain conduct of the Nicaraguan *Contras* (rebels against the Nicaraguan government) could be attributed to the United States, which had provided 'planning, direction, and support' to the *Contras*, including financing, arming and training them.[32] The ICJ determined that for the acts of the *Contras* to be attributable to the United States, the United States must exercise 'effective control' over those acts:

> All the forms of United States participation mentioned above, and even the general control by the respondent State over a force with a high degree of dependency on it, would not in themselves mean, without further evidence, that the United States directed or enforced the perpetration of the acts contrary to human rights and humanitarian law alleged by the applicant State. Such acts could well be committed by members of the *contras* without the control of the United States. For this conduct to give rise to legal responsibility of the United States, it would in principle have to be proved that that State had effective control of the military or paramilitary operations in the course of which the alleged violations were committed.[33]

The ICJ thus set a considerably high threshold for control,[34] requiring more than just a 'general situation of dependence and support'; rather, it must be shown that the state had specifically given directions for and had control over the conduct.[35] On the facts the ICJ found that the

---

28    Ibid.
29    *ARSIWA Commentary* (n 8) 46 (Draft Article 7 Commentary [7]).
30    Ibid 46 (Draft Article 7 Commentary [8]).
31    Ibid 46 (Draft Article 7 Commentary [2]).
32    *Military and Paramilitary Activities in and against Nicaragua (Nicaragua v United States) (Merits)* [1986] ICJ Rep 14, 50 [86], 64–5 [115] ('*Nicaragua*'). See also Chapter 8, Sections 8.3.4 and 8.3.5.
33    *Nicaragua* (n 32) 64–5 [115].
34    Indeed, the high threshold has been criticised as being almost impossible to meet: see, eg, Gleider Hernández, *International Law* (Oxford University Press 2019) 256.
35    *ARSIWA Commentary* (n 8) 47 (Draft Article 8 Commentary [4]).

United States did not exercise that level of control. The ICJ affirmed the 'effective control' test in *Application of the Convention on the Prevention and Punishment of the Crime of Genocide*,[36] noting that it was customary international law, as reflected in art 8 of *ARSIWA*.[37]

## 7.3.1.4   Adoption by the state

The conduct of non-state actors can also be attributed to a state if the state post facto 'acknowledges and adopts the conduct in question as its own' under art 11 of *ARSIWA*.[38] This is most clearly illustrated by *United States Diplomatic and Consular Staff in Tehran*.[39] Following the overthrow of the government during the Iranian revolution in 1979, militant students entered and occupied the US Embassy in Tehran, taking US diplomatic and consular staff hostage. Iranian authorities failed to take steps to compel the militants to withdraw from the Embassy, placing Iran in breach of its obligation to protect the inviolability of the embassy under the *Vienna Convention on Diplomatic Relations* and the *Vienna Convention on Consular Relations*.[40] In response, the United States brought a case against Iran, claiming that it was responsible for the acts of the students in seizing and occupying the Embassy. The Court held that Iran's initial failure to act during the revolutionary unrest did not engage its responsibility. However, once the new revolutionary government became established, it endorsed the actions of the militants, and ultimately issued a decree which expressly approved of their continuing actions – and this *did* entail its responsibility.[41] As the ICJ explained:

> The policy thus announced by the Ayatollah Khomeini, of maintaining the occupation of the Embassy and the detention of its inmates as hostages for the purpose of exerting pressure on the United States Government was complied with by other Iranian authorities and endorsed by them repeatedly in statements made in various contexts. The result of that policy was fundamentally to transform the legal nature of the situation created by the occupation of the Embassy and the detention of its diplomatic and consular staff as hostages. The approval given to these facts by the Ayatollah Khomeini and other organs of the Iranian State, and the decision to perpetuate them, translated continuing occupation of the Embassy and detention of the hostages into acts of that State.[42]

What is therefore needed for art 11 of *ARSIWA* to apply is more than mere support or endorsement; it must be 'acknowledgement and adoption' of the non-state actor's actions as '[t]he language of "adoption" ... carries with it the idea that the conduct is acknowledged by the State as, in effect, its own conduct'.[43]

---

36   *Application of the Convention on the Prevention and Punishment of the Crime of Genocide (Bosnia and Herzegovina v Serbia and Montenegro) (Judgment)* [2007] ICJ Rep 43 ('*Genocide*').

37   Ibid 208–9 [401]. The effective control test has also been applied by other international courts and tribunals: see, eg, *Jan de Nul NV v Egypt (Award)* (ICSID Arbitral Tribunal, Case No ARB/04/13, 6 November 2008) [173].

38   *ARSIWA* (n 10) art 11.

39   *United States Diplomatic and Consular Staff in Tehran (United States of America v Iran) (Judgment)* [1980] ICJ Rep 3.

40   Ibid 32–3 [67]–[68].

41   Ibid 33–4 [71]–[73].

42   Ibid 35 [74].

43   *ARSIWA Commentary* (n 8) 53 (Draft Article 11 Commentary [6]).

## 7.3.1.5    Joint responsibility

Customary international law also recognises that more than one state might be responsible for an internationally wrongful act: first, where there is a plurality of responsible states; and secondly, 'because one State is implicated in the internationally wrongful act of another'.[44]

Beginning with the first of these categories, there may be more than one responsible state, as envisaged in art 47 of *ARSIWA*, where the wrongful conduct can be attributed to each of the states concerned: 'Where several States are responsible for the same internationally wrongful act, the responsibility of each State may be invoked in relation to that act.'[45] For example, two or more states might invade a third state, contrary to the prohibition on the use of force. Article 47(2) clarifies that this 'does not permit an injured State to recover, by way of compensation, more than the damage that it has suffered', and it also confirms that recovery against one state is 'without prejudice to any right of recourse against the other responsible States'.[46]

The second category consists of instances of 'derived responsibility', arising either through the voluntary provision of aid or assistance to the responsible state (art 16), or by the exercise of control or coercion over the responsible state (art 17).[47] In both cases the aiding or controlling state must have 'knowledge of the circumstances of that internationally wrongful act', and the act would have to be internationally wrongful if it were committed by that state.[48] Aid or assistance under art 16 could arise, for example, by knowingly providing an essential facility or financing the activity in question,[49] as where one state permits another to use an airbase on the first state's territory to unlawfully attack a third state. As the ILC explains, the assisting state will be responsible only to the extent of the assistance:

> Under article 16, aid or assistance by the assisting State is not to be confused with the responsibility of the acting State. In such a case, the assisting State will only be responsible to the extent that its own conduct has caused or contributed to the internationally wrongful act. Thus, in cases where that internationally wrongful act would clearly have occurred in any event, the responsibility of the assisting State will not extend to compensating for the act itself.[50]

Article 17 provides that a state which 'directs and controls another State in the commission of an internationally wrongful act' is responsible *for that act*.[51] During a military occupation, for example, the occupying state might have control over the police or armed forces of the occupied state, and would be responsible for their actions.[52]

---

44    See, eg, ibid 68 (Draft Article 17 Commentary [1]); James Crawford, *State Responsibility: The General Part* (Cambridge University Press, 2013) 333.

45    *ARSIWA* (n 10) art 47(1).

46    Ibid art 47(2).

47    Crawford, *State Responsibility* (n 44) 333.

48    *ARSIWA* (n 10) art 16. This means the obligation must be owed by both states – and would therefore exclude, for example, an obligation owed only by the other state under a bilateral treaty. The ILC notes '[t]he essential principle is that a State should not be able to do through another what it could not do itself': *ARSIWA Commentary* (n 8) 69 (Draft Article 17 Commentary [9]).

49    *ARSIWA Commentary* (n 8) 66 (Draft Article 16 Commentary [1]).

50    Ibid.

51    *ARSIWA* (n 10) art 17.

52    *ARSIWA Commentary* (n 8) 68 (Draft Article 17 Commentary [5]). The Commentary notes that, in such an example, the controlled state might itself be held responsible for breaching international law: 'the mere

## 7.3.2   Breach

The second ingredient of an internationally wrongful act (the first being attribution) is that the act must be a breach of a rule of international law.[53] Whether the act is illegal, permitted or even mandated under *domestic* law is not relevant to its legality under *international* law.[54] The breach can be of a rule of a treaty or of custom.[55] However, a treaty or customary rule in a particular area may contain rules about the consequences of breaches which displace *ARSIWA* or any general rules of customary law relating to state responsibility.

## 7.3.3   Admissibility of claims

The most important issues of admissibility of claims against states arise in diplomatic protection claims. They are the requirement for a satisfactory link of nationality between the claimant state and the injured person, and the requirement that the injured person has exhausted local remedies under the law of the respondent state. These two issues are dealt with in Section 7.4.[56]

## 7.3.4   Circumstances precluding wrongfulness

International law provides that there may be circumstances that preclude the wrongfulness of the act attributable to the state; the circumstances do not operate as general exceptions to the wrongful act, but rather as a justification for conduct that has occurred in a specific situation. Likewise, the circumstances do not suspend or terminate the underlying obligation, and cannot justify the violation of a rule of *jus cogens*.[57] Six circumstances precluding wrongfulness are outlined in Chapter V of *ARSIWA*: consent, self-defence, countermeasures, *force majeure*, distress and necessity.

### 7.3.4.1   Consent

Article 20 of *ARSIWA* provides that '[v]alid consent by a State to the commission of a given act by another State precludes the wrongfulness of that act in relation to the former State to the extent that the act remains within the limits of that consent'.[58] Consent therefore precludes the wrongfulness of an act that would otherwise be contrary to international law. Thus Julian Assange enjoyed diplomatic asylum for seven years in the Ecuadorian embassy in London,[59]

---

fact that it was directed to carry out an internationally wrongful act does not constitute an excuse ... If the conduct in question would involve a breach of its international obligations, it is incumbent upon it to decline to comply with the direction': at 68 (Draft Article 17 Commentary [9]).

53    *ARSIWA* (n 10) art 2.
54    Ibid art 3.
55    Ibid art 12.
56    There are other grounds on which a court or tribunal might find that a claim is inadmissible. See further Chapter 9.
57    *ARSIWA* (n 10) art 26.
58    See also Crawford, *State Responsibility* (n 44) 283–9.
59    Fabia Veçoso, 'International Law, Diplomatic Asylum and Julian Assange', *The University of Melbourne* (Blog Post, 14 April 2019) <https://pursuit.unimelb.edu.au/articles/international-law-diplomatic-asylum-and-julian-assange>.

and could only be lawfully arrested when the Ecuadorian Ambassador officially invited the UK authorities to enter the embassy to do so in 2019.[60]

Once given, the state to whom consent has been granted must operate within the limits of that consent. This was illustrated in *Armed Activities on the Territory of the Congo*,[61] where Uganda claimed that its armed forces were operating in territory of the Democratic Republic of the Congo ('DRC') with the DRC's consent. The ICJ held:

> [T]he consent that had been given to Uganda to place its forces in the DRC, and to engage in military operations, was not an open-ended consent. The DRC accepted that Uganda could act, or assist in acting, against rebels on the eastern border and in particular to stop them operating across the common border. Even had consent to the Ugandan military presence extended much beyond the end of July 1998, the parameters of that consent, in terms of geographic location and objectives, would have remained thus restricted.[62]

Consent cannot be granted *ex post facto* – it must be granted before or during the act.[63]

### 7.3.4.2   Self-defence

Article 21 of *ARSIWA* provides:

> The wrongfulness of an act of a State is precluded if the act constitutes a lawful measure of self-defence taken in conformity with the *Charter of the United Nations*.

The reference to 'lawful' in art 21 indicates that the act in self-defence must comply with the law on self-defence, as outlined in art 51 of the *Charter of the United Nations* ('*UN Charter*'), and with customary rules on self-defence, such as requirements of necessity and proportionality.[64] An example of a claim of self-defence as a circumstance precluding wrongfulness arose in the *Oil Platforms* case, where the United States argued that, notwithstanding a treaty with Iran aimed at securing 'firm and enduring peace and sincere friendship',[65] its attacks against Iranian oil platforms were permissible in self-defence.[66]

In this instance, the Court did *not* find in favour of the United States, stating that the initial acts to which the United States was purportedly responding in self-defence did not amount to an 'armed attack', as required by art 51 of the *UN Charter*.[67] Self-defence cannot, however, preclude wrongfulness of some acts, such as violations of the law of armed conflict or human rights law.[68]

---

60    'Julian Assange: Wikileaks Co-Founder Arrested in London', *BBC News* (online, 12 April 2019) <www.bbc.com/news/uk-47891737>.

61    *Armed Activities on the Territory of the Congo (Democratic Republic of the Congo v Uganda) (Judgment)* [2005] ICJ Rep 168.

62    Ibid 198 [52].

63    See further Crawford, *State Responsibility* (n 44) 287; *ARSIWA Commentary* (n 8) 74 (Draft Article 20 Commentary [9]). If a state were to fail to protest or act in response to a wrongful act, this would be better characterised as acquiescence or waiver.

64    For a more complete analysis of the law on self-defence, see Chapter 8.

65    *Treaty of Amity, Economic Relations, and Consular Rights*, signed 15 August 1955, 284 UNTS 93 (entered into force 16 June 1957) art I.

66    *Oil Platforms (Islamic Republic of Iran v United States of America) (Merits)* [2003] ICJ Rep 161, 183–5 [43], [45], [48].

67    Ibid 191 [64]. See further Crawford, *State Responsibility* (n 44) 289–92.

68    *ARSIWA Commentary* (n 8) 74 (Draft Article 20 Commentary [3]).

### 7.3.4.3   Countermeasures

Article 22 of *ARSIWA* provides that a countermeasure, validly taken, will preclude wrongfulness. Countermeasures are non-forcible measures taken against a state committing a wrongful act. Countermeasures are 'intrinsically unlawful, but are justified by the alleged failing to which they were a response'[69] and aim to bring an end to the initial wrongful act.[70] Countermeasures, and the conditions for their lawful exercise, were examined by the ICJ in *Gabčíkovo-Nagymaros Project*.[71] The Court had to examine whether Czechoslovakia's unilateral modification of a dam project along the Danube River was a lawful countermeasure in response to Hungary's cessation of its obligations under a treaty with Czechoslovakia relating to the dam project:

> In the view of the Court, an important consideration is that the effects of a countermeasure must be commensurate with the injury suffered, taking account of the rights in question. . . .
>
> The Court considers that Czechoslovakia, by unilaterally assuming control of a shared resource, and thereby depriving Hungary of its right to an equitable and reasonable share of the natural resources of the Danube – with the continuing effects of the diversion of these waters on the ecology of the riparian area of the Szigetköz – failed to respect the proportionality which is required by international law.[72]

### 7.3.4.4   *Force majeure*

*Force majeure* relates to situations where a state is not able to fulfil its obligations due to the occurrence of an irresistible force or unforeseen event. Under art 23 of *ARSIWA*, earthquakes, floods or human-created events such as armed conflict may amount to *force majeure*, making it materially impossible for a state to prevent a breach. However, the state pleading *force majeure* cannot have contributed to creating the *force majeure*, or have assumed the risk of the situation occurring. Key to *force majeure* is that the state had no choice but to commit the act, and that situation of *force majeure* was unforeseen. Given the requirements of lack of choice and unforeseeability, the threshold for *force majeure* is high.

Attempts to argue *force majeure* have usually been unsuccessful. One attempt at an argument of *force majeure* came with the *Rainbow Warrior* arbitration.[73] In July 1985, French state security personnel bombed the Greenpeace ship *Rainbow Warrior* while it was berthed in Auckland, New Zealand. The ship was bombed on orders from the French authorities to prevent it from sailing to French Polynesia to protest French nuclear testing on Mururoa Atoll. The bombing killed a member of the crew and sank the vessel. Ultimately, the

---

69   Denis Alland, 'Countermeasures of General Interest' (2002) 13 *European Journal of International Law* 1221, 1221.

70   See generally Nigel White and Ademola Abass, 'Countermeasures and Sanctions' in Malcolm Evans (ed), *International Law* (Oxford University Press, 5th ed, 2018) 521.

71   *Gabčíkovo-Nagymaros Project (Hungary v Slovakia) (Judgment)* [1997] ICJ Rep 7.

72   Ibid 56 [85]; see also 55–7 [83]–[84], [87].

73   *Difference between New Zealand and France concerning the Interpretation or Application of Two Agreements Concluded on 9 July 1986 between the Two States and Which Related to the Problems Arising from the Rainbow Warrior Affair (New Zealand v France) (Decision)* (1990) 20 RIAA 215 ('*Rainbow Warrior: Interpretation or Application*').

dispute between France and New Zealand was taken to an arbitral tribunal where, inter alia, it was agreed that the two special forces agents who carried out the bombing were to be held in French custody, which included no less than three years on an isolated French military base in the Pacific. The agreement between France and New Zealand provided that the agents were prohibited from leaving the island military base for any reason, except with the mutual consent of the two governments.[74] Both agents were, at separate times, repatriated to France without the consent of the New Zealand government, with the French government claiming that, for one of the agents, medical factors amounted to *force majeure* necessitating immediate repatriation. The Tribunal disagreed, stating that the test for *force majeure* is material impossibility, not that the *force majeure* has made fulfilling the obligation burdensome or difficult.[75]

### 7.3.4.5   Distress

Under art 24 of *ARSIWA*, a wrongful act may be precluded if the author of the act 'had no other reasonable way, in a situation of distress, of saving the author's life or the lives of other persons entrusted to the author's care'. Distress cannot be claimed by a state if it contributed to the situation of distress, nor if 'the act in question is likely to create a comparable or greater peril'.[76] Distress is distinguishable from *force majeure*: 'whereas *force majeure* requires material impossibility, in distress the author of the act has no real choice than to breach an obligation'.[77] In contrast, with distress there is a choice, but the situation requires that the 'unlawful' act is the one chosen. For example, in 1975, the United Kingdom informed the Security Council that its naval vessels had entered Icelandic territorial waters without permission, to seek shelter from a severe storm.[78] Though not specifically acknowledged by the United Kingdom as such, this is a clear example of distress.[79]

### 7.3.4.6   Necessity

Article 25 of *ARSIWA* provides:

1. Necessity may not be invoked by a State as a ground for precluding the wrongfulness of an act not in conformity with an international obligation of that State unless the act:
   (a) is the only way for the State to safeguard an essential interest against a grave and imminent peril; and
   (b) does not seriously impair an essential interest of the State or States towards which the obligation exists, or of the international community as a whole.
2. In any case, necessity may not be invoked by a State as a ground for precluding wrongfulness if:
   (a) the international obligation in question excludes the possibility of invoking necessity; or
   (b) the State has contributed to the situation of necessity.

---

74   *Differences between New Zealand and France Arising from the Rainbow Warrior Affair (New Zealand v France) (Ruling)* (1986) 19 RIAA 199, 214 ('*Rainbow Warrior*').
75   *Rainbow Warrior: Interpretation or Application* (n 73) 253.
76   *ARSIWA* (n 10) art 24(2)(b).
77   Crawford, *State Responsibility* (n 44) 301.
78   UN SCOR, 13th year, 1866th mtg, UN Doc S/PV.1866 (16 December 1975) 3 [24].
79   Crawford, *State Responsibility* (n 44) 302.

Necessity, like distress, involves a choice by a state to breach its obligations. However, necessity requires that the act must only be done to protect an essential interest of the state (unlike with distress, which relates to the protection of human life). The threshold for necessity is therefore high, and was not accepted in several cases, including *Gabčíkovo-Nagymaros Project*.[80] One possible example is the incident involving the *SS Torrey Canyon*, a Liberian oil tanker which ran aground off the coast of Cornwall in the United Kingdom but outside UK territorial waters. The resultant oil spill posed a threat to coastal wildlife. After unsuccessful attempts to mitigate the damage, the United Kingdom bombed the vessel.[81] Though the United Kingdom did not expressly claim necessity for its action in destroying foreign national property, the act was not objected to, and is now regarded as an example of necessity.[82]

## 7.3.5   Consequences of an internationally wrongful act

A state that has committed an internationally wrongful act must cease the wrongful act and take steps to, as far as possible, wipe out its consequences. It is also not relieved of any continuing obligations to perform the obligation breached.[83]

### 7.3.5.1   Cessation

Under art 30 of *ARSIWA*, the wrongdoing party must cease the wrongful act (if it is a continuing act) and offer assurances and guarantees of non-repetition, if circumstances so require. The form that such guarantees should take was examined by the ICJ in *LaGrand*.[84] In 1982, two German nationals, Walter and Karl LaGrand, were tried and sentenced to death in Arizona. The brothers had not been informed of their rights to consular assistance, as required under art 36 of the *Vienna Convention on Consular Relations*. The Court examined the nature of the US assurances of non-repetition:

> [T]he Court observes that it has been informed by the United States of the 'substantial measures [which it is taking] aimed at preventing any recurrence' of the breach of Article 36, paragraph 1 (b). ... [including inter alia] that 'the Department of State is working intensively to improve understanding of and compliance with consular notification and access requirements throughout the United States, so as to guard against future violations of these requirements'. The United States points out that '[t]his effort has included the January 1998 publication of a booklet entitled *Consular Notification and Access: Instructions for Federal, State and Local Law Enforcement and Other Officials Regarding Foreign Nationals in the United States and the Rights of Consular Officials to Assist Them*, and development of a small reference card designed to be carried by individual arresting officers'.[85]

---

80   *Gabčíkovo-Nagymaros Project* (n 71) 40–1 [51]–[52].
81   See further John Sheail, '"Torrey Canyon": The Political Dimension' (2007) 42(3) *Journal of Contemporary History* 485.
82   Crawford, *State Responsibility* (n 44) 309.
83   *ARSIWA* (n 10) art 29.
84   *LaGrand (Germany v United States of America) (Judgment)* [2001] ICJ Rep 466.
85   Ibid 511 [121].

Germany disputed that these assurances were adequate,[86] but the ICJ disagreed, stating that the measures adopted by the United States would amount to a general assurance of non-repetition.[87]

## 7.3.5.2    Reparation

Article 31 of *ARSIWA* outlines the obligation on the wrongdoing party to make full reparation for any injury caused by the wrongful act. The classic statement on reparation comes from the Permanent Court of International Justice ('PCIJ') in *Factory at Chorzów*, where it noted that '[i]t is a principle of international law, and even a general conception of law, that any breach of an engagement involves an obligation to make reparation'[88] and further:

> The essential principle contained in the actual notion of an illegal act . . . is that reparation must, as far as possible, wipe out all the consequences of the illegal act and reestablish the situation which would, in all probability, have existed if that act had not been committed. Restitution in kind, or, if this is not possible, payment of a sum corresponding to the value which a restitution in kind would bear; the award, if need be, of damages for loss sustained which would not be covered by restitution in kind or payment in place of it – such are the principles which should serve to determine the amount of compensation due for an act contrary to international law.[89]

Injury, in this respect, refers to both material harm or damage (such as damage to property or persons) as well as 'moral' harm: '"Material" damage here refers to damage to property or other interests of the state and its nationals which is assessable in financial terms. "Moral" damage includes such items as individual pain and suffering, loss of loved ones or personal affront associated with an intrusion on one's home or private life.'[90] The extent of reparation will be affected if the wronged party fails to mitigate the damage from the wrongful act.[91] As noted in the commentary on the draft articles: 'Even the wholly innocent victim of wrongful conduct is expected to act reasonably when confronted by the injury. Although often expressed in terms of a "duty to mitigate", this is not a legal obligation which itself gives rise to responsibility. It is rather that a failure to mitigate by the injured party may preclude recovery to that extent.'[92]

Article 34 of *ARSIWA* outlines three forms of reparation: restitution, compensation and satisfaction.

### RESTITUTION

Restitution involves re-establishing the situation that would have existed prior to the wrongful act. Restitution is not necessary if it is materially impossible – for instance, if property has been destroyed.[93] Additionally, restitution is not necessary if it would 'involve a burden out of all

---

86    Ibid 512 [122].
87    Ibid 513 [124].
88    *Factory at Chorzów (Germany v Poland) (Jurisdiction) (Judgment No 8)* [1927] PCIJ (ser A) No 9, 21.
89    *Factory at Chorzów (Germany v Poland) (Merits)* [1928] PCIJ (ser A) No 17, 47.
90    *ARSIWA Commentary* (n 8) 91–2 (Draft Article 31 Commentary [5]).
91    *ARSIWA* (n 10) art 39.
92    *ARSIWA Commentary* (n 8) 93 (Draft Article 31 Commentary [11]).
93    *ARSIWA* (n 10) art 35(a).

proportion to the benefit deriving from restitution',[94] which the ILA states would exist where 'there is a grave disproportionality between the burden which restitution would impose on the responsible State and the benefit which would be gained, either by the injured State or by any victim of the breach'.[95] The commentary on the draft articles gives no example of what this disproportionality would be; however, a possible situation might be where the financing and construction by the wrongful state of a piece of infrastructure (such as an airport) jeopardised the economic stability of the wrongful state, but offered no significant benefit to the wronged state because it already maintained several similar operational airports. Where restitution is considered inappropriate, compensation is considered the more appropriate form of reparation. Restitution is 'best suited to certain types of claims'[96] such as those involving return of property or the release of persons from detention.[97]

## COMPENSATION

Compensation, under art 36, requires that the wrongdoing state 'compensate for the damage caused thereby, insofar as such damage is not made good by restitution',[98] and that 'compensation shall cover any financially assessable damage including loss of profits'.[99] Compensation relates to the material damage suffered as a result of the wrongful act; compensation, under international law, is not punitive – so-called 'exemplary' damages were rejected by the ILC as having 'no place in international law, either as a matter of compensation or satisfaction'.[100] ARSIWA does not set out a formula for assessing compensation and particular rules have developed in relation to different kinds of breaches, whether violations of human rights or damage to property, for example.[101]

## SATISFACTION

In some instances, reparation can be symbolic; it can be a remedy 'for those injuries, not financially assessable, which amount to an affront to the State'.[102] Satisfaction may take the form of an apology for wrongdoing, or an acknowledgement of wrongdoing by way of a declaratory judgment.[103] For example, in the *Rainbow Warrior* arbitration, the question of

---

94    Ibid art 35(b).
95    *ARSIWA Commentary* (n 8) 98 (Draft Article 35 Commentary [11]).
96    Hernández (n 34) 271.
97    See, eg, *United States Diplomatic and Consular Staff in Tehran* (n 39), where the ICJ ordered that Iran must immediately 'terminate the unlawful detention of the United States Chargé d'affaires and other diplomatic and consular staff and other United States nationals now held hostage in Iran, and must immediately release each and every one': at 44 [95].
98    *ARSIWA* (n 10) art 36(1).
99    Ibid art 46(2).
100   James Crawford, *Brownlie's Principles of Public International Law* (Oxford University Press, 9th ed, 2019) 560; *ARSIWA Commentary* (n 8) 99 (Draft Article 36 Commentary [4]), 107 (Draft Article 37 Commentary [8].
101   Crawford, *Brownlie's Principles* (n 100) 558–60.
102   *ARSIWA Commentary* (n 8) 106 (Draft Article 37 Commentary [3]).
103   See, eg, the finding by the ICJ that Serbia breached its obligations under the *Convention on the Prevention and Punishment of the Crime of Genocide*, opened for signature 9 December 1948, 78 UNTS 277 (entered into force 12 January 1951), where the very act of finding the breach was considered appropriate satisfaction since the case was 'not one in which an order for payment of compensation, or ... a direction to provide assurances and guarantees of non-repetition, would be appropriate': *Genocide* (n 36) 239 [471]. In such instances, a declaratory judgment is considered appropriate because

appropriate reparation for the bombing was considered, including reparation for the use of violence on New Zealand's territory:

> The violation of New Zealand territory by France did not in itself cause any material damage to New Zealand. On the other hand it may be admitted that it has caused it moral damage which, according to international law, may be compensated by the offer of regrets or apologies. The Government of New Zealand requests the French Government to offer it such apologies. The French Government is prepared to make compensation in this manner for the moral damage suffered by New Zealand and the French Prime Minister is ready, therefore, to address to the New Zealand Prime Minister a formal and unconditional letter of apology for the attack carried out on 10 July 1985.[104]

Satisfaction is a well-established remedy in international law; however, measures ordered in satisfaction, such as an apology, may not take forms which are humiliating or excessive for the responsible state.[105]

## 7.3.6    Consequences for a breach of a *jus cogens* norm

As noted in Chapter 2 on sources of international law, peremptory norms of international law are rules that occupy a 'superior normative rank'[106] relative to other international rules. Given the seriousness of *jus cogens* norms, and the fact that they may not be derogated from, there has been, in both the ILC[107] and in the literature generally,[108] debate over whether there should be different, more serious consequences that follow a breach. Ultimately, *ARSIWA* did not embrace the idea of imposing criminal liability on a wrongdoing state, but instead, in arts 40 and 41, outlined additional special consequences of a 'serious' breach of a *jus cogens* norm. A 'serious' breach is defined as a 'gross or systematic failure by the responsible State'[109] to fulfil its obligations. Under art 41, all states have a duty to cooperate to bring about an end to the breach. Additionally, states must not recognise as lawful situations created by a serious breach, or aid or assist the wrongdoing state to maintain the breach. The obligations in arts 40 and 41 were alluded to in *Legal Consequences of the Construction of a Wall in the Occupied Palestinian Territory*.[110] This advisory opinion arose from a request by the UN General Assembly regarding the legality of Israel's construction of a security barrier partially within Palestinian territory. Construction began in 2000 during the Second Intifada (a popular uprising by Palestinians against the Israeli occupation) and Israel hoped that the barrier would

---

to order any other type of reparation may 'risk reigniting or aggravating a conflict': Crawford, *Brownlie's Principles* (n 100) 563.

104    *Rainbow Warrior* (n 74) 209.

105    *ARSIWA Commentary* (n 8) 107 (Draft Article 37(3) Commentary [8]).

106    Crawford, *Brownlie's Principles* (n 100) 565.

107    See debates in the ILC over the course of the drafting of *ARSIWA*, particularly under the stewardship of Special Rapporteurs Ago, Arangio-Ruiz and Riphagen: 'Analytical Guide to the Work of the International Law Commission: State Responsibility', *International Law Commission* (Web Page) <https://legal.un .org/ilc/guide/9_6.shtml>.

108    See generally Crawford, *State Responsibility* (n 44) 362–78.

109    *ARSIWA* (n 10) art 40(2).

110    *Legal Consequences of the Construction of a Wall in the Occupied Palestinian Territory* (*Advisory Opinion*) [2004] ICJ Rep 136.

reduce acts of violence within Israel. However, concerns were raised by the international community that the barrier effectively dispossessed Palestinian residents, amounted to de facto annexation of territory, and infringed the Palestinian right of self-determination (a *jus cogens* right).[111] The ICJ stated:

> Given the character and the importance of the rights and obligations involved, the Court is of the view that all States are under an obligation not to recognize the illegal situation resulting from the construction of the wall in the Occupied Palestinian Territory, including in and around East Jerusalem. They are also under an obligation not to render aid or assistance in maintaining the situation created by such construction. It is also for all States, while respecting the *United Nations Charter* and international law, to see to it that any impediment, resulting from the construction of the wall, to the exercise by the Palestinian people of its right to self-determination is brought to an end.[112]

The consequences that follow from the breach of a peremptory norm can be considered 'not so much a regime of *aggravated* consequences as one of *additional* consequences'.[113]

## 7.3.7 Invocation

Article 42 of *ARSIWA* deals with invocation and provides:

> A State is entitled as an injured State to invoke the responsibility of another State if the obligation breached is owed to:
> (a)   that State individually, or
> (b)   a group of States including that State, or the international community as a whole, and the breach of the obligation:
>> (i)    specially affects that State; or
>> (ii)   is of such a character as radically to change the position of all the other States to which the obligation is owed with respect to the further performance of the obligation

The ILC presents as an example of a specially affected state the obligations under the *United Nations Convention on the Law of the Sea*:

> For example a case of pollution of the high seas in breach of article 194 of the *United Nations Convention on the Law of the Sea* may particularly impact on one or several States whose beaches may be polluted by toxic residues or whose coastal fisheries may be closed. In that case, independently of any general interest of the States parties to the Convention in the preservation of the marine environment, those coastal States parties should be considered as injured by the breach ... For a State to be considered injured, it must be affected by the breach in a way which distinguishes it from the generality of other States to which the obligation is owed.[114]

---

111    See generally Daphne Barak-Erez, 'Israel: The Security Barrier – Between International Law, Constitutional Law, and Domestic Judicial Review' (2006) 4 *International Journal of Constitutional Law* 540.
112    *Construction of a Wall in the Occupied Palestinian Territory* (n 110), 200.
113    Crawford, *Brownlie's Principles* (n 100) 565 (emphasis in original).
114    *ARSIWA Commentary* (n 8) 119 (Draft Article 42 Commentary [12]).

Examples of art 42(b)(ii) obligations suggested by the ILC are disarmament or nuclear-free zone treaties, or the *Antarctic Treaty*, 'or any other treaty where each party's performance is effectively conditioned upon and requires the performance of each of the others' – that is, where a breach by one party would materially affect all the other parties.[115]

It is possible for several states to separately invoke the responsibility of another state for a wrongful act[116] – a single wrongful act may injure several states, and all states injured are entitled to invoke the responsibility of the wrongdoing state. Likewise, several states may have contributed to a wrongful act – in such cases, the responsibility of each of the wrongdoing states may be invoked.[117]

A more complicated question is whether a state can invoke responsibility if it has *not* been directly injured by the breach. Article 48 of *ARSIWA* operates in conjunction with art 42, and is 'based on the idea that in case of breaches of specific obligations protecting the collective interests of a group of States or the interests of the international community as a whole, responsibility may be invoked by States which are not themselves injured in the sense of article 42'.[118]

Article 48 distinguishes between two types of 'collective' obligations. Article 48(1)(a) refers to obligations owed to a group of states and adopted to protect a collective interest of the group. An example might be a regional treaty established for the protection of human rights – such as the European *Convention for the Protection of Human Rights and Fundamental Freedoms*. Such collective obligations have sometimes been called *obligations erga omnes partes* – obligations owed to all parties. Article 48(1)(b) is broader, and refers to obligations owed to the international community, sometimes referred to as obligations *erga omnes* – obligations owed to *all* (not just to parties to a treaty establishing group obligations). An example of an obligation *erga omnes* would be the customary prohibition against genocide. While the terms are often found in the literature and in cases, *ARSIWA* does not use either *erga omnes* or *erga omnes partes*.

The ICJ looked at this issue in the case relating to the former president of Chad, Hissène Habré.[119] While president, Habré allegedly oversaw numerous illegal acts including torture. After he was ousted from power, Habré was granted asylum in Senegal. Attempts to bring Habré before the Senegalese courts failed on jurisdictional grounds, prompting Belgian authorities to issue an arrest warrant. Extradition was sought on several occasions, without success, which led to Belgium bringing a case before the ICJ, arguing that Senegal had breached its obligations under the *Convention against Torture and Other Cruel, Inhuman or Degrading Treatment or Punishment* by failing to 'prosecute or extradite' Habré. Senegal disputed that Belgium had standing to bring a case, and the ICJ was asked to determine whether the responsibility of Senegal could be invoked by Belgium. The Court stated:

---

115    Ibid.
116    *ARSIWA* (n 10) art 46.
117    Ibid art 47. See also *Certain Phosphate Lands in Nauru (Nauru v Australia) (Preliminary Objections)* [1992] ICJ Rep 240 regarding the joint responsibility of Australia, New Zealand and the United Kingdom for environmental damage to Nauru.
118    *ARSIWA Commentary* (n 8) 126 (Draft Article 48 Commentary [2]).
119    *Questions Relating to the Obligation to Prosecute or Extradite (Belgium v Senegal) (Judgment)* [2012] ICJ Rep 422 ('*Belgium*').

> The States parties to the Convention have a common interest to ensure, in view of their shared values, that acts of torture are prevented and that, if they occur, their authors do not enjoy impunity. The obligations of a State party to conduct a preliminary inquiry into the facts and to submit the case to its competent authorities for prosecution are triggered by the presence of the alleged offender in its territory, regardless of the nationality of the offender or the victims, or of the place where the alleged offences occurred. All the other States parties have a common interest in compliance with these obligations by the State in whose territory the alleged offender is present. That common interest implies that the obligations in question are owed by any State party to all the other States parties to the Convention. All the States parties 'have a legal interest' in the protection of the rights involved. These obligations may be defined as 'obligations *erga omnes partes*' in the sense that each State party has an interest in compliance with them in any given case.[120]

As yet unresolved is the question whether states can have standing before a tribunal in cases of obligations *erga omnes* (under customary international law), in addition to obligations *erga omnes partes* (under a treaty). At the time of writing, it probably cannot be said that international law recognises a right of standing for obligations owed *erga omnes* under customary international law, though it remains a theoretical possibility.[121]

Finally, note should be made of art 55 of *ARSIWA*, which states: 'These articles do not apply where and to the extent that the conditions for the existence of an internationally wrongful act or the content or implementation of the international responsibility of a State are governed by special rules of international law.' In essence, this means that if states have agreed between themselves, in a treaty or customary rule, for breaches of the treaty to be governed by special rules (*lex specialis*), then *ARSIWA* will operate in a 'residual way'.[122] Thus states may agree between themselves to 'exclude a State from relying on *force majeure* or necessity'[123] to excuse a breach. For example, the *lex specialis* of the primary law on the use of force contains its own exhaustive exceptions (such as the rule on self-defence) and does not admit necessity as a circumstance precluding wrongfulness.[124]

# 7.4   Diplomatic protection

Connected to the rules on state responsibility are those rules relating to diplomatic protection, which deal with how a state may raise a claim against another state for a wrong committed against one of its nationals (persons, corporations or entities). As stated by the PCIJ in 1924 in *Mavrommatis Palestine Concessions*:

> It is an elementary principle of international law that a State is entitled to protect its subjects, when injured by acts contrary to international law committed by another State, from whom they have been unable to obtain satisfaction through the ordinary channels. By taking up the case of one of its subjects and by resorting to diplomatic action or

---

120   *Belgium* (n 119) 449 [68]–[69] (citations omitted).
121   See further Priya Urs, 'Obligations Erga Omnes and the Question of Standing before the International Court of Justice' (2021) 34(2) *Leiden Journal of International Law* 505.
122   *ARSIWA Commentary* (n 8) 140 (Draft Article 55 Commentary [2]).
123   Ibid 140 (Draft Article 55 Commentary [3]).
124   Ibid 84 (Draft Article 25 Commentary [21]).

international judicial proceedings on his behalf, a State is in reality asserting its own rights – its right to ensure, in the person of its subjects, respect for the rules of international law. … Once a State has taken up a case on behalf of one of its subjects before an international tribunal, in the eyes of the latter the State is sole claimant.[125]

The development and codification of the rules on diplomatic protection were, for a long time, tied up with the development and codification of the general rules on state responsibility. As noted in Section 7.2, it was only in 1996 that the ILC decided that diplomatic protection should be the subject of its own specialised articles, culminating in the adoption in 2006 of the Draft Articles on Diplomatic Protection ('*ADP*')[126] and commentary.[127] These set out the rules on when and how diplomatic protection may be exercised.

Diplomatic protection is a right of the state, and not a duty – if a natural or legal person suffers an injury that can be attributed to a state, the state of nationality of the injured person may, but does not have to, espouse a claim on their behalf.[128] This was noted by the ICJ in *Barcelona Traction, Light and Power Company*:

> The Court would here observe that, within the limits prescribed by international law, a State may exercise diplomatic protection by whatever means and to whatever extent it thinks fit, for it is its own right that the State is asserting. …
>
> The State must be viewed as the sole judge to decide whether its protection will be granted, to what extent it is granted, and when it will cease. It retains in this respect a discretionary power the exercise of which may be determined by considerations of a political or other nature, unrelated to the particular case. Since the claim of the State is not identical with that of the individual or corporate person whose cause is espoused, the State enjoys complete freedom of action.[129]

Domestic law in different states can, however, confer greater rights on citizens. There is also some indication that the law may be beginning to change, so that states may eventually be obligated to protect their nationals by way of a claim in diplomatic protection. Article 19 of *ADP* recommends that a state which is entitled to exercise a right of diplomatic protection should give due consideration to exercising that right, especially where a significant injury has occurred, and consult with the injured person, to take into account their views on resort to diplomatic protection and possible reparation. There is state practice to suggest that 'although a State has a discretion whether to exercise diplomatic protection or not, there is an obligation on that State, subject to judicial review, to do something to assist its nationals, which may include an obligation to give due consideration to the possibility of exercising diplomatic protection'.[130]

---

125    *Mavrommatis Palestine Concessions (Greece v Great Britain) (Jurisdiction)* [1924] PCIJ (ser A) No 2, 12.
126    'Draft Articles on Diplomatic Protection' [2006] II(2) *Yearbook of the International Law Commission* 1, 23 ('*ADP*').
127    'Draft Articles on Diplomatic Protection, with Commentary' [2006] II(2) *Yearbook of the International Law Commission* 1, 26 ('*ADP Commentary*').
128    *ADP* (n 126) art 1.
129    *Barcelona Traction, Light and Power Company Ltd (Belgium v Spain) (Judgment)* [1970] ICJ Rep 3, 44 [77]–[78] ('*Barcelona Traction*').
130    *ADP Commentary* (n 127) 54 (Draft Article 19 Commentary [3]). Cf the limitations of the law of diplomatic protection, highlighted in particular regarding people detained in Guantanamo Bay by US

# 7.5    Content of a state's obligation regarding the treatment of foreign nationals

International law on the obligations of states regarding the treatment of foreign nationals (also known as the 'treatment of aliens') has been controversial. The principal areas of disagreement have included the standard of treatment owed to foreign nationals (or 'aliens'),[131] as well as the standard of compensation which states have to pay in the event of expropriation or nationalisation of the property of foreign nationals.

## 7.5.1    National standard vs international minimum standard

Historically, the 'national treatment' standard held that foreign nationals should be treated equally with the state's own nationals; this standard was accepted by numerous states (particularly developing and newly independent states).[132] In contrast, proponents of the 'international minimum standard' considered that states had a duty to treat foreign nationals in accordance with a standard set by international law, rather than their own domestic law. It was promoted by developed states to protect their nationals abroad, including the foreign investment and international trading activities of their nationals and companies. With the expansion of Western economic powers, the international minimum standard became dominant.

## 7.5.2    International minimum standard of treatment

The most frequently cited arbitral decision in support of the international minimum standard is the award of the US–Mexican Claims Commission in *Neer v Mexico* ('*Neer*'), which concerned the murder of a US national in rural Mexico.[133] A claim was brought before the Commission on behalf of Mr Neer's widow and his estate, in which it was argued that Mexico had not done enough to apprehend or punish those responsible for his death, resulting in a denial of justice. In discussing the legal standard for assessing Mexico's conduct, the Commission held that 'the propriety of governmental acts should be put to the test of international standards',[134] articulated as follows:

---

authorities: see further Natalie Klein and Lise Berry, 'A Human Rights Perspective on Diplomatic Protection: David Hicks and his Dual Nationality' (2007) 13(1) *Australian Journal of Human Rights* 1; *R (Abbasi) v Secretary of State for Foreign and Commonwealth Affairs* [2002] EWCA Civ 1598; *R (Al Rawi) v Secretary of State for Foreign and Commonwealth Affairs* [2008] QB 289.

131    See, eg, Crawford, *Brownlie's Principles* (n 100) 597–600; Chester Brown, 'The Evolution of the Regime of International Investment Agreements: History, Economics, and Politics' in Marc Bungenberg et al (eds), *International Investment Law: A Handbook* (Nomos, 2013) 153, 158–60.

132    Eg, Crawford, *Brownlie's Principles* (n 100) 597 n 39, referring to Carlos Calvo, *Derecho internacional teórico y práctico de Europa y América* (1868).

133    *Neer (United States v Mexico) (Award)* (1926) 4 RIAA 60 ('*Neer*').

134    Ibid 61.

[T]he treatment of an alien, in order to constitute an international delinquency, should amount to an outrage, to bad faith, to wilful neglect of duty, or to an insufficiency of governmental action so far short of international standards that every reasonable and impartial man would readily recognize its insufficiency. Whether the insufficiency proceeds from deficient execution of an intelligent law or from the fact that the laws of the country do not empower the authorities to measure up to international standards is immaterial.[135]

This dictum has been understood by subsequent international courts and tribunals as having set the minimum standard of treatment under customary international law.[136]

## 7.5.3  Responsibility for direct and indirect injury to foreign nationals

Under the law of diplomatic protection, it is possible for a state to both directly injure a foreign national (through act or omission) and to cause indirect injury to a foreign national. The *Neer* case is more appropriately understood as setting the standard in cases of *indirect* injury, such as denial of justice, where there is a failure of the state to exercise its functions in response to conduct which is not attributable to the state (the murder of Mr Neer by private actors). By contrast, the US–Mexican Claims Commission in *Roberts v Mexico* affirmed a different minimum standard of treatment for state conduct which causes *direct* injury to foreign nationals.[137] In this case, a US national had been arrested and detained without trial for a period of 19 months, and kept in conditions which the Commission described in the following terms:

[T]he jail in which he was kept was a room thirty-five feet long and twenty feet wide with stone walls, earthen floor, straw roof, a single window, a single door and no sanitary accommodations, all the prisoners depositing their excrement in a barrel kept in a corner of the room; ... thirty or forty men were at times thrown together in this single room; ... the prisoners were given no facilities to clean themselves; ... the room contained no furniture except that which the prisoners were able to obtain by their own means; ... they were afforded no opportunity to take physical exercise; and ... the food given them was scarce, unclean, and of the coarsest kind.[138]

The Commission held that the conditions in which Mr Roberts had been held constituted a violation by Mexico of its obligation to treat foreign nationals in accordance with an international standard, expressly rejecting the national standard. The Commission set the test for the international minimum standard for direct injury as treatment 'in accordance with ordinary standards of civilisation'.[139] This appears to be somewhat subjective, but in any event seems to be a stricter obligation than assessing merely whether the state had acted in a way

---

135    Ibid 61–2.
136    See, eg, *Glamis Gold Ltd v United States (Award)* (NAFTA Chapter 11 Arbitral Tribunal, IIC 380, 8 June 2009) [614]–[616].
137    *Roberts (United States v Mexico)* (1926) 4 RIAA 77.
138    Ibid 80.
139    Ibid.

which was 'an outrage', in 'bad faith' or in 'wilful neglect of duty', as in the Commission's award in *Neer*.[140]

## 7.5.4 Obligation to provide physical protection for foreign nationals

Other cases provide guidance on the obligation of states to provide physical protection to foreign nationals who are faced with threats by third parties. In *Home Frontier and Foreign Missionary Society v Great Britain*, British colonial authorities had imposed a 'hut tax' in the colony of Sierra Leone in 1898 which had caused outrage among the population, leading to an uprising.[141] A number of missions of the Home Frontier and Foreign Missionary Society were attacked, and several of the missionaries (who were US nationals) were murdered. The United States argued that the loss had been caused by the British authorities' imposition of the 'hut tax' which, it was submitted, they should have foreseen would lead to the rebellion. The United States argued that British authorities 'failed to take proper steps for the maintenance of law and order and the protection of life and property' and that 'the loss of life and damage to property was the result of this neglect and failure of duty'.[142] The Commission rejected the claim, finding that there was 'no evidence to support the contention that [the British authorities] failed in [their] duty to afford adequate protection for life and property'.[143] The British authorities had taken 'every measure available' for the repression of the insurrection, including ensuring that 'troops in the area of revolt were continually increased'.[144] The Commission confirmed that the obligation on the British authorities was one of due diligence rather than one of strict liability, finding that 'it was impossible at a few days' or a few hours' notice to afford full protection to the buildings and properties in every isolated and distant village'.[145] A more recent decision, *Asian Agricultural Products Ltd v Sri Lanka*, affirmed that states must comply with due diligence obligations under the minimum standard of customary international law.[146]

## 7.5.5 International minimum standard and obligations under investment treaties

In relation to international investment law, the international minimum standard of treatment arising from the cases discussed in Sections 7.5.2–7.5.4 is today frequently subsumed in treaty-

---

140   *Neer* (n 133) 61–2. See also *Youmans (United States v Mexico)* (1926) 4 RIAA 110, which concerned both a direct injury to a foreign national and a failure of the state's authorities to punish persons involved in the commission of a crime.
141   *Home Frontier and Foreign Missionary Society (United States v Great Britain)* (1920) 6 RIAA 42.
142   Ibid 43.
143   Ibid 44.
144   Ibid.
145   Ibid.
146   *Asian Agricultural Products Ltd v Sri Lanka (Award)* (ICSID Arbitral Tribunal, Case No ARB/87/3, 27 June 1990) [67].

based standards of the obligation to provide fair and equitable treatment, and the obligation to provide full protection and security. These obligations are discussed in Chapter 16.

## 7.5.6   Expropriation of the property of foreign nationals

As discussed in Chapter 6, states have sovereignty over their territory, which gives them powers over private property, including the taking (or 'expropriation') of private property. The international law rules concerning expropriation have been controversial, and have revealed a difference of approach.[147] Developed (and usually capitalist) states have tradition-ally argued that expropriation measures must comply with conditions set by international law (such as the payment of compensation) in order to be lawful, whereas developing (and socialist) states have typically argued that such measures are lawful so long as they comply with domestic law.[148] An early example of this disagreement can be seen in the 1940 corres-pondence of US Secretary of State Cordell Hull addressed to the Mexican government following the expropriation of property owned by US nationals. Proposing what came to be known as the 'Hull formula', Hull wrote that

> the right to expropriate property is coupled with and conditioned on the obligation to make adequate, effective and prompt compensation. The legality of an expropriation is in fact dependent upon the observance of this requirement.[149]

The Draft Convention on the International Responsibility of States for Injuries to Aliens ('*Harvard Draft Convention*') sought to codify customary international law on the protection of foreign nationals.[150] With respect to expropriation, it provided in art 10(1) that '[t]he taking, under the authority of the state, of any property of an alien, or of the use thereof, is wrongful (a) if it is not for a public purpose clearly recognized as such by a law of general application in effect at the time of the taking, or (b) if it is in violation of a treaty.' Article 10(2) further provided that the taking of any property for a public purpose would be unlawful if it were not accompanied by 'the prompt payment of compensation'.[151] Article 10(3)(a) of the *Harvard Draft Convention* recognised that an expropriation could consist of an 'outright taking of property' (which has become known as a 'direct' expropriation), as well as the 'unreasonable interference with the use, enjoyment or disposal' of property (which has become known as an 'indirect' expropriation). Article 10(3)(a) stated:

> A 'taking of property' includes not only an outright taking of property but also any such unreasonable interference with the use, enjoyment, or disposal of property as to justify an inference that the owner thereof will not be able to use, enjoy, or dispose of the property within a reasonable period of time after the inception of such interference.[152]

---

147    See also David Harris and Sandesh Sivakumaran, *Cases and Materials on International Law* (Sweet & Maxwell, 9th ed, 2020) 495 ff.
148    Ibid 497; Crawford, *Brownlie's Principles* (n 100) 605–6.
149    Green Haywood Hackworth, *Digest of International Law* (GPO, 1942) vol 3.
150    'Draft Convention on the International Responsibility of States for Injuries to Aliens' (1961) 55 *American Journal of International Law* 548 ('*Harvard Draft Convention*').
151    Ibid.
152    Ibid art 10(3)(a).

In the case of a 'direct' expropriation, the foreign national would lose title to the property, while in the case of an 'indirect' expropriation, the foreign national would still own the property, but would have lost the ability to 'use, enjoy or dispose' of it. For example, a state may impose measures that make it 'impossible for an alien to operate a factory ... by blocking the entrances on the professed ground of maintaining order'.[153] The Iran–United States Claims Tribunal confirmed the possibility of an indirect expropriation in *Starrett Housing Corporation v Iran*:

> [I]t is recognised in international law that measures taken by a State can interfere with property rights to such an extent that these rights are rendered so useless that they must be deemed to have been expropriated, even though the State does not purport to have expropriated them and the legal title to the property formally remains with the original owner.[154]

Modern investment treaties also typically define expropriation as including both 'direct' and 'indirect' expropriations.[155]

As for the conditions which must be met for an expropriation to be lawful, it appears that customary international law requires that the expropriation must be for a public purpose and non-discriminatory, and compensation must be paid to the foreign national. The requirement of a public purpose was recognised by the PCIJ in *Certain German Interests in Polish Upper Silesia*, where it noted that international law did not prohibit 'expropriation for reasons of public utility, judicial liquidation and similar measures'.[156] In 1962, the UN General Assembly adopted Resolution 1803 (XVII) *Permanent Sovereignty over Natural Resources*, in which it declared: 'The rights of peoples and nations to permanent sovereignty over their natural wealth and resources must be exercised in the interest of their national development and of the well-being of the people of the State concerned.'[157] It also declared:

> Nationalisation, expropriation or requisitioning shall be based on grounds or reasons of public utility, security or the national interest which are recognised as overriding purely individual or private interests, both domestic and foreign. In such cases the owner shall be paid appropriate compensation in accordance with the rules in force in the State taking such measures in the exercise of its sovereignty and in accordance with international law.[158]

153    Explanatory note to the 1961 *Harvard Draft Convention* (n 150) art 10 in Louis B Sohn and RR Baxter, 'Responsibility of States for Injuries to the Economic Interests of Aliens: II. Draft Convention on the International Responsibility of States for Injuries to Aliens' (1961) 55 *American Journal of International Law* 558–9.
154    *Starrett Housing Corporation v Iran* (1983) 4 Iran-US CTR 122, 154.
155    *Metalclad Corporation v Mexico (Award)* (ICSID Arbitral Tribunal, Case No ARB(AF)/97/1, 30 August 2000) [103].
156    *Certain German Interests in Polish Upper Silesia (Germany v Poland) (Merits)* [1926] PCIJ (ser A) No 7, 22.
157    *Permanent Sovereignty over Natural Resources*, GA Res 1803 (XVII), UN Doc A/RES/1803(XVII) (14 December 1962) [1].
158    Ibid [4].

The Iran–United States Claims Tribunal also observed 'the progressive recognition of the right of States to nationalise foreign property for a public purpose' in *Amoco International Finance Corporation v Iran* ('*Amoco*').[159] There is, however, uncertainty concerning what is required. In *Amoco*, the Tribunal noted that 'a precise definition of the "public purpose" for which an expropriation may be lawfully decided has neither been agreed upon in international law nor even suggested', but it acknowledged that 'as a result of the modern acceptance of the right to nationalize, this term is broadly interpreted, and that States, in practice, are granted extensive discretion'.[160]

The requirement that the measure be non-discriminatory has been affirmed in numerous cases such as *BP Exploration Co (Libya) Ltd v Libya*[161] and *Amoco*. In *Amoco* the Tribunal noted that '[d]iscrimination is widely held as prohibited by customary international law in the field of expropriation'.[162] As with the notion of public purpose, there is debate about what exactly 'discrimination' means in this context. Developed states 'insist that discrimination against or between foreigners'[163] renders an expropriation unlawful, even though Resolution 1803 does not mention non-discrimination as a requirement, and some case law[164] suggests that discrimination against or between foreign nationals may be permissible if it is 'reasonably related to the public purpose of the expropriation'.[165]

Turning to the requirement that expropriation be accompanied by compensation in order to be lawful, as noted the standard of compensation has been contested. With many claims for expropriation today being brought under bilateral investment treaties ('BITs'), it is most relevant to consider the particular requirement of the applicable treaty. Many BITs provide for the Hull formula, or a variant of it, for the expropriation to be lawful, with the standard of compensation being further defined as the 'fair market value' of the expropriated asset valued immediately before the expropriation took place or became publicly known.[166]

The foregoing discussion concerns the compensation that is to be paid for the expropriation to be lawful. In the case of an unlawful expropriation, the standard of compensation is set by customary international law, which was articulated by the PCIJ in *Factory at Chorzów* and discussed in Section 7.3.5. This is also the standard of compensation which arbitral tribunals apply where a state has breached an obligation under a BIT, because the treaty-based standard of compensation only applies in the case of a lawful expropriation. For unlawful expropriations (or any other breach of the obligations in the BIT), the customary international law standard applies.[167]

---

159    *Amoco International Finance Corporation v Iran* (1987) 15 Iran-US CTR 189 [113] ('*Amoco*').
160    Ibid [145]; see also [146].
161    *BP Exploration Co (Libya) Ltd v Libya* (1974) 53 ILR 297.
162    *Amoco* (n 159) [140].
163    Harris and Sivakumaran (n 147) 508.
164    See, eg, *Saudi Arabia v Arabian American Oil Company (Aramco)* (1963) 27 ILR 117 [142].
165    Harris and Sivakumaran (n 147) 508.
166    See, eg, *Energy Charter Treaty*, signed 17 December 1994, 2080 UNTS 95 (entered into force 16 April 1998) art 13(1). See also Chapter 16, Section 16.3.2.3.
167    See, eg, *ADC Affiliate Ltd v Hungary (Award)* (ICSID Arbitral Tribunal, Case No ARB/03/16, 2 October 2006) [481].

# 7.6    Additional requirements for a claim in diplomatic protection

In addition to there being a breach of an obligation, for a claim in diplomatic protection to proceed, two other requirements must be fulfilled. As outlined in art 44 of *ARSIWA*:

> The responsibility of a State may not be invoked if:
>
> (a)    the claim is not brought in accordance with any applicable rule relating to the nationality of claims;
>
> (b)    the claim is one to which the rule of exhaustion of local remedies applies and any available and effective local remedy has not been exhausted.

## 7.6.1    Nationality of claims: natural persons

The nationality of claims requirement means that only the state of the injured national may bring a claim in diplomatic protection,[168] unless that person is stateless or a refugee.[169] Nationality is not determined by international law – rather, it is for the municipal law of the state to determine how nationality is granted (that is, through birth, descent, nationalisation, marriage, etc).[170] There is no need for a state to prove that there is a 'genuine and effective link'[171] between itself and the person – it is possible to gain nationality of a state even if one has no connection to it. For example, some states have a system of citizenship through investment, which entitles a person to gain citizenship after a relatively short period of time, provided they have invested a significant sum of money into a local business.[172] Nationality must exist at the date of both the injury and the claim.

Where the national has dual or multiple nationalities, art 6 of *ADP* provides that any state or states who claim nationality over an injured person may exercise diplomatic protection (including jointly) against a state of which the person is not a national.[173] More complicated

---

168    *ADP* (n 126) art 3.

169    Ibid art 8. In such cases, a state may exercise diplomatic protection in respect of a stateless person, or a person recognised as a refugee by that state under international refugee law, so long as the person, at the date of injury and at the date of the official presentation of the claim, is lawfully and habitually resident in that state. However, a state may not claim in respect of an injury caused by an internationally wrongful act of the state of nationality of the refugee.

170    Notwithstanding this, nationality can be neither granted nor stripped from a person contrary to international law. For example, the forcing of nationality on women due to marriage is prohibited by the *Convention on the Elimination of All Forms of Discrimination against Women*, signed 18 December 1979, 1249 UNTS 13 (entered into force 3 September 1981) art 9.

171    *Nottebohm (Liechtenstein v Guatemala) (Judgment)* [1955] ICJ Rep 4; see also *ADP Commentary* (n 127) 29–30 (Draft Article 4 Commentary [5]). While *Nottebohm* is where the notion of 'genuine and effective nationality' first arose (and was the basis of the decision), the reasoning in this instance was contextual, and it has since been considered unlikely that the ICJ intended to establish a general principle of a requirement of 'genuine and effective' nationality.

172    See further Salome Garnier, 'Citizenship by Investment: Transactions of National Identity' (2020) 41(1) *Harvard International Review* 15, 15–18; Odile Ammann, 'Passports for Sale: How (Un)Meritocratic Are Citizenship by Investment Programmes?' (2020) 22(3) *European Journal of Migration and Law* 309.

173    See *Mergé Claim* (1955) 22 ILR 443, 456 (Italian–United States Conciliation Commission); *Salem (Egypt v United States)* (1932) 2 RIAA 1161.

is where an injured person with dual or multiple nationality has a claim brought by one state of nationality against another state of nationality – for instance, if an Australian–New Zealand dual national has a claim brought on their behalf by Australia against New Zealand. Under art 7 of *ADP*:

> A State of nationality may not exercise diplomatic protection in respect of a person against a State of which that person is also a national unless the nationality of the former State is predominant, both at the date of injury and at the date of the official presentation of the claim.

It is for the claiming state to prove predominant nationality. Courts and tribunals have looked at differing facts to ascertain predominant nationality – such as

> habitual residence; the amount of time spent in each country of nationality; date of naturalization ... place, curricula and language of education; employment and financial interests; place of family life; family ties in each country; participation in social and public life; use of language; taxation, bank account, social security insurance; visits to the other State of nationality; possession and use of passport of the other State; and military service.[174]

It may be in certain circumstances that a tribunal cannot establish a predominant nationality, which would result in the case being unable to be heard.[175]

## 7.6.2   Nationality of claims: corporations and shareholders

States may also claim in diplomatic protection over other legal persons – like corporations. Article 9 of *ADP* provides that the state of nationality of a corporation is the state under whose law the corporation was incorporated. However, if the corporation is controlled by nationals of another state (or states) and 'has no substantial business activities in the State of incorporation, and the seat of management and the financial control of the corporation are both located in another State',[176] then *that* state shall be regarded as the state of nationality. The leading case on point is *Barcelona Traction, Light and Power Company*. A dispute arose between Belgium and Spain regarding a company established in Canada in 1911. The company produced electricity in Spain, but most shareholders were Belgian. Following World War II, the Spanish government enacted several measures that ultimately led to the company declaring bankruptcy in 1948. After Canada declined to exercise diplomatic protection, Belgium took up the claim of its shareholders. In the ICJ, the Court agreed with Spain that Belgium lacked standing to bring the claim, noting that the injury had been to the company, and not the shareholders:

> Notwithstanding the separate corporate personality, a wrong done to the company frequently causes prejudice to its shareholders. But the mere fact that damage is sustained by both company and shareholder does not imply that both are entitled to claim compensation.
>
> . . .

---

174    *ADP Commentary* (n 127) 35 (Draft Article 7 Commentary [5]).
175    *Mergé Claim* (n 173) 455.
176    *ADP* (n 126) art 9.

[E]vidence that damage was suffered does not *ipso facto* justify a diplomatic claim. Persons suffer damage or harm in most varied circumstances. This in itself does not involve the obligation to make reparation. Not a mere interest affected, but solely a right infringed involves responsibility, so that an act directed against and infringing only the company's rights does not involve responsibility towards the shareholders, even if their interests are affected.[177]

Because no shareholder *rights* (such as the right to attend meetings or receive dividends) had been infringed by the Spanish government, Belgium lacked standing to proceed.[178] The question of shareholder rights was revisited in *Diallo*,[179] where the ICJ affirmed: '[T]here is no general exception to the general rule governing the protection of companies by which the national state of a shareholder may offer that shareholder protection where, as on the facts of the *Diallo* case, the national state of an existing company is the state against which protection is sought.'[180]

The Draft Articles on Diplomatic Protection recognise the rights of shareholders as distinct from the right of the corporation, but only in specific circumstances. Article 11 provides:

A State of nationality of shareholders in a corporation shall not be entitled to exercise diplomatic protection in respect of such shareholders in the case of an injury to the corporation unless:
(a)  the corporation has ceased to exist according to the law of the State of incorporation for a reason unrelated to the injury; or
(b)  the corporation had, at the date of injury, the nationality of the State alleged to be responsible for causing the injury, and incorporation in that State was required by it as a precondition for doing business there.

If one of these conditions is found, then '[t]o the extent that an internationally wrongful act of a State causes direct injury to the rights of shareholders as such, as distinct from those of the corporation itself, the State of nationality of any such shareholders is entitled to exercise diplomatic protection in respect of its nationals'.[181]

## 7.6.3    Exhaustion of local remedies

The remaining element for a claim in diplomatic protection is the requirement that all local remedies are exhausted before a claim is brought in an international forum. Article 14 of *ADP* affirms the customary obligation stated in the *Ambatielos* arbitration:[182] 'a state may not present an international claim in respect of an injury to a national or other person'[183] unless they have exhausted all local remedies. Local remedies are understood to include any available legal

177    *Barcelona Traction* (n 129) 35 [44], 36 [46].
178    The right of shareholders was acknowledged in *Barcelona Traction*: ibid 26 [47].
179    *Diallo (Republic of Guinea v Democratic Republic of the Congo) (Preliminary Objections)* [2007] ICJ Rep 582.
180    Harris and Sivakumaran (n 147) 549; *Diallo* (n 179) 615 [89].
181    *ADP* (n 126) art 12.
182    *Ambatielos Claim (Greece v United Kingdom) (Award)* (1956) 12 RIAA 83.
183    *ADP* (n 126) art 14.

remedies before judicial or administrative bodies of the state alleged to be responsible for the injury. However, the requirement to exhaust local remedies only applies to available effective remedies – that is, by bringing a case to courts or bodies able to provide a binding resolution, as opposed to purely discretionary or optional dispute resolution mechanisms. As affirmed by the ICJ in *Elettronica Sicula*:

> [F]or an international claim to be admissible, it is sufficient if the essence of the claim has been brought before the competent tribunals and pursued as far as permitted by local law and procedure, without success.[184]

If an appeal against judgment would not affect the basic outcome of the case (for instance, because the court could not order the necessary remedies), failure to appeal would not run afoul of this rule.[185] Likewise, pursuant to art 15 of *ADP*, local remedies do not need to be exhausted if any of the following circumstances exist: 'there are no reasonably available local remedies to provide effective redress'; local remedies provide no reasonable possibility of redress; there is undue delay in the remedial process attributable to the alleged responsible state; there is no relevant connection between the injured person and the alleged responsible state at the date of injury; the injured person is manifestly precluded from pursuing local remedies; or the state alleged to be responsible has waived the requirement that local remedies be exhausted.

# 7.7    State responsibility in the era of international human rights law

In some respects the international minimum standard on the treatment of foreign nationals has been significantly overtaken by developments in other areas of international law. For example, modern international human rights law (see Chapter 10) now itself provides minimum international standards in relation to the subject matter of many of the cases considered above, including conditions in detention, freedom from torture, fair trial and the state's duty to diligently investigate and prosecute violations of the right to life. Human rights law is usually more specific and detailed in its content, comprises standards owed to all (not only foreign nationals), is arguably customary in many areas, and often provides procedures by which to make claims. Claims to protect foreign nationals are now routinely framed by states as violations of concrete human rights, or where relevant as violations of international humanitarian law or international criminal law, rather than as violations of the *Neer* or *Roberts* principles. The law on the treatment of nationals may still have a role to play where wrongdoing states are not parties to particular treaties and the rules concerned are not customary.

In contrast, the era of BITs and investment treaty claims has confirmed the ongoing relevance and vitality of the international minimum standard of treatment (and the standard of fair and equitable treatment), even in the days of the expansion of treaty-based human rights law protecting property rights. It may be thought that states' obligations under international human rights law may well have overtaken the protection afforded by customary international law as exemplified

---

184    *Elettronica Sicula SpA (ELSI) (United States of America v Italy) (Judgment)* [1989] ICJ Rep 15, 46 [59].
185    *Claim of Finnish Shipowners against Great Britain in Respect of the Use of Certain Finnish Vessels during the War (Finland v United Kingdom) (Award)* (1934) 3 RIAA 1479.

in claims such as *Neer* and its modern-day counterparts, such as *Saluka Investments BV v Czech Republic*.[186] Yet the remedies provided by most BITs (in the form of a right to commence international arbitration proceedings against the host state, usually without the need to exhaust local remedies before bringing the claim, and which will result in a binding award) have ensured their attractiveness when compared with remedies under human rights treaties. The ICJ has observed that traditional diplomatic protection claims have become far less frequent in light of the existence of BITs which give companies and individuals standing to present claims. As it noted in *Diallo*:

> [I]n contemporary international law, the protection of the rights of companies and the rights of their shareholders, and the settlement of the associated disputes, are essentially governed by bilateral or multilateral agreements for the protection of foreign investments, such as the treaties for the promotion and protection of foreign investments, and the *Washington Convention of 18 March 1965 on the Settlement of Investment Disputes between States and Nationals of Other States*, which created an International Centre for Settlement of Investment Disputes (ICSID), and also by contracts between States and foreign investors. In that context, the role of diplomatic protection somewhat faded, as in practice recourse is only made to it in rare cases where treaty régimes do not exist or have proved inoperative.[187]

As the ICJ explained, this does not mean that instruments for the protection of human rights are not utilised in this field. The *Diallo* case is an example of a diplomatic protection claim on behalf of an individual who was arrested, detained and expelled from the Democratic Republic of the Congo contrary to the *International Covenant for Civil and Political Rights* and the *African Charter on Human and People's Rights*.[188] The responsibility of states for internationally unlawful acts can be implemented through the vehicle of diplomatic protection claims for breach of rights protected by customary international law (such as the protection against expropriation, and the minimum standard of treatment), and such claims might also be brought in respect of breaches of human rights obligations. The interrelationship between human rights law and diplomatic protection remains a live issue, with both bodies of law bringing unique strengths to the settlement of disputes involving injury to foreign nationals.[189]

## DISCUSSION QUESTIONS

(1) In an age when international human rights law increasingly offers avenues for individuals to seek redress at international law, has the law of diplomatic protection lost some of its value?

---

186    *Saluka Investments BV v Czech Republic (Partial Award)* (ICSID Arbitral Tribunal, Case No 2001-04, 17 March 2006).
187    *Diallo* (n 179) 614–5 [88].
188    Ibid 606 [63].
189    See further John Dugard, 'Diplomatic Protection and Human Rights: The Draft Articles of the International Law Commission' (2005) 24 *Australian Year Book of International Law* 75; Noura Karazivan, 'Diplomatic Protection: Taking Human Rights Extraterritorially' (2007) 44 *Canadian Yearbook of International Law* 299; Frédéric Mégret, 'The Changing Face of Protection of the State's Nationals Abroad' (2020) 21(2) *Melbourne Journal of International Law* 450.

**(2)**   The threshold for attribution in the *Articles on Responsibility of States for Internationally Wrongful Acts* ('*ARSIWA*') and in customary international law – that of effective control – has been criticised as being so high as to prevent it ever being applicable. Do you agree?

**(3)**   Should *ARSIWA* and the Draft Articles on Diplomatic Protection be adopted by states as conventions, as was done in the case of the International Law Commission's work on the law of treaties?

**(4)**   Does the Commission's formulation of the defence of 'necessity' set too high a bar in requiring that the state demonstrate that the action it took was 'the only way' for it 'to safeguard an essential interest against a grave and imminent peril'?

**(5)**   Should the *Nottebohm* test of requiring the establishment of a 'genuine connection' between a state and a person claiming to have that state's nationality still play a role in the law of nationality?

# 8

# USE OF FORCE

Alison Pert

# 8.1    Introduction

This chapter covers the international law governing the use of force between states – the *jus ad bello*. This is in contrast to the *jus in bello* – the law of armed conflict, or international humanitarian law – which regulates the conduct of hostilities once under way (see Chapter 11). Since at least 1945 the use of force by states has been prohibited, except in self-defence or when authorised by the UN Security Council. This chapter analyses the prohibition, the two exceptions, and the controversial issue of humanitarian intervention and its close relative, the 'responsibility to protect'.

# 8.2    Pre-1945

In the 19th century, war was not prohibited in international law, and territory could be lawfully acquired by conquest.[1] As weapons increased in number and sophistication, tentative steps were taken at the end of the century to place modest limits on this unfettered right to go to war. The Hague Peace Conferences of 1899 and 1907 produced treaties requiring parties to attempt peaceful settlement of disputes,[2] not use armed force to recover certain debts[3] and not commence hostilities without warning.[4]

The carnage of World War I led to further, limited constraints on the legality of war, in the *Covenant of the League of Nations* ('*League Covenant*') – that part of the *Treaty of Versailles* creating the League of Nations.[5] But these constraints were procedural only: members of the League were required to submit disputes to arbitration, judicial settlement or the League Council, and war was only prohibited against a state complying with any resulting decision.[6] The first major step towards outlawing war was the *Kellogg–Briand Pact* of 1928,[7] in which 'substantially all the nations of the world' renounced war;[8] thereafter war was prohibited unless conducted in self-defence or pursuant to a 'recommendation' by the League Council.[9] The Pact was hailed as rendering war 'illegal throughout practically the entire world'.[10] But it only applied to war, and

1    See, eg, William Edward Hall, *International Law* (Oxford University Press, 1880) 52; Ian Brownlie, *International Law and the Use of Force by States* (Oxford University Press, 1963) 19 and (for an overview of the attitudes to war of different civilisations over the millennia) ch 1.

2    *Hague Convention (I) for the Pacific Settlement of International Disputes*, opened for signature 29 July 1899, [1901] ATS 130 (entered into force 4 September 1900).

3    *International Convention respecting the Limitation of the Employment of Force for the Recovery of Contract Debts*, opened for signature 18 October 1907, [1910] ATS 6 (entered into force 26 January 1910).

4    *International Convention Relative to the Opening of Hostilities*, opened for signature 18 October 1907, [1910] ATS 7 (entered into force 26 January 1910).

5    *Treaty of Peace between the Allied and Associated Powers and Germany*, opened for signature 28 June 1919, [1920] ATS 1 (entered into force 10 January 1920) pt 1 ('*League Covenant*').

6    Ibid arts 12–15.

7    *General Treaty for Renunciation of War as an Instrument of National Policy*, opened for signature 7 August 1928, 94 LNTS 57 (entered into force 24 July 1929).

8    Henry Stimson, 'The Pact of Paris: Three Years of Development' (Speech, Council on Foreign Relations, 8 August 1932) in 36(6) *Current History* (1932) 760, 761.

9    Ibid; *League Covenant* (n 5) art 16.

10    Stimson (n 8) 761.

not to any use of force short of a formal war. And neither the *League Covenant* nor the Pact prevented the major armed conflicts of the 1930s, culminating in World War II.

# 8.3    The *Charter of the United Nations*

The drafters of the *Charter of the United Nations* ('*UN Charter*')[11] sought to remedy these shortcomings. As recorded in the Preamble to the Charter, they had lived through two world wars, and were determined to avoid another. The first purpose of the Charter is 'to maintain international peace and security',[12] and this is supported by 'the Charter system' relating to the use of force:

- art 2(3) – the obligation on members to settle disputes peacefully;
- art 2(4) – the prohibition on the unilateral use of force;
- Chapter VI – preventing international disputes from escalating into war; and
- Chapter VII – collective measures to maintain or restore international peace and security.

Article 2(4) is 'a cornerstone'[13] of the Charter:

> All Members shall refrain in their international relations from the threat or use of force against the territorial integrity or political independence of any state, or in any other manner inconsistent with the Purposes of the United Nations.

## 8.3.1    'Force', 'in their international relations', 'any state'

Several elements in art 2(4) should be noted. First, it refers not to war, but to 'force'; what this encompasses is discussed in Section 8.3.3. Second, it prohibits force by member states only 'in their international relations' – it does not apply to civil war or other intra-state conflict. Third, force is prohibited against 'any state', and not just members of the United Nations; this has little practical effect today, as nearly all states are UN members. Fourth, the threat of force is equally prohibited – what this means is considered in Section 8.3.8.

## 8.3.2    'Territorial integrity or political independence'

Force is prohibited against 'the territorial integrity or political independence' of another state, 'or in any other manner inconsistent with the Purposes of the United Nations'.[14] These words have given rise to debate over whether they enlarge, or restrict, the prohibition. This question becomes particularly relevant when considering the right of self-defence (see Section 8.4), and whether humanitarian intervention is permitted (see Section 8.6). Some writers argue that art 2(4) does not prohibit a use of force which is, for example, not directed at seizing another

---

11    The term 'United Nations' was coined in 1941 by President Roosevelt to describe the United States, Great Britain and their allies; it was used formally in the 'Declaration by United Nations' of 1 January 1942 in (1942) 36 (S3) *American Journal of International Law* 191, 191–2.

12    *Charter of the United Nations* ('*UN Charter*') art 1(1).

13    *Armed Activities on the Territory of the Congo (Democratic Republic of the Congo v Uganda)* *(Judgment)* [2005] ICJ Rep 168, 223–4 [148] ('*Armed Activities*').

14    *UN Charter* art 2(4).

state's territory (territorial integrity) or overthrowing its government (political independence).[15] They further argue that force which is broadly consistent with the purposes of the United Nations, such as to protect human rights, does not violate the final part of art 2(4).

The overwhelming body of opinion, however, supported by decisions of the International Court of Justice ('ICJ'), is that art 2(4) should be read as a whole, and that the prohibition is comprehensive.[16] The *UN Charter* was drafted at a conference in San Francisco from April to June 1945, using as a basis a draft agreed between the United States, the United Kingdom, the USSR and China at Dumbarton Oaks the previous year.[17] The Dumbarton Oaks draft of art 2(4) read simply:

> All members of the Organization shall refrain in their international relations from the threat or use of force in any manner inconsistent with the purposes of the Organization.

Australia, New Zealand and at least a dozen other states considered this insufficient, and proposed amendments to refer specifically to territorial integrity and political independence;[18] these were familiar terms that had been used in other treaties including art 10 of the *League Covenant*. The Australian wording was accepted and became art 2(4).[19] As the US delegate noted, 'the intention of the authors of the original text was to state in the broadest terms an absolute all-inclusive prohibition; the phrase "or in any other manner" was designed to insure that there should be no loopholes'.[20]

## 8.3.3   What is prohibited?

Several different but related terms are used in the *UN Charter* – 'armed force' (Preamble), 'force' (art 2(4)), 'aggression' (art 39) and 'armed attack' (art 51) – but none is defined. It is broadly accepted that 'force' in art 2(4) means 'armed force' and not, for example, political or economic pressure. Delegates at the San Francisco conference rejected an amendment proposed by Brazil to include the words 'and from the threat or use of economic measures' in art 2(4). There is no record of the reason for the rejection but despite the drafting committee's somewhat vague reference to 'use of force or similar coercive measures',[21] the conference discussions, negotiations and decisions that are recorded strongly suggest that the delegates had armed force in mind.[22]

This lack of clarity in art 2(4) led the smaller and less-developed members of the UN General Assembly to seek more detailed descriptions of what the article encompassed, two important results being the *Friendly Relations Declaration* in 1970[23] and the *Definition of Aggression*

15      See, eg, Derek Bowett, *Self-Defence in International Law* (Praeger, 1958) 150–2, 185–6.
16      See, eg, Brownlie, *International Law and the Use of Force by States* (n 1) 265–8.
17      'Dumbarton Oaks Proposals' (1945) 39 (S1) *American Journal of International Law* 42, 42–56.
18      See *Documents of the UN Conference on International Organisation* (1945) vol 3.
19      Ibid vol 6, 334, 342.
20      Ibid vol 6, 335.
21      Ibid.
22      See, eg, ibid vol 6, 70, 304, 334–5, 342–6, 356, 368, 400, 459.
23      *Declaration on Principles of International Law concerning Friendly Relations and Co-operation among States in accordance with the Charter of the United Nations*, GA Res 2625 (XXV), UN Doc A/RES/2625 (24 October 1970) annex ('*Friendly Relations Declaration*').

in 1974,[24] both of which reflect customary international law.[25] Principle 1 of the *Friendly Relations Declaration* imposes on all states a number of duties, including to refrain from:

> ... the threat or use of force to violate the existing international boundaries of another State or as a means of solving international disputes, including territorial disputes and problems concerning frontiers of States.
>
> ... organizing or encouraging the organization of irregular forces or armed bands including mercenaries, for incursion into the territory of another State.
>
> ... organizing, instigating, assisting or participating in acts of civil strife or terrorist acts in another State or acquiescing in organized activities within its territory directed towards the commission of such acts, when the acts referred to in the present paragraph involve a threat or use of force.

The Declaration makes it clear that not only direct force by a state's armed forces, but also indirect force is prohibited – for example, organising non-state actors in one state for incursion into another, or one state fomenting conflict in another.

The *Definition of Aggression* contains a long list of 'acts of aggression', also both direct and indirect in nature. Those which could be described as direct aggression include invasion, attack, occupation, annexation, bombardment or blockade of another state; examples of indirect aggression include allowing territory to be used for perpetrating aggression against a third state, or 'the sending by or on behalf of a State of armed bands, groups, irregulars or mercenaries, which carry out acts of armed force against another State of such gravity as to amount to the acts listed above, or its substantial involvement therein'.[26]

## 8.3.4 The prohibition is customary international law, and *jus cogens*

The prohibition on the use of force was confirmed as part of customary international law in *Military and Paramilitary Activities in and against Nicaragua* ('*Nicaragua*'). It is also said to be a norm of *jus cogens*.[27]

### 8.3.4.1 The *Nicaragua* case

In the *Nicaragua* case, brought by Nicaragua against the United States, the ICJ confirmed that the prohibition on the use of force, as elaborated in the *Friendly Relations Declaration*, was customary international law.[28] In 1979, the (right-wing) Somoza government in Nicaragua was overthrown by the (left-wing) *Sandinistas*. According to the United States, the new regime was allowing Soviet arms to pass through Nicaraguan territory en route to guerrillas

---

24 *Definition of Aggression*, GA Res 3314 (XXIX), UN Doc A/RES/3314(XXIX) (14 December 1974) annex ('*Definition of Aggression*').

25 *Military and Paramilitary Activities in and against Nicaragua (Nicaragua v United States of America) (Merits)* [1986] ICJ Rep 14, 99–100 [188], 101 [191] ('*Nicaragua*'); *Armed Activities* (n 13) 226–7 [162], 268 [300].

26 *Definition of Aggression* (n 24) art 3.

27 Report of the International Law Commission *on the Work of Its Seventy-First Session*, UN GAOR, 74th sess, Supp No 10, UN Doc A/74/10 (2019) 141–208.

28 *Nicaragua* (n 25) 99–100 [188].

in El Salvador, fighting against the US-supported government there. The United States took various actions in the early 1980s to stop this, from economic measures to the use of force both directly, through its own agents, and indirectly, through the *Contras*.[29] The *Contras* were originally a small organisation of anti-*Sandinista* rebels, which the US government built up, funded, equipped and trained.

In its claim before the ICJ, Nicaragua argued that these activities violated the United States' international legal obligations, including under art 2(4) of the *UN Charter*. The United States disputed the Court's jurisdiction to hear the claim because its submission to jurisdiction under art 36(2) of the *Statute of the International Court of Justice* excluded claims arising under a multilateral treaty.[30] The *UN Charter* being a multilateral treaty, the Court's jurisdiction was excluded. The Court accepted this argument, but also accepted Nicaragua's argument that the use of force was equally prohibited in customary international law, which was not excluded by the United States' reservation.[31]

The way in which the Court identified the requisite state practice and *opinio juris* was rather opaque, and heavily criticised at the time.[32] In summary, state practice was to be found in the many agreements and resolutions prohibiting force,[33] and *opinio juris* was to be 'deduced from, *inter alia*, the attitude of the Parties and the attitude of States towards certain General Assembly resolutions, and particularly resolution 2625 (XXV)'.[34] But the conclusion that the prohibition existed both in treaty law (art 2(4) of the *UN Charter*) and customary law was accepted and has been confirmed on numerous occasions since.[35]

The Court was satisfied that the United States had engaged in a range of actions constituting the unlawful use of force. These included:

- laying mines in Nicaraguan ports and waters – these operations were conducted by US personnel or persons in its pay;[36]
- attacking Nicaraguan oil installations – 'agents of the United States participated in the planning, direction and support and execution of the operations', which were therefore attributable to the United States;[37] and
- arming and training the *Contras*: this violated the prohibition as described in the *Friendly Relations Declaration*, by 'organizing or encouraging the organization of irregular forces or armed bands ... for incursion into the territory of another State', and 'participating in acts of civil strife [involving the use of force] in another State'.[38]

---

29    For a history of the US intervention see William M LeoGrande, *Our Own Backyard: The United States in Central America, 1977–1992* (UNC Press, 1998).
30    The exclusion applied unless all parties to the treaty were also parties to the case: *Nicaragua* (n 25) 31 [42], 34–8 [47]–[56]. See also Chapter 9 on dispute settlement.
31    *Nicaragua* (n 25) 38 [56], 97 [182].
32    See, eg, Hilary Charlesworth, 'Customary International Law and the *Nicaragua Case*' (1991) 11 *Australian Year Book of International Law* 1.
33    *Nicaragua* (n 25) 98–100 [183]–[188].
34    Ibid 100 [188].
35    See, eg, *Armed Activities* (n 13) 226–7 [162], 268 [300].
36    *Nicaragua* (n 25) 118 [227].
37    Ibid 50–1 [86].
38    Ibid 118–19 [228]. This is an example of an indirect use of force – the force was used directly by the *Contras*, but the United States violated the prohibition by organising and encouraging it.

Other findings of the Court included:

- generally, 'assistance to rebels in the form of the provision of weapons or logistical or other support' may be a threat or use of force;[39]
- however, 'the mere supply of funds to the *Contras*, while undoubtedly an act of intervention in the internal affairs of Nicaragua ... [did] not in itself amount to a use of force';[40] and
- the United States' military manoeuvres near the Nicaraguan border, 'in the circumstances in which they were held', did not constitute a threat or use of force.[41]

## 8.3.5   Indirect use of force vs 'effective control'

The *Nicaragua* case illustrates the distinction between the indirect use of force – using force through non-state actors – and state responsibility for the conduct of those actors in the course of their operations. As explained in Chapter 7 on state responsibility, the conduct of private individuals will be attributable to a state 'if the state directed or controlled the specific operation, and the conduct complained of was an integral part of that operation', known as 'effective control'.[42] This follows the ICJ's ruling in *Nicaragua*, that the alleged violations of international humanitarian law by the *Contras* could not be attributed to the United States, because there was no evidence that the United States had directed or controlled the specific *Contra* operations in which the violations had occurred.[43] So the United States was not responsible in international law for those violations; it did not contravene international humanitarian law. But the United States *did* contravene the prohibition on the use of force, by arming and training the *Contras*.[44]

## 8.3.6   What is not a use of force?

Apart from 'the mere supply of funds', there is little authority on what will not constitute a prohibited use of force.[45] Incursion into a state's airspace or territorial waters by the armed forces of another state, where no actual use or threat of force occurs, would clearly be a violation of sovereignty[46] but would probably not violate the prohibition of force. More difficult is the mere presence of troops on another state's territory, such as occurred when Nicaraguan troops were stationed in disputed territory which was subsequently found by the ICJ to be part of Costa Rica. The Court confirmed Nicaragua's violation of Costa Rican sovereignty, but found it unnecessary to consider whether it also constituted a threat or use of force.[47] In his separate opinion, Judge Robinson asserted that when regard was had to

---

39      Ibid 103–4 [195].
40      Ibid 118–19 [228]; see Section 6.1 on intervention.
41      Ibid 118 [227].
42      'Draft Articles on Responsibility of States for Internationally Wrongful Acts, with Commentaries' [2001] II(2) *Yearbook of the International Law Commission* 1, 20 (Draft Article 8 Commentary [3]).
43      *Nicaragua* (n 25) 64–5 [115].
44      Ibid 118–19 [228].
45      See, eg, Tom Ruys, 'The Meaning of Force and the Boundaries of the Jus ad Bellum: Are Minimal Uses of Force Excluded from UN Charter Article 2(4)?' (2014) 108(1) *American Journal of International Law* 159.
46      *Corfu Channel (United Kingdom v Albania) (Merits)* [1949] ICJ Rep 4, 28.
47      *Certain Activities Carried out by Nicaragua in the Border Area (Costa Rica v Nicaragua) and Construction of a Road in Costa Rica along the San Juan River (Nicaragua v Costa Rica) (Merits)* [2015] ICJ Rep 665, 704 [97], 705 [99].

Nicaragua's purpose in occupying the territory, and the gravity of its actions, the Court should have found that it had violated art 2(4).[48]

Authors such as Oscar Schachter have argued that measures akin to 'law enforcement' are not caught by the prohibition:

> There is no question about the right of a territorial sovereign to enforce its laws, with force if necessary, against an intruding vessel, plane or land vehicle that has violated the national domain. The use of such force is limited, not by the general language of article 2(4), but by customary law principles requiring that force be limited in manner and amount to that reasonable in the circumstances. The sweeping prohibition against force does not apply in such cases of 'enforcement' by states, because the act of force does not fall within the proscribed categories of article 2(4).[49]

This view finds some support in the 1998 *Fisheries Jurisdiction* case, in which the ICJ found that '[b]oarding, inspection, arrest and minimum use of force [against a foreign fishing vessel] . . . are all contained within the concept of enforcement of conservation and management measures'.[50] Another tribunal affirmed in principle 'the argument that in international law force may be used in law enforcement activities provided that such force is unavoidable, reasonable and necessary'.[51]

Sixty years ago, Ian Brownlie doubted that actions such as 'the deliberate and forcible expulsion of population over a frontier, release of large quantities of water down a valley and the spreading of fire through a built-up area or woodland across a frontier' would constitute unlawful force.[52] This view assumes that the use of arms – a weapon – is a necessary ingredient of unlawful force, and an unanswered question is what exactly constitutes a 'weapon'. For example, it is widely accepted that commercial passenger aircraft were used as weapons in the '9/11' attacks in the United States in 2001.[53] Similar challenges to traditional views arise in spheres such as cyber-warfare, as discussed in the next section.

## 8.3.7    New challenges: cyber-attacks

The use of computers rather than physical force to cause damage – cyber-attacks – is a recent and growing phenomenon. An example of the damage these attacks can cause occurred in Estonia in 2007. Following a row about moving a Soviet-era statue, Estonia was hit by a series of cyber-attacks which paralysed banks, media outlets and government bodies for several weeks.[54]

---

48    Ibid 807.
49    Oscar Schachter, 'The Right of States to Use Armed Force' (1984) 82(5–6) *Michigan Law Review* 1620, 1626 (citations omitted).
50    *Fisheries Jurisdiction (Spain v Canada) (Jurisdiction)* [1998] ICJ Rep 432, 466 [84]. This finding was for the purposes of interpreting the reservation in Canada's art 36(2) declaration submitting to the jurisdiction of the Court. The Court stressed that this conclusion was a separate question to the legality of the actual actions undertaken, a question which was unnecessary to decide as the Court found it had no jurisdiction: at 456 [55].
51    *Guyana v Suriname (Award)* (2007) 139 ILR 566, 696 [445].
52    Ian Brownlie, 'International Law on the Use of Force by States Revisited' (2000) 21 *Australian Year Book of International Law* 21, 256.
53    See Section 8.3.5.
54    Damien McGuinness, 'How a Cyber Attack Transformed Estonia', BBC *News* (online at 27 April 2017) <www.bbc.com/news/39655415>.

Russia was suspected of orchestrating the attacks,[55] but a key problem with cyber-attacks is attribution: the very nature of the attacks makes it difficult, and often impossible, to trace their real source.

The Estonian attack led to the founding of the NATO Cooperative Cyber Defence Centre of Excellence in Tallinn, which in 2009 convened an International Group of Experts to consider the international law implications of cyber-operations.[56] These experts produced the Tallinn Manual on how existing international law applies to cyberspace.[57] The experts concluded that cyber-operations could amount to a use of force in certain situations,[58] taking into account eight factors:

> severity, immediacy, directness, invasiveness, measurability of effects, military character, state involvement, and presumptive legality. . . .
>
> The more immediate, direct, invasive, and measurable the attendant effects, the more liable states are to style the operation in question as a use of force.[59]

## 8.3.8    What is a threat of force?

Article 2(4) of the *UN Charter*, and customary international law, prohibit not only the use of force but also the threat of force. There are few decided cases on threats. As to when a threat will be unlawful, the ICJ in its *Legality of the Threat or Use of Nuclear Weapons* advisory opinion stated that 'if the use of force itself in a given case is illegal – for whatever reason – the threat to use such force will likewise be illegal'.[60] While logical, a difficulty with this test is ascertaining, in advance, the legality of the force which is threatened – for example, whether it would be justified as self-defence, or necessary and proportionate (see Section 8.4.1); these factors could only be assessed after the fact. But some threats would be clearly unlawful, such as an ultimatum to seize territory if the other state did not accede to certain demands.[61]

To be unlawful, the threat must also be reasonably specific: 'a signalled intention to use force if certain events occur', or 'the declared readiness of a State to use force',[62] as opposed to generally belligerent rhetoric or the mere possession of weapons.[63] The surrounding

55    See, eg, Rain Ottis, 'Analysis of the 2007 Cyber Attacks against Estonia from the Information Warfare Perspective' (NATO Cooperative Cyber Defence Centre of Excellence, October 2018) <https://ccdcoe .org/uploads/2018/10/Ottis2008_AnalysisOf2007FromTheInformationWarfarePerspective.pdf>.

56    Ibid.

57    Michael Schmitt (ed), *Tallinn Manual 2.0 on the International Law Applicable to Cyber Operations* (Cambridge University Press, 2017).

58    Ibid rules 68–75.

59    Michael Schmitt, 'The Use of Cyber Force and International Law' in Marc Weller (ed), *The Oxford Handbook of the Use of Force in International Law* (Oxford University Press, 2015) 1110, 1113–14 (citations omitted).

60    *Legality of the Threat or Use of Nuclear Weapons (Advisory Opinion)* [1996] ICJ Rep 226, 246 [47] ('*Nuclear Weapons*').

61    See Anne Lagerwall, 'Threats of and Actual Military Strikes against Syria: 2013 and 2017' in Tom Ruys, Olivier Corten and Alexandra Hofer (eds), *The Use of Force in International Law: A Case-Based Approach* (Oxford University Press, 2018) 828.

62    *Nuclear Weapons* (n 60) 246 [47].

63    Ibid 246–7 [48].

circumstances will also be relevant. For example, the threats by the United States and the United Kingdom in 2002–03 to use force against Saddam Hussein, if he did not fully comply with his United Nations–imposed disarmament obligations, were widely regarded as unlawful threats because there was no Security Council approval for that force.[64] In 2007 an arbitral tribunal found that an incident, in which Surinamese Navy gunboats demanded that a Guyanese-licensed oil rig in disputed waters 'leave the area in 12 hours [or] the consequences will be yours', constituted a threat of force.[65] Conversely, as mentioned in Section 8.3.4.1, the ICJ in *Nicaragua* did not consider that US military manoeuvres near the Nicaraguan border, in the particular circumstances, were a threat of force.[66]

# 8.4   Self-defence

Apart from consent,[67] there are two exceptions to the prohibition on the use of force: self-defence, and authorisation by the Security Council.

The right of self-defence is, on one level, a simple proposition: the right of a state to 'defend itself against an attack, to repel the attackers and expel them from its territory'.[68] But in the contemporary world, there are many unresolved questions about when, and how, the right of self-defence applies.

The natural starting point is art 51 of the *UN Charter*:

> Nothing in the present Charter shall impair the inherent right of individual or collective self-defence if an armed attack occurs against a Member of the United Nations, until the Security Council has taken measures necessary to maintain international peace and security. Measures taken by Members in the exercise of this right of self-defence shall be immediately reported to the Security Council and shall not in any way affect the authority and responsibility of the Security Council under the present Charter to take at any time such action as it deems necessary in order to maintain or restore international peace and security.

The reference in art 51 to the 'inherent right' of self-defence is to customary law, which was preserved and not displaced by art 51; as the ICJ said in *Nicaragua*:

> It cannot therefore be held that Article 51 is a provision which 'subsumes and supervenes' customary international law. It rather demonstrates that in the field in question, the importance of which for the present dispute need hardly be stressed, customary international law continues to exist alongside treaty law. The areas governed by the two sources of law thus do not overlap exactly, and the rules do not have the same content.[69]

---

64   See, eg, François Dubuisson and Anne Lagerwall, 'The Threat of the Use of Force and Ultimata' in Marc Weller (ed), *The Oxford Handbook of the Use of Force in International Law* (Oxford University Press, 2015) 910, 918–20.
65   *Guyana v Suriname* (n 51) 691–6 [432]–[445].
66   *Nicaragua* (n 25) 118 [227].
67   Consent can be viewed as precluding the operation of *UN Charter* art 2(4) in the first place, or as a defence to the prohibition.
68   Robert Jennings and Arthur Watt (eds), *Oppenheim's International Law* (Oxford University Press, 9th ed, 1996) 417–18.
69   *Nicaragua* (n 25) 94 [176].

Lawful self-defence requires:

- the existence of an 'armed attack' (analysed in Section 8.4.3);
- a response which is no more than is necessary and proportionate;
- (under art 51) reporting to the Security Council; and
- (for collective self-defence) a declaration by the victim state and a request for assistance.

## 8.4.1   Necessity and proportionality

Although not mentioned in art 51, the ICJ has confirmed that for any action to be lawful self-defence under either art 51 or customary international law it must be 'proportional to the armed attack and necessary to respond to it'.[70]

The US–UK correspondence following the *Caroline* incident is often cited as an early example of this requirement. In 1837 during the Canadian rebellion against British rule, US vessel *The Caroline* was used to transport men and supplies across the Niagara River from the United States to the rebels in Canada. After British protests to the United States failed to stop this activity, a UK force entered US territory at night, seized and set fire to *The Caroline*, and sent it over Niagara Falls; two US citizens were killed.[71] In the ensuing US–UK correspondence, the two states agreed on the criteria for justifying the United Kingdom's actions:

> It will be for [the British] Government to show a necessity of self-defence, instant, over-whelming, leaving no choice of means, and no moment for deliberation', and 'that the [British force] did nothing unreasonable or excessive; since the act justified by the necessity of self-defence, must be limited by that necessity, and kept clearly within it.[72]

'Necessary' in this context[73] means that the action taken must be a last resort – 'no alternative response [is] possible'[74] – while 'proportional' means that the force used must be the minimum required to stop or, if anticipatory self-defence is accepted (see Section 8.4.3.2), avert the attack.[75] The better view is that proportionality is measured not against the scale or nature of the armed attack – a tit-for-tat response – but against what is required to stop it,[76] although such a distinction is not always obvious in the decided cases.

If a state, claiming self-defence, uses force which is not necessary and proportionate, it will itself violate art 2(4) of the *UN Charter*. In the following cases, the ICJ rejected the plea of self-defence but noted that, in any event, the response was not necessary or proportionate. In *Nicaragua*, the US attacks on ports and oil installations were not a proportionate or necessary response to Nicaragua's alleged aid to the armed opposition in El Salvador.[77] In *Oil Platforms*,

---

70    Ibid.
71    'British–American Diplomacy: The Caroline Case', *Avalon Project: Documents in Law, History and Diplomacy* (Web Page) <https://avalon.law.yale.edu/19th_century/br-1842d.asp>.
72    Ibid.
73    Not to be confused with, for example, the doctrine of necessity in state responsibility (see Chapter 7).
74    Christine Gray, *International Law and the Use of Force* (Oxford University Press, 4th ed, 2018) 159.
75    *Nicaragua* (n 25) 94 [176], 103 [194]; *Nuclear Weapons* (n 60) 245 [41]; *Oil Platforms (Islamic Republic of Iran v United States of America) (Merits)* [2003] ICJ Rep 161, 198 [76]; *Armed Activities* (n 13) 223 [147], 269 [304]; Gray (n 74) 157–65.
76    *Nuclear Weapons* (n 60) 583–4 [5]. This was a dissenting opinion of Judge Higgins.
77    The United States' actions were not necessary because the alleged armed attack against El Salvador had ceased months earlier: *Nicaragua* (n 25) 122–3 [237].

the United States' destruction of oil platforms and Iranian naval vessels was not a proportionate or necessary response to Iran's alleged rocket attack and laying of sea mines.[78] In *Armed Activities*, the ICJ doubted that the taking of airports and towns far from the border was a proportionate or necessary response to trans-border attacks.[79] The Court has also commented that even nuclear weapons might be proportionate in extreme circumstances.[80]

## 8.4.2    Procedural requirements for lawful self-defence

### 8.4.2.1    Reporting to the Security Council

Article 51 of the *UN Charter* requires acts of self-defence to be reported to the Security Council. In the *Nicaragua* case, the ICJ accepted that this was not a requirement in customary international law, but the fact that the United States had not reported any of its actions to the Security Council undermined the credibility of its claim to have been acting in self-defence.[81] Reporting to the Security Council is now commonplace.[82]

### 8.4.2.2    Declaration by victim state: collective self-defence

Also emerging from *Nicaragua* is a requirement that before one state can defend another – collective self-defence – the attacked state must declare that an armed attack has occurred, and request assistance from the other state. The United States had claimed that it was acting in defence of El Salvador, but the Court found no evidence of any declaration by El Salvador that it had been attacked, nor a request to the United States for assistance:[83]

> [T]he Court finds that in customary international law ... there is no rule permitting the exercise of collective self-defence in the absence of a request by the State which regards itself as the victim of an armed attack. The Court concludes that the requirement of a request by the State which is the victim of the alleged attack is additional to the requirement that such a State should have declared itself to have been attacked.[84]

## 8.4.3    'Armed attack'

Probably the most contentious issue in the law of self-defence is what exactly is meant by the words in art 51 'if an armed attack occurs'. There are divisions of opinion on what is an armed attack, and when (or even if) it must occur.

---

78    The United States' actions were not necessary because it had not complained to Iran about the platforms being used for military activities, and the destruction was disproportionate to the mining of a single US warship: *Oil Platforms* (n 75) 196–9 [73]–[77].
79    *Armed Activities* (n 13) 223 [147].
80    *Nuclear Weapons* (n 60) 245 [42], 263 [97].
81    *Nicaragua* (n 25) 105 [200].
82    See 'Actions with Respect to Threats to the Peace, Breaches of the Peace, and Acts of Aggression', *Repertoire of Security Council Practice* (Web Page) <www.un.org/securitycouncil/content/repertoire/actions>; Loraine Sievers and Sam Daws, *The Procedure of the UN Security Council* (Oxford University Press, 4th ed, 2014) ch 7 section 12 website ('A Historical Overview of Reporting under Article 51 on Actions Taken in Self-Defence') <www.scprocedure.org/chapter-7-section-12b>.
83    *Nicaragua* (n 25) 103–5 [195]–[199].
84    Ibid 105 [199].

### 8.4.3.1   Meaning of 'armed attack'

Only an 'armed attack' will justify the use of force in self-defence.[85] The ICJ in *Nicaragua* held that an armed attack is an operation which, because of its 'scale and effects', is the 'most grave' form of the use of force – in contrast to, for example, a 'mere frontier incident'.[86] Thus an act can be a use of force, violating art 2(4) of the *UN Charter*, but not so serious as to be an 'armed attack' justifying a forcible response in self-defence. This view has been criticised because it leaves a state unable to respond lawfully to a use of force which is below the threshold of an armed attack.[87] A contrary argument is that it discourages escalation of the conflict, and particularly third-state involvement in cases of collective self-defence.[88]

Examples of what might constitute an armed attack appear in the UN General Assembly's *Definition of Aggression*. They include an invasion, bombardment, blockade and

> [t]he sending by or on behalf of a State of armed bands, groups, irregulars or mercenaries, which carry out acts of armed force against another State of such gravity as to amount to the acts listed above, or its substantial involvement therein.[89]

Article 3(g) reflects customary international law.[90]

In *Armed Activities*, the ICJ held implicitly that Ugandan military assaults resulting in the taking of several towns in the Democratic Republic of the Congo ('DRC') were armed attacks.[91] The vast size of the DRC and chronic instability in its remote eastern regions led the DRC government to invite military assistance from several states, including Uganda, to suppress rebel activity in the east. The Court found that in August 1998, the DRC's consent to Uganda's presence was withdrawn, but Uganda remained in the DRC and continued its military operations. The Court rejected Uganda's claims that it was acting in self-defence against anti-Ugandan rebels, finding that:

> The unlawful military intervention by Uganda was of such a magnitude and duration that the Court considers it to be a grave violation of [art 2(4)][92] ... [T]he Court considers that the DRC was entitled to use force in order to repel Uganda's attacks.[93]

The Court has commented that an attack on a single military vessel could, possibly, amount to an armed attack.[94] During the Iran–Iraq War in the 1980s, the United States deployed naval vessels and reflagged merchant ships in an effort to protect vital oil shipping from being attacked in the Persian Gulf. During these operations a US warship struck a mine, and a US-flagged oil tanker was hit by a missile. The United States claimed that Iran was responsible for these and other attacks and, in response, destroyed several Iranian oil platforms. The ICJ

---

85   Ibid 110–11 [211]. See also *Oil Platforms* (n 75) 186–7 [51].
86   *Nicaragua* (n 25) 101 [191], 103 [195]. Provision of arms to the opposition in another state is also not an armed attack: at 119 [230]. See also *Oil Platforms* (n 75) 186–7 [51].
87   See, eg, the separate opinion of Judge Simma in *Oil Platforms* (n 75) 333 [13]; Gray (n 74) 155–6.
88   Gray (n 74) 156–7.
89   *Definition of Aggression* (n 24) art 3(g).
90   *Nicaragua* (n 25) 103 [195].
91   *Armed Activities* (n 13) 269 [304].
92   Ibid 227 [165].
93   Ibid 269 [304].
94   *Oil Platforms* (n 75) 195–6 [72].

concluded that the actions of the United States could not be justified as self-defence: the Court was not satisfied on the evidence that the attacks were attributable to Iran, nor that they qualified as a 'most grave' form of the use of force.[95]

Further, the Court found no evidence that the attacks on the US vessels were 'aimed specifically at the United States',[96] implying that an additional requirement for an 'armed attack' is that it must be intended to strike a particular target, or at least a particular state.[97]

## 8.4.3.2  Timing of 'armed attack'

Article 51 of the *UN Charter* preserves the right of self-defence 'if an armed attack occurs'. This simple phrase has given rise to vigorous debate about timing: a state can clearly respond in self-defence against an attack that is in progress, but can it also respond to a past attack, or even an attack that is anticipated?

### PAST ATTACKS

The use of force in response to a past attack is retaliatory or punitive, not defensive – if the attack is truly over, there is nothing to defend against. Such measures, known as 'armed reprisals', were lawful in the 19th century but, despite occasional arguments to the contrary, are now accepted as prohibited by art 2(4) and customary law.[98]

### ANTICIPATORY SELF-DEFENCE

Much more controversial is whether a state can use force against an anticipated armed attack.[99] Anticipatory self-defence is the term generally applied when the anticipated attack is 'imminent'; pre-emptive self-defence, discussed in the next section, is action taken where it is not known when or even if an armed attack will occur.

### BROAD VIEW OF SELF-DEFENCE

Those who support a broad view of self-defence, which permits anticipatory self-defence, argue that the wording of art 51 ('inherent right') shows that the *UN Charter* intended to preserve, not restrict, the existing customary law on self-defence in response to an imminent threat of force. They point to the *Caroline* incident for support, where it seemed to be accepted that if the criteria of necessity and proportionality had been met, the United Kingdom's actions would have been justified to prevent further anticipated 'attacks' by the *Caroline*.

They also argue that the nature of conflict and of security threats has changed radically since 1945. The *UN Charter* was drafted even before the first atom bomb had been deployed, whereas we now have weapons of mass destruction that can reach their target within minutes. Interpretation of the Charter can and must adapt over time – as has happened, for example,

---

95    Ibid 191–2 [64].
96    Ibid.
97    See Gray (n 74) 151–3.
98    See, eg, *Friendly Relations Declaration* (n 23) Principle 1. See generally Gray (n 74) 205–6; Shane Darcy, 'Retaliation and Reprisal' in Marc Weller (ed), *The Oxford Handbook of the Use of Force in International Law* (Oxford University Press, 2015) 879.
99    See, eg, Gray (n 74) 170–5; Noam Lubell, 'The Problem of Imminence in an Uncertain World' in Marc Weller (ed), *The Oxford Handbook of the Use of Force in International Law* (Oxford University Press, 2015) 697.

with art 27 and Security Council voting.[100] Finally, there is the policy argument that a state should not have to wait until the enemy strikes before it can take action to defend itself, when it might be too late – 'the UN Charter is not a suicide pact'.[101]

The ICJ has expressly reserved its opinion on anticipatory self-defence;[102] UN reports have stated that self-defence is available in the face of an imminent threat,[103] and over the last 20 years jurists have developed the doctrine further.[104] In 2017, the Australian government stated its support for the doctrine:

> [A] State may act in anticipatory self-defence against an armed attack when the attacker is clearly committed to launching an armed attack, in circumstances where the victim will lose its last opportunity to effectively defend itself unless it acts.[105]

This neatly addresses one of the major criticisms of anticipatory self-defence: the meaning of 'imminent'.

## NARROW VIEW OF SELF-DEFENCE

The contrary view is that the customary right of self-defence was qualified by art 51, which should be interpreted as a narrow exception to the broad prohibition in art 2(4); the wording of art 51 ('occurs') is clear and requires an actual armed attack.[106] This view is shared by the Non-Aligned Movement – a significant proportion of the international community – which has regularly declared that 'Article 51 of the UN Charter is restrictive and should not be re-written or re-interpreted'.[107]

---

100    For a Security Council resolution to pass, art 27 requires nine votes including the 'concurring votes' of all five permanent members; however, consistent practice has been to require only that there be no negative vote by a permanent member: *Legal Consequences for States of the Continued Presence of South Africa in Namibia (South West Africa) notwithstanding Security Council Resolution 276 (1970) (Advisory Opinion)* [1971] ICJ Rep 16, 22 [22].

101    George Shultz, Department of State (US), 'Low Intensity Warfare: The Challenge of Ambiguity' (1986) 2018 (March) *Department of State Bulletin* 15, 17.

102    *Nicaragua* (n 25) 103 [194]; *Armed Activities* (n 13) 222 [143].

103    *A More Secure World: Our Shared Responsibility – Report of the High-Level Panel on Threats, Challenges and Change,* UN Doc A/59/565 (2 December 2004) [188]; *In Larger Freedom: Towards Development, Security and Human Rights for All – Report of the Secretary-General,* UN Doc A/59/2005 (21 March 2005) [124].

104    See, eg, *Chatham House Principles of International Law on the Use of Force by States in Self-Defence* (Royal Institute of International Affairs, October 2005); Daniel Bethlehem, 'Principles Relevant to the Scope of a State's Right of Self-Defense against an Imminent or Actual Armed Attack by Non-State Actors' (2012) 106(4) *American Journal of International Law* 769. See also (mostly critical) commentaries: Michael J Glennon, 'Law, Power, and Principles' (2013) 107(2) *American Journal of International Law* 378 and Dapo Akande and Thomas Liefländer, 'Classifying Necessity, Imminence, and Proportionality in the Law of Self-defence' (2013) 107(3) *American Journal of International Law* 563.

105    George Brandis QC, 'The Right of Self-Defence against Imminent Armed Attack in International Law' (2017) 35 *Australian Year Book of International Law* 55 (public lecture delivered by the Attorney-General of Australia at the TC Beirne School of Law, University of Queensland on 11 April 2017).

106    See, eg, Brownlie, *International Law and the Use of Force by States* (n 1) 275–8 (published in 1963); he was 'unrepentant' of this view in 2000: Brownlie, 'International Law on the Use of Force by States Revisited' (n 52) 26.

107    See, eg, 18th Summit of Heads of State and Government of the Non-Aligned Movement, *Final Document,* NAM 2019/CoB/Doc.1 (26 October 2019) [37.2].

To illustrate the continuing division of opinion, in 2021, 33 states made statements to the Security Council at an informal meeting on the use of force in international law, non-state actors and legitimate self-defence; of these, six explicitly, and two implicitly, supported anticipatory self-defence, while four implicitly opposed it.[108]

## 'ACCUMULATION OF EVENTS' THEORY

A potential solution in some situations is the so-called 'accumulation of events' theory, according to which a state that is subject to a series of attacks is able to treat the series as one continuing armed attack. If accepted, this cures several problems. First, even if each individual attack would be below the level of an armed attack, the series as a whole might have the requisite scale and effects to cross that threshold. Second, it solves the timing problem: a forcible response in self-defence at any point during the series of attacks is a response to a continuing, existing attack, and is neither a response to a past attack, and therefore unlawful retaliation, nor in anticipation of a future attack, which as discussed is still an unsettled issue.

The ICJ has acknowledged the theory without expressing a view on its validity.[109]

## 8.4.3.3   Pre-emptive self-defence

Pre-emptive self-defence describes action taken against a perceived threat which may, or may not, materialise. Examples include Israel's destruction of nuclear facilities and chemical weapons precursors in Iraq and Syria, because of Israel's fear that such weapons would be used against it in the future.[110] Pre-emptive self-defence is rarely claimed as a legal right, the exception being the 'Bush doctrine' promulgated by US president George W Bush in the aftermath of the 9/11 attacks.[111]

The US National Security Strategy published in 2002 (and repeated in 2006) openly asserted the right to attack rogue states and terrorists threatening the United States wherever they were located, and before any actual attack.[112] Australia was one of the very few countries that supported this doctrine, but had changed its view by 2004; most states rejected it outright.[113]

---

108   *Letter Dated 8 March 2021 from the Permanent Representative of Mexico to the United Nations Addressed to the Secretary-General and the President of the Security Council*, UN Doc S/2021/247 (16 March 2021). The other states expressed no opinion.

109   *Nicaragua* (n 25) 119–20 [231]; *Oil Platforms* (n 75) 191–2 [64]; *Armed Activities* (n 13) 222–3 [146].

110   Israel has struck nuclear facilities in Iraq (1981) and Syria (2007), and chemical facilities in Syria (several times since 2011): see, eg, 'Israeli Jets Said to Strike Iranian-Run Missile Production Facility in Syria', *The Times of Israel* (online at 22 July 2018) <www.timesofisrael.com/israel-jets-said-to-strike-chemical-weapons-site-in-syria>; Ashley Deeks, 'Taming the Doctrine of Pre-Emption' in Marc Weller (ed), *The Oxford Handbook of the Use of Force in International Law* (Oxford University Press, 2015) 661.

111   See Christopher Greenwood, 'International Law and the Pre-emptive Use of Force: Afghanistan, Al-Qaida, and Iraq' (2003) 4 *San Diego International Law Journal* 7.

112   *National Security Strategy of the United States of America* (September 2002) <https://nssarchive.us/wp-content/uploads/2020/04/2002.pdf>.

113   See generally Michael Reisman and Andrea Armstrong, 'The Past and Future of the Claim of Preemptive Self-Defense' (2006) 100(3) *American Journal of International Law* 525. The Non-Aligned Movement maintains its opposition, for example declaring '[Members] Oppose and condemn . . . the adoption of the doctrine of pre-emptive attack, . . . which is inconsistent with international law': 18th Summit of Heads of State and Government of the Non-Aligned Movement (n 107) [38.6].

The United States toned down its language in later National Security Strategies but has not foresworn the right to take pre-emptive action against terrorist threats.[114]

The main objections to pre-emptive self-defence are that it is not accommodated by even the most expansive interpretation of art 51; there is next to no state practice or *opinio juris* to support a customary rule; any assessment of the threat is wholly subjective; it is therefore too open to abuse; and it is impossible to apply the essential criteria of necessity and proportionality because there is no attack against which they can be assessed.[115]

## 8.4.4    Protection of nationals abroad

Some states claim the right to use force to protect or rescue their nationals in other countries.[116] This was relatively common in the 19th century and is occasionally claimed today, for example by Russia in its actions in Georgia[117] and Ukraine.[118] Two broad legal justifications have been offered for such actions. The first is that it is a standalone customary right which was not affected by art 2(4) of the *UN Charter* because it is not a use of force against the territorial integrity or political independence of the host state – the familiar argument discussed in Section 8.3.2. The other, more common, argument is that it is a form of self-defence: that 'armed attack' covers an attack on a state's nationals, wherever they may be.[119] Neither argument is generally accepted, and the prevailing view is that such actions are not permitted in international law.[120]

## 8.4.5    Self-defence against terrorism

It is well settled that a state has customary law duties not to sponsor terrorism, or allow its territory to be used for terrorism.[121] It is also accepted that a state can respond in self-defence to a terrorist attack if the host state is deemed to have committed the attack – either because the attack is attributable to the host state under the rules of state responsibility, or because the state has 'sent' the terrorists within the meaning of art 3(g) of the *Definition of Aggression*.[122]

A difficulty arises, however, where there is no such link between the terrorists and the host state: does a victim state have a right of self-defence where the force will be used in, even if not

---

114    See, eg, *National Security Strategy of the United States of America* (December 2017) 11 <http://nssarchive.us/wp-content/uploads/2020/04/2017.pdf>.

115    Sean Murphy, 'The Doctrine of Preemptive Self-Defense' (2005) 50 *Villanova Law Review* 699, 715.

116    See further Gray (n 74) 165–9; Mathias Forteau, 'Rescuing Nationals Abroad' in Marc Weller (ed), *The Oxford Handbook of the Use of Force in International Law* (Oxford University Press, 2015) 947.

117    Independent International Fact-Finding Mission on the Conflict in Georgia ('IIFFMCG'), *Report* (September 2009) vol 1, 24–5 [23] <www.mpil.de/en/pub/publications/archive/independent_international_fact.cfm>.

118    'Ukraine Crisis: Does Russia Have a Case?', *BBC News* (online at 5 March 2014) <www.bbc.com/news/world-europe-26415508>.

119    Forteau (n 116) 955.

120    Ibid 959–61; IIFFMCG (n 117) vol 1, 24–5 [23].

121    *Friendly Relations Declaration* (n 23) Principle 1; *Armed Activities* (n 13) 226 [161]; SC Res 1373, UN Doc S/RES/1373 (28 September 2011) [2].

122    *Definition of Aggression* (n 24). See exchange of views between Christian J Tams, 'The Use of Force against Terrorists' (2009) 20(2) *European Journal of International Law* 359, and Kimberley Trapp, 'The Use of Force against Terrorists: A Reply to Christian J Tams' (2009) 20(4) *European Journal of International Law* 1049.

against, the host state?[123] A key question is whether 'armed attack' in art 51 includes attacks by non-state actors. The ICJ answered this in the negative in its advisory opinion *Legal Consequences of the Construction of a Wall in the Occupied Palestinian Territory*,[124] but this has been roundly criticised.[125] In *Armed Activities*, the Court reserved its opinion on the issue.[126]

Article 51 does not expressly require the attack to be by a state, and Security Council resolutions 1368 and 1373, concerning the 9/11 attacks in 2001, both referred in their pre-ambles to 'the inherent right of individual or collective self-defence'. Judges Kooijmans and Simma in their separate opinions in *Armed Activities* viewed these resolutions as a turning point, and argued that self-defence against non-state actors might be permitted, especially where there was no real governmental authority in the 'host' state, so that attribution of the conduct to the state was not possible.[127]

### 8.4.5.1   The 'unable or unwilling' doctrine

The Syrian civil war, starting in 2011, has focused attention on the 'unable or unwilling' doctrine. The terrorist organisation ISIL,[128] an offshoot of Al Qaeda, took advantage of the civil war to seize large parts of Syria and Iraq, from which it launched attacks on Iraq and elsewhere. The United States and other states, including Australia, bombarded ISIL bases in Syria, claiming that they were acting in either individual or collective self-defence in a situation where the host state – Syria – had lost control of large parts of its territory and was therefore unable or unwilling to prevent the ISIL attacks itself.[129]

Some dozen states have endorsed the doctrine on the basis that customary international law has evolved to permit self-defence against terrorists where the 'host' state is unable or unwilling to prevent those attacks.[130] Many others staunchly oppose it, insisting on a strict interpretation of art 51, and pointing to the lack of sufficient state practice and *opinio juris* to support a new rule of customary law.[131]

---

123    See further Gray (n 74) ch 5.
124    *Legal Consequences of the Construction of a Wall in the Occupied Palestinian Territory (Advisory Opinion)* [2004] ICJ Rep 136, 194 [139].
125    Among countless others, by Judge Higgins in her separate opinion in *Legal Consequences of the Construction of a Wall in the Occupied Palestinian Territory* ibid 215–6 [33] and Judge Kooijmans in his separate opinion: at 229–30 [35].
126    *Armed Activities* (n 13) 223 [147].
127    Ibid 314–15 [29]–[32] (Judge Kooijmans); 337 [11] (Judge Simma).
128    Islamic State of Iraq and the Levant (also known as Islamic State of Iraq and Syria, or Da'esh).
129    See, eg, *Letter dated 23 September 2014 from the Permanent Representative of the United States of America to the United Nations addressed to the Secretary-General*, UN Doc S/2014/695 (23 September 2014) and other examples in Sievers and Daws (n 82).
130    Elena Chachko and Ashley Deeks, 'Which States Support the "Unwilling and Unable" Test?', *Lawfare* (Blog Post, 10 October 2016) <www.lawfareblog.com/which-states-support-unwilling-and-unable-test>.
131    At an informal Security Council meeting held in February 2021 on 'the use of force in international law, non-State actors and legitimate self-defence', the right of self-defence against non-state actors was supported by 17 states and rejected by four; the 'unable or unwilling' doctrine was supported by eight states and rejected by one: *Letter Dated 8 March 2021 from the Permanent Representative of Mexico* (n 108). See, eg, Olivier Corten, 'The "Unwilling or Unable" Test: Has It Been, and Could It Be, Accepted?' (2016) 29(3) *Leiden Journal of International Law* 777.

# 8.5   Collective security: action authorised by the Security Council

The second exception to the prohibition of force is action authorised by the UN Security Council under Chapter VII of the *UN Charter*.[132]

## 8.5.1   Collective security

The Security Council has primary responsibility for maintaining international peace and security (under art 24 of the *UN Charter*), and Chapter VII of the Charter sets out the Council's powers and duties if it determines, under art 39, the existence of a 'threat to the peace, breach of the peace, or act of aggression'.[133]

The Security Council has rarely labelled a situation an act of aggression[134] or a breach of the peace.[135] Much more common is declaring a threat to the peace, in a wide range of situations including illegal testing of nuclear weapons, state involvement in terrorism, actual or threatened armed conflict, and the Ebola outbreak in West Africa.[136] The Security Council is a political body and its decisions are not reviewable, although the ICJ could, in principle, assess whether a particular decision was beyond the Security Council's (very broad) powers.[137]

## 8.5.2   Sanctions

If the Security Council makes a determination under art 39, it may impose sanctions on the relevant state or states, or individuals and entities within those states, under art 41. Sanctions are invariably mandatory, meaning that member states must comply with them under art 25 of the *UN Charter* – a sanctions regime where only some states refused to supply the target state with arms, for example, would not be effective.[138] The regimes typically require member states

---

132   See generally Marc Weller (ed), *The Oxford Handbook of the Use of Force in International Law* (Oxford University Press, 2015) pt 2 ('Collective Security and the Non-Use of Force').

133   *UN Charter* art 39 reads: 'The Security Council shall determine the existence of any threat to the peace, breach of the peace, or act of aggression and shall make recommendations, or decide what measures shall be taken in accordance with Articles 41 and 42, to maintain or restore international peace and security.'

134   Examples include Israel in 1985 (Israeli reprisal against the headquarters of the Palestine Liberation Organisation in Tunis), South Africa from 1976 (aggression towards neighbouring states especially Angola), and Rhodesia in 1979 (aggression against Zambia): 'Actions with Respect to Threats to the Peace, Breaches of the Peace and Acts of Aggression' (n 82).

135   Examples include North Korean aggression against South Korea in 1950, the Argentine seizure of Falkland Islands/Malvinas in 1982, the Iran–Iraq War in 1987, and the Iraqi invasion of Kuwait in 1990: ibid.

136   Ibid. Regarding the Ebola outbreak, see SC Res 2177, UN Doc S/RES/2177 (18 September 2014).

137   *Interpretation and Application of the 1971 Montreal Convention arising from the Aerial Incident at Lockerbie (Libyan Arab Jamahiriya v United Kingdom) (Preliminary Objections)* [1998] ICJ Rep 9, 23–4 [37]–[38]. An example might be if the Security Council were to impose sanctions on a state where there was no threat to the peace or any wrongdoing by that state. See generally Dan Sarooshi, *The United Nations and the Development of Collective Security: The Delegation by the UN Security Council of its Chapter VII Powers* (Oxford University Press, 1999).

138   This lesson was learned from the League of Nations where sanctions were only recommendations. See generally 'Sanctions', *United Nations Security Council* (Web Page) <www.un.org/securitycouncil/sanctions/information>.

to cease arms supplies or prohibit commercial dealings with the target states, or in the case of individuals, to freeze their assets or limit their ability to travel by refusing entry visas. Many states add to these mandatory UN sanctions; Australia, for example, has a system of 'autonomous' sanctions that it imposes as a matter of Australian foreign policy.[139]

## 8.5.3 Peacekeeping

Sometimes the Security Council will authorise a peacekeeping force. Peacekeeping is not mentioned in the *UN Charter*, but evolved during the Cold War (1946–89) when the Security Council was unable to agree on military intervention because of the antipathy between, in particular, the United States and the USSR.[140] It did agree occasionally to send a peacekeeping force, typically to monitor a ceasefire, or patrol a contested border.[141]

Early peacekeeping forces were generally observer missions, lightly armed, and not permitted to use force except in self-defence. Over the years this has changed, and some peacekeeping forces have been very large, with a broad mandate.[142] They are still guided by three basic principles: consent of the parties; impartiality; and non-use of force except in self-defence and defence of the mandate, although on occasion that mandate has been quite robust, for example authorising force to secure humanitarian relief or protect civilians, or exceptionally, to target a particular rebel group.[143] On rare occasions the General Assembly has authorised a peacekeeping force.[144]

---

139    UN sanctions may be considered inadequate or may be blocked by a permanent member of the Security Council, as with sanctions against Russia for its actions in Ukraine: see 'Russia Sanctions Regime', *Department of Foreign Affairs and Trade: Sanctions Regimes* (Web Page) <www.dfat.gov.au/international-relations/security/sanctions/sanctions-regimes/Pages/russia-sanctions-regime>. Australia has also amended its *Autonomous Sanctions Act 2011* (Cth) to allow for targeted sanctions to address human rights abuses.

140    See, eg, Gray (n 74) ch 6; Mark Weisburd, 'The Use of Force in United Nations Peacekeeping Operations' in Marc Weller (ed), *The Oxford Handbook of the Use of Force in International Law* (Oxford University Press, 2015) 347. Because peacekeeping was neither a peaceful measure under ch VI of the *UN Charter*, nor a use of force under ch VII, Dag Hammarskjöld (UN Secretary-General, 1953–61) said it belonged to 'Chapter Six-and-a-Half'.

141    One such force is the United Nations Truce Supervision Organization ('UNTSO'), which has operated in the Middle East since 1948: 'UNTSO, Middle East', *United Nations* (Web Page) <www.un.org/en/ccoi/untso-middle-east>. Another is the United Nations Military Observer Group in India and Pakistan ('UNMOGIP'), which has operated since 1949: 'UNMOGIP Fact Sheet', *United Nations Peacekeeping* (Web Page) <https://peacekeeping.un.org/en/mission/unmogip>.

142    For example in 2021 the United Nations Mission in South Sudan had over 19,000 uniformed personnel. See generally 'Our History', *United Nations Peacekeeping* (Web Page) <https://peacekeeping.un.org/en/our-history>. For current statistics see 'Data', *United Nations Peacekeeping* (Web Page) <https://peacekeeping.un.org/en/data>.

143    'What is Peacekeeping', *United Nations Peacekeeping* (Web Page) <https://peacekeeping.un.org/en/what-is-peacekeeping>. For mandates of all current missions see 'Field Missions Dashboard', *United Nations Security Council* (Web Page) <www.un.org/securitycouncil/content/field-missions-dashboard>. The United Nations Organization Stabilization Mission in the DRC ('MONUSCO'), a peacekeeping force, included an 'Intervention Brigade' authorised to use force to 'neutralize' armed groups: see SC Res 2098, UN doc S/RES/2098 (28 March 2003).

144    The authority of the General Assembly to do this was confirmed in *Certain Expenses of the United Nations (Advisory Opinion)* [1962] ICJ Rep 151.

A perennial problem with peacekeeping is finding the necessary personnel and equipment. The peacekeeping budget of USD6–7 billion a year[145] is funded by a levy on all UN member states apportioned according to gross national income, so the United States and other major economies are the main financial contributors.[146] But many states (principally the United States) are chronically in arrears,[147] while a further difficulty is obtaining the equipment and training required to mount an operation.[148] The top 10 troop contributors are mostly poorer nations such as Bangladesh, Nepal, Pakistan and Ethiopia, along with India, Rwanda and China.[149]

## 8.5.4   Authorisation of force

If the Security Council considers that sanctions have not been, or would not be, effective, it can authorise the use of force under art 42 of the *UN Charter*:

> Should the Security Council consider that measures provided for in Article 41 would be inadequate or have proved to be inadequate, it may take such action by air, sea, or land forces as may be necessary to maintain or restore international peace and security. Such action may include demonstrations, blockade, and other operations by air, sea, or land forces of Members of the United Nations.

The original intention was that pursuant to arts 43–47 of the Charter, there would be a UN 'standby force', comprising deployment-ready, trained and equipped troops placed by states at the disposal of the Security Council. However, the type, quantity and location of arms and personnel had first to be agreed by the permanent members of the Council; for different reasons they could not reach agreement, so the 'standby force' never came into existence.[150]

Thus if the Security Council decides that a situation requires military intervention to maintain or restore international peace and security, it must delegate that task to member states.[151] It did this only three times during the Cold War,[152] in 1990 in response to the Iraqi

---

145    'By way of comparison, this is less than half of one per cent of world military expenditures (estimated at $1,981 billion in 2020)': 'How We Are Funded', *United Nations Peacekeeping* (Web Page) <https://peacekeeping.un.org/en/how-we-are-funded>.

146    Ibid.

147    See, eg, Michelle Nichols, 'UN Members Owe $2 Billion in Debt to Peacekeeping, US Owes a Third', *Reuters* (online, 18 January 2019) <www.reuters.com/article/us-un-peacekeepers-usa-idUSKCN1PB2OD>.

148    Gray (n 74) 301–3.

149    'Troop and Police Contributors', *United Nations Peacekeeping* (Web Page) <https://peacekeeping.un .org/en/troop-and-police-contributors>. Contributing countries are paid USD1,438 per soldier per month. See also 'Forming a New Operation', *United Nations Peacekeeping* (Web Page) <https://peacekeeping.un.org/en/forming-new-operation>.

150    Gray (n 74) 262; Adam Roberts, 'Proposals for UN Standing Forces: A Critical History' in Vaughan Lowe et al (eds), *The United Nations Security Council and War: The Evolution of Thought and Practice since 1945* (Oxford University Press, 2008) 99.

151    See, eg, Sarooshi (n 137) ch 5.

152    These were Korea in 1950, the Republic of the Congo in 1961 (United Nations Operation in the Congo ('UNOC') peacekeeping mission), and Rhodesia in 1966 (to enforce sanctions): Gray (n 74) 265–6, 271–2; Scott Sheeran, 'The Use of Force in United Nations Peacekeeping Operations' in Marc Weller (ed), *The Oxford Handbook of the Use of Force in International Law* (Oxford University Press, 2015) 347, 351.

invasion of Kuwait,[153] and over 20 times thereafter.[154] The last significant operation was in Libya in 2011, when member states were authorised to use force to protect civilians in the civil war.[155] This major NATO-led operation was subsequently criticised for going beyond its authorisation by attacking Libyan government troops and removing the Libyan leader, Colonel Gaddafi.[156] Russia and China were among the critics, and have frequently cited the overreach in Libya as a reason for blocking any action to protect civilians during the Syrian civil war, when arguably the international community should have intervened.[157]

# 8.6  Humanitarian intervention and the responsibility to protect

'Humanitarian intervention' has had different meanings over the years including, in the 19th century, the protection of nationals abroad. Its more common contemporary meaning is the use of force by one state in the territory of another state, without consent or Security Council authorisation, for humanitarian purposes such as halting serious human rights abuses. It appears, therefore, to violate the prohibition on the use of force. Nevertheless, supporters of humanitarian intervention argue that it is lawful. One argument is that it is permitted by the wording of art 2(4) of the *UN Charter* itself, because it does not violate the target state's territorial integrity or political independence, or the purposes of the United Nations – indeed it serves the purposes of the United Nations in protecting human rights.[158] This is the same argument as is made for a narrow view of the scope of art 2(4) and for a right to protect nationals abroad and, as explained in Sections 8.3.2 and 8.4.4, is not widely accepted.

The other argument for the lawfulness of humanitarian intervention is that a customary right of humanitarian intervention has developed since 1945. Simon Chesterman has examined this argument and concludes that only three interventions could be candidates for this purpose: India in East Pakistan (1971), Tanzania in Uganda (1978–79), and Vietnam in Kampuchea (1978–79).[159] In each of these cases, one state invaded the other with the result that a violent and oppressive regime was overthrown: the West Pakistan government that was forcibly suppressing the independence movement in East Pakistan; the brutal president of Uganda, Idi Amin; and the genocidal Pol Pot regime in Cambodia. But each of those regimes had also used force against the intervening state, so it was self-defence, and not humanitarian purposes, that was given as the justification for intervention.[160] So from these examples there is very little state practice, and no *opinio juris*, to support a customary rule.[161]

153    SC Res 678, UN Doc S/RES/678 (29 November 1990).
154    Gray (n 74) ch 7.
155    SC Res 1973, UN Doc S/RES/1973 (17 March 2011).
156    Gray (n 74) 377–80.
157    Global Centre for the Responsibility to Protect, 'Syria', *Populations at Risk* (Web Page, 31 May 2021) <www.globalr2p.org/countries/syria>.
158    JL Holzgrefe and Robert Keohane, *Humanitarian Intervention: Ethical, Legal and Political Dilemmas* (Cambridge University Press, 2003) 39.
159    Simon Chesterman, *Just War or Just Peace: Humanitarian Intervention and International Law* (Oxford University Press, 2002) ch 2.
160    Ibid.
161    Ibid 84–7.

However, since the early 1990s the United Kingdom has asserted that there is not only a right, but also a duty, of humanitarian intervention in situations of extreme humanitarian distress demanding immediate relief, where the host state is unable or unwilling to act, and there is no practical alternative.[162] The initial context was the enforcement of no-fly zones in Iraq, to protect minorities from attack by Iraqi government forces. Later it was asserted to justify the NATO air campaign – without Security Council approval[163] – to halt 'ethnic cleansing' by Serbs in Kosovo. The UK Prime Minister called the latter 'a just war';[164] Belgium also justified it as humanitarian intervention;[165] but other states either objected, or regarded the campaign as 'illegal but legitimate'.[166]

The United Kingdom maintains its views,[167] and has always suggested strict conditions for the exercise of humanitarian intervention,[168] but smaller states (as well as Russia and China) object on the basis that it is too subjective and open to abuse: the Non-Aligned Movement has specifically rejected the 'so-called "right" of humanitarian intervention'.[169]

The debate was also fuelled by the genocides in Rwanda in 1994, and at Srebrenica in 1995, both of which the international community failed to prevent. In 1999 the UN Secretary-General challenged the international community to find a solution to the apparently impossible divide between, on the one hand, the international community saying 'never again' to such atrocities, and on the other, the understandable fear of the smaller states that they would be subject to unjustified intervention.[170]

The call was answered by Canada, which established the International Commission on Intervention and State Sovereignty, a group of independent experts. In its 2001 report, the Commission summarised the problem:

> External military intervention for human protection purposes has been controversial both when it has happened – as in Somalia, Bosnia and Kosovo – and when it has failed to happen, as in Rwanda. For some the new activism has been a long overdue international- ization of the human conscience; for others it has been an alarming breach of an international state order dependent on the sovereignty of states and the inviolability of their territory. For some, again, the only real issue is ensuring that coercive interventions

---

162   See, eg, Foreign and Commonwealth Office (UK), 'The Expanding Role of the United Nations and its Implications for UK Policy' (2 December 1992) in (1993) 63 *British Yearbook of International Law* 825.

163   This was blocked by Russia, an ally of Serbia: Ove Bring, 'Should NATO Take the Lead in Formulating a Doctrine on Humanitarian Intervention?' (1999) 47(3) *NATO Review* 24.

164   Tony Blair, 'Doctrine of the International Community' (Speech, Chicago Economic Club, 24 April 1999).

165   'Oral Submissions by Belgium: Verbatim Record 1999/15', *Legality of Use of Force (Serbia and Montenegro v Belgium)* (International Court of Justice, General List No 105, 10 May 1999) 15–19 (English translation).

166   Independent International Commission on Kosovo, *The Kosovo Report: Conflict, International Response, Lessons Learned* (Oxford University Press, 2000) 4.

167   Minister of State, Foreign and Commonwealth Office (UK), *Letter of 14 January 2014 to Foreign Affairs Committee*, 8th Report, House of Commons 695 in (2016) 85 *British Yearbook of International Law* 628–31.

168   See, eg, Robin Cook, 'Guiding Humanitarian Intervention' (Speech, American Bar Association, 19 July 2000) in (2001) 71 *British Yearbook of International Law* 646; 'UK Paper on International Action in Response to Humanitarian Crises' in (2002) 72 *British Yearbook of International Law* 557, 694–6.

169   See, eg, Thirteenth Conference of Heads of State or Government of the Non-Aligned Countries, Final Document, UN Doc A/57/759 (18 March 2013) 10 [16].

170   Kofi Annan, Speech to UN General Assembly, UN Doc GA/9596 (20 September 1999) <www.un.org/press/en/1999/19990920.sgsm7136.html>.

are effective; for others, questions about legality, process and the possible misuse of precedent loom much larger.[171]

The Commission's solution was to shift the focus away from 'intervention' and instead emphasise a state's own responsibility to protect its population:

> 'The Responsibility to Protect' [is] the idea that sovereign states have a responsibility to protect their own citizens from avoidable catastrophe – from mass murder and rape, from starvation – but that when they are unwilling or unable to do so, that responsibility must be borne by the broader community of states.[172]

The Commission recommended that in the face of such a catastrophe, the international community should be prepared to intervene militarily, guided by detailed principles redolent of the just war doctrine,[173] including a 'just cause' and 'right authority'.[174] The ideal authority would be the Security Council, but the Commission contemplated alternatives, such as the General Assembly, if the Council failed to act.[175] This new concept of the responsibility to protect was endorsed, in much diluted form, by the General Assembly in 2005, and since then has generated reports, books, organisations and journals on how it should be given effect.[176] In its adopted form, however, the authority of the Security Council is necessary for any military intervention,[177] and with the current attitudes of Russia and China, the Security Council will not grant that authority.[178] In that respect, therefore, it does not solve the legal problems posed by humanitarian intervention.

# 8.7    Intervention by invitation

Space permits only a brief mention of this topic: when is it lawful for one state to use force in another where it is invited to do so?[179] As this depends on the principle of non-intervention, that principle is summarised first.

---

171    International Commission on Intervention and State Sovereignty, *The Responsibility to Protect* (Report, December 2001) vii.

172    Ibid viii.

173    The just war doctrine, or theory, has existed in different forms for thousands of years. Its essence is that there are moral, or religious, constraints on the right to wage war, such that war is only justified when certain conditions are satisfied: see, eg, Joachim von Elbe, 'The Evolution of the Concept of the Just War in International Law' (1939) 33(3) *American Journal of International Law* 665.

174    International Commission on Intervention and State Sovereignty, *The Responsibility to Protect* (Report, December 2001) xii–xiii (Principles for Military Intervention, principles 1, 3), chs 4, 6, 7.

175    Ibid 53–5.

176    See, eg, Global Centre for the Responsibility to Protect <www.globalr2p.org>; United Nations Office on Genocide Prevention and the Responsibility to Protect <www.un.org/en/genocideprevention/about-responsibility-to-protect.shtml>.

177    *2005 World Summit Outcome*, GA Res 60/1, UN Doc A/RES/60/1 (24 October 2005) 30 [139].

178    As has been seen during the Syrian civil war: see, eg, Rebecca Barber, 'Syria: The Disgraceful Stain Left by the UN Security Council Veto' (24 September 2019) *The Interpreter* <www.lowyinstitute.org/the-interpreter/syria-disgraceful-stain-left-un-security-council-veto>.

179    For more detail see, eg, Louise Doswald-Beck, 'The Legal Validity of Military Intervention by Invitation of the Government' (1985) 56 *British Yearbook of International Law* 18; Gray (n 74) ch 3; Georg Nolte, 'Intervention by Invitation' in Rüdiger Wolfrum (ed), *The Max Planck Encyclopedia of Public International Law* (Oxford University Press, online, January 2010); Gregory Fox, 'Intervention by Invitation' in Marc Weller (ed), *The Oxford Handbook of the Use of Force in International Law* (Oxford University Press, 2015) 816.

## 8.7.1   The principle of non-intervention

The principle of non-intervention is a rule of customary international law that involves the right of every sovereign state 'to choose its political, economic, social and cultural systems, without interference in any form by another State'.[180] To be unlawful, the intervention must have an element of coercion: 'The element of coercion ... defines, and indeed forms the very essence of, prohibited intervention'.[181] Coercion is 'particularly obvious'[182] when it includes the use of force, but is otherwise difficult to define.

The status of, for example, foreign interference in elections,[183] or espionage,[184] is debated – while some say they are clear examples of prohibited intervention, others say that while they are certainly unwelcome, there is no coercion involved.[185] Intervention can therefore be seen as one point along a continuum ranging from unwelcome, but not unlawful, action such as criticism of a state's policies, through to the use of force.

## 8.7.2   The right to intervene by invitation

If the government of one state freely invites another to use force in the first state's territory, there is clearly no element of coercion, and the intervention is lawful. This occurred in 1997, when the DRC requested assistance from Uganda and Rwanda in quelling the rebel activity in the eastern part of the country,[186] and when the Solomon Islands invited Australia to help suppress inter-ethnic violence in 2003.[187] However, some jurists assert that where an internal conflict has reached the threshold of a civil war, it is not lawful to assist the government.[188] A civil war is said to exist when the outcome of the conflict is uncertain: it is unclear whether the government or the rebels will prevail. That being the case, it is for the people of that state to determine the outcome themselves, free from outside interference.[189] Others deny that there is sufficient state practice to support such an exception, so that foreign intervention in support of a government is permitted even in a civil war.[190]

---

180   *Declaration on the Inadmissibility of Intervention in the Domestic Affairs of States and the Protection of Their Independence and Sovereignty*, GA Res 2131 (XX), UN Doc A/RES/2131(XX) (21 December 1965); *Friendly Relations Declaration* (n 23). See also *Nicaragua* (n 25) 106–7 [202].

181   *Nicaragua* (n 25) 107–8 [205].

182   Ibid.

183   See, eg, Michael Schmitt, 'Foreign Cyber Interference in Elections: An International Law Primer', *EJIL: TALK!* (Blog Post, 16 October 2020) <www.ejiltalk.org/foreign-cyber-interference-in-elections-an-international-law-primer-part-i>.

184   See, eg, literature cited in François Dubuisson and Agatha Verdebout, 'Espionage in International Law' in *Oxford Bibliographies* (Oxford University Press, online, February 2021).

185   Similarly the trade embargo that the United States imposed on Nicaragua was found, on the facts, not to breach the principle: *Nicaragua* (n 25) 126 [245].

186   *Armed Activities* (n 13) 194 [36].

187   'About RAMSI', *Regional Assistance Mission in the Solomon Islands* (Web Page) <www.ramsi.org>.

188   Doswald-Beck (n 179) 243.

189   Ibid. This is an aspect of self-determination (see Chapter 5).

190   See, eg, Michael Wood, 'The Principle of Non-Intervention in Contemporary International Law', Chatham House International Law Discussion Group Meeting (28 February 2007) <https://defence.pk/pdf/threads/can-nonintervention-ist-east-asian-states-reign-in-an-intervention-ist-india.317986/>. Forcible intervention would not, however, be permitted against a 'people' entitled to self-determination: *Friendly Relations Declaration* (n 23) Principles 1, 3.

Two points are agreed: first, it is never lawful for a state to provide assistance to the insurgents in another state;[191] and second, if such assistance is nevertheless provided, it then becomes lawful for another state to assist the government, regardless of whether a civil war exists.[192]

Many other issues are unclear, however. Apart from the difficulty of ascertaining the true facts of a situation – who is involved, in what capacity, at whose invitation – there can be a problem in determining the validity of the invitation. Where more than one warring faction claims to represent the state, who is entitled to issue the invitation? Views differ as to whether it is the effective government (the faction actually in control, if any) or the legitimate government (the lawfully appointed government), for example where a head of state disputes an election result or claims to have been removed from office unconstitutionally.[193] Recognition will often play a significant role here.[194]

A final issue is whether the invitation was made freely, or indeed at all. When the USSR invaded Hungary in 1956, Czechoslovakia in 1968 and Afghanistan in 1979, the international community rejected its claims of invitation as either fabricated or made under duress.[195]

## DISCUSSION QUESTIONS

(1)  'It's time for art 2(4) of the *UN Charter* to be amended – or at least clarified by another General Assembly resolution – to resolve the continuing debates on its meaning, and to ensure it covers new threats to international security such as cyberwarfare and drones.' Do you agree?

(2)  Do you agree with the International Court of Justice's definition of 'armed attack' as requiring a 'most grave' use of force?

(3)  'The international law rules concerning a state's use of force through non-state actors are unclear and unsatisfactory.' Do you agree?

(4)  Could, and should, humanitarian intervention be accommodated within the existing jus ad bellum?

(5)  Is Russian military action in Syria, with the Syrian government's consent, lawful?

---

191   *Nicaragua* (n 25) 126 [246]; Doswald-Beck (n 179) 190.
192   Gray (n 74) 95–100; Fox (n 179) 830–1.
193   Doswald-Beck (n 179) 194–200, 222–39; Fox (n 179) 829–30; Gray (n 74) 100–7.
194   See Chapter 5 on recognition.
195   Gray (n 74) 92–3, 96–7.

# INTERNATIONAL DISPUTE SETTLEMENT

Chester Brown

# 9.1    Introduction

All states have an obligation to settle disputes peacefully in accordance with arts 2(3) and 33 of the *Charter of the United Nations* ('*UN Charter*'), and the purpose of this chapter is to provide an introduction to the methods for the settlement of international disputes. It begins with an overview of international dispute settlement, including a discussion of the concept of a 'dispute', and the distinction between political and legal disputes. It then traces the evolution of the obligation to settle disputes peacefully through its broad phases: the 1899 and 1907 Hague Conventions for the peaceful settlement of international disputes, and the creation of the Permanent Court of Arbitration; the *Covenant of the League of Nations* of 1919, and the creation of the Permanent Court of International Justice ('PCIJ'); and the *Kellogg–Briand Pact* of 1928, and the *UN Charter* of 1945.

The chapter then considers the various methods of international dispute settlement, beginning with the diplomatic methods (negotiation, fact-finding and inquiry, the use of 'good offices', mediation, and conciliation) before turning to the adjudicatory forms of dispute settlement. International arbitration has a long history as a means of settling inter-state disputes, and it has experienced a revival of interest in recent years. The International Court of Justice ('ICJ') has a prominent place in international dispute settlement, given its role as the principal judicial organ of the United Nations; issues concerning its composition, jurisdiction and procedures therefore deserve special attention. The final section of the chapter examines the role of the United Nations and regional organisations in the peaceful settlement of international disputes.

# 9.2    International dispute settlement: an overview

It is usual for legal systems to provide for mechanisms and procedures for the settlement of disputes. In domestic legal systems, there are courts with compulsory jurisdiction for the adjudication of civil disputes, and there are also law enforcement agencies such as the police which have powers to prosecute offenders for noncompliance with the law. The same is, however, not true of the international legal system. There is no international court with compulsory jurisdiction over all states; rather, states have to opt in and accept the jurisdiction of the ICJ, and even where states accept the ICJ's jurisdiction, they can do so subject to reservations. As for law enforcement in the international legal order, the UN Security Council has the authority under Chapter VII of the *UN Charter* to adopt enforcement measures to secure compliance by states with its resolutions, although the Security Council can only act in circumstances where none of its five permanent members exercise the right of veto against the proposed resolution.

Against this backdrop of the differences between domestic legal systems and the international legal order, the purposes of the United Nations, as expressed in art 1(1) of the *UN Charter*, include bringing about 'by peaceful means, and in conformity with the principles of justice and international law, adjustment or settlement of international disputes or situations which might lead to a breach of the peace'. In addition, art 2(3) of the *UN Charter* places an obligation on states to settle their disputes peacefully: 'All Members shall settle their international disputes by peaceful means in such a manner that international peace and security, and justice, are not endangered.' Article 33 of the *UN Charter* provides further detail:

1.  The parties to any dispute, the continuance of which is likely to endanger the maintenance of international peace and security, shall, first of all, seek a solution by negotiation, enquiry, mediation, conciliation, arbitration, judicial settlement, resort to regional agencies or arrangements, or other peaceful means of their own choice.
2.  The Security Council shall, when it deems necessary, call upon the parties to settle their dispute by such means.

Article 33 is located within Chapter VI of the *UN Charter*, which is entitled 'Pacific Settlement of Disputes'. The methods for the peaceful settlement of international disputes identified in art 33(1) include diplomatic means (negotiation, enquiry, mediation and conciliation) and adjudicatory means (arbitration and judicial settlement), as well as the possibility of involving regional organisations.

## 9.2.1   Existence of a 'dispute'

The ICJ is concerned with settling 'disputes', as explained in art 38(1) of the *Statute of the International Court of Justice* ('*ICJ Statute*'), which forms an integral part of the *UN Charter*.[1] Article 38(1) not only sets out the sources of international law, but also states the ICJ's function, which is 'to decide in accordance with international law such disputes as are submitted to it'. This provision is substantially identical to art 38 of the *Statute of the Permanent Court of International Justice* ('*PCIJ Statute*'). The PCIJ was the predecessor of the ICJ, and it and the ICJ have both treated the existence of a 'dispute' as necessary for them to exercise their jurisdiction; in the absence of a 'dispute', the ICJ has declined to decide cases.[2]

The PCIJ and the ICJ have given guidance as to how a 'dispute' is to be identified, and this has proved to be relevant before other international adjudicatory bodies. In *Mavrommatis Palestine Concessions*, the PCIJ held: 'A dispute is a disagreement on a point of law or fact; a conflict of legal views or of interests between two persons.'[3] The ICJ gave further content to the concept of a 'dispute' in its advisory opinion in *Interpretation of Peace Treaties with Bulgaria, Hungary and Romania*: 'whether there exists an international dispute is a matter for objective determination. The mere denial of the existence of a dispute does not prove its non-existence.'[4] In the *South West Africa* case, the ICJ went further, stating that

> it is not sufficient for one party to a contentious case to assert that a dispute exists with the other party. A mere assertion is not sufficient to prove the existence of a dispute any more than a mere denial of the existence of the dispute proves its non-existence. Nor is it adequate to show that the interests of the two parties to such a case are in conflict. It must be shown that the claim of one party is positively opposed by the other.[5]

1   *Charter of the United Nations* ('*UN Charter*') art 92.
2   See, eg, *Nuclear Tests (Australia v France) (Judgment)* [1974] ICJ Rep 253, 270–1 [55]; *Northern Cameroons (Cameroon v United Kingdom) (Preliminary Objections)* [1963] ICJ Rep 15, 33–4.
3   *Mavrommatis Palestine Concessions (Greece v Great Britain) (Jurisdiction)* [1924] PCIJ (ser A) No 2, 11.
4   *Interpretation of Peace Treaties with Bulgaria, Hungary and Romania (Advisory Opinion) (First Phase)* [1950] ICJ Rep 65, 74.
5   *South West Africa (Ethiopia v South Africa) (Preliminary Objections)* [1962] ICJ Rep 319, 328 ('*South West Africa Preliminary Objections*').

The ICJ has since put a gloss on the stated requirement that the claim of one party be 'positively opposed by the other', noting that 'the position or the attitude of a party can be established by inference, whatever the professed view of that party'.[6]

In *Obligations concerning Negotiations Relating to Cessation of the Nuclear Arms Race and to Nuclear Disarmament*, the ICJ summarised the requirements for the demonstration of the existence of a 'dispute'.[7] It confirmed its previous jurisprudence which required that 'the two sides must hold clearly opposite views concerning the question of the performance or non-performance of certain international obligations',[8] and went on to explain that 'a dispute exists when it is demonstrated, on the basis of the evidence, that the respondent was aware, or could not have been unaware, that its views were "positively opposed" by the applicant'.[9]

## 9.2.2   Legal and political disputes

It is evident from the ICJ's description of the requirements for a 'dispute' that such disputes are to be characterised as 'legal disputes', in that (for instance) 'the claim' of one party must be 'positively opposed by the other'.[10] This is also the case in requests for advisory opinions from the ICJ, which must concern (in the language of the *ICJ Statute*) a 'legal question'. In international adjudicatory proceedings, respondent states have often sought to characterise the dispute out of which a claim is made against them as a 'political' rather than a 'legal' dispute. This is of no import where one of the diplomatic means of dispute settlement is engaged, but it is relevant in the context of adjudicatory proceedings, such as before the ICJ.

The ICJ has been largely resistant to arguments that the dispute is 'political' and therefore non-justiciable. In *United States Diplomatic and Consular Staff in Tehran*, the United States claimed that Iran was in breach of its obligations under the *Vienna Convention on Consular Relations* and the *Vienna Convention on Diplomatic Relations* in light of the forcible occupation of the US Embassy in Tehran and the detention of diplomatic and consular staff. Iran argued that it was inappropriate for the ICJ to decide the United States' claims in view of the political nature of the dispute. The ICJ was, however, unmoved, stating that

> legal disputes between sovereign States by their very nature are likely to occur in political contexts and often form only one element in a wider and long-standing political dispute between the States concerned. Yet never has the view been put forward before that, because a legal dispute submitted to the Court is only one aspect of a political dispute, the Court should decline to resolve for the parties the legal questions at issue between them ... if the Court were, contrary to its settled jurisprudence, to adopt such a view, it would impose a far-reaching and unwarranted restriction upon the role of the Court in the peaceful settlement of international disputes.[11]

---

6    *Land and Maritime Boundary between Cameroon and Nigeria (Cameroon v Nigeria) (Preliminary Objections)* [1998] ICJ Rep 275, 315 [89].
7    *Obligations concerning Negotiations Relating to Cessation of the Nuclear Arms Race and to Nuclear Disarmament (Marshall Islands v United Kingdom) (Preliminary Objections)* [2016] ICJ Rep 833, 846–7 [26]–[29].
8    Ibid 849 [37].
9    Ibid 850–1 [41]. For a summary of the ICJ's position on the existence of a dispute, see especially the declaration of President Abraham: at 858 [1]–[5].
10   *South West Africa Preliminary Objections* (n 5) 328.
11   *United States Diplomatic and Consular Staff in Tehran (United States of America v Iran) (Judgment)* [1980] ICJ Rep 3, 20.

# 9.3    Evolution of the obligation to settle disputes peacefully and the *UN Charter* framework

The existence of an obligation on states to settle disputes peacefully is a relatively modern development. It emerged against a backdrop of any formal adjudication of international disputes being very rare, and largely unavailable given the absence of international institutions through which formal dispute settlement proceedings could be facilitated. It followed that the typical means for states to settle disputes was through bilateral negotiations, and if the negotiations were unsuccessful in resolving the dispute, states would typically resort to coercive (or 'self-help') means of dispute settlement; this could include gunboat diplomacy involving the imposition of a naval blockade or the use of force. That is not to say that third-party means of settling disputes are completely novel – there was a practice of third-party dispute settlement for disputes among the city states of Ancient Greece;[12] and during the Middle Ages, foreign sovereigns and the Pope were occasionally appointed to decide international disputes.[13] However, a disadvantage of this form of arbitration was that it was common for sovereign arbitrators to decide disputes without giving any reasons for their decision, and it was therefore not possible to know the extent to which the decision was based on the application of legal rules.[14]

The *Jay Treaty* of 1794 is typically referred to as marking the origins of modern international adjudication.[15] It was concluded between the United States and Great Britain to decide claims concerning losses suffered by nationals of each state which arose from the American War of Independence. The *Jay Treaty* provided for the constitution of mixed commissions which consisted of members appointed by the United States and Great Britain, with an impartial umpire deciding claims in the event of disagreement.[16] The next major watershed was the conclusion of the *Washington Treaty* of 1871, another treaty concluded by the United States and Great Britain.[17] This provided for the constitution of an arbitral tribunal to decide claims by the United States against Great Britain concerning its conduct during the US Civil War, including *Alabama Claims*.[18] The tribunal constituted under the *Washington Treaty* followed an 'essentially judicial process'; it issued 'a reasoned decision

---

12    See, eg, Derek Roebuck, *Ancient Greek Arbitration* (Holo, 2001). See also John Bassett Moore, *International Adjudications: Ancient and Modern – History and Documents* (Oxford University Press, 1929); Marcus Niebuhr Tod, *International Arbitration amongst the Greeks* (Clarendon Press, 1913).

13    JG Merrills, *International Dispute Settlement* (Cambridge University Press, 6th ed, 2017) 88–9.

14    Ibid 89.

15    *Treaty of Amity, Commerce and Navigation*, Great Britain–United States, signed 19 November 1794, 8 Stat 116 (entered into force 28 October 1795) ('*Jay Treaty*'). See generally Chester Brown, *A Common Law of International Adjudication* (Oxford University Press, 2007) 17.

16    Brown, *A Common Law of International Adjudication* (n 15) 17; John Collier and Vaughan Lowe, *The Settlement of Disputes in International Law: Institutions and Procedures* (Oxford University Press, 1999) 32.

17    *Treaty for an Amicable Settlement of All Causes of Difference between the Two Countries*, Great Britain–United States, signed 8 May 1871, 17 Stat 863 (entered into force 17 June 1871) ('*Washington Treaty*').

18    *Alabama Claims (United States v Great Britain) (Award)* (1872) 29 RIAA 125.

clearly based on law', which was a significant development.[19] The *Alabama Claims* arbitrations were widely heralded as a success, and as having successfully avoided armed conflict between the United States and Great Britain. This success was followed in further inter-state arbitrations.[20] It was shortly after the *Alabama Claims* arbitrations that an international institution was established to assist in the peaceful settlement of international disputes: the Permanent Court of Arbitration ('PCA'), which was established by the 1899 *Hague Convention for the Pacific Settlement of International Disputes* ('1899 Convention').[21]

The next development came in the *Covenant of the League of Nations* which was adopted at the Paris Peace Conference in 1919 following the end of World War I. In the Covenant, the members of the League of Nations agreed to submit international disputes which may lead to 'a rupture' either 'to arbitration or judicial settlement' or to enquiry by the Council of the League of Nations. The Covenant did not prohibit warfare as a means of settling international disputes, but member states agreed not to resort to war 'until three months after the award by the arbitrators or the judicial decision, or the report by the Council'.[22] Member states also agreed in art 13 to submit disputes 'suitable for submission to arbitration or judicial settlement and which cannot be satisfactorily settled by diplomacy', to arbitration or judicial settlement.[23] Such disputes included 'the interpretation of a treaty, ... any question of international law, ... the existence of any fact which if established would constitute a breach of any international obligation, or ... the extent or nature of the reparation to be made for any such breach'.[24] The Covenant did not therefore mark the clear emergence of an obligation to settle disputes peacefully, and there were evident difficulties in distinguishing between disputes in relation to which states were ultimately permitted to use force, and those which they were obliged to submit to arbitration or judicial settlement for final resolution.

The 1928 *General Treaty for Renunciation of War as an Instrument of National Policy* (also known as the *Kellogg–Briand Pact*) marked the first time that states agreed to 'condemn recourse to war for the solution of international controversies', and to 'renounce it, as an instrument of national policy in their relations with one another'.[25] The 43 contracting parties also agreed that 'the settlement or solution of all disputes or conflicts of whatever nature or of whatever origin they may be, which may arise among them, shall never be sought except by pacific means'.[26] But the *Kellogg–Briand Pact* ultimately did not avert the outbreak of World War II in 1939. Shortly before the conclusion of World War II, the *UN Charter* was negotiated and opened for signature at the San Francisco Peace Conference. It confirmed in arts 2(3) and 33(1) that states have an obligation to settle disputes peacefully.

---

19      Collier and Lowe (n 16) 32.
20      See, eg, *Rights of Jurisdiction of United States in the Bering's Sea and the Preservation of Fur Seals (United States v United Kingdom) (Award)* (1893) 28 RIAA 263; *Boundary Dispute (British Guiana v Venezuela) (Award)* (1899) 28 RIAA 331.
21      *Hague Convention (I) for the Pacific Settlement of International Disputes*, opened for signature 29 July 1899, [1901] ATS 130 (entered into force 4 September 1900) ('*1899 Convention*').
22      *Covenant of the League of Nations* art 12.
23      Ibid art 13(1).
24      Ibid art 13(2).
25      *General Treaty for Renunciation of War as an Instrument of National Policy*, opened for signature 27 August 1928, 94 LNTS 57 (entered into force 25 July 1929) art I.
26      Ibid art II.

This obligation has been affirmed in various General Assembly resolutions, such as Resolution 1815 (XVII) of 1962,[27] Resolution 2625 (XXV) of 1970 (also known as the *Friendly Relations Declaration*)[28] and Resolution 37/10 of 1982 (*Manila Declaration on the Peaceful Settlement of International Disputes between States*).[29]

# 9.4 Diplomatic methods for the peaceful settlement of international disputes

Many textbooks on public international law deal with the subject of international dispute settlement merely by reference to the function of the ICJ. But international dispute settlement is much broader than this, as is evident from the methods of settling international disputes referred to in art 33(1) of the *UN Charter*. These contain methods of settling international disputes which are diplomatic (eg, negotiation, inquiry, mediation and conciliation) and adjudicatory (arbitration and judicial settlement) in nature. This section considers the more prominent diplomatic methods while Section 9.5 will consider the adjudicatory methods.

## 9.4.1 Negotiation

The use of negotiation as a method of international dispute settlement is the most common, and the principal, means of settling such disputes. It is usual that states which have a dispute will first seek to resolve that dispute by negotiation, and many bilateral and multilateral treaties provide for the settlement of disputes concerning the interpretation or application of the treaty by negotiation.[30] It has been noted that negotiation is 'employed more frequently than all of the other methods put together'.[31] Even where other methods of dispute settlement are employed, negotiation remains a key method of resolving practical matters such as the method of appointing an arbitral tribunal, the questions that are put to a fact-finding inquiry, or the modalities for arranging site visits to gather evidence.

Various approaches can be taken to negotiation. Negotiation can begin after a dispute has arisen, and can then be carried out through the diplomatic channel or in other ways discussed in Sections 9.4.2–9.4.5. Alternatively, negotiations can prevent disputes arising in the first place, and may even be required in certain circumstances.[32] This is known as 'consultation': when a

27    *Consideration of Principles of International Law concerning Friendly Relations and Co-operation among States in accordance with the Charter of the United Nations*, GA Res 1815 (XVII), UN Doc A/RES/1815(XVII) (18 December 1962).

28    *Declaration on Principles of International Law concerning Friendly Relations and Co-operation among States in accordance with the Charter of the United Nations*, GA Res 2625 (XXV), UN Doc A/RES/2625(XXV) (24 October 1970).

29    *Manila Declaration on the Peaceful Settlement of International Disputes between States*, GA Res 37/10, UN Doc A/RES/37/10 (15 November 1982).

30    See, eg, *United Nations Convention on the Law of the Sea*, opened for signature 10 December 1982, 1833 UNTS 397 (entered into force 16 November 1994) ('*UNCLOS*'). 'When a dispute arises between States Parties concerning the interpretation or application of this Convention, the parties to the dispute shall proceed expeditiously to an exchange of views regarding its settlement by negotiation or other peaceful means': at art 283(1).

31    Merrills (n 13) 2.

32    See, eg, *Lake Lanoux (Spain v France) (Award)* (1957) 12 RIAA 281. See also Merrills (n 13) 4.

state considers that a 'decision or proposed course of action' may lead to an inter-state dispute, it can hold discussions with the other state to explain the decision and examine whether any adjustments might be made which respect that state's interests.[33]

In the *Land Reclamation* case, Malaysia alleged that Singapore's land reclamation activities in the Straits of Johor were a breach of its obligations under the *United Nations Convention on the Law of the Sea* ('*UNCLOS*'), because they had been initiated and continued 'without due notification and full consultation with Malaysia'.[34] The International Tribunal for the Law of the Sea prescribed provisional measures, in which it ordered (inter alia) that Malaysia and Singapore 'shall cooperate, and shall, for this purpose, enter into consultations forthwith' to establish a group of experts to carry out studies on the effects of Singapore's land reclamation works, and to propose measures to address any adverse effects.[35]

Another case in which a duty to consult arose from the terms of a treaty is *Pulp Mills on the River Uruguay*, in which Uruguay commissioned the construction of two paper mills on the river which forms the international boundary between Argentina and Uruguay.[36] The *Statute of the River Uruguay* of 1975, being a bilateral treaty between the two states, provided for the establishment of a bilateral commission concerning the use of the river to which the states were required to report if it proposed 'to carry out any ... works which are liable to affect navigation, the régime of the river or the quality of its waters'.[37] The ICJ concluded that Uruguay had indeed breached its obligations under the Statute by failing to inform the commission of the planned works before authorising the construction of the two pulp mills.[38] It is not uncommon for bilateral and multilateral treaty regimes to provide for the creation of a joint commission (as is the case under the *Statute of the River Uruguay*) which provides a regular forum for the states parties to exchange views on the implementation of the treaty regime.[39]

The usual way in which states negotiate is through 'diplomatic channels', which would typically involve the respective states' Ministries of Foreign Affairs, diplomatic missions, and officials of relevant government departments.[40] Such negotiations can take place behind closed doors, but they can also be escalated to involve government ministers, and also the head of government or head of state, who may attend a 'summit' at which the outstanding issues are sought to be resolved.[41] Another method of negotiation involves public ventilation of the issues in a multilateral forum, such as the UN General Assembly. This can be a productive way for a state to gain broader support for its position from other states, but such

33    Merrills (n 13) 2–3.
34    *Land Reclamation by Singapore in and around the Straits of Johor (Malaysia v Singapore) (Order of 8 October 2003)* [2003] ITLOS Rep 10, [22] ('*Land Reclamation*'). See also Merrills (n 13) 4–5.
35    *Land Reclamation* (n 34) [106(1)(a)(i)].
36    *Pulp Mills on the River Uruguay (Argentina v Uruguay) (Judgment)* [2010] ICJ Rep 14.
37    *Statute of the River Uruguay*, signed 26 February 1975, 1295 UNTS 331 (entered into force 18 September 1976). The relevant provisions (arts 7–12) are set out in *Pulp Mills on the River Uruguay* (n 36) 49–51 [80].
38    *Pulp Mills on the River Uruguay* (n 36) 58 [111].
39    See, eg, *Comprehensive and Progressive Agreement for Trans-Pacific Partnership*, opened for signature 8 March 2018, [2018] ATS 23 (entered into force 30 December 2018) art 27.1 (which establishes the Trans-Pacific Partnership Commission).
40    Merrills (n 13) 8–9.
41    Ibid 10–11.

public statements can also serve to entrench a state's position which may limit the scope for flexibility in its stance.[42]

Negotiation does of course have its limitations, most obviously in circumstances where the states concerned refuse to deal with each other and have broken off diplomatic relations, or do not even recognise the other as a legitimate interlocutor (for example, because one state does not formally recognise the other). This has hampered Arab–Israeli relations for many years,[43] as well as those between China and Taiwan. Negotiations are also unlikely to succeed where the two states' negotiating positions are too far apart to be capable of reconciliation.[44]

It is also relevant to note the role that negotiation can play as a pre-condition to one state making use of adjudicatory methods of dispute settlement. For instance, the compromissory clause in many treaties provides that the states have an obligation to seek to resolve the dispute by negotiation. The ICJ has held that where there is such a precondition, the state instituting proceedings must demonstrate that it has made a 'genuine attempt' to settle the dispute through negotiations, and 'the subject-matter of the negotiations must relate to the subject-matter of the dispute which, in turn, must concern the substantive obligations contained in the treaty in question'.[45]

## 9.4.2  Fact-finding and inquiry

The next method of settling international disputes listed in art 33(1) is 'enquiry', also known as 'fact-finding'. Fact-finding involves the objective ascertainment and elucidation of facts, which is important because it is the varied perceptions of facts that often give rise to international disputes in the first place.[46] Fact-finding has a venerable history as a means of international dispute settlement, having been included in the *1899 Convention*.[47]

The idea that an 'impartial and conscientious investigation' of the sort contemplated by the *1899 Convention* could result in the settlement of an international dispute had been given impetus by the episode involving the battleship *USS Maine*, which had been destroyed in an explosion while at anchor in Havana harbour, Cuba, in 1898.[48] The United States and Spain conducted their own inquiries, which reached quite different conclusions. This dispute was reportedly one of the causes of the Spanish–American war of 1898–1902, and perhaps it might have been avoided, had there been an independent inquiry by an international body.[49]

The fact-finding procedures of the *1899 Convention* were successfully used in the inquiry into the Dogger Bank incident of 1905, in which a Russian naval vessel opened fire on a fleet of

---

42    Ibid.
43    Ibid 22–3.
44    Ibid.
45    *Application of the International Convention for the Suppression of the Financing of Terrorism and of the International Convention on the Elimination of All Forms of Racial Discrimination (Ukraine v Russian Federation) (Preliminary Objections)* [2019] ICJ Rep 558, 588 [69], referring to *Application of the International Convention on the Elimination of All Forms of Racial Discrimination (Georgia v Russian Federation) (Preliminary Objections)* [2011] ICJ Rep 70, 133 [161].
46    See also Merrills (n 13) 43.
47    *1899 Convention* (n 21).
48    Merrills (n 13) 43–4.
49    Ibid.

British fishing trawlers, having mistaken them for Japanese torpedo boats.[50] The 1907 *Hague Convention for the Pacific Settlement of International Disputes* ('*1907 Convention*') gave further elaboration to the fact-finding regime,[51] and its procedures were put to use in the early part of the 20th century in a number of further disputes.[52] Following these early instances of fact-finding, it was not for another 40 years that the next Commission of Inquiry was constituted in the *Red Crusader* incident. This was another maritime incident, concerning a British registered fishing vessel which was caught by the Danish coast guard while allegedly fishing illegally off the Faroe Islands in 1961.[53] The United Kingdom and Denmark accepted the Commission's report and ultimately agreed to a settlement of the dispute.[54]

In recent years, fact-finding has been used by UN organs – most notably the Human Rights Council – to investigate allegations of the violation by states and non-state actors of international human rights and international humanitarian law obligations, with fact-finding inquires being instituted into the Gaza conflict and the conflict in Yemen.[55] More recently, the World Health Assembly adopted Resolution WHA 73/1 on 19 May 2020, in which it requested the Director-General of the World Health Organization ('WHO') to initiate a process of 'impartial, independent and comprehensive evaluation' to review 'experience gained and lessons learned from the WHO-coordinated international health response to COVID-19'.[56] The Independent Panel for Pandemic Preparedness and Response issued its final report in May 2021.[57]

## 9.4.3   Good offices

'Good offices' is not expressly referred to in art 33(1) of the *UN Charter*. The term refers to a situation where a third party intervenes in the dispute to assist in 'breaking an impasse and producing an acceptable solution', by encouraging the states to 'resume the negotiations', or by providing them with 'an additional channel of communication'.[58] The term can also be understood more broadly 'as referring to any non-structured form of assistance given by a

---

50    Ibid 44–6.
51    *Hague Convention (I) for the Pacific Settlement of International Disputes*, opened for signature 18 October 1907, 36 Stat 2199 (entered into force 26 January 1910) art 22 ('*1907 Convention*').
52    These concerned incidents involving *The Tavignano*, *The Tubantia* and *The Tiger*: see Merrills (n 13) 46–9.
53    *Investigation of Certain Incidents Affecting the British Trawler Red Crusader (Report of the Commission of Inquiry)* (1962) 29 RIAA 521, 524.
54    Merrills (n 13) 53.
55    See, eg, Human Rights Council, *Human Rights in Palestine and Other Occupied Arab Territories: Report of the UN Fact-Finding Mission on the Gaza Conflict*, UN Doc A/HRC/12/48 (25 September 2009); Human Rights Council, *Situation of Human Rights in Yemen, Including Violations and Abuses since September 2014: Report of the Group of Eminent International and Regional Experts on Yemen*, UN Doc A/HRC/45/6 (28 September 2020).
56    *COVID-19 Response*, WHA Res 73.1 (19 May 2020) [9(10)]. See generally Chester Brown et al, 'Getting Ready for Next Time: The Work of the Independent Panel for Pandemic Preparedness and Response', *Opinio Juris* (Blog Post, 18 May 2021).
57    Independent Panel for Pandemic Preparedness and Response, *COVID-19: Make it the Last Pandemic* (Report, May 2021) <https://theindependentpanel.org/wp-content/uploads/2021/05/COVID-19-Make-it-the-Last-Pandemic_final.pdf>.
58    Merrills (n 13) 26. See also Ruth Lapidoth, 'Good Offices' in Rüdiger Wolfrum (ed), *The Max Planck Encyclopedia of Public International Law* (Oxford University Press, online, December 2006).

third party'.[59] The *1899 Convention* and *1907 Convention* envisaged the use of 'good offices', both providing that '[i]n case of serious disagreement or conflict, before an appeal to arms the Signatory Powers agree to have recourse, as far as circumstances allow, to the good offices or mediation of one or more friendly Powers'.[60] States which are not involved in the dispute were encouraged under the Hague Conventions to 'offer their good offices' even 'during the course of hostilities', which was 'not to be regarded as an unfriendly act'.[61] The *Pact of Bogotá* of 1948 also provided for states not involved in a controversy 'to bring the parties together, so as to make it possible for them to reach an adequate solution between themselves'.[62]

The consent of the parties is necessary in order for a third party (whose identity is known to them) to provide their good offices to assist in resolving a dispute. It is often a highly respected person in a position of some influence who fulfils this role, such as the UN Secretary-General, although it could also be a state which is not involved in the dispute.[63] The UN Secretary-General has provided good offices in the attempted settlement of various international disputes, including the withdrawal of Soviet troops from Afghanistan in 1988; the design and implementation of the Central American peace process beginning in 1989 involving Nicaragua, El Salvador and Guatemala; and the status of Kosovo in the 2000s.[64]

## 9.4.4 Mediation

Mediation, which is mentioned in art 33(1) of the *UN Charter*, is another form of dispute settlement which involves a third party who seeks to facilitate a settlement of the dispute. The *1899 Convention* and the *1907 Convention* include it together with 'good offices' in arts 2 and 3 as a form of dispute settlement involving a 'friendly Power' which is a 'stranger to the dispute', but art 4 goes on to explain the role of mediator as consisting in 'reconciling the opposing claims and appeasing the feelings of resentment which may have arisen between the States at variance'.[65] Merrills observes that the mediator is an active participant in the process, and may 'advance fresh proposals and ... interpret, as well as transmit, each party's proposals to the other'.[66] Mediation requires the consent of the parties (to the process, as well as to the identity of the mediator, which may be a state or a respected individual acting independently). In this respect, the mediator's proposals are not binding on the states in dispute, and can only be regarded as having the character of advice.[67] The mediator's functions come to an end if

59    Lapidoth, 'Good Offices' (n 58).
60    *1899 Convention* (n 21) art 2; *1907 Convention* (n 51) art 2.
61    *1899 Convention* (n 21) art 3; *1907 Convention* (n 51) art 3.
62    *American Treaty on Pacific Settlement*, opened for signature 30 April 1948, 30 UNTS 55 (entered into force 6 May 1949) art IX (commonly known as the *Pact of Bogotá*).
63    *UN Charter* art 99.
64    Lapidoth, 'Good Offices' (n 58). See also Teresa Whitfield, 'Good Offices and "Groups of Friends"' in Simon Chesterman (ed), *Secretary or General? The UN Secretary-General in World Politics* (Cambridge University Press, 2007) 86; Thomas Franck, 'The Secretary-General's Role in Conflict Resolution: Past, Present and Pure Conjecture' (1995) 6(3) *European Journal of International Law* 360; BG Ramcharan, 'The Good Offices of the United Nations Secretary-General in the Field of Human Rights' (1982) 76(1) *American Journal of International Law* 130.
65    *1899 Convention* (n 21) art 4; *1907 Convention* (n 51) art 4.
66    Merrills (n 13) 26. See also Francisco Orrego Vicuña, 'Mediation' in Rüdiger Wolfrum (ed), *The Max Planck Encyclopedia of Public International Law* (Oxford University Press, online, December 2010).
67    Merrills (n 13) 26.

one of the states concerned or the mediator itself declares that the proposals made have not been accepted.[68] It can be difficult in practice to distinguish between someone providing 'good offices' and acting as a mediator, and the distinction between mediation and conciliation can also be blurred.[69]

Mediation is frequently used as a form of dispute settlement, and numerous examples can be noted. In the Falkland Islands conflict in 1982, the US Secretary of State Alexander Haig offered to serve as mediator between the United Kingdom and Argentina, and the UN Secretary-General offered his services as well.[70] In the break-up of the former Yugoslavia in the early 1990s, a combination of states and supranational and international organisations lent their services as mediators, including the United States, the European Communities and the United Nations.[71] Further examples where mediation has been employed include Afghanistan, South Sudan, Syria and Yemen.[72]

Recent years have seen a renewed focus on mediation as a form of settlement for international disputes. In 2011, the General Assembly adopted Resolution 65/283, entitled 'Strengthening the Role of Mediation in the Peaceful Settlement of Disputes, Conflict Prevention and Resolution', in which it invited member states 'to optimize the use of mediation and other tools mentioned in Chapter VI of the Charter for the peaceful settlement of disputes, conflict prevention and resolution'.[73]

## 9.4.5   Conciliation

Conciliation is another method for the peaceful settlement of international disputes that is listed in art 33(1) of the *UN Charter*. It is understood as a method for the settlement of international disputes which involves the constitution of a commission by the disputing states, which carries out an 'impartial examination of the dispute and attempts to define the terms of a settlement susceptible of being accepted by them or affording the Parties, with a view to its settlement, such aid as they may have requested'.[74] A conciliation commission makes non-binding recommendations to the disputing parties, which they can then consider implementing.

Conciliation was not mentioned in the *1899 Convention* or the *1907 Convention*, and it appears to have emerged as a form of settling international disputes from a combination of elements of mediation and international commissions of enquiry.[75] Conciliation was first included

---

68    *1899 Convention* (n 21) art 5; *1907 Convention* (n 51) art 5.

69    Merrills (n 13) 26.

70    Ibid 27–8.

71    Ibid 28–9.

72    For a more complete list, see *Strengthening the Role of Mediation in the Peaceful Settlement of Disputes, Conflict Prevention and Resolution: Report of the Secretary-General*, UN Doc A/66/811 (25 June 2012) [22]–[28].

73    *Strengthening the Role of Mediation in the Peaceful Settlement of Disputes, Conflict Prevention and Resolution*, GA Res 65/283, UN Doc A/RES/65/283 (22 June 2011).

74    See, eg, Institute of International Law, 'Regulations on the Procedure of International Conciliation' (1961) 49 *Annuaire de l'Institut de Droit International* 385 (art 1). See also Jean-Pierre Cot, 'Conciliation' in Rüdiger Wolfrum (ed), *The Max Planck Encyclopedia of Public International Law* (Oxford University Press, online, April 2006).

75    See, eg, Jean-Pierre Cot, *La Conciliation Internationale* [International Conciliation] (Pedone, 1968) 29–57; *Timor Sea Conciliation (Timor-Leste v Australia) (Report and Recommendations)* (Permanent Court of Arbitration, Case No 2016-10, 9 May 2018) [52].

as the method of dispute settlement in bilateral treaties in the 1920s.[76] It was notably included in the Locarno Treaties of 1925, which Germany entered into with Belgium, France, Czechoslovakia and Poland as a final part of the post–World War I settlement.[77] Numerous conciliations were held during the 20th century, seeking to resolve disputes including a boundary dispute between Bolivia and Paraguay (the Chaco Commission, in the 1920s), France and Siam (in the 1940s), and Italy and Switzerland (in the 1950s).[78] Inter-state conciliations have been comparatively rare in recent decades, but conciliation remains a form of dispute settlement under many bilateral and multilateral treaties; thus, disputes under the *Framework Convention on Climate Change* can be referred to conciliation, if the states have not agreed to refer the dispute to arbitration or to the ICJ.[79] Other multilateral treaties provide for compulsory conciliation, including the *Vienna Convention on the Law of Treaties*,[80] and *UNCLOS* (under which states can formulate a reservation to the dispute settlement procedures of pt XV in respect of maritime boundary delimitation disputes, but such states must accept compulsory conciliation).[81]

In April 2016, the compulsory conciliation procedures of *UNCLOS* were invoked by Timor-Leste against Australia in a dispute concerning the delimitation of the maritime boundary in the Timor Sea.[82] The Conciliation Commission in the *Timor Sea Conciliation* took a flexible view of its mandate, noting that

> conciliation proceedings may differ in the extent to which they seek to mediate an agreement between the parties or to leave the parties with a report containing the commission's recommendations and conclusions. Historically, conciliation procedures have set out differing expectations regarding a commission's role in the course of proceedings, and conciliation commissions have taken different approaches with respect to this aspect of their mandate.[83]

The Commission noted that although the parties had expressed an intention to reach agreement, it 'considered it to be of great importance' that 'the Commission have the opportunity to offer conclusions and recommendations, whether in the course of discussions or in the report'.[84] For '[e]ven where both parties are actively engaged, an agreement may prove elusive and the willingness to make the difficult decisions and compromises necessary to secure agreement may rise and fall over the course of the proceedings. The report is a necessary component of this conciliation process'.[85]

76   See, eg, *Treaty between Sweden and Chile concerning the Establishment of a Permanent Enquiry and Conciliation Commission*, signed 26 March 1920, available by search at *UN Archives Geneva* (Web Page) <https://archives.ungeneva.org>. See also Merrills (n 13) 62–3.
77   Merrills (n 13) 63–4.
78   Ibid 64–9. See also Sven Koopmans, *Diplomatic Dispute Settlement: The Use of Inter-State Conciliation* (Cambridge University Press, 2008); Cot, *La Conciliation Internationale* (n 75).
79   *United Nations Framework Convention on Climate Change*, opened for signature 19 May 1992, 771 UNTS 107 (entered into force 21 March 1994) art 14.
80   *Vienna Convention on the Law of Treaties*, opened for signature 23 May 1969, 1155 UNTS 331 (entered into force 27 January 1980).
81   *UNCLOS* (n 30) art 298(1)(a)(i).
82   See, eg, *Timor Sea Conciliation* (n 75).
83   Ibid [63].
84   Ibid [64].
85   Ibid [63]–[64].

The Timor Sea Conciliation, which continued throughout 2016–18, proved to be successful, and on 6 March 2018, the *Treaty between Australia and the Democratic Republic of Timor-Leste Establishing their Maritime Boundaries in the Timor Sea* was signed.[86] On 9 May 2018 the Commission issued its report which provides a record of the conciliation and the flexible procedures used by the Commission to facilitate the settlement of the dispute.

# 9.5    International arbitration

This chapter has thus far considered the political or diplomatic means for the peaceful settlement of international disputes. It now turns to arbitration, which is an adjudicatory method of settling international disputes. As noted in Section 9.3, arbitration has a long history of being used as a method of settling international disputes, having been used for the settlement of disputes in Ancient Greece,[87] as well as during the Middle Ages.[88]

At the First Hague Peace Conference, the *1899 Convention* was adopted which saw the establishment of the PCA, 'with the object of facilitating an immediate recourse to arbitration for international differences, which it has not been possible to settle by diplomacy'.[89] The PCA was also declared to be 'competent for all arbitration cases, unless the parties agree to institute a special Tribunal'.[90] Article 15 of the *1899 Convention* provides that '[i]nternational arbitration has for its object the settlement of differences between States by judges of their own choice, and on the basis of respect for law.' In art 16, the contracting states recognised that in 'questions of a legal nature', international arbitration was 'the most effective, and at the same time the most equitable, means of settling disputes which diplomacy has failed to settle'. The arbitral tribunal was to be appointed by the agreement of the parties. In the absence of agreement, each state was to appoint two arbitrators, and the party-appointed arbitrators were to appoint an 'Umpire'. If the party-appointed arbitrators could not agree on the identity of the 'Umpire', it would be appointed by a 'third Power', or by two 'Powers' in concert.[91] These provisions were restated in the *1907 Convention*, which also contained more elaborate provisions on the applicable procedure.[92]

International arbitration has evidently predated the creation of the PCIJ (and its successor, the ICJ), and has remained an enduringly popular method for the settlement of international disputes. In the early 20th century, arbitral tribunals decided cases such as *Pious Fund*,[93] *Norwegian Shipowners' Claims*[94] and *Island of Palmas*.[95] The PCA admittedly had a quieter period after the creation of the PCIJ in 1922, but inter-state disputes were still submitted to

86    *Timor Sea Treaty between the Government of Australia and the Government of East Timor*, signed 6 March 2018, [2019] ATS 16 (entered into force 30 August 2019).
87    See, eg, Roebuck (n 12). See also Moore (n 12); Tod (n 12).
88    Merrills (n 13) 88–9.
89    *1899 Convention* (n 21) art 20.
90    Ibid art 21.
91    Ibid art 31.
92    *1907 Convention* (n 51).
93    *Pious Fund Case (United States v Mexico) (Award)* (1902) 9 RIAA 1.
94    *Norwegian Shipowners' Claims (Norway v United States) (Award)* (1922) 1 RIAA 307.
95    *Island of Palmas (Netherlands v United States of America) (Award)* (1928) 2 RIAA 829.

arbitration,[96] and the PCA has seen a remarkable renaissance in recent years. The PCA has served as registry for 30 inter-state arbitrations since the mid-1990s, including numerous arbitrations under *UNCLOS*, and a number of arbitrations involving Australia.[97]

# 9.6   International Court of Justice (ICJ)
## 9.6.1   History

The ICJ was established by art 7 of the *UN Charter* as one of the six main organs of the United Nations. Article 92 provides that it 'shall be the principal judicial organ of the United Nations' and that it 'shall function in accordance with the annexed Statute, which is based upon the *Statute of the Permanent Court of International Justice* and forms an integral part of the present Charter'.[98] The ICJ is essentially the successor to the PCIJ, which was the judicial body that was established pursuant to art 14 of the *Covenant of the League of Nations*. That article relevantly provided that the Council of the League of Nations was to 'formulate and submit to the Members of the League for adoption plans for the establishment of a Permanent Court of International Justice'. The formulation of those plans was delegated to an advisory committee of jurists, which met during 1920 and prepared the court's statute, which was then adopted by the members of the League of Nations. The PCIJ functioned between 1922 and 1945; it decided 38 contentious cases and delivered 27 advisory opinions.

## 9.6.2   Composition

The question of the composition of the ICJ, including the manner of selecting the judges, is an issue that had blocked previous efforts to create a permanent international court. Different approaches ranged from 'full representation', where every member state could appoint a judge (which would be rather unwieldy), to 'selective representation', whereby only certain states could have a judge of their nationality on the bench. The framers of the *ICJ Statute* chose the selective representation model; originally under the *PCIJ Statute*, there were only nine judges, but that number was expanded. Article 3 of the ICJ Statute provides that the ICJ shall consist of 15 judges 'no two of whom may be nationals of the same state'.[99] The judges are 'independent' and are elected 'regardless of their nationality from among persons of high moral character, who possess the qualifications required in their respective countries for appointment to the highest judicial offices, or are jurisconsults of recognized competence in international law'.[100] They serve a nine-year term, and may be re-elected.[101] Under art 4(1), the judges are elected by the General Assembly and the Security Council, and are chosen from a list of persons

96   See, eg, Christine Gray and Benedict Kingsbury, 'Developments in Dispute Settlement: Inter-State Arbitration since 1945' (1992) 63 *British Yearbook of International Law* 97.
97   See, eg, *Arbitration under the Timor Sea Treaty (Timor-Leste v Australia)* (Permanent Court of Arbitration, Case No 2013-16); *Arbitration under the Timor Sea Treaty (Timor-Leste v Australia) (II)* (Permanent Court of Arbitration, Case No 2015-42).
98   *UN Charter* art 92.
99   *Statute of the International Court of Justice* ('*ICJ Statute*') art 3(1).
100  Ibid art 2.
101  Ibid art 13(1).

nominated by the various 'national groups' of the PCA, each of which consists of up to four people nominated by the contracting parties of the PCA.[102] The election of the judges by the General Assembly and the Security Council is usually a political exercise, although under art 9 of the *ICJ Statute*, the General Assembly and the Security Council are to bear in mind 'not only that the persons to be elected should individually possess the qualifications required, but also that in the body as a whole the representation of the main forms of civilization and of the principal legal systems of the world should be assured'.[103]

If a state is a party to a contentious case before the ICJ and there is a judge of its nationality on the Bench, that judge retains his or her right to sit in the case.[104] If a state is a party to a contentious case before the ICJ but does not have a judge of its nationality on the bench, it has the right to appoint an ad hoc judge for that particular case. This means that in some cases, where both states appoint an ad hoc judge, the bench of the ICJ may expand to 17 members.[105] Ad hoc judges are independent of the state which appointed them to sit in the particular case. It has been understood that 'the institution of the *ad hoc* judge was created for the purpose of giving a party, not otherwise having upon the Court a judge of its nationality, an opportunity to join in the work of this tribunal', but ad hoc judges are to remain independent and impartial in the exercise of their functions.[106]

## 9.6.3  Access to the Court

Under arts 34 and 35 of the *ICJ Statute*, only member states of the United Nations can be parties in cases to the ICJ. Article 93(1) of the *UN Charter* provides that all member states of the United Nations are states parties to the *ICJ Statute*, although art 93(2) provides that a state which is not a member of the United Nations can become a party to the *ICJ Statute*, as determined by the General Assembly on the recommendation of the Security Council. This procedure was used by Switzerland, Liechtenstein, San Marino, Japan and Nauru, before they became member states of the United Nations.[107]

---

102    See, eg, *1907 Convention* (n 51) art 44: 'Each Contracting Power selects four persons at the most, of known competency in questions of international law, of the highest moral reputation, and disposed to accept the duties of Arbitrator. The persons thus elected are inscribed, as Members of the Court, in a list which shall be notified to all the Contracting Powers by the Bureau.'

103    There have been three Australian judges of the ICJ: Judge Sir Percy Spender, who was Minister for External Affairs in the Menzies Government, and subsequently Australia's Ambassador to the United States, who was a judge from 1958 to 1967, and President of the ICJ from 1964 to 1967; Judge James Crawford, who was Challis Professor of International Law and Dean of the University of Sydney Law School, and then Whewell Professor of International Law at the University of Cambridge, and a judge of the ICJ from 2015 until his untimely passing in 2021; and Judge Hilary Charlesworth, who was Harrison Moore Chair in Law (2021) and Melbourne Laureate Professor at Melbourne Law School, University of Melbourne (2016–21) prior to her appointment to the Court in 2021, to fill the position left open by Judge Crawford's passing.

104    *ICJ Statute* art 31(1).

105    Ibid art 31(2)–(3).

106    *Application of the Convention on the Prevention and Punishment of the Crime of Genocide (Bosnia and Herzegovina v Yugoslavia (Serbia and Montenegro)) (Provisional Measures)* [1993] ICJ Rep 325, 407, 409 (Judge Ad Hoc Elihu Lauterpacht).

107    These procedures were established in SC Res 9, UN Doc S/RES/9 (15 October 1946).

## 9.6.4   Jurisdiction of the Court

The ICJ has two forms of jurisdiction: its jurisdiction over contentious inter-state disputes, and its jurisdiction to issue advisory opinions.

### 9.6.4.1   Contentious jurisdiction

Beginning with the ICJ's contentious jurisdiction, it is important to note that the ICJ does not have compulsory jurisdiction over states. Rather, states have to give their consent to the ICJ's jurisdiction in one of several ways. The first method is for states to make a declaration accepting the ICJ's jurisdiction under art 36(2) of the *ICJ Statute*, which is known as the 'optional clause'. This provides:

> The States parties to the present Statute may at any time declare that they recognize as compulsory *ipso facto* and without special agreement, in relation to any other State accepting the same obligation, the jurisdiction of the Court in all legal disputes concerning:
>
> (a)   the interpretation of a treaty;
>
> (b)   any question of international law;
>
> (c)   the existence of any fact which, if established, would constitute a breach of an international obligation;
>
> (d)   the nature or extent of the reparation to be made for the breach of an international obligation.

Article 36(3) further provides that such declarations 'may be made unconditionally or on condition of reciprocity on the part of several or certain states, or for a certain time'.

Of the 193 member states of the United Nations, 73 states have, as at the time of writing, made an optional clause declaration,[108] with the most recent declaration having been made by Latvia on 24 September 2019.[109] Many of these declarations are subject to certain reservations. Such reservations might exclude from the scope of the declaration disputes over certain subject-matter (eg, the status of territory, or boundary delimitation);[110] disputes with certain states (eg, members of the British Commonwealth);[111] disputes under certain treaties (eg, multilateral treaties, unless all of the states parties to the treaty are parties to the ICJ proceeding);[112] or disputes in which the applicant state has accepted the ICJ's jurisdiction only in relation to or for the purpose of the dispute, or where the applicant's acceptance of the ICJ's jurisdiction was deposited less than 12 months before the filing of the application bringing the case to the ICJ.[113]

---

108   International Court of Justice, *Declarations Recognising the Jurisdiction of the Court as Compulsory* (Web Page) <https://icj-cij.org/en/declarations> ('*Declarations*').

109   This replaced the earlier declaration Latvia had made on 31 January 1935 which accepted the jurisdiction of the PCIJ: 'Latvia' (24 September 2019), *Declarations* (n 108).

110   See, eg, 'India' (27 September 2019), *Declarations* (n 108).

111   See, eg, 'United Kingdom' (22 February 2017), *Declarations* (n 108).

112   See, eg, *Military and Paramilitary Activities in and against Nicaragua (Nicaragua v United States of America) (Jurisdiction and Admissibility)* [1984] ICJ Rep 392.

113   See, eg, 'Germany' (30 April 2008), *Declarations* (n 108).

Australia has made such a declaration; it was originally made in 1975, and was replaced on 22 March 2002. The substantive part reads as follows:

> The Government of Australia declares that it recognises as compulsory *ipso facto* and without special agreement, in relation to any other State accepting the same obligation, the jurisdiction of the International Court of Justice in conformity with paragraph 2 of Article 36 of the Statute of the Court, until such time as notice may be given to the Secretary-General of the United Nations withdrawing this declaration. This declaration is effective immediately.
>
> This declaration does not apply to:
>
> (a)   any dispute in regard to which the parties thereto have agreed or shall agree to have recourse to some other method of peaceful settlement;
>
> (b)   any dispute concerning or relating to the delimitation of maritime zones, including the territorial sea, the exclusive economic zone and the continental shelf, or arising out of, concerning, or relating to the exploitation of any disputed area of or adjacent to any such maritime zone pending its delimitation;
>
> (c)   any dispute in respect of which any other party to the dispute has accepted the compulsory jurisdiction of the Court only in relation to or for the purpose of the dispute; or where the acceptance of the Court's compulsory jurisdiction on behalf of any other party to the dispute was deposited less than 12 months prior to the filing of the application bringing the dispute before the Court.[114]

It is important to understand that a state's optional clause declaration is only effective to found the jurisdiction of the ICJ over a contentious dispute if both states have made such a declaration, and both declarations accept the ICJ's jurisdiction over that dispute. This appears from the language of art 36(2) of the *ICJ Statute*, which provides that such declarations apply 'in relation to any other state accepting the same obligation'. This condition of reciprocity has been interpreted to apply also to the reservations which states may formulate and attach to their optional clause declarations. Thus, in *Certain Norwegian Loans*, France commenced proceedings against Norway and sought to base the ICJ's jurisdiction on the two states' optional clause declarations.[115] France's optional clause declaration contained the following reservation: 'This declaration does not apply to differences relating to matters which are essentially within the national jurisdiction as understood by the Government of the French Republic'.[116] Norway raised a preliminary objection to the ICJ's jurisdiction, in which it sought to rely on France's 'national jurisdiction' reservation, which was also self-judging (or 'automatic') in character.[117] The ICJ confirmed the position that

> since two unilateral declarations are involved, such jurisdiction is conferred upon the Court only to the extent to which the Declarations coincide in conferring it. A comparison between the two Declarations shows that the French Declaration accepts the Court's jurisdiction within narrower limits than the Norwegian Declaration; consequently, the

---

114    'Australia' (22 March 2002), *Declarations* (n 108).
115    *Certain Norwegian Loans (France v Norway) (Preliminary Objections)* [1957] ICJ Rep 9.
116    Ibid.
117    Ibid 21–2.

common will of the Parties, which is the basis of the Court's jurisdiction, exists within these narrower limits indicated by the French reservation.[118]

The consequence of this was that Norway was also entitled to exclude from its acceptance of the ICJ's jurisdiction 'disputes understood by Norway to be essentially within its national jurisdiction', and the ICJ upheld Norway's preliminary objection.[119] The ICJ did not consider it appropriate to examine the validity of the French reservation, and whether it was compatible with art 36(6) of the *ICJ Statute*, which confirms the principle of *compétence de la compétence* as follows: 'In the event of a dispute as to whether the Court has jurisdiction, the matter shall be settled by the decision of the Court.' However, Judge Hersch Lauterpacht wrote a separate opinion in which he explained that France's declaration, including its 'automatic' reservation, was invalid and incapable of producing legal effects:

> [N]ot only [is it] contrary to one of the most fundamental principles of international – and national – jurisprudence according to which it is within the inherent power of a tribunal to interpret the text establishing its jurisdiction. It is also contrary to a clear specific provision of the Statute of the Court as well as to the general Articles 1 and 92 of the Statute and of the Charter, respectively, which require the Court to function in accordance with its Statute.[120]

Nonetheless, as the validity of the French declaration was not challenged by either state, the ICJ did not rule on this issue. A number of years later, in the *Interhandel* case, the ICJ also found it unnecessary to rule on the validity of the United States' declaration which excluded from its acceptance of the ICJ's jurisdiction any '[d]isputes with regard to matters which are essentially within the domestic jurisdiction of the United States of America as determined by the United States of America'.[121]

The second method by which the ICJ can exercise jurisdiction over a contentious case is by the states submitting the dispute to the ICJ by special agreement (also known as a *compromis*).[122] By entering into such an agreement which submits an existing dispute to the ICJ, the disputing states can identify the issues they wish the ICJ to decide, and can also specify the rules that the ICJ should apply in deciding the dispute. These rules will usually be the sources of international law in accordance with art 38 of the *ICJ Statute*,[123] but states parties to the dispute have in at least one case concerning the delimitation of a maritime boundary requested that the ICJ 'take account of equitable principles and the relevant circumstances which characterise the area as well as the recent trends admitted at the Third Conference on the Law of the Sea'.[124]

---

118   Ibid 23–4.
119   Ibid 24.
120   Ibid 44 (Judge Hersch Lauterpacht).
121   *Interhandel (Switzerland v United States of America) (Preliminary Objections)* [1959] ICJ Rep 6, 15, 25–6. Again, Judge Hersch Lauterpacht issued a dissenting opinion: at 95.
122   *ICJ Statute* art 36(1).
123   See, eg, *Special Agreement for Submission to the International Court of Justice of the Dispute between Indonesia and Malaysia concerning Sovereignty over Pulau Ligitan and Pulau Sipadan*, signed 31 May 1997, 2023 UNTS 245 (entered into force 14 May 1998) art 4. See also *Special Agreement for Submission to the International Court of Justice of the Differences concerning the Gabčíkovo-Nagymaros Project*, Slovakia–Hungary, signed 7 April 1993, 1725 UNTS 225 (entered into force 28 June 1993) art 2.
124   *Continental Shelf (Tunisia v Libyan Arab Jamahiriya) (Judgment)* [1982] ICJ Rep 18, 21 [2].

The third method by which the ICJ can take jurisdiction over a contentious case is through the invocation of a dispute settlement clause (or 'compromissory clause') in a treaty. Such clauses typically provide that all disputes concerning the 'interpretation or application' of the treaty may be submitted by either of the disputing states to the ICJ, if those disputes are not settled by negotiation; an example is art 22 of the *International Convention on the Elimination of All Forms of Racial Discrimination*.[125] The treaty may be a bilateral treaty or a multilateral treaty. The ICJ website reports that there are 298 treaties that contain clauses 'relating to the jurisdiction of the Court' and states that these 'generally provide that disputes concerning the application or interpretation of the instrument may be referred to the Court for decision'.[126]

The fourth method for the ICJ to take jurisdiction over a contentious case is through the transferred jurisdiction of the PCIJ. Under art 36(5) of the *ICJ Statute*, optional clause declarations made by states under the *PCIJ Statute* 'and which are still in force' are deemed 'to be acceptances of the compulsory jurisdiction' of the ICJ 'for the period which they still have to run and in accordance with their terms'. In addition, art 37 of the *ICJ Statute* provides that where a compromissory clause in a treaty 'provides for reference of a matter to a tribunal to have been instituted by the League of Nations, or to the Permanent Court of International Justice', the dispute shall be referred to the ICJ. This was one of the bases of the ICJ's jurisdiction in *Military and Paramilitary Activities in and against Nicaragua*, in which the ICJ held that Nicaragua's declaration accepting the jurisdiction of the PCIJ was 'still in force'.[127]

The final way in which the ICJ can take jurisdiction is through the doctrine of *forum prorogatum*. This is the extension of the ICJ's jurisdiction by the agreement of the parties in a case which would otherwise be outside the Court's jurisdiction. This doctrine formed the basis of the ICJ's jurisdiction in *Corfu Channel*.[128] That case was brought by the United Kingdom against Albania following the passage of several Royal Navy vessels through the Corfu Channel in which two vessels struck submerged mines and suffered serious damage. Albania had not deposited an optional clause declaration, and there was no special agreement or applicable treaty which contained a compromissory clause conferring jurisdiction on the ICJ. Albania wrote to the ICJ, stating that it 'would be within its rights in holding that the Government of the United Kingdom was not entitled to bring the case before the Court by unilateral application, without first concluding a special agreement with the Albanian Government'.[129] However, Albania went on to state that it was 'prepared, notwithstanding this irregularity in the action taken by the Government of the United Kingdom, to appear before the Court'.[130] In doing so, it emphasised that 'its acceptance of the Court's jurisdiction for this case cannot constitute a precedent for the future'.[131] The ICJ considered that this letter constituted 'a voluntary and indisputable acceptance of the Court's jurisdiction', observing: 'While the consent of the parties confers jurisdiction on the Court, neither the Statute nor the

---

125    *International Convention on the Elimination of All Forms of Racial Discrimination*, opened for signature 7 March 1966, 660 UNTS 195 (entered into force 4 January 1969) art 14.

126    See, eg, 'Treaties', *International Court of Justice* (Web Page) <www.icj-cij.org/en/treaties>.

127    *Military and Paramilitary Activities in and against Nicaragua* (n 112) 403–15.

128    *Corfu Channel (United Kingdom v Albania) (Preliminary Objections)* [1948] ICJ Rep 15.

129    Ibid 18–19 (Albanian letter dated 2 July 1947).

130    Ibid 19.

131    Ibid.

Rules require that this consent should be expressed in any particular form.'[132] It added that 'there is nothing to prevent the acceptance of jurisdiction, as in the present case, from being effected by two separate and successive acts, instead of jointly and beforehand by a special agreement'.[133]

The doctrine of *forum prorogatum* is now recognised in art 38(5) of the ICJ's *Rules of Court*.[134] This was applied by the ICJ in *Certain Criminal Proceedings in France*, in which the Republic of the Congo commenced proceedings against France and proposed to found the ICJ's jurisdiction on art 38(5), to which France agreed.[135]

### 9.6.4.2 Admissibility of claims

Even if the ICJ has jurisdiction over a contentious case, it may decide not to exercise that jurisdiction if it finds that the claim is inadmissible. There are a number of reasons why the ICJ may decline to exercise its jurisdiction. One such reason is that it would not be in keeping with the ICJ's judicial function to give a judgment in a case which would not be capable of effective implementation. As the ICJ explained in *Northern Cameroons*:

> The Court's judgment must have some practical consequence in the sense that it can affect existing legal rights or obligations of the parties, thus removing uncertainty from their legal relations. No judgment on the merits in this case could satisfy these essentials of the judicial function.[136]

A related situation in which the ICJ has found that a claim is inadmissible is where there is no longer a live dispute between the disputing states, and the issue has become moot. In the *Nuclear Tests* case, the ICJ explained:

> The Court, as a court of law, is called upon to resolve existing disputes between States. Thus the existence of a dispute is the primary condition for the Court to exercise its judicial function; it is not sufficient for one party to assert that there is a dispute, since 'whether there exists an international dispute is a matter for objective determination' by the Court ... The dispute brought before it must therefore continue to exist at the time when the Court makes its decision. It must not fail to take cognizance of a situation in which the dispute has disappeared because the object of the claim has been achieved by other means.[137]

The ICJ's judgment in *Nuclear Tests* is controversial, since it exercised an inherent power to reformulate the claims of Australia and New Zealand, who were seeking a declaration that France's program of atmospheric nuclear testing in the South Pacific was contrary to their rights

132    Ibid 27.
133    Ibid 28.
134    Article 38(5) provides: 'When the applicant State proposes to found the jurisdiction of the Court upon a consent thereto yet to be given or manifested by the State against which such application is made, the application shall be transmitted to that State. It shall not however be entered in the General List, nor any action be taken in the proceedings, unless and until the State against which such application is made consents to the Court's jurisdiction for the purposes of the case.'
135    *Certain Criminal Proceedings in France (Republic of the Congo v France) (Provisional Measures)* [2003] ICJ Rep 102, 103 [3], [6].
136    *Northern Cameroons* (n 2) 33–4.
137    *Nuclear Tests* (n 2) 270–1.

under international law[138] In the ICJ's view, the true object of the proceedings was to secure an end to France's nuclear weapons testing program, which was reached by the French Government giving a unilateral undertaking to this effect.[139] The ICJ thus managed to avoid determining the substance of a controversial dispute concerning the testing of nuclear weapons.

The ICJ might also find that a claim is inadmissible if the claim is being brought by the state under the doctrine of diplomatic protection, and the individual concerned has failed to exhaust the local remedies available to it in the state which is responsible for the internationally wrongful act. The rule of exhaustion of local remedies was discussed by the ICJ in *Elettronica Sicula*, where it said that 'it [was] sufficient if the essence of the claim has been brought before the competent tribunals and pursued as far as permitted by local law and procedures, and without success'.[140] The ILC has sought to codify this rule in the Draft Articles on Diplomatic Protection (discussed in Chapter 7). Another reason why the ICJ might find that a diplomatic protection claim is inadmissible is that the individual or company concerned does not have the nationality of the state bringing the proceedings (as in the *Nottebohm* case, and *Barcelona Traction, Light and Power Company*);[141] the nationality of claims is also discussed in Chapter 7.

A further reason why the ICJ might find a claim inadmissible is that the applicant state lacks 'standing' to bring the claim because it is not the injured state. This was the outcome in the *South West Africa* case.[142] Liberia and Ethiopia commenced proceedings against South Africa for its implementation of the policy of apartheid in the territory of South West Africa, over which South Africa had been declared the trustee. By a split decision, with the President of the ICJ exercising his casting vote, the ICJ held that Ethiopia and Liberia lacked standing to bring the claim because they lacked a legal interest. As the ICJ held:

> [T]he argument amounts to a plea that the Court should allow the equivalent of an '*actio populari*', or right resident in any member of a community to take legal action in vindication of a public interest. But although a right of this kind may be known to certain municipal systems of law, it is not known to international law as it stands at present: nor is the Court able to regard it as imported by the 'general principles of law' referred to in Article 38, paragraph 1 (c), of its Statute.[143]

Another reason for the ICJ to decline to exercise jurisdiction over a contentious case is because deciding the legal issues in dispute would require it to make determinations of the rights and obligations of a third state which is not a party to the proceedings.[144] This rule was applied by the ICJ in the proceedings brought by Portugal against Australia concerning East Timor, and in particular Australia's conduct in entering into a treaty with Indonesia (the *Timor Gap Treaty* of 1989)[145] to share the hydrocarbon resources of the Timor Sea. Australia objected to the admissibility of

---

138    Ibid 256–8, 263.
139    Ibid 263.
140    *Elettronica Sicula SpA (ELSI) (United States of America v Italy) (Judgment)* [1989] ICJ Rep 15, 46 [59].
141    *Nottebohm (Liechtenstein v Guatemala) (Second Phase)* [1955] ICJ Rep 4; *Barcelona Traction, Light and Power Company Ltd (Belgium v Spain) (Judgment)* [1970] ICJ Rep 3.
142    *South West Africa (Ethiopia v South Africa) (Second Phase)* [1966] ICJ Rep 6.
143    Ibid 88.
144    See, eg, *Monetary Gold Removed from Rome (Italy v France) (Preliminary Objection)* [1954] ICJ Rep 19.
145    *Treaty between Australia and the Republic of Indonesia on the Zone of Cooperation in an Area between the Indonesian Province of East Timor and Northern Australia*, signed 11 December 1989, [1991] ATS 9 (entered into force 9 February 1991).

Portugal's claim on the basis that Indonesia was not a party to the proceedings, and the ICJ would inevitably also have to rule on whether Indonesia's conduct in entering into the treaty was a breach of its international obligations. The ICJ agreed, holding that

> in the view of the Court, Australia's behaviour cannot be assessed without first entering into the question why it is that Indonesia could not lawfully have concluded the 1989 Treaty, while Portugal allegedly could have done so; the very subject-matter of the Court's decision would necessarily be a determination whether, having regard to the circumstances in which Indonesia entered and remained in East Timor, it could or could not have acquired the power to enter into treaties on behalf of East Timor relating to the resources of its continental shelf. The Court could not make such a determination in the absence of the consent of Indonesia.[146]

The ICJ thus found that Indonesia was an indispensable third party, with the result that Portugal's claim was inadmissible.

### 9.6.4.3  Provisional measures

Like many domestic courts and tribunals, the ICJ has the power to grant provisional measures, which have the purpose of preserving the status quo, and the rights of the parties, pending the ICJ's judgment on the merits of the case. Article 41(1) of the *ICJ Statute* provides that the ICJ has 'the power to indicate, if it considers that circumstances so require, any provisional measures which ought to be taken to preserve the respective rights of either party'. For many years, some doubt attended the question as to whether provisional measures which were 'indicated' under art 41 had binding force, but this question was answered by the ICJ in the affirmative in the *LaGrand* case.[147]

The ICJ has demonstrated considerable flexibility in the provisional measures that it has granted, although it can only grant such measures to preserve the rights of the parties which form the subject-matter of the dispute. The ICJ has also set out certain criteria that have to be established before it will exercise its power to indicate provisional measures. First, the ICJ must be satisfied that there is a prima facie basis on which it can exercise jurisdiction over the merits of the dispute, although it does not need to be definitively satisfied that it has jurisdiction as regards the merits of the case.[148] Secondly, the rights claimed in the applicant state's claim must be at least 'plausible'.[149] Thirdly, the applicant state must establish that there is a risk that 'irreparable prejudice' will be done to the rights of the parties in dispute if the provisional measures are not granted.[150] Fourthly, the applicant state must demonstrate that there is

---

146  *East Timor (Portugal v Australia) (Judgment)* [1995] ICJ Rep 90, 102 [28].

147  *LaGrand (Germany v United States of America) (Judgment)* [2001] ICJ Rep 466.

148  *Application of the International Convention on the Elimination of All Forms of Racial Discrimination (Qatar v United Arab Emirates) (Order of 23 July 2018)* [2018] ICJ Rep 406, 413 [14]; *Seizure and Detention of Certain Documents and Data (Timor-Leste v Australia) (Provisional Measures)* [2014] ICJ Rep 147, 151 [18] (*'Documents and Data'*); *Military and Paramilitary Activities in and against Nicaragua (Nicaragua v United States of America) (Provisional Measures)* [1984] ICJ Rep 169, 179 [24].

149  See, eg, *Qatar v United Arab Emirates* (n 148) 88 [43]; *Documents and Data* (n 148) 152 [22].

150  See, eg, *Qatar v United Arab Emirates* (n 148) 91–2 [60]; *Documents and Data* (n 148) 154 [31]; *Application of the International Convention on the Elimination of All Forms of Racial Discrimination (Georgia v Russian Federation) (Provisional Measures)* [2008] ICJ Rep 353, 396 [142] (*'Georgia v Russian Federation (Provisional Measures)'*).

'urgency' in the sense that there is a real and imminent risk that irreparable prejudice will be caused to the rights in dispute before the Court gives its final decision.[151]

#### 9.6.4.4   Third-party intervention

One of the features of ICJ proceedings which distinguishes them from inter-state arbitration is the possibility of the intervention by third parties in the dispute, which is provided for under arts 62 and 63 of the *ICJ Statute*. Under art 62, if a state considers that it has 'an interest of a legal nature which may be affected by the decision in the case, it may submit a request to the Court to be permitted to intervene', and the ICJ decides on the request. In accordance with the ICJ's practice concerning art 62, it is for the state seeking to intervene in the proceedings 'to identify the interest of a legal nature which it considers may be affected by the decision in the case, and to show in what way that interest may be affected'.[152] The state seeking to intervene only has to show 'that its interest "may" be affected, not that it will or must be affected'.[153] The ICJ has also confirmed that if the state seeking to intervene does not wish to become a party to the case, it can intervene as a 'non-party', with the result that it does not need to establish a basis of jurisdiction between it and the disputing parties.[154]

Article 63 provides for third-party intervention in another situation, namely where 'the construction of a convention to which states other than those concerned in the case are parties is in question'. Any other states are notified by the ICJ Registrar, and such states have the right to intervene in the proceedings, but if they exercise that right, any judgment will be binding on them. This right has been exercised relatively sparingly by states, although New Zealand intervened on the basis of art 63 in the *Whaling in the Antarctic* case between Australia and Japan.[155]

#### 9.6.4.5   Advisory jurisdiction

In addition to its contentious jurisdiction, the ICJ also has the power under art 65 of the *ICJ Statute* to issue advisory opinions 'on any legal question'. Article 96 of the *UN Charter* provides that the General Assembly and the Security Council are empowered to make such a request of the ICJ; also, '[o]ther organs of the United Nations and specialized agencies, which may at any time be so authorized by the General Assembly, may also request advisory opinions of the Court on legal questions arising within the scope of their activities'. The basis of the ICJ's jurisdiction to issue advisory opinions is found in art 65 of the *ICJ Statute*, and as such, it does

---

151    *Qatar v United Arab Emirates* (n 148) 92 [61]; *Documents and Data* (n 148) 154 [31]; *Georgia v Russian Federation (Provisional Measures)* (n 150) 396 [143].

152    *Jurisdictional Immunities of the State (Germany v Italy) (Order on Application by Hellenic Republic for Permission to Intervene)* [2011] ICJ Rep 494, 501 [22]. See also *Land, Island and Maritime Frontier Dispute (El Salvador v Honduras) (Application by Nicaragua for Permission to Intervene)* [1990] ICJ Rep 92, 117 [61].

153    *Jurisdictional Immunities of the State* (n 152) 501 [22]. See also *Land, Island and Maritime Frontier Dispute* (n 152) 117–18 [61].

154    *Jurisdictional Immunities of the State* (n 152) 501 [22]; *Sovereignty over Pulau Ligitan and Pulau Sipadan (Indonesia v Malaysia) (Application by the Philippines for Permission to Intervene)* [2001] ICJ Rep 575, 588 [35]; *Land, Island and Maritime Frontier Dispute* (n 152) 133–5 [96]–[101].

155    *Whaling in the Antarctic (Australia v Japan) (Judgment)* [2014] ICJ Rep 226.

not depend on the consent of states. As the Court explained in *Interpretation of Peace Treaties with Bulgaria, Hungary and Romania*:

> The consent of States, parties to a dispute, is the basis of the Court's jurisdiction in contentious cases. The situation is different in regard to advisory proceedings even where the Request for an Opinion relates to a legal question actually pending between States. The Court's reply is only of an advisory character: as such, it has no binding force. It follows that no State, whether a Member of the United Nations or not, can prevent the giving of an Advisory Opinion which the United Nations considers to be desirable in order to obtain enlightenment as to the course of action it should take.[156]

In its 2004 advisory opinion *Legal Consequences of the Construction of a Wall in the Occupied Palestinian Territory*,[157] the ICJ faced an objection to its jurisdiction to issue an advisory opinion – namely, that this was a political rather than a 'legal question'. The ICJ rejected this view, saying

> the fact that the legal question also has political aspects . . . 'does not suffice to deprive it of its character as a "legal question" and to "deprive the Court of a competence expressly conferred on it" . . .'[158]

Nor is it a bar to the ICJ issuing an advisory opinion that the issue is the subject of debate before the Security Council. In its advisory opinion on *Accordance with International Law of the Unilateral Declaration of Independence in respect of Kosovo*, the ICJ explained that

> the purpose of the advisory jurisdiction is to enable organs of the United Nations and other authorised bodies to obtain opinions from the Court which will assist them in the future exercise of their functions. The Court cannot determine what steps the General Assembly may wish to take after receiving the Court's opinion or what effect the opinion may have in relation to those steps . . . The fact that, hitherto, the declaration of independence has been discussed only in the Security Council and that the Council has been the organ which has taken action with regard to the situation in Kosovo does not constitute a compelling reason for the Court to refuse to respond to the request from the General Assembly.[159]

Where the ICJ is requested to give an advisory opinion, all states entitled to appear before the ICJ, as well as relevant international organisations, are notified by the ICJ and can make written and oral submissions.[160]

## 9.6.5   Judgments

Judgments of the ICJ are binding on the states parties to the dispute, which is confirmed by art 59 of the *ICJ Statute*, although the principle is expressed in the negative, being that '[t]he

---

156    *Interpretation of Peace Treaties with Bulgaria, Hungary and Romania* (n 4) 71.
157    *Legal Consequences of the Construction of a Wall in the Occupied Palestinian Territory (Advisory Opinion)* [2004] ICJ Rep 136.
158    Ibid 155 [41] (citations omitted).
159    *Accordance with International Law of the Unilateral Declaration of Independence in Respect of Kosovo (Advisory Opinion)* [2010] ICJ Rep 403, 420 [41].
160    *ICJ Statute* art 66.

decision of the Court has no binding force except between the parties and in respect of that particular case'. This confirms that there is no doctrine of precedent in the jurisprudence of the ICJ, although the Court strives to decide cases consistently.[161] Article 60 of the *ICJ Statute* provides that the ICJ's judgment is 'final and without appeal'. This is not to say there are no post-judgment procedures available; art 60 provides that if there is a dispute concerning the 'meaning or scope of the judgment', the ICJ can issue an interpretation. In addition, art 61 provides for a power of revision, which can be made 'upon the discovery of some fact of such a nature as to be a decisive factor, which fact was, when the judgment was given, unknown to the Court and also to the party claiming revision, always provided that such ignorance was not due to negligence'. Such an application must be made within six months of the discovery of the new fact, and no later than 10 years after the date of the judgment.[162]

Member states of the United Nations also have the obligation to comply with the ICJ's judgments under art 94 of the *UN Charter*, which states that they undertake 'to comply with the decision of the International Court of Justice in any case to which it is a party'.[163] If any member states do not comply with their obligations under an ICJ judgment, the other state party to the dispute 'may have recourse to the Security Council, which may, if it deems necessary, make recommendations or decide upon measures to be taken to give effect to the judgment'.[164]

## 9.6.6   Australia and the ICJ

Australia has a good record of participation in the work of the ICJ, and has demonstrated an interest in the ICJ's successful operation.[165] Australia is among the minority of states which have maintained an optional clause declaration accepting the ICJ's jurisdiction since 1975, and it also accepts the ICJ's jurisdiction through bilateral and multilateral treaties. Australia has been involved in several contentious proceedings before the ICJ, participating as the applicant or respondent state at different times. It was the applicant state in *Nuclear Tests*, which Australia brought against France,[166] and in *Whaling in the Antarctic*, against Japan.[167] Australia was the respondent state in *Certain Phosphate Lands in Nauru*, which was brought by Nauru; in the *East Timor* case, instituted by Portugal;[168] and in the *Documents and Data* case, brought by Timor-Leste. Australia has also has made submissions in a number of requests for advisory opinions.[169] It has demonstrated a commitment to the ICJ's role in the peaceful settlement of

---

161    See, eg, Chester Brown, 'Article 59' in Andreas Zimmermann et al (eds), *The Statute of the International Court of Justice: A Commentary* (Oxford University Press, 3rd ed, 2019) 1561.

162    *ICJ Statute* art 61.

163    *UN Charter* art 94(1).

164    Ibid art 94(2).

165    See, eg, Bill Campbell QC, 'Australia's Engagement with the International Court of Justice: Practical and Political Factors' (2021) 21(3) *Melbourne Journal of International Law* 596.

166    *Nuclear Tests* (n 2).

167    *Whaling in the Antarctic* (n 155).

168    *East Timor* (n 146) 102 [28].

169    For example, in *Legal Consequences of the Separation of the Chagos Archipelago from Mauritius in 1965 (Advisory Opinion)* [2019] ICJ Rep 95; *Legal Consequences of the Construction of a Wall in the Occupied Palestinian Territory* (n 157); *Legality of the Threat or Use of Nuclear Weapons (Advisory Opinion)* [1996] ICJ Rep 226: see Hilary Charlesworth and Margaret Young, 'Australian Encounters with the Advisory Jurisdiction of the International Court of Justice' (2021) 21(3) *Melbourne Journal of International Law* 698.

international disputes and three Australian nationals have been elected judges of the ICJ, as has been discussed above.

# 9.7   Role of the United Nations and regional organisations in the settlement of international disputes

The peaceful methods of settling international disputes which have been discussed in this chapter are chiefly those found in art 33(1) of the *UN Charter*. Article 33 is located within Chapter VI of the Charter, which contains a number of provisions which explain the functions of the United Nations' political organs in the peaceful settlement of international disputes. For instance, art 34 confers on the Security Council the ability to investigate any 'dispute, or situation which might lead to international friction or give rise to a dispute, in order to determine whether the dispute or situation is likely to endanger the maintenance of international peace and security'. Article 35(1) provides that any member of the United Nations can bring any 'dispute or situation referred to in article 34' to the attention of the General Assembly or Security Council. Under art 36, the Security Council may, 'at any stage of a dispute of the nature referred to in article 33 or of a situation of like nature', make recommendations to the parties with respect to 'appropriate procedures or methods of adjustment'. And under art 37, if the parties to a dispute 'of the nature referred to in article 33' fail to settle it by the means indicated in art 33, 'they shall refer it to the Security Council'.

Chapter VIII of the *UN Charter* addresses the role of regional organisations, which are also referred to in art 33. Article 52(1) provides that nothing in the Charter precludes 'the existence of regional arrangements or agencies for dealing with such matters relating to the maintenance of international peace and security as are appropriate for regional action'. Article 52(2) provides that member states of the United Nations that enter into such regional organisations are to 'make every effort to achieve pacific settlement of local disputes through such regional arrangements or by such regional agencies before referring them to the Security Council'. The Security Council is also able to make use of regional organisations for any enforcement action, which is action taken under Chapter VII of the *UN Charter* such as the imposition of sanctions or the use of force.[170]

## DISCUSSION QUESTIONS

(1)   Why is the jurisdiction of the International Court of Justice ('ICJ') optional?

(2)   How can international law be enforced if the ICJ does not have compulsory jurisdiction?

(3)   What are the advantages of choosing international arbitration over the ICJ?

(4)   What is the role of the UN Secretary-General in the peaceful settlement of international disputes?

(5)   Can the ICJ review decisions of the United Nation's political organs?

---

170   *UN Charter* art 53.

# 10

# INTERNATIONAL HUMAN RIGHTS LAW

Irene Baghoomians and
Jacqueline Mowbray

# 10.1   Introduction

International human rights law ('IHRL') provides minimum standards which states must observe in their treatment of individuals under their jurisdiction. In this respect, it differs from many other areas of international law which focus on regulating international relations between states. The human rights recognised in international instruments are considered to be fundamental rights which all human beings are entitled to enjoy, regardless of their personal circumstances or the state in which they reside.

## 10.1.1   Histories of international human rights law

Contemporary IHRL is generally considered to have its foundations in the *Charter of the United Nations* ('*UN Charter*') of 1945 and the *Universal Declaration of Human Rights* ('*UDHR*')[1] of 1948. Against the background of World War II and the Holocaust, the United Nations sought to prevent future atrocities through an international system for the protection of human rights. The *UN Charter* proclaims the importance of 'fundamental human rights'[2] and the Declaration sets out a list of the rights to which individuals are entitled. These sources established a principle that was (and remains) 'radical'[3] for international law: that states have international obligations to guarantee certain rights to individuals.

Other histories of human rights start much earlier, noting how ideas of human dignity and fundamental rights can be found in religious thought going back many centuries, and in ancient legal texts.[4] These histories generally present a linear progress narrative, in which developments in thought and legal practice over time led to the evolution of IHRL.[5] Key elements in this narrative include the adoption of the Magna Carta in 1215, the English *Bill of Rights* in 1689, the French *Declaration of the Rights of Man and of the Citizen* of 1789, and the US *Constitution* and Bill of Rights in 1791.[6] These histories also identify developments in legal thought which enabled these events, particularly the role of Enlightenment thinkers – such as Thomas Hobbes, John Locke and Jean-Jacques Rousseau – in developing the idea that individuals have natural rights which it is the role of the state to protect.[7] More recently, other scholars have located the origins of IHRL in one particular event or period in history,[8] such as the movement to abolish slavery;[9] British responses to humanitarian crises in the late 19th century;[10] or (more recently and

---

1    *Universal Declaration of Human Rights*, GA Res 217A (III), UN GAOR, UN Doc A/810 (10 December 1948) ('*UDHR*').

2    *Charter of the United Nations* Preamble. See also arts 1, 13, 55, 56, 62(2), 68, 76.

3    Hilary Charlesworth, 'Universal Declaration of Human Rights' in Rüdiger Wolfrum (ed), *The Max Planck Encyclopedia of Public International Law* (online, February 2008) [10].

4    Ed Bates, 'History' in Daniel Moeckli, Sangeeta Shah and Sandesh Sivakumaran (eds), *International Human Rights Law* (Oxford University Press, 2010) 17, 18.

5    Philip Alston, 'Does the Past Matter? On the Origins of Human Rights' (2013) 126(7) *Harvard Law Review* 2043, 2063–4.

6    Ibid.

7    Bates (n 4) 19–20.

8    Alston (n 5) 2064.

9    Jenny S Martinez, *The Slave Trade and the Origins of International Human Rights Law* (Oxford University Press, 2012).

10    Gary J Bass, *Freedom's Battle: The Origins of Humanitarian Intervention* (Alfred A Knopf, 2008).

controversially) the emergence of the international human rights movement in the 1970s, led by non-governmental organisations ('NGOs') such as Amnesty International.[11]

Ultimately, there is no single history of international human rights. Each of the narratives above identifies different precursors to the modern system. At the same time, these histories may not capture the full range of antecedents: most focus on developments in Europe and North America. As discussed later in this chapter, this has given rise to claims that international human rights are ultimately Western constructs which do not reflect other cultures or traditions of thought.

With these arguments in mind, this chapter provides an overview of the contemporary legal architecture for the international protection of human rights. It describes the rules of international law relating to human rights, as well as the international institutions responsible for overseeing the implementation and enforcement of those rules. It considers this framework at the universal (or global) and regional levels, as well as the implementation of IHRL within domestic legal systems – particularly in Australia.

# 10.2   Substantive content of international human rights law

## 10.2.1   The major international human rights instruments

The content of contemporary IHRL is primarily found in treaties and other instruments, both international and regional, starting with the *UDHR*.

### 10.2.1.1   The *Universal Declaration of Human Rights*

The *UDHR* was adopted by the UN General Assembly in December 1948. Australia played a unique role in its drafting and adoption: it was one of only eight states involved in the drafting[12] and the Declaration was adopted at the time that HV Evatt – Foreign Minister, Attorney-General and head of Australia's delegation to the United Nations – was elected President of the General Assembly.[13] Though only a General Assembly resolution, and therefore not legally binding in itself, the resolution has been hugely influential and many of its provisions have been adopted in later treaties or are considered customary law.[14]

The Declaration consists of 30 articles establishing rights to which all human beings are entitled. These include what many would consider 'traditional' rights, such as rights to life and

---

11   Samuel Moyn, *The Last Utopia: Human Rights in History* (Harvard University Press, 2010); Naomi Klein, *The Shock Doctrine: The Rise of Disaster Capitalism* (Penguin, 2007) 118–28.

12   See 'Drafters of the Declaration', *United Nations* (Web Page) <www.un.org/en/about-us/udhr/drafters-of-the-declaration>.

13   Michael Kirby, 'Herbert Vere Evatt, the United Nations and the Universal Declaration of Human Rights after 60 Years' (2009) 34(2) *University of Western Australia Law Review* 238.

14   Charlesworth, 'Universal Declaration of Human Rights' (n 3) [14]–[16]; Hurst Hannum, 'The Status of the Universal Declaration in National and International Law' (1995) 25(2) *Georgia Journal of International and Comparative Law* 287.

liberty,[15] as well as others that may be considered more progressive, such as rights to education,[16] social security[17] and 'leisure'.[18]

### 10.2.1.2 The *ICCPR* and the *ICESCR*

On adopting the *UDHR*, the General Assembly asked the UN Commission on Human Rights to draft a binding treaty protecting the rights in the Declaration. However, the drafting process, affected by political tensions of the Cold War, revealed different approaches to different groups of rights.[19] Civil and political rights – such as rights to life, privacy and freedom of expression – are largely freedoms from state interference. Economic, social and cultural rights – such as rights to health, education and work – generally require states to take positive action to realise them. The United Kingdom initially proposed that the treaty include only civil and political rights; socialist states and others objected.[20] The final compromise was to draft two separate treaties, with as many common provisions as possible: the *International Covenant on Civil and Political Rights* ('*ICCPR*')[21] and the *International Covenant on Economic, Social and Cultural Rights* ('*ICESCR*').[22] Taken together with the *UDHR*, these treaties make up what is known as the 'International Bill of Human Rights'.

The *ICCPR* and the *ICESCR* were opened for signature in 1966 but did not enter into force until 1976. These two Covenants set out most of the rights contained in the *UDHR* in greater detail[23] and elaborate on the nature of state obligations, including when the rights can be limited or derogated from. There is an important difference between the two Covenants in terms of the actions required of states. Article 2 of the *ICCPR* obliges states parties to 'respect and ensure' *ICCPR* rights, whereas art 2 of the *ICESCR* obliges a state only to 'take steps . . . to the maximum of its available resources, with a view to achieving progressively the full realization' of *ICESCR* rights. Although the *ICESCR* imposes some immediate obligations on states, such as to ensure that rights are realised on a non-discriminatory basis,[24] the obligation of 'progressive realisation' foresees the realisation of rights over time rather than immediately.

Australia ratified the *ICESCR* in 1975 and the *ICCPR* in 1980. It has also ratified the two Optional Protocols to the *ICCPR*, the first providing for an individual complaints mechanism

---

15    *UDHR* (n 1) art 3.
16    Ibid art 26.
17    Ibid art 22.
18    Ibid art 24.
19    See Maya Hertig Randall, 'The History of the Covenants: Looking Back Half a Century and Beyond' in Daniel Moeckli, Helen Keller and Corina Heri (eds), *The Human Rights Covenants at 50: Their Past, Present, and Future* (Oxford University Press, 2018) 7, 10–17.
20    Ibid.
21    *International Covenant on Civil and Political Rights*, New York, 16 December 1966, 993 UNTS 3 (entered into force 24 March 1976) ('*ICCPR*').
22    *International Covenant on Economic, Social and Cultural Rights*, New York, 19 December 1966, 999 UNTS 171) (entered into force 3 January 1976) ('*ICESCR*').
23    With some exceptions, including the right to property (*UDHR* (n 1) art 17) which was not included in the *ICCPR*.
24    *ICESCR* (n 22) art 2(2). See also Committee on Economic, Social and Cultural Rights, *General Comment No 3: The Nature of States Parties' Obligations*, UN Doc E/1991/23 (14 December 1990).

(see Section 10.3.1.2) and the second concerning abolition of the death penalty. As at February 2023, Australia was not a party to the Optional Protocol to the *ICESCR*, which provides for an individual complaints mechanism for violations of rights under that Covenant.

### 10.2.1.3   Other international human rights instruments

While the *ICCPR* and the *ICESCR* are the two primary IHRL treaties, several more specialised treaties offer further protection for particular groups or with respect to particular situations. Treaties dealing with the rights of particular groups include the *International Convention on the Elimination of All Forms of Racial Discrimination* ('*CERD*'),[25] the *Convention on the Elimination of All Forms of Discrimination against Women* ('*CEDAW*'),[26] the *Convention on the Rights of the Child* ('*CRC*'),[27] the *International Convention on the Protection of the Rights of All Migrant Workers and Members of Their Families* ('*CMW*')[28] and the *Convention on the Rights of Persons with Disabilities* ('*CRPD*').[29] Treaties addressing particular human rights concerns include the *Convention against Torture and Other Cruel, Inhuman or Degrading Treatment or Punishment* ('*CAT*')[30] and the *International Convention for the Protection of All Persons from Enforced Disappearance* ('*CED*').[31] Australia is party to all the core human rights treaties, with the exception of the *CMW* and the *CED*.

In addition to these nine core treaties,[32] several other treaties have human rights implications. These include the *Convention Relating to the Status of Refugees* ('*Refugee Convention*')[33] (discussed in Section 10.2.1.4) and the *Convention on the Prevention and Punishment of the Crime of Genocide*.[34] The numerous treaties concluded under the auspices of the International Labour Organization protect labour rights, but also extend to protect human rights more generally. The Organization's 1989 *Convention concerning Indigenous and Tribal Peoples in Independent Countries*[35] remains the only binding treaty specifically addressing the human rights of Indigenous peoples. Other fields of international law, such as international

---

25   *International Convention on the Elimination of All Forms of Racial Discrimination*, opened for signature 21 December 1965, 660 UNTS 195 (entered into force 4 January 1969) ('*CERD*').

26   *Convention on the Elimination of All Forms of Discrimination against Women*, opened for signature 18 December 1979, 1249 UNTS 13 (entered into force 3 September 1981 ('*CEDAW*').

27   *Convention on the Rights of the Child*, opened for signature 20 November 1989, 1577 UNTS 3 (entered into force 2 September 1990) ('*CRC*').

28   *International Convention on the Protection of the Rights of All Migrant Workers and Members of Their Families*, opened for signature 18 December 1990, 2220 UNTS 3 (entered into force 1 July 2003) ('*CMW*').

29   *Convention on the Rights of Persons with Disabilities*, opened for signature 13 December 2006, 2515 UNTS 3 (entered into force 3 May 2008) ('*CRPD*').

30   *Convention against Torture and Other Cruel, Inhuman or Degrading Treatment or Punishment*, opened for signature 10 December 1984, 1465 UNTS 85 (entered into force 26 June 1987) ('*CAT*').

31   *International Convention for the Protection of All Persons from Enforced Disappearance*, opened for signature 20 December 2006, 2716 UNTS 3 (entered into force 23 December 2010) ('*CED*').

32   *ICCPR* (n 21), *ICESCR* (n 22), *CERD* (n 25), *CEDAW* (n 26), *CRC* (n 27), *CMW* (n 28), *CRPD* (n 29), *CAT* (n 30), *CED* (n 31).

33   *Convention Relating to the Status of Refugees*, opened for signature 28 July 1951, 189 UNTS 137 (entered into force 22 April 1954) ('*Refugee Convention*').

34   *Convention on the Prevention and Punishment of the Crime of Genocide*, opened for signature 9 December 1948, 78 UNTS 277 (entered into force 12 January 1951).

35   *Convention concerning Indigenous and Tribal Peoples in Independent Countries (No 169)*, opened for signature 27 June 1989, 1650 UNTS 383 (entered into force 5 September 1991).

humanitarian law (see Chapter 11) and international criminal law (see Chapter 12), are also relevant to protecting human rights and suppressing serious violations of them such as war crimes and crimes against humanity.

Other IHRL instruments do not take the form of binding treaties but are nonetheless influential and may reflect customary international law. Most notable of these is the *UDHR*. Other important General Assembly resolutions concerning human rights include the *Declaration on the Right to Development*[36] and the *Declaration on the Rights of Indigenous Peoples*.[37]

### 10.2.1.4   International refugee law

International refugee law is an important complementary source of human rights for refugees and asylum seekers. Under the *Refugee Convention*, modified by the 1967 *Protocol Relating to the Status of Refugees*,[38] states have obligations in relation to their treatment of refugees – that is, individuals who cannot return to their own country 'owing to a well-founded fear of being persecuted for reasons of race, religion, nationality, membership of a particular social group or political opinion'.[39]

In addition to granting refugees extensive rights – civil and political, as well as economic, social and cultural – the *Refugee Convention* prohibits states from returning 'a refugee in any manner whatsoever to the frontiers of territories where his life or freedom would be threatened'.[40] This obligation of *non-refoulement* complements the right to 'seek and enjoy' freedom from persecution under art 14 of the *UDHR*, giving rise to a right to seek asylum under international law.[41]

International human rights law extends the obligation of *non-refoulement* beyond persecution to address situations where a person would be subject to other serious human rights violations, such as torture or arbitrary deprivation of life.[42] In this way, the provisions of international refugee law and IHRL work together to provide a comprehensive scheme of rights protection for asylum seekers. Australia has implemented elements of international refugee law in domestic law but has controversially excluded other aspects.

### 10.2.1.5   Regional human rights treaties

In addition to the universal or global IHRL treaties, there are several regional treaties. The earliest regional instrument was the *American Declaration of the Rights and Duties of Man*, adopted at the International Conference of American States in 1948.[43] This Declaration

---

36   *Declaration on the Right to Development*, GA Res 41/128, UN Doc A/RES/41/128 (adopted 4 December 1986).
37   *Declaration on the Rights of Indigenous Peoples*, GA Res 61/295, UN Doc A/RES/61/295 (2 October 2007, adopted 13 September 2007).
38   *Protocol Relating to the Status of Refugees*, opened for signature 31 January 1967, 606 UNTS 267 (entered into force 4 October 1967).
39   *Refugee Convention* (n 33) art 1A(2).
40   Ibid art 33(1).
41   See Daniel Ghezelbash and Nikolas Feith Tan, 'The End of the Right to Seek Asylum? COVID-19 and the Future of Refugee Protection' (2020) 32(4) *International Journal of Refugee Law* 668, 669–70.
42   See *CAT* (n 30) art 3(1), (2).
43   Ninth International Conference of American States, *Final Act* (adopted 2 May 1948) resolution XXX.

predated the *UDHR* and can thus be considered the world's first IHRL instrument. It is not formally binding. However, it was followed in 1969 by the binding *American Convention on Human Rights*,[44] which entered into force in 1978. While the Convention itself focuses on civil and political rights, the San Salvador Protocol,[45] which entered into force in 1999, is dedicated to economic, social and cultural rights. More than 20 states within the Organization of American States ('OAS') are parties to the Convention.

Within Europe, the *Convention for the Protection of Human Rights and Fundamental Freedoms*,[46] developed under the auspices of the Council of Europe, entered into force in 1953. More than 45 European states are now parties. The Convention primarily includes civil and political rights, although the right to education was included in Protocol 1 to the Convention.[47] The *European Social Charter*,[48] which entered into force in 1965, and the Revised Social Charter,[49] which entered into force in 1999, deal more comprehensively with economic and social rights.

The *African Charter on Human and Peoples' Rights* ('*African Charter*')[50] was adopted in 1981 under the auspices of the Organization of African Unity (now the African Union). More than 50 African Union member states are parties to the Charter, which recognises civil and political rights, as well as economic, social and cultural rights. The Charter differs from earlier international and regional instruments in explicitly recognising the rights not only of individuals but also of 'peoples',[51] and in providing for duties of the individual to society.[52]

The *Arab Charter on Human Rights*[53] was adopted by the Council of the League of Arab States in 2004 and has more than 20 states parties. The Charter recognises civil and political rights, as well as economic, social and cultural rights, but has been criticised as falling short of international standards.[54]

The regions of Asia and Oceania do not have a binding human rights treaty. However, the Association of Southeast Asian Nations ('ASEAN') adopted the *ASEAN Human Rights Declaration* in 2012.[55] This Declaration and the issue of regional protection of human rights within Asia are discussed in Section 10.3.2.1.

---

44    *American Convention on Human Rights*, 22 November 1969, 1144 UNTS 123 (entered into force 18 July 1978) ('*ACHR*').

45    *Additional Protocol to the American Convention on Human Rights in the Area of Economic, Social and Cultural Rights*, opened for signature 17 November 1988, OAS 69 (entered into force 16 November 1999).

46    *Convention for the Protection of Human Rights and Fundamental Freedoms*, opened for signature 4 November 1950, 213 UNTS 221 (entered into force 3 September 1953).

47    *Protocol to the Convention for the Protection of Human Rights and Fundamental Freedoms*, opened for signature 20 March 1952, 213 UNTS 262 (entered into force 18 May 1954) art 2.

48    *European Social Charter*, opened for signature 18 October 1961, 529 UNTS 89 (entered into force 26 February 1965).

49    *European Social Charter (Revised)*, opened for signature 3 May 1996, 2151 UNTS 277 (entered into force 1 July 1999).

50    *African Charter on Human and Peoples' Rights*, opened for signature 27 June 1981, 1520 UNTS 217 (entered into force 21 October 1986) ('*African Charter*').

51    Ibid arts 19–24.

52    Ibid arts 27–29.

53    *Arab Charter on Human Rights*, opened for signature 22 May 2004 (entered into force 15 March 2008) reproduced in (1997) 18 *Human Rights Law Journal* 151.

54    Mervat Rishmawi, 'The Arab Charter on Human Rights and the League of Arab States: An Update' (2010) 10(1) *Human Rights Law Review* 169, 170–2.

55    Twenty-First ASEAN Summit, *ASEAN Human Rights Declaration* (adopted 18 November 2012).

## 10.2.2   Overview of rights and obligations

### 10.2.2.1   Who has obligations under international human rights law?

States are the primary duty-bearers under IHRL. With very few exceptions,[56] only states are parties to the international human rights treaties, so only states have direct obligations under those treaties. States are also the primary subjects of customary international law obligations. But, more recently, there has been discussion of the human rights obligations of other entities, including non-state armed groups,[57] international intergovernmental organisations,[58] and international and transnational corporations.[59] For the most part, however, these entities are only *indirectly* made accountable under IHRL, as a result of obligations imposed on the state to prevent such entities from violating human rights.[60] In addition there are 'soft law' initiatives, such as the UN *Guiding Principles on Business and Human Rights* of 2011, and a Human Rights Council initiative since 2014 to negotiate a treaty on corporations and human rights.

### 10.2.2.2   Who has rights under international human rights law?

Generally, only individuals have rights under IHRL.[61] As a result, corporations and other entities do not have rights under IHRL, although European regional human rights law has recognised them as having standing to make claims on their own behalf concerning violations of certain rights.[62] International law does, however, recognise some group rights, such as the right to self-determination[63] and the more expansive 'peoples' rights' under the *African Charter*.[64]

### 10.2.2.3   Jurisdictional scope

Each state is obliged to guarantee international human rights to 'all individuals within its territory and subject to its jurisdiction'.[65] It is therefore clear that states owe obligations to all individuals currently within their territories.

The question of extraterritorial jurisdiction is more complex. However, jurisprudence recognises that states owe extraterritorial human rights obligations where they exercise 'effective control' outside their own territory, as in situations of occupation or with respect to military operations,[66] or through physical custody of an individual. Thus, the Inter-American

---

56   For example, the European Union (an international organisation) is a party to the *CRPD* (n 29).

57   See Andrew Clapham, *Human Rights Obligations of Non-State Actors* (Oxford University Press, 2006) ch. 7.

58   See Olivier De Schutter, 'Human Rights and the Rise of International Organisations' in Jan Wouters and Eva Brems (eds), *Accountability for Human Rights Violations by International Organizations* (Intersentia, 2011).

59   See, eg, Denis Arnold, 'Corporations and Human Rights Obligations' (2016) 1(2) *Business and Human Rights Journal* 255.

60   For exceptions, see, eg, Sarah Joseph, *Corporations and Transnational Human Rights Litigation* (Hart, 2004) 48–9.

61   See, eg, *ICCPR* (n 21) art 2(1) ('all individuals'); *ACHR* (n 44) art 1(2) ('every human being').

62   See, eg, *Sunday Times v United Kingdom* (1980) EHRR 317, concerning the right to freedom of expression.

63   *ICCPR* (n 21) art 1; *ICESCR* (n 22) art 1.

64   *African Charter* (n 50) arts 19–24.

65   *ICCPR* (n 21) art 2(1).

66   See *Legal Consequences of the Construction of a Wall in the Occupied Palestinian Territory (Advisory Opinion)* [2004] ICJ Rep 136; *Al-Skeini v United Kingdom* (2011) 53 EHRR 18.

Commission on Human Rights found admissible a complaint against the United States concerning the apprehension of an alleged Taliban fighter in Pakistan and his treatment at a US base in Afghanistan and then in Guantánamo Bay, Cuba:

> Regarding the extraterritorial application of the *American Declaration [of the Rights and Duties of Man]*, the [Inter-American Commission on Human Rights] has held that even though a State's duty to protect the rights of any person is based on its territory, that duty may, under given circumstances, refer to conduct with an extraterritorial locus where the person concerned is present in the territory of one State, but subject to the control of another State, usually through the acts of the latter's agents abroad. In these cases, the inquiry turns on whether the alleged victim was subject to the authority and control of the acting State.
>
> In regard to the apprehension of Mr Ameziane, the [Commission] observes that those actions implied an exercise of physical power and control over the person in question performed by agents of the United States ... [who,] even though operating outside its territory, brought Mr Ameziane under US jurisdiction when taking him into their custody.[67]

It is also increasingly argued that states have extraterritorial human rights obligations where acts taken within their territory have foreseeable consequences outside their territory.[68]

### 10.2.2.4    Nature of obligations: respect, protect, fulfil

International human rights law imposes three types of obligations on states: to respect, protect and fulfil human rights.[69] The obligation to *respect* requires states to refrain from taking measures which would limit enjoyment of a right. So, for example, states should not ban public demonstrations as this would be contrary to their obligation to respect freedom of assembly. The obligation to *protect* requires states to take measures to prevent third parties from violating human rights. Thus, states should ensure, through regulation, that employers provide fair wages and safe working conditions for their employees, to protect the right to just and favourable conditions of work. The obligation to *fulfil* requires the state to take positive measures to ensure that individuals enjoy the right in question, including by fulfilling the right directly if necessary. States are therefore required to provide, for example, a public education system to ensure that individuals realise their right to education.

### 10.2.2.5    Derogations and limitations

Most human rights can be restricted under particular circumstances. First, some human rights treaties, such as the *ICCPR*, allow states to derogate from their human rights obligations in

---

67    *Ameziane v United States* (Inter-American Commission on Human Rights, Merits Report 29/20, 22 April 2020) [30]–[31].

68    See, eg, *State Obligations in Relation to the Environment in the Context of the Protection and Guarantee of the Rights to Life and to Personal Integrity (Advisory Opinion)* (Inter-American Court of Human Rights, Series A No 23, 15 November 2017) [95]. See also *Maastricht Principles on Extraterritorial Obligations of States in the Area of Economic, Social and Cultural Rights* (28 September 2011) principle 9(b).

69    See, eg, Committee on Economic, Social and Cultural Rights, *General Comment No 13: The Right to Education*, UN Doc E/C.12/1999/10 (8 December 1990) [46].

times of emergency.[70] States must officially inform other parties to the *ICCPR* that they are derogating from their obligations,[71] and only derogations which are strictly necessary, proportionate, and applied in a non-discriminatory manner are permissible.[72] Further, some rights, such as the right to life and the right not to be subject to torture, can never be derogated from.[73] These are known as 'non-derogable rights'.

Secondly, it is generally possible to limit rights in particular cases. Some rights – including the rights not to be subject to torture, slavery and retrospective criminal laws – can never be limited.[74] These rights are known as 'absolute rights'. All other rights may be limited provided that certain standards are met. Some rights have express limitation clauses setting out when they may be limited;[75] others have implied limitations;[76] and some treaties contain a general limitation clause.[77] In general, any limitation must meet three requirements: it must be prescribed by law; it must pursue a legitimate aim – that is, it must respond to a 'pressing social need';[78] and it must be necessary and proportionate, in that there are no less restrictive ways of achieving the legitimate aim and the burden imposed on individuals' rights is proportionate to the benefit of achieving the aim. So, for example, in the case of *Big Brother Watch v United Kingdom*,[79] discussed further in Section 10.3.2, the European Court of Human Rights found that the limitation on the right to privacy imposed by mass electronic surveillance of individuals pursued the legitimate aim of protecting national security, but the lack of safeguards to protect individuals' rights in the regulatory scheme authorising such surveillance meant that the limitation could not be said to be 'prescribed by law', necessary and proportionate.

### 10.2.2.6   Reservations to human rights treaties?

As discussed in Chapter 3, states may enter reservations to treaties to 'exclude or modify the legal effect of certain provisions of the treaty in their application to that state',[80] unless the treaty prohibits such a reservation or the reservation is incompatible with the 'object and purpose' of the treaty.[81] Very few human rights treaties specifically exclude reservations and hundreds of reservations have been made.[82] Australia, for example, entered a reservation to art 4(a) of the *CERD*, indicating that it was not, at the time of ratification, able to comply with

---

70    *ICCPR* (n 21) art 4.
71    Ibid art 4(3).
72    Ibid art 4(1).
73    Ibid art 4(2).
74    Ibid arts 7, 8, 11, 15(1), 16.
75    See, eg, ibid art 18(3).
76    See, eg, ibid art 17.
77    See, eg, *ICESCR* (n 22) art 4.
78    *Handyside v United Kingdom* (1979–80) 1 EHRR 737 [48] (European Court of Human Rights).
79    *Big Brother Watch v United Kingdom* (European Court of Human Rights, Grand Chamber, Application No 58170/13, 25 May 2021).
80    *Vienna Convention on the Law of Treaties*, opened for signature 23 May 1969, 1155 UNTS 331 (entered into force 27 January 1980) art 2.
81    Ibid art 19.
82    Regarding the *ICCPR*, see Human Rights Committee, *General Comment No 24: Issues Relating to Reservations Made upon Ratification or Accession to the Covenant or the Optional Protocols thereto, or in Relation to Declarations under Article 41 of the Covenant*, UN Doc CCPR/C/21/Rev.1/Add.6 (4 November 1994) [1] ('*General Comment 24*').

the requirement to criminalise 'all dissemination of ideas based on racial superiority or hatred and incitement to racial discrimination'.[83]

Scholars and international bodies have raised concerns about whether reservations can ever be compatible with the 'object and purpose' of human rights treaties. Jurisprudence from regional human rights courts, and *General Comment No 24* of the UN Human Rights Committee,[84] indicate that many reservations to human rights treaties will be considered impermissible.[85] Many states, however, contest this approach.[86]

### 10.2.2.7  Generations of rights?

Human rights are sometimes classified as belonging to different 'generations', suggesting their chronological sequence and/or a hierarchy of normative precedence. This draws on Karel Vasak's description of three 'generations' of rights,[87] the first being civil and political rights and the second being economic, social and cultural rights. The term 'third generation' is used to describe new categories of rights, which Vasak describes as 'solidarity' or collective rights, including the right to development, minority rights, the right to a healthy environment, and the right to peace. This idea of generations of rights has been much criticised.[88] In 1993, the World Conference on Human Rights in Vienna declared that '[a]ll human rights are universal, indivisible and interdependent and interrelated'.[89] Nonetheless, the terminology remains pervasive.

# 10.3    The institutional framework: international human rights bodies

## 10.3.1    International bodies

The Office of the High Commissioner for Human Rights, established by the General Assembly in 1993,[90] has overall responsibility for human rights within the UN system and provides advice and support to all UN bodies. Human rights are relevant to the work of most UN bodies,[91]

---

83    *CERD* (n 25) art 4(a). This was because there was, at that point, no framework for such legislation. The reservation indicated that '[i]t is the intention of the Australian Government, at the first suitable moment, to seek from Parliament legislation specifically implementing the terms of article 4(a)', but, at the time of writing, no such legislation has been successfully passed by the Parliament and the reservation has never been withdrawn.

84    *General Comment 24*, UN Doc CCPR/C/21/Rev.1/Add.6 (n 82).

85    See, eg, *Loizidou v Turkey* (1997) 23 EHRR 513; *Belilos v Switzerland* (1988) 88 ILR 635.

86    See the observations of the United States and the United Kingdom in relation to *General Comment 24* in Human Rights Committee, *Nineteenth Annual Report*, UN Doc A/50/40 (3 October 1995) annex VI.

87    Karel Vasak, 'A 30 Year Struggle', *UNESCO Courier* (November 1977) 29.

88    See, eg, Patrick Macklem, 'Human Rights in International Law: Three Generations or One?' (2015) 3(1) *London Review of International Law* 63.

89    World Conference on Human Rights, *Vienna Declaration and Programme of Action*, UN Doc A/CONF.157/23 (12 July 1993, adopted 25 June 1993) art 5.

90    *High Commissioner for the Promotion and Protection of All Human Rights*, GA Res 48/141, UN Doc A/RES/48/141 (7 January 1994, adopted 20 December 1993).

91    See generally António Guterres, UN Secretary-General, *The Highest Aspiration: A Call to Action for Human Rights* (24 February 2020).

including the General Assembly[92] and the Security Council,[93] as well as many specialised bodies, such as the International Labour Organization, the UN Educational, Scientific and Cultural Organization ('UNESCO'), the UN Development Programme, the UN Children's Fund, the UN Permanent Forum on Indigenous Issues, and UN peacekeeping operations. However, the main UN bodies responsible for monitoring and implementing IHRL are the Human Rights Council and the treaty bodies established under the main human rights treaties.

## 10.3.1.1   Human Rights Council

The Human Rights Council was established in 2006 as a subsidiary body of the General Assembly.[94] It replaced the much-criticised UN Commission on Human Rights, which had been created by the Economic and Social Council in 1946.[95] The Council comprises 47 UN member states, elected by the General Assembly. It is 'responsible for promoting universal respect for the protection of all human rights and fundamental freedoms'.[96]

The Human Rights Council carries out its mandate through a variety of working mechanisms,[97] including regular sessions; special sessions to examine particular human rights situations; commissions of inquiry and fact-finding missions; consideration of individual complaints under a confidential procedure; and subsidiary mechanisms, such as the Social Forum, Forum on Minority Issues, and Expert Mechanism on the Rights of Indigenous Peoples. Arguably, however, the two most significant mechanisms from the perspective of IHRL are the 'universal periodic review' process and the 'special procedures'.

### UNIVERSAL PERIODIC REVIEW

The universal periodic review ('UPR') process, the main innovation of the Human Rights Council, involves all states being regularly peer-reviewed.[98] States report periodically, approximately every five years, on their human rights performance, which is then subject to review. The review is conducted by the UPR Working Group, which consists of the 47 members of the Council, but any state can take part in the discussion and issue recommendations to the state under review, to which that state must respond. The review is conducted on the basis of the report provided by the state, as well as reports of UN bodies and submissions from other stakeholders, such as civil society organisations. The process reviews the extent to which states fulfil all human rights, not only those contained in treaties to which the state is a party. The process aims to constructively influence state behaviour in order to improve conformity with IHRL.

Australia submitted its most recent UPR report in December 2020. In January 2021, the review, including 'interactive dialogue' with 122 states,[99] was held and the Working Group

---

92    See *Charter of the United Nations* art 13.
93    Bardo Fassbender (ed), *Securing Human Rights? Achievements and Challenges of the UN Security Council* (Oxford University Press, 2011).
94    *Human Rights Council*, GA Res 60/251, UN Doc A/RES/60/251 (3 April 2006) ('*Resolution 60/251*').
95    See Nazila Ghanea, 'From UN Commission on Human Rights to UN Human Rights Council' (2006) 55 *International and Comparative Law Quarterly* 695.
96    *Resolution 60/251*, UN Doc A/RES/60/251 (n 94) para 2.
97    See generally Human Rights Council, *Institution-Building of the United Nations Human Rights Council*, HRC Res 5/1, UN Doc A/HRC/RES/5/1 (18 June 2007).
98    Ibid annex ('*United Nations Human Rights Council: Institution Building*') paras 1–38.
99    *Human Rights Council, Report of the Working Group on the Universal Periodic Review: Australia*, UN Doc A/HRC/47/8 (24 March 2021) [9].

adopted its report. Australia received 344 recommendations, including that it ratify human rights treaties to which it is not yet a party;[100] raise the minimum age of criminal responsibility from 10 to at least 14 years;[101] protect freedom of expression for journalists and whistle-blowers;[102] address discrimination against persons with disabilities;[103] address the disadvantage faced by Indigenous peoples;[104] and protect the rights of migrants, refugees and asylum seekers,[105] including by ending mandatory detention and offshore processing.[106] In its response, Australia accepted a large number of these recommendations, although it rejected some – such as to implement the UN *Declaration on the Rights of Indigenous Peoples*,[107] and to review policies of mandatory detention and offshore processing of asylum seekers.[108] Australia also made five voluntary human rights commitments, including to hold 'a referendum to recognize Aboriginal and Torres Strait Islanders in the Constitution', which the Government will support 'when it has the best chance of succeeding'.[109]

## SPECIAL PROCEDURES

The system of 'special procedures' is made up of independent human rights experts – Special Rapporteurs, Independent Experts, or Working Groups – who hold mandates to report to the Human Rights Council on human rights issues. There are currently more than 10 special procedures focused on particular countries and more than 40 focused on particular human rights themes (such as trafficking in persons, the right to food, or the rights of particular groups such as migrants). The special procedures contribute to the monitoring of IHRL in a number of ways. Mandate holders 'undertake country visits; act on individual cases and concerns of a broader, structural nature … conduct thematic studies and convene expert consultations; contribute to the development of international human rights standards; engage in advocacy; raise public awareness; and provide advice for technical cooperation'.[110]

Australia has issued a standing invitation to all thematic special procedures.[111] Between 2016 and mid-2022, for example, Australia was visited by the Special Rapporteurs on the rights of Indigenous peoples;[112] contemporary forms of racism;[113] and the human rights of

---

100    Ibid [146.1]–[146.37].

101    Ibid [146.140]–[146.169].

102    Ibid [146.175]–[146.180].

103    Ibid [146.236]–[146.252].

104    Ibid [146.253]–[146.291].

105    Ibid [146.292]–[146.340].

106    Ibid [146.325], [146.326], [146.328], [146.336].

107    *Human Rights Council, Report of the Working Group on the Universal Periodic Review: Australia: Addendum: Views on Conclusions and/or Recommendations, Voluntary Commitments and Replies Presented by the State under Review*, UN Doc A/HRC/47/8/Add.1 (2 June 2021) [19].

108    Ibid [51].

109    *Human Rights Council, Report of the Working Group* (n 99) [158].

110    'Special Procedures', *Human Rights Council* (Web Page) <www.ohchr.org/en/hr-bodies/hrc/special-procedures>.

111    See 'Standing Invitations', *Office of the High Commissioner for Human Rights* (Web Page) <https://spinternet.ohchr.org/StandingInvitations.aspx>.

112    See *Human Rights Council, Report of the Special Rapporteur on the Rights of Indigenous Peoples on Her Visit to Australia*, UN Doc A/HRC/36/46/Add.2 (8 August 2017).

113    See *Human Rights Council, Report of the Special Rapporteur on Contemporary Forms of Racism, Racial Discrimination, Xenophobia and Related Intolerance on his Mission to Australia*, UN Doc A/HRC/35/41/Add.2 (9 July 2017).

migrants.[114] At the time of writing, the most recent report on Australia is from the Special Rapporteur on violence against women, who raised a number of concerns, particularly relating to domestic violence and violence against women in detention and women with disabilities.[115] She also raised concerns about violence against Indigenous women and the associated removal of Indigenous children from their mothers:

> In comparison with non-indigenous women, indigenous women are up to 35 times more likely to experience domestic and family violence …
>
>    …
>
> [There is] an excessive and inappropriately punitive and judgmental approach towards Aboriginal victims/survivors of family violence that blames victims for exposing their children to violence, rather than supporting them to safely care for their children and live free from violence. Across Australia, indigenous children now account for almost 35 per cent of all children in care, despite comprising only 4.4 per cent of the child population. … Child removal in itself constitutes a form of violence against women.[116]

The Special Rapporteur suggested a number of measures which Australia should take to rectify this situation, including the adoption of a 'specific national action plan'.[117]

Most special procedures also allow for individual complaints. This means that victims of rights violations can complain directly to the mandate holder, who is then able to raise concerns with the state. Individual complaints have been brought against Australia, particularly to the Working Group on Arbitrary Detention. The vast majority of these have related to individuals held in immigration detention; in almost all cases, the Working Group has found their detention to be arbitrary and contrary to IHRL. One recent case concerned a Tamil man who arrived by boat on Christmas Island in 2010, was found to be a genuine refugee, but was refused a visa on the basis of an adverse security assessment.[118] Although that assessment was subsequently revised, he remained in immigration detention. In 2019, the Working Group found that the man's continued detention was arbitrary, as 'during his nine years of detention, no judicial body has ever been involved in the assessment of the legality' of his detention.[119] It further emphasised that seeking asylum is a human right; that immigration detention must be a last resort where alternatives to it are not feasible; and that mandatory detention of asylum seekers under Australian law violates international law.[120]

### 10.3.1.2   Human rights treaty bodies

In addition to the Human Rights Council, which has general responsibility with respect to all human rights, each of the nine core IHRL treaties[121] has its own committee for monitoring its

---

114   See *Human Rights Council, Report of the Special Rapporteur on the Human Rights of Migrants on His Mission to Australia and the Regional Processing Centres in Nauru*, UN Doc A/HRC/35/25/Add.3 (24 April 2017).

115   *Human Rights Council, Report of the Special Rapporteur on Violence against Women, Its Causes and Consequences on Her Mission to Australia*, UN Doc A/HRC/38/47/Add.1 (17 April 2018).

116   Ibid [42], [46].

117   Ibid [92(a)].

118   Human Rights Council, Working Group on Arbitrary Detention, *Opinion No 1/2019 concerning Premakumar Subramaniyam (Australia)*, UN Doc A/HRC/WGAD/2019/1 (12 June 2019).

119   Ibid [80]–[86].

120   Ibid [93]–[95].

121   *ICCPR* (n 21), *ICESCR* (n 22), *CERD* (n 25), *CEDAW* (n 26), *CRC* (n 27), *CMW* (n 28), *CRPD* (n 29), *CAT* (n 30), *CED* (n 31).

implementation. The Human Rights Committee is responsible for the *ICCPR*; other treaty bodies (such as the Committee on Economic, Social and Cultural Rights) take their names from the treaties for which they are responsible. While the composition, mandate and procedures of each treaty body are slightly different, they share some common features. The most significant is that committee members are independent experts – that is, they do not represent their states of nationality. This is an important difference between the treaty bodies and the intergovernmental Human Rights Council, where members are representatives of their states.

Treaty bodies supervise the implementation of their respective treaties through three main mechanisms: monitoring periodic state reports; issuing general comments or general recommendations; and receiving individual complaints. First, each human rights treaty requires states to report periodically to its committee on 'measures they have adopted which give effect to the rights . . . and on the progress made in the enjoyment of those rights'.[122] These reports, together with 'shadow reports'[123] provided by other groups, particularly NGOs, form the basis for a 'constructive dialogue'[124] regarding the state's implementation of the treaty. The committee then adopts concluding observations, which note where the state has made progress, identify issues of concern, and recommend improvements. Although these are not binding, they are influential, as statements of both how the committee interprets the treaty and how the state could improve.

The most recent treaty body report on Australia is from the Committee on the Rights of Persons with Disabilities.[125] Its concluding observations noted a number of concerns, including issues with accessibility under art 9 of the *CRPD*:

> (b)  The significant proportion of the existing built environment that is inaccessible and the lack of mandated national access requirements for housing in the *National Construction Code*;
>
> (c)  The lack of comprehensive and effective measures to implement the full range of accessibility obligations under the Convention, including the lack of information and communications technologies and systems.[126]

Secondly, treaty bodies issue general comments or general recommendations, setting out their interpretation of treaty provisions and related human rights issues. These usually draw on the committee's work in monitoring state reports and are an important distillation of the committee's views. While not formally binding, they are authoritative statements and have been transformative in developing IHRL. For example, the Committee on Economic, Social and Cultural Rights has issued *General Comment 15* on the right to water, which effectively establishes a human right to water – although no such right is specifically articulated in the text of the *ICESCR*.[127]

---

122   *ICCPR* (n 21) art 40(1). There are similar provisions in the other treaties: see, eg, *ICESCR* (n 22) art 16(1).

123   Andrew Clapham, 'The Use of International Human Rights Law by Civil Society Organisations' in Scott Sheeran and Sir Nigel Rodley (eds), *Routledge Handbook of International Human Rights Law* (Routledge, 2014) 159.

124   See, eg, Committee on Economic, Social and Cultural Rights, *Report on the Forty-Fourth and Forty-Fifth Sessions*, UN Doc E/2011/22–E/C.12/2010/3 (2010) [29].

125   Committee on the Rights of Persons with Disabilities, *Concluding Observations on the Combined Second and Third Periodic Reports of Australia*, UN Doc CRPD/C/AUS/CO/2-3 (15 October 2019).

126   Ibid [17].

127   Committee on Economic, Social and Cultural Rights, *General Comment No 15: The Right to Water*, UN Doc E/C.12/2002/11 (20 January 2003). The Committee derives the right from *ICESCR* (n 22) arts 11 and 12 (on the right to an adequate standard of living and the right to health).

Thirdly, treaty bodies can hear complaints from individuals who claim that their rights under a treaty have been violated.[128] Some treaty bodies can also hear inter-state complaints.[129] For complaints against a state to be admissible, the state must have accepted the complaints mechanism, either by making a declaration under the treaty[130] or by ratifying an Optional Protocol.[131] Australia has accepted individual complaints mechanisms with respect to all the treaties to which it is a party, with the exception of the *ICESCR* and the *CRC*.

The complaints process is initiated when a victim makes a communication to the treaty body. The committee seeks written submissions from the state against which the complaint is made and from the individual concerned. It generally bases its decision solely on these submissions. In urgent cases, the committee may order interim protective measures before reaching a final decision.[132] The committee's decision is not formally binding. However, decisions can lead to substantial changes in law and practice. The first complaint brought against Australia to the Human Rights Committee, *Toonen v Australia*,[133] is a good example. This complaint concerned Tasmania's laws criminalising homosexual conduct in private between consenting adults. The Committee found that the law constituted an arbitrary interference with Mr Toonen's right to a private life under art 17 of the *ICCPR*. As a result, the federal government passed legislation overriding the Tasmanian law[134] and Tasmania ultimately repealed its law.[135]

The majority of individual complaints against Australia have been to the Human Rights Committee, which has been able to hear such complaints since 1991. There have been 52 cases to various treaty bodies in which adverse findings have been made against Australia (many concerning refugees); of these 52, it is estimated that Australia provided full remedies in six cases, partial remedies in 12 cases, and failed to provide remedies in 34 cases (65%).[136] The Human Rights Committee has criticised Australia for repeatedly failing to implement its views.

Recent decisions of treaty bodies concerning Australia include the finding of the Committee on the Rights of Persons with Disabilities that Australia was in violation of several provisions of the *CRPD* for not providing sign language interpreters to allow the complainant, who was deaf,

---

128    Although in the case of the *CMW* (n 28), the complaint mechanism has not yet entered into force. It will do so when 10 states have made a declaration under art 77 of the *CMW* to accept the individual complaints mechanism.

129    See *ICCPR* (n 21) arts 41–43; *CERD* (n 25) arts 11–13; *CAT* (n 30) art 21; *CMW* (n 28) art 74.

130    *CERD* (n 25) art 14; *CAT* (n 30) art 22; *CED* (n 31) art 31.

131    *Optional Protocol to the International Covenant on Civil and Political Rights*, opened for signature 16 December 1966, 999 UNTS 171 (entered into force 23 March 1976); *Optional Protocol to the International Covenant on Economic, Social and Cultural Rights*, opened for signature 10 December 2008, 2922 UNTS 29 (entered into force 5 May 2013); *Optional Protocol to the Convention on the Elimination of All Forms of Discrimination against Women*, opened for signature 6 December 1999, 2131 UNTS 83 (entered into force 22 December 2000); *Optional Protocol to the Convention on the Rights of the Child on a Communications Procedure*, opened for signature 19 December 2011, 2983 UNTS 131 (entered into force 14 April 2014); *Optional Protocol to the Convention on the Rights of Persons with Disabilities*, opened for signature 13 December 2006, 2518 UNTS 283 (entered into force 3 May 2008).

132    See, eg, Human Rights Committee, *Rules of Procedure*, UN Doc CCPR/C/3/Rev.12 (4 January 2021) r 94.

133    Human Rights Committee, *Views: Communication No 488/1992*, UN Doc CCPR/C/50/D/488/1992 (31 March 1994) ('*Toonen v Australia*').

134    *Human Rights (Sexual Conduct) Act 1994* (Cth) s 4.

135    *Criminal Code Amendment Act 1997* (Tas) ss 4, 5.

136    'Complaints Upheld against Australia', *Remedy Australia* (Web Page) <https://remedy.org.au/cases>.

to perform jury service;[137] a number of decisions of the Committee against Torture which found that the allegations that asylum seekers would face torture if deported were not substantiated;[138] and a decision of the Human Rights Committee concerning David Hicks, an Australian who was held in Guantánamo Bay for five years.[139] In the last of those cases, the Committee found that Australia was not responsible for Hicks's treatment while in US custody, but that his imprisonment on return to Australia, under the terms of a transfer agreement with the United States, violated his art 9 right to liberty, since his sentence was imposed by the US Military Commission in violation of his right to a fair trial:

> The Committee observes that, by the time the transfer of the author took place, there was abundant information in the public domain that raised serious concerns about the fairness of the procedures before the United States Military Commission and that should have been enough to cast doubts among Australian authorities as to the legality and legitimacy of the author's sentence. . . .
>
> States parties cannot be bound to execute a sentence when there is ample evidence that it was handed down following proceedings in which the defendant's rights were clearly violated. In the Committee's view, giving effect, under a transfer agreement, to sentences resulting from a flagrant denial of justice constitutes a disproportionate restriction of the right to liberty, in violation of article 9(1) of the Covenant.[140]

## 10.3.2  Regional bodies and mechanisms

Whereas IHRL mechanisms tend to rely on 'soft' measures such as supervision and monitoring, some regional human rights mechanisms confer binding remedies on individuals for violations of rights (through a court), often alongside soft mechanisms (such as a commission or committee).

The Inter-American Commission on Human Rights was established in 1959[141] and consists of seven independent experts elected by OAS member states. Its role is to monitor and promote human rights in OAS states, including by receiving individual and inter-state complaints of violations of the *American Declaration of the Rights and Duties of Man*, the *American Convention on Human Rights*, and other regional treaties.[142] The Inter-American Court of Human Rights, which consists of seven independent judges, hears complaints which

---

137    Committee on the Rights of Persons with Disabilities, *Views: Communication No 35/2016*, UN Doc CRPD/C/20/D/35/2016 (20 December 2018) ('*JH v Australia*').

138    Committee against Torture, *Views: Communication No 855/2017*, UN Doc CAT/C/68/D/855/2017 (10 December 2019) ('*SWR v Australia*'); Committee against Torture, *Views: Communication No 718/2015*, UN Doc CAT/C/68/D/718/2015 (26 December 2019) ('*SP v Australia*'); Committee against Torture, *Views: Communication No 723/2015*, UN Doc CAT/C/67/D/723/2015 (21 August 2019) ('*VM v Australia*'); Committee against Torture, *Views: Communication No 761/2016*, UN Doc CAT/C/65/D/761/2016 (17 January 2019) ('*SH v Australia*').

139    Human Rights Committee, *Views: Communication No 2005/2010*, UN Doc CCPR/C/115/D/2005/2010 (19 February 2016) ('*Hicks v Australia*').

140    Ibid [4.8]–[4.9].

141    Organization of American States, Fifth Meeting of Consultation of Ministers of Foreign Affairs, *Final Act* (adopted August 1959) Resolution VIII *Human Rights* pt II. See further *ACHR* (n 44) arts 34–51.

142    *ACHR* (n 44) arts 44 (individual complaints), 45(2) (inter-state complaints).

are referred to it by states or by the Commission,[143] and gives advisory opinions at the request of OAS organs or member states.[144] The Court has jurisdiction in relation to those states (currently 20) that have accepted its compulsory jurisdiction under art 62 of the *American Convention on Human Rights*. The jurisprudence of the Court (and the Commission) is extensive and influential, including recent groundbreaking judgments finding the state responsible for domestic violence[145] and holding that the Convention provides for a right to same-sex marriage.[146] In 2018, the Court issued a landmark advisory opinion finding that the right to a healthy environment protects the environment itself, and not only the interests of individuals:

> The Court considers it important to stress that, as an autonomous right, the right to a healthy environment, unlike other rights, protects the components of the environment, such as forests, rivers and seas, as legal interests in themselves, even in the absence of the certainty or evidence of a risk to individuals. This means that it protects nature and the environment, not only because of the benefits they provide to humanity or the effects that their degradation may have on other human rights, such as health, life or personal integrity, but because of their importance to the other living organisms with which we share the planet that also merit protection in their own right. In this regard, the Court notes a tendency, not only in court judgments, but also in Constitutions, to recognize legal personality and, consequently, rights to nature.[147]

Within Europe, the 47-member-state Council of Europe has general responsibility for the protection and promotion of human rights. The European Court of Human Rights hears individual and inter-state complaints of violations of rights protected by the *Convention for the Protection of Human Rights and Fundamental Freedoms*. The Court has 47 judges (one from each state party to the Convention) and, since its first session in 1959, has developed an enormous body of jurisprudence which has had a profound influence on IHRL. Recently, the Court has issued important judgments on the treatment of victims of human trafficking,[148] as well as on same-sex marriage[149] and the compatibility of electronic mass surveillance with the rights to privacy and freedom of expression.[150] In *Big Brother Watch v United Kingdom*, the Court found that while bulk interception of communications did not per se violate the right to privacy, it needed to be accompanied by safeguards protecting individual rights:

> In the context of bulk interception the importance of supervision and review will be amplified, because of the inherent risk of abuse and because the legitimate need for

143    Ibid art 61.
144    Ibid art 64.
145    *López Soto v Venezuela (Judgment)* (Inter-American Court of Human Rights, Series C No 362, 26 September 2018).
146    *State Obligations concerning Change of Name, Gender Identity, and Rights Derived from a Relationship between Same-Sex Couples (Advisory Opinion)* (Inter-American Court of Human Rights, Series A No 24, 24 November 2017).
147    *State Obligations in Relation to the Environment* (n 68) [62].
148    *VCL v United Kingdom* (European Court of Human Rights, Fourth Section, Application Nos 77587/12 and 74603/12, 16 February 2021).
149    *Fedotova v Russia* (European Court of Human Rights, Third Section, Application No 40792/10, 13 July 2021).
150    *Big Brother Watch v United Kingdom* (n 79); *Centrum för rättvisa* [Centre for Justice] *v Sweden* (European Court of Human Rights, Grand Chamber, Application No 35252/08, 25 May 2021).

secrecy will inevitably mean that, for reasons of national security, States will often not be at liberty to disclose information concerning the operation of the impugned regime.

Therefore, in order to minimise the risk of the bulk interception power being abused, the Court considers that the process must be subject to 'end-to-end safeguards', meaning that, at the domestic level, an assessment should be made at each stage of the process of the necessity and proportionality of the measures being taken; that bulk interception should be subject to independent authorisation at the outset, when the object and scope of the operation are being defined; and that the operation should be subject to supervision and independent ex post facto review.[151]

State compliance with the *European Social Charter* is monitored by the European Committee of Social Rights, primarily through reviewing annual state reports. This Committee can also hear collective complaints of violations from certain NGOs and trade unions.[152] Separately, the 27-member-state European Union has its own *Charter of Fundamental Rights and Freedoms*, which is justiciable before the Court of Justice of the European Union.

The African Commission on Human and Peoples' Rights, which commenced in 1987, was established under the *African Charter* and consists of 11 independent members.[153] It protects and promotes human rights in Africa, primarily through reviewing biennial state reports[154] and hearing individual[155] and inter-state[156] complaints. The African Court on Human and Peoples' Rights was established under a Protocol to the Charter, in force in 2004.[157] The Court can hear complaints referred by the Commission or by states.[158] It can also accept complaints from individuals and NGOs if the state concerned has made a declaration allowing them[159] and can issue advisory opinions on request of an organ of the African Union or any member state.[160] Decisions of the Commission and the Court have made important contributions to the protection of human rights. Landmark decisions include the Commission's finding that the Democratic Republic of Congo, supported by the Australian mining company Anvil Mining, was responsible for the massacre of 400 civilians near a copper and silver mine;[161] and a decision of the Court that the right to freedom of expression requires states to prosecute crimes against journalists.[162] The Court has also made important decisions regarding the nature of customary international law. In 2018, the Court found that arbitrary deprivation of nationality,

151    *Big Brother Watch v United Kingdom* (n 79) [349]–[350].
152    *Additional Protocol to the European Social Charter Providing for a System of Collective Complaints*, opened for signature 9 November 1995, 2045 UNTS 224 (entered into force 1 July 1998).
153    *African Charter* (n 50) art 30.
154    Ibid art 62.
155    Ibid arts 55–59.
156    Ibid arts 47–52.
157    *Protocol to the African Charter on Human and Peoples' Rights on the Establishment of an African Court on Human and Peoples' Rights*, opened for signature 9 June 1998 (entered into force 25 January 2004).
158    Ibid art 5.
159    Ibid arts 5(3), 34(6).
160    Ibid art 4.
161    African Commission on Human and Peoples' Rights, *Communication No 393/10* (9–18 June 2016) ('*Institute for Human Rights and Development in Africa v Democratic Republic of the Congo*').
162    *Zongo v Burkina Faso* (African Court on Human and Peoples' Rights, Application No 13/2011, 28 March 2014).

leading to statelessness, is contrary to the *Universal Declaration of Human Rights* and therefore to customary international law.[163]

The Arab Human Rights Committee was established in 2009 pursuant to art 45 of the *Arab Charter on Human Rights*. Its role is to monitor compliance with the Charter, primarily through reviewing triennial state reports.[164] There have been proposals to establish an Arab Court of Human Rights; however, the 2014 Statute of the Court[165] has not been ratified by any state and has been criticised by a number of NGOs.[166]

## 10.3.2.1   ASEAN case study

Until the 21st century, Asia had no regional human rights system. Indeed, a number of Asian countries opposed the application of IHRL to Asian states on the basis that human rights were Western constructs. They argued that individual civil and political rights did not reflect 'Asian values' which instead prioritise the interests of communities and focus on economic development and political stability.[167] The 'Asian values' debate came to a head at the 1993 World Conference on Human Rights in Vienna. Prior to the conference, more than 40 Asian states signed the *Bangkok Declaration*,[168] which was critical of the international human rights regime,[169] expressed concern at the focus on civil and political rights,[170] and called for cultural particularities to be taken into account in applying IHRL.[171]

The 'Asian values' argument has been challenged, including by local NGOs,[172] as reflecting not genuine cultural difference but rather the desire of ruling elites to justify authoritarianism and prevent scrutiny of their rights records.[173] Scholars have also critiqued its coherence, noting the way that it essentialises 'Asian identity' and fails to account for diversity within Asia.[174] Nonetheless, the argument was influential at the Vienna Conference. Its *Final Declaration and Programme of Action* acknowledges cultural particularities[175] and addresses concerns about the perceived priority given to civil and political rights by noting that '[a]ll human rights are universal, indivisible and interdependent and interrelated'.[176]

---

163   *Anudo v United Republic of Tanzania* (African Court on Human and Peoples' Rights, Application No 12/ 2015, 22 March 2018).
164   *Arab Charter on Human Rights* (n 53) art 48(2).
165   Approved by the Ministerial Council of the League of Arab States on 7 September 2014.
166   See International Commission of Jurists, *The Arab Court of Human Rights: A Flawed Statute for an Ineffective Court* (Report, April 2015).
167   See Ben Saul, Jacqueline Mowbray and Irene Baghoomians, 'The Last Frontier of Human Rights Protection: Interrogating Resistance to Regional Cooperation in the Asia-Pacific' (2011) 18 *Australian International Law Journal* 23, 30–1.
168   Regional Meeting for Asia of the World Conference on Human Rights, *Final Declaration* (29 March– 2 April 1993).
169   Ibid para 3.
170   Ibid Preamble.
171   Ibid para 8.
172   See the Bangkok NGO Declaration submitted to the Preparatory Committee for the Vienna World Conference, in UN General Assembly, *Report by the Secretariat: Bangkok NGO Declaration on Human Rights*, UN Doc A/Conf.157/PC/83 (19 April 1993).
173   See Yash Ghai, 'Asian Perspectives on Human Rights' (1993) 23(3) *Hong Kong Law Journal* 342, especially at 343.
174   Ibid 342–4.
175   *Vienna Declaration and Programme of Action* (n 89) art 5.
176   Ibid.

The Declaration also notes the need for 'regional and subregional arrangements for the promotion and protection of human rights where they do not already exist'.[177] In response, the Foreign Ministers of ASEAN stated that ASEAN should 'consider the establishment of an appropriate regional mechanism'.[178]

Over the next 10 years, NGOs and civil society lobbied for such a mechanism, without success.[179] However, in 2007, ASEAN member states amended the *Charter of the Association of Southeast Asian Nations* to require ASEAN to 'establish an ASEAN human rights body'.[180] In 2009, the ASEAN Intergovernmental Commission on Human Rights was established.[181] In 2012, ASEAN member states unanimously adopted the *ASEAN Human Rights Declaration*, thus giving Southeast Asia a regional system. Like all systems, it has its own peculiarities. It is influenced by the so-called 'ASEAN way' (or 'Asian value') of non-interference in the internal affairs of states. The intergovernmental nature of the Commission means that it is not independent: its members represent their governments. It also lacks the power to hear individual complaints or investigate specific countries. Further, the *ASEAN Human Rights Declaration* is not a binding treaty and it contains 'clawback clauses'[182] that qualify certain rights by indicating that they are subject to national law. On the other hand, the Declaration provides a comprehensive list of rights, including civil and political rights; economic, social and cultural rights; and 'third generation' rights, such as the right to development and the right to peace.

While there are important limitations on this system, scholars argue that it has nonetheless made progress in promoting human rights in the region. It has integrated the language of human rights into national and regional policies and debates[183] and enabled the 'development of new political forms that engage with rights standards ... in, around, and beyond ASEAN's regime'.[184] Australia, however, is not part of ASEAN or any other regional system.

## 10.3.3   Civil society

The term 'civil society' generally refers to non-government, non-commercial actors mobilising around common interests and concerns.[185] This includes NGOs, charities, advocacy networks, unions and professional organisations. It covers individuals and bodies operating at the grassroots level, as well as organisations and coalitions at the national and transnational levels.

Civil society contributes to the development and implementation of IHRL in a number of ways. At the grassroots level, civil society organisations mobilising in response to violations is

---

177   Ibid art 37.
178   Twenty-Sixth ASEAN Ministerial Meeting, *Joint Communiqué* (23–24 July 1993).
179   Hao Duy Phan, 'Promotional versus Protective Design: The Case of the ASEAN Intergovernmental Commission on Human Rights' (2019) 23(6) *International Journal of Human Rights* 915, 916–17.
180   *Charter of the Association of Southeast Asian Nations*, signed 20 November 2007, 2624 UNTS 223 (entered into force 15 December 2008) art 14(1). See further Phan ibid 917.
181   Association of Southeast Asian Nations, *Terms of Reference of ASEAN Intergovernmental Commission on Human Rights* (July 2009).
182   Phan (n 179) 922.
183   Yuyun Wahyuningrum, 'A Decade of Institutionalizing Human Rights in ASEAN: Progress and Challenges' (2021) 20(2) *Journal of Human Rights* 158, 172.
184   Anthony J Langlois, 'Human Rights in Southeast Asia: ASEAN's Rights Regime after Its First Decade' (2021) 20(2) *Journal of Human Rights* 151, 153.
185   See Office of the High Commissioner for Human Rights, *Working with the United Nations Human Rights Programme: A Handbook for Civil Society* (2008) vii–viii.

often the first step in bringing IHRL to bear, including through fact-finding, publicising violations, advocacy, and domestic and international litigation (resulting in important jurisprudence).

Civil society also contributes to the implementation of human rights law through participation in international human rights institutions. Most of these institutions have formal processes through which civil society can participate, such as the process for NGOs to contribute to the UPR process.[186] Further, important changes to the legal and institutional framework of IHRL have resulted from the preparatory work and lobbying of civil society. Prominent examples include the role of Amnesty International and others in campaigning for, and drafting, the *Convention against Torture*,[187] and the crucial role played by the NGO Coalition for an Optional Protocol to the ICESCR in establishing an individual complaints procedure.[188]

# 10.4 Domestic implementation of international human rights law

## 10.4.1 International overview

As Andrew Byrnes and Catherine Renshaw have noted, IHRL is generally implemented within domestic legal orders in one of four ways.[189] The first is by incorporation of human rights treaties or customary international law into domestic law. In monist states (see Chapter 4) such as Brazil, Namibia and the Netherlands, this can occur more or less automatically. In dualist states, treaties must be adopted by a domestic legislative act. So, for example, the *Human Rights Act 1998* (UK) incorporates the *Convention for the Protection of Human Rights and Fundamental Freedoms* into UK law by reference.

Secondly, most state constitutions include guarantees of human rights. Most of these do not implement IHRL per se; indeed, many constitutions predate the International Bill of Human Rights. However, the content of more recent constitutions, such as that of South Africa, tends to reflect IHRL. The third means of implementing IHRL is through the adoption of specific legislation (other than comprehensive incorporation of a treaty, mentioned earlier) and the fourth is through common law protections. As discussed in Section 10.4.2, these are the primary mechanisms through which Australia implements IHRL.

States also rely on different institutions to domestically monitor and enforce IHRL. Where IHRL has been domestically incorporated, courts have an important role to play in interpreting the law, adjudicating claims that rights have been violated, and ordering binding remedies. Some countries also have parliamentary bodies which scrutinise legislation for compliance with IHRL before it is passed. The UK Joint Committee on Human Rights, established in 2001, is a prominent example.

---

186    See Clapham, 'Use of International Human Rights Law' (n 123).
187    Ibid 164.
188    See Gamze-Erdem Türkelli, Wouter Vandenhole and Arne Vandenbogaerde, 'NGO Impact on Law-Making: The Case of a Complaints Procedure under the *International Covenant on Economic, Social and Cultural Rights* and the *Convention on the Rights of the Child*' (2013) 5(1) *Journal of Human Rights Practice* 1.
189    Andrew Byrnes and Catherine Renshaw, 'Within the State' in Daniel Moeckli, Sangeeta Shah and Sandesh Sivakumaran (eds), *International Human Rights Law* (Oxford University Press, 2010) 499.

Most states also have some form of national human rights institution. These are 'State bodies with a constitutional and/or legislative mandate to protect and promote human rights' which 'are part of the State apparatus and are funded by the State'.[190] The mandate and functions of national human rights institutions are determined by domestic law. However, the *Principles Relating to the Status of National Institutions* (also known as the *Paris Principles*), first adopted in 1991 and endorsed by the General Assembly in 1993,[191] set out the minimum standards for these institutions to be legitimate. The Principles establish six main criteria: a broad mandate based on universal standards; autonomy from government; independence guaranteed by statute or constitution; pluralism; adequate resources; and adequate investigative powers.[192] The Principles further provide that national human rights institutions shall make recommendations to government, promote laws consistent with rights, encourage treaty ratification, contribute to UN monitoring and international cooperation, assist with human rights teaching and research, and publicise human rights.[193]

## 10.4.2   Human rights law in Australian law

### 10.4.2.1   Federal law

As noted in Chapter 4, Australia is a dualist state, which requires treaties to be implemented through domestic legislation. However, Australia has not legislated to implement, as a whole, any of the IHRL treaties to which it is a party. While the *Australian Constitution* protects some rights, explicitly or by implication, they are 'limited in scope, and have been interpreted narrowly by the courts'.[194] The implementation of IHRL within federal law instead occurs through a 'patchwork'[195] of legislation protecting particular rights, most notably the four federal anti-discrimination statutes;[196] legislation which indirectly protects or promotes particular rights; policy measures; and the common law. As a result, although Australia is a party to seven of the nine core IHRL treaties, the rights in these treaties are not, with limited exceptions, enforceable under domestic law.

### 10.4.2.2   State and territory human rights legislation

Although Australia has no federal human rights legislation, some states and territories have introduced their own legislation. The first to do so was the Australian Capital Territory, which passed the *Human Rights Act 2004* (ACT). Victoria followed with the *Charter of Human Rights and Responsibilities Act 2006* (Vic) and Queensland with the *Human Rights Act 2019* (Qld).

---

190    Office of the High Commissioner for Human Rights, *National Human Rights Institutions: History, Principles, Roles and Responsibilities* (2010) 13 <www.ohchr.org/sites/default/files/Documents/Publications/PTS-4Rev1-NHRI_en.pdf>.

191    *National Institutions for the Promotion and Protection of Human Rights*, GA Res 48/134, UN Doc A/RES/48/134 (20 December 1993) annex ('*Principles Relating to the Status of National Institutions*').

192    See Office of the High Commissioner for Human Rights, *National Human Rights Institutions* (n 190) 31.

193    *Principles Relating to the Status of National Institutions* (n 191) principle 3.

194    National Human Rights Consultation Committee, *National Human Rights Consultation Report* (September 2009) 349.

195    Ibid.

196    These are the *Racial Discrimination Act 1975* (Cth), the *Sex Discrimination Act 1984* (Cth), the *Disability Discrimination Act 1992* (Cth) and the *Age Discrimination Act 2004* (Cth).

There are some differences between these pieces of legislation, but they have a number of common features. In particular, all three adopt a 'dialogue model', which gives courts the power to find that legislation is inconsistent with human rights, but the legislation remains valid and in force until amended by Parliament.[197] This model, which is also used in the United Kingdom and New Zealand, seeks to avoid (contested) concerns that human rights legislation would encroach on parliamentary sovereignty if the courts could strike down legislation – despite the courts already having such powers in other areas. All three Acts require public authorities to act in a way which is compatible with the rights in the relevant Act and to give proper consideration to those rights when making any decision.[198] The Acts also give individuals certain rights to bring proceedings where their rights have been violated.[199]

### 10.4.2.3    A federal human rights Act?

There has been ongoing debate over whether Australia should have a federal human rights law, as recommended in 2009 by the National Human Rights Consultation Committee.[200] The Committee recommended that any Human Rights Act should follow the 'dialogue model',[201] as used in the state and territory human rights legislation and in the United Kingdom (discussed in Section 10.4.2.2). Other recommendations made by the Committee included that the Act require Commonwealth public authorities to act in a manner compatible with human rights[202] and that the Act provide individuals with an independent cause of action against public authorities for breach of human rights.[203] The Committee favoured including civil and political rights, controversially opining that if economic, social and cultural rights were included, they should not be justiciable by the courts.[204]

The Australian government responded to the report in 2010 by launching Australia's Human Rights Framework.[205] While the government adopted a number of the recommendations in the report, the Framework did not include a Human Rights Act. Instead, it focused on measures such as human rights education; community engagement; developing a National Action Plan on Human Rights; establishing a Parliamentary Joint Committee on Human Rights (discussed in Section 10.4.3.1); reviewing laws, policies and practices for compatibility with IHRL; and harmonising and consolidating anti-discrimination laws.[206] From a legal perspective, the only element of this Framework which remains is the Parliamentary Joint Committee. Attempts to reform anti-discrimination legislation were abandoned

---

197    See *Human Rights Act 2004* (ACT) s 32; *Charter of Human Rights and Responsibilities Act 2006* (Vic) s 36; *Human Rights Act 2019* (Qld) ss 53, 54.
198    *Human Rights Act 2004* (ACT) s 40B; *Charter of Human Rights and Responsibilities Act 2006* (Vic) s 38; *Human Rights Act 2019* (Qld) s 58.
199    *Human Rights Act 2004* (ACT) s 40C; *Charter of Human Rights and Responsibilities Act 2006* (Vic) s 39; *Human Rights Act 2019* (Qld) s 59.
200    *National Human Rights Consultation Report* (n 194) recommendation 18.
201    Ibid recommendation 19.
202    Ibid recommendation 30.
203    Ibid recommendation 31.
204    Ibid recommendation 22.
205    Commonwealth, *Australia's Human Rights Framework* (April 2010).
206    Ibid 3.

following drafting and consultation,[207] and the 2012 National Action Plan was discarded after the change of government in 2013.[208]

## 10.4.3   Australian institutions for the protection and promotion of human rights

### 10.4.3.1   Parliamentary Joint Committee on Human Rights

The Parliamentary Joint Committee on Human Rights was established by the *Human Rights (Parliamentary Scrutiny) Act 2011* (Cth) ('the Act') to 'examine Bills for Acts, and legislative instruments, that come before either House of the Parliament for compatibility with human rights'.[209] 'Human rights' is defined in the Act as the seven key human rights treaties to which Australia is a party.[210] The Committee is composed of 10 Members of Parliament: five from the government and five from non-government parties.[211]

The Committee reports its findings to Parliament.[212] In theory, this gives Parliament the opportunity to amend legislation to comply with IHRL. The Act does not, however, require Parliament to amend legislation which the Committee has concluded may be incompatible with human rights; in practice, very few pieces of legislation are amended.[213] This has led some commentators to conclude that the Committee is ineffective.[214] Other scholars, however, have argued that the Committee's influence is more nuanced and substantial. They point to its 'deliberative impact' on the work of the Parliament and the take-up of its findings in the media and by UN human rights bodies.[215] For example, the Committee's recommendations in 2019 to better regulate the use of restraints in residential aged care facilities influenced amendments to the legislative instrument,[216] as well as the findings of a Royal Commission on aged care[217] which led to further amendments.[218]

### 10.4.3.2   Australian Human Rights Commission

The Australian Human Rights Commission (formerly the Human Rights and Equal Opportunity Commission, established in 1986) is Australia's national human rights institution. It has a

---

207    Following this report into the exposure draft: Senate Legal and Constitutional Affairs Legislation Committee, *Exposure Draft of the Human Rights and Anti-Discrimination Bill 2012* (February 2013).

208    See Adam McBeth, Justine Nolan and Simon Rice, *International Law of Human Rights* (Oxford University Press, 2017) 384.

209    *Human Rights (Parliamentary Scrutiny) Act 2011* (Cth) s 7(a).

210    Ibid s 3(1).

211    Commonwealth, *Parliamentary Debates*, House of Representatives, 4 July 2019, 14 (Christian Porter, Attorney-General).

212    *Human Rights (Parliamentary Scrutiny) Act 2011* (Cth) s 7(a).

213    Daniel Reynolds, Winsome Hall and George Williams, 'Australia's Human Rights Scrutiny Regime' (2020) 46(1) *Monash University Law Review* 256, 299.

214    Ibid.

215    See, eg, Zoe Hutchinson, 'The Role, Operation and Effectiveness of the Commonwealth Parliamentary Joint Committee on Human Rights after Five Years' (2018) 33 *Australasian Parliamentary Review* 72.

216    *Quality of Care Amendment (Minimising the Use of Restraints) Principles 2019* (Cth).

217    *Royal Commission into Aged Care Quality and Safety* (Final Report, February 2021).

218    See Parliamentary Joint Committee on Human Rights, Aged Care and Other Legislation Amendment (Royal Commission Response No 1) Bill 2021; *Aged Care Legislation Amendment (Royal Commission Response No 1) Principles 2021* (Cth); Parliamentary Joint Committee on Human Rights, Parliament of Australia, *Tenth Report of 2021* (Report, 25 August 2021).

number of statutory functions, including promoting human rights, undertaking research and education, conducting inquiries, advising on the compatibility of legislation, preparing guidelines and intervening in legal proceedings.[219] The Commission is also able to hear and conciliate complaints concerning unlawful discrimination under the four federal anti-discrimination statutes.[220] Individuals who wish to commence proceedings for unlawful discrimination in the courts must first bring these claims to the Commission.

The Commission also has the power to 'inquire into any act or practice that may be inconsistent with or contrary to any human rights'.[221] The 'act or practice' in question must be by the Commonwealth or its agencies[222] and the 'human rights' which the Commission has the power to consider include those in the *ICCPR*, the *CERD* and the *CRC*[223] – but not the *ICESCR*. The Commission can also inquire into 'any act or practice (including any systemic practice) that may constitute discrimination'[224] in employment.[225]

The Commission has the power to investigate complaints and attempt conciliation.[226] If conciliation is unsuccessful, the Commission will either decline the complaint or make a finding of a breach and will report to the Attorney-General. The report will be tabled in Parliament.[227] So, for example, in 2019, the Commission conducted an inquiry into the use of force in immigration detention, in response to 14 separate complaints by detainees. The following extract is from the Commission President's letter to the Attorney-General:

> In relation to nine of the complaints, I found that there was a use of force that was contrary to the requirements of article 10 of the *International Covenant on Civil and Political Rights (ICCPR)*. This article provides that all persons deprived of their liberty shall be treated with humanity and with respect for the inherent dignity of the human person. Some of these complaints related to the use of handcuffs. In one case, handcuffs were applied to a detainee for 8 and a half hours over a significant wrist wound while he was transferred between detention centres.
>
> . . .
>
> In relation to the remaining five complaints, I did not find that a breach of human rights had been established.
>
> I made recommendations aimed at remedying the loss or damage caused by the breaches of human rights. I also made a range of systemic recommendations aimed at reforming the way in which force is used in immigration detention.
>
> The department provided its response to my findings and recommendations on 2 April 2019. It did not agree that any of the conduct complained of involved a breach

219  *Australian Human Rights Commission Act 1986* (Cth) s 11(1) ('*AHRC Act*').
220  Ibid s 11(1)(aa).
221  Ibid s 11(1)(f).
222  Ibid s 3(1).
223  Ibid (see the definitions of 'human rights', 'Covenant', 'Declarations' and 'relevant international instrument').
224  Ibid s 31(b).
225  As defined in *Convention concerning Discrimination in Respect of Employment and Occupation (No 111)*, opened for signature 25 June 1958, 362 UNTS 31 (entered into force 15 June 1960). See *AHRC Act* (n 219) s 3(1).
226  *AHRC Act* (n 219) ss 11(f), 31(b).
227  Ibid s 29.

of human rights. Nevertheless, it noted that since receiving my preliminary views in this inquiry it had made amendments to its internal policies which were directed to many of the issues that were the subject of my recommendations.[228]

As this extract demonstrates, the Commission's report may contain recommendations as to remedies, as well as more general recommendations to ensure that breaches do not occur again. However, the party in breach is not required to comply with the recommendations or provide remedies (such as compensation), and a finding of breach is a judicially reviewable decision.[229]

It should also be mentioned that all Australian states and territories have agencies responsible for hearing complaints of discrimination under the relevant state or territory anti-discrimination laws, through similar processes of investigation and non-binding conciliation.

# 10.5   Human rights as a discourse and critiques

The laws and institutions for the protection of IHRL at the international, regional and domestic levels may not always be legally effective. Some instruments are not binding, while others lack effective enforcement mechanisms; some regional systems, such as ASEAN's, are deliberately weak; and the implementation of IHRL within the domestic legal systems of some states, such as Australia, is limited. Nonetheless, IHRL certainly influences the behaviour of governments and other actors. States undertake commitments as part of the UPR process; stronger regional systems fill gaps in the international system; and civil society uses the language of rights to hold governments accountable. In this sense, IHRL is more than a set of legal principles and institutions for enforcing them; it also functions as a 'discourse' – a legal language for affirming the fundamental value of human dignity and for shaping public policy. Understanding IHRL in this way gives us a broader sense of its possibilities and limitations.

When considering its broader relevance, however, it is important also to be aware of significant critiques of the concept of human rights, particularly its manifestation in IHRL. While a comprehensive survey of critiques is beyond this chapter, it is useful to identify some of the main strands in this growing literature.

The first critique questions the *effectiveness* of human rights. It views human rights as largely futile, both because of ambiguities within the law and because international law lacks the means to enforce rights. As early as the 18th century, Jeremy Bentham criticised the French *Declaration of the Rights of Man and of the Citizen* as 'nonsense upon stilts'.[230] Today, this critique emphasises the difficulty of asserting rights against 'the countervailing power of the market and state'[231] and the lack of effective forms of accountability.[232]

---

228    Australian Human Rights Commission, *Use of Force in Immigration Detention* (Report No 130, May 2019).

229    Under the *Administrative Decisions (Judicial Review) Act 1977* (Cth): *Commonwealth v Human Rights and Equal Opportunity Commission* (1999) 95 FCR 218.

230    See Marie-Bénédicte Dembour, 'Critiques' in Daniel Moeckli, Sangeeta Shah and Sandesh Sivakumaran (eds), *International Human Rights Law* (Oxford University Press, 2010) 64, 68–9.

231    Malcolm Langford, 'Critiques of Human Rights' (2018) 14 *Annual Review of Law and Social Science* 69, 75.

232    Eric Posner, *The Twilight of Human Rights Law* (Oxford University Press, 2014).

The Marxist critique of human rights also has a long history. Karl Marx argued that while the French Declaration led to the political emancipation of the individual, it left intact the basic structures of society which cause injustice, including material and economic inequality and oppression.[233] This concern is reflected in contemporary critiques which argue that human rights discourse obscures the role of the economy in producing injustice[234] and that human rights cannot challenge existing relations of power and wealth to achieve redistributive change.[235] A prominent recent contribution is Samuel Moyn's *Not Enough: Human Rights in an Unequal World*, which argues that human rights discourse lacks the resources to challenge the material inequality associated with the rise of neoliberalism and market fundamentalism.[236]

From the opposite direction, libertarians argue that human rights do *too much* to constrain individual freedom and that they interfere with the economy. For them, many rights – and particularly economic and social rights, which underpin the welfare state – represent an unjustifiable interference with the operation of free markets and individual liberty.[237]

Other critiques question the claim that human rights are universal. The cultural relativist critique (as in the 'Asian values' debate discussed in Section 10.3.2.1) argues that human rights are not universal but rather are a specific product of the cultural and intellectual traditions of Western Europe and North America. In particular, by focusing on individual rights, IHRL fails to take account of the fact that humans do not 'function outside the societies of which they form a part'.[238]

Taking this critique further, postcolonial critiques highlight how human rights perpetuate a colonial logic. For these critics, the idea of human rights continues the 'civilising mission' of colonialism, imposing Western ideas of how society should be structured on the 'Other' of the Third World.[239] At the same time, structural features of the human rights system disadvantage those from the global South – '[t]he *ad nauseam* talk of human rights does not today translate into entry rights for asylum seekers'[240] – and the language of international human rights displaces other, local forms of resistance to injustice.[241]

Feminist scholars also challenge the universalism of human rights, arguing that the liberal assumptions underlying IHRL are inherently gendered:[242] 'Because the law-making institutions of the international legal order have always been, and continue to be, dominated by men, IHRL

233   Karl Marx, 'On the Jewish Question' in David McClellan, *Karl Marx: Selected Writings* (Oxford University Press, 2nd ed, 2000) 46.

234   David Kennedy, 'International Human Rights Movement: Part of the Problem?' (2002) 15 *Harvard Human Rights Journal* 101, 109–10.

235   See Langford (n 231) 81.

236   Samuel Moyn, *Not Enough: Human Rights in an Unequal World* (Harvard University Press, 2018).

237   'Libertarianism' in *Stanford Encyclopedia of Philosophy* (online, January 2019) <https://plato.stanford .edu/entries/libertarianism>.

238   American Anthropological Association, *Statement on Human Rights* (1947) 49(4) *American Anthropologist* 539, 539.

239   See Makau Mutua, *Human Rights: A Political and Cultural Critique* (University of Pennsylvania Press, 2002), especially at 155.

240   BS Chimni, 'The Past, Present and Future of International Law: A Critical Third World Approach' (2007) 8(2) *Melbourne Journal of International Law* 499, 507.

241   See generally Balakrishnan Rajagopal, *International Law from Below: Development, Social Movements and Third World Resistance* (Cambridge University Press, 2003).

242   See generally Hilary Charlesworth and Christine Chinkin, *The Boundaries of International Law: A Feminist Analysis* (Manchester University Press, 2000) ch 7.

has developed to reflect the experiences of men and largely to exclude those of women'.[243] Feminist scholars note how the legal concept of 'equality' fails to address the deep structural disadvantage suffered by women and the systemic perpetuation of gender hierarchies.[244] They have also noted how the 'public–private divide', as a result of which the law regulates activity in the putative 'public' and not 'private' sphere, disadvantages women by making forms of injustice in the private sphere, such as domestic violence, invisible.[245]

Each of these critiques has been contested, rebutted and debated. Different scholars have different views on their resonance for IHRL. However, each of these critiques raises important questions about the nature of IHRL and its limitations. For scholars and practitioners of IHRL, these critiques present an opportunity to think about how human rights law can be made more effective, more inclusive and better able to contribute to justice for all. As David Kennedy has noted, '[t]here is no question that the international human rights movement has done a great deal of good'.[246] These critiques raise the question of whether it could do even better.

## DISCUSSION QUESTIONS

(1)    Are human rights universal? Are they the rights of everyone, everywhere?

(2)    'Economic, social, and cultural rights are not "real" rights; human rights law cannot be used to challenge how economic and social resources are allocated within society.' Discuss.

(3)    'International human rights sound good in theory, but in practice they are meaningless because they are unenforceable.' Do you agree?

(4)    Does international human rights law only protect individuals?

(5)    Do you think Australia should have a national Human Rights Act?

---

243    Hilary Charlesworth, 'Human Rights as Men's Rights' in Julie Peters and Andrea Wolper (eds), *Women's Rights, Human Rights: International Feminist Perspectives* (Routledge, 1995) 103, 103.

244    See, eg, Rebecca J Cook, 'Women's International Human Rights Law: The Way Forward' (1993) 15(2) *Human Rights Quarterly* 230, 238–40.

245    See, eg, Donna Sullivan, 'The Public/Private Distinction in International Human Rights Law' in Julie Peters and Andrea Wolper (eds), *Women's Rights, Human Rights: International Feminist Perspectives* (Routledge, 1995) 126.

246    Kennedy (n 234) 101.

# 11

# INTERNATIONAL HUMANITARIAN LAW

Emily Crawford

# 11.1   Introduction

International humanitarian law ('IHL'), also known as the law of armed conflict ('LOAC'), is a branch of international law that regulates the behaviour of participants in armed conflicts and encompasses rules on the military targeting of persons and objects, the means and methods of warfare, the protection of persons and objects, and the implementation and enforcement of the law. International humanitarian law is also one of the most highly codified fields of international law, with numerous treaties adopted over the last 150 years; many of these have also attained customary status.[1]

In developing IHL, states have recognised that, while the ultimate aim of society should be to strive to prevent war, wars will nonetheless occur, and that while 'war will always constitute suffering and personal tragedy ... rules of warfare are intended to prevent *unnecessary* suffering that yields little or no military advantage'.[2] This balance between humanitarian aims and military objectives serves as the basic underpinning of all the modern laws of armed conflict.

# 11.2   Sources of international humanitarian law

Modern IHL comprises numerous treaties on nearly all aspects of armed conflict. The primary treaties of IHL are the four *Geneva Conventions*, the three *Additional Protocols to the Geneva Conventions* ('*Additional Protocols*') and the *Hague Conventions*. The four *Geneva Conventions* adopted in 1949 address, respectively, wounded and sick military personnel on land[3] and at sea,[4] prisoners of war,[5] and the protection of civilians.[6] These Conventions were joined by the three *Additional Protocols* in later decades, adding more rules on international conflicts,[7] non-international conflicts,[8] and the protection of

---

1    See further International Committee of the Red Cross ('ICRC'), *Customary International Humanitarian Law Database* (Web Page) <https://ihl-databases.icrc.org/customary-ihl/eng/docs/home?opendocument>.

2    Gary Solis, *The Law of Armed Conflict: International Humanitarian Law in War* (Cambridge University Press, 3rd ed, 2021) 5 (emphasis in original).

3    *Geneva Convention (I) for the Amelioration of the Condition of the Wounded and Sick in Armed Forces in the Field*, opened for signature 12 August 1949, 75 UNTS 31 (entered into force 21 October 1950) ('*Geneva Convention I*').

4    *Geneva Convention (II) for the Amelioration of the Condition of Wounded, Sick and Shipwrecked Members of Armed Forces at Sea*, opened for signature 12 August 1949, 75 UNTS 85 (entered into force 21 October 1950) ('*Geneva Convention II*').

5    *Geneva Convention (III) Relative to the Treatment of Prisoners of War*, opened for signature 12 August 1949, 75 UNTS 135 (entered into force 21 October 1950) ('*Geneva Convention III*').

6    *Geneva Convention (IV) Relative to the Protection of Civilian Persons in Time of War*, opened for signature 12 August 1949, 75 UNTS 287 (entered into force 21 October 1950) ('*Geneva Convention IV*').

7    *Protocol Additional (I) to the Geneva Conventions of 12 August 1949, and Relating to the Protection of Victims of International Armed Conflicts*, opened for signature 8 June 1977, 1125 UNTS 3 (entered into force 7 December 1978) ('*Additional Protocol I*').

8    *Protocol Additional (II) to the Geneva Conventions of 12 August 1949, and Relating to the Protection of Victims of Non-International Armed Conflicts*, opened for signature 8 June 1977, 1125 UNTS 609 (entered into force 7 December 1978) ('*Additional Protocol II*').

humanitarian emblems.[9] The *Hague Conventions* include the 1899 *Convention (II) with Respect to the Laws and Customs of War on Land* ('*Hague II 1899*') and 1907 *Convention (IV) respecting the Laws and Customs of War on Land* ('*Hague IV 1907*'), both known as the *Hague Regulations*.[10]

In addition, there are numerous treaties on permissible means and methods of warfare, including prohibitions on chemical[11] and biological weapons,[12] blinding laser weapons,[13] incendiary weapons,[14] landmines[15] and booby-traps,[16] cluster munitions,[17] nuclear weapons,[18] weaponising the natural environment,[19] and other conventional weapons.[20] These have been joined by treaties protecting cultural property during armed conflicts,[21]

9    *Protocol Additional (III) to the Geneva Conventions of 12 August 1949, and Relating to the Adoption of an Additional Distinctive Emblem*, opened for signature 8 December 2005, 2404 UNTS 261 (entered into force 14 January 2007) ('*Additional Protocol III*').

10   *Hague Convention (II) with Respect to the Laws and Customs of War on Land*, opened for signature 29 July 1899, 187 CTS 403 (entered into force 4 September 1900) ('*Hague II 1899*'); *Hague Convention (IV) respecting the Laws and Customs of War on Land*, opened for signature 18 October 1907, USTS 539 (entered into force 26 January 1910) ('*Hague IV 1907*'). The Conventions are also referred to as the '*Hague Regulations*'.

11   *Protocol for the Prohibition of the Use of Asphyxiating, Poisonous or Other Gases, and of Bacteriological Methods of Warfare*, opened for signature 17 June 1925, 94 LNTS 65 (entered into force 8 February 1928); *Convention on the Prohibition of the Development, Production, Stockpiling and Use of Chemical Weapons and on Their Destruction*, opened for signature 3 September 1992, 1975 UNTS 45 (entered into force 29 April 1997) ('*Chemical Weapons Convention*').

12   *Convention on the Prohibition of the Development, Production and Stockpiling of Bacteriological (Biological) and Toxin Weapons and on Their Destruction*, opened for signature 10 April 1972, 1015 UNTS 163 (entered into force 26 March 1975).

13   *Additional Protocol to the Convention on Prohibitions or Restrictions on the Use of Certain Conventional Weapons Which May Be Deemed to Be Excessively Injurious or to Have Indiscriminate Effects (Protocol (IV), Entitled Protocol on Blinding Laser Weapons)*, opened for signature 13 October 1995, 2024 UNTS 163 (entered into force 30 July 1998).

14   *Protocol on Prohibitions or Restrictions on the Use of Incendiary Weapons (Protocol III)*, opened for signature 10 October 1980, 1342 UNTS 171 (entered into force 2 December 1983).

15   *Protocol on Prohibitions or Restrictions on the Use of Mines, Booby-Traps and Other Devices (Protocol II)*, opened for signature 10 October 1980, 1342 UNTS 168 (entered into force 2 December 1983); *Convention on the Prohibition of the Use, Stockpiling, Production and Transfer of Anti-Personnel Mines and on Their Destruction*, opened for signature 18 September 1997, 2056 UNTS 211 (entered into force 1 March 1999).

16   *Protocol on Prohibitions or Restrictions on the Use of Mines, Booby-Traps and Other Devices* (n 15).

17   *Convention on Cluster Munitions*, opened for signature 30 May 2008, 2688 UNTS 39 (entered into force 1 August 2010).

18   *Treaty on the Prohibition of Nuclear Weapons*, opened for signature 7 July 2017, UN Doc CNCN/475/2017 (entered into force 22 January 2021).

19   *Convention on the Prohibition of Military or Any Other Hostile Use of Environmental Modification Techniques*, opened for signature 10 December 1976, 1108 UNTS 151 (entered into force 5 October 1978) ('*ENMOD Convention*').

20   *Convention on Prohibitions or Restrictions on the Use of Certain Conventional Weapons Which May Be Deemed to Be Excessively Injurious or to Have Indiscriminate Effects*, opened for signature 10 October 1980, 1342 UNTS 137 (entered into force 2 December 1983) ('*Conventional Weapons Convention*').

21   *Convention for the Protection of Cultural Property in the Event of Armed Conflict*, opened for signature 14 May 1954, 249 UNTS 295 (entered into force 7 August 1956); *Second Protocol to the Hague Convention of 1954 for the Protection of Cultural Property in the Event of Armed Conflict*, opened for signature 26 March 1999, 2253 UNTS 172 (entered into force 9 March 2004).

prohibiting the recruitment of children into combat roles,[22] and creating the International Criminal Court to prosecute, inter alia, war crimes.[23]

State participation in many of these treaties is widespread.[24] The *Geneva Conventions* are universally ratified by all states – the first treaties in history to achieve this.[25] Most, if not all, of the provisions of the *Geneva Conventions* are considered as having attained customary status, and many of the provisions of the *Additional Protocols*, the *Hague Regulations* and the weapons treaties are also considered customary.[26] Australia is party to all of the major IHL treaties,[27] including the *Rome Statute of the International Criminal Court*. Australian military training manuals recognise Australia's participation in the various IHL regimes[28] and many of their obligations have been implemented in domestic legislation.[29]

Joining these binding sources are numerous instruments that are of less-than-treaty status, but are still immensely influential as sources of 'soft' law. These include reports and conclusions of meetings of states, and of groups of experts, on topics such as naval warfare,[30] the use of private military and security companies,[31] the treatment of detainees,[32] and cyberwarfare.[33] Australian government officials and experts have been involved in many of these processes, and a number of these instruments have been incorporated into Australian military manuals. The latter acknowledge that some documents, like the *San Remo Manual on International Law Applicable to Armed Conflicts at Sea*, are 'a restatement of the law

---

22    *Optional Protocol to the Convention on the Rights of the Child on the Involvement of Children in Armed Conflict*, opened for signature 25 May 2000, 2173 UNTS 222 (entered into force 12 February 2002).

23    *Rome Statute of the International Criminal Court*, opened for signature 17 July 1998, 2187 UNTS 3 (entered into force 1 July 2002).

24    'National Implementation of International Humanitarian Law', *International Committee of the Red Cross* (Web Page) <https://ihl-databases.icrc.org/applic/ihl/ihl-nat.nsf>.

25    Philip Spoerri, 'The Geneva Conventions of 1949: Origins and Current Significance' (Speech, Ceremony to Celebrate the 60th Anniversary of the Geneva Conventions, 12 August 2009) <www.icrc.org/en/doc/resources/documents/statement/geneva-conventions-statement-120809.htm>; Adam Beaumont, 'ICRC Hails Ratification of Geneva Conventions', *SWI swissinfo.ch* (22 August 2006) <www.swissinfo.ch/eng/icrc-hails-ratification-of-geneva-conventions/3716>.

26    Jean-Marie Henckaerts and Louise Doswald-Beck (eds), *Customary International Humanitarian Law* (Cambridge University Press, 2005) ('*ICRC Customary IHL Study*'). The rules and practices identified in the study are available at *Customary International Humanitarian Law Database* (n 1).

27    With the exception of the *Treaty on the Prohibition of Nuclear Weapons* (n 18) which, at the time of writing, Australia has not signed/ratified or acceded to. See further the position of the Department of Foreign Affairs and Trade on nuclear weapons: 'Nuclear Weapons', *Department of Foreign Affairs and Trade* (Web Page) <www.dfat.gov.au/international-relations/security/non-proliferation-disarmament-arms-control/nuclear-issues>.

28    See *Law of Armed Conflict* (Australian Defence Doctrine Publication 6.4, June 2006) ch 1.

29    See, eg, *Geneva Conventions Act 1957* (Cth); *Criminal Code Act 1995* (Cth) (specifically s 228, which gives effect to Australian obligations under the *Rome Statute of the International Criminal Court* (n 23) in relation to war crimes).

30    Louise Doswald-Beck (ed), *San Remo Manual on International Law Applicable to Armed Conflicts at Sea* (Cambridge University Press 1995).

31    *Montreux Document on Pertinent International Legal Obligations and Good Practices for States related to Operations of Private Military and Security Companies during Armed Conflict* (Swiss Federal Department of Foreign Affairs, 2009).

32    The Copenhagen Process on the Handling of Detainees in International Military Operations, *The Copenhagen Process: Principles and Guidelines* (October 2012) <https://iihl.org/wp-content/uploads/2018/04/Copenhagen-Process-Principles-and-Guidelines.pdf>.

33    Michael Schmitt (ed), *Tallinn Manual 2.0 on the International Law Applicable to Cyber Operations* (Cambridge University Press, 2017).

in part, and [that] certain provisions of the manual are widely recognised as representing principles of customary international law'.[34]

# 11.3    Types of armed conflict and scope of application of international humanitarian law

International humanitarian law applies as soon as an armed conflict commences and does not depend on whether the international law on the resort to force (*jus ad bellum*) has been observed by the parties to the conflict.[35] Determining whether an armed conflict exists depends on several factors, including whether the conflict is between two or more states (international armed conflict, or 'IAC'), or between a state and one or more non-state armed groups, or between non-state armed groups without the involvement of a state (non-international armed conflict, or 'NIAC').

Determining what *kind* of armed conflict is taking place is critical for the application of the law. It affects the categorisation of both people and objects, which itself has consequences for the law on rights and protections, targeting, detention and weaponry. Due to the historical reluctance to allow international law to apply to domestic conflicts,[36] IHL treaties distinguish between IACs and NIACs, with more rules applicable in IACs. That being said, the gap is narrowing, with treaties being drafted or amended to apply to all types of armed conflict.[37] In addition, state practice is bringing about a convergence of law.[38]

However, despite the necessity of determining the type of armed conflict, IHL treaties do not define what constitutes an armed conflict. In practice, states have adopted the reasoning in *Prosecutor v Tadić* ('*Tadić*'), where the International Criminal Tribunal for the Former Yugoslavia ('ICTY') held that 'an armed conflict exists whenever there is a resort to armed force between states or protracted armed violence between governmental authorities and organized armed groups or between such groups within a state'.[39]

## 11.3.1    International armed conflicts

The *Geneva Conventions* in their entirety and *Additional Protocol I* regulate IACs. Common Article 2[40] states that the Conventions apply to 'all cases of declared war or of any other armed

---

34    *Law of Armed Conflict* (n 28) [1.46].
35    See Chapter 8 on the use of force.
36    For a concise summary, see, eg, Emily Crawford and Alison Pert, *International Humanitarian Law* (Cambridge University Press, 2nd ed, 2020) 62–4.
37    See, eg, *Second Protocol to the Hague Convention of 1954 for the Protection of Cultural Property in the Event of Armed Conflict* (n 21).
38    *Prosecutor v Tadić (Decision on the Defence Motion for Interlocutory Appeal on Jurisdiction)* (International Criminal Tribunal for the Former Yugoslavia, Appeals Chamber, Case No IT-94-1, 2 October 1995) ('*Tadić Jurisdiction*') [117]–[126]; Sandesh Sivakumaran, *The Law of Non-International Armed Conflict* (Oxford University Press, 2015) 55–61.
39    *Tadić Jurisdiction* (n 38) [70]. This is the formulation adopted by the Australian Defence Force: see *Law of Armed Conflict* (n 28) [1.51]–[1.52].
40    Each of the four *Geneva Conventions* has the same arts 1, 2 and 3 – hence, 'Common Article 1', 'Common Article 2' and 'Common Article 3'.

conflict which may arise between two or more of the High Contracting Parties, even if the state of war is not recognized by one of them', as well as 'all cases of partial or total occupation of the territory of a High Contracting Party, even if the said occupation meets with no armed resistance'.[41] An inter-state conflict may involve combat or merely the hostile deployment of state military forces[42] (even if the other state does not resist). Occupation is considered separately in Section 11.7.2.

The adoption of *Additional Protocol I* in 1977, at a time when many colonies were striving for independence and apartheid was at its height, added a new type of IAC: 'armed conflicts in which peoples are fighting against colonial domination and alien occupation and against racist régimes in the exercise of their right of self-determination'.[43] That these 'wars of national liberation' were being fought in pursuance of the international right of self-determination was considered sufficient to elevate such conflicts from their previous classification as NIACs to IACs,[44] since they were not really the same as other classic internal 'civil wars'. States which are not party to *Additional Protocol I* may, however, still treat conflicts with liberation movements as NIACs.

## 11.3.2   Non-international armed conflicts

Non-international armed conflicts are regulated in IHL treaty law primarily in Common Article 3 of the *Geneva Conventions* and in *Additional Protocol II*. The accepted test for the existence of a NIAC, from *Tadić*, is whether the armed violence is sufficiently *intense* and the parties are sufficiently *organised*.[45] These criteria aim to distinguish NIACs from other serious forms of violence – such as internal disturbances and tensions, riots, or acts of banditry – which remain subject only to domestic law enforcement. In *Prosecutor v Limaj*, the ICTY identified factors relevant to assessing intensity and organisation as including

> the seriousness of attacks and whether there has been an increase in armed clashes, the spread of clashes over territory and over a period of time, any increase in the number of government forces and mobilisation and the distribution of weapons among both parties to the conflict, as well as whether the conflict has attracted the attention of the United Nations Security Council, and, whether any resolutions on the matter have been passed. With respect to the organisation of the parties to the conflict Chambers of the Tribunal have taken into account factors including the existence of headquarters, designated zones of operation, and the ability to procure, transport, and distribute arms.[46]

---

41  *Geneva Convention I* (n 3) art 2.
42  See, eg, International Committee of the Red Cross, *Commentary on the First Geneva Convention: Convention (I) for the Amelioration of the Condition of the Wounded and Sick in Armed Forces in the Field* (2016) [225] <https://ihl-databases.icrc.org/ihl/full/GCI-commentary>.
43  *Additional Protocol I* (n 7) art 1(4).
44  For the drafting history of *Additional Protocol I*, see *Official Records of the Diplomatic Conference on the Reaffirmation and Development of International Humanitarian Law Applicable in Armed Conflicts, 1974–77* (1978). For a summary of the debates on art 1(4), see, eg, Anthony Cullen, *The Concept of Non-International Armed Conflict in International Humanitarian Law* (Cambridge University Press, 2010) 66–86.
45  *Tadić Jurisdiction* (n 38) [70]; *Prosecutor v Tadić (Opinion and Judgment)* (International Criminal Tribunal for the Former Yugoslavia, Trial Chamber, Case No IT-94-1-T, 7 May 1997) [562].
46  *Prosecutor v Limaj (Judgment)* (International Criminal Tribunal for the Former Yugoslavia, Trial Chamber II, Case No IT-03-66-T, 30 November 2005) [90].

There is no 'combatant' or 'prisoner of war' ('POW') status for non-state participants in NIACs. However, parties to the conflict must observe fundamental minimum rules regarding persons who are not, or are no longer, taking direct part in the hostilities (including 'members of armed forces who have laid down their arms and those placed "*hors de combat*" or out of combat due to sickness, wounds, detention, or any other cause'[47]). These rules include humane treatment and non-discrimination, protection for the wounded and sick, fair trial guarantees, and prohibitions on murder, mutilation, cruel treatment, torture, hostage-taking and humiliating or degrading treatment.[48] *Additional Protocol II* builds on these protections, adding expanded protections for the wounded, sick and shipwrecked,[49] and persons detained in relation to the armed conflict,[50] as well as protections for the civilian population in the form of rules on targeting and other methods of warfare.[51]

Where Common Article 3 applies to all armed conflicts 'not of an international character',[52] *Additional Protocol II* applies only to NIACs 'which take place in the territory of a High Contracting Party between its armed forces and dissident armed forces or other organized armed groups which, under responsible command, exercise such control over a part of its territory as to enable them to carry out sustained and concerted military operations and to implement this Protocol'.[53] For an *Additional Protocol II* conflict to exist, a non-state armed group must be fighting state armed forces, and the non-state group must control a portion of state territory and demonstrate a degree of organisation over their armed personnel.[54] Very few conflicts would satisfy these criteria. By contrast, a Common Article 3 conflict can involve a state and non-state group(s) or only non-state armed groups, without the state being involved, and without any evidence of territorial control by the non-state group(s). The complexity of characterising armed conflicts was noted in the *Afghanistan Inquiry Report* (also known as the *Brereton Report*):

> [9] The stated legal basis for Australia's presence in Afghanistan, in support of NATO-led military operations in the global struggle against violent extremism, and in order to enhance international peace and security, has changed over time. The United States (US) treated the events of 11 September 2001 as an armed attack upon it, which it said justified the invocation of both the inherent right of self-defence enshrined in Article 51 of the *Charter of the United Nations* and, for the first time, Article IV of the *Australia, New Zealand, United States Security (ANZUS) Treaty*.
>
> [10] The legal bases for Operation SLIPPER were the invitation to NATO by the Government of the Islamic Republic of Afghanistan (GIRoA) and the series of United Nations (UN) Security Council resolutions which provide a *UN Charter* Chapter VII

---

47   *Geneva Convention I* (n 3) art 3.
48   Ibid.
49   *Additional Protocol II* (n 8) arts 7–12.
50   Ibid arts 4–6.
51   Ibid arts 13–18.
52   Common Article 3.
53   *Additional Protocol II* (n 8) art 1(1).
54   See further Yves Sandoz, Christophe Swinarski and Bruno Zimmerman (eds), *Commentary on the Additional Protocols of 8 June 1977 to the Geneva Conventions of 12 August 1949* (ICRC and Martinus Nijhoff, 1987) [4461]–[4469]; Sivakumaran (n 38) 175.

mandate for the NATO-led security mission in Afghanistan, in particular Resolution 1386 in December 2001. . . .

[11] The Government of Australia rightly considered the conflict in Afghanistan to be an armed conflict not of an international character; that is, a conflict between the sovereign Afghan Government on the one hand and insurgents, foreign fighters and remnants or supporters of the former Taliban regime on the other. Thus, Common Article 3 of the *Geneva Conventions* applies as a matter of legal obligation. In addition, certain provisions of the *Geneva Conventions* are applicable as a matter of customary international law. As established customary international law, Common Article 3 applied to all [International Security Assistance Force] members, as was recognised by the US Supreme Court in 2005, in *Hamdan v Rumsfeld*.[55]

## 11.3.3 Parallel conflicts

It is possible for an armed conflict to be simultaneously characterised as both an IAC and a NIAC. For example, during the conflict in the Balkans in the 1990s, at times there were both IACs and NIACs taking place, sometimes in the same geographical region, depending on the parties to the hostilities at the time.[56] Further, there can be multiple parallel NIACs, as in recent conflicts in Syria or the Democratic Republic of Congo, where multiple armed groups have fought each other as well as government forces.

## 11.3.4 Transformation of conflicts and internationalised, transnational, hybrid and spillover conflicts

International humanitarian law recognises only two types of armed conflict: IACs and NIACs. However, in practice, some armed conflicts can demonstrate qualities of both IACs and NIACs at various stages of their existence, sometimes even simultaneously. A NIAC can also be transformed into an IAC; likewise, an IAC can become a NIAC. For example, one state may fight a non-state armed group on the territory of another state (whose forces are not involved in the conflict), as in the conflicts between the United States and Al Qaeda in Afghanistan in 2001, Israel and Hezbollah in southern Lebanon in 2006, and periodically between Turkey and the Kurdish PKK in Iraq. In another example, a NIAC could be 'internationalised' by the involvement of a state on behalf of a non-state party, such as when a foreign state intervenes in a civil war on behalf of the rebel movement.[57]

Depending on the nature and extent of the intervention, the intervening state could become a party to the conflict and thus could generate an IAC between the two states, in parallel with the ongoing NIAC between the armed group and the territorial state, or remain a NIAC where foreign state support to the rebels is more indirect. The withdrawal of a state's

---

55    Inspector-General of the Australian Defence Force, *Afghanistan Inquiry Report* (November 2020) 266–7 [9]–[11] (citations omitted) ('*Brereton Report*').

56    *Tadić Jurisdiction* (n 38) [72]–[78].

57    As was the case during the Balkans Wars in the 1990s. See further *Prosecutor v Tadić (Appeal against Conviction)* (1999) 124 ILR 61, [84] for a specific discussion of the Balkans conflict. For a general outline on internationalised armed conflict, see further Crawford and Pert (n 36) 76–84.

involvement may result in an IAC transforming into a NIAC.[58] For example, in the above-mentioned situation in Afghanistan, the hostilities between the US-led coalition and the Taliban government of Afghanistan after the terrorist attacks of 11 September 2001 were initially an IAC. When the Taliban government was ousted from power in 2002, the conflict was trans-formed into a NIAC between the new Afghan government, supported by coalition forces, and the Taliban – now a non-state armed group.[59]

A NIAC may also 'spill over'[60] into another state's territory or traverse international borders (for example, if a non-state armed group uses that other state's territory for a base).[61] This will not necessarily mean that the other state becomes a party to the NIAC centred in the first state, unless, for example, its own forces engage the armed group (or the other state, in which case there may be an IAC). Ultimately, 'transnational' and 'spillover' are descriptive terms, as there is no legal definition or category of 'transnational' or 'spillover' armed conflict.

## 11.3.5    Scope of application of international humanitarian law

As already noted, IHL applies as soon as an armed conflict – IAC or NIAC – exists. International humanitarian law then applies to all areas of the state or states involved,[62] even if there are no active hostilities (for example, in occupied territory in an IAC[63] or peaceful areas of the state in a NIAC) or the territory is outside the jurisdictional control of a party (for example, on the high seas[64] or in areas designated as neutral zones[65]). This principle of 'unity of territory'[66] applies in both IACs[67] and NIACs.[68]

In IACs, IHL will generally cease to apply when there is a close of military operations;[69] an end of captivity or detention under *Geneva Convention III* relating to POWs;[70] and/or an end of military occupation, which may be one year after the general close of military operations.[71]

58    For example, the conflicts in Afghanistan and Iraq were both 'de-internationalised' when US/coalition forces withdrew from the conflicts. See further Siobhan Wills, 'The Legal Characterization of the Armed Conflicts in Afghanistan and Iraq: Implications for Protection' (2011) 58(2) *Netherlands International Law Review* 173.

59    Jens David Ohlin, 'The Nature and Scope of the War in Afghanistan', *Opinio Juris* (Blog Post, 28 May 2015) <http://opiniojuris.org/2015/05/28/the-nature-and-scope-of-the-war-in-afghanistan/>.

60    As seen in the conflict in Syria, which started in 2011. See Daniel Byman, 'Civil Wars and Spillover', *The Brookings Institute* (Blog Post, 3 June 2015) <www.brookings.edu/blog/markaz/2015/06/03/civil-wars-and-spillover>.

61    Sylvain Vité, 'Typology of Armed Conflicts in International Humanitarian Law: Legal Concepts and Actual Situations' (2009) 91 *International Review of the Red Cross* 69.

62    Robert Kolb and Richard Hyde, *The International Law of Armed Conflicts* (Hart 2008) 94.

63    *Geneva Convention IV* (n 6) art 2.

64    See Jann Kleffner, 'Scope of Application of International Humanitarian Law' in Dieter Fleck (ed), *The Handbook of International Humanitarian Law* (Oxford University Press, 3rd ed, 2013) 43, 56–7.

65    *Geneva Convention IV* (n 6) art 15.

66    Kolb and Hyde (n 62) 95.

67    *Tadić Jurisdiction* (n 38) [68].

68    *Prosecutor v Akayesu (Judgment)* (International Criminal Tribunal for Rwanda, Trial Chamber I, Case No ICTR-96-4-T, 2 September 1998) [635].

69    *Geneva Convention IV* (n 6) art 6(2); *Additional Protocol I* (n 7) art 3(b).

70    *Geneva Convention III* (n 5) art 5(1).

71    *Geneva Convention IV* (n 6) art 6(1).

In occupied territory, however, IHL continues to apply for as long as the occupying power continues to exercise government functions.[72] For NIACs, *Additional Protocol II* refers to the 'end of the armed conflict',[73] though in the *Tadić* case it was stated that IHL ceases to apply in NIACs only when a 'peaceful settlement is achieved'.[74]

# 11.4 Fundamental principles of international humanitarian law

The treaty and customary law of armed conflict is based on several fundamental principles, including distinction, proportionality, military necessity, humanity, and the prohibition on causing unnecessary suffering and superfluous injury. These are discussed in the following sections.

## 11.4.1 Distinction

The principle of distinction is codified in art 48 of *Additional Protocol I*:

> Parties to the conflict shall at all times distinguish between the civilian population and combatants and between civilian objects and military objectives and accordingly shall direct their operations only against military objectives.

The principle of distinction is considered customary law[75] and is one of the 'cardinal principles'[76] of IHL. Connected to it is the prohibition on launching indiscriminate attacks. Article 51(4) of *Additional Protocol I* defines these as attacks which are not directed at a specific military objective, which employ a means or method which cannot be directed at a specific military objective, or which employ a means or method the effects of which cannot be limited, and which are 'of a nature to strike military objectives and civilians or civilian objects without distinction'. An indiscriminate attack would be an attack which is not aimed at a specific military target, or which treats a number of distinct military targets as a single target – for example, through the practice of carpet bombing an area that contains both military installations and civilian property, without specifically aiming the bombs at the military installations.

## 11.4.2 Proportionality

The principle of proportionality requires that the military advantage anticipated from a particular operation outweighs the damage caused to civilians and civilian objects. Proportionality is codified in art 51(5)(b) of *Additional Protocol I*, which states that 'an attack which may be

---

72    Ibid art 6(3). Compare *Hague IV 1907* (n 10) art 42, which holds that the *Hague Regulations* apply for as long as there is de facto occupation of territory.

73    *Additional Protocol II* (n 8) art 2(2).

74    *Tadić Jurisdiction* (n 38) [70].

75    See Geoffrey Best, 'The Restraint of War in Historical and Philosophical Perspective' in Astrid Delissen and Gerard Tanja (eds), *Humanitarian Law of Armed Conflict: Challenges Ahead* (Martinus Nijhoff, 1991) 17 (the principle of distinction was 'no doubt customary law before it received positive formulation in the 1860s').

76    *Legality of the Threat or Use of Nuclear Weapons (Advisory Opinion)* [1996] ICJ Rep 226, 257 [78].

expected to cause incidental loss of civilian life, injury to civilians, damage to civilian objects, or a combination thereof, which would be excessive in relation to the concrete and direct military advantage anticipated', should be considered 'indiscriminate'. The assessment is based on all information reasonably available to the party at the time, including taking precautions to verify that the target is a military and not a civilian one and to minimise civilian casualties. Not all civilian injury or damage to civilian objects is necessarily disproportionate – only that which is considered excessive relative to the military advantage. Therefore, some intentional collateral damage to civilians or civilian objects is permissible.[77] An example of how proportionality assessments are made was seen in the final report to the Prosecutor of the ICTY by the Committee established to review the NATO bombing campaign against Yugoslavia.[78] During the 1999 Kosovo conflict between NATO member states and Yugoslavia, NATO aircraft bombed the Serb TV and Radio Station in Belgrade, killing between 10 and 17 civilians. Although it was a civilian station, the facility was used at the time for Yugoslav military communications. The report explored the question of whether the attack was proportionate:

> [77] Assuming the station was a legitimate objective, the civilian casualties were unfortunately high but do not appear to be clearly disproportionate. ... [I]t is possible that casualties among civilians working at the [Serbian TV and Radio Station ('RTS')] may have been heightened because of NATO's apparent failure to provide clear advance warning of the attack [although advance warning may not have been given because it would have endangered the pilots] ... On the other hand, foreign media representatives were apparently forewarned of the attack ... [I]t would also appear that some Yugoslav officials may have expected that the building was about to be struck ...
>
> [78] Assuming the RTS building to be a legitimate military target, it appeared that NATO realised that attacking the RTS building would only interrupt broadcasting for a brief period. Indeed, broadcasting allegedly recommenced within hours of the strike, thus raising the issue of the importance of the military advantage gained by the attack *vis-à-vis* the civilian casualties incurred. The [Yugoslav] command and control network was alleged by NATO to comprise a complex web and that could thus not be disabled in one strike. ... The proportionality or otherwise of an attack should not necessarily focus exclusively on a specific incident. ... With regard to these goals, the strategic target of these attacks was the Yugoslav command and control network. The attack on the RTS building must therefore be seen as forming part of an integrated attack against numerous [other] objects [which were also targeted, including other transmission towers and electricity grids, which were] ... an integral part of the strategic communications network which enabled both the military and national command authorities to direct the repression and atrocities taking place in Kosovo ...[79]

77    Judith Gardam, 'Necessity and Proportionality in Jus ad Bellum and Jus in Bello' in Laurence Boisson de Chazournes and Philippe Sands (eds), *International Law, the International Court of Justice and Nuclear Weapons* (Cambridge University Press, 1999) 283.
78    International Criminal Tribunal for the Former Yugoslavia, *Final Report to the Prosecutor by the Committee Established to Review the NATO Bombing Campaign against the Federal Republic of Yugoslavia* (2000).
79    Ibid [77]–[78].

### 11.4.3   Military necessity

Military necessity requires that the parties to the conflict adopt only those measures necessary to weaken the enemy and achieve its surrender; it is not necessary to bring about excessive or total destruction of the enemy, its armed forces or its property.[80] Military necessity was first codified in art 14 of the *Lieber Code* and 'consists in the necessity of those measures which are indispensable for securing the ends of the war, and which are lawful according to the modern law and usages of war'.[81]

Military necessity is not codified in either the *Geneva Conventions* or *Additional Protocol I*, but it is closely linked to the principle and rules on proportionality and the prohibition on causing superfluous injury or unnecessary suffering to combatants.[82]

### 11.4.4   Humanity

The principle of humanity operates as a further limiting factor on conduct in armed conflict. It is the concept underlying the prohibition on causing unnecessary suffering and superfluous injury, as well as the rules that prohibit the targeting of persons *hors de combat*. The principle is most obviously seen in the Martens Clause,[83] which states that, in addition to other IHL rules, the parties must abide by 'the principles of international law, as they result from the usages established between civilised nations, from the laws of humanity, and the requirements of the public conscience'.[84] The Martens Clause has had a profound influence on the development of more specific IHL rules; it is included in the *Geneva Conventions* and *Additional Protocols*, and it has been cited in numerous tribunals and courts as an important foundational principle of IHL.[85]

### 11.4.5   Prohibition on causing unnecessary suffering and superfluous injury

Parties to an armed conflict are also prohibited from using means or methods of warfare that result in superfluous injury or unnecessary suffering to combatants,[86] meaning the causing of any injuries which are greater than what is strictly necessary to achieve the military objectives

---

80    See generally Burrus Carnahan, 'Lincoln, Lieber and the Laws of War: The Origins and Limits of the Principle of Military Necessity' (1998) 92(2) *American Journal of International Law* 213.

81    Department of War (US), *Instructions for the Government of Armies of the United States in the Field*, General Orders No 100 (24 April 1863) art 14 (also known as the *Lieber Code*).

82    *Additional Protocol I* (n 7) art 36.

83    The Martens Clause is included in *Geneva Convention I* (n 3) art 63(4), *Geneva Convention II* (n 4) art 62(4), *Geneva Convention III* (n 5) art 142(4), *Geneva Convention IV* (n 6) art 158(4), *Additional Protocol I* (n 7) art 1(2) and *Additional Protocol II* (n 8) Preamble. It is also found in *Conventional Weapons Convention* (n 20) para 5.

84    See further Antonio Cassese, 'The Martens Clause: Half a Loaf or Simply Pie in the Sky?' (2000) 11(1) *European Journal of International Law* 187, 193–8; Jean Pictet (ed), *Commentary to the Third Geneva Convention Relative to the Treatment of Prisoners of War* (ICRC, 1960) 46–7.

85    See *Legality of the Threat or Use of Nuclear Weapons* (n 76) 226, 257 [78]. See also, eg, *Prosecutor v Kupreškić (Judgment)* (International Criminal Tribunal for the Former Yugoslavia, Appeals Chamber, Case No IT-95-16-T, 14 January 2000) [527].

86    *Hague IV 1907* (n 10) art 23; *Additional Protocol I* (n 7) art 36.

and which 'uselessly aggravate the sufferings of disabled men, or render their death inevitable'.[87] For a particular means or method to be prohibited under this principle, the injury or suffering caused must be 'substantially disproportional to the military advantage gained'.[88] Examples of weapons that have been banned on the grounds of causing unnecessary suffering or superfluous injury include blinding laser weapons, chemical weapons, and biological weapons, discussed in more detail in Section 11.6.2.

# 11.5   Persons and objects under international humanitarian law

International humanitarian law categorises and protects a wide range of people and objects, with specialised protection regimes for some of them (see Section 11.7). As a starting point, IHL distinguishes between persons (and objects) directly participating in or contributing to the armed conflict, and persons (and objects) taking no part in the hostilities. Depending on the categorisation of a person (or object), they may be lawfully targeted with lethal or destructive force, or such targeting may violate IHL.

## 11.5.1   Combatants and attached non-combatants

In an IAC, persons who are permitted to take direct part in the hostilities[89] (for instance, by using a weapon or weapons system), and who are entitled to the benefits of POW status if captured, are known as combatants under IHL. Combatants are also entitled to the 'combatant's privilege', which means that they cannot be prosecuted in any court simply for having taken part in the conflict.[90]

The *Geneva Conventions* and *Additional Protocols* do not define the term 'combatant'; instead, the meaning is derived from art 4A(1) of *Geneva Convention III*, which grants POW status to regular '[m]embers of the armed forces of a Party to the conflict as well as members of militias or volunteer corps forming part of such armed forces'.[91] Added to this category are members of irregular forces, such as other militia and volunteer corps, provided they fulfil certain conditions: that of being commanded by a person responsible for their subordinates, wearing a fixed distinctive emblem recognisable at a distance, carrying arms openly, and conducting operations in accordance with the laws and customs of war.[92] These criteria aim to ensure that combatants are clearly distinguishable from civilians, so that the latter are not regarded suspiciously as possible fighters, and so that both parties can equally recognise one another's fighters. Also included as combatants are participants in *levées en masse*:

---

87    *Declaration Renouncing the Use, in Time of War, of Explosive Projectiles under 400 Grammes Weight,* Saint Petersburg, 29 November/11 December 1868.

88    Solis (n 2) 292.

89    *Additional Protocol I* (n 7) art 43(2).

90    Michael Bothe et al (eds), *New Rules for Victims of Armed Conflicts: Commentary on the Two 1977 Protocols Additional to the Geneva Conventions of 1949* (Martinus Nijhoff, 2nd ed, 2013) 277.

91    *Geneva Convention III* (n 5) art 4A(1).

92    *Hague Regulations* (n 10) art 1.

inhabitants of a non-occupied territory who, on the approach of the enemy, spontaneously take up arms to resist the invading forces, without having had time to form
themselves into regular armed units, provided they carry arms openly and respect the
laws and customs of war.[93]

*Additional Protocol I* added a new category in the definition of combatant:

> all organized armed forces, groups and units which are under a command responsible to
> that Party for the conduct of its subordinates, even if that Party is represented by a
> government or an authority not recognized by an adverse Party. Such armed forces shall
> be subject to an internal disciplinary system which … shall enforce compliance with the
> rules of international law applicable in armed conflict.[94]

*Additional Protocol I* expanded the definition of combatant to include persons fighting in wars
of national liberation; controversially, the Protocol also relaxed the requirements for national
liberation fighters to be classified as combatants:

> Recognizing … that there are situations in armed conflicts where, owing to the nature of
> the hostilities an armed combatant cannot so distinguish himself, he shall retain his status
> as a combatant, provided that, in such situations, he carries his arms openly:
> (a)  during each military engagement, and
> (b)  during such time as he is visible to the adversary while he is engaged in a military
>      deployment preceding the launching of an attack in which he is to participate.[95]

The provision is a concession to the challenges faced by guerrilla-type forces, while also
ensuring that civilians are distinguishable and the enemy can still recognise guerrilla fighters.

Also entitled to POW protections, but not classified as combatants who can be attacked, are
the categories of non-combatants who are closely attached to combatant forces, which include
'[p]ersons who accompany the armed forces without actually being members thereof, such as
civilian members of military aircraft crews, war correspondents, supply contractors, members
of labour units or of services responsible for the welfare of the armed forces',[96] as well as
'[m]embers of crews, including masters, pilots and apprentices of the merchant marine and the
crews of civil aircraft of the Parties to the conflict'.[97]

Certain persons are denied combatant and POW status outright (although they are still
entitled to fundamental guarantees applicable to everyone). These include spies who are
captured while engaging in acts of espionage while wearing civilian clothing (whether such
persons are civilians or members of the armed forces wearing civilian clothes).[98] However, a
member of the armed forces who engages in acts of espionage while in uniform will retain
their combatant and POW status. Mercenaries are also pre-emptively denied combatant and
POW rights. The definition of a mercenary has elements of financial reward ('soldiers of
fortune') and absence of allegiance to the state ('gun for hire'): a person who takes part in

---

93    *Geneva Convention III* (n 5) art 4A(6).
94    *Additional Protocol I* (n 7) art 43(1).
95    Ibid art 44(3).
96    *Geneva Convention III* (n 5) art 4A(4).
97    Ibid art 4A(5).
98    *Hague Regulations* (n 10) art 29; *Additional Protocol I* (n 7) art 46.

active hostilities having been promised 'material compensation substantially in excess of that promised or paid to combatants of similar rank and function in the armed forces of that party'[99] and who is, inter alia, neither a member of the armed forces of a state party to the conflict nor a national or resident of a party to the conflict.[100]

Although there is no combatant or POW status for non-state actors in NIACs, persons who take direct part in hostilities (including the fighters of non-state armed groups) are not left entirely unprotected. The rules in Common Article 3, *Additional Protocol II*, and customary IHL provide fundamental safeguards for persons detained in NIACs,[101] supplemented by applicable standards of international human rights law.

## 11.5.2 Civilians (including those taking direct part in hostilities)

In IACs, civilians are defined in art 50 of *Additional Protocol I* as any persons who do not fulfil the conditions for combatant status. If there is any doubt, the person will be presumed to be a civilian.[102] Civilians are not to be made the object of attack,[103] meaning that they cannot be directly targeted unless they directly participate in hostilities.[104] The same principles apply in NIACs. Deliberately targeting civilians is a war crime in both IACs and NIACs,[105] as well as under Australian law.[106]

Civilians who take a direct part in hostilities lose their immunity from attack for the duration of their direct participation; they become legitimate targets (the rules on targeting are explored in Section 11.6.1). There is no treaty definition of what amounts to direct participation in hostilities ('DPH'), though the Commentary to the *Additional Protocols*[107] indicates that it means 'hostile acts ... which by their nature and purpose are intended to cause actual harm to the personnel and equipment of the armed forces'.[108] There is controversy in IHL about the meaning of 'direct' (versus 'indirect') participation in hostilities, as well as how to measure the duration of participation, including in relation to the use of contemporary military technologies such as pilotless

99    *Additional Protocol I* (n 7) art 47(2)(c).
100   Ibid art 47(2)(d)–(e); *International Convention against the Recruitment, Use, Financing and Training of Mercenaries*, opened for signature 4 December 1989, 2163 UNTS 75 (entered into force 20 October 2001).
101   See further Emily Crawford, *The Treatment of Combatants and Insurgents under the Law of Armed Conflict* (Oxford University Press, 2010) specifically ch 3; Lawrence Hill-Cawthorne, *Detention in Non-International Armed Conflict* (Oxford University Press, 2016). See also *Brereton Report* (n 55) 29 [17].
102   *Additional Protocol I* (n 7) art 50(1).
103   Ibid art 51(2).
104   Ibid art 51(3).
105   *Rome Statute of the International Criminal Court* (n 23) art 8(2)(b)(i) (attacking civilians in an IAC) and art 8(2)(e)(i) (attacking civilians in a NIAC).
106   *Criminal Code Act 1995* (Cth) sch 1 s 268.35 (attacking civilians in an IAC), s 268.77 (attacking civilians in a NIAC). See also *Brereton Report* (n 55) 29 [17].
107   The International Committee of the Red Cross has published 'Commentaries' on the *Geneva Conventions* and the *Additional Protocols*, written by experts in the field, which explain the background to the treaties and their intended meaning. All are available on the website of the ICRC. See 'Geneva Conventions of 1949 and Additional Protocols, and Their Commentaries', *Treaties, States Parties and Commentaries* (Web Page) <https://ihl-databases.icrc.org/applic/ihl/ihl.nsf/vwTreaties1949.xsp>.
108   Sandoz, Swinarski and Zimmerman (n 54) [1942].

aircraft ('drones') and the targeting of 'terrorists'.[109] The Australian Defence Force position on DPH essentially mirrors foreign case law[110] and state practice,[111] acknowledging that

> [w]hether or not a civilian is involved in hostilities is a difficult question, which must be determined by the facts of each individual case. Civilians bearing arms and taking part in military operations are clearly taking part in hostilities; civilians working in a store on a military air base may not necessarily be taking such a direct part.[112]

The International Committee of the Red Cross suggests that indirect participation in hostilities – for which a civilian cannot be targeted – includes activities that are part of, or sustain, the general war effort but which are not of themselves directly hostile acts:

> [T]he general war effort could be said to include all activities objectively contributing to the military defeat of the adversary (eg, design, production and shipment of weapons and military equipment, construction or repair of roads, ports, airports, bridges, railways and other infrastructure outside the context of concrete military operations), while war-sustaining activities would additionally include political, economic or media activities supporting the general war effort (eg, political propaganda, financial transactions, production of agricultural or non-military industrial goods).[113]

The *Brereton Report* also addressed the question of how to determine DPH situations:

> [23] LOAC sets out separate tests for assessing the targetability of people in each of these two categories (DPH and OAG [organised armed groups]). Whilst there are some similarities, the tests differ as to content given that the indicia, emphasis, and consequences of each categorisation differ.
>
> [24] This distinction as to indicia and targetability criteria was necessary because under LOAC, the liability to targeting of each type of enemy fighter (DPH on one hand, OAG on the other) differs. In short, civilians who are assessed as DPH are considered 'ad hoc' enemy whose connection or otherwise to an organised military force is unknown or merely suspected. Consequently, their liability to targeting is only within the 'bubble' of time bound by the lead up to their attack on ADF and friendly forces, during that attack, and for a period of time after that attack. Once the DPH has concluded, however, that person once again re-gains the protections that attend their underlying status as 'civilians' – including the protection from being made the target of an attack. By contrast, people who are considered under the OAG criteria are 'full-time' enemy OAG members. Consequently, they are targetable at all times unless and until they clearly dissociate

---

109    See generally Emily Crawford, *Identifying the Enemy: Civilian Participation in Armed Conflict* (Oxford University Press, 2015).

110    See, eg, *Public Committee against Torture in Israel v Israel* (Supreme Court of Israel, Case No HCJ 769/02, 14 December 2006) [35]–[40]; *Prosecutor v Strugar (Judgment)* (International Criminal Tribunal for the Former Yugoslavia, Appeals Chamber, Case No IT-01-42-A, 17 July 2008). For a more detailed analysis of cases examining direct participation, see *ICRC Customary IHL Study* (n 26) 'Practice Relating to Rule 6'; Crawford ibid 63–72.

111    See generally *ICRC Customary IHL Study* (n 26) 'Practice Relating to Rule 6'.

112    *Law of Armed Conflict* (n 28) [5.36].

113    International Committee of the Red Cross, *Interpretive Guidance on the Notion of Direct Participation in Hostilities under International Humanitarian Law* (2009) 53.

themselves from the OAG and cease hostilities (or are out of the fight due to injuries, surrender, capture, or similar reasons in accordance with LOAC – see below). These indicia are described in general terms below.

**Key indicia regarding the identification of enemy forces who were liable to lethal targeting in accordance with LOAC**

[25] **Set A indicia for DPH**. This test essentially focusses upon observable conduct aimed at causing harm to ADF, friendly forces, and local civilians. Conduct in this category could include, for example, attacking ADF [personnel and materiel] with weapons, laying an improvised explosive device (IED), manoeuvring into an attacking or ambush position, manoeuvring to access a weapons cache, or departing from a position after an attack or after laying an IED.

[26] **Set B indicia for DPH**. This test covers DPH that was indicated by intelligence and other sources. For example, this test could apply when intelligence indicated that an individual was planning an attack or operation against the ADF, friendly forces, or civilians, and this attack or operation was intended to cause harm to those targeted.[114]

## 11.5.3 Objects

As with persons in armed conflicts, objects can also be designated as civilian or military. The categories are not always immutable and can change depending on, inter alia, their use, purpose or location.

### 11.5.3.1 Military objects and objectives

Under art 52(2) of *Additional Protocol I*, attacks may only be directed against military objectives – things which 'by their nature, location, purpose or use make an effective contribution to military action and whose total or partial destruction, capture or neutralisation ... offers a definite military advantage'. Not all military objects will necessarily be military objectives – a military barracks is clearly a military object by its nature and use, but the destruction, capture or neutralisation of the barracks may not always offer a direct military advantage in the circumstances of a particular armed conflict. How to determine what constitutes a military objective, and a direct military advantage, is covered in more detail in Section 11.6.1 on the law of targeting.

### 11.5.3.2 Civilian objects

A civilian object is any object that is not a military objective.[115] However, a civilian object can still be transformed into a military objective if it is used in such a way as to contribute militarily to the armed conflict – for instance, a school or religious building that is used for launching attacks may be considered a military objective if it fulfils the test in art 52(2) of *Additional Protocol I*. However, an object is presumed to be civilian if there is uncertainty about whether the 'object which is normally dedicated to civilian purposes, such as a place of worship,

---

114 *Brereton Report* (n 55) 291–2 [23]–[26].
115 As defined under *Additional Protocol (I)* (n 7) art 52(1).

a house or other dwelling or a school, is being used to make an effective contribution to military action'.[116] Essentially, this means that if there is doubt as to whether a prima facie civilian building is being used to support the military effort, then the presumption should be that it is not: any doubt is resolved in favour of protecting civilians.

# 11.6   The law of targeting and the rules on means and methods of warfare

The rules on the conduct of hostilities, primarily found in the *Hague Regulations* and the *Additional Protocols*, outline the permissible means and methods of attack, and set out the rights and duties to be observed when engaging in offensive or defensive operations. Under IHL, the concept of 'attack' encompasses 'acts of violence against the adversary, whether in offence or in defence'.[117] In this respect, 'attack' as used in IHL is defined more broadly than its conventional dictionary meaning,[118] which suggests an aggressive, offensive action. Rather, as the Commentaries make clear, 'attack' is meant to encompass acts undertaken in both offence and defence in military operations.[119]

The general principles of proportionality,[120] distinction,[121] the prohibition on indiscriminate attacks or weapons,[122] military necessity, humanity, and the prohibition on causing unnecessary suffering or superfluous injury, discussed earlier, must be complied with in the conduct of hostilities. In addition to the specific rules on targeting (outlined in Section 11.6.1), attacks should also endeavour to spare the civilian population as far as possible from the deleterious effects of the conflict;[123] the means and methods of attack chosen must spare the civilian population as far as possible;[124] and certain critical civilian infrastructure[125] should not be targeted, unless certain strict criteria are met.[126]

---

116     Ibid art 51(3).
117     Ibid art 49.
118     Attack: '(n.) An aggressive military action against a place, or enemy forces, equipment, etc, with weapons or armed forces; a joining of battle; an offensive operation; a military assault. Also: the action of making of such an assault': *Oxford English Dictionary Online* (Oxford University Press, December 2020).
119     Sandoz, Swinarski and Zimmerman (n 54) [1879]–[1880].
120     *Additional Protocol I* (n 7) art 57(2).
121     Ibid arts 48, 51(2), 52.
122     Ibid art 51(4)–(5). See Section 11.3.
123     Ibid art 57.
124     Ibid art 57(2)(a)(ii).
125     Including objects considered indispensable to the survival of the civilian population, such as foodstuffs, agricultural areas for the production of foodstuffs, crops, livestock, drinking water installations and supplies, and irrigation works (ibid art 54(2)), as well as works and installations containing dangerous forces, such as dams, dykes, and nuclear power generating stations (ibid art 56).
126     Objects indispensable to the survival of the civilian population (such as water supplies and crops) should not be targeted 'for the specific purpose of denying them for their sustenance value to the civilian population or to the adverse Party, whatever the motive, whether in order to starve out civilians, to cause them to move away, or for any other motive' (ibid art 54); works and installations containing dangerous forces (such as large dams or nuclear power stations) are not to be targeted 'even where these objects are military objectives, if such attack may cause the release of dangerous forces and consequent severe losses among the civilian population' (ibid art 56).

Additional to these requirements for attacks, parties to the conflict must also undertake to respect IHL in their defensive operations, including not using individual civilians or the civilian population as human shields[127] and not locating military objectives in proximity to civilian populations.[128]

## 11.6.1   The law of targeting

As noted, under art 52 of *Additional Protocol I*, deliberate targeting is permissible only against military objectives. An object becomes a military objective if it is being used for military purposes (for example, to store munitions or to launch attacks), if it is inherently military in nature (for example, a military installation such as a barracks or artillery emplacement), if its location offers a military advantage (for example, if a narrow mountain path is the only way to enter a particular territory of high military value, or a hilltop is strategically important) or if the future purpose of the object renders it militarily significant (for example, a military facility that has been constructed but not yet used). While art 52 does not make specific reference to *people* (that is, combatants) being lawful military objectives, a purposive reading of the Protocols would support such an interpretation[129] so as to permit deliberately targeting combatants.

The law on targeting, while seemingly straightforward, is immensely complex – the 2009 Australian Defence Force manual on the law of targeting (a publication separate from the manual on IHL) is over 100 pages long.[130] In addition to the rules contained in *Additional Protocol I*, there are numerous additional considerations, such as who is authorised to make targeting decisions, the role of legal officers in targeting decisions, the approval processes for targeting, the methodology for collateral damage estimations, lists of approved and non-targetable objects, and instructions for post-operation reporting.[131]

## 11.6.2   Prohibited means and methods of warfare

In addition to the rules on targeting, the parties are restricted in the means and methods of warfare they are permitted to employ. The basic rule is contained in art 35 of *Additional Protocol I*, which reiterates the prohibition on causing unnecessary suffering and superfluous injury, and states that 'in any armed conflict, the right of the Parties to the conflict to choose methods or means of warfare is not unlimited'.[132]

### 11.6.2.1   Weapons

Pursuant to the prohibition on causing unnecessary suffering, numerous weapons have been prohibited from use (or are otherwise subject to strict regulation). These include anti-personnel landmines, cluster munitions, booby-traps, weapons that injure by means of fragmentation in

---

127   Ibid art 51(7).
128   Ibid art 58.
129   See in particular ibid arts 37, 41–44, 51(3), 52(2). See also Bothe et al (n 90) 325; Laurie Blank and Gregory Noone, *International Law and Armed Conflict: Fundamental Principles and Contemporary Challenges in the Law of War* (Wolters Kluwer, 2nd ed, 2019) 462.
130   *Targeting* (Australian Defence Doctrine Publication 3.14, 2009).
131   Ibid [3.26]–[3.36].
132   *Additional Protocol I* (n 7) art 35(1). See also a similar provision in *Hague Regulations* (n 10) art 22.

the human body that is undetectable by X-ray, blinding laser weapons, exploding and expanding bullets, chemical and biological weapons, and nuclear weapons.[133] Some of these prohibitions are, however, limited to states parties to particular treaties (as is the case for landmines, cluster munitions, and nuclear weapons), whereas others are universal (such as those concerning chemical and biological weapons). Some treaties also impose wider obligations on states parties, even outside armed conflict – for example, not to develop, produce, acquire, stockpile, retain or transfer certain weapons; prepare for their use; or assist other states in using them – and states must also destroy weapons stockpiles and submit to international supervision.[134]

For parties to *Additional Protocol I*, an additional obligation exists: 'in the study, development, acquisition or adoption of a new weapon, means or method of warfare, a High Contracting Party is under an obligation to determine whether its employment would, in some or all circumstances, be prohibited by this Protocol or by any other rule of international law'.[135] States parties must thus assess the legality of new weapons – whether those that are entirely new inventions, or pre-existing weapons that are new to the arsenal of the acquiring state.

### 11.6.2.2  Methods

In addition to specifically prohibited weapons, there are obligations regarding specific methods of warfare. These include prohibitions on ordering that there are to be no survivors or prisoners taken (known as orders of 'no quarter');[136] prohibitions on acts of pillage[137] against protected persons and objects;[138] and strict limitations on sieges (for example, trying to force a town to surrender by blocking all food supplies and starving the population)[139] and naval blockades.[140]

Also prohibited are perfidious attacks,[141] meaning those that invite 'the confidence of an adversary to lead him to believe that he is entitled to, or is obliged to accord, protection under the rules of international law applicable in armed conflict, with intent to betray that confidence'.[142] Examples include feigning surrender or incapacitation by wounds or sickness (that

---

133    See Section 11.2 for a full listing of weapons treaties.
134    See, eg, *Chemical Weapons Convention* (n 11) art 2.
135    *Additional Protocol I* (n 7) art 36.
136    *Hague Regulations* (n 10) art 23(d); *Additional Protocol I* (n 7) art 40; *Additional Protocol II* (n 8) art 4.
137    Defined in the International Criminal Court as 'the appropriation of certain property by an individual. The act of "appropriation" has been held to imply that "property has come under the control of the perpetrator". The Chamber concurs with other chambers of the Court that pillaging extends to the appropriation of all types of property, private or public, movable or immovable. . . . [T]he appropriation [must] occur without the consent of the owner. The Chamber notes that the Court's legal framework does not include any requirement of violence as an element of the appropriation. In this respect, the Chamber is of the view that in certain circumstances lack of consent can be inferred from the absence of the rightful owner from the place from where property was taken. Lack of consent may be further inferred by the existence of coercion': *Prosecutor v Bemba (Judgment Pursuant to Article 74 of the Statute)* (International Criminal Court, Trial Chamber III, Case No ICC-01/05-01/08, 21 March 2016) [115]–[116] (citations omitted).
138    *Geneva Convention I* (n 3) art 15; *Geneva Convention II* (n 4) art 18; *Geneva Convention IV* (n 6) art 16; *Hague Regulations* (n 10) arts 28, 47; *Additional Protocol II* (n 8) art 4(2)(g).
139    *Geneva Convention IV* (n 6) art 17; *Additional Protocol I* (n 7) art 54.
140    *Additional Protocol I* (n 7) arts 54, 70.
141    Ibid art 37(1); *Hague Regulations* (n 10) art 23(b).
142    *Additional Protocol I* (n 7) art 37(1).

is, pretending to be wounded or dead); feigning civilian or non-combatant status; and feigning protected status by the use of signs, emblems or uniforms of the United Nations or of neutral or other states that are not parties to the conflict.[143] Central to a perfidious act is the intent to misuse a protected symbol or protected status for the purpose of deceiving an adversary to believe that the perfidious actor is entitled to immunity from attack, only for that actor to exploit that status to launch an attack. Such conduct not only gives the attacker an unfair advantage, but also endangers genuine protected persons or objects.

Connected to the rules on perfidy is the obligation on parties to the conflict not to misuse the emblems of the Red Cross, Red Crescent and Red Crystal – internationally[144] and domestically[145] protected emblems used by the International Committee of the Red Cross when providing aid to parties to the conflict.

# 11.7 Special protection regimes

In addition to the general protections outlined in the Conventions and Protocols, there are specific classes of persons and object that enjoy additional protections.

## 11.7.1 Prisoners of war

The fundamental purpose of POW status is not the punishment of captured combatants; rather, it is preventative administrative detention without charge, designed to stop persons from continuing to participate in hostilities[146] for as long (or short) as the conflict persists. At the cessation of hostilities, POWs are to be released and repatriated.[147]

POW detention is subject to numerous conditions in *Geneva Convention III*. POWs are entitled to humane treatment and protection from mistreatment;[148] they must not be murdered, tortured or subjected to ill-treatment;[149] they must be appropriately housed, fed and clothed;[150] and they are to be given necessary medical treatment.[151] As persons out of combat, they are not to be directly targeted or used as human shields.[152] Extensive protections also exist for POWs who work while in captivity:[153] to ensure that POWs have contact with the outside world, such as

---

143    Ibid.
144    *Geneva Convention I* (n 3) art 38; *Geneva Convention II* (n 4) art 41; *Additional Protocol I* (n 7) art 8(1); *Additional Protocol II* (n 8) art 12; *Additional Protocol III* (n 9) art 2(2).
145    In Australia, the emblems are protected under *Geneva Conventions Act 1957* (Cth) s 15. Use of any of the protected emblems without the consent of the Minister for Defence or other authorised person is a strict liability offence.
146    The International Military Tribunal in Nuremberg noted that POW status is 'neither revenge, nor punishment, but solely protective custody, the sole purpose of which is to prevent the prisoners of war from further participation in the war': see 'Judgment of the International Military Tribunal at Nuremberg 1946' in (1947) 41(1) *American Journal of International Law* 172, 172, 229.
147    *Geneva Convention III* (n 5) arts 109–121.
148    Ibid arts 12–13.
149    Ibid arts 12–14.
150    Ibid arts 19–28.
151    Ibid arts 29–32.
152    Ibid art 23.
153    Ibid arts 49–57.

their family and state of origin;[154] and to guarantee fair criminal trial[155] for any offences not related to their prior lawful participation in hostilities (for example, war crimes). Fair trial standards under IHL are roughly equivalent to those under international human rights law.[156]

## 11.7.2   The law of occupation

Occupation is a type of IAC. Foreign territory is considered occupied when it is actually placed under the authority of the hostile army[157] which has displaced that territory's own government. Examples include the post–World War II allied occupations of Germany and Japan, as well as Uganda's occupation of parts of the Democratic Republic of Congo in the late 1990s. There is no concept of occupation in NIACs: a non-state armed group is not recognised as having any authority to rule, even if it in fact administers territory and controls a population.

The law of occupation aims to balance the security needs of the occupying power with the protection of civilians. An occupying power does not acquire sovereignty over occupied territory. Occupation is presumed to be temporary, pending the resumption of the territory's own government when peace is restored. The occupying power must respect the existing laws and institutions of the occupied territory so far as possible, maintain law and order, not alter local demography, and safeguard its resources for the benefit of the local population.[158]

*Geneva Convention IV* contains detailed rules regarding the treatment of civilians who find themselves in the hands of an adverse party or belligerent either because their home territory has been occupied, or because they find themselves on the territory of an enemy state. Much like the protections that accrue to POWs, civilians are also protected in occupied territory – for example, the wounded and sick are to be protected and cared for;[159] civilians must not be subject to ill-treatment or hostage-taking;[160] protections regarding employment, health, food supplies and fundamental infrastructure must be observed;[161] and humanitarian relief must be allowed and facilitated. The law of occupation was one of the issues examined in the *Armed Activities on the Territory of the Congo* case in the ICJ:

> [T]he Court considers that it has credible evidence sufficient to conclude that the UPDF troops [for whom Uganda was legally responsible] committed acts of killing, torture and other forms of inhumane treatment of the civilian population [of the Democratic Republic of Congo], destroyed villages and civilian buildings, failed to distinguish between civilian and military targets and to protect the civilian population in fighting with other combatants, incited ethnic conflict and took no steps to put an end to such conflicts, was involved in the training of child soldiers, and did not take measures to ensure respect for human rights and international humanitarian law in the occupied territories.
>
> . . .

---

154    Ibid arts 8–10, 69–77.

155    Ibid arts 82–108.

156    For example, compare *Additional Protocol I* (n 7) art 75 and *International Covenant on Civil and Political Rights*, opened for signature 16 December 1966, 999 UNTS 171 (entered into force 23 March 1976) art 14.

157    *Hague Regulations* (n 10) art 42.

158    Ibid arts 48–56; *Geneva Convention IV* (n 6) arts 27, 47–75.

159    *Geneva Convention IV* (n 6) arts 13–26.

160    Ibid arts 31–34.

161    Ibid arts 47–63.

> Uganda is internationally responsible for acts of looting, plundering and exploitation of the DRC's natural resources committed by members of the UPDF in the territory of the DRC, for violating its obligation of vigilance in regard to these acts and for failing to comply with its obligations under Article 43 of the *Hague Regulations* of 1907 as an occupying Power in Ituri in respect of all acts of looting, plundering and exploitation of natural resources in the occupied territory.[162]

Civilians in IACs can be administratively detained for security reasons, but, if they are, they are entitled to expansive protections largely similar to those afforded to POWs.[163] However, unlike POWs, they may only be detained based on an individual assessment of the risk they pose, subject to a right of review, and only for as long as they are dangerous (and not automatically until the end of the conflict).

While the law of occupation does not exist in relation to NIACs, there are limited rules regarding the treatment of detainees in NIACs.[164] However, unlike the IAC rules on occupation, the grounds and procedures of detention of persons in NIACs are not expressly set out in IHL treaties and there is controversy regarding whether IHL or national law governs. That being said, under international law, all detention must be non-arbitrary and subject to independent review.[165]

## 11.7.3   Wounded, sick and shipwrecked

International humanitarian law contains extensive protections for members of the armed forces who find themselves out of combat due to wounding or sickness. The protections in *Geneva Convention II* and the *Additional Protocols* provide that relief must be given to the wounded and sick, without distinction or discrimination on any grounds other than medical necessity – factors such as status, allegiance, nationality and gender are irrelevant.[166] Medical personnel, installations and transports are to be protected from attack,[167] respected and protected.[168] They must not be punished for their medical activities.[169] These rules apply in IACs and NIACs; however, medical installations and personnel still find themselves subject to attack, with recent examples being the bombings of the Médecins Sans Frontières facilities in Yemen in 2018[170] and Afghanistan in 2015.[171]

---

162    *Armed Activities on the Territory of the Congo (Democratic Republic of the Congo v Uganda) (Judgment)* [2005] ICJ Rep 168, 241 [211], 253 [250].

163    *Geneva Convention IV* (n 6) arts 42, 79–135.

164    Common Article 3; *Additional Protocol II* (n 8) arts 4–6.

165    See generally *International Covenant on Civil and Political Rights* (n 156) art 9.

166    *Geneva Convention II* (n 4) arts 12–21; *Additional Protocol I* (n 7) arts 8–20; Common Article 3; *Additional Protocol II* (n 8) arts 7–8; *ICRC Customary IHL Study* (n 26) 'Rule 110'.

167    *Geneva Convention II* (n 4) arts 36–40; *Additional Protocol I* (n 7) arts 21–31; Common Article 3; *Additional Protocol II* (n 8) arts 10–11; *ICRC Customary IHL Study* (n 26) 'Rule 30'.

168    *ICRC Customary IHL Study* (n 26) 'Rule 25', 'Rule 28', 'Rule 29'.

169    Ibid 'Rule 26'.

170    Médecins Sans Frontières, 'Unacceptable Investigation Findings into Abs Health Centre Bombing' (Press Release, 6 February 2019) <https://www.msf.org/report-bombing-msf-facility-unacceptable-and-contradictory-abs-yemen>.

171    Médecins Sans Frontières, 'MSF Demands Explanations after Deadly Airstrikes Hit Hospital in Kunduz' (Press Release, 3 October 2015) <https://www.msf.org/afghanistan-msf-demands-explanations-after-deadly-airstrikes-hit-hospital-kunduz>.

## 11.7.4   Cultural property

Cultural property – 'moveable or immovable property of great importance to the cultural heritage of every people'[172] – is specially protected under IHL,[173] including under the standalone *Convention for the Protection of Cultural Property in the Event of Armed Conflict*,[174] due to its cultural significance to humankind. These instruments protect a vast array of items and objects.[175]

The general rule is that the parties to an armed conflict must not target cultural property and must refrain from using it in such a way as to render it liable for targeting (for example, by using it as a military base).[176] The protection of cultural property is an obligation in both IACs and NIACs, and is considered customary international law.[177] A recent successful prosecution for destruction of cultural property was the case *Prosecutor v Al Mahdi*.[178] The defendant was a member of Ansar Eddine, an armed group in Mali listed by the Security Council as a terrorist entity. The case concerned the destruction of several historic mausolea and mosques in Timbuktu, Mali, in 2012. The International Criminal Court found Mr Al Mahdi guilty, as a co-perpetrator, of the war crime of intentionally directing attacks against historic monuments and buildings dedicated to religion. He was sentenced to nine years' imprisonment.

## 11.7.5   The natural environment

The natural environment is protected in the same way as other civilian objects and must not be attacked unless it becomes a military objective or its destruction is required by imperative military necessity. Any incidental harm to the environment resulting from an attack on a military objective must also not be disproportionate.[179]

Although the natural environment also enjoys special protections in IHL, the thresholds for protection are very high. Article 35 of *Additional Protocol I* states that it is 'prohibited to employ methods or means of warfare which are intended, or may be expected, to cause widespread, long-term and severe damage to the natural environment'.[180] This is reaffirmed in art 55. In addition, under the 1976 *Convention on the Prohibition of Military or Any Other Hostile Use of Environmental Modification Techniques*,[181] it is prohibited to manipulate or

---

172    *Convention for the Protection of Cultural Property in the Event of Armed Conflict* (n 21) art 1(a).

173    *Hague Regulations* (n 10) arts 26, 56; *Additional Protocol I* (n 7) art 53.

174    Which includes two protocols: the *Protocol to the Hague Convention for the Protection of Cultural Property in the Event of Armed Conflict*, opened for signature 14 May 1954, 249 UNTS 358 (entered into force 7 August 1956), and the *Second Protocol to the Hague Convention of 1954 for the Protection of Cultural Property in the Event of Armed Conflict* (n 21).

175    *Convention for the Protection of Cultural Property in the Event of Armed Conflict* (n 21) art 1(a).

176    Ibid art 4(1); *Additional Protocol I* (n 7) art 53.

177    *ICRC Customary IHL Study* (n 26) 'Rule 38'; *Tadić Jurisdiction* (n 38) [127].

178    *Prosecutor v Al Mahdi (Judgment and Sentence)* (International Criminal Court, Trial Chamber VIII, Case No ICC-01/12-01/15-171, 27 September 2016).

179    *ICRC Customary IHL Study* (n 26) 'Rule 43'. See also *Protocol on Prohibitions or Restrictions on the Use of Incendiary Weapons (Protocol III)* (n 14) art 2(4) (incendiary attacks on forests or other plant cover).

180    *Additional Protocol I* (n 7) art 35(3).

181    *ENMOD Convention* (n 19).

modify the natural environment for the purpose of weaponising environmental processes, such as through the creation of tsunamis or earthquakes.[182]

Limitations to the protection of the environment during armed conflict prompted the International Law Commission to undertake the drafting of principles for that purpose,[183] which were published in 2019.[184]

# 11.8   Implementation and enforcement of international humanitarian law

Common Article 1 of the *Geneva Conventions* requires states parties to 'respect and ensure respect' for the Conventions. In essence, this means that parties must observe the rules of the treaties at all times, both during armed conflicts and in peacetime. This includes implementing the Conventions into domestic law,[185] engaging in education and dissemination of the law to military and civilian populations,[186] and ensuring that the law is respected by those who plan and execute armed conflicts, including through the maintenance of military discipline and the legal responsibility of commanders. It may also require states to act to ensure that other states parties respect IHL.

Under IHL,[187] all members of the armed forces must be trained in IHL, such as by military lawyers or IHL experts.[188] States are also required to have legal advisers in the field with their armed forces[189] and must distribute rules-of-engagement ('ROE') cards (palm-sized cards providing a summary of the relevant rules of engagement for the deployment, including the relevant IHL principles) to members of the armed forces.[190] Such methods are also available to non-state armed groups to ensure compliance with IHL, in addition to unilateral declarations, agreements with states, and internal codes to apply IHL.

---

182   Ibid art 1(1). See also *Report of the Conference of the Committee on Disarmament*, UN Doc A/31/27 (1976) vol 1, annex I ('*Report of the Working Group on the Prohibition of Military or Any Other Hostile Use of Environmental Modification Techniques*') 91.

183   'Analytical Guide to the Work of the International Law Commission: Protection of the Environment in Relation to Armed Conflicts', *International Law Commission* (Web Page) <https://legal.un.org/ilc/guide/8_7.shtml>.

184   'Summaries of the Work of the International Law Commission: Protection of the Environment in Relation to Armed Conflicts', *International Law Commission* (Web Page) <https://legal.un.org/ilc/summaries/8_7.shtml>.

185   See *Geneva Convention I* (n 3) arts 48, 50; *Geneva Convention II* (n 4) arts 49, 51; *Geneva Convention III* (n 5) arts 128, 130; *Geneva Convention IV* (n 6) arts 145, 147; *Additional Protocol I* (n 7) arts 11(4), 84, 85.

186   *Geneva Convention I* (n 3) art 47; *Geneva Convention II* (n 4) art 48; *Geneva Convention III* (n 5) art 127; *Geneva Convention IV* (n 6) art 144. See also *Additional Protocol I* (n 7) arts 80, 83, 87(2); *Additional Protocol II* (n 8) art 19.

187   See *Hague II 1899* (n 10) art 1.

188   See *Additional Protocol I* (n 7) art 6. See also Blank and Noone (n 129) 634–5.

189   *Additional Protocol I* (n 7) art 82 states that parties 'shall ensure that legal advisers are available, when necessary, to advise military commanders at the appropriate level on the application of the Conventions and this Protocol and on the appropriate instruction to be given to the armed forces on this subject'. See also art 6; Michael Kramer and Michael Schmitt, 'Lawyers on Horseback? Thoughts on Judge Advocates and Civil-Military Relations' (2008) 55(5) *UCLA Law Review* 1407–36.

190   See Solis (n 2) 501–4 for examples of the information included on rules-of-engagement cards, as well as a critique of some of the drawbacks of the cards.

In the field during armed conflict, the International Committee of the Red Cross is central to ensuring that the Conventions and Protocols, as well as other rules of armed conflict, are respected – for example, by visiting the detained and interned, carrying out relief operations in occupied territory, and administering the Central Tracing Agency for the purpose of tracking missing persons.[191] It has a mandate to act in IACs, whereas in NIACs it may only 'offer' its services to the parties.[192]

Criminal accountability is also vital in enforcing IHL. States must criminalise war crimes in domestic law, establish universal jurisdiction over them, and investigate and prosecute or extradite alleged perpetrators. In recent years, a robust permanent system of accountability has developed in international criminal law, not least of which is the creation of the International Criminal Court. This is explored in more detail in Chapter 12.

Other international institutions can also play a role in accountability, such as scrutiny or action by the UN Security Council, UN General Assembly or UN Human Rights Council – including to establish special investigative mechanisms (as has been done recently in relation to conflicts in Iraq, Syria and Yemen). In this context, it should be noted that international human rights law can be an important means of accountability for IHL violations. It applies concurrently with IHL in armed conflict.[193] International human rights law enables individual victims to seek remedies directly in national or international courts for violations of human rights law which are connected to violations of IHL. In contrast, while IHL provides for war crimes prosecutions and inter-state reparations, it does not generally provide individuals with an enforceable right to claim compensation.

# DISCUSSION QUESTIONS

(1)   What are the benefits and drawbacks of the modern international humanitarian law ('IHL') approach of 'restraint in warfare'?

(2)   Should video games like Call of Duty be required to compel players to observe the laws of armed conflict while playing?

(3)   Should mental harm be considered in the context of proportionality assessments?

(4)   Some publicists have argued that the only way to ensure the enforcement of and accountability for IHL is to introduce an individual complaints mechanism, similar to ones that exist in international human rights law. Do you agree?

(5)   Are the terms 'international humanitarian law' and 'law of armed conflict' interchangeable, or do they relate to different but overlapping fields?

---

191   For some of the protected tasks of the International Committee of the Red Cross, see, eg, *Geneva Convention III* (n 5) art 126; *Geneva Convention IV* (n 6) arts 23, 55, 143.

192   See, eg, *Additional Protocol I* (n 7) art 81, which refers to the right of the International Committee of the Red Cross to provide assistance, as opposed to *Additional Protocol II* (n 8) art 18, which states that relief societies '*may* offer their services' (emphasis added).

193   See, eg, the statements of the International Court of Justice to that effect in *Legality of the Threat or Use of Nuclear Weapons* (n 76) 240 [25] and *Legal Consequences of the Construction of a Wall in the Occupied Palestinian Territory (Advisory Opinion)* [2004] ICJ Rep 136, 177–8 [102]–[106].

# 12

# INTERNATIONAL CRIMINAL LAW

Rosemary Grey

# 12.1    Introduction

Under international criminal law ('ICL'), individuals can be prosecuted and punished for conduct that is criminalised under customary international law and/or treaty. This differs from most branches of international law, which concern the rights and obligations of states. The rationale for holding individuals to account for such crimes was articulated in 1946 by the International Military Tribunal at Nuremberg, which stated: 'Crimes against international law are committed by [people], not by abstract entities, and only by punishing individuals who commit such crimes can the provisions of international law be enforced.'[1]

This chapter introduces this branch of international law, citing examples involving Australia as well as many other states. The chapter commences with an overview of some of ILC's key principles and aims. It then gives an overview of the historical development of ICL, starting with the creation of international criminal tribunals in Nuremberg and Tokyo after World War II, through to the establishment of ad hoc international criminal tribunals in response to the conflicts in the former Yugoslavia and Rwanda in the 1990s. Next, the chapter explains how ICL is currently being enforced. This section includes key details about the International Criminal Court ('ICC'), and also considers the role of national courts and 'hybrid' courts that are partly international and partly domestic in character. Turning to the core crimes in ICL, the chapter first considers war crimes, and then crimes against humanity, genocide and aggression. In the final section, the focus turns to individual criminal responsibility and defences.

# 12.2    International criminal law and its aims

Currently, ICL enables the prosecution of four categories of crimes: war crimes, crimes against humanity, genocide (and incitement thereto), and aggression.[2] Such offences are also increasingly recognised under domestic law, enabling their prosecution in national courts (see Section 12.4.2). International criminal law can be distinguished from 'transnational criminal law', which refers to treaties that impose obligations on states to extradite or prosecute individuals for certain crimes such as torture, terrorism, drug trafficking, people trafficking, environmental crimes, and corruption.[3]

Under the laws of state responsibility, states may be held accountable for failing to prevent and punish certain international crimes. The ongoing case in the International Court of Justice between The Gambia and Myanmar, which relates to Myanmar's alleged violations of the 1948 *Genocide Convention*,[4] illustrates this possibility. However, this chapter focuses on the criminal responsibility of *individuals*, as distinct from state responsibility.

---

1    'International Military Tribunal (Nuremberg), Judgment and Sentences' (1947) 41(1) *American Journal of International Law* 172, 221 ('*Nuremberg Judgment*').

2    Certain international criminal courts can also prosecute individuals for offences against the integrity of the judicial process: see, eg, *Rome Statute of the International Criminal Court*, opened for signature 17 July 1998, 2187 UNTS 3 (entered into force 1 July 2002) art 70 ('*Rome Statute*').

3    See Robert Cryer, Darryl Robinson and Sergey Vasiliev, *An Introduction to International Criminal Law* (Cambridge University Press, 4th ed, 2018) 5–6; Carsten Stahn, *A Critical Introduction to International Criminal Law* (Cambridge University Press, 2019) 105–13.

4    *Convention on the Prevention and Punishment of the Crime of Genocide*, opened for signature 9 December 1948, 78 UNTS 277 (entered into force 12 January 1951) ('*Genocide Convention*').

International criminal law incorporates concepts from national criminal law. For example, in ICL, the standard of proof to convict is 'beyond reasonable doubt'; a defendant is entitled to a presumption of innocence; the prosecutor must establish both the conduct elements (*actus reus*) and mental elements (*mens rea*) of a crime; there are defences that exclude criminal responsibility; and there are detailed rules of evidence. And yet, ICL is also unlike national criminal law in many respects, including that its rules are derived from custom and treaty. Thus, ICL is at once a type of international law *and* a type of criminal law.

International criminal law is said to have several aims.[5] One aim is *accountability* or *ending impunity*: that is, holding individuals to account for conduct that constitutes a crime under international law when states cannot, or will not, do so. Another aim is *expressivism*, meaning that ICL's power lies in expressing certain values to which states are committed.[6] A third aim is *deterrence*, referring to the hope that the threat of prosecution will dissuade would-be perpetrators from committing crimes.[7] The enforcement of ICL is also said to contribute to international peace and security. For instance, in the 1990s, the UN Security Council created two ad hoc international criminal tribunals to prosecute crimes in the conflicts in the former Yugoslavia[8] and in Rwanda,[9] using its powers to maintain or restore international peace and security. All of these aims are alluded to in the preamble to the 1998 *Rome Statute of the International Criminal Court* ('*Rome Statute*').

Some commentators also regard international criminal courts as serving broader aims, such as creating historical records of events of international and national concern, and contributing to 'transitional justice' (that is, peace, stability and reconciliation following a conflict).[10] Others hope that ICL can deliver justice to victims and survivors of crimes, such as by recognising their ordeals as legal wrongs or by awarding reparations in the event of a conviction, although this hope has proved very hard to achieve in practice.[11] International criminal law can also serve political aims. States can (and do) instrumentalise ICL to advance their interests, such as by creating courts that will render 'victors' justice' in the wake of a conflict, or by referring their political enemies to the ICC.[12] In short, ICL is a tool that can be deployed for numerous uses, some of them more 'justice oriented' than others.

---

5       See, eg, Cryer, Robinson and Vasiliev (n 3) 28–43; Stahn (n 3) 174–82; Jean Galbraith, 'The Pace of International Criminal Justice' (2009) 31(1) *Michigan Journal of International Law* 79.

6       See, eg, Stahn (n 3) 181–2; Cryer, Robinson and Vasiliev (n 3) 31; Margaret deGuzman, 'An Expressive Rationale for the Thematic Prosecution of Sex Crimes' in Morten Bergsmo (ed), *Thematic Prosecution of International Sex Crimes* (Torkal Opsahl, 2012) 11.

7       Cryer, Robinson and Vasiliev (n 3) 31, 32–5.

8       SC Res 827, UN Doc S/RES/827 (25 May 1993), as amended by SC Res 1877, UN Doc S/RES/1877 (7 July 2009) ('*ICTY Statute*').

9       SC Res 955, UN Doc S/RES/955 (8 November 1994) annex ('*Statute of the International Tribunal for Rwanda*') ('*ICTR Statute*').

10      Lawrence Douglas, *The Memory of Judgment: Making Law and History in the Trials of the Holocaust* (Yale University Press, 2001); Galbraith (n 5) 88–90.

11      Eric Stover, *The Witnesses: War Crimes and the Promise of Justice in The Hague* (University of Pennsylvania Press, 2005); Julie Mertus, 'Shouting from the Bottom of the Well' (2004) 6(1) *International Feminist Journal of Politics* 110; Rachel Killean and Luke Moffett, 'Victim Legal Representation before the ICC and ECCC' (2017) 15(4) *Journal of International Criminal Justice* 713; Mariana Goetz, 'Victims' Experiences of the International Criminal Court's Reparations Mandate in the Democratic Republic of the Congo' in Carla Ferstman and Mariana Goetz (eds), *Reparations for Victims of Genocide, War Crimes and Crimes against Humanity* (Brill Nijhoff, 2nd ed, 2020) 414.

12      Sarah Nouwen and Wouter Werner, 'Doing Justice to the Political: The International Criminal Court in Uganda and Sudan' (2010) 21(4) *European Journal of International Law* 941.

# 12.3 The development of international criminal law

International criminal law evolved out of the laws of war, which can be traced back many centuries (see Chapter 11). However, it was not until the 20th century that states established international courts with power to enforce ICL. Though there was the intention to create a 'special tribunal' following World War I,[13] no such tribunal eventuated.[14] However, the idea of an international criminal tribunal would be revived within a generation, in the aftermath of World War II. On 8 August 1945, three months after Germany's surrender, representatives from the United Kingdom, the United States, France and the USSR gathered in London to create the first ad hoc international criminal court. The International Military Tribunal, as it was known, would be based in Nuremberg and would charge 22 of the surviving Nazi leaders for crimes committed before and during World War II. Its jurisdiction encompassed crimes against peace (now known as aggression), war crimes and crimes against humanity.[15]

The creation of the International Military Tribunal marked the start of contemporary ICL, for it was in that courtroom at Nuremberg that many of the central principles of ICL were first put into practice. These included the principle that criminal liability under ICL lies with individuals (as opposed to states, which under international law are not capable of committing crimes); that such liability exists under international law even if the relevant conduct is not punishable under domestic law; and that a defendant has a right to a fair trial, among others.[16]

Complementing the Nuremburg Tribunal was the International Military Tribunal for the Far East in Tokyo, which had jurisdiction to prosecute Japanese military and political leaders for crimes against peace, war crimes and crimes against humanity.[17] Neither the Nuremberg Tribunal's charter ('*Nuremberg Charter*') nor the Tokyo Tribunal's charter ('*Tokyo Charter*') referred to sexual violence crimes, notwithstanding evidence that all of the warring parties committed such crimes during World War II.[18] Theoretically, sexual crimes could have been charged under various heads in both Charters, such as ill-treatment, enslavement, inhumane acts, or persecution. Yet, reflecting the priorities of legal practitioners at the time, sexual crimes received scant attention in the Nuremberg Tribunal, and patchy coverage in the Tokyo Tribunal.[19]

---

13    *Treaty of Peace between the Allied and Associated Powers and Germany*, signed 28 June 1919, 225 ConTS 188 (entered into force 10 January 1920) art 227 (also known as the *Treaty of Versailles*).

14    M Cherif Bassiouni, 'World War I: The War to End All Wars and Birth of a Handicapped International Criminal Justice System' (2002) 30(3) *Denver Journal of International Law and Policy* 244, 268–72.

15    *Agreement for the Prosecution and Punishment of the Major War Criminals of the European Axis*, 82 UNTC 280 (signed and entered into force 8 August 1945) annex 1 ('*Charter of the International Military Tribunal*') art 6 ('*Nuremberg Charter*').

16    Antonio Cassese, 'Affirmation of the Principles of International Law Recognized by the Charter of the Nürnberg Tribunal: General Assembly Resolution 95(I) New York, 11 December 1946', *United Nations Audiovisual Library of International Law* (2009) <https://legal.un.org/avl/ha/ga_95-I/ga_95-I.html>.

17    *Special Proclamation by the Supreme Commander for the Allied Powers: Establishment of an International Military Tribunal for the Far East* (19 January 1946) annex ('*Charter of the International Military Tribunal for the Far East*') ('*Tokyo Charter*').

18    Kelly Askin, *War Crimes against Women: Prosecution in International War Crimes Tribunals* (Martinus Nijhoff, 1997); Rhonda Copelon, 'Gender Crimes as War Crimes: Integrating Crimes against Women into International Criminal Law' (2000) 46(1) *McGill Law Journal* 217.

19    Rosemary Grey, *Prosecuting Sexual and Gender-Based Crimes at the International Criminal Court* (Cambridge University Press, 2019) 76.

In this same post-war period, many other German and Japanese defendants were prosecuted in national courts, using legislation and legal principles modelled on the Nuremberg and Tokyo Charters.[20] In addition, states also adopted treaties of importance to ICL. These included the 1948 *Genocide Convention*, which defined genocide as a crime for which individuals could be prosecuted and which states were obligated to prevent (see Section 12.5.3), and the 1949 *Geneva Conventions*, certain grave breaches of which constitute war crimes (see Section 12.5.1 and Chapter 11). Thus, the 1940s marked the start of a new era in ICL, one in which the idea of accountability for certain crimes under international law started to become a reality. Such crimes were also prosecuted by domestic courts following World War II, including in Australia.[21]

Cold War politics precluded the creation of any international criminal tribunals over the following decades. Nonetheless, ICL continued to develop, with the International Law Commission preparing a draft statute for an international criminal court and a draft list of offences,[22] as requested by the UN General Assembly.[23] Meanwhile, crimes of the kind defined in the *Genocide Convention* and the Nuremberg and Tokyo Charters continued to be prosecuted under national law. An example is the prosecution of former Nazi official Adolf Eichmann in Israel in 1961–62.[24]

Egregious violations of international humanitarian law prompted the Security Council to create the International Criminal Tribunal for the Former Yugoslavia ('ICTY') in 1993 and the International Criminal Tribunal for Rwanda ('ICTR') in 1994. These tribunals marked the start of a new chapter: a '(re-) creation of international criminal justice'.[25] Both tribunals handled a large case load. By the time of its closure in 2015, the ICTR had indicted 93 people, convicted and sentenced 62 and acquitted 14, and 3 fugitives remained. The remaining cases were referred to national jurisdictions or discontinued, and one was transferred to a residual mechanism created by the United Nations.[26] The ICTY closed in 2017, having indicted 161 people, convicted and sentenced 90, and acquitted 18. The remaining cases were referred to national courts or discontinued, and 3 defendants were transferred to a residual UN mechanism.[27] No fugitives remained.

The ICTY and ICTR made major contributions to the development of ICL. Among other things, they were the first international criminal tribunals to interpret and apply the crime of

---

20    Dan Plesch, *Human Rights after Hitler: The Lost History of Prosecuting Axis War Crimes* (Georgetown University Press, 2017); Georgina Fitzpatrick, Tim McCormack and Narelle Morris, *Australia's War Crimes Trials: 1945–51* (Brill Nijhoff, 2016).
21    Fitzpatrick, McCormack and Morris (n 20).
22    UN Committee on International Criminal Jurisdiction, 'Draft Statute for an International Criminal Court' (1952) 46(S1) *American Journal of International Law* 1; 'Draft Code of Offences against the Peace and Security of Mankind' [1951] II *Yearbook of the International Law Commission* 1, 134 [59].
23    *Study by the International Law Commission of the Question of an International Criminal Jurisdiction*, GA Res A/RES/260 (III) B, UN Doc A/RES/260(III)B (9 December 1948).
24    *A-G (Israel) v Eichmann* (1968) 36 ILR 18 (District Court, Jerusalem, 12 December 1961); *Eichmann v A-G (Israel)* (1968) 36 ILR 277 (Supreme Court of Israel, 29 May 1962). See generally Hannah Arendt, *Eichmann in Jerusalem: A Report on the Banality of Evil* (Viking, 1963).
25    Alex Whiting, 'Could the Crime of Aggression Undermine Deterrence?' (2021) 19(4) *Journal of International Criminal Justice* 1017, 1021.
26    'About the ICTR', *International Criminal Tribunal for Rwanda* (Web Page) <https://unictr.irmct.org/en/tribunal>.
27    'Key Figures of the Cases', *International Criminal Tribunal for the Former Yugoslavia* (Web Page) <www.icty.org/en/cases/key-figures-cases>.

genocide,[28] and they produced a detailed jurisprudence on sexual violence crimes.[29] They also developed techniques for collecting evidence, generated detailed guidance on fair trial rights, produced a new generation of ICL scholars and practitioners, and provided new impetus for the development of the permanent International Criminal Court.

Following its revival in the 1990s, ICL has developed into a detailed branch of international law. Since its early enforcement in the tribunals in Nuremberg and Tokyo, ICL has become more victim oriented and gender sensitive, and has moved from a system based primarily in customary international law to one that is highly codified. It has not ended impunity for war crimes, crimes against humanity, genocide or aggression; nor has it ended the commission of the crimes themselves. Nor does it pose a serious challenge to the structural conditions that contribute to the commission of crimes under international law, such as the ongoing impact of colonial legacies, the unequal distribution of wealth and resources on a local and global scale, and hierarchies of race, ethnicity, gender and so forth that fuel violence against particular groups.[30] And yet, ICL has provided a new means of condemning crimes that, to quote the *Rome Statute*'s Preamble, 'deeply shock the conscience of humanity'.

# 12.4 The enforcement of international criminal law today

## 12.4.1 International Criminal Court

The ICC was created by the *Rome Statute*, a multilateral treaty adopted in 1998 by 120 states, which entered into force on 1 July 2002. The Court sits in The Hague, a short distance from the International Court of Justice and the building that housed the ICTY, although it can theoretically hold proceedings outside this 'Hague bubble'.[31] As of May 2022, a total of 123 states are parties to the *Rome Statute*, including Australia, which ratified it on 1 July 2002 and enacted legislation to facilitate cooperation with the ICC and to enable the domestic prosecution of ICC crimes the same year.[32] Yet several of the world's most powerful and populous states are not parties, including China, the United States and Russia, to name a few.

---

28    See, eg, *Prosecutor v Akayesu (Judgment)* (International Criminal Tribunal for Rwanda, Trial Chamber I, Case No ICTR-96-4-T, 2 September 1998); *Prosecutor v Akayesu (Judgment)* (International Criminal Tribunal for Rwanda, Appeals Chamber, Case No ICTR-96-4-A, 1 June 2001); *Prosecutor v Nahimana (Judgment)* (International Criminal Tribunal for Rwanda, Appeals Chamber, Case No ICTR-99-52-A, 28 November 2007).

29    Kelly Askin, 'Prosecuting Wartime Rape and Other Gender-Related Crimes' (2003) 21(3) *Berkeley Journal of International Law* 288; Helen Brady, 'The Power of Precedents: Using the Case Law of the Ad Hoc International Criminal Tribunals and Hybrid Courts in Adjudicating Sexual and Gender-Based Crimes at the ICC' (2012) 18(1) *Australian Journal of Human Rights* 75; Serge Brammertz and Michelle Jarvis (eds), *Prosecuting Conflict-Related Sexual Violence in the ICTY* (Oxford University Press, 2016).

30    Tor Krevor, 'International Criminal Law: An Ideology Critique' (2013) 26(3) *Leiden Journal of International Law* 701; Kamari Maxime Clarke, 'Negotiating Racial Injustice: How International Criminal Law Helps Entrench Structural Inequality', *Just Security* (Blog Post, 24 July 2020) <www.justsecurity .org/71614/negotiating-racial-injustice-how-international-criminal-law-helps-entrench-structural- inequality>.

31    *Rome Statute* (n 2) art 3.

32    *International Criminal Court Act 2002* (Cth); *International Criminal Court (Consequential Amendments) Act 2002* (Cth).

Victims and survivors have a greater role in ICC proceedings compared to previous international criminal tribunals. Under the *Rome Statute*, victims and survivors are not limited to participating as witnesses for the prosecution or defence. Rather, they also have independent standing to present their views in the proceedings, through their legal representatives,[33] and are entitled to receive reparations following a conviction.[34] These innovations were intended to make the ICC more victim centred or 'restorative' than its predecessors.[35] However, many commentators query whether the ICC is capable of realising this aspiration.[36]

### 12.4.1.1  Jurisdiction of the ICC

The ICC can prosecute individuals for genocide, crimes against humanity and war crimes committed after 1 July 2002.[37] As of 17 July 2018, it can also prosecute the crime of aggression.[38]

The ICC's jurisdiction *ratione loci* (territorial or geographical jurisdiction) depends on how the relevant situation came before the Court. If a situation involving war crimes, crimes against humanity and/or genocide was referred by the Security Council, the ICC has jurisdiction regardless of where the alleged crimes were committed. Thus, following the Security Council's referral of situations in Darfur (Sudan) and Libya, the ICC Prosecutor has opened investigations into crimes allegedly committed in those states,[39] although neither Sudan nor Libya is a state party to the *Rome Statute*. If there is *no* UN Security Council referral, there are two ways that a situation can come before the ICC: it can be referred by a state party to the *Rome Statute*,[40] or the ICC Prosecutor can initiate an investigation *proprio motu* (on one's own motion).[41] In such circumstances (that is, where there is no Security Council referral), the ICC can only exercise jurisdiction if the crimes were committed on the territory or vessel of, or by a national of, a state that either is a party to the *Rome Statute* or has made a declaration accepting the ICC's jurisdiction pursuant to art 12(3) of the *Rome Statute*.[42]

---

33    *Rome Statute* (n 2) art 68(3).
34    Ibid art 75. Where the convicted person lacks the means to fund the reparations, funding from member states of the International Criminal Court is used (if available).
35    Ban Ki-moon, 'An Age of Accountability' (Address to the Review Conference on the International Criminal Court, Kampala, 31 May 2010).
36    See, eg, Mariana Pena and Gaelle Carayon, 'Is the ICC Making the Most of Victim Participation?' (2013) 7(3) *International Journal of Transitional Justice* 518; Christine Van den Wyngaert, 'Victims before International Criminal Courts: Some Views and Concerns of an ICC Trial Judge' (2011) 44(1–2) *Case Western Review of International Law* 475.
37    For additional details about the temporal jurisdiction of the International Criminal Court, see *Rome Statute* (n 2) arts 11, 15 *bis*.
38    International Criminal Court, Assembly of States Parties, *Activation of the Jurisdiction of the Court over the Crime of Aggression*, Doc No ICC-ASP/16/Res.5, 16th sess, 1st plenary mtg, 14 December 2017 ('*Resolution on Activation of Jurisdiction*').
39    SC Res S/RES/1593, UN Doc S/RES/1593 (31 March 2005); SC Res S/RES/1970, UN Doc S/RES/1970 (26 February 2011).
40    *Rome Statute* (n 2) art 13(a).
41    Ibid art 13(c). The Prosecutor's power to initiate an investigation *proprio motu* is subject to art 15, which requires the Prosecutor to conduct a 'preliminary examination' and then obtain authorisation from the Pre-Trial Chamber before the investigation can proceed: Sara Wharton and Rosemary Grey, 'The Full Picture: Preliminary Examinations at the International Criminal Court' (2019) 56 *Canadian Yearbook of International Law* 1.
42    *Rome Statute* (n 2) art 12(2).

For example, in 2020, the ICC Appeals Chamber authorised the ICC Prosecutor's investigation regarding Afghanistan.[43] This situation was initiated *proprio motu* by the Prosecutor in 2006.[44] It involves crimes allegedly committed in Afghanistan by the Afghan National Security Forces and by the Taliban, as well as by members of the United States' Central Intelligence Agency based in Poland, Romania and Lithuania.[45] As Poland, Romania and Lithuania are all states parties to the *Rome Statute*, the ICC can theoretically exercise jurisdiction over *Rome Statute* crimes that occurred in those states, even though the United States is not a state party.[46]

The ICC's jurisdiction with regard to aggression is more limited, and has the effect of excluding acts of aggression committed in 2022 by Russian actors in Ukraine.[47]

## 12.4.1.2   The ICC's admissibility rules

For cases to be admissible to the ICC, two conditions must be met. First, the prospective case must be of sufficient gravity; second, the ICC can only exercise its jurisdiction in the absence of genuine criminal proceedings at the national level.[48] The latter principle is known as the principle of 'complementarity'. It is embedded in art 17 of the *Rome Statute* and involves a two-step test.[49] First, the ICC must ascertain whether a state with jurisdiction is taking (or has taken) concrete steps toward investigating or prosecuting the same case as the ICC Prosecutor.[50] If it is, the ICC must then assess whether the state is unable or unwilling to conduct the proceedings 'genuinely'.[51]

---

43  *Appeal against the Decision on the Authorisation of an Investigation into the Situation in the Islamic Republic of Afghanistan (Judgment)* (International Criminal Court, Appeals Chamber, Case No ICC-02/17-138, 5 March 2020).

44  *Request for Authorisation of an Investigation Pursuant to Article 15* (International Criminal Court, Office of the Prosecutor, Case No ICC-02/17-7-Red, 20 November 2017) [24].

45  Ibid [43]–[49].

46  However, Prosecutor Karim Khan has indicated that if the Afghanistan investigation resumes, he will 'deprioritise' certain aspects of the investigation, including the crimes allegedly committed by the Central Intelligence Agency: 'Statement of the Prosecutor of the International Criminal Court, Karim AA Khan QC, Following the Application for an Expedited Order under Article 18(2) Seeking Authorisation to Resume Investigations in the Situation in Afghanistan' (27 September 2021) <www.icc-cpi.int/news/statement-prosecutor-international-criminal-court-karim-khan-qc-following-application>.

47  In the absence of a Security Council resolution, the ICC can only prosecute the crime of aggression if the state on whose territory the crime occurred *and* the state whose nationals committed it are both parties to the *Rome Statute*: *Rome Statute* (n 2) art 15 *bis*(5). This provision has the effect of keeping Russia's acts of aggression in Ukraine outside the jurisdiction of the ICC because neither Ukraine nor Russia is a state party, and a Security Council referral is not a realistic possibility given Russia's veto power in the Security Council. See Carrie McDougall, 'Why Creating a Special Tribunal for Aggression against Ukraine is the Best Available Option: A Reply to Kevin Jon Heller and Other Critics', *Opinio Juris* (Blog Post, 15 March 2022) <https://opiniojuris.org/2022/03/15/why-creating-a-special-tribunal-for-aggression-against-ukraine-is-the-best-available-option-a-reply-to-kevin-jon-heller-and-other-critics/>.

48  *Rome Statute* (n 2) art 17(1)(a)–(b).

49  *Prosecutor v Katanga (Judgment on the Appeal against the Oral Decision of Trial Chamber II of 12 June 2009 on the Admissibility of the Case)* (International Criminal Court, Appeals Chamber, Case No ICC-01/04-01/07-1497, 25 September 2009) [78].

50  The 'same case' means the same person, for substantially the same conduct: *Prosecutor v Kenyatta (Appeal Judgment on Admissibility)* (International Criminal Court, Appeals Chamber, Case No ICC-01/09-02/11-274, 30 August 2011) [1], [39].

51  *Rome Statute* (n 2) art 17(2)–(3).

As of May 2022, the ICC Office of the Prosecutor has publicly initiated cases against 39 individuals for war crimes, crimes against humanity, and (in one case) genocide.[52] All but one of these defendants are male, and all are African nationals, although that may change in future years given the ICC's ongoing activities in other regions.[53] Final judgment has been rendered in seven cases, resulting in three acquittals[54] and four convictions.[55] An eighth individual has been convicted of war crimes and crimes against humanity, and his appeal judgment was handed down in December 2022.[56]

Several factors have contributed to the ICC's relatively slow completion rate. Each case is large in scale, often involving thousands of victims. Victims have standing to participate in the proceedings, which prolongs the duration of each case. The ICC works across many different conflicts and hence cannot use the same cumulative investigation and prosecution strategies as the ICTY or ICTR. Moreover, the ICC depends on states to provide assistance, such as enabling access to evidence and arresting suspects. Yet such cooperation is not always forthcoming; unlike the ICTY and ICTR, the ICC is not a product of the Security Council, with the result that the Council has been disinclined to compel states to assist the ICC – even in matters that the Council referred to the Court.[57]

Like the ICTY and ICTR, the ICC has contributed to the jurisprudence on sexual and gender-based crimes, including being the first international court to prosecute gender-based persecution and forced pregnancy, and the first to affirm that the sexual abuse of child soldiers by their commander is a war crime.[58]

---

52    The arrest warrants for Sudan's former president Omar Al-Bashir refer to genocide as well as war crimes and crimes against humanity. Cases have also been initiated against eight individuals for offences against the administration of justice, such as bribing or intimidating witnesses.

53    As of May 2022, these include preliminary examinations in the Philippines, Venezuela and Bolivia, and investigations in Ukraine, Georgia, Myanmar/Bangladesh, Afghanistan, Venezuela and Palestine.

54    *Prosecutor v Chui (Judgment on the Prosecutor's Appeal against the Decision of Trial Chamber II Entitled 'Judgment Pursuant to Article 74 of the Statute')* (International Criminal Court, Appeals Chamber, Case No ICC-01/04-02/12-271-Corr, 7 April 2015); *Prosecutor v Gbagbo (Judgment in the Appeal of the Prosecutor against Trial Chamber I's Decision on the No Case to Answer Motions)* (International Criminal Court, Appeals Chamber, Case No ICC-02/11-01/15-1400, 31 March 2021).

55    *Prosecutor v Katanga* (International Criminal Court, Trial Chamber II, Case No ICC-01/04-01/07-3436-tENG, 7 March 2014); *Prosecutor v Lubanga (Judgment on the Appeal against Conviction)* (International Criminal Court, Appeals Chamber, Case No ICC-01/04-01/06-3121-Red, 2 December 2014); *Prosecutor v Al Mahdi (Judgment and Sentence)* (International Criminal Court, Trial Chamber VIII, Case No ICC-01/12-01/15-171, 27 September 2016); *Prosecutor v Ntaganda (Judgment on Appeal against the Decision of Trial Chamber VI of 8 July 2019 Entitled 'Judgment')* (International Criminal Court, Appeals Chamber, Case No ICC-01/04-02/06-2666-Red, 20 March 2021).

56    See *Prosecutor v Ongwen (Appeal Judgment)* (International Criminal Court, Appeals Chamber, Case No ICC-02/04-01/15-2022-Red, 15 December 2022) ('*Ongwen*').

57    For example, in relation to Sudan and Libya, the ICC has made 15 findings of non-cooperation by states parties to the *Rome Statute*. The Prosecutor reported all 15 instances to the Security Council but received no response: see *Independent Expert Review of the International Criminal Court and the Rome Statute System* (Final Report, 30 September 2020) [767] <https://asp.icc-cpi.int/iccdocs/asp_docs/ASP19/IER-Final-Report-ENG.pdf>.

58    Grey (n 19) 19. As of January 2023, three trials for gender-based persecution are ongoing: see defendants Abd-al-Rahman, Al Hassan and Said at <www.icc-cpi.int/cases>. The Appeals Chamber upheld the ICC's first conviction for the crime of forced pregnancy in December 2022: see *Ongwen* (n 56).

## 12.4.2  National courts

The ICC is a court of last resort. The primary role in prosecuting war crimes, crimes against humanity, genocide and aggression lies with national courts.[59] Under public international law, a state has jurisdiction to prosecute crimes committed in its territory, or by its nationals, or against its nationals or its national interests, or if the crime is of the type that attracts universal jurisdiction.[60] In many states, including Australia, the crime must also be recognised in national law to be prosecuted by a national court.[61]

In recent years, there have been numerous 'universal jurisdiction' prosecutions for war crimes, crimes against humanity, torture, and genocide.[62] Australian courts can exercise universal jurisdiction over genocide, crimes against humanity and war crimes (but not aggression) under the *Criminal Code Act 1995* (Cth),[63] if the Attorney-General has given consent.[64] Such consent has been sought on two occasions: in 2011 in relation to Sri Lanka's President Mahinda Rajapaksa, and in 2019 in relation to Myanmar's Foreign Minister Aung San Suu Kyi. However, in both matters, the Attorney-General denied consent on the basis that the suspect had immunity from prosecution in a foreign state.[65] Thus, Australia is yet to prosecute crimes akin to those listed in the *Rome Statute* using universal jurisdiction.

However, Australia is taking action in accordance with *nationality* jurisdiction for war crimes allegedly committed by members of the Australian Defence Forces in Afghanistan between 2005 and 2016.[66] In 2020, an internal inquiry into these allegations found credible evidence that Defence Forces personnel in Afghanistan had committed acts amounting to the war crimes of murder and cruel treatment under Australian law.[67] In response, the government created the Office of the Special Investigator and tasked it with gathering relevant evidence of these crimes, with a view to referring any resultant briefs to the Commonwealth Director of Public Prosecutions.[68]

---

59    Such prosecutions are an exercise in domestic criminal law, not international criminal law. However, decisions of international criminal tribunals are often cited in these domestic cases as persuasive precedent: see, eg, Ciara Laverty and Dieneke De Vos, '"Ntaganda" in Colombia: Intra-Party Reproductive Violence at the Colombian Constitutional Court', *Opinio Juris* (Blog Post, 25 February 2020) <http://opiniojuris.org/2020/02/25/ntaganda-in-colombia-intra-party-reproductive-violence-at-the-colombian-constitutional-court/>.

60    See Chapter 6 at Section 6.2.4.6.

61    *Nulyarimma v Thompson* (1999) 96 FCR 153 (Wilcox J and Whitlam J) ('*Nulyarimma*').

62    TRIAL International, *Universal Jurisdiction: Annual Review 2021* (2021) <https://trialinternational.org/wp-content/uploads/2021/04/TRIAL_International_UJAR-2021.pdf>.

63    *Criminal Code Act 1995* (Cth) sch 1 ('*Criminal Code*') ss 15.4, 268.117(1).

64    Ibid s 268.121(1).

65    Anna Hood and Monique Cormier, 'Prosecuting International Crimes in Australia: The Case of the Sri Lankan President' (2012) 13(1) *Melbourne Journal of International Law* 1; Rawan Arraf, 'Before the High Court of Australia: The Case of Aung San Suu Kyi', *Opinio Juris* (Blog Post, 10 June 2019) <http://opiniojuris.org/2019/06/10/before-the-high-court-of-australia-the-case-of-aung-sang-suu-kyi/>.

66    See Chapter 6 at Section 6.2.4.3.

67    Inspector-General of the Australian Defence Force, *Afghanistan Inquiry Report* (November 2020) 28–9.

68    Prime Minister, Minister for Home Affairs and Minister for Defence, 'Joint Statement on IGADF Inquiry' (Press Release, 12 November 2020); Minister for Home Affairs, 'Office of the Special Investigator' (Press Release, 16 December 2020); Human Rights Watch, 'Australia: Follow Up Afghan Report with Prosecutions' (Web Page, 18 November 2020) <www.hrw.org/news/2020/11/19/australia-follow-afghan-report-prosecutions>.

Holding perpetrators to account for crimes of the type described in the *Rome Statute* is not only a *right* of states; in some instances there is also an *obligation* to extradite or prosecute.[69] For instance, states parties to the 1949 *Geneva Conventions* have a duty to search for all perpetrators of grave breaches, and either prosecute them or deliver them to another state party for trial,[70] and the 1948 *Genocide Convention* obliges states parties to prosecute perpetrators of genocide that occurs on their territory, or to surrender such persons to a competent international criminal tribunal.[71]

## 12.4.3   'Hybrid' criminal tribunals

War crimes, crimes against humanity and genocide have also been prosecuted in 'hybrid' criminal tribunals: that is, tribunals that are partly international and partly national in their sources of law, their staffing and their funding.[72]

An example is the Special Court for Sierra Leone, which was established in 2002 pursuant to an agreement between the Security Council and the Government of Sierra Leone, following Sierra Leone's decade-long civil war.[73] The Court had jurisdiction to prosecute 'persons who bear the greatest responsibility for serious violations of international humanitarian law and Sierra Leonean law committed in the territory of Sierra Leone since 30 November 1996' and, in limited circumstances, transgressions by peace-keeping forces in Sierra Leone as well.[74] Its trials were held in Freetown, Sierra Leone, with the exception of the trial of Liberia's former president Charles Taylor, who was tried in The Hague.

Another example is the Extraordinary Chambers in the Courts of Cambodia ('ECCC'), which was created pursuant to a 2003 agreement between the Cambodian government and the United Nations to prosecute crimes under Cambodian and international law between 1975 and 1979, when Cambodia was ruled by the Democratic Party of Kampuchea (the Khmer Rouge).[75] Still exercising some residual functions (such as declassifying documents), although having completed its final trial in September 2022, the ECCC sits in Phnom Penh and is staffed by both Cambodian and foreign UN-appointed personnel.[76]

---

69    See Chapter 6 at Section 6.2.6.
70    *Geneva Convention (I) for the Amelioration of the Condition of the Wounded and Sick in Armed Forces in the Field*, opened for signature 12 August 1949, 75 UNTS 31 (entered into force 21 October 1950) art 49; *Geneva Convention (II) for the Amelioration of the Condition of Wounded, Sick and Shipwrecked Members of Armed Forces at Sea*, opened for signature 12 August 1949, 75 UNTS 85 (entered into force 21 October 1950) art 50; *Geneva Convention (III) Relative to the Treatment of Prisoners of War*, opened for signature 12 August 1949, 75 UNTS 135 (entered into force 21 October 1950) art 129; *Geneva Convention (IV) Relative to the Protection of Civilian Persons in Time of War*, opened for signature 12 August 1949, 75 UNTS 287 (entered into force 21 October 1950) art 146.
71    *Genocide Convention* (n 4) art VI.
72    Sarah Williams, *Hybrid and Internationalised Criminal Tribunals* (Hart Publishing, 2012).
73    Ibid 68–70.
74    *Agreement between the United Nations and the Government of Sierra Leone on the Establishment of a Special Court for Sierra Leone*, signed 16 January 2002, 2178 UNTS 137 (entered into force 12 April 2002) annex ('*Statute of the Special Court for Sierra Leone*') art 1.
75    *Agreement between the United Nations and the Royal Government of Cambodia concerning the Prosecution under Cambodian Law of Crimes Committed during the Period of Democratic Kampuchea*, signed 6 June 2003, 2329 UNTS 117 (entered into force 29 April 2005).
76    *Law on the Establishment of Extraordinary Chambers in the Courts of Cambodia for the Prosecution of Crimes Committed during the Period of Democratic Kampuchea, with Inclusion of Amendments as Promulgated on 27 October 2004* (NS/RKM/1004/006) ('*ECCC Statute*').

# 12.5   Crimes under international law

## 12.5.1   War crimes

To understand the law of war crimes, one must first have knowledge of international humanitarian law. As detailed in Chapter 11, international humanitarian law regulates the behaviour of participants in armed conflicts. Key principles include the obligation to distinguish between civilian and military targets, the prohibition on indiscriminate attacks on civilian populations, and the prohibition on causing unnecessary suffering and superfluous injury (see Section 11.4). International humanitarian law applies to all parties to an armed conflict, including states and non-state actors. When the its rules are violated, those parties are in breach of international humanitarian law. But the individuals responsible for causing serious violations of international humanitarian law can also be prosecuted and punished – in which case, the violation is considered a 'war crime'.[77]

In many countries, national courts are involved in prosecuting war crimes. Beginning with the Nuremberg and Tokyo Tribunals, international courts have also played a major role in prosecuting war crimes. The most extensive codification of war crimes to date is art 8 of the *Rome Statute*. It lists over 65 war crimes and covers both international armed conflicts ('IACs') and non-international armed conflicts ('NIACs'). For all of these war crimes, the Prosecutor must establish that the particular act of murder, torture or other prohibited act 'took place in the context of and was associated with' the relevant armed conflict.[78] This is the so-called 'nexus' requirement for war crimes: that is, the requirement of a nexus between the state of war and the commission of the crimes.[79]

The *Rome Statute*'s war crimes provision goes further than previous instruments of ICL. For example, it is the first to expressly criminalise the recruitment and use of child soldiers (previous instruments prohibited similar conduct but did not expressly impose individual criminal liability for it).[80] It also expressly recognises a wider range of sexual crimes than previous instruments of ICL.[81]

Interestingly, the lists in art 8 of war crimes in IACs and NIACs are not identical. For example, it is a war crime in an IAC only to intentionally launch an attack in the knowledge that it will cause 'widespread, long-term and severe damage to the natural environment which would be clearly excessive in relation to the concrete and direct overall military advantage anticipated'.[82] However, the ICC's governing body, the Assembly of States Parties, is taking steps to harmonise the war crimes provisions in IACs and NIACs. In 2019, it amended the *Rome Statute* to make the practice of intentionally starving civilians as a method of war, which was already listed as a war crime in an IAC,[83] a war crime in a NIAC also.[84]

---

77    *Prosecutor v Tadić (Decision on the Defence Motion for Interlocutory Appeal on Jurisdiction)* (International Criminal Tribunal for the Former Yugoslavia, Appeals Chamber, Case No IT-94-1, 2 October 1995) [94]; Cryer, Robinson and Vasiliev (n 3) 263–4.

78    International Criminal Court, *Elements of Crimes* (2011) art 8.

79    Antonio Cassese, 'The Nexus Requirement for War Crimes' (2012) 10(5) *Journal of International Criminal Justice* 1395.

80    *Rome Statute* (n 2) arts 8(2)(b)(xxvi), (e)(vii). The same acts are defined as crimes against humanity in art 7(1)(g).

81    Ibid arts 8(2)(b)(xxii), (e)(vi).

82    Ibid art 8(2)(b)(iv).

83    Ibid art 8(2)(b)(xxv).

84    International Criminal Court, Assembly of States Parties, *Resolution on Amendments to Article 8 of the Rome Statute of the International Criminal Court*, Doc No ICC-ASP/18/Res.5, 18th sess, 9th plenary mtg, 6 December 2019.

## 12.5.2 Crimes against humanity

The concept of a 'crime against humanity' developed to fill a gap in war crimes law. As Robert Cryer, Darryl Robinson and Sergey Vasiliev explain:

> In the wake of World War II, the drafters of the *Nuremberg Charter* were confronted with the question of how to respond to the Holocaust and the massive crimes committed by the Nazi regime. The classic definition of war crimes did not include crimes committed by a government against its own citizens. The drafters therefore included 'crimes against humanity', defined in Article 6(c) as:
>
>> murder, extermination, enslavement, deportation, and other inhumane acts committed against any civilian population, before or during the war; or persecutions on political, racial or religious grounds in execution of or in connection with any crime within the jurisdiction of the Tribunal, whether or not in violation of the domestic law of the country where perpetrated.[85]

The reference to 'any civilian population' includes the offending state's own citizens. The phrase 'in connection with any crime within the jurisdiction of the Tribunal' required a connection either to war crimes or crimes against peace (aggression). The *Tokyo Charter* included the same requirement.[86]

The concept of crimes against humanity was further developed in the ICTY and ICTR Statutes. The relevant article of the *ICTY Statute* referred to various acts, such as murder, torture and rape, 'when committed in an armed conflict, whether international or internal in character, and directed against any civilian population'.[87] The ICTY interpreted the latter test ('directed against any civilian population') as meaning that the crimes 'must comprise part of a pattern of widespread or systematic crimes directed against a civilian population'.[88] The *ICTR Statute* listed the same acts as crimes against humanity as the *ICTY Statute*. It required no such link to conflict for crimes against humanity, but it required that the acts be committed 'as part of a widespread or systematic attack against any civilian population on national, political, ethnic, racial or religious grounds'.[89]

The *Rome Statute* drops both the armed conflict requirement and the discriminatory animus for crimes against humanity, and includes a longer list of acts than the ICTY and ICTR Statutes. The relevant provision is art 7, which defines 'crimes against humanity' as

> the following acts when committed as part of a widespread or systematic attack directed against any civilian population, with knowledge of the attack:
> (a)  Murder;
> (b)  Extermination;
> (c)  Enslavement;
> (d)  Deportation or forcible transfer of population;

85    Cryer, Robinson and Vasiliev (n 3) 228.
86    *Tokyo Charter* (n 17) art 5(c).
87    *ICTY Statute* (n 8) art 5.
88    *Prosecutor v Tadić (Appeal against Conviction)* (1999) 124 ILR 61, [248] ('*Tadić Appeal Judgment*').
89    *ICTR Statute* (n 9) art 3.

(e)   Imprisonment or other severe deprivation of physical liberty in violation of funda-
       mental rules of international law;

(f)   Torture;

(g)   Rape, sexual slavery, enforced prostitution, forced pregnancy, enforced sterilization,
       or any other form of sexual violence of comparable gravity;

(h)   Persecution against any identifiable group or collectivity on political, racial, national,
       ethnic, cultural, religious, gender as defined in paragraph 3, or other grounds that
       are universally recognized as impermissible under international law, in connection
       with any act referred to in this paragraph or any crime within the jurisdiction of
       the Court;

(i)   Enforced disappearance of persons;

(j)   The crime of apartheid;

(k)   Other inhumane acts of a similar character intentionally causing great suffering, or
       serious injury to body or to mental or physical health.[90]

As of May 2022, crimes against humanity have been charged in every ICC case (except those
cases concerning witness tampering and other offences against the administration of justice).
Reflecting on this trend, Alex Whiting (former ICTY and ICC prosecutor, and now Head of
Investigations, Kosovo Specialist Prosecutor's Office) has observed:

> At Nuremberg, the seed of crimes against humanity was planted ... *Today, crimes against
> humanity represent the principal crime charged at the modern tribunals, in particular at
> the ICC.*[91]

## 12.5.3   Genocide

The term 'genocide' was coined by Raphael Lemkin, an Eastern European jurist of Jewish
descent, as World War II was unfolding. In his 1944 book *Axis Rule in Occupied Europe*,
Lemkin wrote:

> By 'genocide' we mean the destruction of a nation or of an ethnic group. This new word,
> coined by the author to denote an old practice in its modern development, is made from
> the ancient Greek word *genos* (race, tribe) and the Latin *cide* (killing) ... Generally
> speaking, genocide does not necessarily mean the immediate destruction of a nation,
> except when accomplished by mass killings of all members of a nation. It is intended
> rather to signify a coordinated plan of different actions aiming at the destruction of
> essential foundations of the life of national groups, with the aim of annihilating the groups
> themselves.[92]

Lemkin's crime of 'genocide' was not included in the *Nuremberg Charter*. However, Lemkin
persuaded Robert Jackson, the United States' lead prosecutor, to use this term in the indictment
in relation to the war crimes count, and the United Kingdom's lead prosecutor Hartley

---

90   *Rome Statute* (n 2) art 7(1).
91   Whiting (n 25) 3 (emphasis added).
92   Raphael Lemkin, *Axis Rule in Occupied Europe* (Carnegie Endowment for International Peace, 1994) 79.

Shawcross to use it in his closing statement.[93] Although the *Nuremberg Judgment* did not refer to 'genocide', the concept continued to have resonance beyond Nuremberg. In 1946, the newly-formed UN General Assembly declared genocide to be a 'crime under international law', invited states to enact legislation to prosecute this crime domestically, and set in motion a draft convention on the crime.[94] The draft convention was published the following year, with input from Lemkin and other experts.[95] Article 1(2) defined 'genocide' as certain acts – including causing death or injury to members of the group, restricting births and destroying the group's specific characteristics – when committed for the purpose of destroying a 'racial, national, linguistic, religious or political group' in whole or in part, or preventing that group's preservation or development.[96]

Within art 1(2), [1] covered what Lemkin called 'physical' genocide (that is, destruction of individuals); [2] covered what he called 'biological' genocide (that is, prevention of births); and [3] described the destruction of the language and traditions that give a mass of individuals their shared identity – a phenomenon that Lemkin called 'cultural genocide'.[97] Although Lemkin regarded cultural genocide as integral to the definition of genocide, the other experts considered this to be an 'undue extension' of the crime.[98]

The notion of cultural genocide continued to be contentious throughout the convention's drafting period. The USSR, China, Poland, Venezuela and Lebanon supported its inclusion in the definition of the genocide, but a larger bloc including the United States, France, United Kingdom, Belgium, Sweden, Iran, India, Peru, the Netherlands, Brazil, New Zealand, South Africa and Canada were opposed.[99] As William Schabas observes, 'it was clear that the issue [of cultural genocide] had hit a nerve with several countries who were conscious of problems with their own policies towards minority groups, specifically indigenous peoples and immigrants'.[100] Consequently, the paragraph on cultural genocide was excluded from the 1948 *Genocide Convention*.[101] The Convention obliges states parties to prevent and punish genocide[102] and further provides for the punishment of individuals who commit, conspire to

---

93    International Military Tribunal, *Trial of the Major War Criminals before the International Military Tribunal: Nuremberg, 14 November 1945 – 1 October 1946* (1951) vol 1, 43; Philippe Sands, *East West Street: On the Origins of Genocide and Crimes against Humanity* (Weidenfeld & Nicolson, 2016).

94    *The Crime of Genocide*, GA Res 96 (I), UN Doc A/RES/96(I) (11 December 1946) [4].

95    The other two experts were Henri Donnedieu de Vabres, the primary French judge at the International Military Tribunal, and Vespasian V Pella, a Romanian law professor who was president of the International Association for Penal Law.

96    Economic and Social Council, *Draft Convention on the Crime of Genocide*, UN Doc E/447 (16 June 1947) art 1(2) ('*Draft Genocide Convention*').

97    Ibid 17, 25–28. Regarding 'cultural genocide', see also William Schabas, *Genocide in International Law: The Crime of Crimes* (Cambridge University Press, 2nd ed, 2009) 207–21; Melanie O'Brien and Gerhard Hoffstaedter, '"There We Are Nothing, Here We Are Nothing!" – The Enduring Effects of the Rohingya Genocide' 11(9) *Social Sciences* 209.

98    *Draft Genocide Convention* (n 96) 27.

99    Schabas (n 97) 207–21.

100    Ibid 212.

101    Attacking the language and traditions that bind individuals together as a group was addressed under human rights law roughly 20 years later: see *International Covenant on Civil and Political Rights*, opened for signature 16 December 1966, 999 UNTS 171 (entered into force 23 March 1976) art 27.

102    *Genocide Convention* (n 4) art I.

commit, directly and publicly incite, attempt to commit, or are complicit in, the crime of genocide.[103] It defines 'genocide' as:

> any of the following acts committed with intent to destroy, in whole or in part, a national, ethnical, racial or religious group, as such:
> (a)  Killing members of the group;
> (b)  Causing serious bodily or mental harm to members of the group;
> (c)  Deliberately inflicting on the group conditions of life calculated to bring about its physical destruction in whole or in part;
> (d)  Imposing measures intended to prevent births within the group; [or]
> (e)  Forcibly transferring children of the group to another group.[104]

This same definition is used in the statutes of the ICTY, ICTR, ICC and ECCC.[105] For all five acts enumerated in this definition, the mental element is the same: the perpetrator must act with 'intent to destroy, in whole or in part, a national, ethnical, racial or religious group'. This special intent (*dolus specialis*) distinguishes genocide from other crimes under international law.

Of those five acts, the first four come from Lemkin's categories of 'physical' and 'biological' genocide, while the fifth comes from his category of 'cultural genocide'. Despite that, the International Law Commission considers that *all five acts* enumerated in the *Genocide Convention* relate to physical or biological genocide, and that the word 'destruction' in this Convention 'must be taken only in its material sense, its physical or biological sense'.[106]

The jurisprudence on the crime of genocide comes primarily from national proceedings, including genocide trials after World War II, and from the ICTY and ICTR.[107] This jurisprudence indicates that the international crime of genocide excludes cultural genocide,[108] although there are some exceptions.[109] The ICC has issued one arrest warrant for

---

103   Ibid art III.
104   Ibid art II.
105   *ICTY Statute* (n 8) art 4; *ICTR Statute* (n 9) art 2; *Rome Statute* (n 2) art 5; *ECCC Statute* (n 76) art 4. The English language version of the *ECCC Statute* uses the term 'such as' rather than 'as such'. However, the ECCC Trial Chamber has attached no weight to this apparent drafting error: see *Case 002/02 (Trial Judgment)* (2020) 59 ILM 159 (Extraordinary Chambers in the Courts of Cambodia, Trial Chamber) [793] ('*Case 002/02 Trial*'); separate opinion at [4474] (Judge You Ottara).
106   'Draft Code of Crimes against the Peace and Security of Mankind' [1996] II(2) *Yearbook of the International Law Commission* 1, 45–6 (Draft Article 17 Commentary [12]).
107   Melanie O'Brien, 'Defining Genocide' (2020) 22 *Journal of International Peacekeeping* 149; Schabas (n 97) ch 8.
108   See, eg, *Prosecutor v Krstić (Judgment)* (International Criminal Tribunal for the Former Yugoslavia, Trial Chamber, Case No IT-98-33-T, 2 August 2001) [580]; *Prosecutor v Krstić (Appeal Judgment)* (International Criminal Tribunal for the Former Yugoslavia, Appeals Chamber, Case No IT-98-33-A, 19 April 2004) [25] ('*Krstić Appeal Judgment*'); *Application of the Convention on the Prevention and Punishment of the Crime of Genocide (Bosnia and Herzegovina v Serbia and Montenegro) (Judgment)* [2007] ICJ Rep 43, 181–2 [334].
109   See, eg, the dissenting opinion in *Krstić Appeal Judgment* (n 108) [48]–[54] (Judge Shahabuddeen); *Prosecutor v Blagojević (Judgment)* (International Criminal Tribunal for the Former Yugoslavia, Trial Chamber I, Case No IT-02-60-T, 17 January 2005) [569]–[560]; *Prosecutor v Krajišnik (Judgment)* (International Criminal Tribunal for the Former Yugoslavia, Trial Chamber I, Case No IT-00-39-T, 27 September 2006) [854]. See also *Jorgić*, Bundesverfassungsgericht [German Constitutional Court],

genocide, against Sudan's former president Omar Al-Bashir, but has heard no trials on this crime.[110]

The definition of 'genocide' in international law often conflicts with popular conceptions of the term. This tension between the legal definition and popular definitions of genocide raises questions about whether lawyers should have a monopoly over the meaning of genocide, and what are the social and political consequences when legal and popular conceptions of genocide do not align.

For example, in Cambodia, the term 'genocide' is widely used to describe the large-scale murders, disappearances, sexual violence, torture, forced labour and displacement that occurred during the Khmer Rouge regime (1975–79).[111] However, the bulk of these crimes were not labelled 'genocide' in the ECCC. They were instead charged as crimes against humanity and war crimes, and only those acts aimed at eliminating the country's Vietnamese and Cham ethnic monitories were charged as genocide.[112] This strategy was challenged by one of the Cambodian judges, Judge You Ottara, in the ECCC's major case. In his view, it would have been possible to charge the crimes committed against Cambodian people at large as genocide, on the basis that these crimes were aimed at the destruction of a substantial part of a 'national group'.[113]

### 12.5.3.1   Genocide in Australia?

The term 'genocide' is also contentious in Australia. Indigenous Australians have described their experience of dispossession, slaughter, neglect and child removal following colonisation as 'genocide', including in the cases of *Kruger v Commonwealth* ('*Kruger*')[114] and *Nulyarimma v Thompson* ('*Nulyarimma*').[115] In both cases, the Court rejected the plaintiffs' claims of genocide, finding inter alia that there was insufficient evidence that relevant acts were committed with a genocidal intent.[116] Reflecting on these cases, Larissa Behrendt has observed:

> While legal technicalities have seen claims of Indigenous peoples that genocide has been committed by the state defeated, these legal pronouncements do nothing to erase the conviction that Indigenous communities feel about 'genocide' being the word and the concept that describes the colonial legacy inherited and still pervasive.[117]

The *Kruger* and *Nulyarimma* cases were part of a broader public debate in the late 1990s and early 2000s about genocide in Australia. A flashpoint in this debate was the publication in

---

2 BvR 1290/99, 30 April 1999; *Jorgić v Germany* [2007] III Eur Court HR 263; both cases cited in O'Brien and Hoffstaedter (n 97) 211.

110    *Prosecutor v Al-Bashir (Second Decision on the Prosecution's Application for a Warrant of Arrest)* (International Criminal Court, Pre-Trial Chamber I, Case No ICC-02/05-01/09-95, 12 July 2010) ('*Al-Bashir Second Decision*').

111    Rachel Hughes, Christoph Sperfeldt and Maria Elander, 'Cambodians Await Crucial Tribunal Finding into 1970s Brutal Khmer Rouge Regime', *The Conversation* (online at 15 November 2018) <https://theconversation.com/cambodians-await-crucial-tribunal-finding-into-1970s-brutal-khmer-rouge-regime-106078>.

112    *Case 002/02 Trial* (n 105) [16].

113    Ibid [2234] (Judge You Ottara).

114    *Kruger v Commonwealth* (1997) 190 CLR 1.

115    *Nulyarimma* (n 61).

116    Larissa Behrendt, 'Genocide: The Distance between Law and Life' (2002) 25 *Aboriginal History* 132.

117    Ibid 146.

1997 of the *Bringing Them Home* report by Australia's human rights commission.[118] The report considered the state-orchestrated removal of Aboriginal children from their families throughout Australia during the 20th century. Officials had claimed that such removals were for the children's benefit, although in practice they caused immense grief to Indigenous people, displaced generations of children from their culture, put many children in settings where they were abused, and resulted in ongoing, intergenerational suffering. Among other things, the *Bringing Them Home* report considered whether these child removals constituted 'genocide'. It concluded:

> [T]he predominant aim of Indigenous child removals was the absorption or assimilation of the children into the wider, non-Indigenous, community so that their unique cultural values and ethnic identities would disappear, giving way to models of Western culture. In other words, the objective was 'the disintegration of the political and social institutions of culture, language, national feelings, religion, and the economical existence of' Indigenous peoples [quoting Raphael Lemkin, *Axis Rule in Occupied Europe* (1944) 79]. Removal of children with this objective in mind is genocidal because it aims to destroy the 'cultural unit' which the [*Genocide*] *Convention* is concerned to preserve ... The policy of forcible removal of children from Indigenous Australians to other groups for the purpose of raising them separately from and ignorant of their culture and people could properly be labelled 'genocidal' in breach of binding international law from at least 11 December 1946 [when the General Assembly declared genocide a crime under international law]. The practice continued for almost another quarter of a century.[119]

The report's conclusions regarding genocide have been widely debated. Historian Keith Windschuttle argued that Indigenous Australians had not been mistreated in the ways described in the report and that Indigenous children were not 'stolen'.[120] By contrast, historian Henry Reynolds concluded that the practices documented in the report 'have to be seriously considered as genocidal in effect, if not necessarily in intention'.[121] Historian and anthropologist Inga Clendinnen challenged the report's use of the term 'genocide', arguing that the removal of Aboriginal children from their families, while causing serious harm, bore little resemblance to practices with which she associated the term 'genocide' such as 'Gypsies and Jews being herded into trains' and 'the shadowy figures of Armenian women and children being marched into the desert by armed men'.[122]

An international lawyer might argue that the *Bringing Them Home* report appeared to conclude that child removal amounted to cultural genocide, as distinct from genocide as defined in the 1948 *Genocide Convention*. And yet, a finding that Australia's Indigenous people experienced cultural genocide does not preclude a finding that they have *also*

---

118    Australian Human Rights and Equal Opportunity Commission, *Bringing Them Home: National Inquiry into the Separation of Aboriginal and Torres Strait Islander Children from Their Families* (Report, April 1997).

119    Ibid 236–8.

120    Keith Windschuttle, *The Fabrication of Aboriginal History* (Macleay Press, 2009) vol 3, 17.

121    Henry Reynolds, *The Question of Genocide in Australia's History: An Indelible Stain?* (Viking, 2001).

122    Inga Clendinnen, 'Quarterly Essay 1: In Denial: Correspondence', *Quarterly Essay* (Black Inc, 2001) (first published in *The Australian's Review of Books*, 9 May 2001) <www.quarterlyessay.com.au/correspondence/correspondence-inga-clendinnen-0>.

experienced genocide as defined in the Convention, taking into account the child removals as well as the killings and inhumane conditions to which they have been subjected since colonisation. Some experts have indeed taken this position. For example, law professor Irene Watson has argued:

> The state in refusing to speak of the genocide instead uses other words which nullify any obligation to cease the genocide or to compensate Nungas [Indigenous Australians] for the destruction of life. The assumption is that, if you don't have Auschwitz-style extermination centres, you don't really have genocide. And yet the missions or reservations performed the same function as a Nazi concentration camp, with the same purpose, to constrain and cause the death of the Nungas. The full bloods were to die, the mixed blood was to provide a servant class that was ultimately to become absorbed into whiteness.[123]

A similar approach was taken by the late genocide scholar Colin Tatz, who regarded the Australian experience as a genocide, albeit a 'unique' one because it essentially involved only two of the five genocidal acts (killing and forced transfer of children). These acts of genocide have occurred over at least 200 years, 'quite unlike Europe's forty-five frenetic months between December 1941 and May 1945, or Rwanda's one hundred days in 1994', because the killing was usually done by small groups, and because much of the killing was 'a private genocide, committed by released convicts and settlers, unhindered by the colonial authorities'.[124]

One of the most powerful responses to Australia's genocide question has been voiced by Wadjularbinna Nulyarimma, one of the four Indigenous Australians who in 1998 attempted to initiate genocide proceedings against Australia's Prime Minister and other political leaders, but was thwarted by the fact that Australia was yet to enact the crime of genocide under domestic law.[125] Ms Nulyarimma argued:

> We invoke your own criminal law primarily to get your people to stop the genocide – penalties, if any, are of secondary importance ... [I]t was recognised [in the 1948 *Genocide Convention*] that genocide is not simply murdering people. It is destroying the people through various ways such as sterilising women, removing children, causing serious physical and mental harm and forcibly imposing on the people conditions of life calculated to destroy the people in whole or in part. All of these things have happened to us or our relations and are still happening now.[126]

## 12.5.4  Aggression

'Aggression' refers to the unlawful use of force between states. A state that commits aggression will be responsible for an internationally wrongful act (see Chapter 8), and certain individuals

---

123    Irene Margaret Watson, 'Rule Law: The Coming of the Muldarbi and the Path to Its Demise' (PhD Thesis, University of Adelaide, 1999) 194.
124    Colin Tatz, 'The Destruction of Aboriginal Society in Australia' in Samuel Totten and Robert Hitchcock (eds), *Genocide of Indigenous Peoples* (Routledge, 2011) 87, 88–9.
125    *Re Thompson; Ex parte Nulyarimma* (1998) 136 ACTR 9, [2], [51]–[52]; *Nulyarimma* (n 61); Reynolds (n 121) 199–204.
126    Affidavit of Wadjularbinna Nulyarimma, sworn on 8 July 1998, Supreme Court of the Australian Capital Territory (on file).

who initiate the act of aggression will be responsible for a crime under international law. The criminalisation of aggression reflects a paradigm shift in international relations. Until the early 20th century, the use of force by states was generally considered a lawful tool of foreign policy. However, the devastation caused by World War I helped to accelerate a shift in views, leading to the 1928 *Kellogg–Briand Pact*, which condemned recourse to war as an instrument of national policy, and committed to settling conflicts by pacific (peaceful) means.[127]

The victors of World War II defined aggression as a crime attracting individual criminal responsibility (referred to as 'crimes against peace' in the Nuremberg and Tokyo Charters).[128] In both the Nuremberg and Tokyo Tribunals, defendants were convicted of this crime. At Nuremberg, some defendants argued that this charge violated the principle of legality (*nullum crimen sine lege*), which mandates that a person cannot be prosecuted for conduct that was not clearly defined as a crime at the time of its commission.[129] The tribunal rejected that argument. It held that initiating a war of aggression 'is not only an international crime; it is the supreme international crime'.[130] Citing the *Kellogg–Briand Pact*, among other sources, it concluded:

> [T]he solemn renunciation of war as an instrument of national policy necessarily involves the proposition that such a war is illegal in international law; and that those who plan and wage such a war, with its inevitable and terrible consequences, are committing a crime in so doing.[131]

The Tokyo Tribunal likewise accepted that aggression amounted to a crime under international law, although Judge Pal (India) and Judge Röling (the Netherlands) both dissented on this point.[132]

The ICTY and ICTR did not have jurisdiction over aggression, but the ICC does. This was the most controversial crime in the *Rome Statute*. Key issues included how 'aggression' should be defined (including whether it would include the use of force by 'freedom fighters' seeking to achieve national self-determination) and whether the ICC's jurisdiction over the crime of aggression should be contingent on the Security Council first deciding that an act of aggression had occurred.[133] To overcome this impasse, the delegations at Rome decided to include the crime of aggression in the *Rome Statute*, while leaving the task of defining that crime to a later date.[134]

---

127    *General Treaty for Renunciation of War as an Instrument of National Policy*, opened for signature 27 August 1928, 94 LNTS 57 (entered into force 24 July 1929).

128    *Nuremberg Charter* (n 15) art 6(a); *Tokyo Charter* (n 17) art 5(a).

129    Claus Kreß, 'Introduction' in Claus Kreß and Stefan Barriga (eds), *The Crime of Aggression: A Commentary* (Cambridge University Press, 2016) 1, 4.

130    *Nuremberg Judgment* (n 1) 186.

131    Ibid 218. The International Military Tribunal has been criticised for prosecuting crimes against peace when such conduct had not previously been defined as a crime under international law: see, eg, Carrie McDougall, 'The Crimes against Peace Precedent' in Claus Kreß and Stefan Barriga (eds), *The Crime of Aggression: A Commentary* (Cambridge University Press, 2016) 49, 50–2.

132    Kirsten Sellars, 'The Legacy of the Tokyo Dissents on "Crimes against Peace"' in Claus Kreß and Stefan Barriga (eds), *The Crime of Aggression: A Commentary* (Cambridge University Press, 2016) 113.

133    Roger Clark, 'Negotiations on the Rome Statute, 1995–98' in Claus Kreß and Stefan Barriga (eds), *The Crime of Aggression: A Commentary* (Cambridge University Press, 2016) 244.

134    Ibid 266–7.

That date came in June 2010, at the Review Conference of the Rome Statute in Kampala, Uganda. There, states negotiated art 8 *bis*, which defines the crime of aggression for the purposes of the ICC. Several features of this definition are of note. First, art 8 *bis* defines an 'act of aggression' as certain uses of armed force by 'a State', thus excluding analogous acts by non-state actors such as the so-called Islamic State (or Da'esh).[135] Second, it limits the ICC's jurisdiction over aggression to people in leadership positions: namely, 'persons in a position effectively to exercise control over or to direct the political or military action of a State'.[136] Third, the act of aggression must constitute a '*manifest* violation of the *Charter of the United Nations*', which seems to exclude any borderline cases.[137] This threshold requirement was essential to reaching the compromise at Kampala.[138] There is some debate as to whether 'manifest' describes the character, gravity and scale of the aggressive act, or the degree of its unlawfulness under the *Charter*.[139]

Fourth, the ICC's powers with respect to aggression are largely independent of the Security Council. For example, there is no requirement that the Council must deem an incident to constitute aggression under art 39 of the *Charter of the United Nations* before the ICC Prosecutor can investigate and charge this crime.[140] Moreover, even if the Security Council *did* make such a declaration, it would not be binding on the ICC.[141] However, the *Rome Statute* makes some concessions to the Security Council's role vis-à-vis aggression. It states that, in the absence of a Council referral, the Prosecutor must give the Security Council six months to consider making a determination that an act of aggression has occurred before the Prosecutor can proceed with an investigation into this crime.[142] Furthermore, when there is no Security Council referral, the ICC cannot exercise its jurisdiction over the crime of aggression when committed by nationals of a state that is not a party, or on territory of a state that is not a party, whereas it could for genocide, war crimes or crimes against humanity.[143] In addition, for all crimes, the Security Council has the power to defer ICC proceedings for a renewable period of 12 months.[144]

The ICC's jurisdiction over the crime of aggression was activated on 17 July 2018,[145] in respect of states that ratified the 2010 Kampala amendment.[146] As of May 2022, a total of 43 states have taken that step, not including Australia.[147]

---

135   *Rome Statute* (n 2) art 8 *bis*(2); Kreß (n 129) 9.
136   *Rome Statute* (n 2) arts 8 *bis*(1), 25(3) *bis*.
137   Ibid art 8 *bis* (emphasis added).
138   Kreß (n 129) 10.
139   Cryer, Robinson and Vasiliev (n 3) 309–11.
140   Kreß (n 129) 131.
141   *Rome Statute* (n 2) arts 15 *bis*(9), 15 *ter*(4).
142   Ibid art 15 *bis*(6)–(8). For all crimes (including aggression), the Prosecutor must first obtain Pre-Trial Chamber authorisation before the investigation can proceed.
143   *Rome Statute* (n 2) art 15 *bis*(5).
144   Ibid art 16.
145   *Resolution on Activation of Jurisdiction* (n 38).
146   International Criminal Court, Assembly of States Parties, *Amendments on the Crime of Aggression to the Rome Statute of the International Criminal Court*, Doc No ICC-ASP/16/Res.5, 16th sess, 13th plenary mtg, 14 December 2017.
147   *Amendments to the Rome Statute of the International Criminal Court: Adoption of Amendments on the Crime of Aggression*, C.N.651.2010.TREATIES (11 June 2010) (Web Page) <https://treaties.un.org/pages/ViewDetails.aspx?src=TREATY&mtdsg_no=XVIII-10-b&chapter=18&clang=_en>.

# 12.6    Individual criminal responsibility

For prosecutors in ICL, establishing individual criminal responsibility is among the most challenging tasks.[148] Even if it can be proved beyond reasonable doubt that the crimes occurred, it remains necessary to show that the accused person was criminally responsible for those crimes. Broadly speaking, ICL recognises two types of individual criminal responsibility.[149] A person may be responsible because of the actions that they took toward the commission of the crimes, and/or because of their failure to prevent, repress or punish the crimes. These two conceptions of criminal responsibility (or 'modes of liability') are discussed next.

## 12.6.1    Commission

In some cases, the accused is charged as a direct perpetrator. But mostly, the accused is a senior political or military figure who did not physically commit the offence, but is charged with other forms of commission such as indirectly perpetrating the crimes; ordering, soliciting or inducing the crimes; aiding and abetting the crimes; intentionally contributing to the commission of the crimes by a group of people acting with a common purpose; or attempting to commit the crime.[150]

In the *Tadić* case, the Appeals Chamber held that the notion of 'commission' encompasses three types of joint criminal enterprise. For all three, it is required that there was a plurality of people, a common plan that involved the commission of a crime under the *ICTY Statute*, and participation of the accused person in the execution of that plan.[151] However, the *mens rea* for each type of joint criminal enterprise (or 'JCE') differs. For 'JCE I', the accused must share with the other group members an intent to commit the relevant crime(s); for 'JCE II', the accused must know of a system of ill-treatment such as a concentration camp, and must intend to further that system; and for 'JCE III', the accused must intend to participate in the group's criminal activity, and is responsible for crimes committed by group members if there was a foreseeable risk that such crimes would occur, and the accused willingly took that risk.[152]

Applying that analysis, the Appeals Chamber held that the accused, Dusko Tadić, was responsible for the murder of five civilians by members of an armed group of which he was a member.[153] Tadić did not personally commit these murders. However, they occurred during an attack on the Prijedor region of Bosnia and Herzegovina by Tadić and his fellow group members. The purpose of that attack was to rid the region of the non-Serb population by committing inhumane acts against them. The Appeals Chamber convicted Tadić of these murders under JCE III, reasoning:

> That non-Serbs might be killed in the effecting of this common aim was, in the circumstances of the present case, foreseeable. The Appellant [Tadić] was aware that the actions of the group of which he was a member were likely to lead to such killings, but he nevertheless willingly took that risk.[154]

---

148    See, eg, Grey (n 19) 270–2.
149    Jérôme de Hemptinne, Robert Roth and Elies van Sliedregt (eds), *Modes of Liability in International Criminal Law* (Cambridge University Press, 2019).
150    See, eg, *ICTY Statute* (n 8) art 7(1); *ICTR Statute* (n 9) art 6(1); *Rome Statute* (n 2) art 25(3).
151    *Tadić Appeal Judgment* (n 88) [227].
152    Ibid [228].
153    Ibid [230]–[232].
154    Ibid [232].

The ICTY's conception of joint criminal enterprise has been adopted by the ICTR, the Special Court for Sierra Leone and the ECCC to varying extents[155] (for example, the ECCC did not accept that JCE III had a firm basis under customary international law in the 1970s, when the relevant crimes occurred).[156] However, the ICC does not recognise joint criminal enterprise.[157] Instead, the ICC deals with joint commission of a crime either as 'co-perpetratorship' under art 25(3)(a) of the *Rome Statute*, or as 'contributors' under art 25(3)(d).

Co-perpetrators, in the sense of art 25(3)(a), are those who have *joint control* over the crime. That is, 'co-perpetrators are solely those individuals who provide an "essential" contribution to the commission of the said crime; ie, whose acts were indispensable for the crime's commission, in that without them the common plan would have collapsed'.[158] Each co-perpetrator must be aware, and must accept, that implementing their common plan will result in the commission of the crimes as a certainty, or at least, in the ordinary course of events.[159] By contrast, a 'contributor' in the sense of art 25(3)(d) is an accessory who intentionally provides a 'significant' (but not essential) contribution to the commission of the crime by a group of persons acting with a common purpose.[160] For example, in *Prosecutor v Katanga*, the majority of the Trial Chamber applied this article to convict the accused of crimes committed during an attack on a village in the Democratic Republic of Congo, primarily due to his role in supplying the weapons used in that attack[161] with the knowledge that crimes against civilians would be committed in that attack.[162]

The ICC also recognises the notion of 'indirect perpetratorship' and 'indirect co-perpetratorship' pursuant to art 25(3)(a) of the *Rome Statute*. These 'indirect' forms of commission apply where the accused controls the will of the physical perpetrator(s) of the crime and has the *mens rea* for the crime.[163] For example, in 2009 and 2010, the ICC issued arrest warrants in respect of Sudan's president Omar Al-Bashir on the basis that he was liable as an indirect perpetrator or indirect co-perpetrator for war crimes, crimes against humanity and genocide. This was based on the Court's finding that there was a reasonable basis to believe that as president of Sudan, Al-Bashir controlled the state apparatus, including the Sudanese armed

---

155    Lachezar Yanev, 'Joint Criminal Enterprise' in Jérôme de Hemptinne, Robert Roth and Elies van Sliedregt (eds), *Modes of Liability in International Criminal Law* (Cambridge University Press, 2019) 121.

156    *Case 002/01 (Appeal Judgment)* (Extraordinary Chambers in the Courts of Cambodia, Supreme Court Chamber, Case No 002/19-09-2007-ECCC-SC, 23 November 2016) [791].

157    Stefano Manacorda and Chantal Meloni, 'Indirect Perpetration versus Joint Criminal Enterprise: Concurring Approaches in the Practice of International Criminal Law?' (2011) 9(1) *Journal of International Criminal Justice* 159.

158    Elies van Sliedregt and Lachezar Yanev, 'Co-Perpetration Based on Joint Control over the Crime' in Jérôme de Hemptinne, Robert Roth and Elies van Sliedregt (eds), *Modes of Liability in International Criminal Law* (Cambridge University Press, 2019) 85, 90.

159    *Prosecutor v Katanga (Decision on the Confirmation of Charges)* (International Criminal Court, Pre-Trial Chamber I, Case No ICC-01/04-01/07-717, 30 September 2008) [533].

160    *Prosecutor v Katanga (Judgment)* (International Criminal Court, Trial Chamber II, Case No ICC-01/04-01/07-3436-tENG, 7 March 2014) [1632].

161    Ibid [1670]–[1681].

162    Ibid [1684]–[1691].

163    Ibid [1399].

forces and the allied *janjaweed* militia who physically perpetrated the crimes, and that he intended the commission of the relevant crimes.[164]

## 12.6.2   Command responsibility

Under the doctrine of command responsibility (also known as 'superior responsibility'), a person in a position of authority is criminally responsible for failing to take sufficient action to prevent, stop or punish crimes committed by their subordinates.[165] Professor Diane Marie Amann, the ICC Prosecutor's Special Advisor on Children in and Affected by Armed Conflict, explained:

> Command responsibility doctrine recognizes war's awful consequences, and so imposes extra duties of care upon officers who accept to lead others in the use of lethal, armed force.[166]

While command responsibility originated in a military setting,[167] it now applies also to crimes committed in peacetime and is not limited to those who wield military (as opposed to civilian) authority.[168]

There are three elements of command responsibility. These can be analysed using the ICC's provision on command responsibility (art 28(a)) as a guide. First, the accused must be in a superior–subordinate relationship with the physical perpetrators of the crime, and must have 'effective control' over them.[169] For example, art 28(a)(i) of the *Rome Statute* refers to the responsibility that lies with 'a military commander or person effectively acting as a military commander' for crimes committed 'by forces under his or her effective command and control, or effective authority and control'. Second, the accused must have actual or constructive knowledge of the relevant crimes; they are not criminally responsible for crimes that they could not reasonably have known about. For example, art 28(a)(ii) provides that the accused 'either knew or, owing to the circumstances at the time, should have known that the forces were committing or about to commit such crimes'. Third, the accused must have failed to take sufficient steps to stem the crimes. For example, art 28(b)(iii) requires that the accused 'failed to take all necessary and reasonable measures within his or her power to prevent or repress their commission or to submit the matter to the competent authorities for investigation and prosecution'. The phrase 'within his or her power' means that a commander is not required to do the impossible; they must only take 'all necessary and *reasonable* measures' within their power.[170]

---

164    *Prosecutor v Al-Bashir (Decision on the Prosecution's Application for a Warrant of Arrest)* (International Criminal Court, Pre-Trial Chamber I, Case No ICC-02/05-01/09-3, 4 March 2002) [209]–[223]; *Al-Bashir Second Decision* (n 110) [4]–[5], [41]–[43].

165    See, eg, *ICTY Statute* (n 8) art 7(3); *ICTR Statute* (n 9) art 6(3); *Rome Statute* (n 2) art 28.

166    Diane Amann, 'In Bemba and Beyond: Crimes Adjudged to Commit Themselves', *EJIL Talk!* (Blog Post, 13 June 2018) <www.ejiltalk.org/in-bemba-and-beyond-crimes-adjudged-to-commit-themselves>.

167    Miles Jackson, 'Command Responsibility' in Jérôme de Hemptinne, Robert Roth and Elies van Sliedregt (eds), *Modes of Liability in International Criminal Law* (Cambridge University Press, 2019) 409, 409.

168    See, eg, *Rome Statute* (n 2) art 28(b).

169    Jackson (n 167) 416–19.

170    *Prosecutor v Bemba (Judgment on the Appeal against Trial Chamber III's 'Judgment Pursuant to Article 74 of the Statute')* (International Criminal Court, Appeals Chamber, Case No ICC-01/05-01/08-3636-Red, 8 December 2018) [167]–[168] (emphasis added) ('*Bemba Appeal Judgment*').

The *Bemba* case is the ICC's leading case on command responsibility. It concerned war crimes and crimes against humanity committed by members of an armed group called the Mouvement de Libération du Congo ('Libération du Congo') in the Central African Republic. According to the ICC Prosecutor, Libération du Congo's president and commander-in-chief was Jean-Pierre Bemba Gombo, a politician in the neighbouring state of the Democratic Republic of Congo. In the early 2000s, Bemba sent his troops into the Central African Republic at the request of its president to assist in supressing a coup d'état. There, Libération du Congo soldiers committed multiple acts of rape, murder and pillage against civilians. According to the Prosecutor, Bemba was criminally liable for those acts under art 28(a) of the *Rome Statute* because he had failed to take all necessary and reasonable measures within his power to prevent or punish the crimes.[171]

The Trial Chamber convicted Bemba under art 28(a). It found that as commander of Libération du Congo, he could have taken further measures, including: ensuring that his troops were properly trained in international humanitarian law; ensuring that they were properly supervised in the Central African Republic; initiating 'genuine and full investigations' into the crimes; properly prosecuting and punishing any soldiers suspected of committing crimes; giving his commanders in the Central African Republic further orders to prevent the commission of crimes; altering troop deployment to minimise contact with civilians; removing soldiers who had been found to commit or condone crimes in the Central African Republic; sharing information with that state's authorities; supporting external efforts to investigate the crimes; and withdrawing Libération du Congo from the Central African Republic sooner than he did.[172]

Bemba's conviction was overturned on appeal. The majority of the Appeals Chamber was not satisfied with the Trial Chamber's analysis of command responsibility. In its view, the Trial Chamber had placed insufficient weight on the difficulties that Bemba faced in investigating his troops' misconduct in the Central African Republic, when he himself was a 'remote commander' based in the Democratic Republic of Congo, among other errors.[173] The case illustrates the difficulties of establishing command responsibility and raises moral questions about whether ICL *should* permit commanders to send troops to a foreign country, with little or no means of preventing or punishing serious crimes committed by those troops while abroad.

## 12.6.3  Defences

International criminal law recognises several complete defences, including: mental incapacitation; intoxication; using proportionate means to defend oneself, or another person, or protected property, against an imminent and unlawful use of force; duress resulting from a threat of imminent death or of continuing or imminent serious bodily harm; and a mistake of fact or law.[174] The defences of mental incapacitation and duress were raised by Defence counsel in the ICC's *Ongwen* trial, and were analysed in the appeal judgment.[175]

---

171    *Prosecutor v Bemba (Corrected Version of 'Prosecution's Closing Brief')* (International Criminal Court, Office of the Prosecutor, Case No ICC-01/05-01/08-3079-Corr-Red, 22 April 2016).

172    *Prosecutor v Bemba (Trial Judgment)* (International Criminal Court, Trial Chamber III, Case No ICC-01/05-01/08-3343, 21 March 2016) [729]–[730].

173    *Bemba Appeal Judgment* (n 170) [171].

174    *Rome Statute* (n 2) art 31(1)–(2).

175    See *Ongwen* (n 56).

International criminal law also recognises a defence of 'superior orders', in limited circumstances. The *Nuremberg Charter* indicated that a defendant who acted in accordance with an order from their government or superior was not free of criminal responsibility, although their reliance on the order might be considered a mitigating factor in sentencing.[176] The Nuremberg Tribunal took the view that the availability of the 'superior orders' defence was contingent on whether a 'moral choice [to disobey the order] was in fact possible'.[177] It reasoned:

> [T]he very essence of the [*Nuremberg*] *Charter* is that individuals have international duties which transcend the national obligations of obedience imposed by the individual state. [A person] who violates the laws of war cannot obtain immunity while acting in pursuance of the authority of the state if the state in authorizing action moves outside its competence under international law.[178]

In relation to superior orders, the ICTY and ICTR Statutes followed the *Nuremberg Charter*.[179] However, the *Rome Statute* returns to the pre- International Military Tribunal rule that executing superior orders only relieves a person of criminal responsibility if those orders were not manifestly unlawful.[180]

## DISCUSSION QUESTIONS

(1)  The International Criminal Court ('ICC') has been accused of having an 'Africa bias'. In what ways is this accusation justified? In what ways is it not?

(2)  Does the UN Security Council have too much control over the ICC?

(3)  Should the ICC hold all, or some, of its proceedings outside The Hague?

(4)  What is an offence that is not yet criminalised under international criminal law, but should be?

(5)  Why might it be relevant for contemporary scholars and practitioners of international criminal law to have knowledge of the definitions of crimes used in international tribunals that are no longer operating, such as the Nuremberg and Tokyo Tribunals, the International Criminal Tribunal for the Former Yugoslavia and the International Criminal Tribunal for Rwanda?

---

176    *Nuremberg Charter* (n 15) art 8.
177    *Nuremberg Judgment* (n 1) 221.
178    Ibid.
179    *ICTY Statute* (n 8) art 7(4); *ICTR Statute* (n 9) art 6(4).
180    *Rome Statute* (n 2) art 33; Cryer, Robinson and Vasiliev (n 3) 393–4.

# 13

# INTERNATIONAL LAW OF THE SEA

Tim Stephens

# 13.1   Introduction

The law of the sea, one of the oldest areas of international law, is now substantially codified in the 1982 *United Nations Convention on the Law of the Sea* ('*UNCLOS*'),[1] the 'constitution for the oceans'.[2] *UNCLOS* ushered in the modern law of the sea, providing a comprehensive regime for maritime zones, navigational rights and freedoms, fishing and other uses of the world's oceans that cover approximately 70% of the Earth's surface. As an island country with extensive maritime zones, Australia has a major stake in the law of the sea and has been actively involved in its development and implementation. Australia was one of the original signatories to *UNCLOS* and ratified it in 1994, the year it entered into force generally.[3] The central issues of concern for the law of the sea have traditionally been the extent of maritime jurisdiction and navigational rights. However, a much broader range of matters is addressed in contemporary law and practice, from sustainable fisheries management through to mining of the deep seabed beyond national jurisdiction. There are also major new challenges on the horizon – none more so than climate change, which is driving rapid sea-level rise and damaging marine ecosystems.

# 13.2   Origins and development

As DP O'Connell put it, '[t]he history of the law of the sea has been dominated by a central and persistent theme: the competition between the exercise of governmental authority over the sea and the idea of the freedom of the seas'.[4] The core elements of the law of the sea can be traced to the 17th century when newly emergent states began to extend their sovereign designs beyond their territory and into the oceans. Several maritime powers in Europe viewed the oceans, or at least some parts of them, as indistinguishable from land and subject to ownership and control. Sovereignty over the seas was opposed by other states such as the Netherlands, which had extensive trading interests in Asia and advocated for the 'freedom of the seas' in order to preserve rights of navigation and fishing. The Dutch position gained scholarly support from Hugo Grotius, who set out the case for the 'free seas' in his book *Mare Liberum* in 1609.[5] By reference both to natural law and state practice Grotius maintained that the seas were avenues of commerce and could not be appropriated. This idea of free seas gained a permanent foothold and came to suit the general interests of states.[6]

---

1    *United Nations Convention on the Law of the Sea*, opened for signature 10 December 1982, 1833 UNTS 397 (entered into force 16 November 1994) ('*UNCLOS*').

2    Tommy Koh, 'A Constitution for the Oceans' in *The Law of the Sea: United Nations Convention on the Law of the Sea* (St Martin's Press, 1983) xxxiv.

3    *UNCLOS* (n 1) art 308(1).

4    DP O'Connell, *The International Law of the Sea*, ed Ivan Shearer (Oxford University Press, 1982) vol 1, 1. See further Tullio Treves, 'Historical Development of the Law of the Sea' in Donald Rothwell et al (eds), *The Oxford Handbook of the Law of the Sea* (Oxford University Press, 2015) 1, 1.

5    Hugo Grotius, *The Freedom of the Seas, or The Right Which Belongs to the Dutch to Take Part in the East Indian Trade*, tr Ralph van Deman Magoffin (Oxford University Press, 1916) [trans of: *Mare Liberum* (1633)].

6    Ivan Shearer, *Starke's International Law* (Butterworths, 11th ed, 1994) 218.

While the freedom of the high seas was never seriously challenged, in the 19th and early 20th centuries coastal states began to assert claims of various kinds to their adjacent waters and this practice suggested the need for clear rules. As a result, from the mid-20th century onwards efforts were made to codify existing customary rules and to agree new rules to demarcate ocean space. The International Law Commission was tasked by the UN General Assembly with drafting articles on the law of the sea, and in 1956 the Commission adopted a text it expected would be the basis of a convention. However, at the First UN Conference on the Law of the Sea the text was cleaved apart, and four separate 1958 *Geneva Conventions on the Law of the Sea* were adopted.[7] Although these conventions did deal with a number of fundamental 'law of the sea' issues (for example, the character of the continental shelf), they did not establish an overall scheme or package; they also attracted various levels of membership, and left unresolved some vital matters (such as the extent of the territorial sea). These issues were not addressed at the Second UN Conference on the Law of the Sea in 1960. Moreover, the emergence of many new nations as decolonisation gathered pace soon led to calls for more radical change.

The Third UN Conference on the Law of the Sea was convened in 1973 to address the full gamut of issues, from the breadth of the territorial sea to the internationalisation of the deep seabed. Held over nine years and across 11 sessions, the conference adopted a consensus procedure rather than votes on individual measures and produced the *UNCLOS* text. Unlike earlier efforts at codification, *UNCLOS* was a 'package deal' which had to be taken as a whole and was not subject to reservations (unless expressly permitted by it).[8] After *UNCLOS* was adopted in 1982, the United States and some other industrialised nations withheld their support due to concerns over the deep seabed provisions in pt XI.[9] These were largely addressed by a separate 1994 implementing agreement,[10] which modified some aspects of *UNCLOS*. This paved the way for *UNCLOS* to enter into force in November 1994. In 1995 a further implementing agreement was concluded, the *Fish Stocks Agreement*,[11] which addressed highly

---

7    *Geneva Convention on the High Seas*, opened for signature 29 April 1958, 450 UNTS 11 (entered into force 30 September 1962); *Geneva Convention on the Territorial Sea and the Contiguous Zone*, opened for signature 19 April 1958, 51 UNTS 206 (entered into force 10 September 1964); *Geneva Convention on the Continental Shelf*, opened for signature 19 April 1958, 499 UNTS 311 (entered into force 10 June 1964); *Geneva Convention on Fishing and Conservation of the Living Resources of the High Seas*, opened for signature 19 April 1958, 559 UNTS 285 (entered into force 20 March 1966).

8    *UNCLOS* (n 1) art 309.

9    The United States remains a non-party to *UNCLOS* (due to the refusal of its Senate to ratify the treaty), but has publicly stated that it regards most of the Convention to be customary international law. See Department of State (US), 'Law of the Sea Convention' (Web Page) <www.state.gov/law-of-the-sea-convention/>.

10    *Agreement Relating to the Implementation of Part XI of the United Nations Convention on the Law of the Sea*, opened for signature 28 July 1994, 1836 UNTS 42 (entered into force 28 July 1996) ('*Implementing Agreement 1994*').

11    *Agreement for the Implementation of the Provisions of the United Nations Convention on the Law of the Sea Relating to the Conservation and Management of Straddling Fish Stocks and Highly Migratory Fish Stocks*, opened for signature 4 August 1995, 2167 UNTS 88 (entered into force 11 December 2001) ('*Fish Stocks Agreement*').

migratory and straddling fisheries. There are currently negotiations underway on a third implementing agreement on biodiversity beyond national jurisdiction.[12]

UNCLOS is a lengthy and widely ratified treaty, with 168 states parties. It defines coastal state entitlements to adjacent maritime zones; balances these with the rights and freedoms of the international community at large; safeguards certain maritime spaces (the high seas and the deep seabed beyond national jurisdiction) from state acquisition; and addresses ocean issues of global importance and concern (marine environmental protection, freedom of scientific research and so on). UNCLOS also established three institutions that have roles in implementing the Convention and resolving disputes: the Commission on the Limits of the Continental Shelf ('CLCS'), the International Seabed Authority ('ISA') and the International Tribunal for the Law of the Sea ('ITLOS').

# 13.3    Coastal state maritime zones

One of the main achievements of UNCLOS is to define and delineate maritime zones, both in terms of their spatial reach and in regulating the variety and intensity of permissible activities that may be conducted by coastal and other states within them. The maritime zones codified and elaborated in UNCLOS are the territorial sea, contiguous zone, exclusive economic zone ('EEZ'), continental shelf, archipelagic waters (for states comprising a collection of islands), the deep seabed (known as 'the Area') and the high seas.

**Figure 13.1**    Overview of Australia's maritime zones

Source: Geoscience Australia, 'Maritime Boundary Definitions' (Web Page) <www.ga.gov.au/scientific-topics/marine/jurisdiction/maritime-boundary-definitions>.

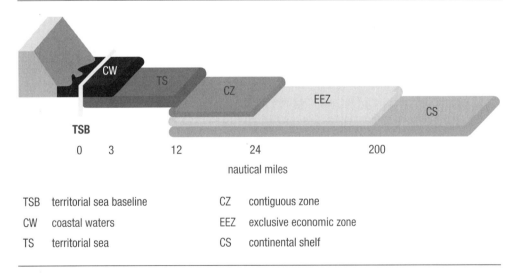

| | | |
|---|---|---|
| TSB | territorial sea baseline | CZ contiguous zone |
| CW | coastal waters | EEZ exclusive economic zone |
| TS | territorial sea | CS continental shelf |

---

12      United Nations, 'Intergovernmental Conference on Marine Biodiversity of Areas beyond National Jurisdiction' (Web Page) <www.un.org/bbnj>.

Coastal maritime zones may only be projected from naturally formed areas of land above water at high tide.[13] Generally, such land areas, including small islands, entitle coastal states to the full range of adjacent maritime zones. However, under art 121 of *UNCLOS*, rocks which cannot sustain human habitation or an economic life of their own may only generate a territorial sea and not the resource zones of the continental shelf and EEZ.[14] This point was made clear in the *South China Sea Arbitration* between the Philippines and China.[15] In that case a key issue in dispute was the geographical status of certain reefs and other maritime features claimed by China. Ascertaining whether these are fully submerged features, low-tide elevations only exposed at high tide, or high-tide features permanently above water is relevant to determining whether they can be appropriated and can generate maritime zones.

The tribunal in the *South China Sea Arbitration* assessed whether coral reefs claimed by China were above water at high tide such that they would generate at least a 12 nautical mile ('M') territorial sea. China has modified many reefs through substantial land reclamation and construction activities but the tribunal observed that under *UNCLOS* it is the natural condition of the feature that is determinative. The evidence before the tribunal established that in their natural condition some of the contested features were high-tide elevations, while others were low-tide elevations that generate no maritime zones. The tribunal also considered whether any of the high-tide features claimed by China were islands and therefore could generate a 200 M EEZ and continental shelf. Importantly, the tribunal set out criteria that features would have to meet to be an island for the purposes of art 121 of *UNCLOS*. These include the objective capacity of a feature, in its natural condition, to sustain either a stable community of people or economic activity that is neither dependent on outside resources nor purely extractive in nature.[16] The tribunal made the following observations on the interpretation of art 121:

> [T]he Tribunal considers that a number of propositions follow from the text itself:
> (a)  First, the use of the term 'rock' does not require that a feature be composed of rock in the geologic sense in order to fall within the scope of the provision.
> (b)  Second, the use of the term 'cannot' makes clear that the provision concerns the objective capacity of the feature to sustain human habitation or economic life. Actual habitation or economic activity at any particular point in time is not relevant, except to the extent that it indicates the capacity of the feature.
> (c)  Third, the use of the term 'sustain' indicates both time and qualitative elements. Habitation and economic life must be able to extend over a certain duration and occur to an adequate standard.
> (d)  Fourth, the logical interpretation of the use of the term 'or' discussed above indicates that a feature that is able to sustain either human habitation or an economic life of its own will be entitled to an exclusive economic zone and continental shelf.[17]

The tribunal detailed application of art 121 was the first close judicial interpretation of this provision. The tribunal noted that although features may have been transformed

13    This follows from *UNCLOS* (n 1) arts 11, 13, 60(8), 80, 121.
14    Ibid art 121.
15    *South China Sea Arbitration (Republic of the Philippines v People's Republic of China) (Award)* (Permanent Court of Arbitration, Case No 2013-19, 12 July 2016).
16    Ibid [475]–[553].
17    Ibid [504].

through land reclamation, and host military personnel, this alone did not substantiate their capacity to sustain, in their natural condition, a stable community. It was concluded that all high-tide features in the Spratly Islands were therefore mere 'rocks' for the purpose of art 121 and could generate no more than a 12 M territorial sea.[18] This included Itu Aba (also known as Taiping Island), the largest feature in dispute (and which is administered by Taiwan).[19]

## 13.3.1 Baselines

In order to establish coastal maritime zones, states must first have regard to the rules concerning the baselines along the coast from which these zones are measured. Baselines are the legal expression of a state's coastal front and serve three key functions. First, they mark the dividing line between the land and internal waters of a coastal state and the territorial sea beyond. For this reason they are called 'territorial sea baselines'. Second, baselines form the lines from which the outer limits of the territorial sea and all maritime zones (with the exception of the continental shelf beyond 200 M) are measured. Third, they are relevant when delimiting maritime boundaries between states with overlapping maritime zones. *UNCLOS* gives coastal states considerable freedom in selecting their baselines. Usually the baseline will be the 'normal' baseline that follows the low-water mark along the coast.[20] However, where the coastal geography is more complex, straight closing lines may be drawn across rivers and bays,[21] and straight baselines may join points along coasts which are deeply indented or have fringing islands.[22] The latter type of straight baselines must follow the general direction of the coast,[23] and cannot be drawn to low-tide elevations unless lighthouses or similar installations permanently above sea level have been built on them.[24]

Australia's baselines are set out in the *Seas and Submerged Lands (Territorial Sea Baseline) Proclamation 2016* and the *Seas and Submerged Lands (Historic Bays) Proclamation 2016*. These proclamations were made under the *Seas and Submerged Lands Act 1973* (Cth), through which the Commonwealth asserted ownership and control over coastal maritime zones from the low-water mark to the extent permitted by international law. Section 6 of the Act declares that 'sovereignty in respect of the territorial sea, and in respect of the airspace over it and in respect of its bed and subsoil, is vested in and exercisable by the Crown in right of the Commonwealth'. The legislation was challenged by all six Australian states as they believed they held title in, and jurisdiction over, a 3 M territorial sea. However, the Act was upheld by the High Court of Australia in the *Seas and Submerged Lands Act* case[25] on the basis that it was supported by the external affairs power under s 51(xxix) of the *Australian Constitution*, as it applied to areas physically external to Australia. Chief Justice Barwick, in the majority, reasoned thus:

---

18    Ibid [625].
19    For further discussion, see Tim Stephens, 'China's Claims Dashed in South China Sea Arbitration' (2016) 25 *Law Society Journal* 73.
20    *UNCLOS* (n 1) art 5.
21    Ibid art 10.
22    Ibid art 7(1).
23    Ibid art 7(3).
24    Ibid art 7(4).
25    *New South Wales v Commonwealth* (1975) 135 CLR 337.

A consequence of creation of the Commonwealth under the Constitution and the grant of the power with respect to external affairs was, in my opinion, to vest in the Commonwealth any proprietary rights and legislative power which the colonies might have had in or in relation to the territorial sea, seabed and airspace and continental shelf and incline. Proprietary rights and legislative powers in these matters of international concern would then coalesce and unite in the nation. That, in my opinion, was the intendment of the Constitution. ...

This result conforms, in my opinion, to an essential feature of a federation, namely, that it is the nation and not the integers of the federation which must have the power to protect and control as a national function the area of the marginal seas, the seabed and airspace and the continental shelf and incline. This has been decided by the Supreme Courts of the United States and of Canada.[26]

Although the Commonwealth thereby gained extensive control over offshore areas, it was accepted that the states were best placed to manage waters close to shore. Accordingly, the Offshore Constitutional Settlement was agreed between the Commonwealth and the states: legislation was passed under which the states were given title to 3 M of 'coastal waters'[27] and jurisdiction over all activities within this area (see Figure 13.1 on page 349).[28]

Partly as a result of the Offshore Constitutional Settlement, and partly due to other issues relating to the division of responsibilities between the Commonwealth and the states and territories, Australia's legal framework for ocean and coastal and management is highly complex.[29]

## 13.3.2   Territorial sea

The territorial sea lies immediately adjacent to the territorial sea baselines. One of the oldest maritime zones (along with the high seas), it is defined in *UNCLOS* as a zone, not exceeding 12 M from the baselines, in which the coastal state has sovereignty over the seabed, subsoil, water column, water surface and airspace.[30] Australia extended its territorial sea from 3 M to 12 M in 1990, consistent with art 3 of *UNCLOS*.[31] Within the territorial sea, coastal states have legislative and enforcement jurisdiction over all local vessels and also over foreign flagged vessels with respect to a range of matters including navigation, the conservation of living resources, the preservation of the environment, marine scientific research and serious criminal matters.[32]

Coastal state sovereignty and jurisdiction in the territorial sea is made subject to the rights of foreign flagged vessels including warships (but not civilian or military aircraft) to exercise innocent passage.[33] Passage means traversing the territorial sea without entering internal

---

26    Ibid 373–4 [53]–[54] (Barwick CJ).
27    *Coastal Waters (State Title) Act 1980* (Cth).
28    *Coastal Waters (State Powers) Act 1980* (Cth).
29    See generally Rachel Baird and Donald Rothwell (eds), *Australian Coastal and Marine Law* (Federation Press, 2011); Donald Rothwell and Stuart Kaye, 'A Legal Framework for Integrated Oceans and Coastal Management in Australia' (2001) 18(3) *Environmental and Planning Law Journal* 278.
30    *UNCLOS* (n 1) arts 2, 3.
31    Commonwealth, *Gazette: Special*, No S 297, 13 November 1990.
32    *UNCLOS* (n 1) arts 21, 27.
33    Ibid art 17.

waters, or proceeding to or from port.[34] It must be continuous and expeditious, with stopping only permitted if incidental to normal navigation, or rendered necessary due to emergency.[35] Passage will be considered innocent so long as it is not prejudicial to the peace, good order or security of the coastal state.[36] *UNCLOS* includes a lengthy list of activities that would be prejudicial to these interests, including any threat or use of force, weapons practice, launching or landing of aircraft, research or surveying, and any fishing activities.[37] Coastal states can take necessary steps to prevent passage which is not innocent,[38] but cannot close the territorial sea to innocent passage except temporarily in specified areas if essential for its security (so as to conduct weapons tests, for example).[39]

Another navigational right central to the law of the sea is transit passage through international straits. Straits are bodies of water used for international navigation that connect one part of the high seas or EEZ and another part of the high seas or EEZ.[40] Ships and aircraft exercising the right of transit passage must proceed without delay, and must refrain from any threat or use of force, and from any activities other than those incidental to their normal modes of navigation.[41] Ships and aircraft must also comply with generally accepted international regulations for safe navigation and overflight.[42] During transit passage, foreign ships may not carry out any marine scientific research or surveys without the prior authorisation of the states bordering the strait.[43]

An example of an international strait is the Torres Strait between Cape York in Australia and Papua New Guinea, which comprises ecologically sensitive territorial sea areas of both states. In 2006 the Australian government extended a compulsory pilotage regime applicable in the Great Barrier Reef to the Torres Strait after Australia and Papua New Guinea successfully proposed that the Torres Strait be recognised as a Particularly Sensitive Sea Area by the International Maritime Organization. However, the compulsory pilotage system was challenged by a number of states, including Singapore and the United States, on the basis that it was inconsistent with *UNCLOS*. Accordingly, Australia now enforces the measure only in respect of foreign vessels that enter Australian ports.[44]

This example illustrates that transit passage is unlike innocent passage in several important respects. First, it gives greater rights to navigating vessels. States bordering straits may not deny, suspend or hamper transit passage.[45] Second, transit passage applies both to ships and aircraft. Third, vessels and aircraft may engage in 'activities ... incidental to their normal modes of continuous and expeditious transit', which suggests that submarines may navigate underwater and naval vessels can launch and take on aircraft (activities which are not permitted in

---

34      Ibid art 18(1).
35      Ibid art 18(2).
36      Ibid art 19(1).
37      Ibid art 19(2).
38      Ibid art 25(1).
39      Ibid art 25(2).
40      Ibid art 37.
41      Ibid art 39(1).
42      Ibid art 39(2).
43      Ibid art 40.
44      Donald Rothwell and Tim Stephens, *The International Law of the Sea* (Hart, 2nd ed, 2016) 264–5.
45      *UNCLOS* (n 1) arts 42(2), 44.

innocent passage).[46] The special status of transit passage was emphasised by the International Court of Justice ('ICJ') in its very first decision, the *Corfu Channel* case.[47] That case related to the passage of British naval vessels through the North Corfu Channel in Albanian territorial waters, where two ships were badly damaged when they struck mines. Albania argued that the United Kingdom had violated Albanian sovereignty; however, the ICJ held that it is

> generally recognized and in accordance with international custom, that States in time of peace have a right to send their warships through straits used for international navigation between two parts of the high seas without previous authorization of a coastal state, provided that the passage is innocent.[48]

The Court also observed that the 'decisive criterion' for determining whether a strait is one in which a right of passage exists is not the volume of traffic passing through the strait but 'rather its geographical situation as connecting two parts of the high seas and the fact of its being used for international navigation'.[49]

## 13.3.3   Contiguous zone

The contiguous zone is addressed in the same part of *UNCLOS* as the territorial sea, and is a zone up to 24 M from the baselines that may be claimed by coastal states for the exclusive purpose of exercising jurisdiction over only customs, fiscal, immigration and sanitary (such as quarantine) matters.[50] Unlike the territorial sea, the contiguous zone is not a zone of sovereignty, but only of jurisdiction. Also unlike the territorial sea, coastal states must expressly claim the contiguous zone if they wish to exercise the four types of jurisdiction it recognises. Australia proclaimed a contiguous zone in 1999.[51]

In the contiguous zone, coastal states may punish foreign ships leaving the territorial sea for breaches in it of regulations relating to customs, fiscal, immigration and sanitary matters. They also have preventative powers against foreign vessels in the contiguous zone that are suspected to be heading to the territorial sea to breach such laws. For instance, a foreign-flagged cruise ship suspected of posing a health risk may be prevented from entering the territorial sea, although this right is conditioned by the binding International Health Regulations[52] adopted by the Health Assembly of the World Health Organization, which are designed to safeguard the health of passengers and crew. Similarly, the preventative powers have been relied upon by Australian authorities to intercept and turn back vessels carrying asylum seekers under Operation Sovereign Borders since 2013,[53] although this has raised issues of consistency with other law of the sea rules (as on rescue and the safety of life at sea) and international refugee law and international human rights law. The powers of Australian government officials in the

---

46      Ibid art 39(1)(c).
47      *Corfu Channel (United Kingdom v Albania) (Merits)* [1949] ICJ Rep 4.
48      Ibid 28.
49      Ibid.
50      *UNCLOS* (n 1) art 33.
51      *Seas and Submerged Lands (Limits of Contiguous Zone) Proclamation 1999* (Cth).
52      World Health Organization, *International Health Regulations* (2005).
53      See Joyce Chia, Jane McAdam and Kate Purcell, 'Asylum in Australia: "Operation Sovereign Borders" and International Law' (2014) 32 *Australian Year Book of International Law* 33.

contiguous zone (and other Australian maritime zones) are set out in the *Maritime Powers Act 2013* (Cth).

The preventative powers in the contiguous zone would likely allow coastal states to stop, detain and inspect a vessel to investigate whether immigration law could be breached by its ongoing passage; however, it is doubtful whether art 33 of *UNCLOS* confers a general power on coastal states to deal with such vessels however they wish (such as by detaining all those on board, or towing the vessel from the contiguous zone into the EEZ and onto the high seas). This issue was raised but not resolved by the High Court in *CPCF v Minister for Immigration and Border Protection*.[54] The plaintiff and 156 other asylum seekers from Sri Lanka were on board a vessel intercepted by Australian border protection officials in Australia's contiguous zone near Christmas Island. The Australian government decided that the asylum seekers should be returned to India from where they had sailed, and they were detained and placed on board an Australian border protection vessel which returned them to India. The plaintiff contended that the detention on an Australian government vessel for over three weeks was unlawful. A majority of the High Court (French CJ and Crennan, Gageler and Keane JJ) held that the detention was authorised under the *Maritime Powers Act 2013* (Cth). The minority held that the detention was not authorised by the Act or by the non-statutory executive powers of the executive. Two of the dissenting judges, Hayne and Bell JJ, found that the detention and taking was not authorised as the plaintiff had no right or permission to enter India. They also made several observations regarding the extent of coastal state powers in the contiguous zone:

> It may be accepted that exercising the control necessary to prevent infringement of laws of the kind described in Art 33 of *UNCLOS* would include a coastal state stopping in its contiguous zone an inward bound vessel reasonably suspected of being involved in an intended contravention of one of those laws. Because there must be a power to stop the vessel, it may be accepted that there is a power to detain the vessel (at least for the purposes of investigating whether there is a threat of a relevant contravention). But whether, for the purposes of international law, Art 33 permits the coastal state to take persons on the vessel into its custody or to take command of the vessel or tow it out of the contiguous zone remains controversial.[55]

## 13.3.4   Exclusive economic zone

The EEZ confers on coastal states sovereign rights for the purposes of exploring and exploiting, conserving and managing the living and non-living resources of the water column, seabed and subsoil to a distance of 200 M from the baseline.[56] Unlike the continental shelf, the EEZ is a claimable zone meaning that coastal states must proclaim the zone and do not automatically possess it. In practice most coastal states have claimed an EEZ.[57]

---

54    (2015) 255 CLR 514.

55    Ibid [79].

56    *UNCLOS* (n 1) arts 55, 56, 57.

57    See United Nations, 'Summary of National Claims', *Maritime Space: Maritime Zones and Maritime Delimitation* (Web Page) <www.un.org/depts/los/LEGISLATIONANDTREATIES/claims.htm>.

Within the EEZ the coastal state has exclusive rights in, and jurisdiction over, fisheries and the mineral and other non-living resources. These resource rights are significant for many coastal states, particularly Australia's South Pacific island neighbours that have small landmasses but very extensive EEZs with highly prized tuna stocks.[58] Coastal states also have jurisdiction with regard to artificial islands, installations and structures for economic purposes, marine scientific research, and the protection and preservation of the marine environment.[59] Balanced against the rights of coastal states in the EEZ are the rights of other states. While coastal states have exclusive rights over resources and artificial islands and structures in the EEZ, other states have rights to exercise high seas freedoms, including the freedom of navigation and overflight and the laying of submarine cables and pipelines.[60] The EEZ is therefore a sui generis zone which is best viewed neither as residual territorial sea nor as residual high seas. This means that coastal state jurisdiction over the EEZ is confined to addressing living and non-living resources, pollution and certain other matters. It is not at large and does not allow coastal states to exercise competence with respect to a broader range of issues such as security or customs.

The EEZ was one of the most important innovations of *UNCLOS*. A major impetus for this zone was the ambition of developing states in the Global South to a fair share of coastal marine resources. Another justification was that the EEZ would lead to more sustainable fisheries management by assigning resource rights to the states best placed to regulate them. The vast majority of the world's fish stocks and most exploitable mineral deposits are located within the EEZ. Australia proclaimed a 200 M EEZ in 1994,[61] covering 8.2 million $km^2$ around the Australian mainland and its offshore territories (an area larger than Australia's total land territory).[62] Australia has the world's third-largest EEZ.[63]

Since *UNCLOS* was adopted there have been a number of disputes over the enforcement of coastal state laws in the EEZ against fishing and other vessels. An example is the ITLOS case *The Volga*,[64] between Australia and Russia, which concerned Australia's arrest of a Russian-flagged vessel for fishing illegally in the EEZ surrounding Australia's Heard and McDonald Islands. The case examined the balance between the rights of coastal states to enforce fisheries laws, and the rights of other states to have vessels released from arrest on the payment of a reasonable bond. The decision substantially upheld the large financial bond set by Australia, having regard to the gravity of alleged offences, the possible penalties under Australian law, and the value of the vessel detained and the cargo seized.

Several ITLOS cases have explored the extent of coastal state legislative jurisdiction in the EEZ. In *The M/V Saiga (No 2)*,[65] Guinean patrol boats arrested an oil tanker flagged to St Vincent and the Grenadines for infringing Guinean customs law. The tribunal held that the

---

58    Tim Stephens, 'Fisheries-Led Development in the South Pacific: Charting a "Pacific Way" to a Sustainable Future' (2008) 365(3) *Ocean Development and International Law* 257–86.

59    *UNCLOS* (n 1) art 56(1)(b).

60    Ibid art 58(1).

61    *Proclamation under the Seas and Submerged Lands Act 1973* (Cth) (26 July 1994).

62    Geoscience Australia, 'Australian Exclusive Economic Zone', *Oceans and Seas* (Web Page) <www.ga.gov.au/scientific-topics/national-location-information/dimensions/oceans-and-seas>.

63    Behind the United States and France. See 'Drops in the Ocean: France's Marine Territories', *The Economist*, 13 January 2016, <https://www.economist.com/graphic-detail/2016/01/13/drops-in-the-ocean-frances-marine-territories>.

64    *The Volga (Russian Federation v Australia) (Prompt Release)* [2002] ITLOS Rep 10.

65    *The M/V Saiga (No 2) (St Vincent and the Grenadines v Guinea) (Judgment)* [1999] ITLOS Rep 10.

arrest was unlawful, including because under *UNCLOS* coastal states may only apply customs laws in the territorial sea and contiguous zone, and not the EEZ (except as regards artificial islands, installations and structures).[66] In a later decision, *The M/V Virginia G*,[67] ITLOS revisited the issue when an oil tanker registered in Panama was arrested by Guinea-Bissau for refuelling fishing vessels in its EEZ. The tribunal affirmed that coastal states may not apply their customs laws in the EEZ, but held:

> The Tribunal is of the view that the regulation by a coastal State of bunkering [ie, refuel-ling] of foreign vessels fishing in its exclusive economic zone is among those measures which the coastal State may take in its exclusive economic zone to conserve and manage its living resources under article 56 of the Convention read together with article 62, paragraph 4, of the Convention. This view is also confirmed by State practice which has developed after the adoption of the Convention.[68]

## 13.3.5 Continental shelf

The continental shelf is the relatively shallow area of the seafloor adjacent to the coast, where what is known as the continental margin slopes down from the landmass into the sea before it drops more sharply towards the deep ocean floor.[69] The origins of this maritime zone lie in the 1945 proclamation of US president Harry Truman which declared that the United States held exclusive rights in the resources of the adjacent seabed beyond the territorial sea out to an unspecified distance.[70]

The continental shelf was recognised and codified in the 1958 *Geneva Convention on the Continental Shelf*.[71] In the *North Sea Continental Shelf* cases,[72] the ICJ concluded that the definition of the continental shelf in this Convention was part of customary international law, and took the concept further by reference to the idea of 'natural prolongation':

> [T]he rights of the coastal State in respect of the area of continental shelf that constitutes a natural prolongation of its land territory into and under the sea exist *ipso facto* and *ab initio*, by virtue of its sovereignty over the land, and as an extension of it in an exercise of sovereign rights for the purpose of exploring the seabed and exploiting its natural resources. In short, there is here an inherent right.[73]

Neither the 1958 *Geneva Convention on the Continental Shelf* nor the *North Sea Continental Shelf* cases clearly resolved the question of where the continental shelf ended. Article 76 of *UNCLOS* answers that coastal states are entitled to a 200 M continental shelf, irrespective of

---

66    Ibid [127].
67    *The M/V Virginia G (Panama v Guinea-Bissau) (Judgment)* [2014] ITLOS Rep 4.
68    Ibid [217].
69    Rothwell and Stephens (n 44) 102.
70    *Policy of the United States with Respect to the Natural Resources of the Subsoil and Sea Bed of the Continental Shelf*, 10 Fed Reg 12303 (28 September 1945) (US Presidential Proclamation No 2667) <https://tile.loc.gov/storage-services/service/ll/fedreg/fr010/fr010193/fr010193.pdf>.
71    *Geneva Convention on the Continental Shelf* (n 7) art 1.
72    *North Sea Continental Shelf (Federal Republic of Germany v Denmark) (Merits)* [1969] ICJ Rep 3.
73    Ibid 22 [19].

whether their continental margin extends that far. Furthermore, states that have a continental margin extending beyond 200 M may delineate the outer limit of their continental shelf by reference to the configuration of the seafloor,[74] so long as this does not extend beyond 350 M from the baselines (or 100 M from the 2,500 m isobath which in some cases will exceed 350 M).[75] However, *UNCLOS* does not leave it to coastal states alone to establish such outer continental shelf limits. Instead, it requires them to submit information to the Commission on the Limits of the Continental Shelf ('CLCS'), an independent scientific and technical body established by *UNCLOS*. Once the CLCS has scrutinised the data, it makes recommendations on the establishment of the outer limits, and the limits so established by the state on the basis of such recommendations become final and binding.[76]

Within the continental shelf, coastal states possess exclusive sovereign rights for the purposes of exploring and exploiting their living and non-living resources. This means that the coastal state has exclusive rights in the mineral resources of the seabed and subsoil together with sedentary living species on the seafloor.[77] Sedentary species are species which 'at the harvestable stage, either are immobile on or under the seabed or are unable to move except in constant physical contact with the seabed or the subsoil',[78] such as oysters. Beyond resources, *UNCLOS* also refers to certain other coastal state rights. These states possess the exclusive rights to authorise and regulate any drilling on the continental shelf,[79] and to construct and authorise the construction of artificial islands, installations and structures.[80] There is therefore a considerable degree of overlap between the continental shelf and the EEZ. However, unlike the EEZ, the continental shelf is inherent and is not dependent on occupation, or any express proclamation.[81] Moreover, as already noted, the continental shelf can in some circumstances extend beyond 200 M.

The continental shelf was the first maritime zone to be proclaimed by Australia, in 1953.[82] When *UNCLOS* entered into force, the definition of 'continental shelf' in the *Seas and Submerged Lands Act 1973* was amended to allow for a new proclamation in line with the expanded definition of the shelf.[83] Australia submitted data to the CLCS in 2004[84] (within the original 10-year deadline stipulated under *UNCLOS*)[85] and the Commission endorsed most of

74    *UNCLOS* (n 1) art 76(4).
75    Ibid art 76(5). An isobath is a line on a map or chart that connects all points having the same depth below the water surface.
76    Ibid art 76(8). See further Ted L McDorman, 'The Role of the Commission on the Limits of the Continental Shelf: A Technical Body in a Political World' (2002) 17(3) *International Journal of Marine and Coastal Law* 301.
77    *UNCLOS* (n 1) art 77.
78    Ibid art 77(4).
79    Ibid art 81.
80    Ibid art 80.
81    Ibid art 77(3).
82    Commonwealth, *Gazette*, No 56, 11 September 1953, 2563.
83    *Seas and Submerged Lands Act 1973* (Cth) s 12.
84    Commonwealth, *United Nations Convention on the Law of the Sea: Submission to the Commission on the Limits of the Continental Shelf on the Outer Limits of Australia's Continental Shelf Extending beyond 200 Nautical Miles from the Territorial Sea Baseline – Executive Summary*, UN Doc AUS-DOC-ES (15 November 2004).
85    *UNCLOS* (n 1) annex II art 4. In 2001 a meeting of states parties resolved that for those states for which *UNCLOS* entered into force before 13 May 1999, the 10-year period would run from that date:

Australia's information in its 2008 recommendations.[86] Australia included data for the Australian Antarctic Territory, but this was not considered as Australia requested that the Commission defer its review 'for the time being'[87] to avoid any perceived conflict with the 1959 *Antarctic Treaty*,[88] which places sovereignty claims to the continent in abeyance.[89] Australia subsequently proclaimed the outer limits of most of its continental shelf in 2012.[90]

## 13.3.6  Archipelagic waters

Another major innovation of *UNCLOS* was the establishment of archipelagic waters as a new maritime zone. It had long been accepted that individual islands could generate a territorial sea and other maritime zones, and also that straight baselines could be used to join islands fringing a mainland coast. However, until *UNCLOS* was concluded it was not clear what entitlements to ocean space could be asserted by states comprising one or several groups of islands. This question of mid-ocean archipelagic states was resolved in *UNCLOS*, which responded directly to the demands of Indonesia, the Philippines and many other archipelagic states for a legal regime that recognises that groups of islands form a single geographic and legal entity in which the sea areas between them ('archipelagic waters') enjoy a special status. In Indonesia this idea is captured in the concept of *wawasan nusantara*, which means that Indonesia's thousands of islands and the waters between and around them form a unified whole. There are many archipelagic states in Australia's region including Indonesia, Fiji, Kiribati, the Marshall Islands, Papua New Guinea, the Philippines, the Solomon Islands, Tuvalu and Vanuatu.

*UNCLOS* defines an 'archipelagic state' to mean a state that is constituted wholly by one or more archipelagos and that may include other islands (that is, islands that are not part of an archipelago).[91] An 'archipelago' is defined as a group of islands, interconnected waters and other natural features so closely interrelated that they form 'an intrinsic geographical, economic and political entity'.[92] Archipelagic states are entitled to draw straight archipelagic baselines joining the outermost islands and drying reefs of archipelagos.[93] It is from these archipelagic baselines that the breadth of the territorial sea and other maritime zones is to be measured.[94] This has the effect of making archipelagos much like a solid land mass for the purposes of

---

United Nations Convention on the Law of the Sea, Meeting of States Parties, *Decision Regarding the Date of Commencement of the Ten-Year Period for Making Submissions to the Commission*, UN Doc SPLOS/72, 11th mtg, 14–18 May 2001.

86  Commission on the Limits of the Continental Shelf, *Recommendations in regard to the Submission Made by Australia on 15 November 2004* (adopted 9 April 2008) <www.un.org/depts/los/clcs_new/submissions_files/aus04/Aus_Recommendations_FINAL.pdf>.

87  'Note from the Permanent Mission of Australia to the Secretary-General of the United Nations Accompanying the Lodgement of Australia's Submission', UN Doc AUS-DOC-ES-attachment (15 November 2004) <www.un.org/depts/los/clcs_new/submissions_files/aus04/Documents/aus_doc_es_attachment.pdf>.

88  *Antarctic Treaty*, opened for signature 1 December 1959, 402 UNTS 71 (entered into force 23 June 1961).

89  Ibid art IV.

90  *Seas and Submerged Lands (Limits of Continental Shelf) Proclamation 2012* (Cth).

91  *UNCLOS* (n 1) art 46(a).

92  Ibid art 46(b).

93  Ibid art 47(1).

94  Ibid art 48.

**Figure 13.2**  Map of Australia's maritime zones

Source: Australian Marine Spatial Information System (AMSIS).

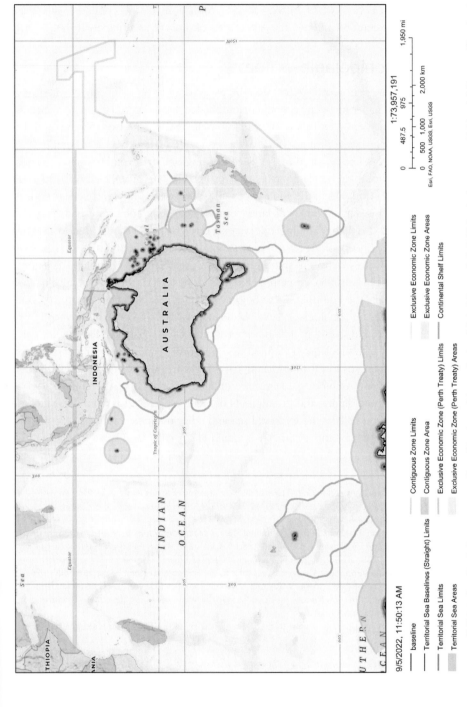

maritime zones seawards of the baselines. There are several conditions for drawing archipelagic baselines. These include that the area of land in comparison with the area of water enclosed by the baselines must fall within a specified ratio (a minimum of 1:9 and maximum of 1:1).[95] Furthermore, archipelagic baselines must not depart to any appreciable extent from the general configuration of the archipelago,[96] and baselines should not exceed 100 M in length, except that up to 3% may be between 100 and 125 M.[97]

Enclosed within these archipelagic baselines are archipelagic waters. This maritime zone is more akin to the territorial sea than internal waters, as innocent passage may be exercised in archipelagic waters. In addition, archipelagic sea lanes passage and archipelagic air routes are available for navigation or overflight. This right applies to archipelagic sea lanes and air routes designated by archipelagic states and, in the absence of designation, to routes normally used for international navigation.[98] Archipelagic sea lanes passage is very similar to transit passage through straits, and likewise may not be hampered or suspended.[99] The designation process for archipelagic sea lanes and air routes occurs through the International Maritime Organization, but this mechanism has not been extensively used. Indonesia has partially designated a number of north–south archipelagic sea lanes though this process.[100]

## 13.4   Maritime boundary delimitation

The proximity of many states inevitably means that there will be overlapping maritime zones. Recognising this, the law of the sea establishes principles for the drawing ('delimitation') of maritime boundaries. This area of the law of the sea gained much greater significance following the conclusion of *UNCLOS* with its greatly expanded maritime zones. Key considerations in maritime boundary delimitation include identifying the relevant parts of the coast (so as to exclude areas outside of dispute), the lengths of the coastlines of the respective states, and the area of overlapping entitlement or claim.

*UNCLOS* contains different rules for delimitation according to which type of maritime zone is overlapping. For overlapping territorial seas, the rule is straightforward. In the absence of agreement between the states, the delimitation line is the median line, every point of which is equidistant from the nearest points on the baselines from which the breadth of the territorial seas of each state is measured.[101] For continental shelf and EEZ delimitation, *UNCLOS* does not apply a geometric rule. Instead, the delimitation 'shall be effected by agreement on the basis of international law ... in order to achieve an equitable solution'.[102] This formulation follows the approach taken by the ICJ in the *North Sea Continental Shelf* cases[103] which rejected

---

95    Ibid art 47(1).
96    Ibid art 47(3).
97    Ibid art 47(2).
98    Ibid art 53.
99    Ibid art 44.
100   Dhiana Puspitawati, 'Indonesia's Archipelagic Sea Lanes (ASLs) Designation: Rights Turning to Obligations?' (2018) 4 *Hasanuddin Law Review* 265.
101   *UNCLOS* (n 1) art 15
102   Ibid arts 74(1), 83(1).
103   *North Sea Continental Shelf* (n 72) 54.

equidistance as a strict rule for continental shelf delimitation. Most maritime boundary disputes have indeed been addressed by negotiation and agreement, which remains the default approach, rather than third-party settlement.

In the absence of a controlling delimitation rule for the continental shelf and EEZ, the ICJ developed a three-stage methodology in *Maritime Delimitation in the Black Sea*.[104] The first step involves using geometrically objective methods to draw a provisional delimitation line that is equidistant between the most appropriate points on the relevant coasts. The second step is to consider whether any factors call for the adjustment or shifting of the provisional line in order to achieve an equitable result. Relevant factors may include the lengths of coasts and the presence of islands. The final step is to verify that the line, which may have been adjusted, does not produce an inequitable result by reason of any marked disproportion between the coastline lengths of the states or between their maritime areas on either side of the line. This methodology has also been adopted by ITLOS.[105] It is usually the case that continental shelf and EEZ boundaries are determined jointly and result in a single delimitation line, but there are some examples where states have agreed upon different delimitation lines for the seabed and the water column. For instance, Australia's maritime boundaries with Indonesia involve separate continental shelf and EEZ boundaries in some places.

Where states have not agreed on a maritime boundary they may enter into provisional arrangements of a practical nature until a boundary is agreed.[106] An example was the joint development zone established in the Timor Sea by Australia and Indonesia via the 1989 *Timor Gap Treaty*.[107] The treaty filled a 'gap' left in the maritime boundary between Australia and Indonesia created by Portuguese sovereignty over East Timor (Portuguese control, but not sovereignty, was interrupted by Indonesia's invasion in 1975). The *Timor Gap Treaty* allowed Australia and Indonesia to exploit the oil and gas resources of the zone without prejudice to any later agreement on a permanent maritime boundary. When Timor-Leste became an independent state in 2002, a new treaty was agreed between Australia and the new nation which had the effect of continuing the joint development arrangement,[108] albeit with adjustments to the revenue sharing provisions. Australia and Timor-Leste also agreed the 2006 *Treaty on Certain Maritime Arrangements* to resolve a dispute over the development of a large oil and gas field, Greater Sunrise, that straddled the joint development area. The treaty included a provision that delayed agreement on a permanent boundary until after 2050.[109]

---

104    *Maritime Delimitation in the Black Sea (Romania v Ukraine) (Judgment)* [2009] ICJ Rep 61.
105    See *Delimitation of the Maritime Boundary in the Bay of Bengal (Bangladesh v Myanmar) (Judgment)* [2012] ITLOS Rep 4.
106    *UNCLOS* (n 1) arts 74(3), 83(3).
107    *Treaty between Australia and the Republic of Indonesia on the Zone of Cooperation in an Area between the Indonesian Province of East Timor and Northern Australia*, signed 11 December 1989, [1991] ATS 9 (entered into force 9 February 1991).
108    *Timor Sea Treaty between the Government of Australia and the Government of East Timor*, signed 20 May 2002, [2003] ATS 13 (no longer in force).
109    *Treaty with the Government of the Democratic Republic of Timor-Leste on Certain Maritime Arrangements in the Timor Sea*, signed 1 December 2006, [2007] ATS 12 (no longer in force) arts 4 and 12.

## 13.4.1 Australia and Timor-Leste's maritime boundary

Timor-Leste believed that the maritime agreements reached with Australia in the aftermath of its independence were unfair and that Australia had misused its power. Indeed, Timor-Leste commenced arbitral provisions seeking to have the *Treaty on Certain Maritime Arrangements* declared invalid on the basis that Australian intelligence officers had placed covert listening devices in Timor-Leste government offices.[110] Timor-Leste continued to press for a permanent maritime boundary, maintaining that it should be drawn according to contemporary principles of delimitation, with the median line between the opposite coasts of Timor-Leste and Australia being the starting point. Australia took a different view, arguing that it was relevant to have regard to the configuration of the seabed, and the deep 'Timor trough' that lies close to the Timor-Leste coast. Timor-Leste was not able to take its claims before an international court or tribunal because in 2002 Australia amended its acceptance of the jurisdiction of the ICJ, and of *UNCLOS* dispute settlement bodies, to exclude disputes concerning maritime boundaries.[111] Timor-Leste therefore turned to conciliation proceedings under annex V of *UNCLOS*, the first ever use of this procedure. Australia's objections to the Conciliation Commission's jurisdiction were rejected, and the Commission proceeded to work with both parties over two years on a durable solution.[112] This ultimately led to the parties agreeing the 2018 *Maritime Boundary Treaty*[113] which follows the median line, establishes permanent maritime boundaries between the two states, recognises both states' sovereign rights, and establishes a special regime for the joint development of the Greater Sunrise gas fields.

The resolution of Australia's maritime boundaries with other states has not been as vexed. In addition to Timor-Leste, Australia has maritime boundary agreements with Indonesia, France, New Zealand, Papua New Guinea and the Solomon Islands.[114] The agreement with Papua New Guinea is of particular interest because of the way it adopts different territorial sea, fisheries and seabed boundaries to account for the unique characteristics of the Torres Strait, in which there are Australian islands close to the Papua New Guinea mainland.[115] Only a few boundaries are yet to be resolved.[116]

---

110  *Arbitration under the Timor Sea Treaty (Timor-Leste v Australia)* (Permanent Court of Arbitration, Case No 2013-16).

111  See International Court of Justice, 'Australia', *Declarations Recognising the Jurisdiction of the Court as Compulsory* (Web Page) <www.icj-cij.org/en/declarations/au>; International Tribunal for the Law of the Sea, 'Australia', *Declarations made by States Parties under Article 298* (Web Page) <www.itlos.org/en/main/jurisdiction/declarations-of-states-parties/declarations-made-by-states-parties-under-article-298/>.

112  *Timor Sea Conciliation (Timor-Leste v Australia) (Report and Recommendations)* (Permanent Court of Arbitration, Case No 2016-10, 9 May 2018).

113  *Timor Sea Treaty between the Government of Australia and the Government of East Timor*, signed 6 March 2018, [2019] ATS 16 (entered into force 26 March 2018).

114  Stuart Kaye and Bill Campbell, 'Australia and the Law of the Sea' in Donald Rothwell and Emily Crawford (eds), *International Law in Australia* (Lawbook Co, 3rd ed, 2017) 433, 443.

115  See Department of Foreign Affairs and Trade, 'The Torres Strait Treaty', *Torres Strait* (Web Page) <www.dfat.gov.au/geo/torres-strait/Pages/the-torres-strait-treaty>.

116  These are the continental shelf boundary between Lord Howe Island and New Caledonia (France), and maritime boundaries from Australia's Antarctic Territory (with France, New Zealand and Norway).

# 13.5   Maritime zones beyond national jurisdiction

## 13.5.1   High seas

The high seas is the maritime zone that largely remains 'free seas' as understood by Grotius. They are defined in pt VII of *UNCLOS* to include all areas not within the EEZ, territorial sea, internal waters or archipelagic waters.[117] *UNCLOS* expressly prohibits states from making sovereign claims to the high seas.[118] On the high seas, all states enjoy the recognised freedoms in art 87 of navigation, overflight, fishing and marine scientific research, and to lay submarine cables and pipelines and construct artificial islands.

A central feature of the high seas regime is the provisions relating to the nationality of, and jurisdiction over, vessels. This reflects the open access nature of the high seas and the corresponding need for 'flag states' to take responsibility for vessels they register as nationals. All states have the right of navigation on the high seas,[119] and may fix conditions for the grant of nationality to ships.[120] There are no substantive prerequisites or conditions that need to be satisfied for this grant of nationality, and hence vessels can be given 'flags of convenience' by states that have few connections with vessels and little interest in overseeing their activities. Article 94 of *UNCLOS* does require states to exercise effective jurisdiction and control over vessels holding their nationality to ensure that they comply with generally accepted international regulations, procedures and practices.[121] As ITLOS explained in *The M/V Virginia G*:

> [O]nce a ship is registered, the flag State is required, under article 94 of the Convention, to exercise effective jurisdiction and control over that ship in order to ensure that it operates in accordance with generally accepted international regulations, procedures and practices. This is the meaning of 'genuine link'.[122]

However, in practice there is no way to force flag states to take these duties seriously.

On the high seas, a vessel is subject to the exclusive jurisdiction of its flag state,[123] subject to several limited exceptions. In the *SS 'Lotus'* case,[124] relating to a high seas collision between French and Turkish vessels, the Permanent Court of International Justice had held that Turkey could exercise criminal jurisdiction over the French master (captain) for his gross negligence. However, *UNCLOS* reversed this position and makes clear in art 97 that in matters of collision, criminal jurisdiction may only be exercised by the flag state. Nonetheless, *UNCLOS* does recognise certain other exceptions to exclusive flag state jurisdiction. Hence, art 110 confers limited rights on warships to board foreign ships on the high seas if there are reasonable grounds for suspecting that a ship was engaged in piracy, the slave trade or unauthorised radio

---

117   *UNCLOS* (n 1) art 86.
118   Ibid art 89.
119   Ibid art 90.
120   Ibid art 91.
121   See also *Request for an Advisory Opinion Submitted by the Sub-Regional Fisheries Commission (Advisory Opinion)* [2015] ITLOS Rep 4 ('*SRFC Advisory Opinion*').
122   *The M/V Virginia G* (n 67) 45.
123   *UNCLOS* (n 1) art 92(1).
124   *SS 'Lotus' (France v Turkey) (Judgment)* [1927] PCIJ (ser A) No 10.

broadcasting, or if the ship is without nationality. Furthermore, under art 111 coastal states have a right of 'hot pursuit' and may pursue and arrest foreign vessels on the high seas if they are detected contravening a valid law applicable in a coastal state maritime zone such as the territorial sea, continental shelf or EEZ. An example is the pursuit of a foreign fishing vessel on to the high seas. Such pursuit must be 'hot' (that is, immediate) and uninterrupted.

There are additional and more detailed provisions relating to the repression of piracy that allow states to seize pirate vessels and arrest pirates,[125] and pirates are subject to universal criminal jurisdiction. Piracy is defined as any illegal acts of violence or depredation (such as attacking or plundering) committed for private ends by the crew or passengers of one private ship against another on the high seas (or in the EEZ).[126] As the definition of piracy is limited in this way, it does not extend to other forms of violence at sea such as maritime terrorism (including where only one ship is involved). In order to address this, the international community adopted the 1988 *Convention for the Suppression of Unlawful Acts against the Safety of Maritime Navigation*.[127]

As the high seas are open to all states and not subject to sovereignty or jurisdiction, there are obvious challenges in monitoring and managing high seas activities from piracy through to pollution and shipping – and not only concerning ships flying flags of convenience. These challenges have been addressed to a significant extent through measures such as regional fisheries management organisations, and by treaties requiring port states to take measures against vessels from other parties suspected of contravening international standards relating to marine pollution or sustainable fishing. Substantial challenges remain in the enforcement of international labour standards, including violence and exploitation against seafarers, as well as against illegal, unreported or unregulated fishing.

## 13.5.2   Deep seabed

One of the most revolutionary features of *UNCLOS* was its designation of the deep seabed beyond national jurisdiction as the 'common heritage' of humankind. Until the 1960s, the deep seabed was treated as a component of the high seas and was therefore open to high seas freedoms including, potentially, the exploitation of its resources. Technological developments and increases in mineral prices raised the prospect that the deep seabed could be a new frontier for resource development, carrying major implications for the many states, especially those in the Global South, which were reliant on terrestrial mining for national income. This led to calls for deep seabed mineral resources to be recognised as common heritage and subject to an international regime that would provide fair access to, and sharing of the benefits from, deep seabed mining. Part XI of *UNCLOS* delivered this outcome.

The Convention introduced a new term, 'the Area', to define the seabed, ocean floor and subsoil beyond the limits of national jurisdiction.[128] The Area and its mineral resources

---

125    *UNCLOS* (n 1) art 105.
126    Ibid art 101.
127    *Convention for the Suppression of Unlawful Acts against the Safety of Maritime Navigation*, opened for signature 10 March 1988, 1678 UNTS 201 (entered into force 1 March 1992).
128    *UNCLOS* (n 1) art 1(a).

are declared to be the common heritage of humankind.[129] No state may claim or exercise sovereignty or sovereign rights over any part of the Area or its resources; nor shall any state or any person appropriate any part of the Area.[130] Part XI also established the ISA, and conferred on it authority to act on behalf of humankind as a whole to manage the resources of the Area.[131] Part XI proved to be controversial when *UNCLOS* was adopted, with the United States and other industrialised states viewing several of its provisions as too favourable to developing states. As the entry into force of *UNCLOS* approached, there were intense diplomatic efforts to agree on an implementing agreement that would modify pt XI so that it would operate according to more market-oriented principles.[132] This paved the way for many developed states, including Australia, to ratify *UNCLOS*.

Since it became operational in 1996, the ISA has sought to discharge its responsibility for managing all activities relating to mining in the Area for the benefit of humankind. The ISA is developing a comprehensive mining code applicable to prospecting, exploration and exploitation of deep seabed mineral resources. Particular attention is being paid to the potential and likely impacts of mining on deep seabed environments which support highly vulnerable ecosystems and unique species. No deep seabed mining has commenced; however, there are exploration activities underway and the ISA has approved over 30 contracts for exploration covering more than 1.3 million km² of the Area.[133] These activities may only occur when they are conducted by states directly or by companies sponsored by states parties to *UNCLOS*.

The nature of this sponsorship system was examined by the Seabed Disputes Chamber of ITLOS in *Responsibilities and Obligations of States Sponsoring Persons and Entities with respect to Activities in the Area* ('*Seabed Mining Advisory Opinion*').[134] This advisory opinion was sought by the ISA after a request by Nauru and Tonga for clarification of their potential liabilities if they sponsored companies to undertake deep seabed mining. They were concerned that they would be exposed to liabilities beyond their capacity as developing countries to meet if they sponsored mining that damaged the marine environment. The Chamber found that the sponsoring states' 'responsibility to ensure' that activities are carried out in conformity with *UNCLOS* was not an obligation of result involving strict liability, but was instead a duty to deploy adequate means and exercise the best possible efforts.[135] Notably, the Chamber advised that the sponsoring obligations applied equally to developed and developing states. This equality of treatment was considered important so as to avoid the problem of 'sponsoring states of convenience', similar to 'flags of convenience' for vessels.

---

129    Ibid art 136.
130    Ibid art 137(1).
131    Ibid arts 137, 157. See *International Seabed Authority* (Web Page) <https://www.isa.org.jm>.
132    *Implementing Agreement 1994* (n 10).
133    See <www.isa.org.jm/frequently-asked-questions-faqs>.
134    *Responsibilities and Obligations of States Sponsoring Persons and Entities with Respect to Activities in the Area (Advisory Opinion)* [2011] ITLOS Rep 10, (2011) 50 ILM 458 ('*Seabed Mining Advisory Opinion*').
135    Ibid [110].

# 13.6  Maritime environmental protection

One of the most important achievements of *UNCLOS* was the inclusion of a dedicated part on marine environmental protection: pt XII. Environmental issues had not attracted much attention at the First and Second UN Conferences on the Law of the Sea, but by the time *UNCLOS* was being negotiated it was clear that there were major pollution threats facing the world's oceans. This was made evident by major maritime disasters and oil spills such as the *Torrey Canyon* shipwreck near England in 1967. *UNCLOS* establishes a comprehensive framework for addressing all sources of marine pollution, and sets an overriding obligation ('to protect and preserve the marine environment')[136] which is given practical effect through a multitude of other treaties and soft law instruments. The treaties adopted by the International Maritime Organization to address pollution from oil and other hazardous materials provides the largest body of these measures.[137] *UNCLOS* effectively incorporates these by reference. For example, art 211, relating to vessel-source pollution, requires states to adopt laws and regulations for the prevention, reduction and control of pollution from vessels flying their flag that 'at least have the same effect as that of generally accepted international rules and standards'.

As a result of *UNCLOS*, and the large body of complementary treaties and instruments, there has been a paradigmatic shift in the approach to marine pollution, from a practice that was tolerated to one which is now generally prohibited.[138] However, the extent of the protections varies greatly according to the source of the pollution. There has been considerable success in addressing pollution from vessels, especially oil. Similarly successful have been measures addressing the dumping of wastes at sea, where a permissive approach has given way to a ban on the dumping of most materials.[139] Other sources of marine pollution have not been addressed so extensively or successfully. There are few if any limits on marine pollution from land or from the atmosphere, even though these together comprise 80% of the pollution entering the world's oceans.[140] For instance, there is no comprehensive regulation of carbon dioxide, which is not only causing climate change but also acidifying the oceans.[141] Similarly lacking is any global agreement on plastics, millions of tonnes of which enter the marine environment each year.[142]

*UNCLOS* exists alongside a large body of other international law relating to environmental protection (see Chapter 14). Key concepts of the latter, such as the precautionary principle, have been referred to and developed in law of the sea cases,[143] and in the ISA's work on

---

136    *UNCLOS* (n 1) art 192.
137    See International Maritime Organization, *List of IMO Conventions* (Web Page) <www.imo.org/en/About/Conventions/Pages/ListOfConventions.aspx>.
138    See James Harrison, *Saving the Oceans through Law* (Oxford University Press, 2017).
139    *Protocol to the London Convention on the Prevention of Marine Pollution by Dumping of Wastes and Other Matter*, opened for signature 8 November 1996 (1997) 36 ILM 1 (entered into force 24 March 2006).
140    National Oceanic and Atmospheric Administration (US), 'What is the Biggest Source of Pollution in the Ocean?', *Ocean Facts* (Web Page) <https://oceanservice.noaa.gov/facts/pollution.html>.
141    David VanderZwaag, Nilufer Oral and Tim Stephens (eds), *Research Handbook on Ocean Acidification Law and Policy* (Edward Elgar, 2021).
142    Jenna Jambeck et al, 'Plastic Waste Inputs from Land into the Ocean' (2015) 347(6223) *Science* 768.
143    See, eg, *Southern Bluefin Tuna (New Zealand v Japan) (Provisional Measures)* [1999] ITLOS Rep 280.

deep seabed mining. An example is the *Seabed Mining Advisory Opinion*, where ITLOS observed:

> [T]he precautionary approach has been incorporated into a growing number of inter-national treaties and other instruments, many of which reflect the formulation of Principle 15 of the *Rio Declaration*. In the view of the Chamber, this has initiated a trend towards making this approach part of customary international law. This trend is clearly reinforced by the inclusion of the precautionary approach in the Regulations and in the 'standard clause' contained in Annex 4, section 5.1, of the *Sulphides Regulations*. So does the following statement in paragraph 164 of the ICJ Judgment in *Pulp Mills on the River Uruguay* that 'a precautionary approach may be relevant in the interpretation and application of the provisions of the Statute' (ie, the environmental bilateral treaty whose interpretation was the main bone of contention between the parties).[144]

The *Whaling in the Antarctic* case[145] decided by the ICJ is another example where connections were made between *UNCLOS* and international environmental law. Australia's main argument in the case was that Japan's Southern Ocean research whaling program breached art VIII of the 1946 *International Convention for the Regulation of Whaling*[146] because it was not undertaken for purposes of scientific research.[147] The Court accepted this argument and found that Japan's whaling violated the Convention's commercial whaling moratorium.[148] Several judges in separate opinions went further and referred to key principles of international environmental law. Judge Cançado Trindade observed:

> When deciding whether a programme is 'for purposes of scientific research' so as to issue a special permit under Article VIII (1), the State party concerned has, in my understanding, a duty to abide by the principle of prevention and the precautionary principle.[149]

He also referred to the principle of intergenerational equity, and considered that this principle was at the centre of the Convention.[150] Judge Ad Hoc Charlesworth in her separate opinion assessed the relevance of the precautionary principle in some detail, concluding that it was relevant to the interpretation of art VIII and to the question whether lethal methods of research should be used:

> The precautionary approach to environmental regulation also reinforces this analysis of the conditions in which lethal research methods may be undertaken. The approach was formulated in Principle 15 of the *Rio Declaration on Environment and Development* in 1992 as '[w]here there are threats of serious or irreversible damage, lack of full scientific certainty shall not be used as a reason for postponing cost-effective measures to prevent environmental degradation'. The precautionary approach entails the avoidance of activities

---

144   *Seabed Mining Advisory Opinion* (n 134) 135 (citations omitted).
145   *Whaling in the Antarctic (Australia v Japan) (Judgment)* [2014] ICJ Rep 226.
146   *International Convention for the Regulation of Whaling*, opened for signature 2 December 1946, 161 UNTS 72 (entered into force 10 November 1948).
147   Ibid art VIII allows states parties to issue special permits to their nationals to take whales for scientific purposes.
148   *Whaling in the Antarctic* (n 145) 298–300 [247].
149   Ibid 356–7 [23] (Judge Trindade) (citations omitted).
150   Ibid 362 [41].

that may threaten the environment even in the face of scientific uncertainty about the direct or indirect effects of such activities. It gives priority to the prevention of harm to the environment in its broadest sense, including biological diversity, resource conservation and management and human health. The essence of the precautionary approach has informed the development of international environmental law and is recognized implicitly or explicitly in instruments dealing with a wide range of subject-matter, from the regulation of the oceans and international watercourses to the conservation and management of fish stocks, the conservation of endangered species and biosafety.[151]

# 13.7    Fisheries

A major focus of the modern law of the sea is the sustainable management of the world's fisheries. Many fisheries are under increasing pressure due to overfishing, and local and global changes to the marine environment such as climate change and ocean acidification.[152] Around 93% of fisheries are fully fished or overfished.[153] The law of the sea seeks to advance sustainable fisheries management in several ways. The first is by giving coastal states primary responsibility for managing their EEZs, which contain the vast bulk of fisheries globally, thus avoiding the 'tragedy of the commons'.[154] Coastal states have considerable discretion in setting total allowable catches and granting fishing licences, but there is an obvious economic incentive for them to manage their own fisheries sustainably in order to maintain fisheries industries. In *Request for an Advisory Opinion Submitted by the Sub-Regional Fisheries Commission*, ITLOS noted that coastal states have 'special rights and responsibilities' over fisheries in their EEZs and must adopt necessary laws and regulations, including enforcement procedures, consistent with *UNCLOS* to conserve and manage living resources.[155] The tribunal observed that the ultimate goal of fisheries management 'is to conserve and develop them as a viable and sustainable resource' and that, accordingly, 'sustainable management' means 'conservation and development' as referred to in art 63(1) of *UNCLOS*.[156] In Australia, responsibility for managing fisheries is shared between the Commonwealth, the states and the Northern Territory. In the area beyond 3 M, the Commonwealth manages over 20 fisheries under the *Fisheries Management Act 1991* (Cth).[157]

For shared stocks (those across multiple EEZs), straddling stocks (those across the EEZ and the high seas) and highly migratory species, where effective cooperation is essential for sustainable fisheries management, a range of new treaties has been adopted, including those establishing regional fisheries management organisations. The most important treaty is the

---

151     Ibid 455 [6] (Judge Ad Hoc Charlesworth).
152     See Food and Agriculture Organization, *The State of World Fisheries and Aquaculture 2020* (SOFIA Series, 2020).
153     Ibid.
154     Bonnie J McCay, 'Enclosing the Fishery Commons: From Individuals to Communities' in Daniel H Cole and Elinor Ostrom (eds), *Property in Land and Other Resources* (Lincoln Institute of Land Policy, 2012) 219, 219.
155     *SRFC Advisory Opinion* (n 121) [104].
156     Ibid [190]–[191].
157     See Robin Warner, 'Australia's Marine Resources' in Warwick Gullett, Clive Schofield and Joanna Vince (eds), *Marine Resources Management* (LexisNexis Butterworths, 2011) 59.

1995 *Fish Stocks Agreement*, an implementing agreement under *UNCLOS* which seeks to achieve the long-term conservation and sustainable use of straddling and highly migratory fish stocks. Among other things, it requires parties to join existing regional fisheries management organisations or to create one if there is none applicable to a straddling or highly migratory fishery. The *Fish Stocks Agreement* operates according to 12 fundamental principles, and requires states to apply the precautionary and ecosystem approaches. This means that governments must use the best scientific evidence and set cautious stock reference points,[158] and assess the impact of fishing not just on targeted species but on associated and dependent ecosystems as a whole.[159] Its adoption marked the introduction into international fisheries law of a strong environmental focus that had previously been absent.

## 13.8   Dispute resolution

It was noted at the start of this chapter that *UNCLOS* has been described as a 'constitution for the oceans', and this characterisation has influenced the way in which states and commentators have approached it. *UNCLOS* has several innate constitutional attributes, including its comprehensive coverage of oceans issues, its 'package deal' character in which reservations are impermissible[160] and the hurdles it places in the way of amendment.[161] In order to hold this constitution or 'package deal' together, *UNCLOS* establishes a sophisticated dispute settlement system which is comprehensive and mostly mandatory, but also quite flexible. This system, set out in pt XV, helps to ensure that *UNCLOS* disputes are resolved, and that the Convention is subject to authoritative rather than unilateral interpretation. As the ICJ noted in *Maritime Delimitation in the Indian Ocean*:

> The dispute settlement provisions of Part XV of UNCLOS are an integral part of the Convention, rather than being in the form of an optional protocol. Given that the Convention does not permit reservations (Art 309), all States parties are subject to Part XV. However, the Convention gives States parties considerable flexibility in the choice of means to settle disputes concerning its interpretation or application. Section 1 permits them to agree either to procedures that do not lead to a binding result (Arts 280 and 281) or to procedures leading to a binding result (Art 282), and accords priority to such agreed procedures over the procedures of Section 2 of Part XV. The first article in Section 2 of Part XV, entitled 'Application of procedures under this section' (Art 286), provides that the procedures of Section 2 are only available when a dispute has not been settled pursuant to Section 1. Thus, the procedures in Section 2 complement Section 1 in ensuring the integrity of the Convention, by providing a basis for binding dispute settlement (subject to Section 3), but those procedures are residual to the provisions of Section 1. In particular, a procedure that is agreed between States parties and that falls within the scope of Article 282 shall apply 'in lieu' of (ie, instead of) the procedures of Section 2 of Part XV.[162]

158   *Fish Stocks Agreement* (n 11) art 6.
159   Ibid art 5(d), (e).
160   *UNCLOS* (n 1) art 309.
161   Ibid art 312.
162   *Maritime Delimitation in the Indian Ocean (Somalia v Kenya) (Preliminary Objections)* [2017] ICJ Rep 3, 47–8 [125].

Under art 287 of *UNCLOS*, parties are allowed a degree of choice in selecting which court or tribunal is to decide disputes concerning the convention. Parties may express a preference for their disputes to be settled by ITLOS, the ICJ, an arbitral tribunal constituted under annex VII of *UNCLOS*, or a special arbitral tribunal constituted under annex VIII. In the absence of any declaration of preference, or where the preferences of disputing states differ, then annex VII arbitration applies by default. This means that ITLOS, which was established by *UNCLOS*, is not the only forum to which parties may turn. Nonetheless, ITLOS has had a relatively busy docket, deciding 29 cases since it was established in 1996. These have addressed a range of law of the sea issues including the enforcement of fisheries law, marine pollution, deep seabed mining, the immunity of warships, and the delimitation of maritime boundaries. Australia has been party to a number of law of the sea disputes, the most recent being that with Timor-Leste.

## DISCUSSION QUESTIONS

(1)  What do the terms 'free seas' and 'closed seas' mean and what relevance do they have for the contemporary law of the sea?

(2)  What is the exclusive economic zone and why might it be described as one of the most elusive maritime zones under the United Nations Convention on the Law of the Sea ('*UNCLOS*')?

(3)  Why is the law of the sea important to Australia, and has *UNCLOS* been fully implemented under Australian law?

(4)  Why does the law of the sea address the resources of the high seas and those of the deep seabed in such radically different ways?

(5)  How does the dispute settlement system of *UNCLOS* function to hold the Convention's 'package deal' together?

# 14

# INTERNATIONAL ENVIRONMENTAL LAW

Ben Boer

# 14.1   Introduction

International environmental law ('IEL') began to emerge as a distinct subdiscipline of international law in the 1970s. Since then, it has assumed critical importance in helping to maintain the ecological systems upon which all life on planet Earth depends. It is continuing to develop and is relevant to all states and communities, affecting a wide range of human activities and concerns.

This chapter briefly traces the history of IEL and sets out some recent institutional and policy developments, including the United Nations Environment Assembly and the UN Sustainable Development Goals. It also looks at concerted attempts to fill gaps in the field. Given the vastness of the subject matter, the chapter does not purport to be a comprehensive or in-depth analysis. It addresses the main organising principles of IEL, both established and emerging. It provides an overview of treaties (also referred to as multilateral environmental agreements or 'MEAs') in several key subfields, including regimes addressing the atmosphere, transboundary pollution, chemicals and wastes, biodiversity, and land degradation. It also includes a case study on world heritage and its implementation in Australia.

As should be clear from the chapter, the field of IEL continues to expand. The interlinkages between the environmental media (air, water and land) are becoming scientifically better understood, and a more integrated approach to the implementation of the large number of international and regional environmental legal instruments is beginning to be taken. It should be borne in mind that for IEL to achieve maximal effectiveness, obligations, principles and concepts should ideally be incorporated into domestic legislation and policies and implemented through the actions of national and sub-national governmental ministries and departments, the courts, and the private sector, and by civil society.

Further, with greater attention being placed on the issue of environmental rights at international and regional levels, the intersections of IEL with human rights law are becoming increasingly relevant, especially as a result of the recently recognised human right to a clean, healthy and sustainable environment.[1] Lawyers and legislators therefore need to gain a much better comprehension of the social, cultural and economic effects of environmental degradation, not just within their own jurisdictions, but also regionally and internationally. Procedurally, they should also work to ensure that local communities and individuals can participate in decisions concerning development activities affecting their environments, as well as their health, livelihood and wellbeing.

# 14.2   Development of international environmental law

## 14.2.1   International environmental law over five decades

The past 50 years have seen an exponential growth of IEL. In 1968, the UN Economic and Social Council called for an international conference on the problems of the human

---

1    *The Human Right to a Clean, Healthy and Sustainable Environment*, GA Res A/76/L.75, UN Doc A/RES/L.75 (28 July 2022).

environment, in response to the concerns of governments and civil society about 'the continu-ing accelerating impairment of the quality of the human environment caused by such factors as air and water pollution, erosion, and other forms of soil deterioration, secondary effects of biocides, waste and noise'.[2] That call gave rise to the Stockholm Conference on the Human Environment of 1972 ('Stockholm Conference'), the first-ever global meeting of leaders focused on environmental issues, which also involved hundreds of representatives of non-government organisations. The resulting *Stockholm Declaration*[3] is regarded as the progenitor of modern IEL.[4] It is notable that the Stockholm Conference also marked the increasing involvement and influence of developing countries in international environmental law-making, at a time when many states of the South were emerging from the grip of colonialism. The demand for recognition of permanent sovereignty over their natural resources[5] was a coeval factor in the increasing participation of Asian, African and Latin American states in the further development of international environmental law and policy,[6] a trend which has continued to the present time.[7]

From the 1970s, there has been a marked rise in the number of MEAs negotiated and concluded around the world[8] on virtually every environmental issue. Some MEAs are very broad, while others are narrowly focused. They cover wetlands, heritage, international trade in endangered species, migratory animals, air pollution, marine pollution, law of the sea, protec-tion of the ozone layer, hazardous wastes, persistent organic chemicals, biological diversity, climate change, desertification, mercury, Indigenous peoples, nuclear proliferation, and envir-onmental rights. While all of these are global issues, there are also a number of environmental agreements covering specific geographical regions. Further, there is a clear need for an approach in the implementation of IEL that recognises the disparities in capacity of North and South countries to address global and national environmental challenges, embodied in the principle of common but differentiated responsibility.[9]

---

2       *Question of Convening an International Conference on the Problems of Human Environment*, ESC
        Res 1346 (XLV), UN Doc E/RES/1346(XLV) (30 July 1968) para 1.
3       *Report of the United Nations Conference on the Human Environment*, UN Doc A/CONF.48/14/REV.1
        (16 June 1972) annex I ('*Declaration of the United Nations Conference on the Human Environment*')
        ('*Stockholm Declaration*').
4       Pierre-Marie Dupuy and Jorge Viñuales, *International Environmental Law* (Cambridge University Press,
        2nd ed, 2018). The authors refer to the Stockholm Conference as 'the foundational moment of modern
        international environmental law': at 9.
5       See *Permanent Sovereignty over Natural Resources*, GA Res 1803 (XVII), UN Doc A/RES/1803(XVII)
        (14 December 1962).
6       These developments are traced in Parvez Hassan, 'Role of the South in International Environmental Law'
        (2017) 1(2) *Chinese Journal of Environmental Law* 133.
7       See Karin Mickelson, 'The Stockholm Conference and the Creation of the South–North Divide in
        International Environmental Law and Policy' in Shawkat Alam et al (eds), *International Environmental
        Law and the Global South* (Cambridge University Press, 2015) 109.
8       See, eg, 'International Environmental Agreements (IEA) Database Project', *University of Oregon* (Web
        Page) <https://iea.uoregon.edu/what-iea-database-project>.
9       See Sumudu Atapattu, 'The Significance of International Environmental Law Principles in Reinforcing or
        Dismantling the North–South Divide' in Shawkat Alam et al (eds), *International Environmental Law
        and the Global South* (Cambridge University Press, 2015) 74, 93–8.

## 14.2.2   National level implementation

The effectiveness of international and regional environmental law regimes must be measured in terms of their global and regional operation as well as at the national level. There is now a broader recognition that national environmental governance must be strengthened. For example, in the Asia Pacific, 'environmental regimes and institutions are still inadequate in many countries of the region, which leads to inadequate policy responses, weak enforcement of laws and regulations, and poor compliance with MEAs'.[10] The same is true for Africa[11] and West Asia.[12] The pan-European region as a whole performs well in terms of environmental law implementation and enforcement,[13] but major environmental problems are being more slowly addressed in states in Eastern Europe, the Caucasus and Central Asia.[14] In the Latin American states, the picture is also fragmented, with deficiencies in legal authority and institutional capacity for implementation and enforcement in many states.[15]

## 14.2.3   Remedies for violations

The mechanisms available to address violations of international and regional environmental law are relatively weak.[16] Individuals, communities and corporations generally do not have standing in international tribunals to achieve legally binding remedies. Further, in contrast to the field of human rights,[17] there are no regional courts focused on the environment, and, despite attempts, there is no international court on the environment. A Special Environmental Chamber set up within the International Court of Justice ('ICJ') in 1993 was never utilised and ceased to be constituted after 2006.[18]

# 14.3   Sources and drafting of IEL

As recognised in Chapter 2, in addition to the traditional or formal sources of international law (particularly treaties and custom), soft law instruments and declarations of conferences and the

---

10   United Nations Environment Programme, *GEO-6 Regional Assessment for Asia and the Pacific* (Report, 2016) xix, 8, 39, 50, 105 (citations omitted) <https://wedocs.unep.org/handle/20.500.11822/7548>.

11   United Nations Environment Programme, *GEO-6 Regional Assessment for Africa* (Report, 2016) 88, 125 <http://wedocs.unep.org/handle/20.500.11822/7595>.

12   United Nations Environment Programme, *GEO-6 Regional Assessment for West Asia* (Report, 2016) 63, 64, 65, 73, 75 <http://wedocs.unep.org/handle/20.500.11822/7668>.

13   United Nations Environment Programme, *GEO-6 Regional Assessment for the Pan-European Region* (Report, 2016) <http://wedocs.unep.org/handle/20.500.11822/7735>.

14   Ibid 48.

15   See United Nations Environment Programme, *GEO-6 Regional Assessment for Latin America and the Caribbean* (Report, 2016) 19, 28, 78 <https://wedocs.unep.org/handle/20.500.11822/7659>.

16   See, eg, Jona Razzaque, 'Access to Remedies in Environmental Matters and the North–South Divide' in Shawkat Alam et al (eds), *International Environmental Law and the Global South* (Cambridge University Press, 2015) 588, 588–9.

17   For example, the European Court of Human Rights, established in 1959, and the African Court on Human and Peoples' Rights, founded in 2004.

18   See Jorge Viñuales, 'The Contribution of the International Court of Justice to the Development of International Environmental Law: A Contemporary Assessment' (2008) 32(1) *Fordham International Law Journal* 232, 233. See also Tim Stephens, *International Courts and Environmental Protection* (Cambridge University Press, 2009) 38–40.

like have also become increasingly significant, and this is particularly so in IEL. Since the 1970s, an expanding range of non-state actors have contributed to the making of IEL.[19]

Among the most important of these actors is the International Union for the Conservation of Nature ('IUCN'), a longstanding hybrid intergovernmental and non-governmental organisation. It has regularly issued influential statements on environmental principles and generated draft MEAs, leading to some of the most significant international and regional MEAs adopted by states.[20] These include the *African Convention on the Conservation of Nature and Natural Resources* 1968 and its 2013 revised version,[21] the *World Heritage Convention* 1972,[22] the *Convention on International Trade in Endangered Species* 1973 ('*CITES*'),[23] the *ASEAN Agreement on the Conservation of Nature and Natural Resources* 1985,[24] and the *Convention on Biological Diversity* 1992.[25] The IUCN also prepared the *Draft International Covenant on Environment and Development* in 2005[26] (in collaboration with the International Council on Environmental Law[27]) and the *World Declaration on the Environmental Rule of Law* 2016 ('*World Declaration*').[28]

Less formal groups of actors also feed into the making of IEL and associated policy, as can be seen in debates leading up to the Sustainable Development Goals 2015[29] as well as the 2015 *Paris Agreement* on climate change.[30] In addition to their contributions to the making of IEL, these intergovernmental and non-government organisations assist in the national legal implementation of international obligations arising from environmental

---

19    Thilo Marauhn, 'Changing Role of the State' in Daniel Bodansky, Jutta Brunnée and Ellen Hey (eds), *The Oxford Handbook of International Environmental Law* (Oxford University Press, 2007) 738.

20    Drafts of these MEAs were prepared by the IUCN Environmental Law Centre and the World Commission on Environmental Law. Barbara Lausche, *Weaving a Web of Environmental Law* (Erich Schmidt, 2008) traces the history of the IUCN's involvement in the development of international and regional environmental law from the 1960s to the 2000s: at 53–91.

21    Ibid 53–70; *African Convention on the Conservation of Nature and Natural Resources*, opened for signature 15 September 1968, 1001 UNTS 4 (entered into force 16 June 1969). The revised Convention was adopted by the African Union on 11 July 2013.

22    *Convention concerning the Protection of the World Cultural and Natural Heritage*, opened for signature 16 November 1972, 1037 UNTS 151 (entered into force 17 December 1975 ('*World Heritage Convention*').

23    *Convention on International Trade in Endangered Species of Wild Fauna and Flora*, opened for signature 3 March 1973, 983 UNTS 243 (entered into force 1 July 1975) ('*CITES*').

24    *ASEAN Agreement on the Conservation of Nature and Natural Resources*, opened for signature 9 July 1985, ECOLEX TRE-000820 (not yet in force) <www.ecolex.org/details/treaty/asean-agreement-on-the-conservation-of-nature-and-natural-resources-tre-000820>.

25    *Convention on Biological Diversity*, opened for signature 5 June 1992, 1760 UNTS 79 (entered into force 29 December 1993).

26    The Covenant was initially drafted in 1994 and launched at the United Nations Congress on Public International Law in March 1995; its fifth edition was prepared in 2015: <https://sdgs.un.org/publications/draft-international-covenant-environment-and-development-fifth-edition-updated-text>.

27    *International Council of Environmental Law* (Web Page) <http://icelinternational.org>.

28    International Union for Conservation of Nature, *World Declaration on the Environmental Rule of Law* (adopted by IUCN World Congress on Environmental Law, 29 April 2016) ('*World Declaration*') <www.informea.org/en/literature/world-declaration-environmental-rule-law>.

29    *Transforming Our World: The 2030 Agenda for Sustainable Development*, GA Res 70/1, UN Doc A/RES/70/1 (21 October 2015, adopted 25 September 2015) ('*Transforming Our World*') <https://sustainabledevelopment.un.org/post2015/transformingourworld/publication>. The resolution incorporates the 17 Sustainable Development Goals ('SDGs') and 169 associated targets.

30    *Paris Agreement*, opened for signature 22 April 2016, [2016] ATS 24 (entered into force 4 November 2016).

conventions.[31] Also now included in law-making are more intergovernmental bodies, led by the United Nations and its institutions and programs, and the secretariats and conferences of the states parties to environmental conventions.

# 14.4 International institutions

## 14.4.1 United Nations Environment Programme

The United Nations Environment Programme ('UNEP') was established in 1973 as a result of the Stockholm Conference. It is headquartered in Nairobi, with offices in Geneva and Bangkok. It acts as the secretariat of a number of significant MEAs, including those on international trade in endangered species,[32] and migratory animals;[33] the ozone layer (*Vienna Convention*[34] and *Montreal Protocol*[35]); chemicals and wastes (*Basel*,[36] *Rotterdam*[37] and *Stockholm*[38] *Conventions*) and mercury (*Minamata Convention*[39]); and biological diversity.[40]

## 14.4.2 United Nations Environment Assembly

One of the most important institutional developments in recent years has been the establishment of the United Nations Environment Assembly. The Assembly was created in 2012 as part of an effort to strengthen and upgrade UNEP.[41] It has universal membership, comprising all states of the United Nations, in place of the limited rotating membership of the former UNEP Council.[42] It also has broad participation from civil society and private sector representatives, as well as from the scientific and academic communities.

---

31    See further Mark Drumbl, 'Actors and Law-Making in International Environmental Law' in Malgosia Fitzmaurice et al (eds), *Research Handbook of International Environmental Law* (Routledge, 2010) 2; Ben Boer, 'International Law-Making' in Elisa Morgera and Kati Kulovesi (eds), *Research Handbook on International Law and Natural Resources* (Edward Elgar, 2016) 449.

32    *CITES* (n 23).

33    *Convention on the Conservation of Species of Migratory Animals*, opened for signature 23 June 1979, 1651 UNTS 333 (entered into force 1 November 1983).

34    *Vienna Convention for the Protection of the Ozone Layer*, opened for signature 22 March 1985, 1513 UNTS 293 (entered into force 22 September 1988) ('*Vienna Convention*').

35    *Montreal Protocol on Substances That Deplete the Ozone Layer*, opened for signature 16 September 1987, 1522 UNTS 28 (entered into force 1 January 1989) ('*Montreal Protocol*').

36    *Basel Convention on the Control of Transboundary Movements of Hazardous Wastes and Their Disposal*, opened for signature 22 March 1989, 1672 UNTS 57 (entered into force 5 May 1992) ('*Basel Convention*').

37    *Rotterdam Convention on the Prior Informed Consent Procedure for Certain Hazardous Chemicals and Pesticides in International Trade*, opened for signature 10 September 1998, 2244 UNTS 337 (entered into force 24 February 2004) ('*Rotterdam Convention*').

38    *Stockholm Convention on Persistent Organic Pollutants*, opened for signature 22 May 2001, 2256 UNTS 119 (entered into force 17 May 2004) ('*Stockholm Convention*').

39    *Minamata Convention on Mercury*, opened for signature 10 October 2013, 55 ILM 582 (entered into force 16 August 2017).

40    *Convention on Biological Diversity* (n 25).

41    See further 'About the United Nations Environment Assembly', *United Nations Environment Assembly* (Web Page) <www.unep.org/environmentassembly/about-united-nations-environment-assembly>.

42    Ibid.

# 14.5   Principles of international environmental law

## 14.5.1   The importance of principles

While international law in general rests on a wide range of principles, the development of IEL has seen an increasing focus on principles specifically directed to the protection and conservation of the environment. This trend is evidenced by declarations and statements from major international and regional UN conferences, specialised judicial conferences, and conferences of various non-government organisations, by judgments of international courts and tribunals, and by scholarly books in the field,[43] as briefly referred to in the following sections.

## 14.5.2   Established principles

Principles of environmental law can be divided into several categories. The most fundamental principles are associated with the prevention of environmental damage and have been developed in international law cases. These can be further classified into *substantive* and *procedural* principles.[44] Examples are set out in this section.

The substantive principle of prevention is described by Leslie-Ann Duvic-Pavoli as 'the cornerstone of environmental law'.[45] She points out that its early formulation is found in the *Trail Smelter* arbitration, which concerned sulphur dioxide emissions from a zinc and lead smelter in British Columbia which were harming farmers' crops in the United States. The joint arbitral tribunal found that

> no State has the right to use or permit the use of its territory in such a manner as to cause injury by fumes in or to the territory of another or the properties or persons therein, when the case is of serious consequence and the injury is established by clear and convincing evidence.[46]

This principle also found expression in the *Stockholm Declaration* and the *Rio Declaration on Environment and Development* ('*Rio Declaration*').[47] Principle 2 of the latter provides:

> States have, in accordance with the *Charter of the United Nations* and the principles of international law, the sovereign right to exploit their own resources pursuant to their own environmental and developmental policies, and the responsibility to ensure that activities

---

43    See, eg, Philippe Sands and Jacqueline Peel, *Principles of International Environmental Law* (Cambridge University Press, 4th ed, 2018); Eloise Scotford, *Environmental Principles and the Evolution of Environmental Law* (Hart Publishing, 2017); Dupuy and Viñuales (n 4) ch 3; Ludwig Krämer and Emanuela Orlando (eds), *Principles of Environmental Law* (Elgar, 2018); Nicolas de Sadeleer, *Environmental Principles: From Political Slogans to Legal Rules* (Oxford University Press, 2nd ed, 2020).
44    Dupuy and Viñuales (n 4) 61.
45    Leslie-Ann Duvic Paoli, 'Principle of Prevention' in Ludwig Krämer and Emanuela Orlando (eds), *Principles of Environmental Law* (Elgar, 2018) 162.
46    *Trail Smelter (United States of America v Canada) (Awards)* (1938-1941) 3 RIAA 1905, 1905, 1965.
47    *Report of the United Nations Conference on Environment and Development*, UN Doc A/CONF.151/26 (vol I) (12 August 1992) annex I ('*Rio Declaration on Environment and Development*') ('*Rio Declaration*'); *Report of the United Nations Conference on Environment and Development*, GA Res 47/190, UN Doc A/RES/47/190 (adopted 22 December 1992).

within their jurisdiction or control do not cause damage to the environment of other States or of areas beyond the limits of national jurisdiction.[48]

Another substantive principle is that of precaution, first spelled out at the national level in Germany as the *Vorsorgeprinzip*. As explained by Pierre-Marie Dupuy and Jorge Viñuales: 'The underlying idea is that the lack of scientific certainty about the actual or potential effect of an activity must not prevent States from taking appropriate measures when such effects may be serious or irreversible'.[49] Despite many debates concerning its interpretation, the principle has found its way into a range of MEAs and important declarations. Its most common rendering is Principle 15 of the *Rio Declaration*:

> In order to protect the environment, the precautionary approach shall be widely applied by States according to their capabilities. Where there are threats of serious or irreversible damage, lack of full scientific certainty shall not be used as a reason for postponing cost-effective measures to prevent environmental degradation.[50]

In 2011, the International Tribunal for the Law of the Sea, in the *Seabed Mining Advisory Opinion*, on the issue of manganese nodule mining, stated that 'the precautionary approach is ... an integral part of the general obligation of due diligence of sponsoring States, which is applicable even outside the scope of the [relevant prospecting and exploration] Regulations'.[51]

Particular mechanisms of environmental law are also often characterised as principles at the international level. Such principles can be regarded as procedural as opposed to substantive. The procedural principle of environmental impact assessment ('EIA') is one of the most important. As a process, EIA involves collecting and analysing information about the impact of a proposed development activity on the environment. It normally includes public participation, at least of concerned parties, and results in an environmental impact statement, used in giving or withholding consent for an application for development activity or placing specified conditions on such consent. The EIA principle can apply both at the national level as well as transnationally. It was spelled out in Principle 17 of the *Rio Declaration*:

> Environmental impact assessment, as a national instrument, shall be undertaken for proposed activities that are likely to have a significant adverse impact on the environment and are subject to a decision of a competent national authority.[52]

Vice-President Weeramantry in *Gabčíkovo-Nagymaros Project* described the EIA principle as follows with regard to treaties:

> Environmental law in its current state of development would read into treaties which may reasonably be considered to have a significant impact upon the environment, a duty of environmental impact assessment and this means also, whether the treaty expressly so

---

48   Ibid. Principle 21 of the *Stockholm Declaration* (n 3) differs slightly from Principle 2 of the *Rio Declaration*, as it does not include the words 'and developmental' after 'environmental'.
49   Dupuy and Viñuales (n 4) 70.
50   *Rio Declaration* (n 47).
51   *Responsibilities and Obligations of States Sponsoring Persons and Entities with Respect to Activities in the Area (Advisory Opinion)* [2011] ITLOS Rep 10, 46.
52   *Rio Declaration* (n 47).

provides or not, a duty of monitoring the environmental impacts of any substantial project during the operation of the scheme.[53]

The *Pulp Mills on the River Uruguay* case[54] strongly reinforced this perspective, with the ICJ declaring that EIA practice

> in recent years has gained so much acceptance among States that it may now be considered a requirement of the general international law to undertake impact assessment where there is a risk that the proposed industrial activity may have a significant adverse impact in a transboundary context, in particular on a shared resource.[55]

While EIA has often been regarded as a merely technical process concerning the impact of a proposed development activity on the environment,[56] it has come to involve broader social, cultural, political and human rights considerations, both at a national and at a transboundary level. This is particularly the case when an EIA relates to Indigenous and local communities, a field that increasingly engages norms contained in the *United Nations Declaration on the Rights of Indigenous Peoples*, such as the principle of free, prior and informed consent.[57]

This view was followed by the ICJ in *Certain Activities Carried out by Nicaragua in the Border Area*, where it was stated:

> Although the Court's statement in the *Pulp Mills* case refers to industrial activities, the underlying principle applies generally to proposed activities which may have a significant adverse impact in a transboundary context. Thus, to fulfil its obligation to exercise due diligence in preventing significant transboundary environmental harm, a State must, before embarking on an activity having the potential adversely to affect the environment of another State, ascertain if there is a risk of significant transboundary harm, which would trigger the requirement to carry out an environmental impact assessment.[58]

### 14.5.3 Sustainable development

The idea of achieving sustainable development is one of the most aspirational of any global policy goal in the three decades since 1992. Beginning with the *Rio Declaration*, it has been instrumental in shaping successive high-level declarations, statements and resolutions. It has become a lynchpin of international policy and law concerning protection of the environment

---

53    *Gabčíkovo-Nagymaros Project (Hungary v Slovakia) (Judgment)* [1997] ICJ Rep 7, 112.

54    *Pulp Mills on the River Uruguay (Argentina v Uruguay) (Judgment)* [2010] ICJ Rep 14, 83.

55    For further comment, see Donald R Rothwell et al, *International Law: Cases and Materials with Australian Perspectives* (Cambridge University Press, 2018) 587–95; Sands and Peel (n 43) 657–81.

56    See, eg, Ben Boer et al, *The Mekong: A Socio-Legal Approach to River Basin Development* (Routledge, 2016) 114.

57    *United Nations Declaration on the Rights of Indigenous Peoples*, GA Res 61/295, UN Doc A/RES/61/295 (2 October 2007, adopted 13 September 2007). Australia was one of four countries to vote against the resolution at the time, but finally endorsed it in 2009. The other three countries were Canada, New Zealand and the United States. They all subsequently endorsed the Declaration.

58    *Certain Activities Carried out by Nicaragua in the Border Area (Costa Rica v Nicaragua) and Construction of a Road in Costa Rica along the San Juan River (Nicaragua v Costa Rica) (Merits)* [2015] ICJ Rep 665, 706 [104].

and the conservation of natural resources. Its most common definition derives from the 1987 report of the World Commission on Environment and Development, *Our Common Future*: 'Development that meets the needs of the present without compromising the ability of future generations to meet their own needs'.[59]

The report then elaborates on this definition:

> It contains within it two key concepts: the concept of 'needs', in particular the essential needs of the world's poor, to which overriding priority should be given; and the idea of limitations imposed by the state of technology and social organization on the environment's ability to meet present and future needs.[60]

Although most analysts refer to sustainable development as a concept, Vice-President Weeramantry in *Gabčíkovo-Nagymaros Project* had no doubt of its status in his separate opinion, characterising it as a principle and emphasising its importance as 'an integral part of modern international law'.[61]

### 14.5.3.1   Sustainable Development Goals 2015

One of the major contemporary challenges in the environmental debate is how to more rapidly implement sustainable development globally. The challenges are set out in the 2015 UN General Assembly resolution ambitiously entitled *Transforming Our World: The 2030 Agenda for Sustainable Development* ('*Transforming Our World*'). The Agenda includes 17 Sustainable Development Goals ('SDGs') and 169 associated targets,[62] to be achieved between 2015 and 2030. The SDGs replaced the Millennium Development Goals of 2000–15.[63] The UN resolution recognises that 'good governance and the rule of law as well as an enabling environment at national and international levels are essential for sustainable development, including sustained and inclusive economic growth'.[64] The Agenda also reaffirms the principles of the *Rio Declaration*, in particular the principle of 'common but differentiated responsibilities' (whereby all states are deemed to have the same obligations, but the level of responsibility differs according to the capacity of the individual state). The SDGs, building on successive initiatives over the past four decades, can be seen as another important set of milestones on the road to global sustainability.

The SDGs include many matters associated directly or indirectly with the environment. Goals 1 to 11 address poverty; hunger; health; education; gender equality; water; energy; economic growth and work; resilient infrastructure; inequality; and cities, cultural and natural heritage, and human settlements. Several SDGs have direct relevance to the implementation of international and regional environmental law. These include Goal 12 on ensuring sustainable consumption and production patterns, Goal 13 on combating climate change and its impacts, Goal 14 on

---

59    World Commission on Environment and Development, *Our Common Future* (Oxford University Press, 1987) ch 2, [1].

60    Ibid.

61    *Gabčíkovo-Nagymaros Project* (n 53) 92 (Vice-President Weeramantry).

62    *Transforming Our World*, UN Doc A/RES/70/1 (n 29).

63    See *United Nations Millennium Declaration*, GA Res 55/2, UN Doc A/RES/55/2 (18 September 2000); 'News on Millennium Development Goals', *Millennium Development Goals and beyond 2015* (Web Page) <www.un.org/millenniumgoals>.

64    See *Transforming Our World*, UN Doc A/RES/70/1 (n 29).

oceans and marine environment, and Goal 15 concerning the terrestrial environment. Goal 16, on peaceful and inclusive societies, access to justice and institution-building, is a vital element for both the human rights and the environmental spheres. Goal 17 is an overarching one, on strengthening the means of implementation and revitalising the Global Partnership for Sustainable Development. Many states and intergovernmental organisations have started to develop strategies to implement the SDGs. The SDGs will no doubt continue to influence the further development of international, regional and national environmental law and policy.

### 14.5.3.2 Sustainable development in Australia

The advent of sustainable development is an important example of how a widely accepted norm has been transferred from the international to the national level. In Australia, the term acquired an additional descriptor, becoming *ecologically* sustainable development, now often referred to as 'ESD'.[65] The Council of Australian Governments endorsed the *National Strategy for Ecologically Sustainable Development* in 1992 that was reflected in the comprehensive *Intergovernmental Agreement on the Environment* between Australian national, state/territory and local governments.[66] A set of principles associated with ESD began to be incorporated first into Commonwealth legislation and then state and territory legislation from 1991.[67] They were also embodied in s 3A of the *Environment Protection and Biodiversity Conservation Act 1999* (Cth). These principles are similar to ones that have been adopted at Australian state and territory levels.[68]

With regard to the SDGs in the Australian context, the federal government established the Reporting Platform on the SDG Indicators to provide the basis for its Voluntary National Review,[69] a process undertaken by all UN member states that have agreed to deliver SDG reports to the UN High-Level Political Forum on Sustainable Development.[70]

## 14.5.4 Emergence of new principles

### 14.5.4.1 Principles of IEL in a global instrument

In the 1990s, the IUCN World Commission on Environmental Law prepared the *Draft International Covenant on Environment and Development*.[71] It was originally seen as the

---

65  For an early analysis, see Ben Boer, 'Institutionalising Ecologically Sustainable Development: The Roles of National, State, and Local Governments in Translating Grand Strategy into Action' (1995) 31(2) *Willamette Law Review* 307.

66  *Intergovernmental Agreement on the Environment* (May 1992). See also *National Strategy for Ecologically Sustainable Development* (1992) endorsed by the Council of Australian Governments: <https://webarchive.nla.gov.au/awa/20130905024205/http://www.environment.gov.au/about/esd/publications/strategy/index.html>.

67  See *Protection of the Environment Administration Act 1991* (Cth) s 6, which was followed by myriad pieces of legislation in New South Wales and subsequently in the other Australian states and territories; Gerry Bates, *Environmental Law in Australia* (LexisNexis Butterworths, 10th ed, 2019).

68  Bates (n 67) ch 4.

69  *Australian Government's Reporting Platform on the SDG Indicators* (Web Page) <www.sdgdata.gov.au>.

70  United Nations, 'High-Level Political Forum on Sustainable Development', *Sustainable Developments Goals: Knowledge Platform* (Web Page) <https://sustainabledevelopment.un.org/hlpf>. The Forum was established in 2012.

71  *Draft International Covenant on Environment and Development* (n 26).

foundation of a negotiating text for a binding international instrument on environment and development. The fifth edition, published in 2015, aimed to provide governments, parliamentarians and other actors with an authoritative source to ensure that IEL principles and rules were addressed in policies and laws. It was particularly seen 'as a framework for implementing sustainability at all levels of society',[72] in the context of the 2015 SDGs. The momentum for the adoption of the Draft Covenant was overtaken by the push, since 2017, for a binding *Global Pact for the Environment*, initiated by the French Club des Juristes.[73] The Pact aims, inter alia, to 'integrate, consolidate, unify and ultimately entrench many of the fragmented principles of IEL'.[74] Whether negotiations on the Pact or on a similar instrument will eventually result in a legally binding instrument remains to be seen.[75]

## 14.5.4.2  Environmental Rule of Law

A concept that has emerged in recent years is the Environmental Rule of Law ('EROL'). The concept was first recognised in 2013 by UNEP, which called for

> the development and implementation of environmental rule of law with attention at all levels to mutually supporting governance features, including information disclosure, public participation, implementable and enforceable laws, and implementation and accountability mechanisms including coordination of roles as well as environmental auditing and criminal, civil and administrative enforcement with timely, impartial and independent dispute resolution.[76]

The United Nations Environment Programme sees EROL as central to achieving sustainable development, as '[i]t integrates environmental needs with the essential elements of the rule of law and provides the basis for improving environmental governance. It highlights environmental sustainability by connecting it with fundamental rights and obligations.'[77]

The concept was further elaborated in the *World Declaration*:

> The environmental rule of law is understood as the legal framework of procedural and substantive rights and obligations that incorporates the principles of ecologically sustainable development in the rule of law. Strengthening the environmental rule of law is the key to the protection, conservation, and restoration of environmental integrity. Without it, environmental governance and the enforcement of rights and obligations may be arbitrary, subjective, and unpredictable ...[78]

---

72    See ibid xiii.

73    See 'About Us', *Global Pact for the Environment* (Web Page) <https://globalpactenvironment.org/en>.

74    Louis Kotzé and Duncan French, 'A Critique of the Global Pact for the Environment: A Stillborn Initiative or the Foundation for Lex Anthropocenae?' (2018) 18(6) *International Environmental Agreements: Politics, Law and Economics* 811, 816.

75    See Yann Aguila and Lionel Chami, 'The Global Pact for the Environment: Where To?', *Jus Mundi* (Blog Post, 17 March 2022) <https://blog.jusmundi.com/global-pact-for-the-environment-where-to>.

76    UNEP Governing Council/Global Ministerial Environment Forum, Decision 27/9, 27th sess, 17 February 2013 <www.informea.org/en/decision/advancing-justice-governance-and-law-environmental-sustainability>.

77    'Environmental Rule of Law', *United Nations Environment Programme* (Web Page) <www.unep.org/explore-topics/environmental-rights-and-governance/what-we-do/promoting-environmental-rule-law-0>; United Nations Environment Programme, *Environmental Rule of Law: First Global Report* (2019) 8.

78    *World Declaration* (n 28) 2.

The environmental rule of law is intended to apply at the national, regional and international levels, and is likely to become more important in decision-making processes as it is progressively taken up by governments and courts. The Declaration contains 13 principles aimed at promoting and achieving ecological justice through EROL. The most significant emerging principles are briefly canvassed in the following sections.

### 14.5.4.3  *In dubio pro natura*

An important new principle is that of *in dubio pro natura*. Literally translated from Latin, it means 'when in doubt, in favour of nature'. It can also be interpreted as 'resolving ambiguity in favour of nature'.[79] It was first recognised in some Latin American jurisdictions[80] and was adopted at the international level in Principle 5 of the *World Declaration*:

> In cases of doubt, all matters before courts, administrative agencies, and other decision-makers shall be resolved in a way most likely to favour the protection and conservation of the environment, with preference to be given to alternatives that are least harmful to the environment. Actions shall not be undertaken when their potential adverse impacts on the environment are disproportionate or excessive in relation to the benefits derived therefrom.[81]

A subsequent specialised instrument, the 2018 *Brasília Declaration of Judges on Water Justice*, adapted the principle to the water environment – *in dubio pro aqua*.[82]

### 14.5.4.4  Principle of non-regression

The principle of non-regression expresses the idea that when an environmental law is passed, or a standard is set (such as a permissible level of pollution), there should be no 'backsliding'. The *World Declaration* formulation appears in Principle 12:

> States, sub-national entities, and regional integration organisations shall not allow or pursue actions that have the net effect of diminishing the legal protection of the environment or of access to environmental justice.[83]

The principle was championed by French environmental law professor Michel Prieur, who argued that 'environment law has an immutable core content closely linked to the fundamental human right to life. Environmental law is a set of norms that are interdependent of one another.

---

79    Nicholas Bryner, 'A Constitutional Human Right to a Healthy Environment' in Douglas Fisher (ed), *Research Handbook on Fundamental Concepts of Environmental Law* (Edward Elgar, 2016) 180.

80    In particular, Brazil, Chile, Costa Rica and Ecuador. See Alberto Olivares and Jairo Lucero, 'Content and Development of the Principle In Dubio Pro Natura: Towards Comprehensive Protection of the Environment' (2018) 24(3) *Ius et Praxis* 619; Nicholas Bryner, 'In Dubio Pro Natura: A Principle for Strengthening Environmental Rule of Law' (2015) 78 *Revista de Direito Ambiental* [Journal of Environmental Law] 245.

81    *World Declaration* (n 28) 3.

82    *Brasília Declaration of Judges on Water Justice* (March 2018) <www.iucn.org/our-union/commissions/world-commission-environmental-law/our-work/history/foundational-documents-0>. Both of these principles have been applied at the national level in Pakistan: *DG Khan Cement Co Ltd v Government of Punjab* (Supreme Court of Pakistan, Mansoor Ali Shah J, CP.1290-L/2019, 2021).

83    *World Declaration* (n 28) 4.

The concept of standstill protects this complex, fragile and fundamental construct'.[84] The principle became more widely known because of a referendum in California in 2010 when a majority of voters refused to suspend the *California Global Warming Solutions Act of 2006* (on climate change and reduction of greenhouse gas emissions) as proposed by US oil companies.[85] The non-regression principle was incorporated into French law in 2016.[86]

### 14.5.4.5 Principle of progression

The principle of progression is of recent origin and is expressed in Principle 13 of the *World Declaration*:

> In order to achieve the progressive development and enforcement of the environmental rule of law, States, sub-national entities, and regional integration organisations shall regularly revise and enhance laws and policies in order to protect, conserve, restore, and ameliorate the environment, based on the most recent scientific knowledge and policy developments. States, sub-national entities, and regional integration organisations shall not allow or pursue actions that have the net effect of diminishing the legal protection of the environment or of access to environmental justice.[87]

The principle can be seen to build on the principle of non-regression: that is, rather than the law just standing still and not backsliding, the principle contemplates continuous improvement in a particular law or legal standard. An example is in art 4(3) of the *Paris Agreement* concerning reduction of greenhouse gas emissions: 'Each Party's successive nationally determined contribution will represent a progression beyond the Party's then current nationally determined contribution and reflect its highest possible ambition, reflecting its common but differentiated responsibilities and respective capabilities, in the light of different national circumstances.'[88]

### 14.5.4.6 Human right to a safe, clean, healthy and sustainable environment

The connection between human rights and environment protection was first recognised in principle 1 of the *Stockholm Declaration*: 'Man has the fundamental right to freedom, equality

---

84    Michel Prieur, 'De L'urgente Nécessité de Reconnaître le Principe de "Non Régression" en Droit de l'Environnement' ['Urgently Acknowledging the Principle of "Non-Regression" in Environmental Rights'] (summary in English) (2011) 1 *IUCN AEL Journal of Environmental Law* <www.iucnael.org/en/e-journal/previous-issues/157-issue-20111.html>. See also Michel Prieur, 'The Principle of Non-Regression' in Ludwig Krämer and Emanuela Orlando (eds), *Principles of Environmental Law* (Elgar, 2018) 251.

85    Michel Prieur and Gaëll Mainguy, 'Non-Regression in Environmental Law' (2012) 5(2) *SAPIENS* <https://journals.openedition.org/sapiens/1405>. See further Markus Vordermayer-Riemer, *Non-Regression in International Environmental Law* (Intersentia, 2021).

86    *Code de l'environnement* [Environmental Code] (France) art L.110-1(II)(9) <www.legifrance.gouv.fr/codes/article_lc/LEGIARTI000033033501/2018-06-30>.

87    *World Declaration* (n 28) 4.

88    *Paris Agreement* (n 30) art 4(3). Some of the history of the progression principle is traced in Christina Voigt and Felipe Ferreira, 'Dynamic Differentiation': The Principles of CBDR-RC, Progression and Highest Possible Ambition in the Paris Agreement' (2016) 5 *Transnational Environmental Law* 285.

and adequate conditions of life, in an environment of a quality that permits a life of dignity and well-being, and he bears a solemn responsibility to protect and improve the environment for present and future generations.'[89] Since that time, a number of attempts have been made to promote this concept internationally.[90] For example, Vice-President Weeramantry stated in *Gabčíkovo-Nagymaros Project* in 1997: 'The protection of the environment is . . . a vital part of contemporary human rights doctrine, for it is a *sine qua non* for numerous human rights such as the right to health and the right to life itself.'[91]

Further development of the links between human rights and the environment is seen in the UN *Declaration on the Rights of Indigenous Peoples 2007*,[92] which contains a substantive provision on the right to environment: 'Indigenous peoples have the right to the conservation and protection of the environment and the productive capacity of their lands or territories and resources.'[93] While the Declaration is by its nature limited to indigenous communities and individuals, it is important to note that they constitute around 5% of the world's population, numbering between 370 and 500 million worldwide, and make up some 15% of the world's poor.[94] They are also among the most discriminated against, especially with regard to access to their traditional lands and conservation of their cultural and natural environments. Of all the world's people, they depend most directly on the environment, which makes the right to environment and productive capacity of their lands of fundamental significance to them.

Building on previous initiatives, the UN Human Rights Council appointed a Special Rapporteur on the Right to Environment in 2011.[95] The Special Rapporteur's final report presented 16 Framework Principles that set out 'the basic obligations of States under human rights law as they relate to a safe, clean, healthy and sustainable environment',[96] and proposed recognising the human right to a healthy environment in a global instrument.

Principle 3 of the *World Declaration* also includes the right to environment: 'Each human, present and future, has the right to a safe, clean, healthy, and sustainable environment.'[97] At a regional level, the right has been recognised in one form or another, in the African,[98]

---

89    *Stockholm Declaration* (n 3).

90    See further Ben Boer, 'Environmental Principles and the Right to a Quality Environment' in Ludwig Krämer and Emanuela Orlando (eds), *Principles of Environmental Law* (Elgar, 2018) 52.

91    *Gabčíkovo-Nagymaros Project* (n 53) 91–2. This was a separate opinion of Vice-President Weeramantry.

92    *United Nations Declaration on the Rights of Indigenous Peoples*, UN Doc A/RES/61/295 (n 57).

93    Ibid art 29(1).

94    'Indigenous Peoples', *The World Bank* (Web Page) <www.worldbank.org/en/topic/ indigenouspeoples>.

95    'Special Rapporteur on Human Rights and the Environment', *United Nations Human Rights* (Web Page) <www.ohchr.org/en/Issues/environment/SRenvironment/Pages/SRenvironmentIndex.aspx>.

96    John H Knox, Special Rapporteur, *Report on Human Rights Obligations Relating to the Enjoyment of a Safe, Clean, Healthy and Sustainable Environment*, UN Doc A/HRC/37/59 (24 January 2018) annex ('*Framework Principles on Human Rights and the Environment*'); John H Knox, 'The United Nations Mandate on Human Rights and the Environment' (2018) 2(1) *Chinese Journal of Environmental Law* 83, 83–9.

97    *World Declaration* (n 28) 3.

98    *African Charter on Human and Peoples' Rights*, opened for signature 27 June 1981, 1520 UNTS 217 (entered in force 21 October 1986).

Inter-American[99] and Southeast Asian realms.[100] In 2021, the Human Rights Council noted that 'more than 155 States have recognized some form of a right to a healthy environment in, inter alia, international agreements or their national constitutions, legislation or policies'.[101] These developments culminated in a groundbreaking resolution by the Human Rights Council in October 2021 entitled *The Human Right to a Clean, Healthy and Sustainable Environment*.[102] The main operative paragraphs read:

> The Human Rights Council . . .
> 1. *Recognizes* the right to a clean and sustainable environment as a human right that is important for the enjoyment of human rights;
> 2. *Notes* that the right to a clean, healthy and sustainable environment is related to other rights that are in accordance with existing international law.
> 3. *Affirms* that the promotion of the human right to a clean, healthy and sustainable environment requires the full implementation of the multilateral environmental agreements under the principles of international environmental law; . . .

A historic resolution similar to that passed by the Human Rights Council was voted on by the UN General Assembly in July 2022.[103] The operative paragraphs read:

> The General Assembly . . .
> 1. *Recognizes* the right to a clean, healthy and sustainable environment as a human right;
> 2. *Notes* that the right to a clean, healthy and sustainable environment is related to other rights and existing international law;
> 3. *Affirms* that the promotion of the human right to a clean, healthy and sustainable environment requires the full implementation of the multilateral environmental agreements under the principles of international environmental law;
> 4. *Calls upon* States, international organizations, business enterprises and other relevant stakeholders to adopt policies, to enhance international cooperation, strengthen capacity-building and continue to share good practices in order to scale up efforts to ensure a clean, healthy and sustainable environment for all.

The adoption of this resolution is likely to have a marked effect on the future development, implementation and interpretation of many aspects of environmental law as well as human rights law at both international and national levels.

---

99   *Additional Protocol to the American Convention on Human Rights in the Area of Economic, Social and Cultural Rights*, opened for signature 17 November 1998, OAS 69 (entered into force 16 November 1999) art 11.

100   *ASEAN Human Rights Declaration* (adopted 18 November 2012) art 28(f). See Ben Boer, *Environmental Law Dimensions of Human Rights* (Oxford University Press, 2015) 135, 152–6.

101   *Human Rights and the Environment*, GA Res 46/7, UN Doc A/HRC/RES/46/7 (30 March 2021, adopted 23 March 2021).

102   *The Human Right to a Clean, Healthy and Sustainable Environment*, HRC Res 48/13, UN Doc A/HRC/RES/48/13 (adopted 8 October 2021).

103   *The Human Right to a Clean, Healthy and Sustainable Environment*, UN Doc A/RES/L.75 (n 1). See 'UN General Assembly Declares Access to Clean and Healthy Environment a Universal Human Right', *UN News* (Web Page, 28 July 2022) <https://news.un.org/en/story/2022/07/1123482>.

## 14.6 Selected environmental law issues

This section gives an overview of selected IEL instruments and topics in the areas of climate change, transboundary air pollution, chemicals and wastes, the conservation of biodiversity, and land degradation. Marine environmental matters are covered in Chapter 13.

### 14.6.1 Greenhouse gases and climate change

Historically, climate change has been a very slow natural process taking place over many centuries. However, from the beginning of the industrial revolution in the 18th century, the burning of fossils fuels has increased exponentially. Industrial processes, transport, forest clearing, and heating are the main sources of emission of greenhouse gases ('GHGs', often referred to as 'anthropogenic emissions'). These processes have resulted in much more rapid climate change.

All environmental media are detrimentally impacted by climate change: the impacts include increasingly extreme weather events; water scarcity and flooding; degraded land and soil; depletion of biodiversity in general and forest ecosystems in particular; and a variety of impacts on oceans and coasts, including sea-level rise and acidification. Each of these affect people in myriad ways, especially regarding forced migration of entire human communities; agricultural challenges; and food and water security. These effects have also resulted in a variety of associated human rights being affected, such as the right to property, right to shelter, right to livelihood and right to food and water. Of all the world's states affected by sea-level rise up to 2050, seven of the 10 most vulnerable states are in the Asia-Pacific region.[104] Vulnerable states include low-lying Pacific islands and delta states such as Bangladesh, Nigeria and Vietnam. Australia also continues to be seriously affected by climate change, manifested by the intensification of droughts, higher incidence of bushfires, severity of flood events, sea-level rise, and adverse effects on biodiversity, such as on the Great Barrier Reef, alpine areas, and rivers and lakes.

The most recent climate change instrument, intended to address these issues more robustly, is the 2015 *Paris Agreement* on climate change.[105] The Agreement builds on the UN *Framework Convention on Climate Change*[106] and its 1997 *Kyoto Protocol*.[107] The *Kyoto Protocol* placed specific obligations to reduce greenhouse gas emissions only on developed states, but the *Paris Agreement* imposes obligations on *all* states. The Agreement 'aims to strengthen the global response to the threat of climate change, in the context of sustainable development and efforts to eradicate poverty, including by... holding the increase in the global average temperature to well below 2°C above pre-industrial levels and pursuing efforts to limit the temperature increase to 1.5°C above pre-industrial levels'.[108] Although the *Paris Agreement* imposes obligations on all states, it nevertheless recognises the different capacities

---

104     Abstracted from *GEO-6 Regional Assessment for Asia and the Pacific* (n 10) 32.
105     *Paris Agreement* (n 30).
106     *United Nations Framework Convention on Climate Change*, opened for signature 9 May 1992, 1771 UNTS 107 (entered into force 21 March 1994).
107     *Kyoto Protocol to the United Nations Framework Convention on Climate Change*, opened for signature 11 December 1997, 2303 UNTS 148 (entered into force 16 February 2005).
108     *Paris Agreement* (n 30) art 2(1)(a).

of developed and developing states: '[T]his agreement will be implemented to reflect equity and the principle of common but differentiated responsibilities and respective capabilities, in the light of different national circumstances.'[109]

Further, each party is obliged to identify its own emission reduction targets and to pursue them through domestic mitigation measures.[110] The *Paris Agreement* also places more emphasis on adaptation to climate change, with the parties agreeing to 'establish the global goal on adaptation of enhancing adaptive capacity, strengthening resilience and reducing vulnerability to climate change'.[111] The SDGs, also agreed in 2015, complement the Agreement by requiring states to take urgent action to combat climate change and its impacts (SDG 13). Despite this sense of urgency, the *Sustainable Development Goals Report 2021* states: 'The world remains woefully off track in meeting the *Paris Agreement* target of limiting global warming to 1.5°C above pre-industrial levels and reaching net-zero carbon dioxide ($CO_2$) emissions globally by 2050.'[112]

The sixth assessment report of the Intergovernmental Panel on Climate Change[113] in 2021 makes it abundantly clear that much more effort is required with regard to both mitigation and adaptation, with the UN Secretary-General uttering the most strident warning on the environment ever issued at UN level, referring to the report as

> a code red for humanity. The alarm bells are deafening, and the evidence is irrefutable: greenhouse gas emissions from fossil fuel burning and deforestation are choking our planet and putting billions of people at immediate risk. Global heating is affecting every region on Earth, with many of the changes becoming irreversible ... We need immediate action on energy. Without deep carbon pollution cuts now, the 1.5-degree goal will fall quickly out of reach. This report must sound a death knell for coal and fossil fuels, before they destroy our planet.[114]

Notably, in 2021, the UN Human Rights Council passed a resolution setting out the mandate for the first Special Rapporteur to be appointed on the promotion and protection of human rights in the context of climate change.[115] This underlines the importance that this aspect of the effects of climate change has acquired, notwithstanding that the issue of human rights was only mentioned in the Preamble of the *Paris Agreement* and not in the substantive text.[116]

---

109    Ibid art 2(2).
110    Ibid art 4(2).
111    Ibid art 7(1).
112    United Nations Department of Economic and Social Affairs, *The Sustainable Development Goals Report 2021* (2021) 52 <https://unstats.un.org/sdgs/report/2021>.
113    Intergovernmental Panel on Climate Change, *Climate Change 2021: The Physical Science Basis* (Contribution of Working Group I to the Sixth Assessment Report of the IPCC, 2021) <www.ipcc.ch/report/ar6/wg1/#FullReport>.
114    *Secretary-General's Statement on the IPCC Working Group 1 Report on the Physical Science Basis of the Sixth Assessment* (United Nations, 9 August 2021) <www.un.org/sg/en/content/secretary-generals-statement-the-ipcc-working-group-1-report-the-physical-science-basis-of-the-sixth-assessment>.
115    *Mandate of the Special Rapporteur on the Promotion and Protection of Human Rights in the Context of Climate Change*, HRC Res 48/14, UN Doc A/HRC/RES/48/14 (13 October 2021, adopted 8 October 2021).
116    See further Ben Boer, 'The Preamble' in Geert van Calster and Leonie Reins (eds), *The Paris Agreement on Climate Change: A Commentary* (Edward Elgar 2021) 23, 23–5.

## 14.6.2 Transboundary air pollution

In addition to atmospheric pollution from greenhouse gases causing climate change, air pollution is addressed by several global and regional instruments. Since the atmosphere is a single global medium, many different types of air pollution can have transboundary effects on many states, their human communities, and on all other life.

The earliest regional instruments originated in Europe. The most important is the *Convention on Long-Range Transboundary Air Pollution* 1979,[117] negotiated when it was realised in the 1950s that sulphur emissions from industrial processes were acidifying lakes in Scandinavia. The Convention now has eight protocols on specific pollutants.[118] It recognises the need for cooperative monitoring and evaluation of the long-range transmission of air pollutants in Europe.[119] In the Asian region, the *ASEAN Agreement on Transboundary Haze Pollution*[120] is a legally binding instrument for the member states of the Association of Southeast Asian Nations aimed at reducing air pollution from forest fires in Southeast Asia.

## 14.6.3 Chemicals and wastes

The 1985 *Vienna Convention for the Protection of the Ozone Layer*[121] and its 1987 *Montreal Protocol*[122] address the phase-out of the manufacture and use of substances that deplete the ozone layer of the earth's atmosphere. The major ozone-depleting substances include chloro-fluorocarbons, halons and less damaging transitional chemicals such as hydrochlorofluorocarbons . Ozone depletion results in increasing the level of ultraviolet radiation that reaches the earth, leading to increased incidence of skin cancers and other effects on both humans and animals. The ozone regime is regarded as among the most effective and successful in IEL.[123]

The 2016 *Kigali Amendment*[124] is the fifth amendment to the *Montreal Protocol*. It aims to phase-down the use of hydrofluorocarbons ('HFCs'), which are used as substitutes for ozone-depleting substances. While HFCs are not themselves ozone-depleting, they are nevertheless strong greenhouse gases that contribute to global warming and climate change.[125] The *Kigali Amendment* is thus different from the other amendments, as it is not aimed at ozone-depleting substances as such. It sets specific targets and timetables in order to replace the

---

117     *Convention on Long-Range Transboundary Air Pollution*, opened for signature 15 November 1979, 1302 UNTS 217 (entered into force 16 March 1983).

118     See 'Protocols', *United Nations Economic Commission for Europe* (Web Page) <https://unece.org/protocols>.

119     'The Convention and Its Achievements', *United Nations Economic Commission for Europe* (Web Page) <https://unece.org/convention-and-its-achievements>.

120     *ASEAN Agreement on Transboundary Haze Pollution*, opened for signature 10 June 2022, ECOLEX TRE-001344 (entered into force 10 November 2003) <www.ecolex.org/details/treaty/asean-agreement-on-transboundary-haze-pollution-tre-001344>.

121     *Vienna Convention* (n 34).

122     *Montreal Protocol* (n 35).

123     Francesca Romanin Jacur, 'Convention for the Protection of the Ozone Layer 1985' in Malgosia Fitzmaurice et al (eds), *Multilateral Environmental Treaties* (Elgar, 2017) 313, 313–14.

124     *Amendment to the Montreal Protocol on Substances that Deplete the Ozone Layer*, opened for signature 15 October 2016, C.N.872.2016.TREATIES-XXVII.2.f (Depositary Notification) (entered into force 1 January 2019).

125     See United Nations Environment Programme, *Briefing Note: Ratification of the Kigali Amendment* (Ozone Secretariat, February 2017) 1.

use of HFCs with environment-friendly alternatives. It acts to prohibit or restrict parties to the *Montreal Protocol* or its amendments from trading in controlled substances with states that are yet to ratify the Protocol. It also includes agreement by wealthy countries to help finance the transition by poor countries to alternative safer products. The *Kigali Amendment* divides countries into three groups, each with a different target. The wealthiest states, such as EU countries, Australia, Canada and the United States, were required to reduce the production and consumption of HFCs from 2019. Most other states, such as China, Brazil and all states in Africa, are expected to stop the use of HFCs by 2024. A small number of very warm countries such as those in the Middle East, which have high use of air conditioning, must cease by 2028.[126]

The *Basel Convention on the Control of Transboundary Movements of Hazardous Wastes* ('*Basel Convention*')[127] deals with the transboundary transportation and disposal of hazardous wastes. It places specific obligations on states parties to ensure that hazardous wastes are managed and disposed of in an environmentally sound manner. It covers toxic, poisonous, explosive, corrosive, flammable, ecotoxic and infectious wastes. Amendments were adopted in 2019 aimed at improving the control of the transboundary movements of plastic waste, and clarifying the scope of the Convention with regard to plastics.[128]

The *Rotterdam Convention on the Prior Informed Consent Procedure for Certain Hazardous Chemicals and Pesticides in International Trade* ('*Rotterdam Convention*')[129] focuses on processes to obtain and exchange information between states parties concerning certain hazardous chemicals and pesticides in international trade. The Convention is particularly focused on setting out procedures for prior and informed consent with regard to developing countries, which are regarded as vulnerable because they often lack adequate infrastructure to monitor the import and use of the specified chemicals.

The objective of the *Stockholm Convention on Persistent Organic Pollutants* ('*Stockholm Convention*')[130] is to protect human health and the environment from persistent organic pollutants. It includes a range of measures to reduce or eliminate releases from intentional production and use of such pollutants, and to prohibit or limit production and use, and import and export of certain specified chemicals.

Air pollution from the manufacture and use of mercury has been an issue for many years, first highlighted by the effects of mercury poisoning on human health and the environment in Minamata, Japan in the 1950s.[131] Mercury poisoning was the subject of one of the protocols of the *Convention on Long-Range Transboundary Air Pollution*. In recent years, there was significant pressure to conclude a global convention, culminating in the *Minamata Convention on*

---

126    Summarised from 'The Kigali Amendment to the Montreal Protocol: Another Global Commitment to Stop Climate Change', *United Nations Environment Programme* (Web Page) <www.unenvironment.org/news-and-stories/news/kigali-amendment-montreal-protocol-another-global-commitment-stop-climate>.

127    *Basel Convention* (n 36).

128    'Basel Convention Plastic Waste Amendments', *United Nations Environment Programme* (Web Page) <www.basel.int/Implementation/Plasticwaste/Amendments/Overview/tabid/8426/Default.aspx>.

129    *Rotterdam Convention* (n 37).

130    *Stockholm Convention* (n 38).

131    Noriyuki Hachiya, 'The History and the Present of Minamata Disease: Entering the Second Half Century' (2006) 49 *Journal of the Japan Medical Association* 112.

*Mercury* 2013 ('*Minamata Convention*'),[132] the first global environmental agreement of the 21st century. It has 139 parties at the time of writing.[133]

The Convention deals with anthropogenic emissions of mercury, not natural emissions. In this respect it is similar to the *Framework Convention on Climate Change*. It is notable for covering the whole life cycle of this heavy metal. It bans new mercury mines, supports phasing out existing mines, and phasing out and phasing down mercury use in products and processes. It introduces control measures on emissions into the air, on land and in water. It also regulates artisanal and small-scale gold mining operations that use mercury. Further, the Convention addresses interim storage and disposal once the metal becomes waste, as well as sites contaminated by mercury.

The *Minamata Convention* links with the *Basel Convention*, the *Rotterdam Convention* and the *Stockholm Convention*. Together, these conventions provide a global regime covering manufacture, transport, use, storage and disposal of chemicals and hazardous wastes.[134]

## 14.6.4   Conservation of biological diversity

Biological diversity is conserved through a number of global and regional conventions. The most important are the 1971 *Ramsar Convention on Wetlands*,[135] the 1972 *World Heritage Convention*,[136] *CITES*,[137] the 1979 *Convention on the Conservation of Species of Migratory Animals*[138] and the 1992 *Convention on Biological Diversity*.[139] Although these instruments are independent of each other, there is a good deal of liaison to promote cooperation and coherence between them.[140]

Sustainable Development Goal 15 ('SDG 15') is also directly relevant to biodiversity, focusing on sustainable use of terrestrial ecosystems, sustainably managed forests, combating desertification, halting and reversing land degradation, and halting biodiversity loss. All of the above instruments are needed to achieve SDG 15. However, progress with respect to SDG 15 and its targets has been uneven; for example, with respect to forests, 'declining trends in land productivity, biodiversity loss and poaching and trafficking of wildlife remain serious concerns'.[141]

---

132   *Minamata Convention* (n 39).
133   'Party Profiles', *Minamata Convention on Mercury* (Web Page) <www.mercuryconvention.org/en/parties/overview>.
134   See further Dupuy and Viñuales (n 4) 283 ('Integrated Regulation: Mercury'). See also Sands and Peel (n 43) 276.
135   *Convention on Wetlands of International Importance Especially as Waterfowl Habitat*, opened for signature 2 February 1971, 996 UNTS 245 (entered into force 21 December 1975) ('*Ramsar Convention*').
136   *World Heritage Convention* (n 22).
137   *CITES* (n 23).
138   *Convention on the Conservation of Species of Migratory Animals* (n 33).
139   *Convention on Biological Diversity* (n 25).
140   'Liaison Group of Biodiversity-Related Conventions', *Convention on Biological Diversity* (Web Page) <www.cbd.int/blg>; 'COP 7 Decision VII/26: Cooperation with Other Conventions and International Organizations and Initiatives', *Convention on Biological Diversity* (Web Page) <www.cbd.int/decision/cop/default.shtml?id=7763>.
141   See, eg, 'Goal 15: Progress and Info: 2017', *Department of Economic and Social Affairs: Sustainable Development* (Web Page) <https://sdgs.un.org/goals/goal15>.

The *Convention on Biological Diversity*[142] has a complex range of functions, among the most of important of which is in-situ conservation of biodiversity, especially the establishment and maintenance of 'protected areas'. Article 8 obliges states parties 'as far as possible and as appropriate' to establish and manage systems of protected areas or areas requiring special measures needed to conserve biological diversity. Article 9 addresses ex-situ conservation of biodiversity, which is stated 'as far as possible and as appropriate' as being predominantly for the purpose of complementing in-situ conservation measures. Such measures are encouraged to 'establish and maintain facilities for ex-situ conservation of and research on plants, animals and micro-organisms, preferably in the country of origin of genetic resources'. These include zoological gardens, botanical gardens and seedbanks.

Article 15, on access to genetic resources, has become a very important aspect of the Convention, and is the basis for the *Nagoya Protocol on Access and Benefit Sharing*.[143] Article 19 of the Convention focuses on handling of biotechnology and distribution of its benefits, including advance informed agreement for 'the safe transfer, handling and use of any living modified organism resulting from biotechnology that may have adverse effects on the conservation and sustainable use of biological diversity'. This provision was the basis for the *Cartagena Protocol on Biosafety*,[144] aimed at preventing adverse effects of biotechnology on biodiversity and human health.

The world's vast but nevertheless dwindling forests represent the lion's share of terrestrial biodiversity.[145] However, there is no specific convention dealing with forests. Attempts from the 1992 Rio Conference onwards to introduce an MEA to deal with forest conservation have so far been unsuccessful. The current soft-law instrument is the *United Nations Forest Instrument*, so named in 2016.[146] It 'articulates a series of agreed policies and measures at the international and national levels to strengthen forest governance, technical and institutional capacity, policy and legal frameworks, forest sector investment and stakeholder participation'.[147] The UN Forum on Forests[148] meets on an annual basis, and has devised both a Strategic Plan for Forests[149] and an

---

142    *Convention on Biological Diversity* (n 25).

143    *Nagoya Protocol on Access to Genetic Resources and the Fair and Equitable Sharing of the Benefits Arising from Their Utilisation to the Convention on Biological Diversity*, opened for signature 29 October 2010, UN Doc CN 782 2010 TREATIES-1 (entered into force 12 October 2014).

144    *Cartagena Protocol on Biosafety to the Convention on Biological Diversity*, opened for signature 29 January 2000, 2226 UNTS 208 (entered into force 11 September 2003).

145    'Since 1990 it is estimated that 420 million hectares of forest have been lost through conversion to other land uses, although the rate of deforestation has decreased over the past three decades': 'State of the World's Forests 2020', *United Nations Food and Agriculture Organization* (Web Page) <www.fao.org/state-of-forests/en>.

146    *United Nations Forest Instrument*, GA Res 70/199, UN Doc A/RES/70/199 (16 February 2016). See 'UN Forest Instrument', *Department of Economic and Social Affairs: Forests* (Web Page) <www.un.org/esa/forests/documents/un-forest-instrument/index.html>.

147    'UNFI: United Nations Forest Instrument', *Department of Economic and Social Affairs: Forests* (Web Page) <www.un.org/esa/forests/wp-content/uploads/2018/12/UNFI__brochure.pdf>.

148    'UN Forum on Forests', *Department of Economic and Social Affairs: Forests* (Web Page) <www.un.org/esa/forests/forum/index.html>.

149    'United Nations Strategic Plan for Forests 2017–2030', *Department of Economic and Social Affairs: Forests* (Web Page) <www.un.org/esa/forests/documents/un-strategic-plan-for-forests-2030/index.html>.

International Arrangement on Forests to promote the implementation of sustainable forest management and the *Forest Instrument*.[150]

With regard to the conservation of wetlands, the *Ramsar Convention*[151] is of central importance to biodiversity conservation through the establishment of protected areas. It provides 'the framework for national action and international cooperation for the conservation and wise use of wetlands and their resources'.[152] It requires all states parties to declare at least one wetland for the Ramsar List. In 2022, there were 2,471 designated sites covering 255,640,401 hectares.[153] The countries with the most Ramsar sites are the United Kingdom (175) and Mexico (142). Australia has 67 Ramsar-listed wetlands covering around 8.3 million hectares and over 900 wetlands listed as nationally important.

The trafficking of wildlife is addressed by *CITES*.[154] This trade, both legal and illegal, continues to be a major threat to biodiversity worldwide, with millions of transactions recorded annually, worth billions of dollars. *CITES* provides varying degrees of protection via three appendices, relying on domestic legislation for implementation, to over 37,000 species of flora and fauna. It has attracted 184 parties to date.[155]

## 14.6.5  Land degradation

Until recently, land degradation had not attracted as much international legal attention as other environmental issues. However, improved understanding of soil erosion and land pollution has led to an increased focus on laws and policies relating to land degradation and its links to food security and the human right to food. Many of the world's regions suffer from land degradation, but the issue is most prominent on the African continent, where some 500,000 km$^2$ of land is estimated to be degraded. In Australia, 'about two thirds of agricultural land is degraded'.[156]

The causes of land degradation include soil erosion, salinisation, desertification, deforestation, forest fires, overcultivation, inefficient irrigation practices, overgrazing, overexploitation of resources and uncontrolled mining activities.[157] The degradation of land and soils has also become a significant topic because of their relevance to climate change. Land and soils are the second largest reservoir of carbon after the world's oceans, acting as natural carbon sinks; however, they are also a source of greenhouse gas emissions.[158] Because of unsustainable

---

150    'International Arrangement on Forests', *Department of Economic and Social Affairs: Forests* (Web Page) <www.un.org/esa/forests/documents/international-arrangement-on-forests/index.html>.

151    *Ramsar Convention* (n 135).

152    'About the Convention on Wetlands', *Ramsar* (Web Page) <www.ramsar.org>.

153    'Sites Number and Area by Year', *Ramsar Sites Information Service* (Web Page) <https://rsis.ramsar.org/?pagetab=2>.

154    *CITES* (n 23).

155    'What is CITES?', *CITES* (Web Page) <https://cites.org/eng/disc/what.php>.

156    Mick Lumb, 'Land Degradation' (Fact Sheet, The Australian Collaboration) 1 <https://australiancollaboration.com.au/pdf/FactSheets/Land-degradation-FactSheet.pdf>.

157    *GEO-6 Regional Assessment for Africa* (n 11) 45.

158    See Intergovernmental Panel on Climate Change, *Climate Change and Land* (Special Report, 2019): 'Land is simultaneously a source and a sink of CO$_2$ due to both anthropogenic and natural drivers, making it hard to separate anthropogenic from natural fluxes': at 10.

agricultural and grazing practices, land degradation is becoming a significant factor in global[159] and regional climate change policy.[160]

The UN *Convention to Combat Desertification in Countries Experiencing Serious Drought and/or Desertification* is the most significant legal instrument in this field.[161] However, the Convention does not cover all aspects of land degradation, being limited to arid, semi-arid and dry subhumid regions.[162]

An international instrument addressing all forms of land degradation has been called for, but progress continues to be slow.[163] However, target 15.3 of SDG 15 urges countries to address the issue of land and soil using the concept of 'land degradation neutrality', the achievement of which is now seen as an essential part of ecosystem restoration.[164]

# 14.7    Heritage conservation

## 14.7.1    The heritage conventions

Cultural and natural heritage has become a specialised area of study within the general field of environmental law. There are a number of conventions that are relevant to the protection and conservation of heritage. The *Convention for the Protection of Cultural Property in the Event of Armed Conflict*[165] and its two protocols[166] are important instruments in areas of the world where armed conflict occurs between and within countries. More recent instruments, such as the *Underwater Heritage Convention*,[167] the *Intangible Heritage Convention*[168] and the *Convention on Diversity of Cultural Expressions*[169] have also attracted a wide range of

---

159    Charlotte Streck and Agustina Gay, 'The Role of Soils in International Climate Change Policy' in Harald Ginzky et al (eds), *International Yearbook of Soil Law and Policy 2016* (Springer, 2017) 105.

160    Jonathan Verschuuren, 'Towards an EU Regulatory Framework for Climate-Smart Agriculture: The Example of Soil Carbon Sequestration' (2018) 7(2) *Transnational Environmental Law* 301.

161    *United Nations Convention to Combat Desertification in Those Countries Experiencing Serious Drought and/or Desertification Particularly in Africa*, opened for signature 17 June 1994, 1954 UNTS 3 (entered into force 26 December 1996).

162    'The Role of Regions under the UNCCD', *United Nations Convention to Combat Desertification* (Web Page) <www.unccd.int/convention/regions>.

163    See Ben Boer, Harald Ginzky and Irene L Heuser, 'International Soil Protection Law: History, Concepts, and Latest Developments' in Harald Ginzky et al (eds), *International Yearbook of Soil Law and Policy* (Springer, 2017) 50. See also Ben Boer and Ian Hannam, 'Developing a Global Soil Regime' (2015) 1 *International Journal of Rural Law and Policy* 1.

164    Ben Boer and Ian Hannam, 'Restoration of Ecosystems and Land Degradation Neutrality' in Narinder Kakar, Vesselin Popovski and Nicholas Robinson (eds), *Fulfilling the Sustainable Development Goals: On a Quest for a Sustainable World* (Routledge, 2022) 392.

165    *Convention for the Protection of Cultural Property in the Event of Armed Conflict*, opened for signature 14 May 1954, 249 UNTS 24 (entered into force 7 August 1956).

166    *Protocol for the Protection of Cultural Property in the Event of Armed Conflict*, opened for signature 14 May 1954, 249 UNTS 358 (entered into force 7 August 1956); *Second Protocol to the Hague Convention of 1954 for the Protection of Cultural Property in the Event of Armed Conflict*, opened for signature 26 March 1999, 2253 UNTS 172 (entered into force 9 March 2004).

167    *Convention on the Protection of the Underwater Cultural Heritage*, opened for signature 2 November 2001, 2562 UNTS 3 (entered into force 2 January 2009).

168    *Convention on the Safeguarding of the Intangible Heritage*, opened for signature 17 October 2003, 2368 UNTS 1 (entered into force 20 April 2006).

169    *Convention on the Protection and Promotion of the Diversity of Cultural Expressions*, opened for signature 20 October 2005, 2440 UNTS 311 (entered into force 18 March 2007).

membership of states parties. Two further conventions, with respect to illegal dealing in movable cultural heritage property, are the 1970 UNESCO Convention[170] and the 1995 UNIDROIT Convention.[171] Section 14.7.2 focuses on the *World Heritage Convention* as an illustration of the dynamism of the international heritage law field, especially in the Australian context.

## 14.7.2   The *World Heritage Convention*

The *World Heritage Convention*[172] must be read in conjunction with its Operational Guidelines,[173] which are regularly reviewed and revised by the World Heritage Committee. The Guidelines set out in detail how the Convention should be implemented. Importantly, they include 10 criteria for judging whether or not a World Heritage nomination is of 'outstanding universal value'. If the property does not have one or more of such values, it cannot be listed. The first six of these criteria are focused on the cultural heritage and the last four are focused on the natural heritage.[174] Further, a property must also meet the conditions of authenticity and/or integrity, and must have an adequate protection and management system specified.[175] Once a state nominates a property, even if the Committee does not inscribe a property on the list, there is an obligation to protect the property as if it were a World Heritage-listed item.[176]

With regard to the national obligations of states parties to the Convention, art 5 includes an important provision: each state party 'shall endeavour, in so far as possible, and as appropriate for each country: ... (d) to take the appropriate legal, scientific, technical, administrative and financial measures necessary for the identification, protection, conservation, presentation and rehabilitation of this heritage'.[177] The Guidelines also indicate: 'All properties inscribed on the World Heritage List must have adequate long-term legislative, regulatory, institutional and/or traditional protection and management to ensure their safeguarding.'[178] Despite the fact that the Convention has been in force since 1974, only a few states have introduced specific legislation in some form to implement the Convention: these are Australia, Hungary, Italy, Macedonia, Romania, South Africa, Suriname and the United States.

---

170   *Convention on the Means of Prohibiting and Preventing the Illicit Import, Export and Transfer of Ownership of Cultural Property*, opened for signature 14 November 1970, 823 UNTS 231 (entered in force 24 April 1972).

171   *UNIDROIT Convention on Stolen or Illegally Exported Cultural Objects*, opened for signature 20 June 1995, 2421 UNTS 457 (entered into force 1 July 1998).

172   *World Heritage Convention* (n 22).

173   *Operational Guidelines for the Implementation of the World Heritage Convention*, UN Doc WHC.21/01 (31 July 2021) ('*Operational Guidelines*') <https://whc.unesco.org/en/guidelines>.

174   Ibid [77].

175   Ibid [79]–[95] (authenticity and/or integrity), [96]–[119] (protection and management).

176   *World Heritage Convention* (n 22) art 12 provides: 'The fact that a property belonging to the cultural or natural heritage has not been included in either of the two lists mentioned in paragraphs 2 and 4 of Article 11 [World Heritage List and List of World Heritage in Danger] shall in no way be construed to mean that it does not have an outstanding universal value for purposes other than those resulting from inclusion in these lists'. As stated by Dawson J: 'Once identified, even if there is a refusal to enter such a property on the World Heritage List, it does not cease to be part of the cultural or natural heritage and the obligations imposed by the Convention in relation to it remain in force': *Queensland v Commonwealth* (1989) 167 CLR 232, 245–6.

177   *World Heritage Convention* (n 22) art 59(d).

178   *Operational Guidelines* (n 173) [97].

The World Heritage Committee has identified a wide range of threats to listed properties. These include: buildings and development; transportation infrastructure; utilities or service infrastructure; pollution of all kinds; the use and modification of biological resources; extraction of physical resources, such as mining, oil and gas; local environmental conditions affecting the physical fabric of sites; the social and/or cultural uses of heritage items; climate change and severe weather events; ecological or geological events such as fires, avalanches and earthquakes; invasive and/or alien species; and management and institutional factors including adequacy of legal frameworks.[179]

Where threats become 'serious and specific dangers', the Committee can place a property on the List of World Heritage in Danger, under art 11(4). This is a powerful tool to ensure that states protect their World Heritage–listed items. Importantly, such properties can be listed by the Committee without the specific consent of the concerned state. In 2022, the number of 'in danger' listings stood at 55 properties, in a wide range of countries.[180] Placement on the List of World Heritage in Danger may result in increased international attention and pressure directed at the respective state to increase its conservation efforts or reconsider its decisions concerning threatening activities, including development of physical infrastructure, as well as attracting financial and technical assistance that may assist in removing the property from the in-danger list.

As of 2022 there were 194 states parties, with 167 having properties listed. The total number of listed properties stood at 1,157; this comprised 900 cultural properties, 218 natural properties and 39 mixed cultural and natural properties. Some states, such as China, Italy, Germany and Spain, have a high number of inscriptions, others have only one or two, and some states have not yet nominated properties for the list.[181]

### 14.7.2.1    The *World Heritage Convention* in Australia

Australia was one of the earliest jurisdictions to ratify the Convention, in 1974. As of 2022, it had 20 sites listed, ranging from the Great Barrier Reef in 1981 to the Sydney Opera House in 2006 to the Budj Bim Cultural Landscape in 2019. Australia's experience with the *World Heritage Convention* is an important one, having enacted the world's first national legislation specifically for the protection of properties on the World Heritage List. The *World Heritage Properties Conservation Act 1983* (Cth)[182] led to litigation in the Federal Court and the High Court. Australia is one of the only jurisdictions in the world to generate significant jurisprudence on the interpretation of the Convention. From a constitutional law point of view,[183] the most important case was *Commonwealth v Tasmania*, also known as the *Franklin Dam* case.[184] This case examined the extent of Australia's national obligations, the 'federal' clause, and the external affairs power under the *Australian Constitution* (on which, see Chapter 4).

179    'List of Factors Affecting the Properties', World *Heritage Convention* (Web Page) <https://whc.unesco .org/en/factors>.

180    'List of World Heritage in Danger', *World Heritage Convention* (Web Page) <https://whc.unesco.org/ en/danger>.

181    'World Heritage List', *World Heritage Convention* (Web Page) <https://whc.unesco.org/en/list>.

182    This legislation was repealed by the *Environment Protection and Biodiversity Conservation Act 1999* (Cth), which includes extensive provisions on world heritage.

183    See James Crawford, 'The Constitution and the Environment' (1991) 13(1) *Sydney Law Review* 11, 30.

184    *Commonwealth v Tasmania* (1983) 158 CLR 1.

This and several subsequent cases in the High Court and the Federal Court have made it clear that the Australian federal government has broad powers over environmental matters, including decisions concerning world heritage.[185]

Two of Australia's world heritage properties have been considered for in-danger listing. The first of these is Kakadu National Park in the Northern Territory, which was considered for in-danger listing in 2001 as a result of a report from the International Council for Science and the IUCN on the threat of river pollution from the Ranger uranium mine in an enclave of the park.[186] In-danger listing was avoided due to strong international lobbying by the Australian government.[187] The second property, the Great Barrier Reef, was recommended for in-danger listing in 2015 and again in 2021, due to concern about climate change–related rising average temperatures of the waters of the reef which is resulting in coral bleaching; also cited were the effects of pesticides and fertilisers from agricultural run-off. The report of an official UNESCO mission in March 2022 concluded that 'the property meets the criteria for inscription on the List of Word Heritage in Danger', with the consequent recommendation that it be placed on the List of World Heritage in Danger by the World Heritage Committee.[188] The report included 10 'high priority' recommendations 'that require to be implemented with the upmost urgency'[189] to address the more immediate concerns with regard to improvement of water quality. These included recommending that the 'Reef 2050 Plan is strengthened to include clear government commitments to reduce greenhouse emissions consistent with the efforts required to limit the global average temperate increase to 1.5°C above pre-industrial levels'.[190] The response to this report from the newly appointed federal Minister for the Environment noted that the report's criticisms were focused on the previous government's policies, and that governmental targets for reducing Australia's greenhouse emissions had increased significantly.[191]

Further tests of the strength of the resolve of the Australian and relevant state and territory governments to protect Australia's listed and nominated properties under the *World Heritage Convention* will no doubt occur in the future.

---

185    See Ben Boer and Donald R Rothwell, 'From the Franklin to Berlin: The Internationalisation of Australian Environmental Law and Policy' (1995) 17(2) *Sydney Law Review* 242, 258. See further Ben Boer, 'World Heritage Disputes in Australia' (1992) 7 *Journal of Environmental Law and Litigation* 247, 278–9; Ben Boer and Graeme Wiffen, 'The World Heritage Convention in Australia' in *Heritage Law in Australia* (Oxford University Press, 2006) 63.

186    *Joint ICSU/IUCN Mission Report, Kakadu National Park, 3–7 July 2000* (July 2000); Bureau of the World Heritage Committee, United Nations Educational, Scientific and Cultural Organization, *Item 4 on the Provisional Agenda: State of Conservation of Properties Inscribed on the List of World Heritage in Danger and on the World Heritage List*, 24th ordinary sess, UNESCO Doc WHC-2000/CONF.202/5 (22 May 2000) <https://whc.unesco.org/en/documents/307>.

187    William Logan, 'Australia, Indigenous Peoples and World Heritage from Kakadu to Cape York: State Party Behaviour under the World Heritage Convention' (2013) 13(2) *Journal of Social Archaeology* 153, 153–6. See also 'Brereton Accuses Govt of Kakadu Tricks', *PM* (ABC Radio National, 1 July 1999) <www.abc.net.au/pm/stories/s32902.htm>.

188    Eleanor Carter and Hans Thulstrup, *Report on the Joint World Heritage Centre/IUCN Reactive Monitoring Mission to the Great Barrier Reef (Australia)* (March 2022) 5.

189    Ibid 5, 28–9.

190    Ibid 54.

191    Michael Slezak, 'United Nations Recommends Great Barrier Reef Be Added to World Heritage "In-Danger" List', *ABC News* (online, 29 November 2022) <www.abc.net.au/news/2022-11-29/united-nations-queensland-great-barrier-reef-danger-report/101705908>.

# DISCUSSION QUESTIONS

(1)   Which actors are involved in the making of international environmental law?

(2)   How and why has the concept of sustainable development become a central part of international environmental law?

(3)   What are the most fundamental principles in international environmental law?

(4)   How and why are the fields of international environmental law and human rights law linked?

(5)   Is the international environmental law regime complete?

(6)   How can international environmental law be made more effective?

# 15

# INTERNATIONAL ORGANISATIONS

Ben Saul

# 15.1   Introduction

States often need to cooperate with each another to address legal and other issues of common concern across many fields in an interdependent world. International organisations ('IOs') emerged in the 19th century as a means of intensifying and permanently institutionalising international cooperation, through bodies with an international legal personality, and functions and powers, separate from their member states. While the earliest IOs had a narrow technical focus, the League of Nations (1919–46) and United Nations (since 1945) reflect a more ambitious global agenda of broad-spectrum cooperation. The proliferation of IOs has generated some key legal issues which this chapter explores: how to define IOs; the nature, extent and consequences of their international legal personality; their powers, immunities and privileges; and the scope of their legal responsibility for their conduct. There is a special focus on the United Nations, as a universal IO with competence in many areas of international life and human activity, and from whose establishment and practice much of the international law of IOs has emerged.

# 15.2   Origins and purposes of international organisations

The origins of IOs can be traced to more rudimentary forms of cooperation in earlier times, including federations and confederations,[1] conferences or congresses of states,[2] and alliances. The modern development of IOs was spurred in the 19th century by the growth of trade and new transport and communications technologies,[3] as well as pressure from civil society bodies for greater inter-state cooperation on common issues – for instance to outlaw slavery, codify international law, encourage international commerce or develop international humanitarian law.[4]

The emergence of IOs was also stimulated by a long and rich intellectual tradition. Ideas about the universal political unity, as through notions of 'world government', can be traced to ancient thought in China, India, Greece and Rome,[5] certain religious traditions, and thinkers such as the 13th century Italian Christian philosopher Dante Alighieri,[6] the 17th century English philosopher Thomas Hobbes,[7] and the 18th century German philosopher Immanuel Kant.[8]

---

1    Robert Kolb, 'International Organisations or Institutions, History of' in Rüdiger Wolfrum (ed), *The Max Planck Encyclopedia of Public International Law* (Oxford University Press, online, January 2011) [8]–[9].

2    Jan Klabbers, *An Introduction to International Institutional Law* (Cambridge University Press, 2002) 17.

3    Anne Peters and Simone Peter, 'International Organisations: Between Technocracy and Democracy' in Bardo Fassbender and Anne Peters (eds), *The Oxford Handbook of the History of International Law* (Oxford University Press, 2012) 170, 171.

4    Philippe Sands and Pierre Klein, *Bowett's Law of International Institutions* (Sweet & Maxwell, 5th ed, 2001) 5–6.

5    Derek Heater, *World Citizenship and Government: Cosmopolitan Ideas in the History of Western Political Thought* (Macmillan, 1996) ix–x.

6    Dante Alighieri, *Convivio* (bk 4, ch 4, 1304–07) in Cary Nederman and Kate Forhan (eds), *Medieval Political Theory: A Reader, 1100–1400* (Routledge, 1993) 168, 169.

7    Thomas Hobbes, *Leviathan* (Penguin, 1986) 286 (first published in 1651).

8    Immanuel Kant, 'Perpetual Peace: A Philosophical Sketch', tr HB Nisbet in Hans Reiss (ed), *Kant: Political Writings* (Cambridge University Press, 2nd ed, 1991) 93, 104–5, 113–14 [trans of: 'Zum ewigen Frieden: Ein philosophischer Entwurf' (1795)].

Aspirations to world government have often met objections as to their practicality, utopianism, impact on state sovereignty, and risks of tyranny or imperialism.[9]

The earliest modern IOs in the 19th century instead addressed discrete technical issues and avoided overtly 'political' questions or supranational ambitions. An early example is the establishment, by seven riparian states at the Congress of Vienna in 1915, of the Central Commission for the Navigation of the Rhine, with regulatory and judicial powers. Numerous specialised bodies were created in other technical fields in the second half of the 19th century and early 20th century, ranging from postal services to public health, including the predecessors of some of today's IOs.

The powers and degree of institutionalisation differed between organisations. Some possessed 'permanent deliberative or legislative organs working with administrative organs' (as in relation to telegraphy, metrics, and postal services); others operated more restrictively through periodic conferences of states supported by permanent secretariats (as for railway freight); and some exercised judicial power (as with river commissions) or arbitral power (as with railway freight).[10] The operating costs were born by member states. Decisions could often be made by majority not unanimity,[11] enabling effective decision-making.

## 15.2.1   League of Nations 1919

The establishment of the League of Nations in 1919 was a turning point in the evolution of IOs, being a far more ambitious organisation than the technical bodies which preceded it. It was created in response to World War I, which killed perhaps 10 million soldiers and 4–7 million civilians (and wounded many more),[12] redrew state borders and changed the geopolitical world order. There were 32 founding member states (including the British Dominion of Australia, which was not yet fully independent); at its peak (1934–35), it had 58 members (including their colonial territories) – most states in the world at that time (compared to 193 member states of the current United Nations). The League's purposes are set out in the 1919 *Covenant of the League of Nations*, adopted under the *Treaty of Versailles* settling the war:

> [T]o promote international co-operation and to achieve international peace and security
>> by the acceptance of obligations not to resort to war,
>> by the prescription of open, just and honourable relations between nations,
>> by the firm establishment of the understandings of international law as the actual rule of conduct among Governments, and
>> by the maintenance of justice and a scrupulous respect for all treaty obligations in the dealings of organised peoples with one another ...[13]

9     Heater (n 5) 187–200; Catherine Lu, 'World Government' in Edward N Zalta (ed), *Stanford Encyclopedia of Philosophy* (Spring 2021 ed) <https://plato.stanford.edu/archives/spr2021/entries/world-government/>.
10    Sands and Klein (n 4) 8.
11    Ibid 8–9.
12    Norman Davies, *Europe: A History* (Pimlico, 1997) 925, 1328–9; Ian Beckett, *The Great War 1914–1918* (Routledge, 2nd ed, 2007) 438.
13    *Treaty of Peace between the Allied and Associated Powers and Germany*, signed 28 June 1919, 225 CTS 188 (entered into force 10 January 1920) pt I ('*League Covenant*') Preamble ('*Covenant of the League of Nations*').

Progressive disarmament, consistent with national defence, was a core goal of the Covenant and its Disarmament Commission,[14] but this was thwarted by the geopolitical tensions in Europe in the 1920s and the deteriorating security situation in the 1930s.[15] The Covenant restrained the use of military force but did not outlaw war, and its collective security provisions were a step forward but proved too weak in practice (see Chapter 8).

The Covenant also sought to address the structural causes of conflict and injustice which contributed to war. During the war, US president Woodrow Wilson (along with anti-imperialist Russian Bolsheviks) championed the principle of self-determination,[16] meaning the right of national populations to become independent of foreign rule. This idea underlay various elements of the Versailles settlement:[17] the dissolution of the Austro-Hungarian and Ottoman empires, and statehood for their component nations (or 'peoples'); the protection of national minorities in other states; and the Covenant's system of 'mandate' territories,[18] involving international supervision of the governance of some colonial and dependent territories. The mandate system did not, however, guarantee all peoples an ultimate right of independent statehood.

The Covenant also empowered the League, including through technical bodies, to address a wide spectrum of human problems, including fair and humane labour conditions; just treatment of 'native' inhabitants; human trafficking; drug trafficking; the arms trade; freedom of communications, transit and commerce; development; and disease control.[19]

Structurally, the League (based in Geneva) had three principal organs: an Assembly and a Council comprised of state representatives, and a permanent Secretariat of international civil servants. A Permanent Court of International Justice was established by its Statute of 1920,[20] but was independent of the League. All member states were represented in the Assembly.[21] The Council was more exclusive, comprised of the Allied and associated powers who won the war (with Germany added later), plus four elected member states[22] (increased to 11 by 1936). Both the Assembly and the Council had the same competence to address 'any matter within the sphere of action of the League or affecting the peace of the world'.[23] Both normally had to adopt unanimous decisions,[24] although this was moderated in practice in the Assembly.[25] The decisions of the Council and the Assembly were not binding on member states. While this weakened the League's capacity to enforce the Covenant, it was all that states could agree to at the time.

The League was fatally undermined by geopolitical realities, including the refusal of the United States (blocked by its hostile Senate) to become a member; the Great Depression of

---

14    Ibid arts 8–9.
15    FP Walters, *A History of the League of Nations* (Oxford University Press, 1952) 217–30, 361–76, 500–16, 541–55, 763–6.
16    See, eg, Woodrow Wilson, *Address of the President of the United States, Delivered at a Joint Session of the Two Houses of Congress, January 8, 1918* (US GPO, 1918) (the 'Fourteen Points').
17    See generally Margaret Macmillan, *Paris 1919* (Random House, 2001).
18    *Covenant of the League of Nations* (n 13) art 22. See Susan Pedersen, *The Guardians: The League of Nations and the Crisis of Empire* (Oxford University Press, 2015).
19    *Covenant of the League of Nations* art 23(a)–(f).
20    Ibid art 14.
21    Ibid art 3(3).
22    Ibid art 4(1).
23    Ibid arts 3(3), 4(4).
24    Ibid art 5(1).
25    Sands and Klein (n 4) 11.

1929–39 and its political shockwaves (including fascism in Europe and militarism in Japan); and the lawful withdrawal in the 1930s of aggressor states such as Japan, Germany and Italy, and expulsion of the Soviet Union (for invading Finland) in 1939 (it had only joined in 1934).[26] The League was nonetheless a bold and invaluable experiment in the institutionalisation of cooperation, resolving many disputes, developing international law and cooperatively addressing a wide range of technical problems. The League formally dissolved itself in 1946, and was replaced by the United Nations, founded in 1945.

## 15.2.2   Contemporary international organisations

Many lessons were drawn from the League of Nations when designing the *Charter of the United Nations* ('*UN Charter*') of 1945 – including the need to include the great powers, and to make withdrawing from the organisation more difficult; confer binding powers to maintain international security; eliminate colonialism as a cause of conflict; and strengthen international law, development and human rights.[27] The United Nations now has a near-universal membership of 193 member states, and a wide competence to address most common human problems, and is regarded as the 'supreme type' of IO.[28] Many principles of the modern law of IOs flowed from its establishment. The United Nations is discussed in Section 15.7.

Beyond the archetype of the United Nations, now there are at least 289 and as many as 2,140 diverse IOs.[29] At the level of *membership*, some are open to all states, such as the United Nations and the World Trade Organization ('WTO', a body to liberalise trade). Others are limited to states based on geographical regions,[30] identity attributes[31] or common interests.[32]

In terms of *functions*, IOs can have a wide competence (such as the United Nations, charged with addressing the gamut of human problems, except matters exclusively within domestic jurisdiction[33]); more commonly, they have competence in specialised areas such as trade or human rights.

Considering the *powers* exercised, IOs may have powers that are legislative (such as the European Union), judicial (the International Criminal Court), political (the Organization for Security and Co-operation in Europe or 'OSCE'), security-oriented (North Atlantic Treaty Organization or 'NATO'), technical (the World Meteorological Organization) or a mixture (the United Nations).[34]

---

26    In total, seven states either withdrew, ceased to exist, or were expelled.
27    See Daniel-Erasmus Kahn, 'Drafting History' in Bruno Simma et al (eds), *The Charter of the United Nations: A Commentary* (Oxford University Press, 3rd ed, 2012) vol 1, 1.
28    *Reparation for Injuries Suffered in the Service of the United Nations (Advisory Opinion)* [1949] ICJ Rep 174, 179.
29    Union of International Associations, *Yearbook of International Organizations 2020–2021* (Brill, 57th ed, 2020) vol 5, 27, Figure 2.1.
30    Such as the African Union, European Union, Organization of American States, South Asian Association for Regional Cooperation, the Commonwealth of Independent States, the Shanghai Cooperation Organization, the Association of Southeast Asian Nations, or the Pacific Islands Forum.
31    Such as based on identity or history, including the Organization of Islamic Cooperation, League of Arab States, (British) Commonwealth or the *Francophonie*.
32    Such as the Organization for Security Co-operation in Europe ('OSCE'), the Organization of the Petroleum Exporting Countries ('OPEC'), river commissions, or regional or species-specific fisheries arrangements.
33    *Charter of the United Nations* art 2(7) ('*UN Charter*').
34    See Kolb (n 1) [14].

At the level of *institutionalisation*, IOs can be lightly organised, or involve more intensive structures. Since separate international legal personality (discussed in Section 13.3.3) is a necessary element, all IOs must have a structure (such as a plenary political or legislative organ) that is distinct from the member states collectively, and many will also have an executive body and an administrative secretariat. The number, nature, complexity and powers of their organs (and any subsidiary organs established by them) vary between organisations.

The most institutionalised organisations are those of a 'supranational' character, meaning that their organs have the capacity to directly make and enforce laws binding on member states, without the need for states to separately ratify treaties. The European Union is the paradigm, but its authority is still limited in fields such as common foreign and security policy.[35]

# 15.3  What is an international organisation?

It is challenging to generally define IOs to reflect their diversity of purposes and functions, powers, constituent instruments, organs and memberships. A useful starting point is art 2(a) of the International Law Commission's (non-binding) Draft Articles on the Responsibility of International Organizations 2011, which defines an IO as 'an organization established by a treaty or other instrument governed by international law and possessing its own international legal personality. IOs may include as members, in addition to States, other entities'.[36] Each element is discussed in the following sections.

## 15.3.1  Established by international law

International organisations are usually established by treaty. They could, however, be created by another instrument under international law, such as resolutions of an IO (such as the General Assembly resolution granting independence to the UN Industrial Development Organization); or a conference of states (the Organisation for Petroleum Exporting Countries was established by five states at the Baghdad Conference in 1960).[37] The World Trade Organization was established as follows:

> **Marrakesh Agreement Establishing the World Trade Organization 1994**[38]
>
> *Article I: Establishment of the Organization*
>
> The World Trade Organization (hereinafter referred to as 'the WTO') is hereby established.

The International Law Commission's definition does not include entities created purely by domestic law, including inter-governmental commercial or non-profit entities, or private bodies or non-government organisations ('NGOs'), even if states are members, shareholders or directors. An example is the International Union for Conservation of Nature.[39] This limitation

---

35    Ibid [18].

36    'Draft Articles on the Responsibility of International Organizations' [2011] II(2) *Yearbook of the International Law Commission* 1, 40 ('*DARIO*').

37    Ibid.

38    *Marrakesh Agreement Establishing the World Trade Organization*, opened for signature 15 April 1994, 1867 UNTS 3 (entered into force 1 January 1995 ('*WTO Agreement*').

39    'Draft Articles on the Responsibility of International Organizations, with Commentaries' [2011] II(2) *Yearbook of the International Law Commission* 1, 47, 50 (Draft Article 2 Commentary [6]) ('*DARIO Commentary*'); Kolb (n 1) [6].

applies even if the entity is endowed with rights by a treaty but is not created by it, and even if it bears sui generis international personality, such as the International Committee of the Red Cross (established under Swiss law). Nor does the definition include bodies established under treaties and charged with particular functions, but whose members do not include states (such as UN human rights monitoring committees of experts).[40]

## 15.3.2   Membership including states

An essential characteristic of IOs is membership including states. Many IOs are purely inter-governmental, including the United Nations.[41] The fact of being a state does not entitle an applicant to membership of any IO. Eligibility depends on the organisation's constituent instrument and/or the will of the member states. There can also be different classes of membership for states. The State of Palestine, for example, has been a non-member observer state of the General Assembly since 2012,[42] without the status and privileges (including voting rights) of member states.

International organisations may choose to open membership (including of a lesser status) to non-state actors (even if they lack capacity to enter into the constituent treaty[43]). These may include other IOs (such as European Community membership of the WTO,[44] with individual European states simultaneously being members); non-state territorial entities (such as customs territories in the WTO,[45] or dependent territories in the World Meteorological Organization[46]); groups of states (as in the International Coffee Organization[47]); or private entities (such as companies or NGOs as affiliate members of the World Tourism Organization[48]).

Membership of the International Labour Organization is only open to states, but, innovatively, each state must send to the Annual Conference (the Organization's supreme deliberative body) two government representatives, one representative of workers and one representative of employers, all of whom are entitled to vote independently.[49] The International Labour Organization's standing 56-person Governing Body reflects the same weighted 'tripartite' structure.[50]

---

40    Kirsten Schmalenbach, 'International Organisations or Institutions, General Aspects' in Rüdiger Wolfrum (ed), *The Max Planck Encyclopedia of Public International Law* (Oxford University Press, online, October 2020) [10].

41    *UN Charter* art 4.

42    *Status of Palestine in the United Nations*, GA Res 67/19, UN Doc A/RES/67/19 (4 December 2012).

43    *DARIO Commentary* (n 39) 49–50 (Draft Article 2 Commentary [5]).

44    *WTO Agreement* (n 38) art XI.

45    Ibid art XII(1) ('separate customs territory possessing full autonomy in the conduct of its commercial relations').

46    *Convention of the World Meteorological Organization*, opened for signature 11 October 1947, 778 UNTS 143 (entered into force 23 March 1950) art 3(d)–(f).

47    *International Coffee Agreement*, opened for signature 28 September 2007 (entered into force 2 February 2011) art 4.

48    *Statute of the World Tourism Organization*, opened for signature 28 September 1970 (entered into force 2 January 1975) art 7.

49    *Treaty of Peace between the Allied and Associated Powers and Germany*, signed 28 June 1919, 225 ConTS 188 (entered into force 10 January 1920) pt XIII ('*The Constitution of the International Labour Organization*') (as amended) art 3.

50    Ibid art 7.

International organisations may further allow non-state actors to participate as non-member, non-voting observers or partners. For example, over 6,000 NGOs have 'consultative status' with the UN Economic and Social Council.[51]

Membership of an IO generates legal rights and duties for both members and the organisation, including in relation to decision-making and voting, the budget, and implementing constitutional obligations or decisions.[52] Withdrawal from an organisation is normally governed by the organisation's constituent instrument or by the default law-of-treaties rule on denunciation.[53] Suspension or expulsion may also be governed by the constituent instrument.

Occasionally, organisations may change their view on which government represents a member state, as when the United Nations voted to recognise the (communist) People's Republic of China as the representative of the state of China instead of the (nationalist) Republic of China[54] (Taiwan). Where a member state disappears,[55] an organisation may recognise a successor state, such as Russia's continued UN membership in place of the Soviet Union in 1991[56] (the former Soviet Republics became new UN members), or require new states to reapply for membership (as for all states which emerged from the dissolution of Yugoslavia between 1992 and 2006).[57]

## 15.3.3  International legal personality

To constitute an IO an entity must possess international legal personality – a status and capacities distinct from its member states,[58] with a will of its own. As discussed in Chapter 1, the notion of personality originally derives from the core characteristics of states, namely the capacity to enter into treaties, to bring and receive international claims, and to enter into relations with other states. It is now recognised that entities other than states may possess international legal personality, but it is *relative* in that their legal capacities are less than those of states and vary between IOs, as discussed in this section.

---

51    United Nations, Economic and Social Council, *List of Non-Governmental Organizations in Consultative Status with the Economic and Social Council as at 1 September 2019: Note by the Secretary-General*, UN Doc E/2019/INF/5 (2 March 2021).

52    Henry Schermers and Niels Blokker, 'International Organisations or Institutions, Membership' in Rüdiger Wolfrum (ed), *The Max Planck Encyclopedia of Public International Law* (Oxford University Press, online, January 2008) [12]–[14].

53    Namely, *Vienna Convention on the Law of Treaties*, opened for signature 23 May 1969, 1155 UNTS 331 (entered into force 27 January 1980) art 56.

54    *Restoration of the Lawful Rights of the People's Republic of China in the United Nations*, GA Res 2758 (XXVI), UN Doc A/RES/2758(XXVI) (25 October 1971).

55    See Michael Scharf, 'Musical Chairs: The Dissolution of States and Membership in the United Nations' (1995) 28(1) *Cornell International Law Journal* 29.

56    UN Doc 1991/RUSSIA (24 December 1991) appendix ('Letter from President of the Russian Federation, Boris Yeltsin, to the UN Secretary-General').

57    General Assembly resolutions on admission to membership in the United Nations: GA Res 46/238, UN Doc A/RES/46/238 (22 May 1992) (Croatia); GA Res 46/237, UN Doc A/RES/46/237 (22 May 1992) (Bosnia and Herzegovina); GA Res 46/236, UN Doc A/RES/46/236 (22 May 1992) (Slovenia); GA Res 47/225, UN Doc A/RES/47/225 (8 April 1993) (Macedonia); GA Res 55/12, UN Doc A/RES/55/12 (1 November 2000) (Yugoslavia); GA Res 60/264, UN Doc A/RES/60/264 (28 June 2006) (Montenegro).

58    *DARIO Commentary* (n 39) 50 (Draft Article 2 Commentary [7]); *Reparation for Injuries* (n 28) 179.

The constituent instruments of few IOs explicitly claim international personality; examples include those of the European Union,[59] the WTO,[60] the Association of Southeast Asian Nations[61] and the International Criminal Court.[62] The *Marrakesh Agreement Establishing the World Trade Organization* states simply that '[t]he WTO shall have legal personality'.[63] The instruments of most organisations are silent on the issue. The issue arose concerning the United Nations in the International Court of Justice ('ICJ') advisory opinion, *Reparation for Injuries Suffered in the Service of the United Nations* ('*Reparation for Injuries*').[64] The case involved the murder of the UN Security Council's Mediator in Palestine, the Swede Count Folke Bernadotte, by the Zionist terrorist organisation Lehi in 1948. The ICJ was asked by the General Assembly to decide whether the United Nations had the capacity to bring an international claim against a state responsible for damage to a UN agent injured in the performance of his duties.

The Court noted that the *UN Charter* does not expressly address the United Nations' personality,[65] but found that the United Nations is an international legal person: a 'subject of international law and capable of possessing international rights and duties, [with] capacity to maintain its rights by bringing international claims'.[66] The Court explained that personality is 'indispensable' to achieving the United Nations' principles and purposes under the Charter; that the United Nations is not simply a centre for cooperation but has its own organs and tasks, and status distinct from member states, which member states must facilitate; and that the United Nations is endowed by states with domestic legal capacity and privileges and immunities, and can enter into treaties.[67] As such the Court concluded that

> the Organization was intended to exercise and enjoy, and is in fact exercising and enjoying, functions and rights which can only be explained on the basis of the possession of a large measure of international personality and the capacity to operate upon an international plane. It is at present the supreme type of international organization, and it could not carry out the intentions of its founders if it was devoid of international personality. It must be acknowledged that its Members, by entrusting certain functions to it, with the attendant duties and responsibilities, have clothed it with the competence required to enable those functions to be effectively discharged.[68]

The Court distinguished the United Nations' international personality from the fullest personality under international law enjoyed solely by states:

> [T]he Organization is an international person. That is not the same thing as saying that it is a State, which it certainly is not, or that its legal personality and rights and duties are the

---

59    *Treaty on European Union*, opened for signature 7 February 1992, 1755 UNTS 3 (entered into force 1 November 1993) art 47.

60    *WTO Agreement* (n 38) art VIII.

61    *Charter of the Association of Southeast Asian Nations*, signed 20 November 2007, 2624 UNTS 223 (entered into force 15 December 2008) art 3.

62    *Rome Statute of the International Criminal Court*, opened for signature 17 July 1998, 2187 UNTS 91 (entered into force 1 July 2002) art 4.

63    *WTO Agreement* (n 38) art VIII(1).

64    *Reparation for Injuries* (n 28).

65    Ibid 178.

66    Ibid 179. See also Chapter 1.

67    *Reparation for Injuries* (n 28) 179.

68    Ibid.

same as those of a State. Still less is it the same thing as saying that it is 'a super-State', whatever that expression may mean. It does not even imply that all its rights and duties must be upon the international plane, any more than all the rights and duties of a State must be upon that plane. What it does mean is that it is a subject of international law and capable of possessing international rights and duties, and that it has capacity to maintain its rights by bringing international claims.[69]

Personality is thus relative and the degree enjoyed by an IO – including the extent of its rights and duties, powers, immunities and legal responsibility – will depend on its characteristics, including its constitution, functions, powers, organs and so on. Evidence of personality, and indicators of its extent, may include: the rights to enter into treaties,[70] send and receive diplomatic missions, and bring and receive international claims;[71] requirements on members to recognise the organisation's legal capacity,[72] or to confer immunities and privileges,[73] in domestic law; the endowment of the organisation with organs and powers independent of member states;[74] and the conferral of functions which can only be effective if the organisation is understood to bear international personality.[75]

In relation to organisations with near-universal membership such as the United Nations, the ICJ has adopted an 'objective' approach to international legal personality,[76] by which the organisation constitutes a legal person even in respect of non-member states, and thus has the potential to enter into relations with them, or to sue or be sued by them. This is despite the ordinary rule of treaty law that a treaty (such as the *UN Charter*) cannot have legal effects for non-party states without their consent (such as through recognition of the United Nations' personality). Thus, as found in *Reparation for Injuries*, the United Nations could claim even against a non-member state, Israel, because it was created by the 'vast majority' of members of the international community.[77] The position is much less settled in relation to organisations with narrower memberships. For this reason, even where an IO's constituent instrument asserts legal personality, this may be an influential but not determinative indicator of objective personality.

## 15.4   Powers of international organisations

The legal powers of most IOs are set out in their constituent instruments and subsequent agreements, and their scope is foremost defined by the principles of treaty interpretation, albeit with an evolutionary emphasis given the nature of constitutional treaties.[78] Situations may,

---

69    Ibid.
70    See *Vienna Convention on the Law of Treaties between States and International Organizations or between International Organizations*, opened for signature 21 March 1986, UN Doc A/CONF.129/15 (not yet in force).
71    Klabbers (n 2) 44–8.
72    See, eg, *UN Charter* art 104.
73    See, eg, ibid art 105.
74    *Reparation for Injuries* (n 28) 179.
75    Ibid.
76    Ibid 185; *DARIO Commentary* (n 39) 50 (Draft Article 2 Commentary [9]).
77    *Reparation for Injuries* (n 28) 185.
78    Robert Jennings and Arthur Watts, *Oppenheim's International Law* (Oxford University Press, 9th ed, 1992) 1268.

however, arise where a constituent instrument does not explicitly empower an IO to do something that is essential to its functioning or objectives.

One, restrictive, approach is the doctrine of 'attributed powers', whereby an organisation can only exercise the powers conferred by its constituent instrument, so as to respect the limits of powers ceded by member states and not intrude, ultra vires, upon their sovereign jurisdiction.[79] A key drawback of this approach is that it can prevent an organisation from acting in relation to matters which were not addressed by its founders, whether by inadvertent omission or because of the evolution of society and the organisation over time.[80] Requiring formal amendment of a constituent instrument is often impractical, including because of unwieldy amendment procedures and political divisions.

In *Reparation for Injuries* the ICJ instead recognised the doctrine of 'implied powers' of IOs: the United Nations 'must be deemed to have those powers which, though not expressly provided in the Charter, are conferred upon it by necessary implication as being essential to the performance of its duties'.[81] The Court thus held that the United Nations' international personality enabled it to bring international, not merely domestic, legal claims, since this was necessary to discharge its functions, including against a state for reparation for injury to a UN agent in the course of his duties (being an injury to the United Nations itself).[82] The Court further accepted that, by implication, the United Nations could claim reparation on behalf of a UN agent for the injury done to them personally, to assure them they are under UN protection and need not rely on national protection by their state of nationality.[83]

Implied powers has also supported the establishment of a binding UN administrative tribunal to decide UN staff disputes, to ensure the efficient functioning of the UN Secretariat and justice under the *UN Charter* for staff who cannot sue the United Nations in domestic courts due to UN immunity.[84] Another example is the United Nations' establishment of peacekeeping forces,[85] and the Security Council's practice of authorising enforcement action to maintain international security, in the absence of the Charter's original scheme for a UN military force coming into being.[86]

A narrow version of implied powers confines the doctrine to implications drawn from an express power.[87] A wider version – the majority in *Reparation for Injuries* – implies powers from the functions or objectives of an organisation, rather than specific powers. This more flexibly facilitates the dynamic governance needs of organisations. However, it can also create uncertainty about the scope of legal powers, and may be perceived as 'judicial activism', exceeding state consent, or intruding on individual rights.[88]

---

79    See Klabbers (n 2) 63–6.
80    Ibid 66.
81    *Reparation for Injuries* (n 28) 182. See also *Legality of the Use of Nuclear Weapons in Armed Conflict (Advisory Opinion)* [1996] ICJ Rep 66, 78 [25].
82    *Reparation for Injuries* (n 28) 182–4.
83    Ibid 183–4.
84    *Effect of Awards of Compensation Made by the United Nations Administrative Tribunal (Advisory Opinion)* [1954] ICJ Rep 47, 57.
85    *Certain Expenses of the United Nations (Advisory Opinion)* [1962] ICJ Rep 151, 167 ('*Certain Expenses*').
86    Schermers and Blokker (n 52) [6]. See also Chapter 8.
87    As Judge Hackworth suggested in his dissenting opinion in *Reparation for Injuries* (n 28).
88    See Klabbers (n 2) 67–73.

The *Reparation* principle is, however, now broadly accepted and important limitations apply to it. Implied powers must be necessary for the organisation to perform its functions, and be consistent with the IO's object and purpose; they should not intrude on express powers, or disturb the quasi-constitutional allocation of competence between organs of the organisation; and they must not violate fundamental rules of international law.[89]

# 15.5 Immunities from and privileges under national law

International organisations may enjoy legal immunities and privileges but there are no universal rules for all IOs.[90] Broadly speaking these are adapted from state and diplomatic immunities and created by treaty law, rather than from custom as for state immunities (see Chapter 6). 'Immunities' are procedural bars to the exercise of jurisdiction, including all forms of legal process, judicial or executive. 'Privileges' include the inviolability of – that is, non-interference with – certain persons, premises and assets, and exemptions from or adjustments to certain laws, such as tax or immigration.

The immunities and privileges of an organisation may be partly identifiable from its constituent instrument. For example, art 105 of the *UN Charter* establishes the immunity of the United Nations:

1.  The Organization shall enjoy in the territory of each of its Members such privileges and immunities as are necessary for the fulfilment of its purposes.
2.  Representatives of the Members of the United Nations and officials of the Organization shall similarly enjoy such privileges and immunities as are necessary for the independent exercise of their functions in connection with the Organization. . . .

Multilateral agreements may detail the immunities and privileges of an organisation. The key instruments for the United Nations are the 1946 *Convention on the Privileges and Immunities of the United Nations* ('*UN Immunities Convention*')[91] and the 1947 *Convention on the Privileges and Immunities of the Specialized Agencies*.[92] In giving effect to art 105 of the *UN Charter*, the *UN Immunities Convention* confers absolute immunity on the United Nations and its most senior officials, and functional immunity on other UN officials for their conduct performed in an official capacity.

---

89    Schermers and Blokker (n 52) [17]–[20]; Institute of International Law, *Resolution on Limits to Evolutive Interpretation of the Constituent Instruments of the Organizations within the United Nations System by their Internal Organs* (4 September 2021).

90    Mirka Möldner, 'International Organisations or Institutions, Privileges and Immunities' in Rüdiger Wolfrum (ed), *The Max Planck Encyclopedia of Public International Law* (Oxford University Press, online, May 2011) [2].

91    *Convention on the Privileges and Immunities of the United Nations*, opened for signature 13 February 1946, 1 UNTS 15 (entered into force 17 September 1946) ('*UN Immunities Convention*').

92    *Convention on the Privileges and Immunities of the Specialized Agencies*, opened for signature 21 November 1947, 33 UNTS 261 (entered into force 2 December 1948).

## 15.5.1    Immunities of the United Nations

Article II(2) of the *UN Immunities Convention* establishes the foremost rule: 'The United Nations, its property and assets wherever located and by whomsoever held, shall enjoy immunity from every form of legal process except insofar as in any particular case it has expressly waived its immunity.' This provision is normally understood to confer absolute immunity on the United Nations. Thus, UN immunities are wider than those of most states, which enjoy immunity for sovereign governmental acts but not commercial activities ('restrictive immunity').[93] The United Nations also enjoys immunity from execution.[94]

Absolute immunity under the *UN Immunities Convention* does not necessarily deprive aggrieved parties of justice,[95] unlike state immunity, since art VIII(29) of the Convention requires the United Nations to provide for dispute settlement in relation to contractual or private law disputes.[96] Arbitration is commonly used in contractual disputes with private parties; the permanent UN Administrative Tribunal handles UN staff contract disputes, and the United Nations may agree ad hoc to arbitrate other claims (such as under national tort law).[97]

However, the dispute settlement procedures depend on the United Nations establishing them, which it has not always done, and do not necessarily extend to violations of international law. In relation to the key operational area of UN peacekeeping, 'status of forces' agreements with host governments typically refer to a prospective UN Standing Claims Commission, but it has never been established.[98] Instead, ad hoc local UN procedures are usually established, but these are usually post facto, not independent, only advisory and cannot award binding remedies; their findings are non-reviewable; and compensation is limited (except in cases of gross negligence or wilful misconduct).[99]

For example, UN peacekeepers caused the 2010–19 cholera epidemic in Haiti which killed 10,000 people and infected 800,000. While the United Nations apologised in 2016,[100] and pledged USD400 million to combat cholera, it continues to deny legal responsibility or provide individual remedies to victims.[101] United Nations peacekeepers in Haiti and Africa have been accused of sexual exploitation or abuse of women and children, but the United Nations mainly relies on troop-contributing countries to hold their own personnel

---

93    See Chanaka Wickremasinghe, 'International Organisations or Institutions, Immunities before National Courts' in Rüdiger Wolfrum (ed), *The Max Planck Encyclopedia of Public International Law* (Oxford University Press, online, July 2009) [14]–[23].
94    *UN Immunities Convention* (n 91) art II(3).
95    *Difference Relating to Immunity from Legal Process of a Special Rapporteur of the Commission on Human Rights (Advisory Opinion)* [1999] ICJ Rep 62, 88 [66].
96    August Reinisch, 'Convention on the Privileges and Immunities of the United Nations 1946, and Convention on the Privileges and Immunities of the Specialized Agencies 1947', *United Nations Audiovisual Library of International Law* <https://legal.un.org/avl/ha/cpiun-cpisa/cpiun-cpisa.html>.
97    Möldner (n 90) [41].
98    Guglielmo Verdirame, *The UN and Human Rights: Who Guards the Guardians?* (Cambridge University Press, 2011) 225.
99    Ibid 225–7.
100    'Secretary-General Apologizes for United Nations Role in Haiti Cholera Epidemic', SG/SM/18323-GA/ 11862 (1 December 2016).
101    Institute for Justice and Democracy in Haiti, 'Cholera Accountability', *Our Work* (Web Page) <www.ijdh .org/our-work/accountability/cholera-accountability>.

accountable;[102] there is now also an internal UN mechanism for reporting sexual exploitation and abuse.[103] In the Balkans in the 1990s, UN peacekeepers failed to protect civilians in UN 'safe zones' and, while admitting some blame,[104] the United Nations has not accepted formal legal responsibility and provided remedies.

## 15.5.2    Privileges of the United Nations

As in the field of diplomatic relations law, the *UN Immunities Convention* guarantees the inviolability of the premises, property and assets, and archives of the United Nations,[105] thus exempting them from any form of interference (legislative, judicial or executive), such as search or seizure. The United Nations is also exempt from financial controls or regulations on currency; direct taxes (but not charges for public utilities); customs duties; and prohibitions and restrictions on goods for official use.[106] States must also reimburse excise duties and taxes on the sale of movable and immovable property but only where they concern 'important purchases for official use'.[107] Official UN communications must be treated at least equivalently to those of governments, as regards costs and taxes, and must not be censored; and the United Nations is entitled to use codes and enjoy the equivalent of diplomatic inviolability of couriers and bags.[108]

## 15.5.3    Immunities and privileges of UN personnel

The *UN Immunities Convention* affords immunities and privileges to UN officials, experts on UN missions, and representatives of member states at the United Nations. Its principles have influenced numerous 'headquarters' agreements with host states and national laws. All UN officials are entitled to functional immunity 'in respect of words spoken or written and all acts performed by them in their official capacity'.[109] In addition, they enjoy tax exemption on their salaries and emoluments; immunities from national service and immigration law; privileges in exchange facilities, and repatriation facilities during crises, equivalent to diplomats; and duty-free import of furniture and effects.[110]

The most senior UN officials (and their spouses and minor children) additionally enjoy diplomatic privileges and immunities;[111] these include the UN Secretary-General and Deputy/Under/Assistant Secretaries-General, and some others. This entitles them to absolute personal immunity from criminal jurisdiction and wide personal immunity from civil jurisdiction

102    See, eg, *Model Status-of-Forces Agreement for Peacekeeping Operations: Report of the Secretary-General*, UN Doc A/45/594 (9 October 1990) annex ('*Draft Model Status-of-Forces Agreement between the United Nations and Host Countries*') [40]–[45] ('*Draft Model Status-of-Forces Agreement*').

103    Verdirame (n 98) 218.

104    *The Fall of Srebrenica: Report of Secretary-General*, UN Doc A/54/549 (15 November 1999) [501].

105    *UN Immunities Convention* (n 91) art II(3)–(4).

106    Ibid art II(5)–(8).

107    Ibid art II(8).

108    Ibid art II(10).

109    Ibid art V(18)(a).

110    Ibid art V(18).

111    Ibid art V(19).

(excluding certain disputes concerning private property or professional or commercial activities outside their official functions).[112]

In addition, these senior officials enjoy inviolability of the person and their residence, papers, correspondence and property.[113] Inviolability includes protection from direct state interference (such as arrest or detention) as well as a duty on the host state to take all appropriate steps to prevent any attack on the person or their freedom or dignity.[114]

Experts undertaking UN missions (such as members of the International Law Commission ('ILC') or human rights treaty bodies, Special Rapporteurs, or peacekeepers) enjoy more limited functional immunities 'as are necessary for the independent exercise of their functions during the period of their missions', including during travel.[115] These foremost include immunity from arrest or detention and seizure of baggage, and inviolability of all papers and documents.[116] In practice, the immunities and privileges of UN peacekeepers are typically implemented through status-of-forces agreements with the host state.[117]

Separately, immunities and privileges are enjoyed by representatives of member states at the United Nations under the *UN Immunities Convention*,[118] and by international judges under other instruments.[119]

## 15.5.4   Lifting of immunity

The immunities and privileges of UN officials and experts are granted 'in the interests of the United Nations and not for the personal benefit of the individuals' and the UN Secretary-General must waive an immunity if it would 'impede the course of justice and can be waived without prejudice to the interests of the United Nations'.[120] The United Nations must also cooperate with states to facilitate justice and respect for law, and prevent abuse of immunities and privileges.[121] In practice, however, the United Nations rarely waives immunity.[122]

In its advisory opinion *Immunity from Legal Process of a Special Rapporteur*, the ICJ indicated that while the immunity of a UN official must be given 'the greatest possible weight' by domestic courts, it could be set aside by a court 'for the most compelling reasons'.[123] In this respect it may be more limited than the immunities of state officials. Human rights violations could provide one reason in some circumstances. The European Court of Human Rights has found that the right of access to a court may be limited by the legitimate aim of immunities to

---

112    By implicit *renvoi* to the customary rules reflected in the *Vienna Convention on Diplomatic Relations*, opened for signature 18 April 1961, 500 UNTS 95 (entered into force 24 April 1964) art 31.

113    Ibid arts 29–30.

114    Ibid art 29.

115    *UN Immunities Convention* (n 91) art VI(22).

116    Ibid.

117    See, eg, *Draft Model Status-of-Forces Agreement* (n 102) [24]–[34] (privileges and immunities, and entry/exit), [46]–[49] (functional immunity from jurisdiction).

118    *UN Immunities Convention* (n 91) art IV.

119    See, eg, *Statute of the International Court of Justice* art 19; *Rome Statute of the International Criminal Court* (n 62) art 48.

120    *UN Immunities Convention* (n 91) art V(20) (officials), art VI(23) (experts).

121    Ibid art V(21).

122    Verdirame (n 98) 356–7.

123    *Difference Relating to Immunity from Legal Process of a Special Rapporteur of the Commission on Human Rights (Advisory Opinion)* [1999] ICJ Rep 62, 87 [61].

enable an IO to efficiently perform its functions, but such restriction must be proportionate in that there must be reasonable alternative means to protect rights.[124] The availability and adequacy of UN arbitration procedures will be an important consideration.

However, in *Stichting Mothers of Srebrenica v The Netherlands*, the European Court of Human Rights indicated that where international security powers under Chapter VII of the *UN Charter* are concerned, immunities must be upheld to prevent national courts from interfering in the effective conduct of UN military operations, and there is no 'compelling reason' to lift immunity, even if there is no alternative redress.[125] The case concerned failures by UN peacekeepers to prevent the killing of civilians in Bosnia by Serb forces (see Section 15.6.3). As in relation to state immunity, there is no recognised exception to immunity for international crimes or serious human rights violations.[126]

# 15.6   Responsibility and accountability of international organisations and member states

Given the immunities of IOs before national courts, their responsibility on the international plane assumes special importance.[127] Rules on the responsibility of IOs emerged recently, with little past practice.[128] Only rarely do treaties expressly provide for the responsibility of IOs.[129] The bankruptcy of the International Tin Council in 1985, with large debts to creditors, prompted much litigation and effort to clarify the issue.

In 2009 the ILC adopted Draft Articles on the Responsibility of International Organizations ('*DARIO*'), closely modelled on, with necessary adaptations, the Commission's *Articles on Responsibility of States for Internationally Wrongful Acts* 2001. As such, many of its rules are comparable to those concerning state responsibility (discussed in Chapter 7) and are not repeated here. They include circumstances precluding wrongfulness (arts 20–27); legal consequences of a wrong (arts 28–42, including continued performance, cessation and non-repetition, reparation, and *jus cogens* issues); and implementation (arts 43–57, including invocation and countermeasures).

---

124   *Waite v Germany; Beer v Germany* (European Court of Human Rights, Grand Chamber, Application Nos 26083/94 and 28934/95, Judgment, 18 February 1999) [59], [67]–[68], [73].

125   *Stichting Mothers of Srebrenica v The Netherlands* (European Court of Human Rights, Section III, Application No 65542/12, Decision, 11 June 2013) [154], [159], [164]–[165].

126   Ibid [158]. See similarly *Mothers of Srebrenica v The Netherlands* (Dutch Supreme Court, ECLI:NL: HR:2012:BW1999, Judgment, 13 April 2012) [4.3.7]–[4.3.14].

127   See generally Verdirame (n 98).

128   *DARIO Commentary* (n 39) 46 (General Commentary [5]; Matthias Hartwig, 'International Organisations or Institutions, Responsibility and Liability' in Rüdiger Wolfrum (ed), *The Max Planck Encyclopedia of Public International Law* (Oxford University Press, online, May 2011) [5].

129   See, eg, *Convention on International Liability for Damage Caused by Space Objects*, opened for signature 29 March 1972, 961 UNTS 187 (entered into force 1 September 1972); *United Nations Convention on the Law of the Sea*, opened for signature 10 December 1982, 1833 UNTS 397 (entered into force 16 November 1994) annex XI art 5 ('*UNCLOS*').

This section focuses on some rules adapted for IOs, including attribution (arts 6–9),[130] multiple responsibility for an act (art 48), responsibility connected with acts of a state or other IO (arts 14–19), and state responsibility connected with an IO's conduct (arts 58–63).

## 15.6.1   Breach of an international obligation

The central rule is that an IO is responsible for internationally wrongful acts: namely, acts or omissions attributable to it which constitute a breach of an international obligation owed by it (arts 3–4 of *DARIO*) whether under its constitutive instrument, treaties or custom.[131] While this appears straightforward, there can be difficulty identifying which obligations apply to an IO. For example, the United Nations is not a party to important treaties on human rights or international humanitarian law, and many treaties direct their obligations towards states; also, it may be unclear whether their subject matter reflects customary rules binding on IOs. However, organisations may explicitly declare their adherence to norms, as the United Nations has done in relation to compliance of peacekeepers with international humanitarian law.[132]

## 15.6.2   Attribution

Conduct is attributable to an IO if committed by an organ or agent in the performance of its functions (art 6 of *DARIO*). Agents are persons tasked with carrying out the organisation's functions, even if not permanently employed (for instance, as UN officials) or even paid[133] (as for volunteer experts), and irrespective of rank. The rule does not cover acts done in a private capacity.

Conduct remains attributable even if the organ or agent exceeds their authority or contravenes instructions, as long as the conduct was done in an official capacity and within the overall functions of the organisation (art 8). This ensures that third parties are protected from not only valid acts but also acts that are ultra vires.[134]

Where a state organ is placed fully at the disposal of an IO, as where an official is fully seconded to it, art 6 applies.[135] Where a secondment is partial, however, art 7 applies instead: an organisation is responsible for the conduct of the organ of a state or another IO placed at its disposal if it exercises 'effective control' over the conduct. The issue is especially relevant to UN peacekeeping operations, where, by agreement with the United Nations, troop-contributing states place their military forces at the disposal of the United Nations, but normally retain disciplinary powers and criminal jurisdiction over their soldiers, and even some operational command.

The issue of attribution has critical implications for accountability: if the United Nations is responsible, justice may be precluded by the United Nations' immunities before national courts

---

130   *DARIO* (n 36) art 9 is not considered here. Under art 9, conduct may be attributable to the extent that an organisation acknowledges and adopts it as its own.

131   *Interpretation of the Agreement of 25 March 1951 between the WHO and Egypt (Advisory Opinion)* [1980] ICJ Rep 73, 89–90 [37].

132   UN Secretary-General, *Bulletin on Observance by United Nations Forces of International Humanitarian Law*, UN Doc ST/SGB/1999/13 (6 August 1999).

133   *Reparation for Injuries* (n 28) 177.

134   *DARIO Commentary* (n 39) 61 (Draft Article 8 Commentary [5]); *Certain Expenses* (n 85) 168.

135   *DARIO Commentary* (n 39) 55 (Draft Article 6 Commentary [6]).

and the unavailability of international tribunals at which to pursue the United Nations. In contrast, if states are responsible, while they may have immunities before foreign courts (including under status of forces agreements), they may still be sued by individuals in their own courts and often in regional human rights courts.

In the cases of *Behrami v France* and *Saramati v France* ('*Behrami*'),[136] the European Court of Human Rights found that the United Nations was responsible for the conduct of the UN-established security force in Kosovo, known as 'KFOR'. This was because it retained 'ultimate authority and control' over KFOR, which was a UN subsidiary organ authorised by the Security Council and operated through an effective NATO operational chain of command (itself constituting 'effective control') which reported to the Council; and notwithstanding that individual troop-contributing countries retained some authority over their own troops as regards safety, discipline, accountability, and provision of uniforms and equipment.[137] The Court conceded that troop-contributing states could still be responsible for their own conduct in carrying out their obligations under Security Council resolutions, but such claims were inadmissible before the Court since it would interfere with the Council's security powers.[138]

On different facts in *Al-Jedda v United Kingdom* ('*Al-Jedda*'),[139] the same Court found that the United Nations exercised neither ultimate authority and control nor effective control (confusingly using two different standards, in contrast to the ILC's emphasis solely on 'effective control') over UK forces in Iraq, whose conduct remained attributable to the United Kingdom.[140] While a multinational security force in Iraq was authorised by the Security Council, unlike in *Behrami* the force was not created by the United Nations but reflected a continuation of a prior UK/US force structure in Iraq, was not under UN command, and only periodically reported to the United Nations.[141] In *Al-Jedda* the United Kingdom could thus be held responsible before the European Court, whereas the Court had no jurisdiction over the United Nations in *Behrami*.

## 15.6.3 Dual attribution

Whereas the cases of *Behrami* and *Al-Jedda* attribute responsibility to either the United Nations or a state, in principle the separate personality of an IO does not preclude attribution of conduct to both an IO and a state or another IO.[142]

The Dutch court cases of *Nuhanović*[143] and *Mothers of Srebrenica* concerned the failures by Dutch UN peacekeepers in Bosnia, 'Dutchbat', to protect civilians from genocidal killing by

---

136    *Behrami v France; Saramati v France* (European Court of Human Rights, Grand Chamber, Application Nos 71412/01 and 78166/01, Admissibility, 2 May 2007) ('*Behrami*').

137    Ibid [138]–[139], [142]. For criticism of the judgment, see Marko Milanovic and Tatjana Papić, 'As Bad As It Gets: The European Court of Human Right's *Behrami and Saramati* Decision and General International Law' (2009) 58(2) *International and Comprative Law Quarterly* 267.

138    *Behrami* (n 136) [145], [149].

139    *Al-Jedda v United Kingdom* (European Court of Human Rights, Grand Chamber, Application No 27021/08, 7 July 2011).

140    *Behrami* (n 136) [84].

141    For analysis, see Marko Milanovic, 'Al-Skeini and Al-Jedda in Strasbourg' (2012) 23(1) *European Journal of International Law* 121.

142    *DARIO* (n 36) art 48.

143    *The Netherlands v Nuhanović* (Dutch Supreme Court, Case No 12/03324, Judgment, 6 September 2013) ('*Nuhanović*').

Serb forces. Dutchbat was part of the UN mission (a UN subsidiary organ), and the United Nations ordinarily exercised 'effective control', in the sense of command and control, over Dutchbat.[144] However, the Dutch government also had 'effective control'[145] in some situations, meaning 'factual control over specific conduct', even absent full independent Dutch operational command or any overriding of UN command.[146] 'Effective control' did not, however, include the mere power to prevent acts, since it requires 'actual participation of and directions' by the state.[147]

On the facts, the Netherlands had effective control before the fall of Srebrenica to Serb forces when Dutchbat acted on the Dutch government's instructions or beyond UN authority;[148] and after its fall, where the government made decisions with the United Nations about humanitarian relief and evacuations, and where Dutchbat acted in the Dutchbat compound and safe area.[149] It was significant that the Netherlands retained authority over personnel matters such as troop selection, training, discipline and criminal punishment.[150] The courts thus accepted that, in principle, both a state and the United Nations could be responsible for the same conduct (without deciding UN responsibility on the facts). The Netherlands did not, however, have control over most of Dutchbat's conduct before the fall of Srebrenica, or after its fall outside the UN safe area.[151]

## 15.6.4   Responsibility for contributing to the acts of others

Distinct from the attribution of conduct to an IO or state is the responsibility of an IO for contributing to the conduct of a state or another IO. Here an IO is responsible if it knowingly *aids or assists in*, or *exercises direction or control over*, the commission of an internationally wrongful act by a state or IO; or *coerces others* to commit such an act.[152] An example of aiding or assisting is logistical support by UN peacekeepers to government military forces where it is known that the latter are involved in violations of international humanitarian law, human rights law or refugee law.[153]

In addition, an IO is responsible if it circumvents its own obligations by adopting a decision binding on, or authorising, member states or IOs to commit an act that would be wrongful if committed by the IO itself, even if such act is not wrongful for the state or other IO.[154]

---

144    Under *DARIO* (n 36) art 7.
145    Under *Responsibility of States for Internationally Wrongful Acts*, GA Res 56/83, UN Doc A/RES/56/83 (28 January 2002, adopted 12 December 2001) annex ('*Responsibility of States for Internationally Wrongful Acts*') art 8 (where the state effectively controls persons placed at the United Nations' disposal).
146    *Nuhanović* (n 143) [3.11.3]; *Mothers of Srebrenica v The Netherlands* (Hague District Court, ECLI:NL: RBDHA:2014:8562, Judgment, 16 July 2014) [4.34] ('*Mothers of Srebrenica 2014*').
147    *Netherlands v Stichting Mothers of Srebrenica* (Dutch Supreme Court, ECLI:NL:HR:2019:1284, Judgment, 19 July 2019) [3.5.3].
148    *Mothers of Srebrenica 2014* (n 146) [4.62].
149    *Nuhanović* (n 143) [3.11.3], [3.12.2]–[3.12.3]; *Mothers of Srebrenica 2014* (n 146) [4.80], [4.83], [4.91].
150    *Nuhanović v The Netherlands* (Dutch Court of Appeal, Interim Judgment, 5 July 2011 and 26 June 2012) [5.9]–[5.10]; *Mothers of Srebrenica 2014* (n 146) [4.62].
151    *Mothers of Srebrenica 2014* (n 146) [4.87].
152    *DARIO* (n 36) arts 14–16 respectively.
153    *DARIO Commentary* (n 39) 66 (Draft Article 14 Commentary [6]).
154    *DARIO* (n 36) art 17.

The provision aims to prevent an organisation from taking advantage of its separate personality to procure an unlawful act.[155] An example is where an IO, but not its member states, is a party to a treaty with a non-member state.[156]

## 15.6.5   Responsibility of member states for a breach by an international organisation

The separate personality of an IO means that its members cannot normally be held responsible for the organisation's own conduct. There is thus no notion of 'joint and several, concurrent, [or] subsidiary' liability based on membership of an organisation.[157] However, states or other organisations may still bear responsibility for their own acts contributing to the conduct of an organisation, through aid or assistance, direction and control, or coercion (arts 58–60 of *DARIO*).

A member state is itself only responsible for an act of an organisation where it takes advantage of the organisation's competence in an area to circumvent its own international obligation (art 61). An example is where a state uses the organisation to breach human rights.[158] A member state may also be responsible for an act by an organisation if it has either accepted responsibility for it or led an injured party to rely on its putative responsibility (art 62).

## 15.6.6   Dispute settlement procedures

Even if the responsibility of an IO can be invoked, whether a claim can be vindicated may depend on the availability and effectiveness of any modalities of dispute resolution, including rules on jurisdiction and standing. For instance, the ICJ can only hear inter-state disputes and not claims against an IO (and only states can bring claims, not IOs, individuals or entities). Contentious cases between states could, however, concern rights or obligations in relation to an IO, such as the effect or validity of Security Council sanctions on treaty rights at issue in the *Lockerbie* case.[159] A few constituent instruments allow inter-state disputes over their interpretation or application to be submitted to the ICJ or arbitration.[160] In its advisory opinions, the Court may pronounce on issues of responsibility, and IOs can potentially participate in proceedings. As mentioned earlier, UN procedures to provide remedies to individuals or entities are limited, and UN human rights bodies cannot receive individual complaints against the United Nations.

Diplomatic protection by the state of nationality of a victim of breaches by an IO is discretionary and, if asserted, may not be favourably received by the IO. Often, political or executive organs of IOs, rather than legal bodies, may address disputes. Even where an organisation agrees to compensate ex gratia – without admitting responsibility – it may be difficult to raise funds from member states who were not responsible for its wrong. Further,

---

155   *DARIO Commentary* (n 39) 68 (Draft Article 17 Commentary [4]).
156   Ibid.
157   Hartwig (n 128) [32].
158   *DARIO Commentary* (n 39) 99 (Draft Article 61 Commentary [3]–[5]).
159   *Interpretation and Application of the 1971 Montreal Convention arising from the Aerial Incident at Lockerbie (Libyan Arab Jamahiriya v United Kingdom) (Preliminary Objections)* [1998] ICJ Rep 9 ('*Lockerbie*').
160   Sands and Klein (n 4) 341–2.

while IO responsibility is without prejudice to the international responsibility of individuals acting on behalf of an IO or a state,[161] the immunities of officials may apply unless waived.

Some IOs do, however, allow claims to be brought against them. For example, the Court of Justice of the European Union can review the legality (including under treaties such as the EU *Charter of Fundamental Rights and Freedoms*) of EU legislative acts intended to produce effects for third parties.[162] Non-binding procedures may also be available. At the World Bank, an administrative Inspection Panel can hear complaints from groups (not individuals) affected by Bank-financed projects, but only in relation to the Bank's own policies and procedures.[163] These address social and economic impacts and harm to people or the environment, but do not directly apply international legal standards, and Panel findings are non-binding. In relation to counter-terrorism sanctions imposed by the UN Security Council, a quasi-judicial Ombudsperson can hear petitions for delisting by listed persons or entities but can only make recommendations and compensation is unavailable.

Where procedures are unavailable, it cannot be ruled out that individual states could declare an act of an IO ultra vires and treat it as ipso facto invalid, or voidable, but the position under customary international law is unclear.[164]

# 15.7   United Nations 1945

As mentioned earlier, the United Nations is the world's most influential IO and much of the law on IOs in general, as discussed, derives from the law and practice relating to it. This new IO was envisaged by the major Allied powers, led by the United States, during World War II.[165] The resulting *UN Charter* 1945 was adopted by 51 states (then representing most countries) and is open to all states.[166] Article 1 of the Charter sets out the 'Purposes of the United Nations':

1. To maintain international peace and security, and to that end: to take effective collective measures for the prevention and removal of threats to the peace, and for the suppression of acts of aggression or other breaches of the peace, and to bring about by peaceful means, and in conformity with the principles of justice and international law, adjustment or settlement of international disputes or situations which might lead to a breach of the peace;

---

161   *DARIO* (n 36) art 66.
162   *Consolidated Version of the Treaty on the Functioning of the European Union*, opened for signature 13 December 2007, [2012] OJ C 326/47 (entered into force 1 December 2009) art 263.
163   Originally established by the World Bank Board of Executive Directors Resolution No IBRD 93-10 (1993) and Resolution No IDA 93-6 (1993).
164   Schmalenbach (n 40) [51]–[54].
165   In 'The Atlantic Charter' (US–UK Policy Paper, 14 August 1941), the *Declaration by United Nations* (1 January 1942) (26 states), summits during 1943 in Quebec, Moscow, Cairo and Tehran, and, most crucially, the Dumbarton Oaks Proposals of 1944 and the Yalta Conference of 1944. See Jean-Pierre Cot, 'United Nations Charter, History of' in Rüdiger Wolfrum (ed), *The Max Planck Encyclopedia of Public International Law* (Oxford University Press, online, April 2011); Kahn (n 27) 1.
166   *UN Charter* art 4. On the drafting of the *UN Charter*, see Ruth Russell, *A History of the United Nations Charter: The Role of the United States 1940–45* (Brookings Institution, 1958); Evan Luard, *A History of the United Nations: Vols 1–2* (Macmillan, 1982–89). On its interpretation, see Bruno Simma et al (eds), *The Charter of the United Nations: A Commentary* (Oxford University Press, 3rd ed, 2012) vol 1.

2.  To develop friendly relations among nations based on respect for the principle of equal rights and self-determination of peoples, and to take other appropriate measures to strengthen universal peace;

3.  To achieve international co-operation in solving international problems of an economic, social, cultural, or humanitarian character, and in promoting and encouraging respect for human rights and for fundamental freedoms for all without distinction as to race, sex, language, or religion; and

4.  To be a centre for harmonizing the actions of nations in the attainment of these common ends.[167]

Article 2 of the *UN Charter* further outlines UN 'purposes' to include sovereign equality of states; duties on members to fulfil their Charter obligations, and to ensure non-member states respect UN principles where necessary to maintain security; duties to peacefully settle international disputes, refrain from the threat or use of force, and assist the United Nations; and non-intervention in the domestic jurisdiction of states.

The Charter both strengthens the foundations laid by the League of Nations and innovates. First, the threat or use of 'force' between states is stringently prohibited by art 2(4), except in national self-defence against an 'armed attack' under art 51 or if the Security Council has authorised collective security measures under Chapter VII of the Charter.[168] States are relatedly required to peacefully settle any dispute which is 'likely to endanger the maintenance of international peace and security'.[169] Unlike the League Council, the Security Council has binding powers to respond to international security threats and to compel compliance (see Section 15.7.2), even in respect of states which are not members of the United Nations.[170]

Secondly, potential causes of war are addressed by advancing the self-determination of peoples (art 1(2)) as a central principle of the international order. Under the *Charter*, a UN Trusteeship Council supervised progress towards self-governance or independence of international trust territories[171] – 11 in total – which largely comprised the former League mandates. The last trusteeship agreement ended in 1994. Australia administered two trust territories: Nauru (independent in 1968) and Papua and New Guinea (independent in 1975).

In addition, the *Charter* promoted the self-determination of 'non-self-governing territories',[172] by which administering powers accepted 'as a sacred trust the obligation to promote . . . the well-being', development, protection, and self-governance of their inhabitants.[173] The United Nations listed 72 such territories in 1946.[174] A General Assembly Special Committee

---

167    *UN Charter* art 1.
168    See Chapter 8 on the use of force.
169    *UN Charter* art 33, ch VI ('Peaceful Settlement of Disputes'). See Chapter 9.
170    *UN Charter* art 2(1).
171    *UN Charter* ch XII ('International Trusteeship System'), ch XIII ('Trusteeship Council').
172    Ibid ch XI.
173    Ibid art 73.
174    *Information from Non-Self-Governing Territories Transmitted under Article 73e of the Charter*, GA Res 66(1), UN Doc A/RES/66(1) (14 December 1946). Sixty non-self-governing territories were still listed in 1963: *Report of the Special Committee on the Situation with Regard to the Implementation of the Declaration on the Granting of Independence to Colonial Countries and Peoples*, UN Doc A/5446/Rev.1 (30 October 1963) annex 1.

on Decolonization was also established in 1961 to advance self-determination.[175] Australia administered Cocos/Keeling Islands until they elected to permanently integrate with Australia in 1984.

After 1945, a total of 80 former colonies with over 750 million people were decolonised, often peacefully, although some attained independence through wars of national liberation against colonial powers. Decolonisation, along with other manifestations of self-determination (for instance, the dissolution of the Soviet Union and former Yugoslavia), accounts for much of the United Nations' growth from 51 states in 1945, to 193 by 2011. Today there remain only 17 non-self-governing territories[176] (mostly small islands, except Western Sahara); self-determination is disputed in some other situations (see Chapter 5).

Thirdly, more so than the League, the *UN Charter* commits the organisation to advancing social and economic development and human rights (as art 55 indicates), on the basis that these human insecurities can contribute to conflict – as the Great Depression of the 1930s, and oppressive conditions under colonial rule, did before World War II. The Charter establishes an Economic and Social Council as the lead UN body on these issues,[177] under the supervision of the General Assembly.

### Article 55

With a view to the creation of conditions of stability and well-being which are necessary for peaceful and friendly relations among nations based on respect for the principle of equal rights and self-determination of peoples, the United Nations shall promote:

1. higher standards of living, full employment, and conditions of economic and social progress and development;

2. solutions of international economic, social, health, and related problems; and international cultural and educational cooperation; and

3. universal respect for, and observance of, human rights and fundamental freedoms for all without distinction as to race, sex, language, or religion.[178]

During the drafting of the Charter, Australia, led by its Minister for External Affairs, HV Evatt, advocated strongly for these provisions,[179] and for the Economic and Social Council[180] to be elevated to a principal organ.

An important limitation is that the United Nations must not 'intervene in matters which are essentially within the domestic jurisdiction of any state'.[181] The United Nations is not a 'world government' which is sovereign over its members. The Security Council's international security powers may, however, lawfully intrude on domestic jurisdiction.[182] Over time, the Council has

---

175    *The Situation with Regard to the Implementation of the Declaration on the Granting of Independence to Colonial Countries and Peoples*, GA Res 1654 (XVI), UN Doc A/RES/1654(XVI) (27 November 1961).

176    See list at 'Non-Self-Governing Territories', *The United Nations and Decolonisation* (Web Page) <www.un.org/dppa/decolonization/en/nsgt>.

177    *UN Charter* ch X.

178    *UN Charter* art 55.

179    Alan Watt, *The Evolution of Australian Foreign Policy 1938–1965* (Cambridge University Press, 1967) 83.

180    *UN Charter* ch X.

181    Ibid art 2(7).

182    Ibid.

regarded many hitherto 'internal' issues as matters of international security, including colonialism, civil war, human displacement, human rights violations, international crimes, and environmental harm. Further, the scope of 'domestic jurisdiction' itself is nowadays understood to exclude matters arising under treaties[183] and other issues of international concern, including human rights.

To implement the United Nations' ambitious agenda, the *Charter* establishes six 'principal organs'.[184] Three are relatively autonomous and reflect a rudimentary separation of powers: the General Assembly, the Security Council and the International Court of Justice (considered in Chapter 9). The three other organs sit under the authority of the General Assembly: the above-mentioned Economic and Social Council and Trusteeship Council, plus a permanent UN Secretariat.[185] In addition, the United Nations is empowered by the *Charter* to found 'subsidiary organs' as necessary[186] (discussed in Section 15.7.3). Other bodies are also part of the extended UN family.

## 15.7.1 General Assembly

The General Assembly is the United Nations' plenary deliberative organ, comprised of all member states,[187] each enjoying one equal vote.[188] It has a general competence to 'discuss any questions or any matters' under the *UN Charter*.[189] It is specifically mandated to promote international cooperation in the political, economic, social, cultural, educational and health fields; promote human rights, and economic and social development; and progressively develop international law.[190] It also has responsibility for the 54-member state Economic and Social Council,[191] trusteeship system,[192] UN budget,[193] and subsidiary organs and other UN bodies.

The Assembly's mandate extends to addressing international disputes[194] and international peace and security,[195] although it is precluded from making recommendations on the latter if the Security Council 'is exercising' its functions in relation to the situation.[196] In its 1962 advisory opinion, *Certain Expenses of the United Nations*, the ICJ accepted that the Council's security powers are 'primary' but not exclusive under the Charter, and that the Assembly may make security recommendations[197] which do not involve binding enforcement action (a power reserved to the Council under the Charter).[198]

---

183    Sands and Klein (n 4) 26.
184    *UN Charter* art 7.
185    Ibid ch XV.
186    Ibid art 7(2).
187    Ibid art 9(1).
188    Ibid art 18(1). Votes on important questions require a two-thirds majority.
189    Ibid art 10.
190    Ibid art 13, chs IX, X.
191    Ibid ch X.
192    Ibid art 16, chs XII, XIII.
193    Ibid arts 17, 19.
194    Ibid art 14.
195    Ibid arts 11, 15.
196    Ibid art 12(1).
197    As under its resolution *Uniting for Peace*, GA Res 377 (V), UN Doc A/RES/5/377 (3 November 1950), for instance, to recommend peacekeeping.
198    *Certain Expenses* (n 85) 164.

Despite its universal membership and wide competence, the Assembly is not akin to a global 'legislature' since it is only empowered to make non-binding 'recommendations'.[199] Resolutions are only binding on matters internal to the organisation, such as apportionment of budget contributions and admission of members.[200] Nonetheless, the Assembly can stimulate international political consensus and international law making in various ways (discussed in Chapter 2).

## 15.7.2  Security Council

In order to collectively maintain international security, the *UN Charter* establishes an executive-style Security Council of 15 member states. Five are permanent members (the 'P5'), representing the victors in World War II: Republic of China (People's Republic of China, since 1971), France, the USSR (Russia, since 1991), the United Kingdom and the United States. Ten are non-permanent members[201] elected for two-year terms by the General Assembly. The non-permanent members are elected from geographic groups of states. The Council's limited, executive membership is intended to facilitate efficient decision-making. The P5 reflected the 1945 balance of power, ensuring that those states most able to enforce security, and on whom the burden would fall, had a decisive say in decision-making.[202] This lesson was learnt from the League, where great powers were fatefully absent.

The Council has power to make both recommendations and, where acting to enforce international security under Chapter VII of the *Charter*, decisions binding on states. Substantive decisions of the Council require nine affirmative votes, including those of the P5 – effectively giving each of them a veto power (including a 'reverse' veto to prevent rescission of a previous decision) – although, in practice, abstention by a P5 member is treated as an affirmative vote. In contrast to the League of Nations, all UN member states agree to 'accept and carry out the decisions' of the Council,[203] even where these conflict with states' other treaty obligations.[204] However, in discharging its duties the Council must 'act in accordance with the Purposes and Principles' of the United Nations,[205] which include respect for human rights.[206]

Australia has served on the Council five times,[207] including as its first president in 1946. In Australia's last term in 2013–14,[208] it notably led the response to the shooting down of Malaysia Airlines flight MH17 over Ukraine, and brokered agreement on cross-border humanitarian aid into the Syria conflict.[209] Australia has also been continuously involved in UN peacekeeping

---

199    *UN Charter* art 10.
200    Ibid arts 17(1), 4(2).
201    Originally there were six non-permanent members but this was increased to 10 by an amendment in 1965.
202    Sands and Klein (n 4) 41.
203    *UN Charter* art 25.
204    Ibid art 103.
205    Ibid art 24(2).
206    Ibid art 1(3).
207    During 1946–47, 1956–57, 1973–74, 1985–86 and 2013–14.
208    See Department of Foreign Affairs and Trade, 'Australia's Term on the United Nations Security Council 2013–14: Achievements', *International Relations* (Web Page) <www.dfat.gov.au/about-us/publications/international-relations/Pages/australias-term-on-the-united-nations-security-council-2013-14-achievements>.
209    SC Res 2165, UN Doc S/RES/2165 (14 July 2014).

worldwide since the first UN operation deployed in the Dutch East Indies (now Indonesia) in 1947. Over 65,000 Australians have participated in more than 50 UN missions,[210] and Australia led interventions in Cambodia and East Timor.

## 15.7.3   Other UN bodies

Numerous bodies are associated with the United Nations in different ways.[211] First, the United Nations has established many 'subsidiary organs' under the *UN Charter* to advance its mission, whether designated as boards, commissions, committees, councils, panels, working groups or others.[212] These are integral parts of the United Nations. Notable bodies under the Assembly's auspices include the Human Rights Council in Geneva, the International Law Commission, the Disarmament Commission, the UN Commission on International Trade Law ('UNCITRAL') and the UN Administrative Tribunal (an internal judicial body binding only on the United Nations). Many are composed of state representatives, while some (such as the International Law Commission) comprise elected independent experts. Under the Security Council, subsidiary organs include peacekeeping operations, counter-terrorism and sanctions committees, and the international criminal tribunals for the former Yugoslavia and Rwanda. The advisory UN Peacebuilding Commission was jointly established by the Assembly and Council.

Secondly, the UN family includes many 'programs' or 'funds' under General Assembly auspices. Many have operational and technical assistance functions, while some also have legal protection and/or 'soft' standard-setting roles. Examples include the Office of the High Commissioner for Refugees, the UN Children's Fund, the UN Development Programme, the UN Conference on Trade and Development, the UN Environment Programme, the UN Office on Drugs and Crime, UN Women, and the World Food Programme. In addition, the Economic and Social Council oversees its own commissions on women, development, forests, crime and indigenous peoples.

Thirdly, some organisations with greater autonomy in the UN system are classified as 'specialised agencies'; these, unlike subsidiary organs or programmes/funds, enjoy separate international legal personality, but are closely connected to the United Nations by special agreements[213] and coordinated by the Economic and Social Council. They often have a plenary organ, executive body and administrative secretariat.[214] They include some of the earliest IOs from the late 19th and early 20th centuries, including the International Labour Organization ('ILO'), the Food and Agriculture Organization ('FAO'), the World Health Organization ('WHO'), the World Intellectual Property Organization ('WIPO'), the Universal Postal Union ('UPU') and the International Telecommunications Union ('ITU'), as well as post–World War II entities such as the World Meteorological Organization, the World Tourism Organization and the UN Educational, Scientific and Cultural Organizations ('UNESCO'). Other important examples are the World Bank Group and International Monetary Fund

---

210    United Nations Association of Australia, 'UN Peacekeeping' (Fact Sheet) <www.unaa.org.au/wp-content/uploads/2015/07/UNAA_peacekeeping_factsheet_v2.pdf>.

211    See *The United Nations System* <www.un.org/en/pdfs/un_system_chart.pdf>.

212    See 'Subsidiary Organs of the General Assembly', *General Assembly of the United Nations* (Web Page) <www.un.org/en/ga/about/subsidiary/index.shtml>.

213    Sands and Klein (n 4) 77.

214    Ibid 83.

('IMF'), the International Civil Aviation Organization ('ICAO') and the International Maritime Organization ('IMO').

### 15.7.3.1   World Bank and International Monetary Fund

The international economic institutions deserve special mention. The World Bank was founded in 1944, before the United Nations, initially to finance the rebuilding of countries shattered by World War II and subsequently to promote global trade, foreign investment, development and poverty eradication, particularly through loans. The IMF was also established in 1944 to promote international financial stability and monetary cooperation, and likewise aspires to facilitate trade, employment, economic growth and poverty alleviation. Both 'Bretton Woods' institutions (named after the place in the United States where they were founded) have been criticised because their governance structures, despite reforms, continue to favour key Western developed powers; and their operations, despite improvements, have sometimes had negative human rights, labour, social and environmental, and sovereignty impacts.[215]

### 15.7.3.2   Other autonomous UN bodies

Finally, numerous other relatively autonomous bodies, usually established by treaty, are related to the United Nations. Those closer to the United Nations include the human rights treaty committees (elected experts who supervise state implementation of treaties); the International Atomic Energy Agency; three bodies under the *United Nations Convention on the Law of the Sea*;[216] and regimes under environmental agreements. Organisations more distant from the United Nations are the WTO; the Organization for the Prohibition of Chemical Weapons; and organisations with roles related to Antarctic governance, environmental regimes, satellite communications, and commodity arrangements.[217]

### 15.7.3.3   World Trade Organization

The WTO was established in 2005 as the successor to the *General Agreement on Tariffs and Trade* 1947, as a forum to set (through multilateral agreements) international trade rules. It aims to reduce national protectionism while maintaining justifiable national regulation, and to settle trade disputes through binding procedures. The WTO has 164 members, accounting for 98% of global trade. Deep controversies have concerned the balance between liberalisation and national regulation, protectionism in agriculture, tensions between developing and developed states, and inequality.[218]

## 15.7.4   UN Secretariat

The Secretariat is the administrative beating heart of the United Nations, but also develops policy. Its staff has grown from 400 in 1946, to about 36,500 today.[219] Total staff across the

---

215   See, eg, Mac Darrow, *Between Light and Shadow, The World Bank, The International Monetary Fund and International Human Rights Law* (Hart Publishing, 2003).

216   The International Tribunal for the Law of the Sea, the Commission on the Limits of the Continental Shelf, and the International Seabed Authority: *UNCLOS* (n 129).

217   See Sands and Klein (n 4) 128–36.

218   See, eg, Sarah Joseph, *Blame It On the WTO? A Human Rights Critique* (Oxford University Press, 2011).

219   Richard Swift, 'Personnel Problems and the United Nations Secretariat' (1957) 11 *International Organisation* 228, 228; *Composition of the Secretariat: Staff Demographics – Report of the Secretary-General*, UN Doc A/75/591 (9 November 2020).

whole United Nations (including the Secretariat) stands at 114,000 people[220] (60% in the field rather than at headquarters[221]) – modest for a world of 8 billion people and given the breadth of UN responsibilities. In addition, there are about 90,000 UN peacekeepers (mainly national military or police) in 12 missions.[222] United Nations staff serve as members of an international civil service, not as state representatives. Appointments aim to reflect equitable distribution among regions and nationalities (although 56 states are under-represented[223]). The United Nations is headquartered in New York, with major regional offices in Geneva, Vienna and Nairobi.

The Secretariat is led by the United Nations' 'chief administrative officer' – the UN Secretary-General – who is appointed by the General Assembly on the Security Council's recommendation.[224] The first Secretary-General, the Norwegian Trygve Lie, described the role as 'the most impossible job on this earth'.[225] He or she is not merely an apolitical bureaucrat, but must be a moral leader, 'norm entrepreneur', organisational reformer, consummate diplomat, lobbyist, fundraiser, and manager of tens of thousands of people worldwide.[226] All this while maintaining the confidence of 193 diverse member states (especially the P5) and many civil society constituencies. There has never been a woman in the job in over 75 years, and women are very under-represented at senior levels in the United Nations.

## 15.7.5   Criticisms of the United Nations

Like any large, complex organisation, particularly one addressing acute global problems with limited resources under relentless political pressure, the United Nations has always faced criticisms.[227] Some are well founded, while others stem from ignorance or conspiracy theories (such as fears of 'world government'). The United Nations is derided for interfering in state sovereignty; having a 'democratic deficit'; being a 'talk shop' (the General Assembly) or a toothless tiger (the Security Council when paralysed by the veto, ill-equipped peacekeepers, or the International Court of Justice); being too dominated by great powers (the Council, and the major donors) or by small or developing states (the Assembly); involving 'horse trading' not merit or expertise in elections; coddling dictators (as on the Human Rights Council); or being inefficient (in its Secretariat or budget), ineffective (from peacekeeping to human rights to development) or even corrupt (as in the 'Oil for Food' sanctions scandal in Iraq).

The whole United Nations is often tarred with the same brush, when defects may affect only certain parts, thus overlooking its accomplishments as a whole. The United Nations is also

---

220    United Nations System, Chief Executives Board for Coordination, *Personnel Statistics: Data as at 31 December 2019*, UN Doc CEB/2020/HLCM/HR/12 (4 September 2020).

221    United Nations, '#Work4UN: Basic Facts about Working for the United Nations', *Academic Impact* (Web Page) <www.un.org/en/academic-impact/work4un-basic-facts-about-working-united-nations>.

222    'Data', *United Nations Peacekeeping* (Web Page) <https://peacekeeping.un.org/en/data>.

223    Secretary-General, *Composition of the Secretariat* (n 219).

224    *UN Charter* art 97.

225    Shashi Tharoor, '"The Most Impossible" Job Description' in Simon Chesterman (ed), *Secretary or General? The UN Secretary-General in World Politics* (Cambridge University Press, 2007) 33.

226    See generally Simon Chesterman (ed), *Secretary or General? The UN Secretary-General in World Politics* (Cambridge University Press, 2007).

227    For a comprehensive overview of UN issues, see Thomas Weiss and Sam Daws, *The Oxford Handbook on the United Nations* (Oxford University Press, 2nd ed, 2018); Rosalyn Higgins et al, *Oppenheim's International Law: United Nations* (Oxford University Press, 2017).

blamed for failures that are the fault of member states. The United Nations is not sovereign; it can only do what members permit, and too often states thwart its mission, whether by vetoing action, failing to provide or equip peacekeepers, blocking cooperation for self-interested reasons or coercing the United Nations by refusing to pay its budget. At the same time, the United Nations' many achievements often do not make the news, whether settling disputes or preventing conflict, peacekeeping, alleviating poverty and promoting development, advancing human rights, protecting refugees or vaccinating children, conserving the environment or promoting international law. Further, as the second Secretary-General, the Swede Dag Hammarskjöld, wryly and realistically observed, 'the United Nations was not created in order to bring us to heaven, but in order to save us from hell'.[228]

## 15.7.6    Reform of the United Nations

The United Nations has experienced continuous pressure for reform since its inception.[229] Since the end of the Cold War in 1990, and the expansion of UN activities, successive waves of 'internal' reform have focused on management, staffing, budget and efficiency; as well as transparency, integrity, oversight and accountability.[230] There have also been reforms to the Economic and Social Council; a new Human Rights Council in 2006, to replace the discredited Commission on Human Rights, created in 1946; and new UN offices for disarmament and counter-terrorism.

Substantive reforms[231] have centred on preventive diplomacy, peacemaking, peacekeeping and peacebuilding (including the new advisory Peacebuilding Commission in 2005); strengthening collective security (including through the 'responsibility to protect' populations at risk of atrocities,[232] plus a rejection of pre-emptive self-defence[233] after the illegal invasion of Iraq in 2003); and development (through the Millennium Development Goals of 2000–15 and Sustainable Development Goals 2016–30). There have also been initiatives on business and human rights, climate change and LGBTQI rights, among others. Under current Secretary-General António Guterres (of Portugal), since 2017, reform has focused on better coordinating development, improving management, and enhancing peacekeeping and related political missions.[234] The COVID-19 pandemic has reinvigorated interest in governance of global public health and the role of the WHO. After Russia's invasion of Ukraine in 2022, the General

---

228    Address by Secretary-General Dag Hammarskjöld at University of California Convocation, Berkeley, UN Doc SG-382 (13 May 1954) 7.
229    Joachim Miller, *Reforming the United Nations: The Struggle for Legitimacy and Effectiveness* (Brill, 2006) 7.
230    Ibid 8–9. See generally Yves Beigbeder, *The Internal Management of United Nations Organisations: The Long Quest for Reform* (Macmillan, 1997).
231    Major policy initiatives included *A More Secure World: Our Shared Responsibility – Report of the High-level Panel on Threats, Challenges and Change*, UN Doc A/59/565 (2 December 2004) and *In Larger Freedom: Towards Development, Security and Human Rights for All – Report of the Secretary-General*, UN Doc A/59/2005 (21 March 2005), culminating in the *2005 World Summit Outcome*, adopted by General Assembly resolution GA Res 60/1, UN Doc A/RES/60/1 (16 September 2005). See generally Miller (n 229).
232    *2005 World Summit Outcome* (n 231) [138]–[139].
233    Ibid [77]–[80].
234    'United to Reform', *United Nations* (Web Page) <https://reform.un.org/>. See generally Joachim Miller, *Reforming the United Nations: Fit for Purpose at 75?* (Brill, 2021).

Assembly committed to debate, within 10 days, every situation where a veto was exercised on the Security Council.[235]

One of the most pressing areas for UN reform is politically the hardest: the Security Council. There are serious legitimacy problems with its composition, which fossilises the 1945 geopolitical order of war victors and is glaringly unrepresentative in a world of 193 states (not 51 as in 1945), changing demographics and shifting power balances. Reform of the Council has been a perennial issue,[236] aiming to make it more 'representative, efficient and transparent' and thus to enhance its effectiveness and legitimacy.[237] There have been improvements in the transparency of its procedures and the participation of states not on the Council. Since 1993 various proposals have suggested adding new permanent members, non-permanent members (as occurred in 1965) or semi-permanent members, but there are disagreements about which states should be permanent;[238] how to geographically distribute non-permanent members; and whether new or existing permanent members should possess the veto. Australia supports more permanent and non-permanent members; during the drafting of the *UN Charter*, Australia opposed the veto. The problem is that the P5 must agree to amendments[239] – and they will almost certainly not relinquish their advantageous veto.

## DISCUSSION QUESTIONS

(1)  How did the experience of the League of Nations influence the design of the United Nations – and to what extent has the UN Charter stood the test of time?

(2)  What are the similarities and differences between the international legal personalities of states and international organisations?

(3)  Does the doctrine of implied powers create too much uncertainty about the scope of the powers of international organisations, and undermine state sovereignty?

(4)  Do the immunities of the United Nations adequately balance the interests of the organisation with those adversely affected by its actions?

(5)  Are the rules on attributing conduct to international organisations sufficiently clear and workable in practice?

---

235   *Standing Mandate for a General Assembly Debate when a Veto is Cast in the Security Council*, GA Res 76/262, UN Doc A/RES/76/262 (26 April 2022) para 1.
236   See, eg, Peter Nadin, *UN Security Council Reform* (Routledge, 2018); Sebastian von Einsiedel, David Malone and Bruno Stagno Ugarte (eds), *The UN Security Council in the 21st Century* (Lynne Rienner, 2016).
237   *2005 World Summit Outcome* (n 231) [153].
238   Frequent suggestions include Brazil, Germany, India and Japan, and possibly one or two African states.
239   *UN Charter* arts 107–108.

# 16

# INTERNATIONAL ECONOMIC LAW

Chester Brown and
Alison Pert

# 16.1   Introduction

International economic law is an umbrella term with no fixed meaning. At its broadest, it covers all aspects of economic relations between states, including regulation of the conduct of individuals, corporations and international organisations.[1] A narrower meaning is 'the segment of public international law directly governing – rather than merely affecting – economic relations between States or international organizations'.[2] The field also embraces governance arrangements, such as the World Bank, International Monetary Fund and World Trade Organization, as well as the many UN and regional bodies that advance economic development. As space does not permit a discussion of all these aspects, this chapter focuses on two important areas: international trade law and international investment law.[3]

International trade law is the body of law, mainly treaty based, that governs the terms on which states permit the trade in goods and services across their borders. Different states at different times have favoured 'protectionism' (imposing high tariffs on imports, to protect domestic industry from foreign competition) or 'free trade' (lowering or removing tariffs to encourage greater international trade). Prior to Federation, for example, the Australian colonies were highly protectionist, as were some Australian political parties in the early 20th century, but since then Australia has generally adopted more liberal trade policies.[4] Today the World Trade Organization, with 164 members, plays a major role in promoting multilateral trade;[5] it is discussed in Section 16.2.2.

International investment law regulates the conditions on which states admit, and treat, foreign investment. In addition to rules of customary international law on the treatment of aliens and diplomatic protection,[6] there are myriad bilateral and multilateral investment treaties. The main features of international investment law are described in Section 16.3.

# 16.2   International trade law
## 16.2.1   The *General Agreement on Tariffs and Trade* 1947

The Great Depression of the 1930s led many states to impose significant trade barriers in an effort to protect their economies: Australia, for example, imposed tariffs of 50% on some

---

1    For example, Herdegen lists, as part of international economic law, 'international trade law, regional economic integration, international investment law and international monetary law ... international commercial arbitration, double taxation agreements, and international intellectual or industrial property law, as well as international competition law': Matthias Herdegen, 'International Economic Law' in Rüdiger Wolfrum (ed), *The Max Planck Encyclopedia of Public International Law* (Oxford University Press, online, November 2020) [1].
2    Herdegen (n 1) [1].
3    Ibid.
4    See generally Richard Pomfret, 'Trade Policy in Canada and Australia in the Twentieth Century' (2000) 40(2) *Australian Economic History Review* 114.
5    According to the World Trade Organization, 'liberal trade policies – policies that allow the unrestricted flow of goods and services – sharpen competition, motivate innovation and breed success. They multiply the rewards that result from producing the best products, with the best design, at the best price': 'The Case for Open Trade', *World Trade Organization* (Web Page) <www.wto.org/english/thewto_e/whatis_e/tif_e/fact3_e.htm>.
6    See also Chapter 7 on state responsibility.

imports, and prohibited others altogether.[7] These defensive measures are widely held to have worsened the depression by contributing to a severe contraction in world trade and high unemployment.[8] Mindful of these events, after World War II, 23 states entered into the *General Agreement on Tariffs and Trade* ('*GATT*')[9] to effect 'the substantial reduction of tariffs and other trade barriers and ... the elimination of preferences, on a reciprocal and mutually advantageous basis'.[10] They also negotiated the *Havana Charter*[11] which would have created an International Trade Organization ('ITO') to promote and oversee a multilateral international trading system.[12] However, the United States did not ratify the *Charter* and, because US participation was seen as essential, the proposed organisation failed to materialise.[13] Instead the *GATT*, which was intended as an interim arrangement pending establishment of the ITO,[14] remained on foot for nearly 50 years. Its core provisions are described in Section 16.2.2.1.

Pursuant to the *GATT*, states parties submitted schedules of concessions, known as 'bindings' – the maximum tariffs each would impose on imports of specified goods[15] – and agreed to meet regularly to negotiate further reductions in barriers to trade.[16] There were seven subsequent rounds of multilateral negotiations under the agreement: Annecy (1949), Torquay (1951), Geneva (1956), 'Dillon Round' (1960–61), 'Kennedy Round' (1964–67), Tokyo (1973–79) and Uruguay (1986–94).[17] In the later rounds, negotiations expanded beyond tariffs to include other barriers such as dumping,[18] subsidies and technical barriers, and some agricultural products, but the agreement was still limited in scope – it did not cover services, for example. By the 1980s the *GATT* was seen as inadequate for a world trading system that had changed radically since 1947; the 1986–94 Uruguay Round therefore resulted in several major new agreements covering different sectors, to be administered by a new body, the World Trade Organization.[19]

7    Australian Bureau of Statistics, *Year Book Australia, 1937* (Catalogue No 1301.0, December 1937) 984 <www.abs.gov.au/AUSSTATS/abs@.nsf/DetailsPage/1301.01937?OpenDocument>.
8    See generally Barry Eichengreen and Douglas Irwin, 'The Slide to Protectionism in the Great Depression: Who Succumbed and Why?' (Working Paper No 15142, National Bureau of Economic Research, July 2009) <www.nber.org/system/files/working_papers/w15142/w15142.pdf>.
9    *General Agreement on Tariffs and Trade*, opened for signature 30 October 1947, 55 UNTS 187 (entered into force 1 January 1948 ('*GATT*').
10    Ibid Preamble.
11    *Havana Charter for an International Trade Organization*, UN Doc E/Conf. 2/78 (24 March 1948) (not in force) <https://treaties.un.org/doc/source/docs/E_CONF.2_78-E.pdf>.
12    'Bretton Woods–GATT, 1941–1947', *Office of the Historian* (Web Page) <https://history.state.gov/milestones/1937-1945/bretton-woods>.
13    The Charter attracted little support and the US administration decided not to press for Congressional approval to ratify: see, eg, William Diebold Jr, 'The End of the ITO' (Essay No 16, International Finance Section, Department of Economics and Social Institutions, Princeton University, October 1952).
14    *GATT* (n 9) art XXIX.
15    Ibid art II.
16    Ibid art XXVIII*bis*.
17    'The GATT Years – From Havana to Marrakesh', *World Trade Organization* (Web Page) <www.wto.org/english/thewto_e/whatis_e/tif_e/fact4_e.htm> ('The GATT Years').
18    'Dumping occurs when goods are exported at a price less than their normal value, generally meaning they are exported for less than they are sold in the domestic market or third-country markets, or at less than production cost': 'Glossary', *World Trade Organization* (Web Page) <www.wto.org/english/thewto_e/glossary_e/dumping_e.htm>.
19    'The GATT Years' (n 17).

## 16.2.2   The World Trade Organization

The World Trade Organization ('WTO'), created by the *WTO Agreement*,[20] came into existence on 1 January 1995, to 'provide the common institutional framework for the conduct of trade relations among its Members in matters related to the agreements and associated legal instruments included in the Annexes to [the WTO] Agreement'.[21] Membership of the WTO is open to '[a]ny State or separate customs territory possessing full autonomy in the conduct of its external commercial relations'.[22] Its 164 members account for 98% of world trade[23] and, in addition to states, include the European Union, Chinese Taipei, and the Hong Kong and Macao Special Administrative Regions of China.[24]

Annexed to the *WTO Agreement* are a number of multilateral and plurilateral agreements. The latter are binding on the WTO members who accept them, while the multilateral agreements are binding on all members:[25]

> **Annexes to the WTO Agreement**
>
> **Annex 1A –** Multilateral Agreements on Trade in Goods:
>
> General Agreement on Tariffs and Trade 1994
>
> Agreement on Agriculture
>
> Agreement on the Application of Sanitary and Phytosanitary Measures
>
> Agreement on Textiles and Clothing
>
> Agreement on Technical Barriers to Trade
>
> Agreement on Trade-Related Investment Measures
>
> Agreement on Implementation of Article VI of the General Agreement on Tariffs and Trade 1994
>
> Agreement on Implementation of Article VII of the General Agreement on Tariffs and Trade 1994
>
> Agreement on Preshipment Inspection
>
> Agreement on Rules of Origin
>
> Agreement on Import Licensing Procedures
>
> Agreement on Subsidies and Countervailing Measures
>
> Agreement on Safeguards
>
> Trade Facilitation Agreement[26]
>
> **Annex 1B –** General Agreement on Trade in Services and Annexes
>
> **Annex 1C –** Agreement on Trade-Related Aspects of Intellectual Property Rights
>
> **Annex 2 –** Understanding on Rules and Procedures Governing the Settlement of Disputes

---

20    *Marrakesh Agreement Establishing the World Trade Organization*, opened for signature 15 April 1994, 1867 UNTS 154 (entered into force 1 January 1995) ('*WTO Agreement*').

21    Ibid art II.

22    Ibid art XII.

23    'WTO in Brief', *World Trade Organization* (Web Page) <www.wto.org/english/thewto_e/whatis_e/inbrief_e/inbr_e.htm>.

24    Members and Observers', *World Trade Organization* (Web Page) <www.wto.org/english/thewto_e/whatis_e/tif_e/org6_e.htm>.

25    *WTO Agreement* (n 20) art II.

26    *Protocol Amending the Marrakesh Agreement Establishing the World Trade Organization*, WTO Doc WT/L/940 (28 November 2014) (Decision of 27 November 2014) annex ('*Agreement on Trade Facilitation*').

**Annex 3** – Trade Policy Review Mechanism
**Annex 4** – Plurilateral Trade Agreements:
  Agreement on Trade in Civil Aircraft
  Agreement on Government Procurement
  International Dairy Agreement
  International Bovine Meat Agreement

Some of the more important of these agreements are summarised in the following sections.

## 16.2.2.1   The *General Agreement on Tariffs and Trade 1994*

Annex 1A to the *WTO Agreement* contains a number of multilateral agreements on trade in goods, the first being the *General Agreement on Tariffs and Trade 1994*. It is known as '*GATT 1994*' because it is legally distinct from the original *GATT* (now referred to as '*GATT 1947*'), and comprises the provisions of *GATT 1947* as amended over time, together with several 'understandings' on the meaning of certain provisions.[27] If there is a conflict between *GATT 1994* and one of the other multilateral agreements in annex 1A, *GATT 1994* prevails.[28]

### MOST-FAVOURED-NATION TREATMENT

Article I of the *GATT* establishes a general obligation on each member, subject to specified exceptions, to grant 'most-favoured-nation' ('MFN') treatment to the import and export of goods:

**Article I General most-favoured-nation treatment**

1.   With respect to customs duties and charges of any kind imposed on or in connection with importation or exportation or imposed on the international transfer of payments for imports or exports, and with respect to the method of levying such duties and charges, and with respect to all rules and formalities in connection with importation and exportation, and with respect to all matters referred to in paragraphs 2 and 4 of Article III, any advantage, favour, privilege or immunity granted by any contracting party to any product originating in or destined for any other country shall be accorded immediately and unconditionally to the like product originating in or destined for the territories of all other contracting parties. ...

Most-favoured-nation treatment essentially means that all imports and exports of a particular product must be treated equally: if a state decides to, for example, lower the rate of customs duty on imports on a particular product from a particular country, art I of the *GATT* requires the importing state 'immediately and unconditionally' to apply the same lower rate to imports of the like product from other WTO members. Certain preferential arrangements listed in annexes to the *GATT*, such as those pre-dating *GATT 1947*, and regional trade agreements, are excluded from this obligation.[29]

---

27   *WTO Agreement* (n 20) annex 1A ('*General Agreement on Tariffs and Trade 1994*') ('*GATT 1994*'). For a detailed summary of *GATT 1947* and *GATT 1994*, see Wolfgang Benedek, 'General Agreement on Tariffs and Trade (1947 and 1994)' in Rüdiger Wolfrum (ed), *The Max Planck Encyclopedia of Public International Law* (Oxford University Press, online, March 2015).

28   *WTO Agreement* (n 20) General Interpretative Note to Annex 1A.

29   *GATT 1994* (n 27) art I(2)–(4). Exceptions added later are set out in the *WTO Analytical Index: Guide to WTO Law and Practice*: see *GATT 1994 – Article I*, 'GATT Analytical Index (Pre-1995)' IID; *GATT 1994 – Article I*, 'Practice (WTO)' 1.4 <www.wto.org/english/res_e/publications_e/ai17_e/gatt1994_e.htm>.

Also excluded are preferences granted to developing and least-developed countries.[30] International trade law recognises that formally equal treatment of all states would 'perpetuate inequality of competitiveness between industrialized and developing countries'.[31] Developing countries are therefore granted privileges according to their individual needs and capabilities.[32] Australia, for example, removed duties on imports from 49 least-developed countries in 2003.[33] Nonetheless, WTO law still allows developed countries to subsidise their own agricultural industries, to the detriment of developing states.[34] Australia broadly opposes agricultural protectionism.[35]

## NATIONAL TREATMENT

Article III of *GATT* imposes a similarly general obligation, subject to exceptions, to grant 'national treatment' in relation to the internal taxation and regulation of imported products:

> **Article III National treatment on internal taxation and regulation**
> 1. The contracting parties recognize that internal taxes and other internal charges, and laws, regulations and requirements affecting the internal sale, offering for sale, purchase, transportation, distribution or use of products, and internal quantitative regulations requiring the mixture, processing or use of products in specified amounts or proportions, should not be applied to imported or domestic products so as to afford protection to domestic production.
> 2. The products of the territory of any contracting party imported into the territory of any other contracting party shall not be subject, directly or indirectly, to internal taxes or other internal charges of any kind in excess of those applied, directly or indirectly, to like domestic products. . . .

As art III(1) indicates, the purpose of this clause is to prevent states using such laws to protect domestic production from foreign competition.

## OTHER PROVISIONS OF *GATT 1994*

The *GATT* also contains provisions on a wide range of related matters from anti-dumping and subsidies, to marks of origin and safeguards.[36] Many of these are elaborated in separate agreements in annex 1A to the *WTO Agreement*.[37] There are also further exceptions to *GATT*

---

30    *Differential and More Favourable Treatment, Reciprocity and Fuller Participation of Developing Countries*, GATT Doc L/4903 (28 November 1979) (Decision) GATT BISD 26S/203; *Preferential Tariff Treatment for Least-Developed Countries*, WTO Doc WT/L/304 (Decision on Waiver) 15 June 1999.

31    Herdegen (n 1) [35].

32    *WTO Agreement* (n 20) art XI(2).

33    *Duty- and Quota-Free Entry for Least-Developed Countries and East Timor*, WTO Doc WT/COMTD/N/18 (21 January 2004) (Notification from Australia).

34    Herdegen (n 1) [34].

35    See, eg, Dan Tehan, Minister for Trade, 'Economic Statecraft in a Challenging Time' (Speech, National Press Club, 22 September 2021) <www.trademinister.gov.au/minister/dan-tehan/speech/national-press-club-address-economic-statecraft-challenging-time>. At around 0.1% of GDP, Australian support to agricultural producers is among the lowest in the OECD: Organisation for Economic Co-operation and Development, *Agricultural Policy Monitoring and Evaluation 2020* (Report, June 2020) Section 4 ('Australia') <www.oecd-ilibrary.org/agriculture-and-food/agricultural-policy-monitoring-and-evaluation-2020_928181a8-en>.

36    *GATT 1994* (n 27) arts VI, XVI, IX and XIX, respectively.

37    See Section 16.2.2 for the list of multilateral agreements in *WTO Agreement* (n 20) annex 1A.

obligations, in arts XX and XXI, such as measures 'necessary to protect human, animal or plant life or health'[38] and measures necessary to protect a member's 'essential security interests' in certain situations.[39] These exceptions are designed to ensure that international trade standards can be balanced against the regulatory choices of sovereign states.[40] Related issues which have attracted increasing attention in recent years concern the consistency of trade measures with international human rights law and international environmental law generally.[41]

### 16.2.2.2   The *General Agreement on Trade in Services*

Annex 1B to the *WTO Agreement* is the *General Agreement on Trade in Services* ('*GATS*'), which aims to liberalise trade in services.[42] As summarised by the WTO:

> Banks, insurance firms, telecommunications companies, tour operators, hotel chains and transport companies looking to do business abroad enjoy the same principles of more open trade that originally only applied to trade in goods. … WTO members have also made individual commitments under the *GATS* stating which of their service sectors they are willing to open to foreign competition, and how open those markets are.[43]

The *GATS* applies to all services except air traffic rights (and directly related services)[44] and government services, such as social security, public health and education. Like the *GATT*, the *GATS* has some rules of general application, and others that apply only to services specified in the schedule of specific commitments submitted by each member.[45] The principal general rules are the requirements to grant MFN treatment in respect of all services, with exceptions broader than those in the *GATT*, and to promote transparency by, for example, members publishing their measures and providing information when requested.[46] For the services specified in a member's schedule, the obligation is to grant national treatment and market access – again, subject to certain limitations and qualifications.[47]

To ensure the widest coverage, the *GATS* covers four different modes of supplying services.[48] The first is *cross-border trade*, where a service flows across a border from one territory to another, such as online banking. The second is *consumption abroad*, where a consumer moves into another territory to obtain the service, such as in tourism. The third and fourth are referred to as *commercial presence*, and *presence of natural persons*. Here the service supplier either establishes a commercial presence in another territory, such as through a local subsidiary of a foreign company, or enters the other territory to supply the service themselves, such as a medical practitioner or a teacher.[49] The schedules of specific

38   *GATT 1994* (n 27) art XX(b).
39   Ibid art XXI(b).
40   Herdegen (n 1) [41].
41   Ibid [46]–[47].
42   *WTO Agreement* (n 20) annex 1B ('*General Agreement on Trade in Services*') Preamble ('*GATS*').
43   'WTO in Brief' (n 23).
44   *GATS* (n 42) Annex on Air Transport Services.
45   See, eg, *GATS* (n 42) art XX.
46   Ibid arts II, III.
47   Ibid art XVII.
48   'The General Agreement on Trade in Services (GATS): Objectives, Coverage and Disciplines', *World Trade Organization* (Web Page) <www.wto.org/english/tratop_e/serv_e/gatsqa_e.htm>.
49   Ibid.

commitments submitted by members address each mode separately. Australia's schedule, for example, lists in exhaustive detail what limitations on national treatment or market access it will apply for each mode of supply, for every service sector.[50]

### 16.2.2.3    The *Agreement on Trade-Related Aspects of Intellectual Property*

The *Agreement on Trade-Related Aspects of Intellectual Property* ('*TRIPS Agreement*') forms Annex 1C to the *WTO Agreement*. Intellectual property – 'creations of the mind'[51] – is an increasingly important part of international trade. There are several major multilateral treaties on particular kinds of intellectual property, notably the *Paris Convention*[52] on industrial property (patents, trademarks, industrial designs, etc) and the *Berne Convention*[53] on literary and artistic works (essentially, copyright),[54] both administered by the World Intellectual Property Organization ('WIPO').[55] Under these and other WIPO treaties, states can grant, protect and enforce intellectual property rights, particularly the rights of those who create works – such as writers, artists, inventors and designers – to prevent others from using their work, and to 'earn recognition or financial benefit from what they invent or create'.[56]

In the Uruguay Round of *GATT* negotiations from 1986 to 1994, it was recognised that inconsistency between states in the domestic treatment of these rights was hindering international trade.[57] *TRIPS* aims to reduce the inconsistency by applying similar rules to the different types of intellectual property covered: copyright, trademarks, geographical indications (eg, 'Champagne'), industrial designs, patents, layout designs of integrated circuits, protection of undisclosed information, and the control of anti-competitive practices in contractual licences,[58] as described in the following sections.

#### NATIONAL AND MFN TREATMENT

As in the *GATT* and the *GATS*, the *TRIPS Agreement* provides for national and MFN treatment. It obliges WTO members to treat nationals of other members no less favourably than its own nationals with regard to the protection of intellectual property, subject to the exceptions in

---

50    See *Australia: Schedule of Specific Commitments*, WTO Doc GATS/SC/6 (15 April 1994); *Australia: Schedule of Specific Commitments – Supplements*, WTO Docs GATS/SC/6/Suppl.1–Suppl.4) <www.wto .org/english/tratop_e/serv_e/serv_commitments_e.htm>.

51    'Intellectual Property: Protection and Enforcement', *World Trade Organization* (Web Page) <www.wto .org/english/thewto_e/whatis_e/tif_e/agrm7_e.htm>.

52    *Paris Convention for the Protection of Industrial Property*, opened for signature 14 July 1967, WIPO Lex No TRT/PARIS/001 (as amended 28 September 1979, entered into force 3 June 1984) (179 parties) <www.wipo.int/treaties/en/ip/paris>.

53    *Berne Convention for the Protection of Literary and Artistic Works*, opened for signature 9 September 1886, WIPO Lex No TRT/BERNE/001 (as amended 28 September 1979, entered into force 19 November 1984) (181 parties) <https://wipolex.wipo.int/en/treaties/textdetails/12214>.

54    Copyright is the right of the creator of a literary or artistic work to authorise or prevent the use of the work by others. For a summary of the rights included see, eg, 'Copyright', *World Intellectual Property Organization* (Web Page) <www.wipo.int/copyright/en>.

55    See generally 'WIPO-Administered Treaties', *World Intellectual Property Organization* (Web Page) <www.wipo.int/treaties/en>.

56    'What is Intellectual Property?', *World Intellectual Property Organization* (Web Page) <www.wipo.int/ about-it/en>.

57    *WTO Agreement* (n 20) annex 1C ('*Agreement on Trade-Related Aspects of Intellectual Property*') Preamble ('*TRIPS Agreement*').

58    Ibid arts 9–40.

specified treaties including the *Paris Convention* and *Berne Convention*.[59] Most-favoured-nation treatment is guaranteed under art 4 of *TRIPS* – any advantage or favour granted to a national of another country, relating to the protection of intellectual property, must be 'immediately and unconditionally' granted to the nationals of all other members, again subject to exceptions.[60]

The *TRIPS Agreement* also contains a general objective, that of balancing the interests of producers and consumers for the common good:

> **Article 7 Objectives**
> The protection and enforcement of intellectual property rights should contribute to the promotion of technological innovation and to the transfer and dissemination of technology, to the mutual advantage of producers and users of technological knowledge and in a manner conducive to social and economic welfare, and to a balance of rights and obligations.

## COPYRIGHT AND RELATED RIGHTS

The *TRIPS Agreement* requires WTO members to comply with the substantive provisions of the *Berne Convention*,[61] and extends coverage to computer programs and some compilations of data.[62] It also extends copyright protection to include rental rights,[63] a more standardised minimum term of protection,[64] and the right of performers to prevent unauthorised recording or broadcasting of their performances.[65]

## TRADEMARKS

A trademark is 'a sign capable of distinguishing the goods or services of one enterprise from those of other enterprises':[66] for example, a product logo. Trademarks can be registered under domestic law, and the owner of a registered trademark has the exclusive right to use, and prevent others from using, that trademark. Similarly to copyright protection, the *TRIPS Agreement* aims to extend the application of existing treaties on trademarks and related rights,[67] particularly the *Paris Convention*.

Article 2(1) of the *TRIPS Agreement* obliges WTO members to comply with the substantive provisions of the *Paris Convention*.[68] These provisions cover industrial property, defined as 'patents, utility models, industrial designs, trade marks, service marks, trade names [and] indications of source or appellations of origin',[69] and set out the details of the rights granted. However, in relation to trademarks, the *Paris Convention* contains no express requirement to

59    Ibid art 3.
60    Ibid art 4.
61    Ibid art 9, which applies *Berne Convention* (n 53) arts 1–21 (except for art 6 *bis*).
62    *TRIPS Agreement* (n 57) art 10.
63    Ibid art 11.
64    Ibid art 12.
65    Ibid art 14.
66    'Trademarks', *World Intellectual Property Organization* (Web Page) <www.wipo.int/trademarks/en>.
67    See 'Trademarks' ibid for a list of WIPO-administered treaties on patents, trademarks and related rights.
68    The substantive provisions are *TRIPS Agreement* arts 1–12 and 19.
69    *Paris Convention* (n 52) art 1(2).

give trademark holders the right to prevent others from using the trademark. To fill that gap, art 16(1) of *TRIPS* provides:

> The owner of a registered trademark shall have the exclusive right to prevent all third parties not having the owner's consent from using in the course of trade identical or similar signs for goods or services which are identical or similar to those in respect of which the trademark is registered where such use would result in a likelihood of confusion. In case of the use of an identical sign for identical goods or services, a likelihood of confusion shall be presumed.

The *TRIPS Agreement* also extends protection to trademarks for services as well as goods,[70] and sets a minimum term of protection of seven years, renewable indefinitely.[71]

## OTHER PROVISIONS OF *TRIPS*

The *TRIPS Agreement* adopts a similar approach in relation to patents,[72] layout designs of integrated circuits,[73] and trade secrets,[74] incorporating the provisions of relevant treaties[75] and setting minimum standards of protection. Importantly, it also sets a minimum standard for the enforcement of intellectual property rights, requiring WTO members to provide enforcement procedures and remedies for infringement in their domestic legal systems.[76] One area of controversy has been whether patent protection for essential pharmaceuticals is consistent with the human right to health, including access to essential medicines in developing countries.[77]

## 16.2.2.4   The *Understanding on Dispute Settlement*

The final part of the *WTO Agreement* to be considered here is the *Dispute Settlement Understanding* ('*DSU*'), which forms annex 2 to the Agreement.[78] The *DSU* applies to the *WTO Agreement* and all 'covered agreements': that is, those listed in annexes 1, 2 and 4 to the Agreement.[79] There was a dispute settlement procedure in *GATT 1947*, but it was slow, and rulings could easily be blocked as they required adoption by consensus of all members. The *DSU* provides for a faster and more structured process, although, as will be seen, some disputes can still take several years to resolve.

---

70    *TRIPS Agreement* (n 57) art 16.
71    Ibid art 18.
72    Ibid arts 27–34.
73    Ibid arts 35–38.
74    Ibid art 39.
75    For example, art 35 incorporates provisions of the *Treaty on Intellectual Property in Respect of Integrated Circuits*, opened for signature 26 May 1989, WIPO Lex No TRT/WASHINGTON/001 (not yet in force).
76    *TRIPS Agreement* (n 57) arts 41–50.
77    See, eg, Reed F Beall, 'Patents and the WHO Model List of Essential Medicines (18th Edition): Clarifying the Debate on IP and Access' (WIPO Global Challenges Brief, 2016) <www.wipo.int/edocs/mdocs/mdocs/en/wipo_gc_ip_ge_16/wipo_gc_ip_ge_16_brief.pdf>.
78    *WTO Agreement* (n 20) annex 2 ('*Understanding on Rules and Procedures Governing the Settlement of Disputes*') ('*DSU*').
79    Ibid art 1.

A dispute generally arises when one WTO member considers that another is violating its obligations under the *WTO Agreement*, such as by imposing a tariff contrary to its commitments under the *GATT*. The *DSU* creates the Dispute Settlement Body ('DSB'), comprising all members,[80] to oversee a multi-stage procedure, starting with consultations: the disputing parties are required to attempt a settlement through negotiations.[81] If these are not successful within 60 days, either party may request the DSB to establish a panel of (generally) three 'well-qualified' individuals to hear the dispute.[82] The parties can make written and oral submissions to the panel,[83] as can any WTO member having a 'substantial interest' in the matter.[84] By the end of 2020, some 90 members had taken advantage of this right, including Australia in 116 cases.[85]

Ideally within six months, the panel issues a report of its findings and conclusions which is circulated to all WTO members and submitted to the DSB.[86] The DSB decides whether or not to adopt the report, unless a party decides to appeal to the Appellate Body.[87] This is a body established by the DSB comprising seven individuals 'with demonstrated expertise in law, international trade and the subject matter of the covered agreements generally', three of whom sit on each appeal.[88] Appeals can only be made on issues of law and, again, both the disputing parties and interested third parties can make written and oral submissions to the Appellate Body which can uphold, modify or reverse the panel's findings and conclusions.[89] The DSB must adopt the Appellate Body's report unless it decides otherwise, by consensus.[90]

If a complaint is upheld, the noncompliant member must bring the relevant measure into conformity with its WTO obligations.[91] If it fails to do so, the complaining party may seek compensation or request authorisation from the DSB to suspend its obligations under the covered agreements vis-à-vis the noncomplying party.[92]

The whole dispute resolution procedure should take between 9 and 12 months,[93] but many disputes take much longer, such as Australia's complaint against India concerning sugar subsidies: consultations began in early 2019 and the panel report was issued nearly three years later in December 2021.[94] Further, since the end of 2019 the Appellate Body has been

---

80    'Dispute Settlement Body', *World Intellectual Property Organization* (Web Page) <www.wto.org/english/tratop_e/dispu_e/dispu_body_e.htm>.
81    *DSU* (n 78) art 4.
82    Ibid arts 6–8.
83    Ibid app 3.
84    Ibid art 10.
85    'Dispute Settlement Activity: Some Figures', *World Intellectual Property Organization* (Web Page) <www.wto.org/english/tratop_e/dispu_e/dispustats_e.htm>; 'Australia and the WTO', *World Intellectual Property Organization* (Web Page) <www.wto.org/english/thewto_e/countries_e/australia_e.htm>. For a continuously updated list of all disputes since 1995, see 'Current Status of Disputes', *World Intellectual Property Organization* (Web Page) <www.wto.org/english/tratop_e/dispu_e/dispu_current_status_e.htm>.
86    *DSU* (n 78) art 12.
87    Ibid art 16.
88    Ibid art 17.
89    Ibid.
90    Ibid.
91    Ibid arts 19, 21.
92    Ibid art 22.
93    Ibid art 20.
94    Panel Report, *India – Measures concerning Sugar and Sugarcane*, WTO Doc WT/DS580 (14 December 2021) <www.wto.org/english/tratop_e/dispu_e/cases_e/ds580_e.htm>. See also

unable to function: in 2017 the United States began blocking new appointments to the body, citing various grievances in the way the body was operating, and there are now no members remaining.[95]

Overall there is a high level of compliance with the WTO dispute resolution procedure. From 1995 to 2020, some 445 panel reports, appellate reports and arbitral decisions were issued in 598 disputes.[96] In only 37 disputes was there resort to arbitration to determine permissible retaliation for noncompliance with a panel report, resulting in 19 decisions.[97]

### 16.2.2.5  Australia and the WTO

Australia has been actively engaged with the WTO and its dispute settlement procedures since the WPO's inception, participating in 11 cases as complainant and 17 as respondent. Its two most recent cases at the time of writing are complaints against China concerning China's imposition of anti-dumping and countervailing duties on imports of Australian barley and wine.[98]

One of Australia's better known cases was the successful defence of its tobacco plain-packaging legislation. In 2011, Australia was one of the first countries to introduce legislation requiring tobacco products to have plain, uniform packaging, without the usual trademarks and other marketing material. Several WTO members complained that this infringed Australia's WTO obligations, including those relating to trademark rights. The proceedings lasted several years, from 2013 to 2020; the DSB ultimately adopted the panel report finding that the legislation was no more restrictive of trade than was necessary to achieve a legitimate public health objective.[99]

## 16.2.3  Other free trade agreements

Finally, a brief word should be said about the increasing number of trade agreements outside the WTO. Many states' faith in the multilateral trading system represented by the WTO has waned, illustrated by the failed Doha Round of negotiations.[100] These commenced in 2001 but

---

'WTO Disputes', Department of Foreign Affairs and Trade (Web Page) <www.dfat.gov.au/trade/organisations/wto/wto-disputes/summary-of-australias-involvement-in-disputes-currently-before-the-world-trade-organization>.

95  See, eg, European Parliament, Briefing, 'International Trade Dispute Settlement: WTO Appellate Body Crisis and the Multiparty Interim Appeal Arrangement' (April 2021) <www.europarl.europa.eu/RegData/etudes/BRIE/2021/690521/EPRS_BRI(2021)690521_EN.pdf>.

96  'Dispute Settlement Activities: Some Figures', *World Trade Organization* (Web Page) <www.wto.org/english/tratop_e/dispu_e/dispustats_e.htm>.

97  Ibid.

98  See WTO disputes DS598, DS602 and DS603 at 'Chronological List of Disputes Cases', *World Trade Organization* (Web Page) <www.wto.org/english/tratop_e/dispu_e/dispu_status_e.htm>.

99  *Australia – Certain Measures concerning Trademarks, Geographical Indications and Other Plain Packaging Requirements Applicable to Tobacco Products and Packaging*, WTO Cases DS435, DS441, DS458, DS467. For a full summary see World Trade Organization, *WTO Dispute Settlement: One-Page Case Summaries – 1995–2020* (2021 ed) 188 <www.wto.org/english/res_e/booksp_e/dispu_settl_1995_2020_e.pdf>.

100  See, eg, Clete Willems, *Revitalizing the World Trade Organization* (Report, The Atlantic Council, October 2020) <www.atlanticcouncil.org/wp-content/uploads/2020/10/Revitalizing-the-WTO-Report-author-edit.pdf>.

were suspended in 2006 when members could not reach agreement on important issues concerning agriculture, investment and competition policy.[101] More and more states are therefore turning to bilateral or regional free trade agreements.[102] One of the drawbacks of this trend is that such agreements are likely to provide lower economic gains overall than multilateral liberalisation: the agreements usually cover a smaller volume of trade than multi- lateral agreements, and tend to create less trade between the parties than is lost from excluding non-parties.[103]

Australia is party to 16 free trade agreements, many of long standing,[104] including the Regional Comprehensive Economic Partnership Agreement,[105] 'that will complement and build upon Australia's existing free trade agreements with 14 other Indo-Pacific countries'.[106] It came into force for Australia on 1 January 2022 and, according to the Australian government, is the world's largest free trade agreement, with the parties accounting for 30% of the world's population and GDP.[107] Like virtually all 'free' trade agreements, it aims to reduce rather than eliminate all trade barriers: its stated objectives are to facilitate the expansion of regional trade and investment, progressively liberalise trade in goods and services, and enhance investment opportunities among the parties.[108]

# 16.3    International investment law
## 16.3.1    Introduction

International investment law promotes foreign investment in states and protects investments from unlawful interference by the host state.[109] Attracting and maintaining foreign investment in turn make a vital contribution to economic development in many countries.[110]

Modern international investment law has its origins in the customary international law rules concerning the obligations of states regarding the treatment of foreign nationals (also known as the 'treatment of aliens'). Like many other fields of public international law, international

---

101    'Doha Development Agenda', *World Trade Organization* (Web Page) <www.wto.org/english/thewto_ e/whatis_e/tif_e/doha1_e.htm>.

102    See, eg, James McBride and Anshu Siripurapu, 'What's Next for the WTO?', *Council on Foreign Relations* (Blog Post, 13 December 2021) <www.cfr.org/backgrounder/whats-next-wto>.

103    Foreign Affairs, Defence and Trade References Committee, *Opportunities and Challenges: Australia's Relationship with China* (Report, November 2005) [10.17]–[10.18] <www.aph.gov.au/Parliamentary_ Business/Committees/Senate/Foreign_Affairs_Defence_and_Trade/Completed_inquiries/2004-07/ china/report01/index>.

104    'Australia's Free Trade Agreements (FTAs)', *Department of Foreign Affairs and Trade* (Web Page) <www.dfat.gov.au/trade/agreements/trade-agreements>.

105    *Regional Comprehensive Economic Partnership Agreement*, opened for signature 15 November 2020, [2022] ATS 1 (entered into force 1 January 2022) (15 states have signed) ('*RCEP*').

106    'Regional Comprehensive Economic Partnership Agreement (RCEP)', *Department of Foreign Affairs and Trade* (Web Page) <www.dfat.gov.au/trade/agreements/in-force/rcep>. The other parties are Brunei Darussalam, Cambodia, China, Indonesia, Japan, Lao PDR, Malaysia, Myanmar, New Zealand, Philippines, Singapore, South Korea, Thailand and Vietnam.

107    Commonwealth, *Parliamentary Debates*, House of Representatives, 1 September 2021, 9080–81 (Stuart Robert).

108    *RCEP* (n 105) art 1(3).

109    Herdegen (n 1) [7].

110    Ibid.

investment law has been contested, with the principal area of disagreement concerning the content of a state's obligations vis-à-vis foreign nationals. In particular, the debate has centred on whether it is sufficient for states to accord treatment to foreign nationals which is consistent with the treatment they accord to their own nationals (that is, the 'national treatment' standard), or whether states have an obligation to treat foreign nationals in accordance with an 'international minimum standard' of treatment.[111] This debate is discussed in Chapter 7 on state responsibility. As noted there, the international minimum standard became dominant; it was applied in early arbitral decisions such as *Neer v Mexico* ('*Neer*')[112] and *Roberts v Mexico* ('*Roberts*'),[113] and is today frequently included in investment protection treaties as the standard of treatment owed by host states to foreign investors and their investments.

Recent decades have seen rapid developments in international investment law.[114] In January 2022, the United Nations Conference on Trade and Development reported that there were 2,825 bilateral investment treaties ('BITs') in existence (with 2,257 in force), and 420 other treaties with investment provisions (with 324 in force).[115]

The modern precursor to the BIT was the 'treaty of friendship, commerce and navigation', in which states sought to provide protection for the foreign business activities of their nationals.[116] These treaties were negotiated on a bilateral basis, and usually contained guarantees concerning the right of access to the territory of the other state party; MFN treatment with respect to taxes and trade more generally; and sometimes the obligation to accord national treatment to foreign nationals.[117]

In the latter part of the 20th century, proposals were made for the negotiation of a multilateral treaty on investment protection.[118] These efforts did not, however, result in a multilateral convention codifying states' obligations as regards the protection of aliens, largely due to ongoing disagreement on the content of the substantive obligations.

---

111   See, eg, James Crawford, *Brownlie's Principles of Public International Law* (Oxford University Press, 9th ed, 2019) 597–600; Chester Brown, 'The Evolution of the Regime of International Investment Agreements: History, Economics, and Politics' in Marc Bungenberg et al (eds), *International Investment Law: A Handbook* (Beck Hart Nomos, 2015) 153, 158–60; Kate Miles, *The Origins of International Investment Law* (Cambridge University Press, 2013) 49–53.
112   *Neer (United States v Mexico) (Award)* (1926) 4 RIAA 60 ('*Neer*'). See also Chapter 7, Section 7.5.2.
113   *Roberts (United States v Mexico)* (1926) 4 RIAA 77 ('*Roberts*'). See also Chapter 7, Section 7.5.3.
114   See, eg, Chester Brown, 'Introduction: The Development and Importance of the Model Bilateral Investment Treaty' in Chester Brown (ed), *Commentaries on Selected Model Investment Treaties* (Oxford University Press, 2013) 1, 9 ('Model Bilateral Investment Treaty').
115   See United Nations Conference on Trade and Development, 'International Investment Agreements Navigator', *UNCTAD Investment Policy Hub* (Web Page) <https://investmentpolicy.unctad.org/international-investment-agreements>.
116   Brown, 'Model Bilateral Investment Treaty' (n 114) 4–6. See also Kenneth Vandevelde, *The First Bilateral Investment Treaties: US Postwar Friendship, Commerce, and Navigation Treaties* (Oxford University Press, 2017).
117   Brown, 'Model Bilateral Investment Treaty' (n 114) 6.
118   See, eg, Abs–Shawcross Draft Convention on the Protection of Investments Abroad of 1959 (Herman Abs and Hartley Shawcross, 'The Proposed Convention to Protect Private Foreign Investment: A Round Table' (1960) 9(1) *Journal of Public Law* 116); Harvard Draft Convention on the International Responsibility of States for Injuries to Aliens of 1961 (Louis Sohn and Richard Baxter, 'Responsibility of States for Injuries to the Economic Interests of Aliens' (1961) 55(3) *American Journal of International Law* 545); OECD Draft Convention on the Protection of Foreign Property of 1962 (in (1963) 2 ILM 241; 1967 revised version in (1968) 7 ILM 117).

One multilateral initiative which did succeed was the *Convention on the Settlement of Investment Disputes between States and Nationals of Other States* ('*ICSID Convention*') in 1965, and the establishment of the International Centre for Settlement of Investment Disputes ('ICSID'), which sits at the World Bank in Washington DC.[119] The *ICSID Convention* does not contain substantive obligations on states vis-à-vis foreign investors, but rather provides procedures and a facility for the resolution of foreign investment disputes between states and foreign investors.[120]

The failure of the various multilateral initiatives vindicated the approach of those states who had embarked on the negotiation of BITs, starting with the Germany–Pakistan BIT of 1959. Significantly, states began negotiating provisions which would permit the foreign investor to bring a claim in international arbitration directly against the host state of the investment without the need to seek the diplomatic protection of its own state of nationality (or 'home state') or to exhaust domestic remedies in the host state. Australia has negotiated 22 BITs in total, although only 15 of these are currently in force, with some having been terminated and/or replaced by a new BIT or a free trade agreement with an investment chapter.[121]

## 16.3.2   Substantive obligations in investment treaties

This section examines the substantive standards of protection which are typically found in investment treaties. In discussing the content of these obligations, it should be remembered that there is no doctrine of *stare decisis* in international law, and no hierarchical structure between the various arbitral tribunals which are constituted to decide investment disputes. The result is that there is some inconsistency in arbitral practice on the interpretation of the various legal issues.[122]

It should also be noted that many investments are made by the investor entering into an investment contract with the host state (which may be called a 'concession agreement'). Such contracts are typically governed by a system of domestic law, such as the law of the host state, and it is by reference to the governing law of the investment contract that the content of the rights and obligations arising under it are to be determined.[123]

### 16.3.2.1   Fair and equitable treatment

The obligation to accord fair and equitable treatment ('FET') is a substantive protection frequently found in BITs and investment chapters in free trade agreements.[124] It has its origins

119    *Convention on the Settlement of Investment Disputes between States and Nationals of Other States*, opened for signature 18 March 1965, 575 UNTS 159 (entered into force 14 October 1966).
120    See especially Christoph Schreuer et al, *The ICSID Convention: A Commentary* (Cambridge University Press, 2nd ed, 2009).
121    'Australia's Bilateral Investment Treaties', *Department of Foreign Affairs and Trade* (Web Page) <www.dfat.gov.au/trade/investment/australias-bilateral-investment-treaties>.
122    See, eg, Julian Arato, Chester Brown and Federico Ortino, 'Parsing and Managing Inconsistency in Investor–State Dispute Settlement' (2020) 21(2–3) *Journal of World Investment and Trade* 336.
123    See, eg, Christoph Schreuer, 'Investment Disputes' in Rüdiger Wolfrum (ed), *The Max Planck Encyclopedia of Public International Law* (Oxford University Press, online, May 2013) [38].
124    On the FET standard, see, eg, Ioana Tudor, *The Fair and Equitable Treatment Standard in the International Law of Foreign Investment* (Oxford University Press, 2008); Roland Kläger, '*Fair and Equitable Treatment*' in International Investment Law (Cambridge University Press, 2011);

in the obligation on states under customary international law to treat foreigners in accordance with a 'minimum standard of treatment', which must be measured by reference to international standards, rather than those of the national law of the host state. This was explained by the United States–Mexican Claims Commission in the *Neer* claim as meaning that states had to provide treatment to an alien which was not 'an outrage', or conduct which amounted to 'bad faith', or to 'wilful neglect of duty, or to an insufficiency of government action so far short of international standards that every reasonable and impartial man would readily recognise its insufficiency'.[125] As the same Commission explained in the subsequent *Roberts* claim, the ultimate question was 'whether aliens are treated in accordance with ordinary standards of civilisation'.[126]

There is a debate regarding whether the FET standard should be interpreted as providing the equivalent protection for foreign nationals as the minimum standard of treatment. Arbitral tribunals have been divided on this issue, with some interpreting the FET obligation as a requirement to comply with the minimum standard of treatment,[127] and others concluding that the two standards are distinct.[128] This debate has become somewhat arid, with the ICSID tribunal in *Biwater Gauff (Tanzania) Ltd v Tanzania* noting that 'the actual content of the treaty standard of fair and equitable treatment is not materially different from the content of the minimum standard of treatment in customary international law'.[129] Further, various tribunals have expressed the view that conduct required under the customary international law minimum standard of treatment is no longer that articulated in *Neer*, with the result that the standards (if they were ever separate) have converged; in particular, it is no longer necessary for the state to be acting in bad faith.[130] While international human rights law also nowadays provides minimum international standards of treatment, as discussed in Chapter 7 on state responsibility, the remedies under BITs can be more attractive than those under human rights procedures.

Turning to the content of the FET obligation, this too has been somewhat contested. Some tribunals have interpreted the obligation in an expansive way,[131] but others have been able to identify more precisely the content of the obligation. One particularly influential decision is *Waste Management v Mexico (No 2)* ('*Waste Management (No 2)*'),[132] which was a claim

---

Martins Paparinskis, *The International Minimum Standard and Fair and Equitable Treatment* (Oxford University Press, 2013); Chester Brown and Domenico Cucinotta, 'Treatment Standards in Environment-Related Investor–State Disputes' in Kate Miles (ed), *Research Handbook on Environment and Investment Law* (Edward Elgar, 2019) 175, 180–4.

125    *Neer* (n 112) 61–2.

126    *Roberts* (n 113) 80.

127    See, eg, *Genin v Estonia (Award)* (ICSID Arbitral Tribunal, Case No ARB/99/2, 25 June 2001) [367]; *El Paso Energy International Co v Argentina (Award)* (ICSID Arbitral Tribunal, Case No ARB/03/15, 31 October 2011) [337].

128    See, eg, *Biwater Gauff (Tanzania) Ltd v Tanzania (Award)* (ICSID Arbitral Tribunal, Case No ARB/05/22, 24 July 2008) [589]–[591].

129    Ibid [592].

130    See, eg, *Mondev International v United States (Award)* (ICSID Arbitral Tribunal, Case No ARB(AF)/99/2, 11 October 2002) [116]. See also *Crystallex International Corporation v Venezuela (Award)* (ICSID Arbitral Tribunal, Case No ARB(AF)/11/2, 4 April 2016) [545].

131    See especially *Tecmed v Mexico (Award)* (ICSID Arbitral Tribunal, Case No ARB(AF)/00/2, 29 May 2003) [154].

132    *Waste Management v Mexico (No 2) (Award)* (ICSID Arbitral Tribunal, Case No ARB(AF)/00/3, 30 April 2004).

brought under Chapter 11 of the *North American Free Trade Agreement ('NAFTA')*.[133] In that case, the tribunal held:

> [T]he minimum standard of treatment of fair and equitable treatment is infringed by conduct attributable to the State and harmful to the claimant if the conduct is arbitrary, grossly unfair, unjust or idiosyncratic, is discriminatory and exposes the claimant to sectional or racial prejudice, or involves a lack of due process leading to an outcome which offends judicial propriety – as might be the case with a manifest failure of natural justice in judicial proceedings or a complete lack of transparency and candour in an administrative process. In applying this standard it is relevant that the treatment is in breach of representations made by the host State which were reasonably relied on by the claimant.[134]

The tribunal saw the FET standard as covering the range of situations addressed by the minimum standard of treatment under customary international law, including state conduct which is arbitrary or discriminatory, lacking in procedural fairness or natural justice, and treatment which amounts to a denial of justice. This dictum has been cited and applied by multiple investment tribunals, recognising that it provides authoritative guidance. In one such case, *Micula v Romania*, the ICSID tribunal cited *Waste Management (No 2)* with approval, noting that 'conduct that is substantively improper, whether because it is arbitrary, manifestly unreasonable, discriminatory or in bad faith, will violate the fair and equitable treatment standard'.[135]

Consistent with *Waste Management (No 2)*, arbitral tribunals have also agreed that host state conduct which breaches 'legitimate expectations' will also amount to a violation of the FET standard. The tribunal in *Saluka Investments v Czech Republic ('Saluka')* even said that the protection of legitimate expectations formed the 'dominant element' of the FET standard.[136]

On the facts, the tribunal in *Saluka* accepted that the investor had a legitimate expectation that the Czech Republic would provide financial assistance to the leading financial institutions on a non-discriminatory basis.[137] Importantly, though, the tribunal added that the protection of legitimate expectations did not mean that the respondent state was prevented from adopting new regulatory measures:

> No investor may reasonably expect that the circumstances prevailing at the time the investment is made remain totally unchanged. In order to determine whether frustration of the foreign investor's expectations was justified and reasonable, the host State's legitimate right subsequently to regulate domestic matters in the public interest must be taken into consideration as well.[138]

---

133    *North American Free Trade Agreement*, Canada–Mexico–United States, signed 17 December 1992, [1994] CTS 2 (entered into force 1 January 1994) (*'NAFTA'*).
134    *Waste Management v Mexico (No 2)* (n 132) [98].
135    *Micula v Romania (Final Award)* (ICSID Arbitral Tribunal, Case No ARB/05/20, 11 December 2013) [522]. See also *Quiborax SA v Bolivia (Award)* (ICSID Arbitral Tribunal, Case No ARB/06/2, 16 September 2015) [291]; *Philip Morris Brands Sàrl v Uruguay (Award)* (ICSID Arbitral Tribunal, Case No ARB/10/7, 8 July 2016) [323] (*'Philip Morris v Uruguay'*).
136    *Saluka Investments BV v Czech Republic (Partial Award)* (ICSID Arbitral Tribunal, Case No 2001-04, 17 March 2006) [302] (*'Saluka'*).
137    Ibid [322]–[323].
138    Ibid [305].

In this regard, the tribunal agreed that a 'high measure of deference' was to be accorded to 'the right of domestic authorities to regulate matters within their own borders'.[139] As in WTO law, therefore, other public interests – such as human rights, the environment, public health or labour standards – can be balanced against economic interests, although where this balance appropriately lies in particular cases is often contested.

## 16.3.2.2   Full protection and security

The obligation to accord full protection and security ('FPS') is another standard of protection that is typically included in investment treaties, and it requires states to provide physical protection for investors and their investments. The FPS standard is an obligation of 'due diligence', rather than one of strict liability, consistent with early practice of arbitral tribunals and the International Court of Justice on the international minimum standard.[140] The 'due diligence' standard (which has been confirmed in the practice of BIT tribunals) requires the state to take 'all reasonable measures to protect assets and property from threats or attacks which may target particularly foreigners or certain groups of foreigners'.[141]

Tribunals also appear to agree on the relevance of the state's particular circumstances when determining whether it has breached the FPS obligation with respect to a foreign investment.[142] As it has been put by writers: 'An investor investing in an area with endemic civil strife and poor governance cannot have the same expectation of physical security as one investing in London, New York or Tokyo.'[143]

One apparently unresolved issue is whether it is possible for the FPS obligation to extend beyond the provision of physical protection and to require the host state to provide legal protection. There is some authority for this proposition, including in *CME Czech Republic BV (The Netherlands) v Czech Republic*, in which the tribunal held that, under the FPS standard, '[t]he host State is obligated to ensure that neither by amendment of its laws nor by actions of its administrative bodies is the agreed and approved security and protection of the foreign investor's investment withdrawn or devalued'.[144] Likewise, the ICSID tribunal in *Azurix v Argentina* held that FPS was 'not only a matter of physical security; the stability afforded by a

---

139    Ibid [263] (citing *SD Myers Inc v Canada (Partial Award)* (2005) 8 ICSID Rep 3). For an excellent analysis of the multiple ways in which international courts and tribunals have applied the concept of deference, see Esmé Shirlow, *Judging at the Interface: Deference to State Decision-Making Authority in International Adjudication* (Cambridge University Press, 2021).

140    See, eg, *Home Frontier and Foreign Missionary Society (United States v Great Britain)* (1920) 6 RIAA 42 ('*Missionary Society (US) v Great Britain*'); *Noyes (United States v Mexico)* (1933) 6 RIAA 308; *Elettronica Sicula SpA (ELSI) (United States of America v Italy) (Judgment)* [1989] ICJ Rep 15, 63–5.

141    *Saluka* (n 136) [484]. See also *Asian Agricultural Products Ltd v Sri Lanka (Award)* (ICSID Arbitral Tribunal, Case No ARB/87/3, 27 June 1990) [49]–[53]; *Mamidoil Jetoil Greek Petroleum Products SA v Albania (Award)* (ICSID Arbitral Tribunal, Case No ARB/11/24, 30 March 2015) [821].

142    This is consistent with *Missionary Society (US) v Great Britain* (n 140) 44.

143    Andrew Newcombe and Lluis Paradell, *Law and Practice of Investment Treaties* (Kluwer, 2009) 310. See also *Pantechniki SA v Albania (Award)* (ICSID Arbitral Tribunal, Case No ARB/07/21, 30 July 2009) [77]; *Ampal-American Israel Corporation v Egypt (Decision on Liability and Heads of Loss)* (2022) 20 ICSID Rep 406, [241]–[244]; *Strabag SE v Libya (Award)* (ICSID Arbitral Tribunal, Case No ARB(AF)/15/1, 29 June 2020) [234]–[236].

144    *CME Czech Republic BV (The Netherlands) v Czech Republic (Partial Award of 13 September 2001)* (2006) 9 ICSID Rep 113, 238 [613].

secure investment environment is as important from an investor's point of view'.[145] Other tribunals have however disagreed; the tribunal in *Saluka* held:

> The 'full protection and security' standard applies essentially when the foreign investment has been affected by civil strife and physical violence. . . . [T]he 'full security and protection' clause is not meant to cover just any kind of impairment of an investor's investment, but to protect more specifically the physical integrity of an investment against interference by use of force.[146]

### 16.3.2.3   Protection from expropriation

A third standard of protection typically included in BITs is protection from expropriation unless certain conditions are met, including the payment of compensation.[147] This is a longstanding rule of customary international law that has been incorporated into BITs. There is no rule of international law which prohibits expropriation per se. In fact, consistent with the notion of territorial sovereignty, international law accepts in principle the host state's right to expropriate alien property situated on its territory,[148] subject to the satisfaction of certain criteria.[149]

In this respect, there is general acceptance that in order for an expropriation to be lawful, it must be for a public purpose, non-discriminatory and accompanied by the payment of compensation.[150] Modern BITs largely reflect the content of this customary international law rule. For instance, art 9.8 of the *Comprehensive and Progressive Agreement for Trans-Pacific Partnership* ('*CPTPP*') provides:

> No Party shall expropriate or nationalise a covered investment either directly or indirectly through measures equivalent to expropriation or nationalisation (expropriation), except:
> (a)   for a public purpose;
> (b)   in a non-discriminatory manner;
> (c)   on payment of prompt, adequate and effective compensation in accordance with paragraphs 2, 3 and 4; and
> (d)   in accordance with due process of law.[151]

State practice, along with the decisions and awards of arbitral tribunals, has also recognised the distinction between 'direct expropriations' (where the title to movable and immovable

---

145   *Azurix v Argentina (Award)* (ICSID Arbitral Tribunal, Case No ARB/01/12, 14 July 2006) [408]. See also *Siemens AG v Argentina (Award)* (ICSID Arbitral Tribunal, Case No ARB/02/8, 6 February 2007) [303].

146   *Saluka* (n 136) [483]–[484]. See also *UAB E Energija (Lithuania) v Latvia (Award)* (ICSID Arbitral Tribunal, Case No ARB/12/33, 22 December 2017) [840].

147   Brown and Cucinotta (n 124) 176–80. See also Chapter 7, Section 7.5.6.

148   See, eg, FV García-Amador, Special Rapporteur, *Fourth Report on State Responsibility*, UN Doc A/CN/4/ 119 (26 February 1959) 11 [41].

149   See, eg, Crawford (n 111) 603–5; August Reinisch, 'Legality of Expropriations' in August Reinisch (ed), *Standards of Investment Protection* (Oxford University Press, 2008) 171, 173–6; García-Amador, UN Doc A/CN/4/119 (n 148) 11.

150   See, eg, Reinisch, 'Legality of Expropriations' (n 149) 173–5; Christoph Schreuer, 'The Concept of Expropriation under the ECT and Other Investment Protection Treaties' in Clarisse Ribeiro (ed), *Investment Arbitration and the Energy Charter Treaty* (JurisNet, 2006) 108; United Nations Conference on Trade and Development, *International Investment Agreements: Key Issues* (2004) vol 1, 235; American Law Institute, *Restatement (Third) of the Foreign Relations Law of the United States* (1987) § 712.

151   *Comprehensive and Progressive Agreement for Trans-Pacific Partnership*, signed 8 March 2018, [2018] ATS 23 (entered into force 30 December 2018) ch 9 art 9.8 (citations omitted) ('*CPTPP*').

property is compulsorily transferred to the state) and 'indirect expropriations' (where the foreign investor retains title to the property, but the conduct of the host state has the effect that the investor is unable to make use of the property).[152] An example might be found in the cancellation of a mining licence which is required in order to operate a natural resources project; the investor may well retain contractual and proprietary rights over the land, its mining equipment, and other assets, but it is unable to make use of them without the mining licence. The test for an indirect expropriation has been developed in arbitral and state practice, for example by the NAFTA tribunal in *Metalclad Corporation v Mexico*:

> [E]xpropriation under *NAFTA* includes not only open, deliberate and acknowledged takings of property, such as outright seizure or formal or obligatory transfer of title in favour of the host State, but also covert or incidental interference with the use of property which has the effect of depriving the owner, in whole or in significant part, of the use or reasonably-to-be-expected economic benefit of property even if not necessarily to the obvious benefit of the host State.[153]

The ICSID tribunal in *CMS Gas Transmission Co v Argentina* held the 'essential question' was to establish 'whether the enjoyment of the property has been effectively neutralized', and that the correct question was whether there had been a 'substantial deprivation'.[154] The ICSID tribunal in *Electrabel SA v Hungary* sought to synthesise the arbitral practice as follows:

> [T]he Tribunal considers that the accumulated mass of international legal materials, comprising both arbitral decisions and doctrinal writings, describe for both direct and indirect expropriation, consistently albeit in different terms, the requirement under international law for the investor to establish the substantial, radical, severe, devastating or fundamental deprivation of its rights or the virtual annihilation, effective neutralisation or factual destruction of its investment, its value or enjoyment.[155]

A further issue is that customary international law recognises that the obligation not to expropriate the property of foreign investors must be understood in light of the 'police powers' doctrine,[156] under which the state may adopt certain measures for the public welfare (concerning, for instance, currency exchange controls, environmental protection and the protection of public health, among others) without those measures amounting to an indirect expropriation. As the *Saluka* tribunal explained:

> [254] The Tribunal acknowledges that Article 5 of the Treaty in the present case is drafted very broadly and does not contain any exception for the exercise of regulatory power. However, in using the concept of deprivation, Article 5 imports into the Treaty the customary international law notion that a deprivation can be justified if it results from

---

152    Brown and Cucinotta (n 124) 177. See also Rudolf Dolzer and Christoph Schreuer, *Principles of International Investment Law* (Oxford University Press, 2nd ed, 2012) 101–26.

153    *Metalclad Corporation v Mexico (Award)* (ICSID Arbitral Tribunal, Case No ARB(AF)/97/1, 30 August 2000) [103].

154    *CMS Gas Transmission Co v Argentina (Award)* (ICSID Arbitral Tribunal, Case No ARB01/8, 12 May 2005) [262].

155    *Electrabel SA v Hungary (Decision on Jurisdiction, Applicable Law and Liability)* (ICSID Arbitral Tribunal, Case No ARB/07/19, 30 November 2012) [6.62].

156    Brown and Cucinotta (n 124) 179. See also Harvard Draft Convention on the International Responsibility of States for Injuries to Aliens (n 118) art 10(5).

the exercise of regulatory actions aimed at the maintenance of public order. In interpreting a treaty, account has to be taken of 'any relevant rules of international law applicable in the relations between the parties' – a requirement which the International Court of Justice . . . has held includes relevant rules of general customary international law.

[255] It is now established in international law that States are not liable to pay compensation to a foreign investor when, in the normal exercise of their regulatory powers, they adopt in a non-discriminatory manner bona fide regulations that are aimed at the general welfare.[157]

In *Methanex*, the tribunal observed:

[A]s a matter of general international law, a non-discriminatory regulation for a public purpose, which is enacted in accordance with due process and, which affects, inter alios, a foreign investor or investment is not deemed expropriatory and compensable unless specific commitments had been given by the regulating government to the then putative foreign investor contemplating investment that the government would refrain from such regulation.[158]

The police powers doctrine now appears to be reflected in the 'Annex on Expropriation' which is included in similar formulations in many modern treaties, including the *CPTPP*:

Non-discriminatory regulatory actions by a Party that are designed and applied to protect legitimate public welfare objectives, such as public health, safety, and the environment, do not constitute indirect expropriations, except in rare circumstances.[159]

## 16.3.2.4    Most-favoured-nation treatment

A fourth obligation which is contained in many BITs is the MFN provision, which generally requires that the host state provide treatment to foreign investors which is 'no less favourable' than that which is enjoyed by investors from other states.[160] In some investment treaties, the obligation is to accord treatment which is no less favourable to investors from other states who are 'in like circumstances'.[161] The effect of including a MFN clause in BITs is understood as permitting an investor to obtain more beneficial treatment which the host state grants to investors from a third state, including under a different BIT.

Thus, in *Bayindir v Pakistan*, the investor sought to rely on the MFN clause in the Turkey–Pakistan BIT to import the FET clause from one of Pakistan's other BITs, namely the Pakistan–Switzerland BIT.[162] The Turkey–Pakistan BIT did not contain an FET clause, and the investor

---

157    *Saluka* (n 136) [254]–[255].
158    *Methanex Corporation v United States (Final Award on Jurisdiction and Merits)* (2005) 44 ILM 1345 pt IV ch D [7]. See also *Chemtura Corporation v Canada (Final Award)* (North American Free Trade Agreement Chapter 11 Arbitral Tribunal, 2 August 2010); *Philip Morris v Uruguay* (n 135).
159    *CPTPP* (n 151) annex 9-B art 3(b).
160    See, eg, Brown and Cucinotta (n 124) 184–8; August Reinisch, 'Most Favoured Nation Treatment' in Marc Bungenberg et al (eds), *International Investment Law: A Handbook* (Beck Hart Nomos, 2015) 807; Andrew Newcombe and Lluis Paradell, *Law and Practice of Investment Treaties: Standards of Treatment* (Kluwer, 2009) 193–232.
161    See, eg, *NAFTA* (n 133) art 1103(1).
162    *Bayindir v Pakistan (Award)* (ICSID Arbitral Tribunal, Case No ARB/03/29, 27 August 2009) [167]. The claimant also pointed to Pakistan's BITs with France, the Netherlands, China, the United Kingdom, Australia, Switzerland, Lebanon, Sri Lanka and Denmark: at [231]–[232].

argued that it was therefore being treated less favourably than (for instance) Swiss investors in Pakistan. The ICSID tribunal upheld Bayindir's right to rely on the FET provisions in that other BIT.[163]

There is the unresolved issue of whether the obligation to provide MFN treatment also includes procedural protections, such as the investor–state arbitration provisions in a BIT. There are decisions and awards both in favour of permitting MFN treatment for procedural protections such as *Maffezini v Spain*,[164] and against, such as *Plama Consortium Ltd v Bulgaria*.[165] This is ultimately a question of treaty interpretation, as the International Law Commission's Study Group on the Most-Favoured-Nation clause concluded in its Final Report:

> The central interpretative issue in respect of the MFN clauses relates to the scope of the clause and the application of the *ejusdem generis* principle. That is, the scope and nature of the benefit that can be obtained under an MFN provision depends on the interpretation of the MFN provision itself.[166]

### 16.3.2.5  National treatment

A fifth typical standard of protection in BITs is the national treatment standard, pursuant to which foreign investors are to be accorded treatment which is no less favourable than that which the host state accords to its own investors.[167] The general purpose of the clause is to oblige a host state not to discriminate between foreign and national investors when enacting and applying its rules and regulations. Arbitral practice suggests that there are three analytical steps which tribunals undertake to determine whether or not the state has breached the obligation to provide national treatment, which were identified by the tribunal in *United Parcel Service v Canada*: (1) the claimant 'must demonstrate that the Party accorded treatment to it with respect to the establishment, acquisition, expansion, management, conduct, operation, and sale or other disposition of investments'; (2) the claimant or its investment 'must be in like circumstances with local investors or investments'; and (3) it must also be shown that the host state has treated 'the foreign investor or investment less favorably than it treats the local investors or investments'.[168]

---

163    There is, however, some doubt that an MFN clause automatically permits a potential claimant to benefit from the substantive protections available in other BITs, following the ICSID tribunal's decision in *Ickale Insaat v Turkmenistan (Award)* (ICSID Arbitral Tribunal, Case No ARB/10/24, 8 March 2016).

164    *Maffezini v Spain (Decision on Jurisdiction)* (ICSID Arbitral Tribunal, Case No 97/7, 25 January 2000). See also *Siemens AG v Argentina* (ICSID Arbitral Tribunal, Case No ARB/02/8, 3 August 2004); *Teinver SA v Argentina (Decision on Jurisdiction)* (ICSID Arbitral Tribunal, Case No ARB/11/20, 3 July 2013) [186].

165    *Plama Consortium Ltd v Bulgaria (Decision on Jurisdiction)* (ICSID Arbitral Tribunal, Case No ARB/03/24, 8 February 2005). See also *Salini Costruttori SpA v Jordan (Decision on Jurisdiction)* (ICSID Arbitral Tribunal, Case No ARB/02/13, 29 November 2004); *Daimler AG v Argentina (Award)* (ICSID Arbitral Tribunal, Case No ARB/05/1, 22 August 2012) [281].

166    International Law Commission, *Final Report of the Study Group on the Most-Favoured-Nation Clause*, UN Doc A/CN.4/L.852 (29 May 2015) [214].

167    Brown and Cucinotta (n 124) 188–9.

168    *United Parcel Service of America Inc v Canada (Merits)* (North American Free Trade Agreement Chapter 11 Arbitral Tribunal, 24 May 2007) [83].

A further consideration appears to be whether the measure in question can nonetheless be justified on the basis of the pursuit of domestic public policy objectives.[169] In *Bilcon v Canada*, the tribunal held it was possible for a state to demonstrate that treatment otherwise in breach of the national treatment standard could be justified; it observed that this 'would seem to provide legally appropriate latitude for host states, even in the absence of an equivalent of art XX of the *GATT*, to pursue reasonable and non-discriminatory domestic policy objectives through appropriate measures even when there is an incidental and reasonably unavoidable burden on foreign enterprises'.[170] Several modern investment treaties include an explanatory text consistent with the existence of such an exception. For instance, art 9.4 of the *CPTPP* states in a clarificatory footnote: 'For greater certainty, whether treatment is accorded in "like circumstances" ... depends on the totality of the circumstances, including whether the relevant treatment distinguishes between investors or investments on the basis of legitimate public welfare objectives.'[171]

## 16.3.2.6   Umbrella clause

Many BITs also include a provision which is known as an 'observance of undertakings' clause or 'umbrella clause'. An example is found in the United Kingdom–Sri Lanka BIT, art 2(2) of which provides: 'Each Contracting Party shall observe any obligation it may have entered into with regard to investments of nationals or companies of the other Contracting Party.'[172] Australia included such provisions in a number of its earlier BITs, such as the Australia–Poland BIT of 1991: 'A Contracting Party shall, subject to its law, do all in its power to ensure that a written undertaking given by a competent authority to a national of the other Contracting Party with regard to an investment is respected.'[173]

The effect of an umbrella clause has been examined in a number of arbitral awards, the first being those in *SGS v Pakistan*[174] and *SGS v Philippines*,[175] which came to different conclusions as to how the clause was to be interpreted. The *SGS v Pakistan* tribunal rejected the claimant's claims that the umbrella clause in the Switzerland–Pakistan BIT had the effect of elevating the contract claims to the level of treaty protection.[176] In contrast, the *SGS v Philippines* tribunal concluded that the umbrella clause in the Switzerland–Philippines BIT made it 'a breach of the BIT for the host state to fail to observe binding commitments, including contractual commitments, which it has assumed with regard to specific investments'.[177] This

169    *Bilcon v Canada (Award on Jurisdiction and Liability)* (Permanent Court of Arbitration, Case No 2009-04, 17 March 2015) [720].
170    Ibid [723].
171    *CPTPP* (n 151) art 9.4 n 14.
172    *Agreement between the United Kingdom and the Republic of Sri Lanka for the Promotion and Protection of Investments*, signed 13 February 1980, [1981] UKTS 14 (entered into force 18 December 1980).
173    *Agreement between Australia and the Republic of Poland on the Reciprocal Promotion and Protection of Investments*, signed 7 May 1991, [1992] ATS 10 (entered into force 27 March 1992) art 10.
174    *SGS SA v Pakistan (Decision on Jurisdiction)* (ICSID Arbitral Tribunal, Case No ARB/01/13, 6 August 2003).
175    *SGS SA v Philippines (Decision on Jurisdiction)* (ICSID Arbitral Tribunal, Case No ARB/02/6, 29 January 2004).
176    *SGS SA v Pakistan* (n 174) [168].
177    *SGS SA v Philippines* (n 175) [128].

did not mean, however, that the contractual claim was then governed by international law; it remained an issue to be determined in accordance with the law of the contract.[178] This had the practical result that the question of the Philippines' contractual liability had to be determined under the contractually agreed dispute resolution mechanism (which conferred jurisdiction on the Philippines courts); it was only if that obligation remained unfulfilled that the claimant would then be able to present a claim under the BIT.[179]

Subsequent tribunals have arrived at differing interpretations of the umbrella clause, even in circumstances where they claimed to be following one of these approaches. Thus, the tribunal in *Eureko v Poland* found the 'analysis of the Tribunal in *SGS v Republic of the Philippines*, a Tribunal which had among its distinguished members Professor Crawford, cogent and convincing',[180] but then proceeded to determine that Poland was in breach of its obligations (without requiring that the contractual dispute be resolved by the contractually agreed forum). And in another case, *El Paso v Argentina*, the tribunal held that the umbrella clause in the United States–Argentina BIT did 'not extend the Treaty protection to breaches of an ordinary commercial contract entered into by the State or a State-owned entity', but would 'cover additional investment protections contractually agreed by the State as a sovereign – such as a stabilisation clause – inserted in an investment agreement'.[181]

## 16.3.3   Dispute settlement

### 16.3.3.1   Investor–state dispute settlement

One of the innovations introduced by BITs is that many of them not only contain substantive protections for investors, but also procedural protection in the form of an investor–state dispute settlement ('ISDS') clause. Such clauses generally entitle an aggrieved investor to commence international arbitration proceedings against the host state for a breach of the host state's obligations under the BIT, with awards being binding and final.

The inclusion of such provisions avoids one of the adverse consequences of diplomatic protection claims, namely the creation of difficulties in the relations between the two states. The possibility of a direct investor–state claim is thus said to 'depoliticise' the dispute and allow it to be resolved by an arbitral tribunal without affecting the relationship between the two states,[182] including where developing countries would otherwise come under pressure from powerful developed states.[183] From the investor's perspective, it also avoids the risks of their state of nationality deciding not to exercise diplomatic protection, or of having to exhaust domestic remedies in the host state – which the investor may perceive as partial, unfair, lacking

---

178    Ibid.
179    Ibid.
180    *Eureko BV v Poland (Partial Award)* (Ad Hoc Arbitral Tribunal, 19 August 2005) [257].
181    *El Paso v Argentina (Decision on Jurisdiction)* (ICSID Arbitral Tribunal, Case No ARB/03/15, 27 April 2006) [81]. A 'stabilisation clause' may (depending on how it is formulated) have the effect of prohibiting the host state from adopting any measures which would affect the rights and obligations under the contract, or it may require the host state to restore the economic benefits of the contract to the investor if any such measures are adopted: see, eg, Peter Cameron, *International Energy Investment Law* (Oxford University Press, 2nd ed, 2021).
182    See, eg, Aron Broches, 'The Convention on the Settlement of Investment Disputes between States and Nationals of Other States' (1972) 136 *Recueil des cours* 331, 344.
183    Schreuer, 'Investment Disputes' (n 123) [3].

in expertise or marred by delay.[184] There has, however, been controversy over the right of foreign investors to bypass a host state's courts, because domestic investors do not enjoy the same privilege and domestic courts can provide adequate justice in many countries.[185]

These clauses have developed somewhat from the early days of BITs where they simply required an investor to give a certain period of notice of a dispute, and it could then commence arbitration proceedings, under either the *ICSID Convention* or the Rules of Arbitration developed by the United Nations Commission on International Trade Law ('UNCITRAL'),[186] which is a UN legal body that works on the harmonisation and modernisation of international trade law.[187] Modern investment chapters in free trade agreements contain far more detailed investor–state dispute settlement clauses, and make detailed provision for matters such as the bifurcation of preliminary objections, the transparency of the proceedings (including amicus curiae intervention), and the method of appointment of the tribunal.[188]

The current procedures for ISDS have been the subject of some criticism, with concerns being raised in response to perceptions of, for example, inconsistency in the interpretation of legal issues, the excessive cost and duration of ISDS proceedings, and a lack of independence and impartiality of the decision-makers. In 2017, concerned states initiated a process to consider the possibility of ISDS reform before Working Group III of UNCITRAL.[189] As of January 2022, Working Group III had identified concerns with regard to ISDS, and had decided that reform was desirable, although its deliberations are likely to continue for some years.[190] Possible outcomes include the creation of a permanent multilateral investment court and appellate body, as well as more targeted procedural reforms.[191]

### 16.3.3.2   Inter-state dispute settlement

Investment treaties also usually contain provisions for the resolution of state-to-state disputes, although these have only rarely been invoked, given that investors are able to commence dispute settlement proceedings under the ISDS clause. There are, however, a small number of cases in which the investment claims have proceeded as a state-to-state dispute.[192]

---

184     Ibid [3], [15].
185     For discussion see Gabrielle Kaufmann-Kohler and Michele Potestà, 'Why Investment Arbitration and Not Domestic Courts?' (2020) *European Yearbook of International Economic Law* 7.
186     See, eg, *Agreement between the Government of Australia and the Government of Hong Kong for the Promotion and Protection of Investments*, signed 15 September 1993 (entered into force 15 October 1993, terminated 17 January 2020) art 10.
187     See 'About UNCITRAL', *United Nations Commission on International Trade Law* (Web Page) <https://uncitral.un.org/en/about>.
188     See, eg, *CPTPP* (n 151) ch 9 arts 9.18–9.30.
189     See, eg, UNCITRAL, *Report of Working Group III (Investor–State Dispute Settlement Reform) on the Work of its Thirty-Fourth Session (Vienna, 27 November – 1 December 2017)*, UN Doc A/CN.9/930/Rev.1 (19 December 2017).
190     See, eg, UNCITRAL, *Annotated Provisional Agenda (New York, 14–18 February 2022)*, UN Doc A/CN.9/WG.III/WP.211 (3 December 2021).
191     See, eg, Anthea Roberts, 'Incremental, Systemic, and Paradigmatic Reform of Investor-State Arbitration' (2018) 112(3) *American Journal of International Law* 410.
192     See, eg, *Italy v Cuba (Final Award of 1 January 2008)* (2012) 106(2) *American Journal of International Law* 341; *Ecuador v United States (Award)* (Permanent Court of Arbitration, Case No 2012-5, 29 September 2012).

# DISCUSSION QUESTIONS

(1) What are the advantages and disadvantages of 'free' (open) trade and protectionism?

(2) Do the WTO-covered agreements strike the right balance between free trade and protecting the environment?

(3) What is the purpose of bilateral investment treaties and investment chapters in free trade agreements, given that some of their provisions can be said to reflect customary international law?

(4) Do bilateral investment treaties and investment chapters in free trade agreements act as a limitation on state sovereignty?

(5) What are the prospects for reform of investor–state dispute settlement?

# GLOSSARY

**Absolute immunity:** the doctrine that the state and its representatives are absolutely immune from the jurisdiction of a foreign court, regardless of the nature of the relevant act or conduct.

**Absolute rights:** human rights which cannot be limited, under any circumstances. Examples include the rights not to be subject to torture, slavery, and retrospective criminal laws.

**Acceptance:** international acts by which a state expresses its consent to be bound.

**Accession:** international acts by which a state expresses its consent to be bound.

**Act of state doctrine:** a common law doctrine which prevents the courts of one state passing judgment on the validity or effect of another state's laws or executive acts.

**Admissibility:** this concept is closely related to jurisdiction, and concerns whether an international adjudicatory body which has jurisdiction should proceed to exercise its jurisdiction, or whether there are reasons why it should not proceed to decide the dispute.

**Anticipatory self-defence:** the use of force to forestall an imminent armed attack.

**Approval:** international acts by which a state expresses its consent to be bound.

**Arbitration:** a third-party method of international dispute settlement in which the disputing parties appoint an independent arbitral tribunal which decides the dispute in accordance with international law, and the decision (referred to as an 'award') is binding on the disputing parties.

**Archipelagic state:** a state that is constituted wholly by one or more archipelagos and may include other islands (ie, islands that are not part of an archipelago).

**Armed attack:** a 'most grave' use of force.

**Baselines:** the legal expression of a state's coastal front from which maritime zones are projected.

**Bilateral investment treaty ('BIT'):** a treaty between two parties for the promotion and protection of investment.

**Civil and political rights:** also known as 'first generation' rights, these rights reflect traditional political 'freedoms', such as the right to liberty and freedom of expression, and are enshrined in, inter alia, the *International Covenant on Civil and Political Rights*.

**Combatant:** a person lawfully permitted to take part in hostilities under international law.

**Comity:** an act of courtesy or consideration, but not legally required.

**Commission on the Limits of the Continental Shelf ('CLCS'):** an international body of experts established by the *United Nations Convention on the Law of the Sea* to review data submitted by states concerning continental shelf areas beyond 200 M.

**Common but differentiated responsibilities and respective capabilities:** a principle which has its roots in Principle 23 of the *Stockholm Declaration on the Human Environment* and is spelled out in Principle 7 of the *Rio Declaration on Environment and Development* and in art 3.1 of the *UN Framework Convention on Climate Change*. It recognises that, while all states have common responsibilities with regard to the carrying out of globally agreed environmental goals, developed countries have a higher level of obligation in achieving them.

**Compliance theories:** efforts to explain the factors and processes which encourage or impede states from complying with their international legal obligations.

**Conciliation:** a method of international dispute settlement which involves the constitution of an independent conciliation commission, which carries out an impartial examination of the dispute and makes non-binding recommendations for its peaceful settlement, which the parties may then adopt.

**Contiguous zone:** a zone up to 24 M from the baselines that may be claimed by coastal states for the exclusive purpose of exercising jurisdiction over only customs, fiscal, immigration and sanitary (eg, quarantine) matters.

**Continental shelf:** an inherent maritime zone at least 200 M from the coastline in which the coastal state has sovereign rights in the mineral resources of the seabed and subsoil together with sedentary living species on the seafloor.

**Countermeasures:** proportional and unilateral non-forcible measures which an injured state may take in response to another state's wrongful act, undertaken in order to induce the wrongful state to cease its conduct, to make reparation and, where appropriate, offer assurances and guarantees of non-repetition.

**Countervailing measures:** 'action taken by the importing country, usually in the form of increased duties to offset subsidies given to producers or exporters in the exporting country': 'Glossary', *World Trade Organization* <www.wto.org/english/thewto_e/glossary_e/glossary_e.htm> (hereafter, '*WTO Glossary*').

**Crime of aggression:** the offence of initiating, or making certain other contributions to, acts of aggression as defined in international law. Acts of aggression involve the unlawful use of force by one state (or states) against another.

**Crimes against humanity:** generally, certain inhumane acts when committed as part of a widespread or systematic attack against a civilian population, although the definition differs among international courts and tribunals.

***De facto* ('in fact'):** a situation that exists in practice which is not reflected in law.

***De jure* ('in law'):** a legally recognised practice, which may or may not exist in fact.

**Diplomatic immunity:** the privileges and immunities granted to diplomatic personnel, codified in the *Vienna Convention on Diplomatic Relations*.

**Dualism:** the legal theory according to which domestic law and international law respectively exist and operate in spheres that are distinct from one another.

**Dumping:** the practice in which 'goods are exported at a price less than their normal value, generally meaning they are exported for less than they are sold in the domestic market or third-country markets, or at less than production cost' (*WTO Glossary*).

**Economic, social and cultural rights:** also known as 'second generation' rights, these rights, such as the rights to education and health, generally require some sort of positive support from the state. They are enshrined in, inter alia, the *International Covenant on Economic and Social Rights.*

**Exceptions for unlawfulness:** exceptionally, if an entity's creation is tainted by a use of force by an existing state or a breach of a peremptory norm (eg, the prohibition of racial discrimination) that may preclude it from qualifying as a state, regardless of whether it meets the criteria for statehood.

**Exclusive economic zone ('EEZ'):** a claimable maritime zone up to 200 M from the baselines in which coastal states have sovereign rights for the purpose of exploring and exploiting, conserving and managing the living and non-living resources of the water column, seabed and subsoil and jurisdiction in relation to these and several other matters (eg, pollution).

**Expropriation:** the taking (by way of substantial deprivation) by the state of an investor's investments, which is lawful if the measure of expropriation is for a public purpose, is non-discriminatory and is accompanied by compensation.

**External affairs power:** the power of the Commonwealth Parliament under s 51(xxix) of the *Constitution* to legislate with respect to external affairs, including to implement treaties to which Australia is a party.

**External self-determination:** a right held by only certain peoples: namely, colonised peoples, a smaller non-colonial category of peoples, and, debatably, peoples in cases of remedial secession. The right is not a power to create a new state automatically, but it may make qualifying as a state easier.

**Fair and equitable treatment ('FET'):** an obligation usually found in bilateral investment treaties and investment chapters in free trade

agreements under which the states parties generally agree to treat investor and investments from the other state party reasonably and to protect their legitimate expectations.

**Feminism:** critiques of the gendered norms and actors of international law, and an agenda for how to reconstruct a more equal and inclusive international legal order.

***Force majeure:*** situations where a state is not able to fulfill its obligations due to the occurrence of an irresistible force or unforeseen event.

**Foreign state immunity:** the immunity of a state and its representatives from the jurisdiction of a foreign court.

**Free trade agreement ('FTA'):** a bilateral or multilateral treaty which deals with a wide range of issues including trade in goods, trade in services, rules relating to customs procedures, trade in financial services, rules relating to government procurement, and the protection of intellectual property rights.

**Freedom of the seas:** the notion that the ocean is open to all states for free navigation and other high-seas freedoms. As a result of developments in customary international law and treaty law, coastal state maritime zones have expanded such that the high seas is the only area where the traditional high-seas freedoms remain most applicable.

**Full protection and security ('FPS'):** an obligation usually found in bilateral investment treaties and investment chapters in free trade agreements to provide physical protection for foreign investors and their investments.

**Fundamental change of circumstances:** a change in circumstances where the original circumstances were an essential basis of the parties' consent to the treaty, and the effect of the change is to radically transform the parties' remaining obligations (*Vienna Convention on the Law of Treaties* art 62).

**Genocide:** 'any of the following acts committed with intent to destroy, in whole or in part, a national, ethnical, racial or religious group, as such: (a) Killing members of the group; (b) Causing serious bodily or mental harm to members of the group; (c) Deliberately inflicting on the group conditions of life calculated to bring about its physical destruction in whole or in part; (d) Imposing measures intended to prevent births within the group; (e) Forcibly transferring children of the group to another group' (*Convention on the Prevention and Punishment of the Crime of Genocide* art II).

**Good offices:** a third-party form of international dispute settlement in which an independent third party assists in establishing contact and acting as a channel of communication between the disputing parties, and who may propose a solution which may be acceptable to the disputing parties.

**High seas:** all areas not within the exclusive economic zone, territorial sea, internal waters or archipelagic waters and where high-seas freedoms such as the freedom of navigation are enjoyed.

***Hors de combat* ('out of combat'):** a person who does not, or who no longer, takes direct part in hostilities, due to illness, wounding, surrender or any other reason.

**Humanitarian intervention:** the use of force for humanitarian purposes, without the consent of the target state or the approval of the Security Council.

**Immunities of international organisations:** procedural bars to the exercise of national jurisdiction, including legal process, against an international organisation. 'Privileges' include the inviolability of (ie, non-interference with)

certain persons, premises and assets, and exemptions from or adjustments to certain laws, such as tax or immigration.

**Immunity *ratione materiae* (functional immunity):** immunity for official acts.

**Immunity *ratione personae* (personal immunity):** immunity by virtue of the position the person holds (eg, Head of State, Minister for Foreign Affairs).

**Impossibility:** the situation in which it is impossible for the parties to perform the treaty because an object indispensable for the execution of the treaty has permanently disappeared or been destroyed (*Vienna Convention on the Law of Treaties* art 61).

**Incorporation:** a technique through which international law becomes part of domestic law as is or with its own wording.

**Internal waters:** waters landwards of the baselines in which the coastal state has complete sovereignty and jurisdiction.

**International Bill of Rights:** together, the *Universal Declaration of Human Rights*, the *International Covenant on Civil and Political Rights* and the *International Covenant on Economic, Social and Cultural Rights*.

**International Criminal Court:** the international organisation created by the *Rome Statute of the International Criminal Court*, with power to prosecute individuals for war crimes, crimes against humanity, genocide and the crime of aggression in certain circumstances.

**International dispute settlement:** methods and procedures for resolving international legal disputes, such as negotiation, mediation, conciliation, arbitration and adjudication.

**International legal person:** an entity subject to international law, possessing international legal rights and obligations, with a capacity to bring international claims and be held internationally responsible.

**International legal personality of international organisations:** the legal capacity of an international organisation, constituted under international law, to possess international legal rights and obligations, bring international claims and be held internationally responsible.

**International Maritime Organization ('IMO'):** a specialised agency of the United Nations which is responsible for measures to improve the safety and security of international shipping and to prevent pollution from ships.

**International organisation ('IO'):** an organisation usually established by a treaty, comprised mainly of states, governed by international law and possessing separate international legal personality.

**International Seabed Authority ('ISA'):** an international organisation established by the *United Nations Convention on the Law of the Sea* to regulate the exploitation of the mineral resources of the deep seabed beyond national jurisdiction.

**International Tribunal for the Law of the Sea ('ITLOS'):** a permanent international tribunal based in Hamburg, Germany, established by the *United Nations Convention on the Law of the Sea* with jurisdiction over disputes concerning the interpretation or application of the convention.

**Interpretative declaration:** a statement made by a state on signature or ratification etc, clarifying the meaning of a provision of the treaty.

**Invalidity:** a treaty is void if it was procured by threat of force, it violates a *jus cogens* norm or a party's consent to be bound was invalid on one of the grounds in *Vienna Convention of the Law of Treaties* arts 46–51.

**JSCOT:** the Joint Standing Committee on Treaties of the Commonwealth Parliament which scrutinises treaties which the executive proposes to ratify.

**Judicial settlement:** a method of settling a dispute by submitting it to an international court (such as the International Court of Justice) which resolves the dispute by issuing a binding judgment in accordance with a judicial process.

**Jurisdiction:** the competence of an international dispute settlement body which is seised of a dispute (such as an international court or tribunal) to render a decision.

***Jus ad bellum*:** the body of law relating to the right to use force at international law.

***Jus cogens* ('compelling law'):** a peremptory norm of international law, from which no derogation is permitted. A *jus cogens* norm takes precedence over any other rule of international law, whether in treaty or custom.

***Jus in bello*:** the law in war – international humanitarian law and the law of armed conflict.

**Law of state responsibility:** the rules governing the attribution of internationally wrongful conduct to a state and the consequences thereof, including the duty to make reparation.

***Levee en masse*:** an uprising of the civilian population, which springs up spontaneously as the enemy advances on the civilian's territory, but prior to the occupation of said territory.

**Liberalism:** the view that international law shapes state behaviour, whether through international, transnational and/or domestic social processes.

**M:** nautical mile.

**Maritime boundary delimitation:** the rules and processes applicable to the resolution of disputes between states regarding overlapping maritime zones.

**Marxism:** a critique of international law as reflecting and enabling the relations of power, exploitation and exclusion in the national and global economic order.

**Material breach:** breach of a provision of the treaty which is essential to the accomplishment of the object or purpose of the treaty, or a repudiation of the treaty not permitted by the *Vienna Convention of the Law of Treaties* (at art 60).

**Mediation:** a method of international dispute settlement which involves a third party who meets with the parties (including the possibility of meeting the disputing parties separately), and is actively involved in the dispute settlement process by transmitting each party's proposals to the other, and also by making fresh proposals for the settlement of the dispute.

**Monism:** legal theory according to which domestic and international law are part of the same legal order.

**Most-favoured-nation treatment:** 'the principle of not discriminating between one's trading partners' (*WTO Glossary*).

**Multilateral environmental agreement ('MEA'):** refers to all kinds of legally enforceable international environmental instruments generally involving many states parties; conventions, protocols, agreements. The United Nations Environment Programme has provided the central organising framework for global environmental management since 1973, providing secretariat functions for a number of MEAs.

**National treatment:** 'The principle of giving others the same treatment as one's own nationals' (*WTO Glossary*).

**Natural law:** supposedly universal rules inherent in human nature, whether revealed by religious law or emanating from human reason.

**Necessity:** the use of force in self-defence must be necessary to halt or repel the armed attack.

**Non-derogable rights:** rights which cannot be derogated from, even in times of emergency. Examples include the right to life and the right not to be subject to torture.

***Non liquet* ('not clear'):** where a judicial body does not rule due to an insufficiency in the law, because there is an absence of clear legal rules.

***Non-refoulement*:** the principle of international refugee law which prohibits states from returning refugees to states where their life or freedom would be threatened. International human rights law extends the obligation of *non-refoulement* beyond persecution to address situations where a person would be subject to other serious human rights violations, such as torture or arbitrary deprivation of life.

**Obligations *erga omnes*:** obligations owed to all (not just to parties to a treaty establishing group obligations).

**Obligations *erga omnes partes*:** obligations owed to all parties of a treaty regime.

***Opinio juris sive necessitates* ('an opinion of law or necessity'):** the subjective element of customary international law – the belief that a behaviour is legally required.

**Other manifestations of self-determination:** internal, indigenous and economic self-determination and the self-determination of existing states. These do not involve creating new states.

***Pacta sunt servanda* ('agreements must be kept'):** a state's obligation under art 26 of the *Vienna Convention on the Law of Treaties* and under customary international law to execute its treaty obligations in good faith.

**'*Polites* principle':** the principle that, in the absence of express words to the contrary, it is presumed that legislation is intended to be in conformity with international law and should be interpreted as such.

**Positivism:** international law as expressly declared by states (whether in treaty or custom), not deriving from higher religious or natural law sources.

**Postmodernism:** an analysis of the indeterminacy of international law and explanations for its binding force, rendering it prone to political abuse.

**Pre-emptive self-defence:** the use of force to prevent a possible future armed attack.

**Privileges of international organisations:** the inviolability of (non-interference with) certain persons, premises and assets related to international organisations, and exemptions from or adjustments to certain laws, such as tax or immigration.

**Proportionality:** the doctrine that the use of force in self-defence must be proportionate (not excessive) to the purpose of halting or repelling the armed attack.

**Public international law:** a universal system of rules and institutions largely created by states and governing inter-state relations and many subjects and actors within states.

**Ratification:** international acts by which a state expresses its consent to be bound.

**Realism:** the belief that international relations is explained by the pursuit of power and self-interest by states, with international law reflecting power or otherwise being insignificant.

**Recognition:** recognition as a state by other states. On the prevailing view, this is not necessary for statehood, but it is still significant in various ways and may be decisive in special situations.

**Reservation:** a statement made by a state on signature or ratification etc, purporting to exclude or modify the legal effect of a treaty provision in relation to that state.

**Responsibility of international organisations:** the rules governing the attribution of internationally wrongful conduct to an international organisation and the consequences of such attribution, including the duty to make reparation.

**Responsibility to protect:** a doctrine that reminds states of their responsibility to protect their own people; if the state is unable to prevent, or is itself responsible for, atrocities occurring in its territory, the international community has a duty to intervene, with Security Council approval.

**Restrictive immunity:** the doctrine that the state and its representatives are immune from the jurisdiction of a foreign court in relation to official acts and conduct, but not for commercial or non-governmental acts or conduct.

**Retorsion:** an unfriendly, but not unlawful, act by one state in response to another state's breach of an international obligation towards it.

**Safeguard measures:** 'action taken to protect a specific industry from an unexpected build-up of imports' (*WTO Glossary*).

**Self-defence:** a use of force in response to an armed attack.

**Self-determination:** the right of a people to freely determine their political status and freely pursue their economic, social and cultural development.

**Signature:** an international act through which a state expresses an interest in becoming a party to a treaty. Signature is seldom sufficient to express the consent to be bound.

**Soft law:** instruments that are not legally binding as such, but which can form the basis for hard law, or which can be transformed into hard law by recognition as customary law (eg, by the International Court of Justice). The making of international environmental law draws upon traditional sources of international law as well as soft law instruments and declarations of global UN conferences and declarations by non-state environmental actors.

**Special mission immunity:** the privileges and immunities accorded to a visiting delegation of foreign officials.

**Special types of territory:** territories that include Antarctica, maritime zones, airspace and outer space.

**Statehood criteria:** a permanent population, defined territory, effective and independent government, and independence (sometimes called 'capacity to enter into relations with the other states'). Also known as the 'Montevideo criteria'. Generally, an entity that meets these four criteria qualifies as a state.

**Suspension:** where the treaty remains in existence but its operation is suspended in whole or in part.

**Tariff:** a duty (a financial impost) imposed on imports.

**Termination:** where the treaty comes to an end.

**Territorial change:** change that can traditionally occur by any of five methods: (1) avulsion or accretion, (2) conquest (no longer permitted), (3) cession, (4) occupation of terra nullius and (5) prescription.

**Territorial dispute:** where two or more states claim the same territory. In such cases, courts and tribunals tend to apply concepts of effective occupation, the critical date and relativity of title.

**Territorial sea:** a maritime zone, not exceeding 12 M from the baselines, in which the coastal state has sovereignty over the seabed, subsoil, water column, water surface and airspace.

**Transformation:** a technique through which an international norm or rule is given effect domestically by being 'translated' into domestic legislation.

**Treaty:** 'an international agreement concluded between States in written form and governed by international law, whether embodied in a single instrument or in two or more related instruments and whatever its particular designation': *Vienna Convention on the Law of Treaties* art 2(1)(a).

**TWAIL (Third World Approaches to International Law):** approaches that examine how international law both historically enabled colonialism and continues to reflect neo-colonial patterns of dominance and subordination, including through contemporary international economic relations.

***Ultra vires:*** beyond legal authority or competence.

**Umbrella clause:** an obligation usually found in bilateral investment treaties which generally has the effect of making it possible for an investor to assert a claim under the treaty in the case of a breach of contract by the host state.

**United Nations Convention on the Law of the Sea ('UNCLOS'):** the most important treaty in the law of the sea which comprehensively addresses most law of the sea topics and is described as the 'constitution for the oceans'.

**War crimes:** serious violations of international humanitarian law for which individuals can be held criminally responsible.

**Withdrawal:** a party to a multilateral treaty ceasing to be a party to the treaty. Where a party withdraws, the treaty continues in existence among the remaining parties.

# INDEX

*Afghanistan Inquiry Report*, 300–1
    direct participation in hostilities and, 309–10
African Commission on Human and Peoples'
        Rights, 122, 283
African Court on Human and Peoples' Rights,
        283–4
aggression, 338–40
    definition, 338–9
*Agreement on Trade-Related Aspects of Intellectual
        Property, see TRIPS Agreement*
Amnesty International, 267, 286
Arab Human Rights Committee, 284
archipelagic sea lanes passage, 361
archipelagic state, 359
archipelagic waters, 349, 359–61
'armed attack', 223
    meaning of, 224–5
    pre-emptive self-defence, 227–8
    protection of nationals abroad, 228
    self-defence against terrorism, 228–9
    timing of, 225
        'accumulation of events' theory, 227
        anticipatory self-defence, 225
        broad view of self-defence, 225–6
        narrow view of self-defence, 226–7
        past attacks, 225
armed conflict
    international armed conflicts, 298–9
    non-international armed conflicts, 299–301
    parallel conflicts, 301
    transformation of conflicts, 301–2
    types of, 298
Assange, Julian, 162, 188
Association of Southeast Asian Nations (ASEAN),
        271
    Intergovernmental Commission on Human
        Rights, 285
Austin, John, 17
Australia
    continental shelf, 358–9
    exclusive economic zone, 356
    genocide in, 336–8
    International Court of Justice and, 263–4
    maritime boundary with Timor Leste, 363

role of statehood criteria, 111–13
special procedures and, 277–8
Sustainable Development Goals 2015 and, 382
sustainable development in, 382
UN Human Rights Committee complaints
        process and, 280–1
UN Security Council and, 424–5
universal periodic review and, 276–7
*World Heritage Convention* in, 397–8
World Trade Organization and, 441
Australian law
    categorising the influence of international
        law on, 88–90
    customary international law in, 101–4
        crimes in customary international law,
            101–4
    human rights institutions
        Australian Human Rights Commission,
            289–91
        Parliamentary Joint Committee on Human
            Rights, 289
    human rights law in
        federal human rights Act, 288–9
        federal law, 287
        state and territory legislation, 287–8
    international law and constitutional
        interpretation, 100–1
    international law and statutory interpretation,
        97–100
    proof of international law in Australian courts,
        105–6
    separation of powers, 86
    treaties and, 90–1
        constitutional considerations, 92–4
        legislative considerations, 94–6
        treaties and administrative decision-making,
            96–7
        treaty-making process, 91–2

Bangladesh, 127–8
baselines, 351–2
Bentham, Jeremy, 17, 291
bilateral investment treaties, 205, 443–4, 448,
        450–1

biological diversity
  conservation of, 392–4
    *CITES* on wildlife trafficking, 394
    *Convention on Biological Diversity*, 393
    *Ramsar Convention* on wetland
      conservation, 394
    Sustainable Development Goals 2015,
      392
    *United Nations Forest Instrument*, 393–4
Blackstone, William, 17, 103
*Brereton Report, see Afghanistan Inquiry Report*
*Bringing Them Home*, 336–7

Cambodia. *See* Extraordinary Chambers in the
    Courts of Cambodia
*Charter of the United Nations*, 6
  evolution of the obligation to settle disputes
    peacefully and, 242–4
  use of force and, *see* use of force
chemicals and waste
  international environmental law and, 390–2
    *Basel Convention* on hazardous waste
      transportation, 391
    *Kigali Amendment* on hydroflourocarbons,
      390–1
    mercury emissions, 391–2
    *Rotterdam Convention* on hazardous
      chemicals and pesticides, 391
    *Stockholm Convention* on organic
      pollutants, 391
climate change, international environmental law
    and, 388–9
codes of conduct, 52–3
Cold War, 20–1, 23, 52, 117, 231, 268, 428
colonialism, 5, 26, 108, 292, 374, 423
command responsibility, 343–4
Commission on the Limits of the Continental Shelf,
    349, 358
contiguous zone, 354–5
continental shelf, 349, 357–9
copyright and related rights, 438
corporations
  as participants in international law, 10
  diplomatic immunity and, 207–8
Court of Justice of the European Union, 283
Crimea, 23
  Russian annexation of, 120–1
crimes against humanity, 332–3
cultural property, international humanitarian law
    and, 317
customary international law, 34, 225
  in Australian law, 101–4
    crimes in customary international law, 105
  interaction between treaties and custom, 42–3

*jus cogens*, 43–4
  local or regional custom, 40–1
  *opinio juris*, 38–40
  persistent and subsequent objector, 41–2
  prohibition on use of force, 216
  relationship with treaties, 56–7
  'specially affected' states, 38
  state practice, 34–8
cyber-attacks, 219–20

decolonisation, 421–2
deep seabed, 349, 365–7
diplomatic asylum, 40, 162–3, 188
diplomatic immunity, 156
  consular relations, 158
  corporations and shareholders nationality
    claims, 207–8
  diplomatic relations, 157
  *Vienna Convention on Diplomatic Relations*,
    158–9
    appointments, 161
    duties of the sending state, 163–4
    immunities, 159–61
    inviolability, 162–3
diplomatic protection, 198–9
  additional requirements for a claim in, 206
    exhaustion of local remedies, 208–9
    natural persons nationality of claims,
      206–7
Dispute Settlement Board, 440
dualism, 85
  transformation and, 85

*effectivités*, 138, 140
elements of state responsibility
  admissibility of claims, 188
  attribution of conduct, 183
    acts by non-state actors or groups, 185–6
    adoption by the state, 186
    conduct of state organs, and of persons or
      entities exercising governmental
      authority, 183–4
    joint responsibility, 187
    ultra vires or unauthorised acts, 184–5
  breach of a rule of international law, 188
  circumstances precluding wrongfulness, 188
    consent, 188–9
    countermeasures, 190
    distress, 191
    *force majeure*, 190–1
    necessity, 191–2
    self-defence, 189
  consequences of a breach of a *jus cogens* norm,
    195–6

consequences of an internationally wrongful
act, 192
cessation, 192–3
reparation, 193–5
invocation, 196–8
environmental law. *See* international
environmental law
Environmental Rule of Law, 383–4
European Committee of Social Rights, 283
European Court of Human Rights, 282
European Union, 149–50, 283, 404–5
exclusive economic zone, 355–7
extradition, 155–6
Extraordinary Chambers in the Courts of
Cambodia, 330
genocide and, 336
joint criminal enterprise and, 342

feminism, 28–9
fisheries, 369–70
Food and Agriculture Organization, 425
*force majeure*, 190–1
*Rainbow Warrior* arbitration, 190–1
foreign nationals
a state's obligation regarding the treatment of,
200
expropriation of the property of, 203–5
international minimum standard and
obligations under investment treaties,
202–3
international minimum standard of treatment,
200–1
national standard versus the international
minimum standard, 200
obligation to provide physical protection for,
202
responsibility for direct and indirect injury to,
201–2
foreign state immunity, 164–5
absolute versus restrictive immunity, 165–7
*Arrest Warrant* case, 172
personal immunity beyond the Troika,
173
personal immunity from civil proceedings,
172–3
before international tribunals, 177
foreign act of state doctrine, 178–9
immunity for *jus cogens* violations, 173–4
functional immunity of officials for other
crimes, 176
immunity from civil proceedings for torture
and other international crimes, 176
immunity from criminal proceedings for
other *jus cogens* violations, 175

immunity from criminal proceedings for
torture, 174–5
special mission immunity, 177
who or what is entitled to immunity, 272
agencies and instrumentalities, separate
entities, 169
individuals representing the state, 170
personal immunity for certain individuals,
170–2
political subdivisions, 169
the 'state', 168–9
*forum prorogatum*, 257–8

*General Agreement on Tariffs and Trade 1994*
most-favoured-nation treatment, 434–5
national treatment, 435
other provisions, 435–6
genocide
cultural genocide, 334–5
definition, 333–6
in Australia, 336–8
globalisation, 5, 26–7
greenhouse gases, 388
Grotius, Hugo, 4, 43
*Grundnorm*, 20, 84

Hart, HLA, 17–20, 22
*Helsinki Final Act*, 51–2
Henkin, Louis, 22–3
heritage conservation
heritage conventions, 395–6
*World Heritage Convention*, 396–8
Hicks, David, 281
high seas, 349, 364–5
piracy, 365
Hobbes, Thomas, 21, 266, 401
*hors de combat*, 300, 305
human rights
as a discourse and critiques, 291–3
post-war developments, 6–7

immunity *ratione materiae*, 170, 174–5
*in dubio pro natura*, 384
indigenous peoples
right to environment, 386
self-determination, 129
Inter-American Commission on Human Rights, 273,
281
Inter-American Court of Human Rights, 281–2
Intergovernmental Panel on Climate Change, 389
International Centre for the Settlement of
Investment Disputes, 14
International Commission on Intervention and
State Sovereignty, 234–5

International Committee of the Red Cross, 11, 52, 314, 319, 406
  indirect participation in hostilities and, 309
International Court of Justice, 6, 14, 182, 239–40, 251, 375
  access to the Court, 253
  Australia and, 263–4
  composition, 252–3
  existence of a 'dispute' and, 240–1
  history, 252
  judgments, 262–3
  jurisdiction of the Court
    admissibility of claims, 258–60
    advisory jurisdiction, 261–2
    contentious jurisdiction, 254–8
    provisional measures, 260–1
    third-party intervention, 261
  legal and positive disputes and, 241
International Criminal Court, 8, 11, 14, 22, 319, 325–6, 404
  admissibility rules, 327–8
  contributors, 342
  co-perpetrators, 342
  crime of aggression and, 339–40
  'indirect' forms of commission, 342–3
  jurisdiction of, 326–7
international criminal law
  aims, 321–2
  crimes under international law
    aggression, 338–40
    crimes against humanity, 332–3
    genocide, 333–8
    war crimes, 331
  development of, 323–5
  enforcement of
    'hybrid' criminal courts, 330
    International Criminal Court, see
      International Criminal Court
    national courts, 329–30
  individual criminal responsibility, 341
    command responsibility, 343–4
    commission, 341–3
    defences, 344–5
International Criminal Tribunal for Rwanda, 324, 328, 339
  joint criminal enterprise and, 342
International Criminal Tribunal for the Former Yugoslavia, 298, 324, 328, 339
  joint criminal enterprise and, 342
international dispute settlement, 239
  diplomatic methods for the peaceful settlement of international disputes, 244
    conciliation, 249–51
    fact-finding and inquiry, 246–7
    good offices, 247–8
    mediation, 248–9
    negotiation, 244–6
  international arbitration, 251–2
  International Court of Justice, see International Court of Justice
  obligation to settle disputes peacefully and the Charter of the United Nations framework, 242–4
  overview, 239–40
    existence of a 'dispute', 240–1
    legal and political disputes, 241
  role of the United Nations and regional organisations in, 264
international environmental law, 373
  development of, 373–4
    national level implementation, 375
    remedies for violations, 375
  established principles of
    environmental impact assessment, 379–80
    precaution, 379
    substantive principle of prevention, 378–9
  heritage conservation
    heritage conventions, 395–6
    World Heritage Convention, 396–8
  international institutions
    UN Environment Assembly, 377
    UN Environment Programme, 377
  principles of
    new principles, see international environmental law, new principles in
    established principles, 378–80
    importance of principles, 378
    sustainable development, see sustainable development
  selected issues in
    chemicals and waste, 390–2
    conservation of biological diversity, 392–4
    greenhouse gases and climate change, 388–9
    land degradation, 394–5
    transboundary air pollution, 390
  sources and drafting of, 375–7
international environmental law, new principles in
  Environmental Rule of Law, 383–4
  human right to a safe, clean healthy and sustainable environment, 385–7
  in dubio pro natura, 384
  principle of non-regression, 384–5
  principle of progression, 385
  principles of international environmental law in a global instrument, 382–3
international human rights law
  domestic implementation of, international overview, 286–7
  histories of, 266–7
  human rights law in Australia, 287–9

institutional framework
    civil society, 285–6
    human rights treaty bodies, 278–81
    international bodies, 275–6
    UN Human Rights Council, 276–8
major international human rights instruments,
    267
    *ICCPR* and the *ICESR*, 268–9
    international refugee law, 270
    other international human rights
        instruments, 269–70
    regional human rights treaties, 270–1
    *Universal Declaration of Human Rights,*
        267–8
overview of rights and obligations
    derogations and limitations, 273–4
    generations of rights, 275
    jurisdictional scope, 272–3
    nature of obligations, 273
    reservations to human rights treaties,
        274–5
    who has obligations under international
        human rights law, 272
    who has rights under international human
        rights law, 272
regional bodies and mechanisms, 281–4
    ASEAN case study, 284–5
international humanitarian law, 295
    fundamental principles of
        distinction, 303
        humanity, 305
        military necessity, 305
        prohibition on causing unnecessary
            suffering and superfluous injury, 305–6
        proportionality, 303–4
    implementation and enforcement of, 318–19
    law of targeting, *see* law of targeting
    objects under
        civilian objects, 310–11
        military objects and objectives, 310
    persons under
        civilians (including those taking direct part in
            hostilities), 308–10
        combatants and attached non-combatants,
            306–8
    scope of application of, 302–3
    sources of, 295–8
    special protection regimes
        cultural property, 317
        law of occupation, 315–16
        prisoners of war, 314–15
        wounded, sick and shipwrecked, 316
    transformation of conflicts, 301–2
    types of armed conflict, 298
        international armed conflicts, 299

non-international armed conflicts, 299–301
        parallel conflicts, 301
international investment law, 431, 442–4
    dispute settlement
        inter-state dispute settlement, 454
        investor–state dispute settlement, 453–4
    substantive obligations in investment treaties,
        444
        fair and equitable treatment, 444–7
        full protection and security, 447–8
        most-favoured-nation treatment, 450–1
        national treatment, 451–2
        protection from expropriation, 448–50
        umbrella clause, 452–3
International Labour Organization, 11, 14, 269, 276,
        406, 425
international law, 2–3
    Australian law and
        categorising the influence of international
            law on Australian law, 88–90
        international law and constitutional
            interpretation, 100–1
        international law and statutory
            interpretation, 97–100
        proof of international law in Australian
            courts, 105–6
    critical theories
        feminism, 28–30
        Marxism, 26–7
        postmodernism, 30–1
        Third World Approaches to International
            Law, 28
    domestic law and, 84–6
    domestic law in
        deficiencies in municipal law no
            justification for breach of international
            law, 86–8
        municipal law as source of international law,
            86
    historical context
        19th and early 20th centuries, 5–6
        early origins, 3–5
        international order after 1945, 6–7
    implementation and enforcement of, *see*
        international law, implementation and
        enforcement of
    nature of as 'law', 16
        international law as process, 24–5
        law lacking a legal system, 19–20
        not 'law', 17–18
        recognised and treated as law, 22–4
        subordinate to power, 20–2
        theories of compliance with international
            law, 25–6
        voluntarism, 18

international law (cont.)
    participants
        actors with limited personality, 11–12
        corporations, 10
        individuals, 10
        international organisations, 8–9
        non-governmental organisations, 11
        other actors, 9
        peoples, 9
        states, 7–8
    sources of
        custom, *see* customary international law
        general principles of law, 45–7
        *ICJ Statute* art 38, 33
        International Law Commission, 48–9
        judicial decisions and teachings of highly
            qualified publicists, 47–8
        soft law instruments, *see* soft law instruments
        treaties, 34
        unilateral decisions, 117–19
    specialisation of, 7
international law, implementation and
        enforcement of, 12–13
    international level, 13
        diplomatic claims, 13
        dispute settlement methods, 13–14
        enforcement of international security, 14
        other accountability procedures, 14
        self-help, 14–15
        social processes, 15–16
        state responsibility, 13
        treaty law, 15
    national level, 16
International Law Commission, 405, 414–15, 425, 451
    highly qualified publicists, 48–9
    identification of customary international law
        and, 35–6
    *jus cogens* and, 43–4, 49
    law of the sea and, 348
    *opinio juris* and, 39
    state practice and, 34–5
    state responsibility and, 181–2
international law of the sea
    coastal state maritime zones, 349–51
        archipelagic waters, 359–61
        baselines, 351–2
        contiguous zone, 354–5
        continental shelf, 357–9
        exclusive economic zone, 355–7
        territorial sea, 352–4
    dispute resolution, 370–1
    fisheries, 369–70
    maritime boundary delimitation, 361–2
        Australia and Timor Leste maritime
            boundary, 363

maritime environmental protection, 367–9
maritime zones beyond national jurisdiction
    deep seabed, 365–7
    high seas, 364–5
origins and development, 347–9
International Maritime Organization, 353, 361, 367,
    426
International Military Tribunal (Nuremberg), 321,
    323, 331, 339
International Military Tribunal for the Far East, 323,
    331, 339
International Monetary Fund, 425–6, 431
international organisations, 401
    characteristics of, 405
        established by international law, 405–6
        international legal personality, 407–9
        membership by states, 406–7
    immunities from and privileges under
            international law, 411
        immunities and privileges of UN personnel,
            413–14
        immunities of the United Nations, 412–13
        lifting of immunity, 414–15
        privileges of the United Nations, 413
    origins and purposes of, 401–2
        contemporary international organisations,
            404–5
        League of Nations, 402–4
    powers of, 409–11
    responsibility and accountability of
            international organisations and member
            states, 415–16
        attribution, 416–17
        breach of an international obligation, 416
        dispute settlement procedures, 419–20
        dual attribution, 417–18
        responsibility for contributing to the acts of
            others, 418–19
        responsibility of member states for a breach
            by an international organisation, 419
    UN Secretariat, 426–7
    United Nations, 420–3
        criticisms of, 427–8
        other UN bodies, 425–6
        reform of, 428–9
        UN General Assembly, 423–4
        UN Security Council, 424–5
international refugee law, 270
International Seabed Authority, 349, 366
international trade law, 431
    *General Agreement on Tariffs and Trade*,
        431–2
    World Trade Organization, 433–4
        *General Agreement on Tariffs and Trade
        1994*, 434–6

*General Agreement on Trade in Services*,
    436–7
  other free trade agreements, 441–2
  *TRIPS Agreement*, 437–9
  *Understanding of Dispute Settlement*, 439–41
International Trade Organization, 432
International Tribunal for the Law of the Sea, 14,
    245, 349, 379
international tribunals, immunity before, 177
International Union for Conservation of Nature,
    376, 405
investigation *proprio motu*, 326–7
Iraq, invasion of, 22–3

jurisdiction
  accused brought 'unlawfully' before the court,
    154–5
  civil jurisdiction, 146
    *Alien Tort Statute 1789*, 146–7
  criminal jurisdiction, 147–8
    extended territoriality and the 'effects
      doctrine', 148–50
    nationality principle, 150
    passive personality principle, 150–1
    'prosecute or extradite' treaties, 154
    protective principle, 151–3
    territoriality principle, 148
    universal jurisdiction in national courts, 154
    universality principle, 153
  extradition, 155–6
  *Lotus* case, 144–6
  meaning and scope, 143–4
*jus ad bellum*, 213, 298
*jus cogens*, 18–19, 22, 43–4, 74, 81, 119, 188, 216, 415
  consequences of a breach of a *jus cogens* norm,
    195–6
  immunity for *jus cogens* violations, 173–4
    functional immunity of officials for other
      crimes, 176
    immunity from civil proceedings for torture
      and other international crimes, 176
    immunity from criminal proceedings for
      other *jus cogens* violations, 175
    immunity from criminal proceedings for
      torture, 174–5
*jus gentium*, 3

Kant, Immanuel, 4, 401
*Kellogg-Briand Pact*, 132, 213, 239, 243, 339
Kelsen, Hans, 20, 84–5
Kosovo, 118

land degradation, international environmental law
    and, 394–5
law of occupation, 315–16

law of targeting, 311–12
  prohibited means and methods of warfare,
    312
    methods, 313–14
    weapons, 312–13
League of Arab States, 40, 271
League of Nations, 6, 20, 28, 112, 125, 213, 243,
    252, 401–4
*lex specialis*, 19, 198
List of World Heritage in Danger, 397

manuals of instruction, 52–3
Marx, Karl, 292
Marxism, 26–7
monism, 84–5
  incorporation and, 85
Morganthau, Hans, 21
multilateral environmental agreements, 374

natural environment, international humanitarian
    law and, 317–18
natural law, 3–5, 16, 23, 43, 85, 347
Non-Aligned Movement, 226, 234
non-governmental organisations, as participants in
    international law, 11
North Atlantic Treaty Organization, 40, 404
Nuremberg Tribunal, *see* International Military
    Tribunal (Nuremberg)

Office of the High Commissioner for Human
    Rights, 275
Operation Sovereign Borders, 354
*opinio juris*, 34, 38–40, 42, 86, 114, 217, 228–9, 233
Organization for Security and Co-operation in
    Europe, 52, 404

*pacta sunt servanda*, 34, 69, 73
Palestine, 23, 115, 125
peacekeepers, 414
  UN peacekeepers, 412–13
peacekeeping, 231–2
  establishment of peacekeeping forces, 410
  'status of forces' agreements, 412
peoples, as participants in international law, 9
Permanent Court of Arbitration, 6, 14, 239, 243, 251–3
Permanent Court of International Justice, 6, 239,
    251–2, 257, 403
piracy, 365
pluralism, 86, 287
postmodernism, 30–1
pragmatism, 22–4
principle of non-regression, 384–5
principle of progression, 385
prisoners of war, international humanitarian law
    and, 314–15

realism, 20–2
reparation, 193
  compensation, 194
  restitution, 193–4
  satisfaction, 194–5
restitution, 193–4
Rhodesia, 128
Rousseau, Jean-Jacques, 4, 266

sanctions, 230–1
self-defence
  'armed attack', *see* 'armed attack'
  procedural requirements for,
    declaration by victim state, 223
    reporting to the UN Security Council, 223
self-determination, 122–3
  manifestations of self-determination, 128–30
    economic self-determination, 130
    indigenous peoples, 129
    internal self-determination, 128
    will of the people, 129–30
  right to external self-determination, 123
    how self-determination affects statehood,
      126–8
    scope of the right to external self-
      determination, 123–6
self-help, 14–15
  non-forcible self-help
    countermeasures, 15
    retorsion, 15
soft law instruments, 50–1
  codes of conduct and manuals of instruction,
    52–3
  resolutions of international organisations and
    conferences, 51–2
Somalia, 110, 115
Special Court for Sierra Leone, 330
  joint criminal enterprise and, 342
special procedures, 277–8
  Australia, 277–8
state responsibility
  custom and work of the International Law
    Commission and, 181–2
  elements of state responsibility, *see* elements of
    state responsibility
  in the era of international human rights law,
    209–10
statehood, 108
  how self-determination affects statehood, 126–8
  role of recognition, 113
    recognition as a government, 116–17
    recognition as a state, 113–16
  role of the statehood criteria, 108–9
    criterion of independence, 110–11
    example of Australia, 111–13

population, territory and government,
    109–10
  role of unlawfulness, 117
    entities created by breaches of other
      peremptory norms, 121
    entities created by force, 119–21
    entities created by unilateral secession,
      117–19
states, as participants in international law, 8
Stockholm Conference on the Human
    Environment, 374
sustainable development, 380–1
  definition, 381
  in Australia, 382
  Sustainable Development Goals 2015, 376,
    381–3, 389, 392
    Australia and, 382
    *Transforming Our World*, 381
Sustainable Development Goals 2015, 376, 381–2,
    389, 392

Taiwan, 117, 164
  international law and, 12
terra nullius, 45
  territorial change through occupation of, 133–5
territorial sea, 349, 352–4
territory, 130
  initial territory of new states, 130–1
  special types of territory, 140–1
  territorial change, 131
    cession, 132–3
    conquest, 132
    occupation of terra nullius, 133–5
    prescription, 135–7
  territorial disputes, 137
    critical date, 139
    effective occupation, 137–9
    relativity of title, 140
terrorism
  self-defence against terrorism, 228–9
  'unable or unwilling' doctrine, 229
*The Human Right to a Clean, Healthy and*
    *Sustainable Environment*, 387
Third World Approaches to International Law, 28
Tokyo Tribunal, *see* International Military Tribunal
    for the Far East
torture, immunity from criminal proceedings for,
    174–5
trademarks, 438–9
transboundary air pollution, international
    environmental law and, 390
transit passage, 353–4, 361
treaties, 56
  application of, 70
  as source of international law, 34

Australian law and, 90–1
    constitutional considerations, 92–4
    legislative considerations, 94–6
    treaties and administrative decision-making,
        96–7
    treaty-making process, 91–2
bilateral investment treaties, 205, 443–4, 448,
    450–1
compromissory clause, 246, 257
entry into force, 62
expressing the consent to be bound, 61–2
human rights treaties
    reservations to, 64–6
interaction between treaties and custom,
    42–3
interpretation of, 70–1
    general rule, 71–2
    role of resolutions of international
        organisations, 73
    supplementary means of interpretation,
        72–3
invalidity of a treaty, 74
    breach of good faith, 76
    coercion, 75–6
    error, 75
    fraud or corruption, 75
    internal law, 74–5
investment treaties, obligations to foreign
    nationals under, 202–3
legal effects of
    obligation not to defeat the object and
        purpose of a treaty prior to its entry into
        force, 69
    observance of treaties, see treaties
        observance of
multilateral environmental agreements, 374
'prosecute or extradite' treaties, 154
relationship with customary international law,
    56–7
reservations to, 62–3
    allowed reservations, 64–7
    effect of, 67–8
    reservations versus interpretive declarations,
        63–4
termination, withdrawal and suspension, 76
    consequences of invalidity, termination and
        suspension, 81
    denunciation or withdrawal by express or
        implied agreement, 77
    fundamental change of circumstances,
        79–81
    impossibility, 78–9
    material breach, 77–8
    termination by express or implied
        agreement, 77

treaty law, 15
treaty negotiation and conclusion, 60–1
treaties observance of
    internal law and, 70
    pacta sunt servanda, 69
    treaties and third states, 70
TRIPS Agreement, 437
    copyright and related rights, 438
    national and most-favoured-nation treatment,
        437–8
    other provisions, 439
    trademarks, 438–9

Ukraine, Russian aggression in, 22, 228, 327, 428
Uluru Statement from the Heart, 129
UN Administrative Tribunal, 412, 425
UN Children's Fund, 276, 425
UN Commission on Human Rights, 268, 276
UN Commission on International Trade Law, 425,
    454
UN Development Programme, 276, 425
UN Economic and Social Council, 11, 276, 373, 407,
    422–3, 425, 428
UN Educational, Scientific and Cultural
    Organization, 276, 425
UN Environment Assembly, 377
UN Environment Programme, 377, 383, 425
UN Forum on Forests, 393
UN General Assembly, 6, 14, 48, 245, 252–3, 276,
    334, 387, 405, 423–4, 427
    resolutions, 35, 40, 51
UN Human Rights Committee, 14, 275, 279
    complaints process, Australia and, 280–1
UN Human Rights Council, 14, 247, 276, 279, 319,
    386–7, 389, 425, 427–8
    special procedures, 277–8
    universal periodic review, 276–7
UN Industrial Development Organization, 405
UN Peacebuilding Commission, 425
UN Permanent Forum on Indigenous Issues,
    276
UN Secretariat, 60, 426–7
UN Secretary-General, 14, 58, 60, 248
UN Security Council, 6, 13–15, 21, 213, 239, 252–3,
    276, 326, 328, 339–40, 410, 420–2, 424–5,
    427
    collective security, 230
        authorisation of force, 232–3
        peacekeeping, 231–2
        sanctions, 230–1
    reform of, 429
    settlement of international disputes and, 264
UN Trusteeship Council, 421
United Nations, 404, 416, 420–3
    criticisms of, 427–8

United Nations (cont.)
  immunities and privileges of UN personnel,
      413–14
  immunities of, 412–13
  personality, 9
  privileges of, 413
  reform of, 428–9
  role of in international dispute settlement,
      264
universal periodic review, 276–7
  Australia, 276–7
use of force
  *Charter of the United Nations* and, 214
    cyber-attacks, 219–20
    'force', 'in their international relations', 'any
        state', 214
    indirect use of force versus 'effective
        control', 218
    *Nicaragua* case, 216–18
    prohibition is customary international law,
        216
    'territorial integrity or political
        independence', 214–15
    what is a threat of force, 220–1
    what is not a use of force, 218–19
    what is prohibited, 215–16
  collective security, 230
    authorisation of force, 232–3
    peacekeeping, 231–2
    sanctions, 230–1
  humanitarian intervention and the
      responsibility to protect, 233–5
  intervention by invitation, 235
    principle of non-intervention, 236
    right to intervention by invitation, 236–7
  pre-1945, 213–14
  self-defence, 221–2
    necessity and proportionality, 222–3

*uti possidetis*, 130, 137, 139

*Vienna Convention on the Law of Treaties*
  introduction and scope, 57–8
  treaty for purposes of, 58
    agreement between states, 58
    embodied in one or more instruments, 59
    governed by international law, 59
    in written form, 58–9
    whatever its particular designation, 59–60
voluntarism, 18

Waldock, Humphrey, 22, 24
war crimes, 331
  concept of, 332
World Bank, 14, 426, 431
World Food Programme, 425
World Health Organization, 12, 425, 428
World Heritage Committee, 397
World Intellectual Property Organization, 425,
    437
World Meteorological Organization, 404, 406,
    425
World Trade Organization, 8, 12, 14, 22, 117,
    404–5, 426, 431, 433–4
  Australia and, 441
  *General Agreement on Tariffs and Trade 1994*,
      434–6
  *General Agreement on Trade and Services*,
      436–7
  other free trade agreements, 441–2
  *TRIPS Agreement*, 437–9
  *Understanding of Dispute Settlement*,
      439–41
wounded, sick and shipwrecked, international
      humanitarian law and, 316

Yugoslavia, 110, 118, 122